BOTTOM LINE YEAR BOOK 1995

BY THE EDITORS OF

Bottom Line
PERSONAL

Copyright © 1994 by Boardroom® Reports, Inc.

10   9   8   7   6   5   4   3   2   1

Boardroom® Classics publishes the advice of expert authorities in
many fields. The use of a book is not a substitute for legal,
accounting or other professional services. Consult a competent
professional for answers to your specific questions.

Library of Congress Cataloging in Publication Data
Main entry under title:

Bottom Line Yearbook 1995.

    1. Life skills—United States.   I. Bottom line personal.
ISBN 0-88723-090-3

Boardroom® Classics is a registered trademark of
Boardroom® Reports, Inc.
55 Railroad Avenue, Greenwich, CT 06830

Printed in the United States of America

Contents

3 • YOUR FAMILY—YOUR HOME

4 • SMART MONEY MANAGEMENT

5 • INSURANCE SAVVY

6 • TAX SMARTS

7 • SUCCESS IN THE OFFICE

8 • THE WINNING EDGE

9 • INVESTMENT SAVVY

10 • RETIREMENT PLANNING

11 • ENJOYING YOUR LEISURE

12 • ESTATE PLANNING

13 • VERY, VERY PERSONAL

14 • NUTRITION, FITNESS AND EXERCISE

1

Your Health
Your Well-Being

How to Diagnose Yourself—When Your Doctor Can't

Few experiences are as frustrating as having a chronic health problem that your doctor can't identify.

If the doctor cannot diagnose the problem, you must either learn to live with the symptoms …or go on to another doctor.

Trap: The more doctors a patient consults with, the less seriously each new doctor is likely to take the patient's complaints.

Eventually, even the patient begins to doubt the reality of the symptoms…while remaining debilitated by them. The fear that he/she may be neurotic adds to the problem.

I know about this phenomenon first-hand. I came down with a mysterious and incapacitating illness that turned out—after six years and nearly 30 doctors—to be Lyme disease.

In consulting with a seemingly endless procession of specialists, I learned how important it is to take an active role in the search for a diagnosis. I also found out what to do to get respect and cooperation from doctors—many of whom were skeptical of my symptoms.

The lessons I learned during my search for a diagnosis should be helpful to anyone who is sick but doesn't know why—people in what I call the *pre-diagnosis* period of a long illness.

Trust your instincts:

Our society has a need to categorize. We tend to doubt the reality of anything we can't label.

This is certainly true of most doctors. It's also true of friends and relatives, who may have difficulty being supportive of someone whose condition has no name. It helps to know that you're not alone. Many, many illnesses can take months or years to diagnose.

Recently, I surveyed 180 patients in support groups for five different chronic illnesses. *What I found:* The average time between the onset of symptoms and diagnosis was five years.

Lyme disease isn't the only disease that's often misdiagnosed. Others include lupus, colon cancer, ovarian cancer and Parkinson's disease.

Several things changed once I learned to believe in myself—to accept that I had a real illness even though no one knew what it was. I began to feel less desperate. I learned to cope with my mysterious symptoms. And because I no longer had anything to prove, I stopped acting defensive with doctors.

Example: When a doctor suggested that my illness might be psychogenic (originating in the mind), I no longer jumped to deny it. Instead, I calmly said, "I've had psychological problems at certain times in my life, but I can't believe that is what's causing all of these symptoms." The doctor considered my symptoms and my attitude, then replied, "You're right. This is not a psychological problem."

Find the right doctor:

Even if he/she can't diagnose your illness, the right doctor can help you sort out what's wrong.

Your doctor can refer you to specialists, analyze medical opinions and test results and help you manage your symptoms as you await a correct diagnosis and appropriate treatment.

To find the right doctor, get referrals from friends and acquaintances—especially people who work in the medical profession.

Tell them you're looking for a doctor who is compassionate, understanding and willing to take time with patients. Say you want someone who will encourage you to ask questions and be involved in decision-making about your own care.

You're also looking for someone who enjoys being a medical detective. Not every doctor does. You may have to interview several before you find one who takes you seriously and with whom you have a good rapport.

During your first meeting with a prospective doctor, make it clear that you don't expect him/her to have all the answers. Doctors get frustrated, too. If the doctor knows you're looking for someone to help manage your symptoms and guide your search, he/she will be less likely to feel put on the spot—or to brush you off as neurotic.

Examine your records:

Don't assume that you know what's in your medical file. Reviewing your test results and doctors' notes may reveal startling discrepancies...or new avenues to explore.

Problem: Specialists reviewing your file may not always see the big picture—how their findings fit in with those of other specialists. Doctors may record information that's different from what they told you...or from what you meant to relay. Test results may be ambiguous or incomplete.

Example: Three years before my diagnosis, my blood was tested for several illnesses, including Lyme disease. I was told at the time that all the tests came back normal. So, for the next three years I told doctors that I'd tested negative for Lyme. Later, I learned that the Lyme test had never been performed—the state lab had sent a note saying that no such test was available in Minnesota. If I had examined the file, I would have given doctors the correct information and I might have been diagnosed years earlier.

Medical records are usually easy to obtain. Simply request them from the doctor's office or the medical records department of your hospital or clinic. A simple medical dictionary will help you interpret jargon. Some places may ask you to sign a release form and/or pay a small copying fee.

Learn about medications:

Be sure you understand the possible side effects of all drugs prescribed for you. Understand, too, their potential interactions with other medications.

The pamphlets that drug companies put out about their medications are extremely thorough. Ask your pharmacist for copies.

Use the library:

You may discover valuable clues about your illness by doing your own research.

Many hospital and university medical libraries are open to the public. Some general libraries have medical collections. Ask the librarian to steer you toward relevant reference books, journals and databases. Phone the library ahead to find out what times are least busy. Look up your symptoms and their possible causes in diagnostic textbooks.

If your doctor has mentioned possible diagnoses, read about those conditions. Journals frequently include case histories of people with specific diseases or symptoms—the articles are often listed by subject in databases.

Provide your doctor with any scientific article that you think might help him/her with the diagnosis.

For more information on library research, read *Ask Your Doctor, Ask Yourself* by Annette Thornhill Schiffer (Publishing Ltd., 77 Lower Valley Rd., Atglen, Pennsylvania 19310).

Another good source of medical information is the *Health Resource* (209 Katherine Dr., Conway, Arkansas 72032. 501-329-5272). This service will research the relevant medical literature for you, then send you a report of up to 150 pages in length.

Learn to live with uncertainty:

Learn to accept your illness without giving up your search for answers. Acknowledge that your symptoms are real. Don't worry about the future—focus on one day at a time. Try to experience joy even in the midst of uncertainty.

This attitude fosters the relaxed open-mindedness that makes a good detective. It also helps you cope more effectively with your symptoms.

Important: If you stay reasonably relaxed rather than tensing up when symptoms flare up, the discomfort is likely to be of shorter duration and less intense.

Acceptance also helps you notice your body's signals and enables you to respond to them appropriately—whether by eating more nutritiously or taking a nap in the afternoon. You'll be a more effective partner with your body as it works toward healing.

Source: Linda Hanner, coauthor of *When You're Sick and Don't Know Why,* Chronimed Publishing, 13911 Ridgedale Dr., Minneapolis 55343. For information on a national support network now being set up for people with undiagnosed illnesses, write to the author at Box 307, Delano, Minnesota 55328.

Better Help from The Doctor

Be specific when phoning your doctor about your medical problem. Nurses report that when patients are vague—saying they're just not feeling well or have a question—doctors are less likely to return their calls. *Helpful:* Describe the nature, duration and location of symptoms and any medication you have taken. This gives the doctor a "running start" in diagnosing the problem and an idea of how much time the return call will take.

Source: Bruce Yaffe, MD, in private practice, New York.

Choosing a Doctor Made Much Easier

If you think the smartest way to pick a family doctor is to obtain referrals from friends or coworkers, think again. No matter how good their intentions, your friends and coworkers are poorly equipped to evaluate a doctor's medical skills.

After all, a first-rate doctor might be poorly regarded by patients simply because he/she occasionally seems brusque or uncaring. Or a doctor with only marginal skills might come highly recommended just because he has a very pleasant waiting room or a genial bedside manner.

And—a doctor who is ideal for one patient might be wholly inappropriate for another. Doctors are "good" only if they meet your individual needs.

First step:

The most effective way to find a new internist or family doctor (as opposed to a specialist) is to work backward—that is, consider your own medical needs first.

•Think about what particular area of expertise would be of greatest value. This criterion should be based on your age, sex, medical risk factors and medical history.

Example I: A generally healthy person might pick a doctor who is board-certified in one of the four key primary-care specialties: Internal medicine, family practice, pediatrics or gynecology.

Example II: A person who has existing health problems or who is at risk for such problems might want to choose someone who specializes in treating those problems.

•Determine which hospital in your area is best suited to provide this care. In most large communities, this will be a university-affiliated teaching hospital, one with hundreds of beds, sophisticated diagnostic equipment and a large staff of doctors, nurses and medical specialists. Such hospitals are sometimes called "tertiary" hospitals because they accept referrals of difficult or unusual cases.

Even better: A "sentinel" hospital, such as Massachusetts General Hospital in Boston, the Mayo Clinic in Rochester, Minnesota, or Memorial Sloan-Kettering Cancer Center in New York City. These institutions have a range of top-notch doctors on staff and excellent facilities. They can provide you with superb medical care —or refer you to a top-quality doctor and/or hospital in your area.

Problem: Small hospitals with fewer than 100 beds, especially those in rural areas. These are often limited in the type of care they can provide.

•Once you've chosen a hospital, call the appropriate department there and ask to speak to the department chief or head nurse. Explain your situation, then request the names of several board-certified doctors who might be willing to take you on as a patient. Contact each doctor and set up a brief interview, by phone or in person.

Sizing up a doctor:

Because the doctors whose names you've obtained were recommended by experts and are affiliated with a first-rate hospital, they've already been screened. So even the "worst" doctor on the list is no doubt perfectly competent. Nevertheless, the interview gives you a chance to find the best one for your needs. *Consider...*

•Credentials. Though a diploma from a prestigious medical school is no guarantee of stellar medical skills, it is reassuring. So is having completed a fellowship at a distinguished institution.

Note: If the doctor has been practicing for a decade or longer, find out whether he/she has been recertified. Seventeen of the 23 boards of internal medicine nationwide now periodically recertify their members. While recertification is not mandatory—nor is it a definitive indication of a doctor's ability or quality one way or the other—it shows that he cared enough to have it done.

•Professionalism. In most states it's virtually impossible to find out if a particular doctor has

ever been officially sanctioned for misconduct …but it doesn't hurt to call your state medical board to ask.

If the board declines to provide any information, contact the Public Citizen Health Research Group, 2000 P St. NW, Washington, DC 20036. It publishes "10,289 Questionable Doctors," a list of practitioners who have been disciplined by state medical boards.

•Personality. Some patients like a tough, authoritarian doctor who tells them what to do and makes sure they do it. Others prefer a doctor who makes decisions jointly with his patients.

Opportunity: Make sure the doctor is basically optimistic. Pessimism robs patients of hope—and hope is sometimes the only thing that pulls a person through a life-threatening illness or injury.

•Humility. No matter how vast his/her medical knowledge and experience, every doctor eventually confronts an ailment for which he has no solution. In such cases, the doctor should be humble enough to admit uncertainty…and should help "quarterback" patients' exploration of alternative treatments.

Tragic: I've seen too many patients get outdated or even dangerous care simply because their doctors had grown so accustomed to one particular form of treatment that they were unwilling even to consider newer, better forms. Find out what approach the doctor would take if you developed an incurable ailment.

•Experience. All other things being equal, the best doctors generally are those who have the most experience in treating the sorts of medical problems that you're most likely to develop. Ask the doctor if he treats many patients whose circumstances are similar to your own.

•Clout. A good doctor makes sure his patients get the treatment they need when they need it. If you have a heart attack, for instance, you need more than a good cardiologist. You need a good cardiologist capable of immediately summoning the best cardiac surgeons and lining up a bed in a first-rate cardiac intensive care unit. Ask the doctor to describe what would happen if you had such a medical crisis.

Finally, if you belong to a health-maintenance organization (HMO) or managed health-care plan, your options will be more limited.

But the same principles still apply. Choose an HMO on the strength of the doctors and hospitals it permits you to use—not because it's conveniently located or inexpensive or because it pays for comparative "frills" like eyeglasses or dental care.

Source: Robert Arnot, MD, chief medical editor of the *CBS Evening News*, New York City. He is the author of *The Best Medicine: How to Choose the Top Doctors, the Top Hospitals and the Top Treatments*, Addison-Wesley, One Jacob Way, Reading, Massachusetts 01867.

Listing All Medications

List all of the medications you take when giving a doctor your medical history. *Problem:* Many people don't consider vitamin and mineral supplements and herbal preparations to be "drugs"…but some of these remedies may be dangerous. *Examples:* The amino-acid supplement L-tryptophan has been linked to severe muscle pain…and the herb chaparral has been linked to hepatitis.

Source: Stuart L. Nightingale, MD, associate commissioner for health affairs, Food and Drug Administration, Rockville, Maryland. His recommendation was published in the *Journal of the American Medical Association*, 515 N. State St., Chicago 60610.

How to Get the Most for Your Medical Dollar

While it's no surprise that Americans spend too much on medical care, few consumers are aware of just how much money they're wasting on diagnostic tests, drugs, doctor's visits, etc. *Biggest areas of overspending:*

Doctors' fees:

Patients often forget that doctors are businesspeople. While the services they offer are different from those offered by car dealers and real-estate brokers, your goal should be to get the best service for the lowest price.

Every day we negotiate prices with suppliers. The same should be true with those who supply our medical care. Ask questions and nego-tiate with your physician. The more you ask, the more information you'll receive—and the better decisions you'll make.

If you think you're being overcharged by your doctor for office visits or medical procedures, discuss your concerns with the doctor. Try to get a better price. Don't allow yourself to be steered to an assistant or bookkeeper. The physician is supplying the services, and he/she is responsible for what they cost.

Diagnostic tests:

Even the most routine examination often results in the physician suggesting one or more diagnostic tests.

Some tests are useful and necessary—for example, an X ray or MRI scan to check for a broken bone. But 40% are unnecessary. Close to half of the $20 billion a year Americans spend on diagnostic tests is wasted.

Scandal: Many doctors have a financial stake in diagnostic labs, either through direct ownership of the lab or because they may receive a payment for each referral patient.

To protect yourself: Never leave the doctor's office without asking the rationale for the recommended diagnostic test. Find out what the test is intended to find—or to rule out. If you're told that one test might prove inconclusive and that a second test might need to be done, ask your doctor to consider skipping straight to the second test.

Also, make sure you receive a copy of test results directly. Don't let your doctor call you "only if there's trouble." Reviewing test results with your doctor will help ensure that no problems have been overlooked.

Be especially careful if you are hospitalized. When patients check into their rooms, staff doctors often order a new round of diagnostic tests—without first checking to see if these patients have already undergone these tests.

Trap: Hospital patients wind up having to pay for duplicate tests—which can easily cost thousands of dollars.

To avoid duplicate tests, ask your physician to share with the hospital staff the results of all medical tests he/she ordered. And double-check with the hospital physician about what any newly ordered test is supposed to do.

Follow-up office visits:

Doctors often suggest a follow-up visit just to check up on a patient's progress—and they often charge the standard fee even if no additional treatment is necessary.

Example: A pediatrician prescribes a drug to treat your child's ear infection, then tells you to bring the child back for an office visit in 10 days. You pay $40 for the first visit and $20 to $30 for the follow-up—even though it consists of nothing more than a 10-second peek in your child's ear. If that's all there is to the follow-up visit, ask your doctor if he/she would be willing to accept a reduced fee. Rather than haggling, many doctors will agree to look in an ear or listen to a set of lungs for $10 or less—perhaps even for free.

Prescription drugs:

There are several ways to save money here…

•Buy generic drugs. They cost as much as 80% less than brand-name drugs.

Caution: A generic drug may be slightly more or less potent than its brand-name counterpart. If you have a chronic heart condition or another ailment that requires a very precise level of medication in the bloodstream, be sure to ask your doctor if switching medications is safe.

Bottom line: If your doctor insists on a brand name, ask why. If you're not convinced, go generic.

•Buy only a two- to three-day supply of drugs. Doctors often prescribe 10 days or more of a particular drug—even though you might have an adverse reaction to the drug after only a day or two. *Result:* You wind up being stuck with a week's worth of a drug you cannot take. *Lesson:* Don't overbuy.

•Inform your doctor of any medical condition that might affect your tolerance to a particular drug—or if you're taking another drug that might interact with the newly prescribed drug. About $2 billion a year is spent on drugs that treat the adverse effects of other drugs.

•Comparison-shop. Call several pharmacies, especially those in discount stores. Some offer prescriptions below cost to entice customers into the store. Your doctor might have some ideas on finding the best deals.

Medical specialists:

Just because you've used a high-cost specialist in the past doesn't mean you must return in the future.

Examples: If you consult an ear, nose and throat specialist for a difficult sinus problem, there's no need to go back to that specialist for a simple cold or allergy. A general practitioner (GP) can take care of those problems for far less. Women often go to gynecologists for complaints that a GP could easily handle—doubling or even tripling the cost of the office visit.

Bottom line: Pick your doctor on the basis of your problem—see a general practitioner whenever possible. If the GP recommends a specialist, ask why. Doctors occasionally "hand off" patients to specialist colleagues—just to give their friends a little business.

Billing errors:

Although it's easy to check a simple bill from your personal doctor, hospital bills are often so confusing that they defy comprehension. That's too bad, because 90% of these bills contain errors—75% of which favor the hospital.

Common mistakes: Being billed for a private room when you actually had roommates… being billed for a circumcision—when you gave birth to a girl. And hospitals routinely charge thousands of dollars under the category of "pharmacy" with no itemization of the drugs for which they're billing you.

Many patients are so intimidated that they blindly pay bills—squandering hundreds or thousands of dollars.

Better: Delay paying the hospital bill until several days after the day you are discharged. When you check out, tell the billing office you'll pay it after you've had a chance to scrutinize the bill. For any charge you don't understand, call the billing department and request an explanation. Be sure to get an itemized list of all charges—and don't pay up until you're satisfied that all charges are accurate.

Payoff: With some hospital stays costing tens of thousands of dollars, catching just a few errors can produce big savings for you.

Hospital administrators are aware of billing problems, and in many cases they'll adjust your bill when you challenge their fees. If the hospital refuses to adjust your bill, withhold payment for that portion under dispute. If that fails, contact your insurance company and ask for help.

If you're still unhappy, ask your congressional representative to intervene on your behalf. With the health-care industry under fire, insurance companies are particularly sensitive to the threat of negative publicity.

You can also reduce hospital bills by taking a few prudent steps before you check in. Hospitals are notorious for overcharging for simple items —anywhere from $1 for an aspirin to $16 for a plastic water pitcher. To avoid these exorbitant charges, bring your own pitcher, aspirin, pillow, etc. If possible, have your prescriptions filled by a less expensive pharmacy outside the hospital.

Source: Charles B. Inlander, president of the People's Medical Society, a consumer advocacy group based in Allentown, Pennsylvania. His most recent book is *Good Operations, Bad Operations,* Viking Books, 375 Hudson St., New York 10014.

Reduce Hospital Medication Errors

Reduce hospital medication errors by speaking up before treatment…asking for individually wrapped unit-dose medications, when available …taking enough time at discharge to verify and understand all prescriptions…using only one pharmacy and developing a relationship with the pharmacist—to make sure you are not given multiple forms of the same prescription…and being alert to possible drug interactions.

Source: Neil Davis, PharmD, cofounder, Institute for Safe Medication Practices, Huntingdon Valley, Pennsylvania, quoted in *People's Medical Society Newsletter,* 462 Walnut St., Allentown, Pennsylvania 18102.

Aspirin Miracle— Much Better Health For $1.83 a Year

A remarkable, inexpensive key to better health is probably right in your medicine cabi-

net. It's called acetylsalicylic acid—better known as aspirin.

Research suggests that one aspirin tablet, taken every other day, helps reduce risk of heart attack, certain kinds of stroke, cancer of the gastrointestinal tract and possibly Alzheimer's disease, among other serious ailments. All this for $1.83 per year—less than a penny a day.

Caution: Aspirin is not a substitute for healthy habits like eating a balanced diet, exercising regularly or not smoking, nor should it be taken regularly without your doctor's approval.

About aspirin:

Aspirin's active ingredient, salicin, occurs naturally in the willow tree. Willow leaves and bark have been used to relieve pain and inflammation at least since the time of Hippocrates.

Aspirin was first made commercially in Germany at the turn of the century. If it had first been synthesized today instead of a century ago, odds are it would be available only by prescription. *Reason:* Aspirin is far more complex and powerful than many people realize.

Inexpensive generic aspirin is just as effective as more costly brands. In fact, there's less difference than you might imagine. Although there are many brand names of aspirin for sale in the US, all the salicin found in these aspirin formulations is made by just six companies.

How aspirin works:

No one knows exactly how aspirin works. It seems to interfere with the production of prostaglandins, hormones made by the body in response to injury. Aspirin seems to reduce the pain and swelling caused by prostaglandins.

Prostaglandins are also involved in blood-clotting. By blocking prostaglandin synthesis, aspirin acts as an anticoagulant. That probably accounts for its effectiveness against heart attack and stroke.

Aspirin also seems to prevent atherosclerosis, the buildup of fatty deposits in the arteries. However, it cannot reverse atherosclerosis.

Aspirin and heart attack:

In the 1950s, doctors first observed that patients who took aspirin for pain while recovering from a heart attack were less likely to have a second attack.

Supporting data on aspirin's preventive value comes from the *Physicians' Health Study,* a five-year study of more than 22,000 male doctors between the ages of 40 and 84.

Half of the subjects took a standard five-grain aspirin tablet every other day. *Result:* Subjects older than 50 who took aspirin were 44% less likely to suffer a heart attack than were similar men given a placebo (sugar pill).

If the group who took aspirin had also been eating well and getting moderate exercise, even fewer might have had heart attacks.

Researchers looked only at men. However, a subsequent study of female nurses suggests that aspirin also helps prevent heart attacks in women.

Another study found that coronary care unit patients given aspirin immediately after a heart attack were about 25% more likely to survive the attack than patients who did not receive aspirin.

Evidence also suggests that an aspirin a day lowers the risk of a second attack.

Aspirin and stroke:

Most strokes occur as a result of atherosclerosis. When arteries are narrowed, even a tiny blood clot can block blood flow to the brain, thereby depriving the tissue of oxygen.

Aspirin apparently fights stroke by preventing atherosclerosis and thinning the blood, which helps prevent blood clots.

One warning sign of impending stroke—sometimes the only warning—is a transient ischemic attack (TIA). This temporary deficiency of blood in the brain is caused by a blockage of blood flow or by a piece of arterial plaque or a blood clot that lodges in a blood vessel inside the brain. *Symptoms:* Weakness, numbness, dizziness, blurred vision, difficulty in speaking.

A study by Dr. James C. Grottar (published in the January 28, 1988, issue of the *New England Journal of Medicine*) showed that taking aspirin after a TIA cuts the risk of stroke by 25% to 30%. Although aspirin is often prescribed for TIA, it is not usually appropriate for anyone with high blood pressure or an increased risk of hemorrhage.

Aspirin and colon cancer:

Cancers of the colon and rectum account for roughly one out of five cancer deaths in the US.

In 1991, the *Journal of the National Cancer Institute* reported that people who took aspirin or other nonsteroidal anti-inflammatory drugs

at least four days a week for three months halved their risk of colorectal cancer. The results held for men and women across a broad range of ages.

A recent Emory University study suggested that taking one aspirin a week significantly reduces the risk of these cancers. Another study found a 50% reduction in the colon-cancer death rate among daily aspirin takers.

But another study of older subjects (average age 73) showed that frequent aspirin users face a heightened risk of kidney and colon cancer, as well as of heart attack. More research is needed. But—at least for younger patients, the preliminary findings are promising.

Aspirin and Alzheimer's disease:

A University of British Columbia scientist recently observed during autopsies of arthritis patients—who tend to take a great deal of aspirin—that their brains showed fewer than expected signs of Alzheimer's disease.

This observation certainly doesn't prove that aspirin prevents Alzheimer's. However, it does suggest an important avenue for future research. *Also:*

Though aspirin isn't very helpful in relieving migraine pain, it may help prevent migraines. Preliminary research suggests that migraine sufferers who take aspirin regularly may be able to reduce their headaches by as much as 20%.

Aspirin seems to stimulate the production of interferon and interleukin-2—immunity-boosting proteins produced inside the body. This may explain why aspirin may prevent certain kinds of cancer…and suggests that it could be used in the fight against other immune disorders.

Finally, some evidence suggests that aspirin helps prevent cataracts, diabetes and gallstones. As with other possible uses of aspirin, these potential uses of aspirin require further study.

Aspirin precautions:

•If you're thinking about starting an aspirin regimen, check with your doctor first. This is especially important if you're taking anticoagulants…if you have diabetes, gout or arthritis… or if you are taking any other over-the-counter or prescription drug.

Caution: Aspirin should generally be avoided by anyone with asthma…ulcers or other chronic stomach problems…or an allergy to aspirin.

• If you're pregnant or nursing an infant, take aspirin only with a doctor's consent. *Danger:* Aspirin taken during the last three months of pregnancy can injure the fetus or cause birth complications.

• If regular aspirin irritates your stomach, ask your doctor about buffered or coated aspirin. Also, tell your doctor if you experience ringing in the ears or hearing loss while taking aspirin.

• Drink with caution when taking aspirin. Aspirin boosts the concentration of alcohol in the blood. If you want to drive safely after a party, for instance, you may need to drink even less or wait longer than you normally would.

• Children should not be given aspirin without a doctor's approval. *Reason:* Aspirin has been linked to Reye's syndrome, a rare but potentially fatal brain disorder.

Source: Robert S. Persky, coauthor of *Penny Wonder Drug: What the Label on Your Aspirin Bottle Doesn't Tell You,* The Consultant Press, Ltd., 163 Amsterdam Ave. #201, New York 10023.

Stress Tests Aren't Always Reliable

These tests, which are supposed to spot potential heart trouble before it occurs are routinely recommended for men older than 40 and women older than 50 who wish to start an aerobic exercise program. *Problem:* In a recent study, only 4% of exercise-related heart problems were predicted in a group of men with high cholesterol who took the tests. *More:* Misleading results can lead to costly, unnecessary medical procedures. A thorough physical exam and medical history may be all that's required for middle-aged people starting an exercise program. Ask your doctor.

Source: Paul D. Thompson, MD, director, Preventive Cardiology, University of Pittsburgh.

How We Can Slow Our Aging Processes

Today, people are living longer, but enjoying it less. Many of us fear old age as a period of declining powers and failing health. But if we learn to replace that fear with a positive attitude, an enhanced physical and spiritual awareness of our bodies and a sensible pattern of activity, we can expect to enjoy the blessings of a vigorous and healthy old age.

A century ago, less than one person in ten reached the age of 65. Most of those who did live that long had been worn out by a lifetime of inadequate nutrition…widespread disease …backbreaking physical labor. Their remaining years were difficult not because they were old, but because their bodies were in a state of breakdown.

Today, relieved of those harsh external pressures, most of us will live well into our 60s and 70s…and the physical disease and mental breakdown we fear in old age is largely a result of internal stress we can learn to avoid.

People age differently:

Your well-being depends far less on your chronological age—how old you are according to the calendar—than on two other indicators…

• *Biological age* tells how old your body is in terms of critical life signs and cellular processes.

Every individual is affected differently by time…in fact, every cell and organ in your body ages on its own timetable.

Example: A middle-aged marathon runner may have leg muscles, heart and lungs of someone half his age, highly stressed knees and kidneys that are aging rapidly and eyesight and hearing declining on their own individual paths.

Most 20-year-olds look alike to a physiologist …but at 70, no two people have bodies that are remotely alike.

• *Psychological age* indicates how old you feel. Depending on what is happening in your life and your attitude to it, your psychological age can change dramatically within a very short period.

Examples: An old woman recalling her first love can suddenly look and sound as if she has just turned 18…a middle-aged man who loses his beloved wife can become a lonely old man within a few weeks.

Aging is reversible:

It is not news that psychological age can decrease. We all know the old proverb: "You are as old as you feel." And—now scientists have learned that biological aging can be reversed.

Example: Muscle mass is a key factor in the body's overall vitality…and it was believed until recently that it inevitably declined with increasing age. But Tufts University researchers discovered that isn't so. They put 12 men, aged 60–72, on a weight-training program. After three months, the men could lift heavier boxes than the 25-year-old workers in the lab…and milder weight-training programs proved equally successful for people over 95!

That's not all the good news for aging bodies. The Tufts team found that regular physical exercise also reverses nine other typical effects of biological age…

- Reduced strength.
- Lower metabolic rate.
- Excess body fat.
- Reduced aerobic capacity.
- Higher blood pressure.
- Lower blood-sugar tolerance.
- Higher cholesterol/HDL ratio.
- Reduced bone density.
- Poorer body temperature regulation.

To get optimum benefits from exercise, the type and amount have to be expertly tailored to your individual constitution. You don't have to be a fitness freak to gain from exercise…just 20 minutes of walking three times a week improves the cholesterol/HDL ratio. No expert advice is needed to benefit from another important route to longevity…a balanced lifestyle.

A study of 7,000 Southern Californians found that the longest-lived followed seven simple rules:

- Sleep seven to eight hours a night.
- Eat breakfast.
- Don't eat between meals.
- Don't be significantly over- or underweight.
- Engage in regular physical activity…sports …gardening…long walks.
- Drink moderately…not more than two alcoholic drinks a day.
- Don't smoke.

The study found that a 45-year-old man who followed these rules could expect to live another 33 years…but if he followed only three of them or less, he would probably die within 22 years.

Role of stress:

The human body reacts to stress by pumping adrenaline and other powerful hormones into the bloodstream. This "fight or flight" response provides energy for taking rapid action and is vital when you are actually faced with pressing external danger.

But it makes your metabolism work in the direction of breaking your body down instead of building it up.

If it occurs too often or continues too long it produces lasting harmful effects including muscle wasting…diabetes…fatigue…osteoporosis …hypertension…effects typical of aging.

That is why a major contribution to the aging process in modern life comes from situations that do not present real physical dangers but produce dangerous levels of stress.

Example: Our cities are full of unavoidable noise, a serious source of stress. Studies have shown increased levels of mental disorder in people who live under the flight paths near airports…elevated blood pressure in children who live near the Los Angeles airport…more violent behavior in noisy work environments.

Fortunately, we have discovered a number of measures that can reduce the aging effects of stress and other hazards of modern life.

To reduce stress and slow the aging process:

- Experience silence. Research has shown that people who meditate have higher levels of DHEA, a hormone that protects against stress and decreases with age. Spending 20 minutes twice a day in calm silence pays great benefits in detaching you from the mad bustle of the world and finding your true self.

- Avoid toxics…not only foods and drinks that stress your system, but relationships that produce anger and tension.

- Shed the need for approval by others…it's a sign of fear, another stress factor that promotes aging.

- Use relationships with others to learn your own self. People we love provide something we need…those we hate have something we need to get rid of.

•Change your inner dialogue. Change from "What's in it for me?" to "How can I help others?" Selfishness is bad for you. Psychologist Larry Scherwitz found that people who used the words "I," "me," "mine" most often in their conversations had the highest risk of heart disease.

•Be aware of your body's needs. The body only recognizes two signals…comfort and discomfort. You will be healthier if you learn to respond to its signals.

Example: Don't eat by the clock…eat when you're hungry…stop when you're full.

•Live in the moment. Much stress comes from living in the past or the future instead of the present.

Example: If you're angry at something that already happened…or fearful of something that may happen…your stress can't produce any useful result now. When those feelings occur, bring yourself back to the present.

•Become less judgmental. Don't get stressed by other people's decisions…your viewpoint may not be right for them.

•Stay in contact with nature. It will make you feel you want to stay around to enjoy it longer…and your body will respond.

Source: Deepak Chopra, MD, executive director for the Institute for Mind/Body Medicine, San Diego, California. He is the author of *Ageless Body, Timeless Mind: The Quantum Alternative to Growing Old,* Harmony Books, 201 E. 50 St., New York 10022.

Self-Help for Hemorrhoids

Stay regular. Constipation is a leading cause of hemorrhoid pain. *Helpful:* Lots of fiber and fluids, and regular exercise…clean the anal area thoroughly after a bowel movement (use premoistened wipes or toilet paper moistened with warm water)…take a "sitz bath" in plain warm water for ten minutes or so, three or four times daily…apply a water-based ointment, such as Balneol cream, to the area to soothe hemorrhoids and protect against further irritation.

Source: Bruce Yaffe, MD, in private practice, 121 E. 84 St., New York 10028.

Sinusitis Self-Defense

You thought you had recovered from your last cold, but you're still going through a box of tissues a day, trying to clear out the drainage from your nose. This could be sinusitis.

Sinusitis—what it really is:

When you have a cold, the linings of your nose and sinuses become inflamed. With the usual course of events, the linings form lots of clear mucus at first and later yellowish mucus. These secretions gradually disappear after you recover from the cold.

However, if one or more of the tiny openings through which sinuses drain becomes plugged, recovery is delayed and various symptoms appear. These symptoms include localized daytime headache and persistent yellow drainage —the symptoms of acute sinusitis. If the acute sinusitis does not heal, the patient will be left with the chronic form of sinusitis. That condition usually causes only persistent nasal drainage and "postnasal" drip but seldom causes headaches.

Acute sinusitis that does not clear quickly and chronic sinusitis require expert medical attention in order to avoid complications, some of which may be serious. Accurate diagnosis of sinusitis usually requires an X-ray examination.

Remember: Sinusitis does not cause nasal stuffiness and does not produce ordinary headaches. When headaches are caused by sinusitis, they are commonly localized over the affected sinuses, are accompanied by persistent nasal and postnasal drainage and tend to occur only during the daytime.

Other causes of sinusitis:

Sinusitis can be caused by diseases of the upper teeth, facial injuries, nasal polyps or tumors —all of which require medical attention.

Nasal allergies also are a problem, causing nasal stuffiness, drainage, a type of nasal polyp and sometimes headaches. When people with nasal allergies get colds, they are abnormally susceptible to sinusitis.

The differences between pressure inside and outside the sinuses cause some discomfort in daily activities. But when outside pressure changes dramatically, the pain can be excruciating. Divers feel it because water pressure is much higher than air pressure.

Air travelers are apt to experience the same pain when landing or taking off because of the rapid changes in the pressurized atmosphere of the plane.

Medication don'ts…and dos:

Pharmacy shelves bulge with a staggering array of medications for sinusitis.

•Antihistamines and decongestants. These are the popular over-the-counter remedies. But they are generally ineffective for sinusitis and tend to make it worse.

These drugs increase the thickness of mucus and slow the ability of the sinuses to clear themselves. Sometimes the sedative effect of antihistamines and the stimulant effects of oral decongestants balance out, but they usually don't work that way. Because of their ineffectiveness and adverse sinus effects, antihistamines and decongestants should be avoided. *Also:*

•Antihistamines are often recommended by doctors for people with nasal allergies, when they suffer from colds or sinusitis. However, they can cause drowsiness.

•Decongestants alleviate nasal stuffiness by constricting blood vessels and have very limited effects on the sinuses. Worse, they can cause insomnia and nervousness, elevate blood pressure and accelerate the heart.

•Aspirin and other analgesics temporarily relieve mild pain and reduce fever, but they do nothing to help. The physical state of the medication—hot or cold, liquid or solid—also has little effect in treating sinus inflammation, for the same reasons.

•Nasal spray. There is one type of over-the-counter medication that is useful for colds and sinusitis—a nasal spray containing oxymetazoline. It is marketed as Afrin, Duration and Neo-synephrine 12-Hour, among other brands. This spray is also helpful in preventing sinus and ear problems when you are flying and diving.

Important: It is unsafe to use nasal sprays more than twice daily for more than four days. If used too frequently, they cause a "rebound" stuffiness that can be worse than the original problem. If nasal congestion persists, spraying once a day for a few more days can help with-

out harmful rebound effects…but first check with your doctor.

If you need relief from nasal stuffiness, limit medication to nasal sprays—and only those containing oxymetazoline.

Air-travel precautions:

Ideally, you shouldn't fly with a cold or sinusitis, yet that's hardly practical. If it is necessary for you to fly with any condition in which you suspect your sinus cavities may be blocked, try an oxymetazoline spray 15 minutes before take-off.

This should provide relief for six hours or so. If your flight is longer than that, you may want to use the spray again 15 minutes before the plane descends.

Source: Charles P. Lebo, MD, who taught ear, nose and throat surgery at Stanford University and the University of California medical schools before retiring in 1993. He is the medical editor of *The Truth About Sinusitis* audiotape, New Life Options, 14431 Ventura Blvd., Suite 312, Sherman Oaks, California 91423.

Laxative Misuse Reason

Users believe they need daily bowel movements. *Reality:* People can have as few as three a week or as many as three a day, and still be considered regular. *Caution:* Long-term use of stimulative laxatives can cause cathartic bowel—which prevents the colon from contracting or moving properly and results in severe constipation. *Best way to stay regular:* Eat a balanced diet that includes 20 to 30 grams of fiber per day… exercise regularly.

Source: Stephen Collins, MD, chief, clinical division of gastroenterology, McMaster University, Hamilton, Ontario.

Placebo Effect Is Shown To Be Twice as Powerful As Expected

"Hurry, hurry—use the new drugs while they still work!" a 19th-century French physician urged his colleagues. He may not have known why faddish drugs work on credulous patients, but the fact that they do has been borne out by scientists studying the power of the placebo to cure.

Trusted physician power:

New findings show that the *placebo effect*—in which patients given an inactive treatment believe it can cure them—is most powerful when a trusted physician enthusiastically offers a patient a new therapy.

In a study of more than 6,000 patients being given experimental treatments for asthma, duodenal ulcer and herpes, two-thirds improved, at least temporarily, even though rigorous tests later found the treatments medically useless. They were then abandoned.

The old rule of thumb among medical researchers was that only about one-third of patients will show some improvement when given a placebo. The results of the new studies reveal the effect to be twice as powerful as was thought.

These and other findings that the placebo effect can be far stronger than had been widely assumed are leading some researchers to call for stricter standards for testing new medications. Others are proposing that physicians try to capitalize on the placebo effect in treating their patients in order to marshal the body's own healing powers.

"I argue that instead of just trying to control for placebo, we should try to maximize it," said Dr. Frederick Evans, a psychologist at the Robert Wood Johnson School of Medicine in New Brunswick, New Jersey. "If a doctor believes in what he's doing and lets the patient know that, that's good medicine."

While many people think a "placebo" is simply a sugar pill or other medicine with no active ingredients, the term has a broader meaning. The "placebo effect" includes any improvements in a patient not specifically due to a particular ingredient in a treatment, like a drug or surgical procedure. These "nonspecific," or placebo, effects may be due to causes ranging from a patient reporting relief from symptoms in a subconscious effort to please a well-liked physician, to actual biological improvement.

Testing the placebo effect:

To assess the potency of the placebo effect during the burst of enthusiasm for a new medical treatment, researchers reexamined data from initial clinical trials of five procedures that had at first seemed highly promising, and then later were shown to be useless. The procedures included surgical removal of the glomus—a structure near the carotid arteries in the neck—to treat asthma, and gastric freezing for duodenal ulcers. They also included three treatments for herpes simplex virus—the drug levamisole, organic solvents like ether and exposure of dyed herpes lesions to fluorescent light.

"In these studies, the doctors treating were also those evaluating the symptoms, which is what happens in a typical physician's office," said Dr. Alan H. Roberts, a psychologist at the Scripps Clinic and Research Foundation in La Jolla, California, who led the research. The results were published in a recent issue of *Clinical Psychology Review*.

Source: Daniel Goleman, PhD, is the former editor of *Psychology Today* and a fellow of The American Association for the Advancement of Science. He writes about health and human behavior for *The New York Times*.

Cancer Support Groups— To Live Longer... To Live Better

Despite all the hoopla over advances in drugs and surgery, one of the most powerful weapons we have against cancer is simply talking about it.

Study after study has shown that cancer patients who participate in support groups live longer than those who face the illness on their own. If you find that hard to believe, consider our recent study of women with breast cancer.

If detected early, breast cancer is easily treatable. Once the tumor has spread to other parts of the body, however, breast cancer must be thought of as a chronic rather than a curable illness, and the risk of dying from it is much higher. We decided to study how we might help women to face this threat honestly, but in such a way that it enriched their lives and those of their family members.

Our study, which began in 1985, involved 86 patients with advanced breast cancer who had undergone standard medical and surgical treatments for their disease. Fifty of the women were assigned to participate in a support group. Thirty-six "controls" did not participate in a group.

How support groups work:

Our first goal for the women participating in the support group was to help them establish a new social network. These women—many of them new to the process of psychotherapy—were facing death. They were grieving and in pain and feeling isolated.

At first, we worried that talking about their illness might make these women feel worse instead of better. And they were reluctant to discuss their feelings in a room full of people they did not know.

To help break the ice, we tried to foster an atmosphere in which it was possible to talk about the "hard stuff." We encouraged the women to focus on common experiences—things they shared rather than things that set them apart.

Example: Many women discovered they shared a fear of telling their husbands just how frightened they felt.

Living longer—and better:

Watching each other grapple with death helped these women in two ways. First, it showed them how to cope better with the specifics of disease and treatment. Second, it helped them learn to face their own mortality.

The women participating in the group gradually learned to air their true feelings and to accept the support of loving friends and families. They also learned self-hypnosis to "turn down" the pain and anxiety associated with cancer.

Eventually, they reached the point where they could say, "I don't like the idea of dying, and it will sadden me that I can't do what I've wanted to do in the world, and that I will not be with the people in my life I love and care about. However, I am going to make the most of the time I have left."

As a result of their participation, the women were less anxious and depressed. In addition,

they lived significantly longer than women who did not participate in the groups.

In fact, the average survival from diagnosis until death was 18.9 months for women who did not participate in the support group—and 36.6 months for the women who did. Two of the 86 original patients are still alive. Both were in the support group.

Our support group made living with cancer easier. The women in the group found they were not alone. As a result, they felt less fearful and less depressed. They were more likely to adhere to their treatment regimens. They ate better, slept better and exercised more than women not participating in the group—who, despite having a similar disease, tended to feel demoralized and alone.

Bottom line: Health care is more than just drugs, surgery and other methods of physical intervention. It's support from caring doctors and nurses—and often some kind of group counseling with other patients.

Psychological support pays:

In this country, we have long underemphasized compassion, support and stress management and overemphasized costly high-tech procedures. The latter are important, but they are only one portion of medical care.

In managed-care organizations, psychological support for medical illness is often considered an unnecessary expense. The fact is that such psychological support reduces unnecessary office visits and diagnostic tests because it helps patients deal better with a very serious illness.

Source: David Spiegel, MD, professor of behavioral sciences and director of the Psychological Treatment Laboratory, Stanford University School of Medicine, Palo Alto, California. He is the author of *Living Beyond Limits,* Times Books, 206 E. 50 St., New York 10022.

"Phantom" Aches And Pains

"Phantom" aches and pains may be caused by depression. *Background:* Doctors have often "diagnosed" as psychosomatic many fleeting disturbances for which they could not find causes. Now they realize depression causes a drop in neurotransmitter levels, which can bring on symptoms. *How it works:* Depression decreases salivation and slows down gastrointestinal activity. *Result:* Dry mouth, stomachache, gas, constipation. In a sense, the gastrointestinal tract itself is depressed.

Source: *You Mean I Don't Have to Feel This Way? New Help for Depression, Anxiety and Addiction* by Colette Dowling, New York health writer, Bantam Books, 1540 Broadway, New York 10036.

Depression—How to Spot It , How to Beat It

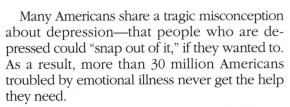

Many Americans share a tragic misconception about depression—that people who are depressed could "snap out of it," if they wanted to. As a result, more than 30 million Americans troubled by emotional illness never get the help they need.

The result is devastating. Sufferers feel hopeless, inadequate and unable to cope with daily life. Their self-esteem is shattered—and so are their ties with family and friends. What's more, depression is often lethal. Up to 30% of people with serious mood disorders kill themselves.

Feeling "blue" from time to time is a normal part of life—we all experience the sadness of failed relationships, the loss of loved ones, etc. Periods of sadness that are mild and short-lived do not require medical help.

Understanding:

But if enjoyable activities, the passing of time and confiding in friends, family or even psychotherapists fail to alleviate emotional pain, you may be suffering from a biological form of depression. Such disorders, triggered by chemical changes in the brain, call for medical treatment. They cannot be cured by talking to a therapist or reading a self-help book.

While the causes of depression are not fully understood, new technology has provided insight. Scientists believe that depressed people have decreased amounts of certain mood-regulating chemicals called neurotransmitters.

In most cases, depressive illness caused by such chemical imbalances is inherited. *Evidence:*

Children of depressed parents have a 20% to 25% risk of having a mood disorder. Children of nondepressed parents have a 5% risk.

Warning signs of depression:

If you have felt sad or down in the dumps in recent weeks, or if you've lost interest in many or all of your normal activities, you may be suffering from depression. *Warning signs:*

•Poor appetite or overeating.

•Insomnia.

•Sleeping more than usual.

•Chronic low energy or fatigue.

•Restlessness, feeling less active or talkative than usual, feeling "slowed down."

•Avoidance of other people.

•Reduced interest in sex and other pleasurable activities.

•Inability to derive pleasure from presents, praise, job promotions, etc.

•Feelings of inadequacy, low self-esteem or an increased level of self-criticism.

•Reduced levels of accomplishment at work, school or home.

•Feeling less able to cope with routine responsibilities.

•Poor concentration, having trouble making decisions.

If you're experiencing four or more of these, consult a doctor immediately.

Kinds of emotional illness:

The most common type of depression is unipolar illness, in which the person's mood is either normal or depressed. *Other common types:*

•Dysthymia. This condition is marked by a chronic mild state of depression. Sufferers of dysthymia experience little pleasure and are chronically fatigued and unresponsive. Sadly, many people suffering from dysthymia mistake their illness for a low-key personality…and never get the help they need.

•Manic depression. Patients whose periods of depression alternate with periods of euphoria are suffering from manic depression (bipolar disorder). During the "high" periods, manic-depressives may also have an inflated sense of self-esteem…a decreased need to sleep…a tendency to monopolize conversations…the feeling that their thoughts are racing…increased activity…impulsive behavior (including buying sprees, promiscuity, rash business decisions).

Though manic episodes sometimes occur when a person has never been depressed, they are frequently followed by severe depression. *Danger:* Manic-depressives often do not realize that they're ill, even though the problem may be obvious to family and friends. As with all forms of biological depression, manic depression calls for immediate treatment.

•Cyclothymia. A variant of manic depression, this disorder is characterized by less pronounced ups and downs. Like manic-depressives, cyclothymics are often unaware of their problem and must be encouraged to seek help.

Diagnosis and treatment:

First, have a complete physical exam to rule out any medical disorders. Certain ailments including thyroid disease and anemia can produce various symptoms that mimic depression.

If the exam suggests no underlying medical problem, ask for a referral to a psychopharmacologist—a psychiatrist who is trained in biological psychiatry. *Caution:* Nonphysician therapists, such as psychologists and social workers, lack medical training and cannot prescribe medication…and may be less adept at distinguishing between biological and psychological forms of depression.

When a biological form of depression is diagnosed, antidepressants should almost always be used as the first line of treatment. They completely relieve or lessen symptoms in more than 80% of people with severe emotional illness… and they are not addictive, nor do they make people "high." Once medications have brought the depression under control, however, psychotherapy often proves helpful—especially to patients embarrassed or demoralized by their illness.

Antidepressants:

Among the oldest and most effective antidepressants are the so-called tricyclics and monoamine oxidase inhibitors (MAOIs). These drugs are often very effective, but they must be used with caution.

Tricyclics have a wide range of side effects, including dry mouth, constipation, blurred vision and sexual difficulties. MAOIs must never be taken in combination with foods containing high levels of tyramine—such as aged cheese. Doing so causes a potentially dangerous rise in blood pressure. Other side effects include low blood pressure, sleep disturbances, weight gain and sexual difficulties.

Although these medications are still valuable in the treatment of depression, newer classes of drugs, including fluoxetine (Prozac), sertraline (Zoloft) and paroxetine (Paxil), are often superior. These new medications have few side effects, although some people who take the drugs complain of drowsiness or anxiety. *Note:* Despite one recent report claiming that Prozac caused some patients to attempt suicide, follow-up studies have not confirmed this finding.

For manic depression, the clear treatment of choice is lithium. Common minor side effects include diarrhea, a metallic taste in the mouth, increased frequency of urination, hand tremor and weight gain.

For seriously depressed or suicidal patients who do not respond to antidepressants, electroconvulsive therapy (ECT) is often a lifesaver. In this procedure, electrical current is applied to the brain via electrodes.

Sad: Many patients who stand to benefit from ECT refuse it altogether—because they consider it a brutal form of treatment. Today, however, patients receive a general anesthetic and a muscle relaxant prior to the application of current, so there's no emotional or physical trauma. Side effects—including slight confusion for several hours after treatment and occasionally memory loss—generally fade with time.

How to find the right help:

If your family doctor cannot recommend a good psychiatrist, contact the nearest medical school or teaching hospital. Many have a special treatment clinic for depression. Local branches of the American Psychiatric Association will provide names of psychiatrists in your area, but they cannot evaluate the psychiatrist's training in biological psychiatry.

The National Foundation for Depressive Illness (800-248-4344) gives referrals to psychiatrists interested in pharmacological treatment of mood disorders. Finally, additional information can be obtained from the National Depressive and Manic-Depressive Association (312-642-0049).

Source: Donald F. Klein, MD, professor of psychiatry at the Columbia University College of Physicians and Surgeons and director of research at the New York State Psychiatric Institute, both in New York City. Dr. Klein is coauthor of *Understanding Depression: A Complete Guide to Its Diagnosis and Treatment,* Oxford University Press, 200 Madison Ave., New York 10016.

Medicine-Bottle Trap

Cotton packed in bottles to keep pills from breaking during shipment can pass germs from one user to the next. This is one way that viruses and other illnesses are passed throughout a household. *Important:* Remove cotton when the medicine bottle is opened.

Source: Bruce Yaffe, MD, an internist in private practice, 121 E. 84 St., New York 10028.

Diabetes Danger

Poor self-testing of blood glucose levels could cause dangerous errors in therapy. Eighty percent of patients studied made procedural testing errors—even though 99% thought their technique was good. And 20% of the mistakes were enough to cause possibly dangerous errors in treatment.

Source: Study of 75 diabetes patients one month after class instruction in self-testing, led by Karen Berkowitz, RN, coordinator of diabetes education, Grady Memorial Hospital Diabetes Clinic, Atlanta, reported in *The Medical Post,* 777 Bay St., Toronto, Ontario M5W 1A7, Canada.

Exhaustion— What to Do When You Are Sick and Tired Of Being Tired

Fatigue runs a broad continuum, from occasional weariness to a debilitating condition known as chronic fatigue immune dysfunction syndrome.

Nearly everyone feels tired at some time… but at least two million Americans are now so fatigued that they are unable to lead productive lives.

Turn around tiredness:

One of the best tools for boosting your energy is a *fatigue diary*—a daily journal in which you jot down all your daily activities and your level of fatigue.

Your fatigue diary should include *everything* that you believe might be contributing to your fatigue. *Most common culprits:*

• Sleep problems. The leading source of fatigue is sleep deprivation—a condition that now affects about 30% of the adult population.

Self-protection: Refuse to let work and family commitments get in the way of a good night's sleep. Make your bedroom a cozy haven, free of drafts—and of reminders of work. Buy a new mattress, pillow, flannel sheets, etc…or do anything else necessary to make your bed more comfortable. Practice rhythmic breathing and other relaxation techniques before bedtime. If possible, take five- to 10-minute "power naps" during the day.

Avoid all sources of caffeine, especially after 5 PM. *Note:* One can of cola contains as much caffeine as half a cup of coffee.

Sleeping pills often make matters worse. *Danger:* Both sedatives (barbiturates) and hypnotics (benzodiazepines) are highly addictive. And they must be taken in increasingly large doses. *To avoid trouble:* If you use sleeping pills, schedule regular "drug holidays" to lessen the danger of addiction. *Even better:* Halve your usual sleeping pill dose. Start with a five-day trial period, then gradually wean yourself off pills entirely.

Best "sleeping pill" ever: Stress reduction.

In addition to insomnia, fatigue is sometimes caused by serious sleep disorders.

Examples: Narcolepsy (a tendency to nod off at inappropriate times) and apnea (a condition—often associated with heavy snoring—in which a sleeping person repeatedly stops breathing).

If you suffer from one of these conditions, ask your doctor to refer you to a sleep specialist. Be sure to take your fatigue diary along to the initial consultation.

•Smoking. Carbon monoxide and other toxins contained in tobacco smoke interfere with the oxygen-carrying capacity of red blood cells. Less oxygen to the cells means less energy.

Smoking also causes accumulation of mucus in the windpipe and bronchial tubes…and constricts blood vessels, impeding blood flow and further reducing the supply of oxygen and nutrients to cells.

Finally, nicotine dependence has also been linked to depression, which results not only in lower energy levels but also in insomnia and other sleep disorders.

Bottom line: Do whatever you need to do to quit smoking—nicotine patch, support group, smoking-cessation program.

•Drinking. Alcohol—a depressant—is a major contributor to chronic fatigue. It impairs coordination, clouds thinking and can cause depression—especially when taken in combination with tranquilizers or antihistamines. In addition, having several drinks can rob you of the essential nutrient thiamine. If you suspect that alcohol is contributing to your fatigue, own up to that possibility—and cut back on your drinking.

•Stress. Psychological stress is enormously draining. While it's not always possible to eliminate the sources of stress in your life, meditation, biofeedback and talking with a therapist or friend can help. *Also helpful:*

•If you hate parties, avoid forcing yourself into tense social situations. Learn how to say *no.*

•If your stress comes from boredom, take a class or learn a new skill.

•If a long commute by car knocks you out, use the time to listen to audiotapes of books.

•To reroute your thoughts away from your problems, donate time and energy to others.

•Negative emotions. Love and joy flood the body with energy-creating chemicals called endorphins. Fear, anger, frustration and other negative emotions drain your energy.

To fight bad feelings: Think of a book, movie or passage of music that has given you a lift—skim the book, rent the film, play the tape. Re-

call a recent mistake that weighs heavily on you—forgive yourself for it and move on. Make time to visit soothing places—an aquarium, zoo, museum, neighbor's house. Rediscover an old friend. Spend time together or initiate a correspondence—perhaps via computer.

In good weather, especially if you work in a sealed building or have no office window, go outside at least briefly during the day. Sunshine helps dispel depression.

•Medications. In many cases, aches and pains will intensify feelings of fatigue. So, one quick way to cut fatigue is to take an occasional aspirin.

On the other hand, many prescription and nonprescription drugs induce fatigue—especially antidepressants, antihistamines and blood-pressure drugs. While you may not be able to stop taking a particular drug, you might be able to find a substitute that does not cause fatigue. Ask your doctor about switching…or about tapering off a drug temporarily to see if that reduces your fatigue.

Fatigue can also be caused by interactions between drugs. *To avoid trouble:* Buy all your prescriptions at the same place. Pharmacists are expert at spotting potentially dangerous drug combinations—but they have to know all the drugs you're taking before they can help.

•Poor nutrition. To avoid fatigue caused by nutrition, eat food in the proper proportion—60% carbohydrates, 20% protein, 20% fat. *Caution:* Too much of the wrong kind of food is more likely to induce fatigue than too little of the right kind.

Strictly limit your intake of alcohol, sugar and fat. Ask your doctor if you should take a daily multivitamin.

•Insufficient exercise. Lack of exercise can cause fatigue just as surely as too much exercise. *For maximum energy:* Develop a fitness plan that pleases and invigorates you. You need not train for a triathlon—simple stretching might do. *Cheapest exercise:* Walking. Or join a health club or a local "Y" and go regularly.

If you have severe fatigue, check with a doctor before beginning an exercise program. The wrong kind or amount of exercise can exacerbate chronic fatigue immune dysfunction syndrome.

Review your diary for clues:

After a month, review your fatigue diary. Look for potential causes of fatigue and take steps to eliminate these causes. If you cannot find evidence linking specific behaviors to your fatigue, or if the changes you make don't help, use the diary instead as a guide for interacting with your doctor. *Note:* Because fatigue is so individualized and complex, doctors have a poor track record for treating it. Your notes should be helpful. In other cases where it's hard to pin down the cause of your fatigue, the answer could lie with a specific illness.

Severe, life-threatening diseases such as cancer and AIDS can cause fatigue. But so can several other easily treatable conditions. *Most widely known:* Anemia, arthritis, Lyme disease, heart disease, thyroid disorders, diabetes, breathing disorders, obesity, anorexia or bulimia.

Chronic infection is another common cause of fatigue. An overtaxed immune system drains energy meant for other endeavors. *Typical culprits:* Allergies…urinary-tract, yeast, fungal and sinus infections…mononucleosis.

See your doctor:

If you suspect you have a fatigue-causing illness, have a thorough physical exam. The examination should last at least 90 minutes and should include a complete blood count (to check for infection or anemia), an erythrocyte sedimentation rate (to check for infection or inflammation), routine chemistry assays (to screen for diseases of the thyroid and other organs) and a chest X ray (to check for tumors.)

If your fatigue is so severe that it makes daily living almost impossible, contact the Chronic Fatigue Immune Dysfunction Syndrome (CFIDS) Association of America, Box 220398, Charlotte, North Carolina 28222. 800-442-3437. It will provide general information about CFIDS, including details about local fatigue support groups.

Source: David S. Bell, MD, a pediatrician with a special interest in chronic fatigue. Affiliated with Harvard Medical School and Cambridge (Massachusetts) Hospital, Dr. Bell is coauthor of *Curing Fatigue: A Step-by-Step Plan to Uncover and Eliminate the Causes of Chronic Fatigue,* Rodale Press, 33 E. Minor St., Emmaus, Pennsylvania 18098, and author of *A Physician's Handbook of Chronic Fatigue Syndrome,* Addison-Wesley.

Always Sleepy?

Of all our body's basic needs, sleep is the most common casualty of our fast-paced culture.

Driven by demanding workday schedules, too many Americans "cheat" by cutting back on sleep during the week, trying to make up the loss on weekends. Others—up to 17% of all adults—suffer from a variety of chronic sleep disorders that remain largely untreated and overlooked.

Result: A sleep-deprived society whose citizens pay a price in reduced resistance to illness, lower energy and vigor, impaired concentration and memory, higher accident rates and lost productivity. Collectively, these problems cost the nation at least $50 billion a year.

People's needs for sleep vary considerably. Some get by with as little as five hours a night, while others need up to ten hours.

While getting an optimal amount is important, so is obtaining quality sleep. Some people lie in bed a sufficient length of time each night but sleep inefficiently, waking up for brief periods throughout the night. The intervals may be so fleeting that sleepers are unaware of them and mistakenly believe they have had an uninterrupted night's sleep.

Some of us sacrifice sleep by choice. Others are haunted by insomnia, finding it hard to fall asleep or return to sleep after waking up too early. Both fitful sleep and insomnia can stem from a variety of causes.

Problem: Doctors often fail to ask patients about their sleeping habits…and patients rarely link their malaise or fatigue to the quality of their sleep.

Spotting sleep problems:

Some people do without sleep better than others, though such tolerance usually declines with age.

Key question: How can you tell how much sleep you need or whether you're getting the right kind of rest?

Answer: Note how refreshed you feel when you awaken. If it takes more than 15 minutes to climb out of bed, you probably did not get quality sleep.

Keep track of how well you function during the day. If you have difficulty focusing, yawn frequently and depend on coffee, you may have to rethink your sleeping behavior.

Causes of poor sleep:

•Psychological stress. Persistent worry, anxiety or depression can leave sleepers' minds in high gear. Professional counseling that targets such underlying distress may result in more tranquil sleep.

•Poor sleep "hygiene." Caffeine, alcohol and nicotine can disrupt sleep. For some people, even one cup of coffee after a late lunch or early dinner leads to nighttime wakefulness. The same effect can also be caused by heavy meals …or by strenuous exercise late in the evening.

While alcohol helps people fall asleep, once it is metabolized it triggers more arousal intervals and ends up disrupting sleep, particularly during the latter part of the night.

•Primary sleep disorders. These can lead to chronic sleep deprivation and generally require medical attention. *Especially common:* Obstructive sleep apnea. This condition occurs when certain respiratory muscles relax too much during sleep, temporarily narrowing or blocking air passages. This restriction in airflow may trigger arousal so brief that the sleeper may be unaware that sleep was disrupted. This pattern may be repeated hundreds of times throughout the night.

As a result of these frequent interruptions, apnea sufferers never achieve continuous, efficient sleep. This failure causes them to feel tired much of the time. Sadly, they don't remember waking up during the night, so they may fail to link their daytime fatigue to sleep problems.

Besides inappropriate sleepiness, loud snoring (possibly accompanied by snorting, choking or gasping) is often a tip-off to sleep apnea. In severe apnea, considerable stress and strain are placed on the heart and lungs.

Apnea is especially common in overweight individuals. In some cases, simply losing weight may solve the problem. In other cases, apnea sufferers must wear a mask linked to a simple air compressor that provides just enough pressure to keep the airway open. Occasionally, surgery to remove excess throat tissue and create a larger airway is an option, as is the use of dental appliances.

Sleep self-defense:

If you're suffering from apnea or another primary sleep disorder, you need medical help. *Otherwise, ways to ensure a good night's sleep…*

•Watch what you eat. Cut back on alcohol, caffeine and nicotine—especially after early evening.

•Get regular aerobic exercise. It not only promotes relaxation but also spurs certain biochemical changes in the body that are conducive to restful sleep. *Caution:* Vigorous workouts before bed can leave you feeling "wired."

•Allow yourself time to unwind—physically and mentally—one to two hours before bedtime. Some people read. Others prefer soothing music or a favorite radio program.

•Unclutter your bedroom. Keep it free of daytime distractions. Fax machines, personal computers, etc., should be covered or kept out of sight—never placed on a nightstand. Screen out late-night business calls. Don't use your bed for eating or working. If you do, you'll find it hard to take a mental break from these activities.

•Keep your bedroom at a comfortable temperature—with adequate ventilation, minimal light and noise. If necessary, use shades and earplugs.

•Establish a regular sleep pattern. Go to sleep and awaken at the same time every day.

•Don't lie in bed awake. If you fail to fall asleep within 30 minutes, get up. Do a crossword puzzle or watch an especially dull TV program until you feel sleepy. Avoid clockwatching. That only heightens tension and anxiety.

•Nap during the early afternoon. Between noon and 2 PM is a "sleep-permissive" time—a secondary quiescent phase when the body has a natural appetite for sleep, even if nighttime rest was fitful.

While napping may make it harder to fall asleep at night, you won't need as much sleep come evening. As long as you meet your sleep quota over a 24-hour period, you'll be adequately rested.

Thus, an eight-hour sleeper may nap for one hour and sleep the remaining seven overnight.

Caution: The "24-hour" rule does not mean that you can simply "bank" lost weekday sleep and save it all for the weekend.

Sleep drugs:

A variety of medications are available. Some are sold over the counter and have few side effects. More potent drugs, including the benzodiazepines, are available only by prescription. Zolpiden, a new drug, is somewhat different from traditional sleeping medications. Such medications are used only for short periods of time.

Besides such common-sense advice, some new drugs show promise as valuable tools in treating sleep problems. One of the most intriguing is melatonin, an experimental drug derived from a natural substance that may be deficient in some elderly individuals.

Some people have also reported success with herbal remedies such as Valerian root, catnip, passion flower, etc. Finally, turkey and milk are good sources of tryptophan, another natural compound believed to have sleep-promoting properties.

Above all, take sleep seriously. Make it a priority in your life. Modify your bedtime behavior and become aware of conditions that might require professional care. That way you can help break undesirable habits and get the sleep you need to stay healthy and alert.

Source: Sanford H. Auerbach, MD, director, Sleep Disorders Center, Boston University Medical Center Hospital, and assistant professor of neurology and psychiatry, Boston University School of Medicine.

Pain-Relieving Ointments

Pain-relieving ointments do little to soothe sore muscles—and nothing to heal muscle strain. Their effect is more psychological than physiological. They work by mildly irritating the skin, and this pain takes your mind off the deeper muscle soreness. *Better remedies:* Ice, most heat and anti-inflammatories, such as aspirin or ibuprofen.

Source: Bill Band, PhD, PT, associate professor of physical therapy, University of Central Arkansas, Conway, Arkansas.

Even a Slightly Elevated Systolic Blood Pressure

Even a slightly elevated systolic blood pressure increases the risk of more advanced hypertension and heart disease. Systolic blood pressure is the top number in blood-pressure readings. Previously, such borderline systolic hypertension was not considered potentially harmful. *Findings:* Patients with systolic blood pressures between 140 and 159 and diastolic readings (the lower numbers) below 90 should be monitored carefully by a physician. These patients are good candidates for nondrug treatments, including exercise and dietary modifications. Further study is needed before drug treatment can be deemed appropriate. Patients with systolic blood pressures of more than 160 may need medication.

Source: Daniel Levy, MD, director of cardiology, Framingham Heart Study, Framingham, Massachusetts. His study was published in *The New England Journal of Medicine*, 10 Shattuck St., Boston 02115.

Maybe It's Yeast That's Causing Your Aches and Fatigue

New evidence suggests that many puzzling, chronic health problems resistant to treatment —from infections and allergies to the aches and exhaustion of chronic fatigue syndrome—are yeast-related.

One type of yeast is regularly found on the body's mucous membranes, especially the intestinal tract and vagina. When we talk about this kind of yeast, we usually mean *Candida albicans*, by far the predominant type found in the body.

In a healthy man or woman, candida (pronounced "can-did-a") is kept under control by so-called friendly bacteria living in the intestinal tract. But several factors can upset the yeast-to-bacteria balance—especially long-term use of broad-spectrum antibiotics. When this happens, yeasts grow out of control—leading to unpleasant symptoms.

Based on my critical review of continuing research, I believe there are three possible mechanisms for yeast's troublesome effects…

•Just as some people are allergic to pollens or mildew, some may be allergic to candida.

•Candida may produce certain toxins that are harmless in small amounts, but that in larger quantities weaken the immune system…leaving the body vulnerable to disease.

•Yeast overgrowth in the intestinal tract (candidiasis) may lead to changes in the intestine. In turn, these changes can cause the body to absorb and react to allergens in food.

The connection between yeast and health problems is highly controversial. Beginning with Dr. C. Orian Truss's article in the late '70s, a number of reports have linked yeast to illness, but the mainstream medical community remains skeptical.

Yet, my experience in treating hundreds of chronically ill patients, as well as similar experiences of a number of colleagues, suggests that a diet designed to curb yeast growth—along with certain antifungal medications—helps alleviate many symptoms that have proven resistant to other forms of treatment.

Do you have a yeast problem?

There is no simple diagnostic test for a yeast-related problem. For this reason, patients must undergo a thorough physical exam to rule out other possible causes of their symptoms. *Next step:* A complete medical history.

You may have a yeast problem if you…

…have used antibiotics repeatedly over a long period of time, such as for control of acne or recurrent infections.

…have taken corticosteroids. One known side effect of nasal cortisone spray is candidiasis of the nose.

…have used birth-control pills. Women on the Pill are far more prone than others to vaginal yeast infection.

…eat a high-sugar diet. A recent study at St. Jude Research Hospital in Memphis found that mice eating large quantities of the sugar glucose had 200 times as much candida in their intestinal tracts as did other mice.

…experience frequent digestive problems, such as abdominal pain, bloating, constipation or diarrhea.

…have a history of vaginal or urinary infections. Women develop yeast-related health problems far more often than men for a number of reasons. These include anatomical differences and hormonal changes associated with the menstrual cycle that promote yeast growth.

…have symptoms involving many parts of the body—for which usual examinations have not found a cause.

Treating a suspected yeast problem:

The cornerstone of treatment is a sugar-free diet. Yeasts in the digestive tract feed on sugar—and multiply. Some patients show remarkable improvement from dietary changes alone. Others need additional help—in the form of over-the-counter anti-yeast preparations sold in health-food stores…and, for more serious cases, from prescription antifungal medications.

The yeast-control diet:

•Eliminate sugar and other simple carbohydrates, such as honey and corn syrup.

•Avoid foods containing yeast or molds, such as cheese, vinegar, wine, beer and other fermented beverages and pickled or smoked meats. Although breads are probably safe, try eliminating yeast-leavened breads for a few weeks.

Note: Yeast-containing foods should be avoided not because intestinal yeast feeds on food yeast—it doesn't. But most people with candida-related problems are sensitive to yeast in foods and can have negative physical reactions. As the candida problem improves, the sensitivity may subside…and yeast can again be included in your diet.

•Strengthen your immune system by boosting your intake of vegetables, minimally processed whole grains and other wholesome foods. Eat lean rather than fatty meats, and cut back on other sources of fat. Avoid potentially harmful additives, including artificial colors and flavors.

Some physicians recommend eliminating fruits from the diet, because fruits are quickly converted to simple sugars inside the body. I believe fruits are safe—unless your yeast-related symptoms are severe. However, I do recommend avoiding commercially prepared fruit juices, which may be contaminated with mold.

Follow this recommended diet for at least three weeks. If your symptoms subside, resume eating forbidden foods one by one. If your symptoms flare up again after you add one of the forbidden foods, stop eating that food for good.

Good news: After they show significant improvement, most people find that they can follow a less rigid diet—and can occasionally consume a bit of sugar.

Over-the-counter remedies:

Many preparations sold in health-food stores can be a useful adjunct to the yeast-control diet...

•Citrus-seed extract, an antimicrobial substance made from tropical plants. Because the extract can irritate mucous membranes, it should be generously diluted with water before drinking.

•Caprylic acid, a saturated fatty acid available in tablet form. It helps keep yeast from reproducing.

Note: Some patients develop digestive problems or notice a slight worsening of yeast-related symptoms during the first week on this medication. If these don't go away within a few days, stop the medication and check with your doctor.

•Lactobacillus acidophilus, a friendly bacterium that helps restore the normal balance of intestinal flora. It is present in yogurt, especially homemade varieties. Store-bought yogurt that contains active cultures will be labeled to that effect. Be sure to buy only unsweetened varieties. Acidophilus is also available as a nutritional supplement.

•Garlic. This herb is known to stimulate the immune system...and at an international medical conference several years ago, researchers reported that garlic also seems to fight candida. Persons wary of the taste of cooked garlic—or its effect on the breath—should consider aged garlic extract (Kyolic), a deodorized supplement. It is widely available in local health-food stores.

Antifungal medications:

When a yeast-related symptom fails to respond to diet or supplements, prescription medication often helps—although the drug may take up to a year to have any effect in severe cases. *Drug options:*

•Nystatin (Mycostatin or Nilstat). In more than 30 years of use, this oral medication has demonstrated no toxic side effects. It knocks out candida in the intestines. It is not absorbed by the bloodstream, however, so it is ineffective against particularly severe cases of candidiasis.

•Fluconazole (Diflucan). This safe, highly effective antiyeast medication has been available in the US for about three years. Unlike nystatin, fluconazole is absorbed into the bloodstream.

•Itraconazole (Sporanox). This medication, a chemical "cousin" of fluconazole, was recently approved for use in the US. Although it appears to be quite safe, a related drug, ketoconazole (Nizoral) has been linked to liver damage.

Source: William G. Crook, MD, a fellow of the American College of Allergy and Immunology, the American Academy of Environmental Medicine and the American Academy of Pediatrics. He is the author of *The Yeast Connection* and *Chronic Fatigue Syndrome and the Yeast Connection,* both published by Professional Books, Inc., Box 3246, Jackson, Tennessee 38303.

Long-Distance Care for an Aging Parent or Relative

In today's highly mobile society, more and more Americans are called on to provide care for aging loved ones—from a distance.

Finding good care for an aging relative can be stressful under the best of circumstances... but it can be particularly worrisome when the caregiver isn't around to provide face-to-face support and follow-up.

Fortunately, there is a way to set up and monitor an effective plan from a distance.

First, discuss care options with the older person—while he or she is still in good health, if possible.

A decline in health and independence can occur quite suddenly. While you may not feel comfortable talking about these issues, it's much easier to discuss them before things have reached a crisis point.

The conversation—or series of conversations—can take place in person or by phone. Be gentle but persistent. Your relative may not want to face the subject any more than you do …or may not be straightforward about preferences for fear of being a burden to you.

Good way to begin: "Mom, I know you're doing great, but we're all getting older. I was just talking to my kids about how I'd like things to be handled if I couldn't take care of myself. If you were to become weak or ill, what would you want to have us do?"

Explore the older person's attitudes about various care arrangements, from in-home assistance to relocation to a partial- or full-care facility.

Also, try to get a sense of your relative's financial resources…and whether savings and insurance are sufficient to pay for future care.

Helpful questions:

• "What happened during your last doctor's visit? Perhaps we should give the pharmacist a list of your medications to make sure there are no dangerous interactions."

• "When was the last time you reviewed your will? It might be a good idea to make sure it is up to date."

• "How do you feel about _____ (a recent life change such as loss of a spouse, retirement, moving to a new home, etc.)?"

• "You look like you've lost/gained a few pounds since my last visit. How is your appetite?"

It's helpful to think of care-planning as a partnership between the older person and the caregiver. As much of the decision-making as possible should rest with the older person…with the goal of preserving his/her independence.

Start a care log:

A care log* is simply a loose-leaf notebook (or whatever filing method you prefer) that allows you to keep all the information about the older person's care in one place. You may want to set up sections for community resources, helpful friends and neighbors, travel (for your own visits), medical information and so on.

In the log, keep all your notes from phone conversations, as well as agency names and contact people, literature on available services and relevant medical, legal, insurance and financial papers.

*To order a care log with preprinted worksheets, send $14.95 (plus $3 postage) to American Source Books, Box 280353, Lakewood, Colorado 80228. 800-530-2080.

Your care log will help the entire planning process go more smoothly. If you're asked to provide eligibility data, such as Social Security cards, proof of income or medical insurance documents, you can get your hands on it quickly. And if you need to make an emergency visit, you can pick up your log and go.

Identify problems and needs:

If you live far away from your aging relative, you must be especially observant, both during phone conversations and when you visit. The older person won't necessarily make an announcement when health begins to decline or needs change.

Watch for potential danger signs, such as weight loss…difficulty in moving around…forgetfulness…decreased ability to perform basic chores like eating, bathing or taking medications properly.

Of course, your relative may be quite open about what the problems are. But one problem could have several possible causes. You may have to do a little digging to find out the best way to address the need.

Example: Your father isn't eating properly and is losing weight. If he's too weak to prepare food, then a Meals-on-Wheels program might be all he needs. But if the problem is ill-fitting dentures…or that he's too depressed and listless to eat…or that he can't see well enough to drive to the grocery store, then the solutions would be very different. You might need to have the dentures adjusted…find someone to sit with him to make mealtime less lonely and make sure he's eating…or arrange for assistance with food shopping.

In addition to your own observations, ask friends or neighbors for their views. Someone who visits often might be able to tell you…

• There's never any food in the house, or

• There's food, but it's not eaten, or

• I've noticed that when he's eating, his dentures keep slipping out.

The informal network:

In most cases, the older person is part of a network of friends, neighbors and associates who are already involved in lending a hand.

Examples: The mail carrier who makes sure your mother picks up her mail every day…a friend from the bridge club who offers a ride when needed…a young mother from the neighborhood who brings her toddler over for friendly visits.

These people can be valuable sources of assistance and reassurance. Ask your relative whom he/she sees on a regular basis.

Also, identify people who might be willing to help but haven't yet gotten involved.

Examples: Members of the person's church, synagogue or social clubs.

Call each person in the network. Introduce yourself, explain the needs that most concern you and find out if they'd be willing to help out on a consistent schedule.

Source: Angela Heath, MGS (master of gerontological studies), a nationally recognized author, lecturer and consultant on caregiving issues. She is the president of Heath and Company, a Washington, DC-based consulting firm that provides aging-related services to corporations, and the author of *Long Distance Caregiving: A Survival Guide for Far-Away Caregivers,* American Source Books, Box 280353, Lakewood, Colorado 80228.

How to Protect Yourself Against Your Drinking Water

Americans are concerned about their drinking water—and rightly so. Roughly 20% of households have dangerous levels of lead in their tap water…and the once sporadic cases of bacterial and industrial-chemical contamination seem to be occurring with increasing frequency.

Yet despite the real and ever-growing threat, there are effective ways to protect yourself and your family.

What's the biggest threat? By far the biggest threat is lead. Ingestion of lead causes a wide variety of serious health problems. Children who drink lead-tainted water often sustain irreversible brain damage—resulting in reduced IQ scores, short attention spans and other mental problems. (These problems are also common among infants born to mothers who drink lead-tainted water while pregnant.)

In adults, lead poisoning can cause kidney damage, high blood pressure and brittle bones. It can also cause brain damage, although adult neurological tissue is less sensitive to lead than children's neurological tissue.

Exposure of skin to lead-containing water—during a bath or shower, for example—is not considered dangerous.

How does lead get into tap water? It leaches into tap water as the water passes through lead-containing pipes or plumbing fixtures. Homes of all ages can show lead contamination from leaded solder joints or lead-alloy pipes.

Even if your water pipes are made of plastic, however, faucets may still be leaching lead into your drinking water. *Reason:* Even faucets touted as "lead-free" are allowed by federal law to contain up to 8% lead.

The lead can also come from outside your home. In some parts of the country—including parts of New York City, Boston, Chicago and the Pacific Northwest—the municipal water systems are built with lead-jointed pipes. Even water from private wells can be contaminated with lead.

Bottom line: Any home can have lead in its water.

What can I do to protect myself? Have your tap water tested. Your local water utility may provide you with a free test kit—or may be able to recommend a water-testing agency in your area.

Test kits are also available from…

•Suburban Water Testing Labs, 4600 Kutztown Rd., Temple, Pennsylvania 19560. 800-433-6595.

•National Testing Laboratories, 6555 Wilson Mills Rd., Cleveland 44143. 800-458-3330.

•Clean Water Lead Testing, 29½ Page Ave., Asheville, North Carolina 28801. 704-251-0518.

A typical test requires two water samples. The first sample is taken early in the morning, when the water has been sitting overnight in your home's pipes. The second is taken after the water has been running for one minute.

Even if the first sample contains dangerous concentrations of lead, the second sample will not in nine out of ten cases.

So I can eliminate the threat of lead simply by purging my water for one minute? Yes, in most cases. But purging your faucet once in the morning—the old advice—is not really valid. *Reason:* Lead leaches into water much more rapidly than previously thought. If it's been more than a few minutes since the last time you drew water, purge the tap again. To save time and water, keep a gallon pitcher of water from a purged tap in your refrigerator.

Can't I just boil my water? No. Although boiling water generally gets rid of bacteria, it does not eliminate lead or other heavy metals.

What if purging my tap water doesn't get rid of lead? Get a water-purification system...
•Cation-exchange filters remove 80% to 90% of lead. *Cost:* Less than $200.
•Reverse-osmosis filters remove 90% to 95% of lead. *Cost:* $300 to $400.
•Distillation units remove nearly 100% of lead. Unlike cation-exchange or reverse-osmosis systems, they do not need periodic filter-element changes. But unlike these other systems, distillation units do require electricity. *Cost:* $200 to $300—plus about $100 a year for electricity.

Caution: Filter makers generally specify a schedule for changing the filter elements on cation-exchange and reverse-osmosis units. But an element that lasts six months in one home might last half as long in a home with higher concentrations of lead.

Self-defense: Until you get a sense of how long the filter element lasts in your home, have your filtered water tested for lead every four months or so. Periodic testing is no longer necessary once you know how long the filter continues to work.

What about bottled water? Bottled water is another safe—and generally less costly—option. We've tested a variety of brands. All have proven safe with respect to lead. Just to be sure you're getting pure water, however, choose bottled spring water over bottled water from a municipal water supply. *Even better:* Distilled water. It's cheaper than spring water and should be absolutely free of lead or any other impurities.

What about germs? Very rarely do water supplies become contaminated with E. coli or other potentially harmful bacteria or parasites. When this happens, local water authorities are generally quick to alert people to the problem —which is easily solved by boiling your tap water or switching to bottled water until the microbes are eliminated.

Bacterial contamination is uncommon in the US because almost all municipal water is now chlorinated. Unfortunately, when chlorinated water comes into contact with dissolved organic matter commonly found in municipal water systems, trihalomethanes (THMs) and related compounds are created.

THMs are suspected of causing cancer of the colon, rectum and bladder. Federal regulations now set the maximum allowable THMs at 100 parts per billion (ppb), and this will likely be reduced to 50 ppb within the next couple of years.

How can I tell if my water contains dangerous levels of THMs? Contact your local water authority. If levels of THMs have approached or exceeded the 50 or 100 ppb level in recent months (or if you're simply worried about the accuracy of the water authority's records), just let water stand in an open container for at least six hours before using. Most of the THMs will dissipate if the water is exposed to air in this fashion.

Another way to get rid of THMs is via a granulated activated carbon (GAC) filter. *Cost:* $80 to $200. GAC filters remove more than 80% to 90% of THMs...and they are equally effective at filtering out most organic industrial pollutants that may have found their way into your tap water.

Caution: GAC filters do not remove lead.

Source: Richard P. Maas, PhD, associate professor of environmental studies, University of North Carolina, Asheville, and director of the university's Environmental Quality Institute, the nation's largest research center on tap water purity.

High Anxiety

High anxiety increases risk of high blood pressure in middle-aged men—but anger does not. *Also:* For middle-aged women, there is no apparent connection between high blood pressure and either anxiety or anger. *Self-defense:* Men who feel tense, nervous or restless should ask their doctors about anxiety-reducing behavioral or relaxation techniques.

Source: Jerome H. Markovitz, MD, assistant professor of medicine, University of Alabama School of Medicine, Birmingham. His 20-year study of 1,123 men and women was published in the *Journal of the American Medical Association,* 515 N. State St., Chicago 60610.

Simple Secrets of Being Healthier and Happier

Did you know that loosening your necktie or collar will improve your vision?

Indeed, according to Cornell University researchers, tightly knotted ties interfere with blood flow to the brain and eyes. So, computer operators, pilots, surgeons and other professionals who must pay close attention to visual detail should avoid confining neckwear. If you must wear a tie, make sure your shirt has plenty of neck room and leave the top button on your collar unfastened. Make the knot loose enough that you can slip a finger between your collar and neck.

Other ways to feel healthier, smarter and safer...

• Exercise in the morning. A recent study showed that 75% of morning exercisers were likely to still be at it one year later, compared to 50% of those who worked out at midday and 25% of the evening exercisers.

Explanation: As the day progresses, people are more apt to think of excuses for avoiding exercise.

• Minimize your exposure to pesticides. They have been linked to birth defects, nerve damage and cancer...yet pesticide use has doubled over the last 20 years. *Self-defense:* Wash fruits and vegetables in hot, soapy water—and rinse thoroughly. Buy US-grown produce whenever possible—imported produce is more apt to contain pesticide residues. Be especially careful when cleaning strawberries, peaches, cherries and apples.

• If you eat bacon, cook it in a microwave. Bacon cooked in a microwave contains lower levels of cancer-causing compounds called nitrites than bacon that is pan-fried or baked. Drain away as much fat as possible—bacon drippings contain twice the level of nitrites as the meat itself.

Vitamin C helps counter the cancer-causing effect of nitrosamines (which are formed when nitrites combine with amino acids in the stomach). People who eat bacon, ham, pepperoni, bologna or other nitrite-preserved meats should be sure to include oranges, tomatoes and other vitamin C-rich foods in their diet.

• Cure hiccups with sugar. Swallowing a teaspoon of sugar almost always does the trick. In a recent study published in the *New England Journal of Medicine*, sugar worked in 19 out of 20 people—some of whom had been hiccupping for as long as six weeks!

Other effective remedies: Grasping your tongue with your thumb and index finger and gently pulling it forward...swallowing a small amount of cracked ice...massaging the back of the roof of the mouth with a cotton swab...and eating dry bread slowly.

Caution: Hiccups that recur frequently or persist for more than a few minutes may be a tip-off to other health problems, including heart disease. Consult a doctor for such hiccups.

• Don't suppress a cough. Coughing is the body's way of clearing mucus and other debris from the lungs.

• To avoid motion sickness, close your eyes. Motion sickness occurs when your eyes and the motion-sensing system of the inner ear receive conflicting signals—the inner ear says you're moving in one direction while your eyes say you're going in another. Keeping eyes closed helps reduce the conflict.

If you're prone to motion sickness in cars, offer to drive. Like closing your eyes, keeping your eyes focused straight ahead on the road helps reduce queasiness. *Also helpful:* Air from the air conditioner or an open window directed toward your face.

• Don't aggravate a strained back. Many people use heat immediately after a minor back injury. But heat increases circulation to the area, causing increased swelling and inflammation. *Better:* To reduce swelling and pain in the first few days following a back strain, use cold compresses made of crushed ice wrapped in a towel. Keep the pack on for 20 minutes, then leave it off for 20. Repeat this cycle for two to three hours a day for three to four days. Only after this interval should heat be applied.

Caution: For severe or persistent back pain, consult a doctor.

• Eat fresh fruit. Fruit juice doesn't give you as much fiber—or vitamins and minerals—as whole fruit. Dietary fiber promotes regularity and helps regulate digestion of carbohydrates. The sugar in fruit is absorbed more slowly than the same sugar in fruit juice. The longer absorption time makes fruit more filling, a boon if you're watching your weight. This keeps your blood sugar levels stable, leaving you feeling more energetic.

• Don't drink tea if your blood is iron-poor. Tea contains tannins, compounds that inhibit iron absorption. (Herbal tea is okay.) *To raise iron levels:* Eat more green, leafy vegetables, lean red meat, poultry, fish, wheat germ, oysters, fruit and iron-fortified cereal. Foods rich in vitamin C help your body absorb iron from other foods.

• Stop snoring—with a tennis ball. Sewn into the back of the snorer's pajama top, it discourages sleeping on the back, a major trigger of snoring. *Also helpful:* Using blocks to raise the head of your bed…or using pillows to elevate the snorer's head.

• Use a cookie jar to lose weight. But—instead of cookies, fill the jar with slips of paper reminding you to do some calorie-burning activity, like going for a walk or gardening.

• Make exercise a game. If you're a swimmer, for example, see how long it takes you to "swim the English Channel." If you swim in a standard 75-foot pool, you'll have to do 1,478 laps to go the 21 miles from Dover to Calais. For stair-climbers, reaching the 29,028-foot summit of Mt. Everest takes 49,762 stairs. Be creative in whatever form of exercise you pursue, and you'll be more apt to stick with it.

• Be careful when shoveling snow. To avoid back injury or heart attack, keep knees bent and both feet firmly planted…push the snow aside instead of lifting it up…protect head and hands from the cold and avoid caffeine or alcohol before going outdoors.

• Develop a "cancer-resistant" personality. Although this finding remains controversial, cancer seems to be more prevalent among people who take a hopeless, helpless view of life, suppress their feelings, allow anger to build and have long-standing unresolved conflicts with loved ones.

A lifetime of built-up emotions may cause a release of hormones that interferes with the body's natural defenses against disease. To reduce the risk, actively try to solve problems within your control. Don't hold grudges.

Researchers have found that people who survive cancer or live longer with the disease tend to be feisty, demanding and emotionally expressive.

Source: Don R. Powell, PhD, president and founder of the American Institute for Preventive Medicine, Farmington Hills, Michigan. A licensed psychologist, he is the winner of numerous awards for his work in the health field and is the author of *365 Health Hints,* Simon & Schuster, 1230 Avenue of the Americas, New York 10020. The book was written in consultation with physicians, dieticians, exercise physiologists and other health-care professionals.

Alzheimer's Early Warning

An inability to name particular odors. A general decline in the sense of smell can also be a sign of the disease…although such a decline can also be the result of normal aging. Diminished sense of smell affects half of those older than 65…and 75% of those older than 80. *Other causes of loss of smell:* Head trauma…recurrent viral illness…Parkinson's disease.

Source: Alan R. Hirsch, MD, neurologic director, The Smell and Taste Treatment and Research Foundation, Chicago.

Coping with Alzheimer's

I was diagnosed with Alzheimer's disease three years ago at age 53, but my symptoms began in my mid-40s.

I started suffering from memory loss, confusion and disorientation. At first the problems were so minor that they were easy to dismiss.

Then one day, I became lost in my own neighborhood—for four hours. I'd lived here for 26 years! That's when I went to see a neurologist.

I'm not alone. Four to five million Americans have Alzheimer's. Perhaps as many as 10% of this number are, like me, "early-onset" patients. We want so much to pass as normal because the disease carries such a stigma, especially when you're young. Here's what I've learned that will help other patients and their families cope…

• Be persistent in your search for a diagnosis. I had a battery of tests—including electro-encephalography (EEG) and magnetic resonance imaging (MRI)—but my doctor couldn't make a diagnosis. He saw how bothered I was and told me to get some counseling for my nerves. And he prescribed tranquilizers. Unfortunately, my problem persisted…so I picked up my lab reports and all other records, then found another doctor. If your doctor is dismissive of your symptoms, you should do exactly the same thing.

• Have someone accompany you to doctor's appointments. The testing procedures for Alzheimer's aren't particularly unpleasant. However, the very fact that you're being tested for this debilitating disease is unnerving. And you're scared because even if you don't know exactly what they're looking for, you know it isn't good.

• Share your diagnosis with family and close friends. Patients like to fool themselves into thinking no one knows anything is wrong. Because of the trauma and emotional upheaval associated with this disease, most try to stay in the closet. I did—at first. I was afraid of being found out, but keeping it a secret only added to my shame. I finally said, "I'm here, and I have nothing to be ashamed of." Letting it out was a tremendous relief.

• Don't expect too much from those around you. Otherwise, you may be disappointed. Caregivers are caught up between denial and compassion—between not wanting to believe it's true and wanting to assure us that everything will be all right.

When I told my family that I had Alzheimer's, they said things like, "I don't think that's true—they've made a mistake," and "You don't have anything to worry about for a long time, you're doing real well." It would have been nicer to hear, "I'm sorry. Is there anything I can do for you?" Denial is very common. My family is still wrestling with it.

All the patients I've spoken to say they thought they had a lot of friends—and found out they had a lot of acquaintances. The family reorganizes itself following a diagnosis of Alz-heimer's. After the reorganization, you seem to have less family than you did before. And it's simply because some people are unable to accept the truth.

• Consider family counseling. If your family reacts poorly or doesn't know how to react, get help as a group—and perhaps, individually.

Like most Alzheimer's patients, I speak slowly and pause frequently while talking. My husband started using a hand gesture to speed me up. He meant to help me…but I found this so unnerving that I eventually developed a stammer. I was reduced to the point where I could barely speak at all.

At first I thought my speechlessness was one more symptom of Alzheimer's. In fact, while Alzheimer's does cause speech problems, mine was an emotional symptom.

• Join a support group. Alzheimer's slowly robs its victims of self-esteem. I felt bad when I had to take early retirement…and because I can't cook the way I once did, I feel like I'm letting my husband down.

That's why it's wonderful to sit in a group of other Alzheimer's patients. It's the only time you feel normal, because no one is going to criticize you, tell you to hurry up or take something out of your hand and say, "I'll do that."

Support groups also give us an opportunity to endure, instead of "terminating"—which is our way of describing suicide. Best of all, we can laugh at ourselves. That's a great help.

• Don't fear changes in your sex drive. Alzheimer's often boosts the libido. For some couples, this is a problem. Others are grateful, because it gives them the chance to be as close and loving as they were as newlyweds. The husband of one patient I know refers to her condition as "good-timer's disease."

The accelerated desire for sex is short-lived. Most men become impotent. That is devastating for many couples—another reason to consider psychotherapy.

• Look into drug therapy. The anti-inflammatory drug I take has made me much sharper and brighter. They don't know why, but Alzheimer's appears to begin with inflammation. My hope is that anti-inflammatory drugs are not only boosting my quality of life now, but also slowing the inevitable progression of the disease.

The newly approved Alzheimer's drug Cognex (tacrine) has been getting a lot of press lately, but my neurologist will not prescribe it for me. He says it helps some patients—but makes others deteriorate faster.

Other drugs are available to relieve the anxiety, depression and insomnia that often accompany Alzheimer's, although they have no direct effect on the disease itself. I take an antidepressant and a nonbarbiturate sleep medication. (Because I'm so forgetful and could easily overdose, a barbiturate is out of the question.)

•Find ways to compensate for your losses. I post notes on the refrigerator reminding me of what I have to do each day. My husband calls to remind me to eat lunch because I frequently forget. I have maps to help me get to my support group meetings…and to my grandchildren's schools, just in case I receive a call that one is ill and needs to be picked up. I can't find my way even though they are in my neighborhood.

Most helpful: Hand-drawn maps. Commercially prepared maps are often useless to Alzheimer's patients because they provide far too much information for us to digest. Curiously, I can go to places that I haven't been to in 20 years because my long-term memory is clear. My short-term memory is what's lagging. My grocery store moved—and I can't find it without a map.

•Plan for your future. I've written a living will. In it, I stipulate that I don't want any medical heroics when I'm near death—no resuscitation, no tracheotomy. I've also stipulated that I should be given intravenous painkillers at the end—to stop the pain. Every Alzheimer's patient should consider drawing up such a will.

You can name who's going to be your guardian, set up a trust for your own care and name a trustee. If you don't do these things, someone else is going to make those decisions for you—and they'll probably be the wrong ones.

I also prepared an open letter to caregivers. I gave a copy to each of my children. The letter spells out exactly what sort of care I want at each stage of my illness.

Because I'm afraid of nursing homes, I want to remain in my own home as long as possible, even if that means someone has to take me to a respite center for the day, like child care. If I need round-the-clock care, I ask that it be provided by a family member—and that this family member be paid for the work.

•Keep your mind active. The more mental stimulation you get, the slower your deterioration. I use the word processor every day. I keep a journal, too. Some people do crossword puzzles or play along with the contestants on *Jeopardy!* or other television game shows.

My plea for myself and all other Alzheimer's patients is simply this—don't count us as dead or dying before we are. Support us. If you take away our dignity, you rob us of our spirit... and that's all that keeps us going.

Source: Diana Friel McGowin, founder of an early-onset Alzheimer's support group in Orlando, Florida, and author of *Living in the Labyrinth: A Personal Journey Through the Maze of Alzheimer's,* Delacorte Press, 1540 Broadway, New York 10036.

The Best Home Medical Tests

Not long ago, fever was about the only medical condition that could be easily diagnosed by a patient at home.

Today—a growing number of medical devices and test kits permit in-home testing of a variety of conditions. *Available now:*

•Thermometers. For low cost and reliability, nothing beats a traditional mercury thermometer. All homes should have one.

Digital thermometers—consisting of an electronic probe and a digital readout—are easier to read and about twice as fast as a mercury thermometer. *Cost:* Less than $10.

Faster still are infrared thermometers, which gauge temperature by bouncing a beam of light off the eardrum. They give readings in seconds. *Cost:* About $120.

Both of these electronic models make sense for families with fidgety children. But keep a mercury thermometer on hand just in case the batteries run down.

Not recommended: Adhesive-strip forehead thermometers. They're notoriously unreliable.

•Blood pressure monitors. Of the several types of monitors available, I recommend any unit that is equipped with an inflatable arm cuff. *Cost:* $20 to $180, depending upon whether the pressure reading is displayed on the traditional column of mercury, a pressure gauge or a digital readout. (The more expensive models can hold multiple readings in computer memory.)

Not recommended: Monitors that measure blood pressure from a finger inserted into a ring. They're usually more expensive and less reliable.

•Urinary-disorder test strips. Persons prone to urinary-tract disorders can often spot an infection in its earliest stages using chemically treated urine test strips.

The user dips the strip into a urine sample. A color change indicates the presence of any of several different substances that often signal trouble. Over-the-counter tests are available for blood sugar and ketones (compounds that suggest uncontrolled diabetes or other severe metabolic disturbances). To check for urine infections, your doctor might provide tests for nitrites, blood or protein. *Cost:* About $40 for 100 strips.

•Colon-cancer screening kits. These kits check for blood in the stool (fecal occult blood), a marker for colon cancer. Though once hailed as a convenient, low-cost screening tool, these kits have proven to be unreliable.

Problem: Not all tumors cause bleeding, and not all blood in the stool is caused by cancer. In addition, the color change intended to signal the presence of blood is often hard to see.

Bottom line: These kits should be used only under a doctor's direct supervision. When properly processed, as in a physician's office, one-third of colon cancers are detected.

•Pregnancy test kits. The latest kits give reliable results within five minutes, and they are effective within just days of a missed menstrual period. *Cost:* Less than $20 for a package of two.

All kits work on the same principle—the user places a urine sample on a test strip and watches for a color change that signals pregnancy.

Note: Single-step kits are easier to use than multistep kits (especially those that require mixing of chemicals). Check the expiration date printed on the box. Out-of-date kits are unreliable.

For maximum accuracy: Use the kit on the first urine specimen of the morning, when hormone levels are at their peak. If the test proves negative, repeat it a day or two later. These tests are 99% accurate.

•Ovulation predictor kits. Designed chiefly for couples having trouble conceiving, these kits pinpoint ovulation by measuring hormone levels in a woman's urine. Though generally reliable, they're far more costly than another reliable method of predicting ovulation—charting the woman's basal body temperature.

Important: Couples having trouble conceiving should see their doctors for thorough physical exams and, if necessary, instructions on keeping a temperature chart. Temperature needs to be taken before getting out of bed in the morning.

•Glucose monitors. These electronic devices give diabetics a fast, reliable method of monitoring the level of glucose in their blood. Several monitors are now available.

Easiest to use: The Johnson & Johnson One-Touch. The user simply inserts a test strip and adds a drop of blood. Glucose levels are indicated by an electronic display. *Cost:* Less than $150 for the monitor, plus $40 for 50 strips.

Source: Paul M. Fischer, MD, University Hospital, Augusta, Georgia. Dr. Fischer serves on an FDA advisory panel that oversees regulation of diagnostic tests and is editor of the *Journal of Family Practice,* 25 Van Zant St., Norwalk, Connecticut 06856.

Time-Released Niacin

Time-released niacin may be toxic when taken in high doses. It should be taken only under a doctor's supervision. In a recent study, the B vitamin—available over-the-counter and used by many to lower elevated LDL (bad) cholesterol levels—caused liver toxicity, fatigue and other side effects. Immediate-release niacin lowered high LDL cholesterol levels with fewer side effects...and was more effective at raising levels of HDL (good) cholesterol.

Source: James M. McKenney, PharmD, professor and chairman of pharmacy, Virginia Commonwealth University, Richmond.

Skin Wrinkles

Skin wrinkles can be removed safely and painlessly via a short burst of laser light. The new "ultra-pulse" laser is also effective against acne...brown spots...blotchy, sun-damaged skin...and scar tissue. The laser vaporizes the sun-damaged top layer of skin and "realigns" the underlying layers. *Cost:* $500 to $3,000, depending on the extent of treatment.

Source: Sand S. Milgraum, MD, clinical assistant professor of dermatology, University of Medicine and Dentistry of New Jersey–Robert Wood Johnson Medical School, New Brunswick. For more information about the ultra-pulse laser, call Dr. Milgraum at 908-613-0300.

It Pays to Prepare For Emergencies

Emergencies, of course, come without warning. But that doesn't mean you can't be prepared when they do arrive. *Steps to take now:*

• Familiarize yourself with the emergency rooms in your area. Look into freestanding urgent-care clinics as well as hospital emergency rooms. Ask your doctor which facility is best for which type of emergency—and chart his/her recommendations on a family bulletin board.

Know where the entrance and parking area are for each emergency facility recommended by your doctor. Go for a visit. Park in a visitor's space and go in and look around. If the admissions clerk is not busy, ask how things work in an emergency.

Call your county health department. Find out the rating of each local emergency room. Level 1 facilities offer only basic emergency care... Level 2 offer more advanced care...and Level 3 are comprehensive trauma centers capable of handling the most severe, life-threatening emergencies. *Caution:* If you go to a Level 3 center for a minor cut, you may have to wait in line behind people with more serious injuries.

• Always carry in your wallet...
  • Health insurance card.
  • Insurance company phone number.
• Your blood type, although it will be tested for verification anyway.
• A list of all medications you take regularly.
• Your doctor's name, address and phone number.
• A brief description—written and signed by your doctor—of any health condition that might affect emergency care.
• The name and phone number of any pharmacy where your medication history is on file—ideally one that is open 24 hours a day.
• Keep handy in your home—and tell everyone the location of...
• A comprehensive first-aid manual, such as the one published by the Red Cross and sold in bookstores. Be sure that it's up-to-date.
• Instructions for doing the Heimlich maneuver.
• A blood-pressure cuff.
• Literature on emergency treatment for any disease or condition relevant to anyone who lives or works regularly in your house—heart disease, epilepsy, asthma, etc.
• Always wear a bracelet or pendant describing any serious medical condition. *Examples:* Diabetes or severe allergies.
• Learn...
  • Basic first aid.
  • Cardiopulmonary resuscitation (CPR) for adults and children—especially if you have a pool.
  • The Heimlich maneuver.
  • How to take blood pressure—even if no one in your family is hypertensive.
• Tape to your telephones the numbers for...
  • Your family doctor and any medical specialists used by your family. List the specialty beside the name and number, just in case the caller doesn't know, for example, that Dr. Jones is a cardiologist.
  • Family dentist, orthodontist, endodontist, periodontist, etc.
  • Police and ambulance. Call ahead to inquire about the normal response time for each.
  • Private ambulance.
  • Fire department—for first aid as well as fires, in case neither your doctor nor your first-aid squad can be reached.
  • Poison-control center. Ask your hospital about the location of the nearest one.

- Emergency room.
- Family veterinarian and animal hospital.
- Neighbors who could be called at any hour, especially those who have a car.
- Read…
- All parts of your health insurance policy pertaining to emergency care. Make sure you know how soon after an emergency you must notify the insurance company…and whether your policy offers better coverage at certain hospitals.
- Your first-aid manual.
- For an elderly or infirm person…
- Sign him/her up with an emergency response system.
- Provide him with a portable telephone. Make sure he keeps the telephone charged and nearby at all times—especially if he is wheelchair-bound.
- Arrange with someone—neighbor, friend or commercial elder-care service representative—to check on the person each day.

Source: Neil Shulman, MD, associate professor of medicine, Emory University School of Medicine, Atlanta. He is the publisher of *Better Health Care for Less,* 2272 Vistamount Dr., Decatur, Georgia 30333. Dr. Shulman is coauthor of *Better Health Care for Less,* Hippocraene Books, 171 Madison Ave., New York 10016. He also wrote the novel *Doc Hollywood,* which was made into a movie.

Dry, Red Eyes

Dry, red eyes aren't always caused by irritation or lack of sleep. *Another possibility:* Rosacea, a progressive skin disease marked not only by facial redness, but occasionally by burning, stinging or a feeling that there's something in the eye. *Danger:* Severe cases of ocular rosacea can cause scarring and even vision loss. Although the condition cannot be cured it can be managed and controlled by oral antibiotics and possibly corticosteroid eye drops. See an ophthalmologist about any eye rash associated with redness, burning or itching that lasts from more than a couple of days.

Source: Jerome Z. Litt, MD, assistant clinical professor of dermatology, Case Western Reserve University School of Medicine, Cleveland.

First Aid Mistakes

One of the most frustrating aspects of working in emergency medicine is coping with people's botched attempts at administering first aid. Often they simply make the situation worse. Yet it's easy to give first aid properly if you learn a few basic rules. *Most common errors:*

- *Mistake:* Smearing butter or lard on a burn. Applying fat only intensifies the injury. Instead, run cold water over the burned area for 10 to 15 seconds. Then wrap it with a handkerchief or other clean, dry dressing. Seek medical care for any burn that is blistered…or in which decreased sensation exists…or which occurs around the mouth, nose, fingers or toes.
- *Mistake:* Moving someone's head after a neck injury. This can cause permanent paralysis. *Sad:* Most cases of paralysis result not from the initial injury, but from moving the injured person. Never move an injured person's head from side to side to "see if they're okay." Instead, tell the victim to lie still while you call an ambulance.
- *Mistake:* Insisting that "it couldn't be a heart attack." Anyone experiencing chest pain, nausea, excessive perspiration or shortness of breath needs immediate medical attention. Delaying treatment to see if symptoms "go away" can turn a survivable heart attack into a fatal one. *Don't drive yourself to the hospital.* Call an ambulance or have someone else drive you.
- *Mistake:* Holding down someone who can't breathe. Encourage the person to sit up. The intestines and diaphragm will descend, giving the lungs more room to expand.
- *Mistake:* Touching an electric shock victim. Always turn off the current *before* touching the victim—or you risk getting shocked yourself. If you cannot turn the current off, use a book, a dry wooden stick or some other nonconducting object (not metallic or wet) to push away the source of the current.

Examples: Hook the heel of a shoe over the wire and pull it off…separate the victim from the wire using a wooden-handled broom or a rolled-up newspaper or magazine.

Drag or gently push the person away from the source of the current. Call for help.

•*Mistake:* Applying a tourniquet to a minor cut. In most cases, bleeding can be controlled simply by applying pressure to the site, then applying a cold compress to help blood vessels constrict.

Tourniquets are appropriate *only* for life-threatening blood loss, as happens with a complete or partial amputation...or for bad cuts sustained in a remote area where help is not nearby.

To apply a tourniquet: Place a clean strip of cloth at least two inches wide between the wound and the rest of the body. Wrap it around the limb twice and tie a knot. Place a stick, pen or other straight, rigid object atop the knot and tie it in place. Twist the stick to tighten the tourniquet until the bleeding stops. Tie the loose ends of cloth around the stick to hold it in the tightened position. Do not loosen or remove the tourniquet while waiting for medical help.

Important: If you use a tourniquet, make sure you have cut off circulation only in the veins—not the arteries. Briefly press on a toenail or fingernail or indent a quarter-inch patch of skin on the "far" side of the tourniquet. If you've applied the tourniquet properly, the skin should turn white, then return to its normal color within a couple of seconds. If it doesn't, loosen the tourniquet slightly.

If a body part has been severed, seal it in a plastic bag and put the bag on ice. Never put the part directly on ice.

•*Mistake:* Overheating frostbitten fingers, toes or ears. Immersing the injured part in hot water only causes additional tissue damage. Instead, thaw it rapidly in water that's between 98°F (normal body temperature) and 110°F. Water that feels uncomfortably hot is too hot.

•*Mistake:* Overtreating a snakebite. A snakebite itself usually poses less of a risk than amateurs' efforts to treat it. They typically cut too deeply into the skin, severing arteries, tendons or nerves. And when they try to suck out the venom, they often contaminate the wound.

Instead: Keep the victim calm and as motionless as possible while he/she is transported to an emergency room. If you suspect the snake was poisonous, use a tourniquet to restrict venous circulation (and venom flow) between the bite and the victim's heart or main part of the body.

•*Mistake:* Hesitating to perform CPR. People often shy away from doing cardiopulmonary resuscitation because they can't remember the technique precisely—especially the ratio of chest compressions to breaths. (For two rescuers, it's five compressions for every "ventilation." For one rescuer, it's fifteen compressions for every two ventilations.)

Good news: Even imperfect CPR will help the person breathe and keep some of his/her blood circulating. Before you start, however, call for help.

•*Mistake:* Squeezing too hard or too long when performing the Heimlich maneuver. Squeezing the chest from the sides can break the person's ribs. *Correct procedure:* Stand behind the choking victim. Shove your fist up and in just above the navel. This will push the diaphragm upward. Then release. Repeat if necessary—but don't stand there squeezing.

Source: Stanley M. Zydlo, Jr., MD, director, department of emergency medicine, Northwest Community Hospital, Arlington Heights, Illinois. He is coauthor of *The American Medical Association Handbook of First Aid and Emergency Care: A Comprehensive Step-by-Step Guide to Dealing with Injuries, Illnesses and Medical Emergencies*, Random House, 201 E. 50 St., New York 10022.

Anti-Inflammatory Drugs

Anti-inflammatory drugs used to treat arthritis may also help prevent Alzheimer's disease. In a recent study, Alzheimer's was four times less common among individuals who used steroids, aspirin, ibuprofen or other anti-inflammatory drugs. *Caution:* Do not begin self-medicating in an effort to avoid Alzheimer's. These drugs can cause serious side effects and should be taken regularly only on the advice of a physician.

Source: John Breitner, MD, MPH, associate professor of psychiatry, Duke University School of Medicine, Durham, North Carolina. His study of 50 pairs of identical and fraternal twins was published in *Neurology*, 7500 Old Oak Blvd., Cleveland 44130.

Arthritis Can Be Controlled

Myths about arthritis abound. Many people assume that arthritis is inevitable with age… that it's invariably crippling…that it can't be treated.

Yet in my 20 years as a rheumatologist, I've rarely seen an arthritic patient who didn't feel much better after following a comprehensive course of treatment. Arthritis refers to inflammation in the joint. There are more than 100 different kinds of arthritis, which fall under two general categories:

•Inflammatory—including rheumatoid arthritis, which afflicts 2.5 million people in this country. This type starts in the membrane that lines the capsule surrounding a joint. Rheumatoid arthritis tends to affect many joints, as well as muscles, nerves or other parts of the body. Inflammatory conditions are systemic in nature and influence other parts of the body. Fatigue and flu-like symptoms are common. It most often has its onset in women between the ages of 30 and 50.

•Degenerative—or osteoarthritis, afflicting 36 million Americans. It is thought to result from natural wear and tear on joints and is more common in older adults…as well as younger people who have suffered sports injuries, accidents or other severe trauma to the joints.

Although we don't know the cause or cure for either type of arthritis, we have many, many resources for controlling it by relieving pain, restoring motion, slowing degeneration and helping patients lead normal and active lives.

Diagnosis and treatment:

Because there is so much prejudice about arthritis in the medical community, the disease is often incorrectly diagnosed. Just because a patient is older and has joint pain doesn't mean he/she has arthritis—and even if arthritis is present, it may not be what's causing the symptoms.

Bursitis (inflammation of the protective sac near a joint) and tendinitis (inflamed tendons) are treatable conditions that are frequently confused with arthritis.

Example: A patient complains that his right hip aches. Because the patient is 65, his doctor assumes he has arthritis. An X ray shows some wear on the hip joint, confirming the doctor's assumption. The physician says, "What do you expect at 65?" and puts him on anti-inflammatory drugs, which don't help him. In fact, the arthritis isn't causing the pain—this patient is actually suffering from bursitis, which could be easily treated with physical therapy or steroid injections.

I urge patients who are diagnosed with arthritis not to accept the attitude that nothing can be done for them. If a primary-care physician isn't sure about the diagnosis, or if treatment isn't successful in relieving symptoms, I recommend consulting a rheumatologist—a specialist in arthritic diseases.

The best approach to treating arthritis is a multi-modal one.

Medications help, but they are far more effective when used in conjunction with other factors, including physical therapy, exercise, adequate sleep, diet and stress management.

Mechanical devices such as splints and canes can also provide relief by resting the affected area.

Many of these elements are surprisingly simple—but often ignored. Common sense remedies the medical establishment once scorned as old wives' tales are now gaining scientific support.

Though new drugs are coming onto the market all the time, I believe the real news in treatment is validation of the old treatments.

Medication:

Physicians have a whole arsenal of drugs to draw from. Mild cases of osteoarthritis may respond to over-the-counter painkillers such as acetaminophen.

More severe cases of degenerative joint diseases and cases of rheumatoid arthritis are usually helped by anti-inflammatory drugs. Most of these can have side effects, such as stomach irritation, but so many varieties are available that doctor and patient can usually find one the patient can tolerate.

Nonprescription anti-inflammatories aren't usually strong enough in recommended doses to be effective against arthritis…and increasing the dose can lead to unpleasant side effects.

Talk to your doctor before taking—or increasing—any medication.

New: Capsaicin, a topical cream originally developed to treat shingles. Capsaicin is rubbed into the skin around the joint. Unlike other topical products, which provide only temporary relief, this cream appears to reduce concentrations of chemicals which lead to the pain response.

It must be used diligently—three to four times a day. Side effects can include a mild burning sensation. Capsaicin is available over the counter, but like any drug it should be used under a doctor's supervision.

For rheumatoid arthritis, gold compounds—taken orally or injected—have long been a mainstay of treatment. But these compounds have been associated with problems including rashes and kidney dysfunction—and must be closely monitored.

Other medications are also helpful for treating rheumatoid arthritis, chiefly antimalarial drugs and immunosuppressive agents—the kind used to treat cancer.

Physical therapy:

Physical therapists are vastly underutilized by physicians in general, and certainly where arthritis is concerned.

A physical therapist will often manipulate the affected area and prescribe therapeutic exercises for the patient to do at home—in order to restore use of the joints and the muscles and tendons supporting them.

Other techniques used by these health-care professionals include massage, application of heat or cold and electrical stimulation of surrounding nerves.

Exercise:

In addition to specific exercises prescribed by a physical therapist, people with arthritis can benefit dramatically from recreational exercise, such as walking, swimming or tennis. The typical patient might respond, "I can't even move without pain—how can I exercise?" But inactivity is likely to make arthritis worse, not better.

When you don't move a painful joint, the muscles around it begin to weaken and atrophy. Scar tissue may form, and you lose mobility.

Everyone—arthritic or not—should exercise 25 to 30 minutes, three or four times a week.

The key is to find the right window—enough exercise to be beneficial, but not so much as to cause great pain. It's a good idea to start very slowly—with ten minutes of walking, for example—and note how your body responds. If your joints hurt severely while you're working out, or you feel very uncomfortable afterward or the next morning, don't give up…just cut back to five minutes for a while. Then gradually increase the length of your workout to 30 minutes. To guard against overuse, consult with a doctor and physical therapist before you begin your program.

Diet:

Changes in diet have not generally been shown to help arthritis. *Exceptions:*

• In rare cases, eliminating certain foods from the diet, especially dairy products, provides relief for sufferers.

• Dark-meat fish—tuna, salmon, mackerel, bluefish, swordfish—are rich in oils that may have a positive anti-inflammatory effect on joints. This, though, hasn't been proven. Eating more fish can't hurt you (though I wouldn't recommend nothing but fish)…and might help.

Sleep:

The value of sleep in controlling pain is often overlooked. Arthritis patients often find themselves in a vicious cycle. Their joint pain makes sleeping difficult, and poor sleep in turn leads to more stiffness and pain.

I have found that very low doses of antidepressant medication can break this cycle by reducing chronic pain enough to ensure sound sleep.

Stress management:

Though there's no evidence that stress causes arthritis, it may make symptoms more noticeable or bothersome. Therefore, learning to deal effectively with stress is an essential part of a comprehensive treatment program.

Meditation, deep breathing or other relaxation techniques can be helpful. Yoga is gaining popularity as a relaxation method that's also good exercise.

Can arthritis be prevented?:

Theoretically, no—but there are steps we can take to reduce risk and slow progression of the disease…

• Maintain ideal weight. Obesity is a risk factor for osteoarthritis, possibly because greater weight causes more wear on the joints.

• Exercise regularly—to keep supporting muscles strong and joints moving smoothly.

• Seek medical attention early. If you notice recurring stiffness in a joint, or if it appears swollen, warm to the touch or red, see your physician. The sooner the problem is identified and treatment begun, the better the prognosis.

Source: Fred G. Kantrowitz, MD, who is on the faculty of the Harvard Medical School and the author of *Taking Control of Arthritis,* HarperPerennial, 10 E. 53 St., New York 10022.

What You May Not Know About High Blood Pressure

More than 40 million Americans—about 75% of whom are adults over age 30—have high blood pressure (hypertension). Yet too few understand what they can do to possibly prevent or treat it.

Many people with mild hypertension ignore the problem or fail to spot it soon enough through medical checkups.

Danger: By the time hypertension causes medical complications, heart health has already been put at risk.

What's normal, what's not:

An initial blood-pressure reading should be taken at about age three and again during adolescence. If your blood pressure is normal during this period, it should be rechecked every two or three years throughout your adult life.

If your blood pressure rises above 140/90, more frequent readings may be needed. Mild high blood pressure or Stage I—from 140/90 to 160/100—usually requires lifestyle changes. Medication may also be necessary.

Here's what you may or may not know about high blood pressure and how to control it…

• Being tense or nervous will not give you high blood pressure. The term hypertension refers to elevated pressure in the arteries, not to someone's personality. Many calm, cool-headed people have hypertension…many anxious, jittery people have perfectly normal blood pressures.

Nervousness may cause a short-term rise in blood pressure because of the adrenaline response. But there's no evidence that a nervous personality or even a stress-filled life causes hypertension.

• Blood pressure is variable. Your blood pressure does not remain constant. It can fluctuate by as much as 20 to 30 points a day.

Your blood pressure is at its highest during the early morning hours—just before and as you awaken—and when extra blood is needed, such as when you exercise.

It is at its lowest during sleep and restful times, dropping to the lowest point from about 1 AM to 4 AM.

• Blood pressure can change with the weather. Generally, your blood pressure drops during hot weather or when you're perspiring a lot. Warm weather causes blood vessels to dilate—and that lowers blood pressure.

In cold weather, blood-pressure readings may rise because blood vessels constrict. Unless weather conditions are extreme, the change isn't enough to be medically significant.

• Excessive alcohol consumption can increase risk. Moderate to heavy drinking (about three to five drinks daily) can raise blood pressure over the long term.

Reason: Though large amounts of alcohol may dilate blood vessels, which can lower blood pressure, drinking also increases the heart rate, which raises blood pressure and cancels the dilation effect. Alcohol can also affect certain hormone systems that regulate blood pressure.

Cutting back on alcohol can bring levels to within normal range in some individuals. One or two drinks daily generally does not affect blood pressure, and some researchers have found that small quantities of alcohol can protect against cardiovascular disease.

Treatment:

• Exercise is good—but not all kinds. For some people, mild, repetitive exercise over time helps reduce blood pressure slightly. For others, it reduces levels significantly. It is not necessary to take up jogging or join an exercise club unless you need or prefer a structured plan. Walking or other leisure activities are satisfactory.

Warning: Isometric (pushing) exercises, like weightlifting (free weights or weight machines), should be avoided by anyone with high blood pressure or heart disease. The tightened muscles constrict blood vessels and can raise blood pressure. Avoid inversion bars and "antigravity boots," from which you hang upside down and do sit-ups. This increases blood-pressure levels.

•Losing weight is the most effective nondrug method to reduce high blood pressure. Excess weight increases the volume of blood in the body, constricting blood vessels and putting extra demands on the heart, which elevates blood pressure. In some cases, losing as little as ten pounds can return blood-pressure levels to normal. If you plan to lose a significant amount of weight (more than 30 pounds), ask your doctor to monitor cardiovascular effects.

•Sex will not dramatically affect hypertension. Though sex can raise blood pressure temporarily—particularly with a new or unfamiliar partner—just minutes after the peak at orgasm, it will drop back to levels equivalent to or lower than before.

•Good nutrition can help keep levels in line. Lowering sodium intake helps some people with high blood pressure—about 20% or 30% of all cases. Others are hardly affected at all. Because most of us have too much salt in our diets, it's a good idea to cut back, regardless of your blood-pressure readings.

Best way: Be aware of salt in cooking and on the table, as well as hidden sources of sodium. Many processed foods that don't taste salty—soft drinks, ice cream, breakfast cereals—are high in sodium.

Other dietary factors: Potassium—found in fresh fruits and vegetables, unprocessed meats and fish—and calcium are thought to have protective effects. Adequate calcium—800 to 1,000 mg a day for adults—rather than high doses is best. The minimum daily intake of potassium is 2,000 mg, but 4,000 mg is optimal. Daily sodium intake should be about half that of potassium.

Source: Marvin Moser, MD, clinical professor of medicine, Yale University School of Medicine. He is the author of *Lower Your Blood Pressure and Live Longer* (Berkley, 200 Madison Ave., New York 10016) and *Week By Week to a Strong Heart* (Rodale Press, 33 E. Minor St., Emmaus, Pennsylvania 18098).

Winter Wellness

To help you get through winter as healthily as possible, three experts in the treatment of colds and flu give their advice…

•Dr. Jack Gwaltney—*virus self-defense:*

Every year when cold and flu season rolls around, we get some new information about the common cold to wonder about, take hope from or fret over.

Recently, both the popular and professional press have served up debate about stress—and how it may affect your susceptibility to the common cold.

First, it's important to understand that there are two distinct phases to the process of catching a cold. The first is becoming infected, and the second is becoming sick. Instead of coming out in a full-blown cold, some people may develop a symptomless or subclinical infection, which is common in many infectious diseases. How they get to you:

I'm not a great believer in the stress theory. I recently reviewed 15 years of clinical case studies in which 94% of individuals exposed to the common cold virus under laboratory conditions became infected.

Although those results do not leave much latitude for stress to play a role, it may still be possible that stress could tip the balance in favor of your becoming infected.

However, I believe it's more likely that, if stress does play a role, it might determine whether, once you become infected, you then develop the actual symptoms of a cold. About 25% of natural rhinovirus (the "common cold" virus) infections are of the "silent," symptomless type.

Why this is good news: If you get one of these subclinical infections, you may then acquire immunity and not develop the symptoms of a cold in response to subsequent exposure to that virus.

The most effective way to avoid catching a cold is to prevent the virus from getting into your eyes, nose or, in some cases, your mouth. Ideally, you should avoid all contact with infected individuals.

But if you are unwilling or unable to become a hermit for several months of the year, simply keep your hands clean…don't touch your face, especially your eyes, and don't put your fingers near your nose when you're around someone who obviously has a cold. No one knows exactly how cold viruses are spread, but the prevailing theories favor skin-to-skin contact or an airborne route via coughs and sneezes.

What if you're forced into close contact with someone—in an elevator, for example, or on public transit—who doesn't cover coughs and sneezes? Is simply turning away from that person an effective defense against infection?

That depends. Uncertainty remains over whether viruses spread through the air are transmitted in small particles (droplets of about one to two microns in diameter) that can float and remain suspended for a time, or in larger particles that are heavier and would therefore drop more quickly. Currently, the best evidence about the transmission of rhinovirus is that it's probably spread via large particles. So turning away from an uncovered cough or sneeze is useful, because those large particles will drop from the air around you.

The whole phenomenon of a "winter cold season" is intrinsically contradictory, because rhinovirus, which thrives in high humidity, is much more prevalent from mid-spring through summer and into early fall.

When the humidity begins to drop (about the beginning of October), the rhinovirus population tends to fall off significantly, and the viruses that do better in low humidity—parainfluenza virus, respiratory syncytial virus, influenza virus and corona virus—become more prevalent.

Bottom line: Whatever the weather conditions, there's a virus out there that's waiting to infect you.

•Dr. Bruce Yaffe—*on colds and flu:*

The simple truth about cold and flu season: The more people you're exposed to, the more likely you are to get a cold. And certain factors can increase your risk of becoming infected—for example, crowded classroom or office settings, indoor environments that are very dry and closed spaces, such as airplanes, in which the air-filtration systems constantly recirculate viruses (as well as lung irritants and indoor pollutants).

Cold and flu viruses may be transmitted through the air by coughs and sneezes, but about 50% of the time, viruses travel via hand-to-hand contact. Shaking hands with someone or sharing a telephone can transfer a dose of live cold virus to your hand.

Stop giving bugs a free ride: Wash your hands frequently, wipe a shared phone with alcohol before using it, and—most important—don't touch your face. (The mucous membranes that line the eyes, nose and mouth transmit viruses efficiently.)

The use of a hot-steam vaporizer at night may help prevent colds. People tend to breathe through their mouths when they sleep, which dries out mucous membranes and makes a person more susceptible to infection. When someone coughs on you in the elevator the next morning, those dry membranes will be more permeable to infecting organisms.

Trap: The use of humidifiers can be counterproductive when fungus and molds are allowed to grow in the water. People with allergies to household molds may develop excessive membrane swelling and increased mucus secretions, thereby decreasing their ability to fight off infection effectively. So if you use humidifiers, keep them meticulously clean.

It may be helpful to change toothbrushes periodically during cold season. You may be harboring a stockpile of viruses and bacteria in your brush. Another sensible thing to do in winter—as always—is to quit smoking. Smokers not only get more frequent viral infections… they get more prolonged and severe viral infections, with more secondary bacterial infections. Flu self-defense:

You can help to prevent influenza infection, of course, with an annual flu shot. Influenza is a type of virus usually prevalent between December and March. An influenza infection is characterized by high fever and a dry cough…it is much more severe than a "common cold." A flu shot can prevent the flu, although a small percentage of people will react to the shot by developing a sore arm and a low-grade viral syndrome that lasts for a day or two.

Helpful: Elderly people and people with chronic medical conditions (including diabetes or chronic respiratory diseases) should strongly consider flu shots. Everyone else should weigh the risk of catching the flu against the risk of developing a reaction to the shot. Reactions are rare and usually very mild. In this upcoming flu season, all adults should strongly consider a flu shot. *The good news:* Should you get an influenza infection, there is a drug—amantadine—that can treat it.

• Dr. Robban A. Sica-Cohen—*self-defense:*

Rather than sitting around waiting for the bug with your name on it to strike, it's important to take steps to increase your resistance to colds and flu when you know that cold season is coming.

I recommend decreasing your intake of sugar and refined carbohydrates, and increasing your intake of garlic, onions and cruciferous vegetables like broccoli and cauliflower. These vegetables contain natural antibiotics, as well as high amounts of vitamins A and C—both of which are important to immune system functioning.

Vitamin and mineral supplements may also be useful additions to your diet during cold and flu season. *Suggested daily dosages:* Vitamin C —2,000 to 4,000 mg/day…zinc, picolinate form (the most absorbable form)—25 mg/day… vitamin A in the form of beta-carotene—do not exceed 50,000 units/day. You should also take a multivitamin tablet with minerals added.

Good idea: Buy your vitamin and mineral supplements from a health-food store or reputable vitamin supplier. The products available in grocery stores and pharmacies are most often chemical-based, and some are bound in a waxy coating that makes the contents of the pills inaccessible to the body.

All your mother used to tell you about not getting chilled or overheated turns out to have significant implications for immune-system functioning. There is a close correlation between temperature and immune-system effectiveness —cold temperatures suppress the immune system. This is why you develop a fever when you get an infection—the body switches into high gear to fight off the invading organisms.

Caution: The benefits of these higher body temperatures level off after about 102.5° F.

I believe that the individual immune response, rather than the strength of the infecting organism, is the key factor in determining why some people get sick after exposure to a virus and some don't. I recommend the use of herbal remedies like echinacea and Golden Seal to strengthen the immune system. These preparations can be found in most health-food stores, and they apparently make you less susceptible to infection and may even be able to boost immune-system functioning after the symptoms of a cold appear. They should be taken in a "pulsed" manner. *Example:* Five days a week/ two days off.

The stress connection:

In view of recent evidence that stress may make you more susceptible to infection, I suggest that if you know you have a problem dealing with stress, you consider taking a course on relaxation exercises, biofeedback, meditation or another stress-management technique to control your body's physiological response to stress.

Flu season:

The duration and severity of the symptoms of influenza can be markedly decreased by a homeopathic remedy, oscillococcinum. Take one to three doses at the onset of symptoms. Available in health-food stores.

Sources: Jack Gwaltney, MD, professor, department of internal medicine, University of Virginia School of Medicine, Charlottesville, Virginia 22908. Bruce Yaffe, MD, internist in private practice, 121 E. 84 St., New York 10028. Robban A. Sica-Cohen, MD, private practitioner at the Center for the Healing Arts, 325 Boston Post Rd., Orange, Connecticut 06477.

Vitamin E

Vitamin E is still a good—and safe—stroke preventive, says Arthur Winter, MD. It's one of several dietary antioxidants—others are vitamins A and C, beta-carotene and selenium—that guard body tissues against deterioration due to age and pollution. While vitamin E is usually safe even at fairly high levels, large doses of vitamin A can be toxic. Before taking any antioxidant in pill form, check with your doctor. *The leading natural sources of vitamin E:* Walnuts, almonds, sunflower seeds…wheat germ…sweet potatoes…spinach.

Source: Arthur Winter, MD, assistant professor of neurosurgery, University of Medicine and Dentistry of New Jersey, Livingston. He is also director of the New Jersey Neurological Institute, Newark.

How to Use Imagery And Inner Wisdom To Conquer Illness

Though it would be overly simplistic to say that the mind causes—or cures—illness, it's clear that our emotions, attitudes and beliefs can influence our health…and that altering those thoughts and emotions can have a powerful effect on health as well.

Surprisingly, the most health-supporting emotional state seems not to be enthusiasm or even optimism, but serenity and peacefulness.

Body, mind and spirit:

In addition to exploring the role of the mind in promoting health, I believe it's equally important to consider the role of the spirit. When we're aware of the spiritual dimension of life, we have access to many powerful resources that aren't available when we limit our focus to mind and body.

It isn't necessary to practice a particular religion—or to hold any special theological views —in order to embrace the concept of spirituality. The dictionary refers to spirit as *life principle*…the force that gives us vitality, drives and motivates us and supports our survival.

I don't view work with the mind and spirit as a substitute for established Western medical practices. Humans are physical, as well as mental and spiritual, beings. All three aspects need to be addressed.

Your innate healing capacity:

At the Simonton Cancer Center, we have developed an effective group of techniques that can help patients mobilize their innate healing capacities. *Essential elements of the program…*

•Social support and communication. Your support system could be a formal group made up of people with problems similar to yours. Or it could be an individual, such as a friend or spouse, who is committed to encouraging your efforts toward healing.

The idea of support can be broadened to include your entire environment—physical surroundings, the people with whom you spend time, your own commitments. How do they make you feel?

When Person X is around, do you tend to feel more hopeful, confident, moving in the direction of better health? Or are you fearful, anxious, depressed?

Evaluate your environment and make a point of spending more time with people and situations that enhance health-promoting feelings… and avoiding those that do the opposite.

There are some people you won't want to banish from your life—and shouldn't. If your spouse is anxious about illness and unable to provide the support you need, don't feel you have to avoid him/her—but do look for other sources of support. And encourage your spouse to get support as well, perhaps through counseling or a group geared to partners' needs.

Caution: Evaluate a support group the same way you do the rest of your environment—by how it makes you feel. If it leaves you more fearful or depressed than before, find another group.

Much stress between loved ones can be avoided through straightforward communication. People tend to assume they know what the ill person needs and attempt to provide it, without checking first.

This leads to frustration—the unwilling recipient may feel manipulated or intruded upon, while the would-be helper feels punished for his efforts. This scenario can be avoided by a simple discussion during which the helper agrees to ask beforehand, "Would it be helpful if I did X?"…and to accept the honest answer.

•Imagery:

Imagery, broadly defined as the way we think about things, can have a powerful effect on the body. Healthy images lead to healthy emotional responses, which stimulate the body to produce chemicals important to the healing process.

Conversely, unhealthy images and emotions can stimulate the production of stress hormones and other chemicals that divert the body's resources away from healing and make it more vulnerable to illness.

We can help ourselves toward health by searching for words and mental pictures that allow us to think about illness and its treatment in ways that promote health.

Example: A patient going in for chemotherapy may be thinking about the procedure with dread, seeing it as a hurtful poison and dwelling on the unpleasant side effects…or, conversely, he may view it as a powerful tool that can help him get well—a healthier image.

There are many kinds of healthy imagery, and patients need to find the images with which they feel comfortable.

Some people like to visualize the body's immune system attacking the disease, picturing the white blood cells as soldiers attacking the hostile invader.

Others prefer less aggressive imagery—such as vividly imagining an arthritic joint with white blood cells exploring joint surfaces, removing debris and soothing any areas of irritation until the joint is imagined as smooth with glistening surfaces.

•Meditation—tapping our inner wisdom. Years ago Albert Schweitzer observed that each person has a wise physician within him. We already possess many of the keys to health and healing, and we can learn to gain greater access to that deep center of wisdom within each of us.

One of the most effective tools for doing so is meditation. There are many forms of meditation, and many excellent books have been written on the subject.

The main element tying these various meditation approaches together is the act of quieting oneself in a ritualized manner, whether through rhythmic breathing, physical movement (as in yoga or tai chi) or contemplation of an image or a sound pattern. Once in this quiet state, we can learn a great deal by asking ourselves for guidance.

Often when we step outside of our usual way of thinking, the mind rebels and stirs up a great deal of mental noise. It can sometimes be difficult to tell whether we've tapped a fount of inspiration or just a new way of kidding ourselves.

Useful guideline: If an inner message produces distressing emotions such as guilt, fear or depression, it's not arising out of inner wisdom. A truly inspiring message creates a feeling of rightness, a sense of peace. (The mental static tends to decrease with practice.)

•Setting goals. Goal-setting skills are useful no matter what the state of your health, but they're especially important for those dealing with serious illness. Since lifestyle changes can be such important healing tools, people are often tempted to make too many drastic changes all at once. *Result:* Stress and discouragement, which are definitely not health-producing emotions.

I suggest making goals for the long term. Look at where you'd like to be in two years and set goals that will help you get there. This will give you a structure for change, but with very little pressure. *Major areas for goal-setting:*

- •Diet
- •Exercise
- •Social support
- •Creative thinking
- •Play
- •Life purpose
- •Meditation

Play and life purpose are often neglected, but they're vital to maintaining a healthy emotional state. It might seem frivolous to set aside more time for fun when you're sick—but that's when you need it most. As for life purpose, that's what mobilizes us to reach for other goals. Ask yourself: "What gives me deep fulfillment? Why am I on the planet today?" Keep answers specific, not global: "I'm here to make sure my kids get fed and loved" is more motivating than "I hope to contribute to world peace"—though that's a worthy desire.

After you assess what you'd like to achieve in these seven areas, prioritize them. Don't try to tackle them all at once. Pick one area to focus on first…then, in two or three months, add the next priority…then the next. Not only will you find it easier to reach more of your goals… you'll have the energy to appreciate them.

Source: Radiation oncologist O. Carl Simonton, MD, medical director of the Simonton Cancer Center in Pacific Palisades, California, and pioneer in the study of mind-body techniques for treating cancer. His most recent book is *The Healing Journey: The Simonton Center Program for Achieving Physical, Mental and Spiritual Health*, Bantam Books, 1540 Broadway, New York 10036.

Healing and the Mind/Body Connection

Over the past century, physicians have learned much about the workings of the various organs in the human body…and have also found effective treatments for many diseases.

This focus on the machine-like aspects of the human body has led many doctors to ignore the many natural ways people can heal themselves when they are aware of the connection between the mind and the body.

The mind-body connection:

The human body is a complex mechanism that regulates itself using naturally occurring chemical substances. When something is wrong in one organ, messenger molecules of various kinds flow through the body and instruct other chemicals to correct the situation.

Example: When you cut your finger, your body reacts by releasing chemical clotting factors, which thicken the blood in the vicinity of the cut, preventing you from bleeding to death from a cut.

Blood clotting occurs unconsciously, but every process that happens in our bodies, including thought, involves chemical reactions.

In recent years, scientists have learned about important chemicals such as peptides—chains of amino acids that transmit chemical messages. And they've learned about endorphins—proteins that are powerful natural painkillers.

Peptides are found throughout the body, not just in the brain. It has become evident that there is no clear distinction between mind and body.

Since antiquity, we have known that chemicals like drugs and alcohol affect both the mind and the body. Changes in the balance of the chemicals in our bodies also affect the way we feel.

Example: When we have a problem in just one part of the body...like a toothache...our whole self tends to feel down.

More surprisingly, the mind-body connection also works the other way. We are finding more evidence every day that the way we feel about life does not simply reflect the state of our health—it also affects it.

Doctors long ago observed that about 30% of patients respond positively even when given a placebo—an inert pill with no curative properties.

The placebo effect occurs because those patients believe that they are being given a useful medicine...and their bodies follow that belief by fighting their sickness better than they would have otherwise.

Unfortunately, many doctors themselves encourage a reverse placebo effect. By emphasizing that a certain treatment has only a small statistical chance of success, they encourage patients to expect failure...and their bodies are likely to get the message.

Better way: Doctors should discuss procedures more positively, encouraging patients to adopt a hopeful attitude, so their bodies will be more likely to react favorably. Patients should not let themselves be convinced by statistics... because every person is a unique human being, not a statistic.

The body's natural wisdom:

Today, a growing number of physicians recognize that their patients have an ally in the body's natural wisdom. Sensitivity to signals sent by our bodies helps us detect emerging health problems before standard medical tests reveal them.

Example: Journalist Mark Barasch had a terrifying dream that he was being tortured by hot coals beneath his chin and thought he had cancer in his throat. Months later, he felt symptoms and went to a doctor, but his blood tests were normal. However, during a later and more complete examination, a thyroid tumor was found.

And, conversely, by sending hopeful signals back to the body, we encourage our bodies to respond with their surprising self-healing capabilities.

Example: In December, Mary was told she had only a few weeks to live. Her daughter, Jane, tried to cheer her up by buying her a new winter nightgown. Mary, who had always been very frugal, said she didn't want the gown, but would like a new summer purse.

This reaction surprised Jane until she interpreted it as a signal that her mother thought she could survive another six months. Jane demonstrated that she shared that belief. Mary recovered enough not only to enjoy her new purse but was active enough to wear it out...and a half dozen more.

One of the most striking examples of the mind-body connection is susceptibility to disease. About 40 years ago, researchers at the University of Rochester found that people who adopted an attitude of helplessness and hopelessness were those most likely to contract a variety of diseases.

Other studies have found that people who repress their emotions because of unhappy childhood relationships with their parents are prone to suffer heart disease, hypertension, mental illness and cancer.

Mental attitudes also affect the ability to overcome disease.

Patients who take an active part in treatment ask doctors and nurses many questions, insist on finding out what lies behind every request before complying and want to be given a choice between a variety of treatment options. They want to be told what the choices and the priorities are for each. But a Yale study showed that the most "difficult" patients were those with the most active immune systems. They survived longer than "good" patients who were quiet and submissive.

How to survive:

You are most likely to survive serious illness if you can answer "yes" to the following questions:

•Does your life have meaning?

•Do you express your anger appropriately— in defense of yourself?

•Are you willing to say "no"?

•Do you make your own choices?

•Are you able to ask for help?

•Do you have enough play in your life?

People who answer "yes" are survivors because their minds give their bodies a good reason to fight for survival. Everyone is eventually going to die. I see life as a labor pain. But like a mother willing to suffer labor pains to give birth to a child, survivors accept the pain of fighting back against disease as part of giving birth to their own renewed life.

Source: Bernie S. Siegel, MD, a surgeon and writer. His latest book is *How to Live Between Office Visits: A Guide to Life, Love and Health,* HarperCollins, 10 E. 53 St., New York 10022.

How Not to Be an Air Pollution Victim

Air pollution irritates us in many different ways. Eyes sting, throats scratch, mouths dry out—and when impaired visibility along roads and highways slows traffic to a standstill, tempers flare.

But air pollution is more than a nuisance. It's a threat to life. According to recent research, long-term exposure to soot, haze, dust and smoke raises the risk of early death by as much as 26%, translating into thousands of premature deaths a year.

Even when it doesn't kill, air pollution compromises health and wellness, especially for people with asthma, bronchitis, emphysema, heart disease or other chronic illnesses. *At special risk:* Elderly people, because their lungs aren't as healthy as they once were…and young people, because their lung tissue is just forming.

Americans live in a world of pollutants—outdoors and indoors. Until the Environmental Protection Agency (EPA) sets stringent standards for all forms of air pollution, it's up to each of us to take steps to protect ourselves.

Airborne enemies:

Particulate matter is just one of the many types of dangerous pollutants in the air we breathe. *Other dangerous pollutants include…*

•Ozone. It causes coughing, shortness of breath and chest pain. It also boosts susceptibility to infection. At high concentrations, ozone can scar the lungs.

•Sulfur dioxide. It irritates the airways, causes asthma attacks and sets the stage for permanent lung damage.

•Nitrogen dioxide. It causes bronchitis and, like ozone, increases susceptibility to infection.

•Carbon monoxide. This odorless, colorless gas reduces oxygen levels in the blood, starving the body's cells. It's especially dangerous for people with heart disease.

•Lead. This heavy metal causes permanent brain, kidney and cardiovascular damage.

Indoor air pollution:

Although Americans tend to fret a great deal about *outside* air quality, most of us underestimate the threat posed by *indoor* pollution.

The average American spends 90% of his/ her time indoors—65% of that time at home. So if your home is polluted, you could have big trouble.

Self-defense:

•Clean air conditioners, humidifiers, dehumidifiers and heat exchangers on a regular basis.

Follow manufacturers' instructions. Fill humidifiers with distilled or demineralized water only.

•Test your home for radon. This colorless, odorless gas—a powerful carcinogen—percolates up into the home from soil beneath the foundation. Pick up from your local hardware store a radon test kit bearing the label, "Meets EPA Requirements."

•Check furnaces once a year before heating season. Be sure the air intake is adequate and that the exhaust system is operating properly. And check flues and chimneys for blockage by debris and for cracks that could allow fumes to enter the house.

•Vent all heaters outside your home. Gas heaters generally produce less pollution than kerosene heaters. If you use a kerosene heater, burn only a low sulfur (1-K) fuel, fill the heater outside and keep it clean and properly adjusted.

•If you cook with gas, fit your range with a hood fan that vents pollutants outside. Or open a window and use an exhaust fan while cooking.

Caution: Never use a gas range or oven to heat your home. Use these appliances only for cooking—they generate too much pollution to be used continuously.

•Choose the right appliances. If you're considering replacing old gas appliances, select models with spark ignition rather than a pilot light. Or choose electric appliances instead. They're "cleaner" than gas appliances.

•Watch out for household products—cleaning agents, pesticides, paints, hobby products, solvents and other potentially dangerous products. Follow label instructions carefully regarding both use and disposal.

Better: Buy nontoxic alternatives and products in a nonaerosol form. *Example:* Use soap instead of phosphate detergents.

If there are no nontoxic alternatives to a particular product, buy only as much as is needed — no matter how good the price for bulk quantities.

•Ban cigarettes, cigars and pipes. Secondhand smoke more than doubles a person's indoor exposure to cancer-causing particles.

At greatest risk: Babies. Those living with a parent or parents who smoke are more likely than other children to have serious lung disease during the first two years of life. And children exposed to secondhand smoke are more likely to cough and wheeze and to have middle ear problems.

•Sweep and vacuum regularly—especially if you have rugs or wall-to-wall carpet. Use a vacuum cleaner with revolving brushes and disposable vacuum bags. Reusable bags tend to collect—and disperse—lots of dust.

If you have new carpet installed, keep your house well-ventilated for at least 48 hours afterward. *Reason:* New carpet releases into the air potentially harmful chemicals called *volatile organic compounds* (VOCs).

These chemical vapors irritate the eyes, nose and throat and trigger rashes and allergies. Recent animal studies have linked them to cancer.

•Place doormats at all entrances—to reduce tracked-in dust. Make sure people use them. *Even better:* Ask your family and guests to remove their shoes when inside.

•Keep windows and inside doors of your house open whenever possible. This will increase ventilation.

Also: Install exhaust fans in bathroom windows or walls. Doing so not only helps keep air free of chemicals from hair spray, deodorants, etc., but also inhibits growth of mold and mildew.

Caution: Tabletop air cleaners—especially those that rely solely on activated charcoal—are relatively ineffective at clearing the air of small particles.

Sick-building checkup:

Because of the materials used in modern construction, new or recently renovated office buildings are likely to contain VOCs.

To cut heating and cooling costs, some employers set their heating/air conditioning systems to use stale, "recirculated" air. In addition, many modern offices have sealed windows.

Danger: Stale air can cause headaches, nausea and fatigue. These symptoms could signify harmful indoor air pollution.

Self-defense: If you experience eye or throat irritation or coughing while at work, tell your building manager. If the system is using recirculated air, ask that more fresh air be pumped into the system.

Any office with sealed windows should have both a supply vent (usually on a windowsill) and an exhaust vent (usually on the ceiling). If your office does not have a ventilation system, call the department of health or speak to the landlord to find out why.

Make sure that air circulation is unimpeded. Walls, partitions, file cabinets and even temporary stacks of cartons can block air flow. If the air in your office is stagnant, talk to your office manager about ways to improve the air circulation.

If you begin to feel tired or dizzy or have headaches, there may be an air-circulation problem. Check with other employees to see if they are experiencing the same symptoms. If they are and the symptoms persist, it may be time to complain to your office manager.

Whatever kind of ventilation system is used in your workplace, your office or building manager should see that it's properly maintained. Every part of the system—including humidifiers and dehumidifiers, air filters, air-circulation pumps and blowers—must be cleaned and disinfected regularly.

The building's mechanical staff should follow the manufacturers' recommendations for maintenance and cleaning of the ventilation system. The building manager should know how often it needs to be cleaned and make sure that this schedule is being followed.

Make sure computer printers and copying machines have adequate space for free circulation of air. *Ideal location:* A large room with an open window.

Exercise self-defense:

During intense exercise, we breathe up to 16 times faster than we do at rest and draw air more deeply into the lungs. We also tend to breathe through our mouths, bypassing the body's first line of defense against pollution—the hair-lined nostrils.

To protect yourself: Time your workouts or walks for the early morning. In most areas, outdoor pollutants start to form shortly after sunrise and become increasingly concentrated until mid-afternoon, tapering off after sundown.

Outdoor exercise: Choose a route that takes you through open, breezy spaces. Avoid running or walking near traffic. Stay as far away as possible from moving automobiles.

Caution: While dust masks may be helpful to those with allergic conditions, they are ineffective at reducing your exposure to harmful pollutants. They also make it harder to breathe and can cause chafing of facial skin.

Source: Alfred Munzer, MD, president of the American Lung Association, 1740 Broadway, New York 10019, 800-586-4872. He is also codirector of pulmonary medicine at Washington Adventist Hospital in Takoma Park, Maryland.

Dental Patients in Need of Root Canal

Dental patients in need of root-canal work are almost always best served by a root-canal specialist instead of a general dentists. *Key:* The specialist's higher level of expertise is vital when the work will be complicated—redoing a failed root canal, canals that are blocked, teeth with more than the average number of canals. A simple root canal can be ably performed by a general dentist. In addition, root canal specialists provide more accurate diagnoses—it can be difficult to identify the precise source of facial pain. *Special problem:* Root canals often arise on short notice. A root-canal practice is designed to accommodate patients with emergencies…but it can be difficult to get in quickly to a general dentist, whose time is booked well in advance.

Source: Sheldon Nadler, DDS, is a dentist in private practice, 25 W. 54 St., New York 10019.

All About Receding Gums

If you're worried about your gums receding —relax. While gum recession can be a cosmetic problem, it does not cause tooth loss, it tends to be self-limiting and it rarely requires treatment.

Gum recession occurs when the gum shrinks from the neck of a tooth, exposing some of the root and giving the appearance of being "long in the tooth." Recession can occur with a single tooth or with many.

Causes of gum recession:

Gum recession can be part of the normal aging process. But age isn't the only thing that causes receding gums.

Other possible causes:

•Heredity. Some people are simply destined to have receding gums. They may have inherited thin, delicate gums...or may have teeth that are "too big" for their jaw—like inheriting grandma's large teeth with grandpa's narrow jaw. If the gums are stretched beyond their limits, recession can occur.

In some cases, recession occurs when the frenum—the band of muscle fibers attaching the upper and lower lips to the gums—attaches too close to the gum line.

•Improper brushing. Scrubbing your teeth with a harsh side-to-side motion damages delicate gum tissue, which can result in recession. Using a toothbrush with hard bristles can make it even worse, so be sure to use one that's labeled "soft."

Hard brushing can also cause the exposed portion of the roots to become notched. This situation can lead to tooth decay...and the need for fillings.

•Braces. As crooked teeth are straightened, they may be moved beyond the edge of the jaw. *Result:* Exposed roots. A skilled orthodontist may be able to avoid this problem in some cases. In others, it's simply the price you pay for having straight teeth.

•Chronic irritation. Anything that irritates the gums—whether it's a poorly placed filling, improper flossing or chronic "picking" with a fingernail, hairpin, paper clip, etc.—can cause recession.

Treatment:

Can gum recession be minimized? Yes. Brush properly (have your dentist or dental hygienist check your technique)...ask your dentist about replacing irritating fillings...and be sure not to pick at your teeth.

Source: Alan A. Winter, DDS, associate clinical professor of dentistry, New York University School of Dentistry, New York City. A board-certified periodontist, he also maintains a private practice at 30 E. 60 St., New York 10022.

Thyroid Disease

When the thyroid gland fails to do its job, other body systems go haywire. A simple, inexpensive blood test for thyroid disease is readily available, and medication is available to control the problem. But—the thyroid gland is often overlooked as a potential source of physical symptoms.

Eleven million Americans have thyroid disease, but only ten million know of their problem. *At greatest risk:* Women. They're at least five times more likely than men to have thyroid disease. But men and children also develop thyroid disease—something that many doctors seem to forget.

The thyroid gland consists of two one-inch lobes located along either side of the windpipe (trachea) and connected via a narrow band of tissue. When the thyroid is healthy, these lobes are soft and difficult to feel. Thyroid disease makes them firmer and easier to feel.

The thyroid is part of the endocrine system, a network of interrelated glands including the pituitary, which governs physical growth, and the ovaries and testes, which govern fertility.

The thyroid secretes two hormones—*thyroxine* (T_4) and *triiodothyronine* (T_3). If too little or too much of these hormones is secreted, the body's organs cannot function properly.

Because these hormones affect so many different organs, thyroid problems can cause a wide variety of symptoms, ranging from irritability to infertility to palpitations of the heart. With such diverse symptoms, it's no surprise that doctors often have trouble diagnosing thyroid disease.

Common thyroid conditions:

•Hyperthyroidism (oversecretion of thyroid hormones) causes body metabolism to accelerate. The heart beats faster, sometimes with thumping, irregular rhythms or chest pain (angina). In severe cases, blood clots form in the heart. These clots can break away and travel to the brain, causing stroke.

Other symptoms: Excessive sweating...hot, trembling hands...nervousness or irritability...a short attention span...disturbed sleep...weight loss...hair loss.

Bowel movements come more frequently. Medications may be eliminated from the body more quickly.

Women may have shorter menstrual periods or none at all. They may become infertile. If they do become pregnant, they're more likely to have a miscarriage. People with advanced hyperthyroidism often have bulging eyes or other eye problems—the result of an immune reaction.

You needn't have *all* these symptoms to suspect hyperthyroidism. If you have a few—or even one, if it's severe—ask your doctor about being tested for thyroid disease.

The most common form of hyperthyroidism is Graves' disease—which is caused by a disorder of the immune system. (It was Graves' that struck George and Barbara Bush a few years ago.)

•Hypothyroidism. Too little thyroid hormone slows the metabolism, blunting the emotions and making it difficult to concentrate.

Other symptoms include feeling cold, constipation, muscle cramps, fatigue and sleepiness. Also, hair may become coarse and brittle as skin grows dry, rough, pale and yellowish.

Women with hypothyroidism often have frequent, heavy menstrual periods. As with hyperthyroidism, they may be infertile or more prone to miscarriage.

Hypothyroidism stunts children's growth. *Reason:* Without sufficient thyroid hormone, the pituitary gland fails to synthesize enough growth hormone.

•Thyroiditis. After a viral illness, your thyroid gland may become inflamed, causing a sore throat, fever, weakness and muscle pain. Turning your head or swallowing may be painful.

This pain—often mistakenly blamed on a sore throat, dental problems or ear infections —usually disappears within a few months.

•Cancer. Thyroid cancer is rare. Only 5% to 15% of thyroid nodules are cancerous. It is usually curable, especially if caught early.

Prevention and risk:

There's little you can do to prevent thyroid trouble. Most cases seem to strike out of the blue…although some can be caused by psychological stress, such as that resulting from the death of a loved family member.

Also: Certain cases of Graves' disease are linked to smoking. And carpal tunnel syndrome and postpartum depression, for example, may have their roots in thyroid disease.

In the elderly, hypothyroidism often goes undetected.

Reason: Its symptoms occur as part of the normal aging process.

Many doctors urge periodic thyroid blood tests for women older than 65—especially those who experience unexplained weight loss, abnormal heart rhythms or chest pain.

Finally, some thyroid conditions seem to have a hereditary basis. Anyone whose parent, grandparent, sibling, aunt or uncle has had thyroid disease should have a blood test every year or two. Any child whose mother or father has had thyroid disease should be carefully examined by a pediatrician.

The office examination:

If you think you might have thyroid disease, tell your doctor right away. To check for an enlarged thyroid (goiter) or for nodules in the thyroid, you'll be asked to swallow as the doctor watches and feels your neck. The doctor will probably use a stethoscope to check your thyroid for *bruits* (noises caused by excessive blood flow). The presence of bruits suggests hyperthyroidism.

The doctor will also take a sample of your blood. It will be tested to determine whether it contains too much or too little thyroid hormone.

Important: Blood tests usually provide all of the information necessary to arrive at a preliminary diagnosis. Yet some doctors order ultrasound ($100 to $200), computer tomography ($300 to $500) or magnetic resonance imaging ($700 to $1,000). If your doctor orders one or more of these costly tests, ask if they're absolutely necessary.

The *radioactive iodide uptake test,* which measures the thyroid's ability to trap iodide, should be used only to distinguish between Graves' disease and other forms of hyperthyroidism.

Source: Martin I. Surks, MD, director, division of endocrinology, Montefiore Medical Center, and professor of medicine, The Albert Einstein College of Medicine, both in Bronx, New York. He is the author of *The Thyroid Book: What Goes Wrong and How to Treat It,* Consumer Reports Books, 101 Truman Ave., Yonkers, New York 10703.

Lyme Disease
Self-Defense Strategies

Almost 20 years after it was first identified, Lyme disease is still perplexing. It's sometimes unrecognized and now more often overdiagnosed.

Misinformation is common, causing many to worry about having it and others to falsely assume that they do not.

What it is:

Difficulties with Lyme disease begin with describing it. Basically, it is an infection that usually starts with an expanding skin lesion. Later, it can affect the joints, nerves or heart.

However, the severity of symptoms varies widely and not all victims experience all of them. Long periods of latent infection may also complicate diagnosis and treatment.

Lyme disease is contracted *only* through the bite of an infected deer tick. Actually, humans are not part of the normal process of the illness. A disease-carrying spirochete is transmitted from tick to mice and back to ticks. The adult stage of the tick prefers to feed on deer, so they are important for the life cycle of the tick. As deer populations grow in what were recently rural areas, more people come into contact with deer—and with their infected tick parasites.

Where it is:

Lyme disease is found primarily in the northeastern United States, in the Midwest in Minnesota and Wisconsin and in Oregon and northern California. But since birds also host infected deer ticks and deer herds are growing elsewhere in the US, Lyme disease will probably spread further.

Symptoms:

•A large circular red rash at the site of the bite is the first—and most characteristic—symptom of Lyme disease. Within weeks, the lesion expands and may be accompanied by symptoms that include fatigue, fever, chills, headaches, stiff neck, muscle and joint aches.

About 20% of victims will have no skin lesions, and some may experience no early symptoms at all.

•The disease's second stage is due to dissemination of the Lyme organism to different sites. In this stage, the nervous system may be affected in several ways, particularly partial or complete facial paralysis, and radiating pain or abnormal sensations at different spots on the body. Symptoms in the second stage may come and go, causing the sufferer to believe he/she is "getting over" whatever he had.

•Months to years after the initial infection, Lyme disease problems may become chronic. In this third stage, arthritis, usually in the knees, and disturbances in memory, mood and sleep may become evident.

Diagnosis and treatment:

Lyme disease is diagnosed by recognition of a characteristic clinical picture and confirmed by blood tests. If diagnosed in its early stages, it is successfully treated with oral antibiotics—usually doxycycline and amoxicillin.

If the disease affects the nervous system, intravenous antibiotic therapy is usually recommended.

A new vaccine is being developed and is currently undergoing testing.

Prevention:

•Even in places where the disease occurs, the tick often needs to be attached to you for at least 24 hours before the infection is transmitted. Checking yourself at the end of a day outdoors greatly reduces the possibility of contracting Lyme disease.

•It's important to know that not every tick bite results in Lyme disease.

•Redness following some tick bites may be a harmless allergic reaction or simple irritation caused by scratching, not the skin lesion of Lyme disease.

•When in the woods, tall grass or marshy areas, wearing long pants tucked into socks and long-sleeved shirts reduces your risk of tick-borne illnesses.

The confusion:

•Lyme disease spirochetes may vary in their virulence, and individual differences in our immune systems may account for the range of severity of the disease's symptoms. This can make diagnosis difficult.

•Blood tests for Lyme disease aren't foolproof or standardized. False-negative and, more commonly, false-positive results have been a great problem.

• Lyme disease is sometimes the diagnosis when the real culprit may be chronic fatigue syndrome or fibromyalgia, two ailments with some symptoms that closely mimic Lyme disease. If treatment for Lyme disease is failing, it could be because you don't have the disease at all.

On the other hand, physicians have mistaken Lyme disease for other illnesses. Don't be afraid to mention the possibility of Lyme disease to your doctor.

• Some individuals suffering from depression, anxiety or other legitimate illnesses may insist they have Lyme disease—in spite of their doctors' assurances to the contrary. *Beware:* There are now clinics catering to these fears, "treating" patients for an illness they do not have.

Source: Allen C. Steere, MD, director of rheumatology and immunology at New England Medical Center and professor of medicine at Tufts University School of Medicine, Boston. Dr. Steere is credited with being the first doctor to identify Lyme disease, in 1975.

How to Reduce the Risk of Heart Disease

Designed to uncover the leading risk factors for heart disease in a typical American community, the Framingham Heart Study has been tracking the daily living and eating habits of thousands of residents of Framingham, Massachusetts since 1948.

Dr. William Castelli, director of the study for 15 years and a popular lecturer on heart disease, discusses the study's most recent findings.

How does the current generation of Americans compare with the original subjects of the Framingham Heart Study? Are we becoming healthier —or are we at greater risk? While many of us are benefiting from lower-fat diets and the greater emphasis that is put on fitness, children today may actually be in worse shape than those of previous generations.

One surprise is that teenage boys and young men in Framingham today weigh more than their fathers did at the same ages and they are not as physically active. Therefore, they may be at higher risk for heart disease and diabetes.

The combination of TV and computer technology has made children more sedentary, and their diets are unacceptably high in saturated fat and cholesterol.

Girls in grammar and high school are now smoking at a much higher rate than ever before. If the present pattern continues, the rate of women's deaths from heart disease and diabetes will match or even exceed that of men. From other studies, we have learned that arterial disease can begin as early as the grade-school years.

What are the most recent findings regarding the links between diet and heart disease? One of the latest discoveries in cardiology is that the newest fat deposit in your arteries—for example, the one that was placed there by the cheeseburger you ate yesterday—may be more likely to break loose, clog your arteries and kill you than the older deposits that have been partially blocking your arteries for years.

These "young" deposits from your most recent high-fat meal don't impede blood flow while attached to artery walls. But they are unstable and can easily snap off and block a coronary vessel.

An estimated 65% to 70% of acute heart attacks are now believed to come from these newer, barely detectable lesions, which are covered by only a thin layer of cells. The older, larger obstructions are covered by thick scar tissue and are rather resistant and stable.

But don't discount big blockages. They are, of course, still undesirable and an indication of widespread disease. In fact, if you have a coronary artery that is at least 50% blocked, the smaller arteries of your heart cannot possibly be free of disease. That would make you a "walking time bomb"—and especially vulnerable to the effects of one fatty meal.

We have all heard that saturated fat is the chief culprit in heart disease. Where does cholesterol fit in? How much of each can we safely consume? While fat is the primary villain in heart disease, cholesterol is definitely an accomplice.

As a nation, we would be better off if every day we each ate no more than 300 milligrams of cholesterol and 35 to 40 grams of total fat—of which 20 grams or less were in the form of saturated fat. This is the "bad" fat that contributes to heart disease.

Once you reach this goal, you can see whether making these changes gets your serum cholesterol down to a level of 200 or less. The closer you get to the 150-to-160 range, the less likely you are to have a heart attack.

If these adjustments don't "straighten out" your cholesterol, then you should aim for a daily quota of no more than 17 grams of saturated fat, 30 grams of total fat and 200 milligrams of cholesterol.

Example: A lunch of a four-ounce steak, coffee with low-fat milk and a pat of butter on a roll is about 150 milligrams of cholesterol and 30 grams of fat—of which 18 grams are saturated.

Are triglycerides the same as "bad" cholesterol? How critical are they as risk factors for heart disease? One of the by-products of the fatty foods we digest are substances called *triglycerides.* They are formed in the liver and are known as Very Low Density Lipoproteins (VLDLs). The familiar LDL, or "bad," cholesterol is not formed directly—it comes from VLDL.

We are now learning that there are four different types of triglycerides, two of which are damaging to arteries and two of which are not. The most dangerous ones are small and dense and associated with diets high in saturated fats. These VLDLs have been linked with very early heart attacks—striking victims in their 20s, 30s and 40s.

Recently, we have discovered that these VLDLs enter the white blood cells in our artery walls even faster than LDLs. This makes them particularly destructive.

Genetic predispositions and unwise eating habits play roles in the formation of these dangerous fats, but the dangers can be curbed by maintaining a healthy lifestyle.

Other types of triglycerides can be raised by eating diets high in whole grains, vegetables and fruits, but these are not the kind that are harmful to our hearts or artery walls.

What are the best ways to raise levels of HDL, or "good," cholesterol? When our Framingham data showed that the relative amount of HDL in our blood is even more important than total cholesterol and that exercise can have a favorable impact on HDL, I began jogging regularly. This raised my HDL level from 49 to 63. A regular routine of brisk walking or any other exercise is fine for most people—but talk with your doctor before beginning a new exercise regimen.

Losing weight also elevates HDLs, and certain foods and nutrients, such as brewer's yeast, garlic, onions, ginseng and chromium, have been credited with boosting them as well.

My advice is to have a test done after eating such wholesome, harmless foods for about a month—as part of a low-fat diet—to see whether they have any measurable effect on your HDLs.

Aim: The ratio of your total cholesterol to HDL should be under 3.5.

How does the risk of heart attack in men compare with that of women? One of the most shocking findings to emerge from the Framingham Heart Study is that one out of every five men has had a heart attack by the time he reaches age 60. The heart attack rate for women is only one in 17 by the same age.

Unless they have diabetes, smoke or have familial hypercholesterolemia (inherited abnormally high serum cholesterol), women are relatively immune to heart disease before menopause because they produce high levels of estrogen, which apparently plays a protective role.

However, within six to 10 years after menopause—when estrogen levels drop off sharply—women's risk becomes similar to that of men. Unfortunately, women tend to have more advanced heart disease by the time they are treated, since physicians still consider them to be less susceptible to coronary problems and often don't diagnose the condition early enough.

How many people survive heart attacks today? Can any of them ever return to "normal"? As the Framingham data have shown, when people get heart attacks, about 85% of them survive.

With the new thrombolytic therapy, in which people having a heart attack are injected with a clot-dissolving drug, we can increase the percentage of survivors to about 93%. Even in the oldest age groups, 75% of first-time heart attack victims survive.

Of those who survive, about half lose the normal pumping ability of their hearts—when we put them on a treadmill, they "flunk." If we subsequently inject them with a radioisotope such as thallium, which allows us to scan the heart, we find that the heart muscle tissue in 30% of these people is "hibernating" but still very much alive—which means it can eventually be restored to normal function.

In the short run, we can't lower the cholesterol levels of these patients sufficiently or fast enough —either through dietary changes or drugs—to shrink the deposits inside their coronary arteries and get their hearts pumping at full capacity again.

Today's "high-tech" treatments, such as coronary bypass surgery, balloon angioplasty or atherectomy, can help restore cardiac function and allow these people to return to work. But in the long run, the only treatment that works is aggressively lowering blood cholesterol through diet and lifestyle changes. If blood cholesterol is lowered within three to five years of the first heart attack, we can markedly reduce the risk of a second heart attack.

What are your latest recommendations for a "healthy heart" diet? When it comes to protecting yourself from heart disease, the best strategy is to become a vegetarian—eating primarily fresh vegetables, legumes, whole grains, fruits and nonfat dairy products.

Vegetarians not only outlive the rest of us, they also aren't prey to other degenerative diseases, such as diabetes, strokes, etc., that slow us down and make us chronically ill.

If you can't *be* a vegetarian, the next best thing is to *eat* a vegetarian from the sea. One type of shellfish fits this description—mollusks (clams and oysters). They loll around on the ocean floor and are filter feeders, sucking in the phytoplankton (the vegetables of the sea). Mollusks have the lowest cholesterol levels of all seafood.

The second best choices are moving shellfish such as shrimp and lobster. While they contain more cholesterol than most meats and cheeses, they are so low in saturated fat that they are a much better bargain nutritionally—more desirable even than skinless white-meat chicken.

Also good, of course, is to eat any fish—even fatty fishes. They are very low in saturated fat and contain fish oils, which also benefit your heart.

If you prefer a more standard American diet, recent changes at your supermarket allow you to have some beef, too. The newest grade of beef available—*select*—contains only 10% saturated fat by weight, or approximately four grams of fat in four ounces of precooked meat. And *ConAgra* now puts out a product called "Healthy Choice Extra Lean Ground Beef" that contains only 1.5 grams of saturated fat per four-ounce serving. That means you could have burgers for breakfast, lunch and dinner and still have plenty of saturated fat to "spend" that day. Similarly, everything from ham to ice cream comes in a low-fat and delicious version at your local market today.

Does heart disease follow a predictable course —and is it ever too late to stop it? Once it begins, atherosclerosis—the hardening and thickening of arteries because of fatty deposits—follows a fairly predictable course.

It starts in the abdominal aorta, spreads to the coronary arteries, the big artery in the chest, then down into the leg, up into the neck and finally inside the head. This is why strokes generally occur later in life than heart attacks do.

Now that we have such diagnostic tools as echocardiography, which uses ultrasound, we can look inside the neck arteries of our Framingham subjects. By the time they are in their 60s, 76% of them have deposits or lesions in that area. This means that the disease is already well advanced elsewhere in their bodies and has been in their coronary arteries for at least ten years.

If these people continue on their present course, about half of them will end up dying from this arterial clogging.

While we can intervene and make a difference even at this point, the earlier one starts the better, so I don't want to exclude children or premenopausal women from good preventive programs.

Twenty-five years from now, when these children are adults and the women are past menopause, they and their families will have already acquired healthy eating habits to keep them well protected from heart disease.

I've yet to meet anyone whose genes are so good that they have license to eat whatever they want—or who can get away with being too sedentary. It's only by altering diet and exercise habits that I can change the destiny of 75% of the people who are headed for heart attacks. The remaining 25% will need lipid-lowering drugs in order to achieve the same result.

At age 62 and as the first man in my family to reach the age of 45 without any coronary symptoms, I'm living proof that a healthful change of lifestyle can definitely work.

Source: William Castelli, MD, director of the Framingham Heart Study, Five Thurber St., Framingham, Massachusetts 01701. Dr. Castelli is credited with coining the terms "good" cholesterol and "bad" cholesterol and is among the nation's preeminent experts on the heart and heart disease prevention.

Women's Heart Disease Risks

Women's heart disease risks differ from men's, says Dr. Edward Diethrich. *Compared with men:* Women's hearts and blood vessels are smaller, so cardiovascular damage can occur faster and from less exposure to risk factors…women have higher fat-to-muscle ratios than men—and that is associated with heart disease…too many women wait until after menopause to take defensive steps against heart disease. *Also:* Heart attack symptoms are different in women and men. The main symptom in men is crushing pain in the chest and down the left arm. *In women:* Pain down the *right* arm, in the jaw, collarbone or upper back (with or without chest pain)…nausea, vomiting, dizziness, sweating. *Important:* Women, like men, must eat a heart-healthy, low-fat diet…exercise…refrain from smoking…and make sure that preventive cardiac care is routinely covered by their doctors.

Source: Edward Diethrich, MD, is medical director for the Arizona Heart Institute & Foundation, Phoenix, and author of *Women and Heart Disease*, Random House, 201 E. 50 St., New York 10022.

New Solutions to Old Sleep Problems

Two decades of research in the US, Europe and Japan by hundreds of specialists in sleep disorders has paid off. There is now little reason for anyone—even executives or professionals in high-stress jobs who frequently travel—to suffer from insomnia, poor-quality sleep or sleep deprivation.

Proven techniques to get to sleep quickly and to get enough deep, refreshing sleep—without medications or alcohol—can be learned by everyone.

Know what you need:

About two-thirds of adults sleep between six and nine hours a night. That is a pretty wide range—but the remaining one-third sleep more or less than this amount.

Common mistake #1: People who think they need eight hours of sleep, but really need only seven often worry unnecessarily about their health when they get, say, only six-and-a-half hours of sleep.

Common mistake #2: Trying to force yourself to get more sleep than you need, simply because you think you need more. This often creates an insomnia problem. About one out of five adults is a short sleeper—someone who needs less than six hours of sleep. Thomas Edison slept four or five hours a night and a few people are fine with even less.

Your "normal" sleep need is largely programmed at birth by hereditary factors. It is possible to alter your sleep needs, but first you must know what those needs are.

If, however, your sleep pattern worsens to a bothersome degree as you get older, try to correct the problem by…

• Keeping to a regular sleep-wake rhythm. Don't linger in bed in the morning if work pressures ease up or when you retire.

• Keeping busy during the day.

• Avoiding daytime naps. If you do nap, however, do it before 3 PM and don't nap more than one hour.

• Staying awake at least until 10 or 11 PM. If you get drowsy earlier, take a brisk walk, do some indoor exercise or listen to the radio or watch TV.

If you find you often don't get back to sleep during the night, develop some activities to do then—videos, craft projects, computer networking.

• Medical conditions. Many illnesses have symptoms that are hardly noticeable during the day but that interfere with sleep at night—such as pain, itching or shortness of breath. Identify and treat the symptoms of disease—rather than focusing on sleep. *Typical problems:*

• Bladder problems. Too-frequent urination during the night can be caused by excessive caffeine use. If avoiding caffeine doesn't help, try retraining your urinating reflexes by progressively delaying urination each time you feel the urge during the day and evening. Try to add fifteen minutes to the interval each week until you increase it to ninety minutes. To strengthen the reflex even further, start drinking more water (though not too close to bedtime).

• Sunday night insomnia. Some people have insomnia only on Sunday night. Or they say insomnia started on Sunday nights but now happens other nights as well. Worries about Sunday night insomnia may also be one of the major causes of the widespread Sunday afternoon blues.

The cause: Going to bed late Friday and Saturday nights and sleeping late Saturday and Sunday mornings—or napping Sunday afternoon—can put your internal clock two, three or four hours behind the actual time you try to go to sleep Sunday night at your "regular" 11 PM bedtime. That's why you can't fall asleep. And because it's Sunday night, you begin to worry about work on Monday as you toss and turn. So you think work stress is causing your insomnia.

The cure: Get up at your regular weekday wake-up time on Saturday and Sunday mornings. If you absolutely must sleep later—make it no more than one hour later than your usual wakeup time. And expose yourself to daylight as soon as you wake up. Don't nap—especially not on Sunday afternoon. Get into the habit of exercising Sunday afternoon or early evening.

Source: James Perl, PhD, a clinical psychologist in private practice, 4761 McKinley Dr., Boulder, Colorado 80303. Dr. Perl is author of *Sleep Right in Five Nights*, William Morrow, 1350 Avenue of the Americas, New York 10019.

2

The Savvy Traveler

Travel:1995...and beyond

Edith Weiner, Weiner Edrich, Brown, Inc.

For leisure travel—the clear trend is toward shorter trips...mini vacations. Constrained by tight work schedules and tight budgets, and dazzled by endless choices of travel packages, people are choosing to take two, three...even four short vacations a year, rather than the traditional once-a-year summer extravaganza.

Related trend: Attaching leisure travel to business travel. To save money, people will increasingly take spouses along on company-paid business jaunts, taking advantage of corporate discounts on hotels, car rentals and other travel services...and rooms don't really cost any more for two than one.

Increasingly—"eco-travel". These are ecologically-intense vacations...white-water rafting, rock climbing, mountain biking and safaris.

The current trend toward "being connected" while away from the workplace will gather momentum in the short term, with cellular phones, faxes and laptops increasingly providing comfort to travelers fearing that being out of touch for too long will cause irreparable career damage.

But by the year 2000, this phase will be gradually replaced by the socially preferable ability to be unconnected. It will be a sign of status if you can be on vacation, *without* a beeper, phone or laptop, while the less professionally advanced remain fused to their electronic umbilical cords.

Contrary to the frequently heard prediction that improvements in teleconferencing technology will diminish the need for business travel, the opposite will occur. As businesspeople increasingly get "acquainted" electronically, they will have an *increased* urge to get to know each other face-to-face.

Result: Teleconferencing will make business communication more efficient, but it will at the same time spur growth in business travel.

But the technology of teleconferencing will seem primitive by the turn of the century when the literally mind-boggling powers of virtual reality are better harnessed and made commercially accessible.

Virtual reality—which currently enables a person to feel almost part of a chosen environment—will soon be perfected to the point where the mind is indeed completely tricked into believing that the body is elsewhere, giving people the sense of total immersion in a reality far removed from that of their own physical space.

This will reduce the need and desire to travel, as people are afforded the opportunity of simply slipping on a headset and "travelling" to outerspace while seated at their kitchen table.

Better Flying

Avoid the sun's glare when flying by reserving a seat on the right side (facing the cockpit) of the plane when traveling east to west…and on the left side when traveling west to east. This keeps you on the plane's shady side. For morning north-south travel—in either direction—book the west side of the plane. For afternoon north-south travel, book the east side.

Source: *Men's Health*, 33 E. Minor St., Emmaus, Pennsylvania 18098.

Advice for Solo Travelers

Traveling alone by air can have its advantages. You don't have to think about anyone but yourself, you can relax, watch a movie, read a book or work in peace. Or can you? What if the traveler next to you won't stop talking? What if your wallet or purse disappears? For trouble-free trips…

• Don't travel without telling someone. Contact a friend or family member. Give him/her your itinerary so someone knows how to find you.

• Streamline your wallet or purse. Avoid having to replace everything—if it's lost or stolen—by only carrying identification and those cards that you may actually use.

• Don't wear fine jewelry. It's dangerous to put it in your luggage, so leave it home.

• Travel light. An overloaded traveler is a vulnerable traveler. Ship bulky items in advance.

• Keep an inventory of items—and put a copy of it and your personal identification inside your suitcase, and keep a copy, too. You'll know by checking the inventory if something's missing and you will increase the odds that you'll see it again if it's lost.

• Wear a wedding ring. You'll discourage unwanted advances.

• Wear headphones. You don't even have to plug them in, but you'll politely tune out chatterers.

• Avoid the bulkhead—the area that separates first class from coach. If there's an unescorted child on board, that's where he/she is most likely to be.

• Have single bills handy. You won't have to get change and attract the wrong kind of attention, and you'll speed your progress through the airport if you need to give a tip.

Source: Natalie Windsor, the author of *How to Fly—Relaxed and Happy From Takeoff to Touchdown*, Cork-Screw Press, Box 833, Old Saybrook, Connecticut 06475.

Reset Your Internal Clock When Flying

Reset your internal clock as well as your watch when flying across time zones. On the plane, immediately adopt the sleeping and waking schedule of your destination. On arrival, nap no more than one hour during the day—preferably not at all. Spend time outdoors at your destination—sunlight helps synchronize your internal clock. Avoid or minimize use of caffeine and alcohol. Do not use sleep medications, which delay the body's adjustment.

Source: James Frost, MD, professor of neurology, Baylor College of Medicine, Houston, quoted in *Mature Outlook*, 1912 Grand Ave., Des Moines, Iowa 50309.

Florida— Off the Beaten Path

Think of Florida, and certain images immediately come to mind—oranges, beaches, golf, Disney World and spring break. While they're accurate, they don't provide the whole picture.

Florida is, in fact, loaded with natural and man-made sights that run from caves and inland rivers to wildlife sanctuaries, funky restaurants, charming towns and castles. Better yet, many of these attractions are relatively unknown.

Natural Florida:

• The Everglades. Truly unique—and that is saying a lot for a state that abounds with natural beauty both along the coastline and inland. As the nation's largest remaining subtropical wilderness, the Everglades (10 miles southwest of Homestead and 35 miles southwest of Miami) are comprised of more than 1.5 million acres that are a haven for fish, plant life, birds and other wildlife, such as panther, bobcat, diamondback terrapin, dolphin and manatee.

The best way to get acquainted is to visit the Main Visitors Center at Everglades National Park on SR 9336.

• The Ten Thousand Islands region in the northwestern section of the park offers the chance to take some great boat tours either independently or with a guide.

• Shark Valley is another nearby park treat that lies off US 41. The valley's 15-mile loop road, used for trams, bikes and hiking, follows a shallow stream—complete with alligators, turtles, snakes and birds—as it empties into the Shark River.

• Homosassa Springs Wildlife Park—60 miles north of Tampa on the Gulf Coast. Visitors can get a close look at manatees—giant but gentle underwater mammals. It also gives visitors the opportunity to realize that Florida's scenic and natural beauties aren't limited to the Everglades.

• Peace River, 40 miles east of Sarasota in southwest Florida, provides an even more remote experience, especially if you're in the mood for a canoe trip. The pristine river, which is too shallow for motorboats, offers an excellent opportunity for daytrips or extended canoe/camping trips. Besides the chance to see deer, armadillos and alligators, the Peace River is also a great place to hunt for shark's teeth, which can be as large as a fist.

Other natural sights:

• Sanibel Island, 20 miles southwest of Fort Myers, is a must for anyone interested in shelling. It is, in fact, reputed to be one of the best shelling beaches in the world.

• Ding Darling National Refuge nearby is a 5,000-acre mangrove wilderness that is an essential stop for any would-be ornithologist. It is home to 200 types of birds, including the endangered brown pelican.

• John Pennekamp Coral Reef State Park is based near Key Largo. A snorkler's paradise, the park has over 21 miles of coral reefs.

• Florida Caverns State Park. A wonderland of underground formations created by centuries of dripping mineral water. The park is off SR 167, three miles north of Marianna and 70 miles north of Tallahassee.

• Bok Tower Garden, three miles north of Lake Wales and 45 miles southwest of Orlando in central Florida, is man-made, but that doesn't diminish the tranquility, beauty and peace of this 128-acre garden of azaleas, camellias and magnolias. The only thing that interrupts the garden's quiet is the wonderful daily bell song from the 205-foot carillon.

Historic sights:

• St. Augustine is the jewel of Florida's historic towns and cities. That is logical considering the town has been continually occupied for more than four centuries. In addition to the restored sections of the old town, St. Augustine's charm revolves around its ancient Spanish fortress, Castillo de San Marcos.

• Key West, the last island on the chain that drips south of Florida, is also worth a visit. The island has a wealth of architectural styles—Spanish, New England, Bahamian and Southern. Other attractions include Ernest Hemingway's house and haunts, the Audubon House, which contains many of John Audubon's original engravings and the Wrecker's Museum, which is the oldest house on the island.

• Amelia Island in the northeast section of the state, 25 miles southwest of Jacksonville, is a particular delight for fans of Victorian architecture. The town has a 30-block old town section,

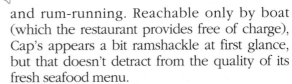

known as Centre Street Fernandina, which includes many restored buildings reflecting Steamboat Gothic and Queen Anne architecture.
Museums and the arts:

•John and Mabel Ringling Museum near Sarasota is only one example of the fine art collections that Florida holds. The Ringling Museum boasts one of the world's finest collections of Baroque art.

•The Salvador Dali Museum in St. Petersburg contains the largest collection of Dali's work in the world, covering his development from 1914 through 1980.

•Thomas Edison's winter residence—on McGregor Blvd. in Fort Myers—has a fascinating selection of many of his inventions and patents.

•John Gorrie Museum may not be as well known as Edison's. This one-room museum in Apalachicola—70 miles southwest of Tallahassee—is a gem. It is dedicated to Gorrie, a physician, who led the way in the development of ice cubes, refrigeration and air conditioning.

•Pensacola Naval Aviation Museum is in a perfect location—at the nation's first naval air station. It follows naval aviation developments from the first plane bought by the service in 1911 to SkyLab. There are 40 full-size aircraft available for inspection.
Shopping:

•Webster Flea Market is a bargain hunter's dream. Set up on Route 471 in Webster, 45 miles west of Orlando, the outdoor affair holds 40 acres and 1,500 vendors that sell everything from junk to fine arts and antiques. The market runs on Monday from 9 AM to 3 PM. (It's only open on Mondays.)

•Tin City in Naples is also worth a visit. Set in an old section of town, Tin City is an old-fashioned shopping bazaar built in historic boat buildings that are connected by cobbled lanes and planked river walks. (Many of the buildings are made of metal.)
Food:

•The Back Porch in Destin offers a wonderful amberjack sandwich.

•Cap's Place, near Boca Raton on the Atlantic Coast, doesn't want for color. The restaurant, which has been frequented by Winston Churchill, Franklin Roosevelt and Jack Dempsey, has been a center for gambling

and rum-running. Reachable only by boat (which the restaurant provides free of charge), Cap's appears a bit ramshackle at first glance, but that doesn't detract from the quality of its fresh seafood menu.

•Capt. Jim's Conch House in St. Augustine is both unique in design and menu. The seafood entrées are usually steamed in special spices and sauces, while other specialties include conch chowder and conch fritters. Beyond this, guests have the option of eating in the main indoor dining room or under thatched huts that are set up on wooden perches.

•The Hopkins Boarding House in the North Hill Preservation District of Pensacola is a perfect way to step back in time, at least in terms of food. The reason is simple. It is the real thing, a boarding house where diners eat with the guests. The fare—fried chicken, cole slaw, corn muffins and black-eyed peas—is good, colorful and nonstop. You have to clear your dishes and pay cash.

Source: Diana Gleasner, a travel writer and photographer who with her husband, Bill, has published 30 books and hundreds of articles on travel in the US and abroad. Their most recent effort is *Florida Off the Beaten Path,* The Globe Pequot Press, Box 833, Old Saybrook, Connecticut 06475.

The Secrets of Better Vacations in the Caribbean

Wonderful vacations and the Caribbean just seem to go together. But spending a few days or longer at some balmy island getaway can be a pretty expensive affair. So—here are some ways to trim costs without sacrificing romance.

Of course, planning a Caribbean vacation can be a daunting task given the number of diverse islands spread across thousands of square miles of sea.

The cost of a vacation can vary widely between each island, or group of islands. There are some approaches and general rules to follow that will help you find that romantic vacation without breaking the bank.

The Caribbean is just like any other vacation destination. It is always cheaper to go in the off-season. That runs from mid-April to mid-November. Vacation prices across the board can be as much as 30% to 40% cheaper in the off-season than during the height of the season.

Prices begin to rise as the high season approaches, but in general there are deals to be had throughout the region right up to the beginning of the high season. What makes the Caribbean different from a lot of vacation spots is the consistency of the weather. There is, in fact, little difference in weather between the high season and the middle of the off-season when temperatures are, at most, 5 to 10 degrees warmer.

Even during the height of the season, there are opportunities to get a price break. There is a three-week period between January 10 and early February when demand slackens somewhat and hoteliers are willing to cut rates by as much as a third.

Watch the headlines:

Another way to tap into a great vacation at an affordable price is to think about going to the Caribbean immediately following a hurricane, storm or some international crisis.

Demand always falls off at these times and hotels and resorts trim prices to encourage vacationers to return. *Catch:* Make sure that the hurricane or storm you're following hasn't disrupted your target island's infrastructure.

The best deals to the Caribbean are usually found on the larger islands with the greatest number of hotels and resorts, particularly Jamaica and the US Virgin Islands. The reason is simple. The greater number of vacation choices provides competition that helps keep prices down. Conversely, smaller, less developed islands, such as St. Barts, Grenada, the Grenadines and Anguilla, are generally more expensive.

Honeymooners forever:

Ask if there are special rates for honeymooners. They are regularly offered special deals, sometimes cutting as much as 50%—but at least 10% to 20%—off the price of a stay. Hotels and resorts do this in hopes that honeymooners will come back repeatedly in future years.

Quality price:

If you're traveling with other couples, it may be worth contacting several hotels to see if they'll give you a special rate for booking at least three rooms at a time.

Villas:

Some of the best deals in the Caribbean don't involve hotels or resorts—but villas. These range in size from one or two bedrooms to small mansions. Depending on the price, they include pools, maid service, cooks, private beaches, tennis courts and other amenities. The cost can be quite reasonable. A small one or two bedroom villa might rent for $1,000 a week during the high season, while the larger villas can go for $5,000 a week.

Even at the upper end of the market, the price can still be reasonable if it's split between three or four couples. Villas are available on most islands. *Good source to check:* Villas and Apartments Abroad Ltd., 212-759-1025 or 800-433-3020.

Floating feast:

Another option, particularly for the more adventurous, is renting a sailboat for a few days or a week. Again, it is an affordable option, especially if several couples are involved. These boats range from 50-footers up. They can come with a crew, including a cook. Sailboats give vacationers the chance to see several islands instead of just one. The only limitations are time and weather. Prices start at $3,000 a week during the high season. There are dozens of chartering services.

A few good ones…
- Bahamas Yachting, 800-327-2276.
- Boat US Travel, 800-477-4427.
- Cruise One, 800-227-8633.

One price for all:

All-inclusive packages (where a single price covers everything) are increasingly popular throughout the Caribbean. Some are offered as an alternative pricing structure at certain resorts, while other resorts are exclusively all-in-one. These packages offer simple yet affordable vacations where one price covers everything from rooms to meals, drinks, entertainment and even sporting activities. The cost of these packages ranges from $1,000 to $3,000 a week. Their value is often determined by how much a guest may eat or drink during a week.

Country retreats:

Puerto Rico leads the way in offering simple yet generally inviting country inns that are extremely affordable. The price for a room for two ranges from $30 to $80 a night. Meals are not included—unless noted. Good ones in Puerto Rico include:

- Parador Baños de Coamo, 809-825-2186.
- Parador Hacienda Gripinas, 809-721-2400.
- Parador Oasis, 809-892-1175.

For information and reservations on other paradores, call 800-443-0266 or 809-721-2884.

Source: Larry Fox, a *Washington Post* reporter, and Barbara Radin-Fox, a social worker and photographer. They are coauthors of several books including *Romantic Island Getaways: The Caribbean, Bermuda and the Bahamas*, John Wiley & Sons, 605 Third Ave., New York 10158.

Off the Beaten Path in The Hawaiian Islands

Hawaii:

- Hawaii Volcanoes National Park encompasses some of the wildest terrain on earth and is the closest that most people will ever get to an active volcano. Visitors can safely view one of the most active volcanoes in the world here —Kilauea. It has erupted continuously since 1983. On occasion, live molten lava can be seen from viewing areas.

More information: 808-967-7311.

- Kilauea Lodge is located just outside Volcanoes National Park. Besides wonderful accommodations, it offers gourmet meals in its lofty central hall.

More information: 808-967-7366.

- Waipio Valley Lookout, situated at the end of Highway 240, is perched above the rim of the valley. Visitors can take in the mile-wide valley below, which is flanked on all sides by cliffs rising vertically from 1,000 to 3,000 feet.

More information: 808-961-5797.

Kauai:

- The Grove Farm Homestead—a sugar plantation homestead founded in 1864 by George Wilcox—gives visitors a glimpse into the lifestyle of the 1860s. View the family's furnishings and personal possessions in the original main house, and stroll the beautifully maintained grounds. Reservations are required.

More information: 808-245-3202.

- Koke's State Park offers some of the most spectacular hiking in Hawaii. The trails pass through dense forests of redwood, cedar and pine…and wetland refuges for endangered native birds. Scenic outlooks include the magnificent Waimea Canyon and remote valleys of the Na Pali coast. To experience the full range, you will have to stay overnight. Koke's Lodge rents comfortably equipped cabins…but you must book well in advance.

More information: 808-335-6061.

Maui:

- Haleakala seems like a crater but is really an eroded valley that is the crowning experience of a visit to this island. Take the 1½-hour drive to this volcano's 10,023-foot summit and peer over the rim and into the 3,000-foot-deep valley. It measures 7.5 miles across at its widest point. Striking rust-colored streaks paint the moonlike slopes of this fascinating place.

More information: 808-572-9306.

- The Road to Hana is one of the more famous adventures in Hawaii. The 52-mile road is tricky with its many curves and one-lane bridges, but the scenery is worth the effort. The Hana Highway (Route 360) runs along the northeast slopes of the Haleakala Mountains. You'll pass isolated valleys, spectacular waterfalls, tropical flowers and stunning ocean overlooks.

More information: 808-244-3530.

- Lahaina is hardly off the beaten path in Maui, but its history makes it worth a visit despite the crowds. The town was once a center of Hawaiian royalty…then it became a raucous whaling port …and finally a quiet sugar plantation. Though it's now a busy tourist center, it has retained its sense of romance and history and is a delight to visit.

More information: 808-667-9175.

Oahu:

- Kole Kole Pass is unknown to most Oahu residents as well as tourists because it is accessible only by way of the Schofield Army Barracks, just south of the town of Wahiawa. The road runs through the Waianae Mountains and offers a cliff-top view at 1,720 feet of the picturesque Lualualei Valley on the Waianae Coast.

More information: 808-524-0722.

•Hoomaluhia Botanical Gardens, near the town of Kaneohe, takes up 400 acres of former farmland and remains more of a forest reserve than a landscaped garden. Towering cliffs create a magnificent backdrop to the varied vegetation, which includes specimens from Africa, India, tropical America, Polynesia and Hawaii.
More information: 808-233-7323.

•Malaekahana State Recreation Area lies on the northern windward shores of the island and consists of deep deposits of white sand piled along a mile-wide bay. Steep hills form a dramatic backdrop to the beach, and Goat Island (just a few hundred yards away through shallow waters) offers a unique glimpse of nesting seabirds.
More information: 808-524-0722.

Source: Sean Pager, long-time resident of Hawaii and avid hiker and windsurfer. He is the author of *Hawaii: Off the Beaten Path*, The Globe Pequot Press, Box 833, Old Saybrook, Connecticut 06475.

Fantastic Learning Vacations

If you've grown weary of the typical vacation activities of golfing, tennis, swimming and sunbathing, it's time to take advantage of one of many vacations that combine learning with relaxation. Your body may arrive home rested and tanned, and your mind will have received quite a workout!

Some great ones to try...

•*Backroads:* Biking trips to 64 destinations in the United States and abroad. The health and fitness trip winds through the California wine country and includes organized runs, hikes, swims and stretch classes, in addition to bicycling. The art lovers' inn trip explores the backroads of the Sonoma and Napa valleys, combining bicycling with visits to two or three of the region's finest artists each day. Other specialty trips are offered as well. Trips last 2 to 16 days.
More information: Backroads, 1516 Fifth St., Berkeley, California 94710. 510-527-1555.

•*Canoe Country Escapes:* Five- to 11-day canoe trips in the magnificent Boundary Waters Canoe Area Wilderness of northeastern Minnesota and southwestern Ontario. No prior paddling experience is needed. "Lodge-to-Lodge" itineraries combine four nights of accommodations with several nights spent at preset campsites (all of which are ready and waiting when you hit the shore). All trips are led by experienced guides, who teach the basics of the sport. You can also hike with a naturalist or fish with a fishing guide.
More information: Canoe Country Escapes, 194 S. Franklin St., Denver 80209. 303-722-6482.

•*The Chautauqua Institution:* A summer learning center with a wonderful mix of programs for all ages. The 750-acre complex borders Chautauqua Lake and encompasses a Victorian village and a 5,500-seat amphitheater. Each of the nine summer weeks focuses on a different political, economic, scientific or religious theme. *Other highlights:* Art exhibits...a symphony orchestra ...theater and opera companies...and a wide array of recreational facilities.
More information: Chautauqua Institution, One Ames St., Chautauqua, New York 14722. 800-836-ARTS.

•*Crow Canyon Archaeological Center:* Links laypeople with professional archaeologists in scientific research. Participants help reconstruct the cultural and natural environment of the Anasazi, the prehistoric people who lived in the "Four Corners Region," where Colorado, New Mexico, Utah and Arizona meet. Each August the center offers a family week in which grandparents and grandchildren (fourth grade or older) can participate in activities together.
More information: Crow Canyon Archaeological Center, 23390 County Rd. K, Cortez, Colorado 81321. 800-422-8975.

•*Hudson River Valley Art Workshops:* Offers a series of five-day workshops taught by nationally recognized artists. These workshops are held from May to October each year at the Greenville Arms, a Victorian country inn located in the northern Catskills. Artists of all levels of accomplishment come here to learn, seek inspiration and enjoy the fellowship of others who share their interest. Classes are offered in water-based media, oil, acrylics, pencil, pastel and charcoal. Recreational activities are also plentiful.
More information: Hudson River Valley Art Workshops, Box 659, Greenville, New York 12083. 518-966-5219.

•*National Habitat Wildlife Adventures:* Incredible trips that enable you to observe animals close up—in their own natural habitats. On most adventures, program leaders are joined by local guides with intimate knowledge of the region visited. North American adventures include a trip to Alaska to observe moose, caribou, Dall sheep, sea lions, whales, porpoises, sea otters, puffins—and the world's largest concentration of bald eagles. The company also operates Sealwatch, a series of 13 tours scheduled from late February through the middle of March. These tours allow people to view the quarter of a million harp seals that enter eastern Canada's Gulf of Saint Lawrence each year to bear their young on the vast floating ice fields off the Magdalen Islands of Quebec.

More information: Natural Habitat Wildlife Adventures, 2945 Center Green St. S., Suite H, Boulder, Colorado 80301. 800-543-8917.

• *The Omega Institute for Holistic Studies:* Offers more than 250 summer workshops focusing on many aspects of music, dance, theater, the fine arts, writing, environmental and social concerns, spiritual understanding, business and work issues and gender, relationship and family subjects. The Omega campus occupies 80 acres of rolling woodlands and lawns in the Hudson River Valley. Its Wellness Center offers massage and body work, nutritional counseling, wellness evaluations, holistic health therapies, sauna and flotation tanks. The institute offers programs year-round as well.

More information: Omega Institute, 260 Lake Dr., Rhinebeck, New York 12572. 914-266-4301.

• *Van Der Meer Tennis Center:* Daily, weekend and week-long clinics year-round for players at all skill levels. Dennis Van Der Meer personally conducts the adult programs and the advanced adult clinics. Students work on mastering a variety of strokes, building stroke consistency and developing mental skills for tennis. Senior citizen programs are also offered.

More information: Van Der Meer Tennis Center, Box 5902, Hilton Head, South Carolina 29938. 800-845-6138.

• *Vermont Off Beat:* Wonderful workshops at lovely country inns throughout Vermont. Topics change from year to year, but typical sessions focus on building techniques, gardening, painting, crafts, music and businesses.

More information: Vermont Off Beat, Box 4366, South Burlington, Vermont 05406. 802-863-2535.

• *Walking The World:* Year-round outdoor adventures in the United States and abroad for those 50 and older. Trips balance activity, rest and personal time. They appeal to a diverse group of people. Programs provide instruction in map and compass/route finding, backpacking, hiking, expedition planning, back-country cooking, hazard evaluation and back-country first aid/emergency procedures. Group gear and meals are supplied.

More information: Walking The World, Inc., Box 1186, Fort Collins, Colorado 80522. 303-225-0500.

Source: Harriet Webster, author of *Great American Learning Adventures,* HarperPerennial, 10 E. 53 St., New York 10022.

How to Have a More Comfortable Flight

If you have flown extensively, you already know the advantages of arriving early at the airport, drinking lots of water during the flight, removing your shoes and bringing a fabulous book to read. *What flight attendants know that you may not know…*

• *Bring your own big coffee mug.* You'll get more coffee from the flight attendant the first time he/she passes by…and it will stay warmer longer.

• *Accept headsets or bring your own.* When you want to get a great deal of work or reading done on a flight—or even if you just want to think undisturbed—headsets politely say "do not disturb" to a chatty neighbor.

• *Count your carry-ons before boarding.* Then recount them as you leave the plane. Passengers often must use two or three overhead compartments when storing carry-ons, making it easy to forget one of these bags when leaving the plane.

• *Wear wrinkle-free or fashionably wrinkled clothes.* Then you won't have to worry about seat-belt marks, and you'll look fresh when you deplane.

• *Bring an inflatable pillow.* This will allow your head to rest firmly in place. You'll snooze more easily and won't wake up with your head on your neighbor's shoulder.

•*Don't overclothe a baby.* Nine times out of ten, babies cry on a plane because they are too hot. *Also:* Be sure to use clothes that can be put on and taken off quickly and easily.

•*Carry your driving glasses with you.* If they go into the suitcase that goes into the baggage compartment, you won't be able to see the movie clearly…or even the flight attendant at the head of the plane. And if your luggage is lost or misplaced for a time, you won't be able to drive yourself from the airport.

Source: Barbara McCain and her daughter, Kelly McCain, flight attendants for Northwest Airlines and Delta Air Lines, respectively.

How to Stay Healthy While Traveling

No matter what your destination or reason for traveling, staying healthy is a prime concern whenever you're far from home.

Fatigue, stress, an upset stomach or worse can spell disaster for your vacation—or sap your business productivity. Fortunately, the wear and tear of travel can be kept to a minimum with some simple advance planning.

Here are some easy ways to make your travel more comfortable—and healthful.

Self-care checklist:

Your chief consideration when packing for a trip will be where you're going, how long you'll be away and what the climate is like at your destination. But no matter what sort of trip you're planning, bring along a well-stocked self-care kit. It should be easily reachable in your carry-on luggage and should contain…

•Antacid. Familiar store-bought remedies such as Maalox, Mylanta, Gelusil, Tums or Rolaids combat stomach upset, heartburn and abdominal cramping sometimes caused by unfamiliar food or drink—or overindulgence in either.

•Diarrhea remedy. Over-the-counter preparations like Imodium AD, Kaopectate or Pepto-Bismol are all effective at stopping diarrhea. Tablets are easier to take along on a trip, although the liquid forms of these medications usually offer faster relief.

•Laxative. On the road, constipation is often more of a problem than diarrhea.

Reason: Your diet while traveling is apt to lack high-fiber foods. Also, it may be difficult while traveling to maintain a regular exercise routine. Take along some Metamucil or Senokot just in case.

•Antihistamine. The over-the-counter medication Benadryl is effective against a host of potential allergens and irritants and is well-tolerated by most people. If you have to stay alert, ask your doctor to prescribe Seldane. It causes little or no drowsiness.

•Antibiotic. For tooth abscesses, severe bronchitis, festering skin wounds or other stubborn bacterial infections, ask your doctor to prescribe an antibiotic in advance.

Caution: Antibiotics should be used only under a doctor's supervision. Call your doctor at home for instructions.

•Motion-sickness remedy. Dramamine or Bonine tablets and scopolamine skin patches (Transderm Scop) are all effective. The patches are especially useful if you'll be spending long periods of time at sea, although they can cause dry mouth and, in the elderly, confusion.

Caution: Dramamine and Bonine can cause drowsiness. Avoid them if you have to stay alert.

•Athlete's foot remedy. Include antifungal foot powder or solutions like Lotrimin, Micatin or Tinactin in your travel kit since showers in hotel rooms and fitness centers aren't always fungus-free. *Also helpful:* Rubber thongs to wear in the shower.

•Sunscreen, sunglasses and hat. These are a must for travel to sunny places or if you intend to be outdoors for extended periods of time. Your sunscreen should have an SPF of at least 15 and should guard against both UVB and UVA rays.

•Insect repellent. Look for one that contains 20% to 30% DEET.

•Aspirin, acetaminophen or ibuprofen.

•Decongestant and facial tissues.

You might also want to bring along a basic first-aid kit containing an antibacterial cream or ointment, bandages, gauze, thermometer, scissors, tweezers and a pocketknife.

If you wear corrective lenses, pack a spare pair of contacts or eyeglasses—plus your prescription.

If you intend to swim in unchlorinated water, take along a remedy for swimmer's ear, an infection marked by redness, itching and pain of the outer ear canal. I recommend an over-the-counter preparation called Vosol.

Fighting jet lag:

Anytime you fly across several different time zones, you disrupt the body's circadian rhythms. The resulting jet lag should be thought of not as a special problem, but as another form of manageable stress. *Ways to control it:*

•Avoid alcohol during your flight. Alcohol, a depressant, can aggravate lethargy and fatigue, two classic symptoms of jet lag. It can also cause restlessness, which can disturb your sleep or keep you from sleeping altogether. And because it acts as a diuretic, alcohol can leave you feeling dehydrated.

•Limit your consumption of caffeine. Like alcohol, caffeine is a diuretic that can leave you feeling dehydrated and out of sorts. Too much caffeine can also cause nervousness, anxiety, tremors and insomnia.

•Drink plenty of water. Recent studies have shown that even slight dehydration can cause listlessness and fatigue and can even make you more prone to mental errors—symptoms similar to those of jet lag.

Bear in mind that you may be dehydrated even before departure. *Reason:* Your eating and drinking patterns may be erratic in the hours before your flight. Breathing dry cabin air only increases this dehydration and all its enervating effects.

To stay hydrated, drink plenty of water or other nonalcoholic beverages before and during your flight—one eight-ounce glass every two to three hours. Don't wait until you feel thirsty—by then you may already be dehydrated.

•Adapt to local time as quickly as possible. *Example:* If you land in Paris the morning after an all-night flight, have no more than a brief 90-minute nap—then stay awake until it's 9 or 10 PM in Paris.

Schedule nonstressful activities and eat light, refreshing meals on your arrival day. Pack a swimsuit and use the hotel's pool or hot tub to help you relax.

Safe food and drink:

Regions of the world fall into three "tiers":

•Europe, North America, Australia.

•Israel and the Caribbean.

•The rest of the Middle East, most of Africa, the Far East and other developing regions.

Anytime you travel to the second or third tier, you must be especially vigilant about what you eat and drink. *Self-defense:*

•Eat cooked food while it is still hot. Make sure meats are well-done. Throughout developing countries, undercooked beef and pork are major sources of tapeworms and other parasites. Likewise, all poultry, seafood and vegetables should be fresh and thoroughly cooked.

•Avoid peeled fruits (and those with broken skin). Watch out for raw vegetable salads, too. They can be contaminated with bacteria from food preparer's hands or from the water used to rinse the vegetables.

•Avoid custards, pastries and other baked desserts. These foods are often contaminated with microbes that trigger gastric distress, especially if improperly refrigerated. *Exception:* Served still hot from the oven, these foods are generally safe. If you want dessert, stick to wrapped candy or fresh fruit that you peel yourself.

•Stick to bottled or canned beverages. And watch out for ice cubes, which might be contaminated. Avoid milk, milk products and foods prepared with them unless you're sure they have been properly pasteurized.

•Avoid bread left lying in open baskets. It may have been exposed to flies and other disease-bearing insects. If you're not certain whether bread has been properly stored, remove the crust and eat only the interior of the loaf.

Watching out for infectious diseases:

If you're planning a trip to the tropics, ask your doctor about protecting yourself against malaria, yellow fever, schistosomiasis and other potential threats. If you'll need immunizations, get them at least a month before your departure. Frantic, last-minute efforts to obtain "shots" only compound the ordinary stress occasioned by an overseas journey. And multiple immunizations require several shots over a period of days or weeks.

A 24-hour hotline run by the Centers for Disease Control and Prevention (CDC) provides recorded messages outlining immunization requirements and recommendations for international travel. Call 404-332-4559.

Health information for overseas travelers is also available from some medical schools and teaching hospitals. For a list of regions where war or political strife might jeopardize travelers, contact the US State Department at 202-647-5225.

Malaria—probably the most serious of all the infectious diseases found in the tropics—used to be easily controlled with medications. *Now:* In many parts of the world, there are drug-resistant strains of malaria. Chloroquine and other anti-malarial drugs are virtually useless against them.

A new drug called mefloquine (Lariam) is often effective against drug-resistant malaria, but even this medication is losing strength in Southeast Asia and parts of Africa. Doxycycline can combat stubborn strains but should not be taken by children or pregnant women.

To avoid malaria, ask your doctor about taking prophylactic drugs. These must be taken one week before you travel to ensure that adequate blood levels of the drug are reached before you arrive—and that any adverse reactions occur while you're still at home. For more information, contact the CDC's 24-hour malaria hotline at 404-332-4555.

Ultimately, no matter where you travel, common sense should prevail. Medications and inoculations are no substitute for adequate rest during a trip, for avoiding excesses in eating and drinking or for following basic hygiene. With these precautions in mind, you should always be able to travel in comfort—and good health.

Source: Karl Neumann, MD, editor and publisher of *Traveling Healthy,* 108-48 70 Rd., Forest Hills, New York 11375. He is also coeditor of *The Business Traveler's Guide to Good Health While Traveling,* Chronimed Publishing, 13911 Ridgedale Dr., Minnetonka, Minnesota 55305.

If Your Flight Is Cancelled

If your flight is cancelled after you reach the airport, find a phone and call the airline's reservation number. Ask to be rebooked on the next scheduled flight to your destination. This avoids waiting in long lines of passengers trying to rebook. *Alternative:* Go to the desk personnel at one of your carrier's other gates, where there is no line. All desks tie into the same computer system—you need not wait at the designated gate.

Source: *Travel & Leisure,* 1120 Avenue of the Americas, New York 10036.

Frequent Fliers

Frequent fliers traveling on free tickets are not guaranteed the same treatment as paying passengers. If their flight is delayed or cancelled, the airline is less likely to endorse the ticket over to another carrier. A stranded traveler may not receive amenities such as hotel and meal vouchers. *Self-defense:* Make sure the gate agent knows you're a very frequent flier. Airlines generally go to great lengths to placate their best customers. Ask to be placed on standby for the carrier's next flight out. If you don't receive the treatment you think you deserve, complain in writing to the airline's customer service department.

Source: *Condé Nast Traveler,* 360 Madison Ave., New York 10017.

Standby Basics

Once a standby passenger boards a plane, he/she has many—but not all—of the same rights as a regularly ticketed passenger. In rare cases, he may be bumped if the regularly scheduled passenger has a series of international connections to make and cannot travel at any other time. Rather than asking the standby passenger to leave, however, most airlines will probably make an announcement asking for volunteers. When a standby passenger is asked to relinquish his seat, it is not required that he be offered compensation—only travelers with confirmed reservations have that right.

Source: Roundup of travel industry experts, reported in *The New York Times.*

Avoiding Rental-Car Penalties

To avoid penalties and higher charges when renting a car, ask the time at which you must return the car. Some companies give a one-hour grace period, some charge an hourly rate for late returns and some charge for an additional *full day* even if you are only an hour late. Also, if you return a weekly rental early, you may be charged the higher day rate instead. When renting at a weekend or weekly rate, find out the earliest and latest times you can return the car.

Source: *Consumer Reports Travel Letter*, 101 Truman Ave., Yonkers, New York 10703.

Rental-Car Breakdown

If a rental car breaks down, the renter is usually not financially responsible. Most rental companies pay for towing and mechanical repairs. *Exception:* Any breakdown caused by off-road or other prohibited use of a vehicle. *What to do:* Follow the company's guidelines from the agreement jacket or glove compartment. Notify the rental location as soon as possible. *Overseas:* In remote locations, you may need to have the car repaired yourself. Save receipts for reimbursement.

Source: *Condé Nast Traveler*, 360 Madison Ave., New York 10017.

Quick Metric Conversion Basics

To convert a two-digit kilometer number into miles, multiply the first digit by six. *Example:* On a road where the speed limit is 90 kilometers per hour, multiply nine times six to get 54 miles per hour...if the kilometer figure is three digits, multiply the first two by six. *Example:* To convert 100 kilometers per hour, multiply 10 times 6 to get 60 miles per hour. *To convert Celsius to Fahrenheit:* Double the Celsius figure and add 30 degrees. *Example:* If it's four degrees Celsius, double that to eight and add 30 to get 38 degrees Fahrenheit. *Important:* While these figures are not exact, they are usually close enough. Four degrees Celsius is actually equal to 39 degrees Fahrenheit.

Source: *Travel Smart*, 40 Beechdale Rd., Dobbs Ferry, New York 10522.

Loss-Proof Luggage

List items contained in each bag...and your home address inside...carry a photo of your luggage for easy identification...check bags at least 30 minutes before domestic and an hour before international flights...never leave bags unattended...always put valuables and a spare set of clothing in a carry-on. *Extra theft protection:* Use a security belt or wallet...when waiting, stand with your back against the wall to discourage pickpockets.

Source: *The Senior Citizens' Guide to Budget Travel in Europe* by Paige Palmer, Pilot Books, 103 Cooper St., Babylon, New York 11702.

Do-It-Yourself Traveler's Diarrhea Relief

In one glass, mix eight ounces fruit juice...½ teaspoon honey...a pinch of salt. In a second glass, mix eight ounces purified water...¼ teaspoon baking soda. Alternate sips from each glass until you've consumed them both.

Source: US Public Health Service, reported in *Natural Health*, 17 Station St., Box 1200, Brookline Village, Massachusetts 02147.

Aisle Seats Are Safest

Aisle seats are safest in plane crashes. Rear seats are best for surviving initial impact. But after the crash, the key to survival is fast escape from smoke and fire—the worst killers in plane crashes. Fire usually blocks exits on one side of the plane and quickly fills the cabin with smoke. *Self-defense:* An aisle seat that gives quick access to exits on both sides and the rear of the plane.

Source: National Transportation Safety Board specialists, reported in *The Safe Travel Book* by Peter Savage, Lexington Books, 866 Third Ave., New York 10022.

House-Swapping

House-swapping is not only an inexpensive way to explore a foreign country...it also offers the comforts of home when you're far from it. *More information:* Vacation Exchange Club, Box 650, Key West, Florida 33041, 800-638-3841...Intervac US, Box 590504, San Francisco 94159, 415-435-3497...Trading Homes International, Box 787, Hermosa Beach, California 90254, 800-877-8723.

Source: *The Mature Traveler*, Box 50820, Reno, Nevada 89513.

Better Outdoor-Market Shopping

Better outdoor-market shopping on international trips: Do not carry valuables or your passport on your person. Bring just the cash that you plan to spend. *Men:* No wallets in side or back pockets. *Women:* No handbags slung behind or at the side. *Also:* Dress conservatively—no beachwear or shorts. Be careful to eat only cooked foods, and only in the cleanest-looking places. Make sure the person handling the food is not also responsible for handling the money.

Source: Diana Kennedy, writing in *Condé Nast Traveler*, 360 Madison Ave., New York 10017.

Better Cruise Ship Tipping

Tip the dining room waiter and cabin steward $3 per day per person...tip the busboy $1.50 per day...tip the headwaiter $2.50 per person for a cruise of three to four days...at your discretion for cruises of seven days or longer...pay gratuities in cash at the end of the cruise. *Also:* Tip bellboys and other service personnel at your discretion as service is given ...add 15% to checks at nightclubs and bars.

Source: *Today's Family*, 27 Empire Dr., St. Paul, Minnesota 55103.

Dance Tours for Solo Travelers

Ballroom Dancers Without Partners sponsors cruises and tours for singles who like to dance. Professional dance instructors accompany each group, and trips cater to beginners and advanced dancers. Trips include at least one man for every five women and one woman for every five men. If enough men don't sign up—gentlemen hosts are invited to come along *free*.

Source: Ira Goldberg, Ballroom Dancers Without Partners, Luxury Worldwide Cruises & Tours, 2750 NE 187 St., North Miami Beach 33180.

Skiing for Seniors

The Over-the-Hill Gang International (OTHG) offers savings on lift tickets at more than 80 ski areas as well as discounts on ski trips and many other adventure travels for people 50 and older.

Source: OTHG, 3310 Cedar Heights Dr., Colorado Springs, Colorado 80904.

Vacation Illness Self-Defense

Get a list of family doctors in the states where you plan to travel. A list of members of the American Academy of Family Physicians is available free from the AAFP, 8880 Ward Pkwy., Kansas City, Missouri 64114.

Source: *American Guidance for Seniors* by Ken Skala, advocate, lecturer and author. The Career Press, 180 Fifth Ave., Box 34, Hawthorne, New Jersey 07507.

Airplane Hijackers

If airplane hijackers demand passports, citizens of the United States should delay presenting them as long as possible. Keep your passport in hand luggage or in the pocket of a coat in an overhead compartment. If terrorists force you to leave your seat, you will not have it with you. If the hijacking continues, you will eventually have to produce it—but the terrorists' initial show of force may be over by then.

Source: *The Safe Travel Book* by Peter Savage, Lexington Books, Inc., 866 Third Ave., New York 10022.

Traveling with Arthritis

Arrange your trip four to six months in advance. This will give you enough time to allow for special arrangements to be made.

If you plan to drive, chart the best route. If you plan to fly or take a train, inform the airline or train personnel that you'll need assistance with baggage and boarding.

Helpful: Ask a travel agent to communicate your special needs and limitations to the appropriate people.

What to ask for: A hotel room on the ground floor…accessible elevators…transportation from the airport…hand rails near toilet and tub…levers instead of knobs on doors and faucets…heated pool or massage…wheelchair accommodations, if necessary.

•Be realistic when picking your destination or tour. If you experience morning stiffness, camping may be difficult, hiking impossible. If you fail to research the trip you intend to take, you could be in for an unpleasant surprise.

Example I: A couple with arthritis was eager to see the French region of Provence, but they didn't anticipate the steep cobblestone lanes or the lack of elevators in medieval castles.

Example II: A woman with arthritis eagerly signed up for a sailing trip—only to find she had to tie knots, climb rope ladders and struggle for footing on deck—activities she found painful and exhausting.

•Make sure your health insurance covers you during travel. Some policies refuse reimbursement for medical costs incurred on cruise ships. If your policy does not cover travel, consider buying special medical trip insurance before you leave.

Caution: Many policies won't pay for treatment of pre-existing conditions—those for which you received medical treatment 90 days prior to purchase or date of travel.

•Pack as lightly as possible. Use nylon luggage with shoulder straps and wheels. Clear out accumulated souvenirs, pamphlets, etc., from purses and totes at the end of each day. Consider using a fanny pack or backpack. They're often more comfortable because they distribute weight across a larger part of the body. Carry small bills to tip skycaps and porters—and use them.

•Pace yourself. Don't expect to do everything, especially in one day. Don't allow yourself to get overtired. Alternate demanding activities and rest. Stop at cafés while sightseeing. While touring museums, sit down to watch video exhibits. Bring a book or plan restful ways to pass time in case you can't keep up with your travel companions.

•Continue your health-maintenance routines. Do range-of-motion exercises to prevent stiffness. When traveling by plane or train, take frequent walks up and down aisles. Stop to stretch frequently when driving. Eat lightly. Take medications on schedule. Hand-carry medications to avoid losing them. Bring snacks if you take medications with food.

•Take along joint-saving devices. A folding cane can be a vacation-saver, even if you don't use one regularly.

Other aids: Soft cervical collar or inflatable pillows for back and neck…rubber lever door handle for hotel rooms…easy-grip utensils and pens…sneakers with Velcro fasteners (be sure to break them in before your trip).

•Use a wheelchair, if necessary. It will help you conserve energy while getting around museums, airports, shopping malls, etc.

•Contact the Arthritis Foundation. Order a free copy of the brochure *Travel Tips for People with Arthritis*. It includes a list of resources for travel information and accessible tours. Ask about its arthritis self-help program and get the address and number of the chapter in your area.

3

Your Family
Your Home

Your Family—Your Home:1995...and beyond

Edith Weiner, Weiner Edrich, Brown, Inc.

The term "family values," the reverberant buzzword of the early 1990s—connoting strong family ties and domestic stability, frugality and normalcy—will become a distant memory, as family traditions gradually blur. The wave of the twenty-first century is already being felt—the wave of career instability, family instability, financial unpredictability and an increasingly fast-paced lifestyle for family members of all ages.

Result: Planning for the future will become all but impossible for most families. Not knowing from one week to the next whether any breadwinner in the family will have a job, or whether the job will be in the same location from one month to the next will be an increasingly widespread source of family anxiety.

So will the continued transience of families themselves, with the high divorce rate throwing hundreds of thousands of families into emotional and financial disarray each year.

For adults of all ages, this challenge strongly suggests the need to improve self-discipline, especially in financial matters—to be prepared for costly upheavals in family life, such as divorce, child support or loss of income.

Learning how to save—not only for retirement but for emergencies that may occur well before retirement—should be a top priority for adults these days.

As for family structure, we can expect to see more and more families headed by grandparents. This is because AIDS, drug addiction, the growing population of unwed mothers and economic hardships are forcing grandparents to redefine their roles in families. They are being forced to take on financial and daily care responsibilities they never expected.

Other home and family trends :

• Increased role of religion in family and personal life. People are becoming more and more anxious about the pace and intensity of change in their personal lives and in society in general. They are therefore searching for anchors of stability—of comforting structure and dogma. They are finding it in religion.

• Growing numbers of "commuter marriages." As jobs are eliminated, job-seeking requires relocating or long-distance commuting, and married working couples will live apart during the week and together on weekends.

• Growing flexibility and changeability in the home. Construction and materials technology will increasingly allow for affordable reconfiguration of rooms, furniture and decoration. This will allow people to upgrade or simply change the design and/or look of their homes at virtually any time for very little money.

How to Organize a Family Reunion

You want to reunite with relatives you haven't seen in years, and meet some you've never even heard about.

You want to have a chance to re-establish relationships—even mend some bridges—and make new friendships. That's what a family reunion is all about.

Keep it simple:

Since putting together a reunion takes lots of time and you must pay attention to detail, it is important that you start off right at the beginning with the motto: "Keep it simple." In order to keep it simple, you need a plan and must be organized. Here's how to begin.

Goal—a big turnout:

One of the easiest ways to generate enthusiasm for a family reunion is to plan it around a 50th wedding anniversary or the 75th (or 100th) birthday of an older, much-loved family member. Knowing that a great-grandmother or grandfather or the family's oldest living great-aunt will be holding court at the reunion adds excitement to the event and attracts the mature—and the younger—family members to be part of what will be a historic family event.

Pulling your team together:

Once you have selected the family relative whom you will fete and a date for the reunion, you'll need to plan three initial mailings:

First mailing: Write to every family member and announce the date and occasion for the reunion…and ask for nominations for chairperson, secretary and treasurer for a Family Reunion Executive Committee.

Enclose a form for each position that includes full name, address, date of birth, phone number and qualifications of nominees.

Request that the form be returned within two weeks so a decision can be made quickly.

Second mailing: Send everyone the names of the nominees, and include a ballot due back in two weeks. This democratic process will imbue the newly elected with legitimate authority.

Third mailing: Announce the names of the Executive Committee, and begin to get the entire family involved by calling for volunteers for the following committees:

•Communications Committee. Develops the mailing list. Keeps track of all the correspondence and forms that will be sent to and received from a growing list of family members, including the introductory letter, mailing list, family address and telephone numbers, birthday list and reservation forms.

•Host Committee. Chooses the ideal location for the reunion, such as an inn, dude ranch, spa, resort or family home.

•Travel Committee. Works with a travel agent to coordinate travel and accommodations…and gets the best price.

•Welcoming Committee. Greets and directs family members upon arrival in the host town.

•Events Committee. Plans raffles, scholarship awards, family-member achievement awards.

•Meals Committee. Organizes the food for formal and informal indoor and outdoor events such as picnics, lunches and dances.

Once you get your committees working, the whole process will take on a life of its own.

Source: Harry McKinzie, author of *Family Reunions: How to Plan Yours*, McKinzie Publishing Co., 11000 Wilshire Blvd., Box 241777, Los Angeles 90024.

How to Disagree With Your Spouse

By observing their parents, children learn how to cope with life—including how to deal with conflict. To be successful parents, fathers and mothers must learn to conduct their disagreements effectively.

If this is done correctly, their children will learn a valuable lesson—that people who love each other can solve their problems in ways that satisfy both sides.

How parental arguments affect children:

No conscientious parent deliberately sets out to argue in front of his/her children…but in a family setting, it is virtually impossible to keep every disagreement hidden from them.

Even when they are too young to understand words, children are remarkably sensitive to the emotional signals of disagreement—such as facial expressions, body language and tone of voice.

Children of all ages are distressed if their parents lose control when disagreeing. The distress is reflected in different behaviors as they develop.

Toddlers who witness shouting matches between their fathers and mothers may become fearful and agitated. Some begin to copy their parents' shouting and table pounding…others suddenly burst into tears. They feel their own security is threatened when their parents show disunity.

Preschoolers understand more of the details of the argument. They may try to stop the fight by diverting their parents' attention to other matters…perhaps even by directing the anger toward themselves.

Example: Jane and her husband were in the front seat of the car bickering about the shortest route to the beach. Five-year-old Suzie started to hug her mother from behind while pointing out the beautiful flowers on the roadside. Meanwhile, three-year-old Sam began calling out in a loud voice, kicking the back of the front seat… and then punching himself.

School-age children are not only worried about their family security…they also feel socially embarrassed. They take sides in arguments.

Example: Martha was angrily accusing her husband of being stingy when eight-year-old Tom joined the fray, telling his father, "…and the last time I asked you for money for a new video game, you turned me down, too."

As Tom's case points out, sometimes children try to manipulate parental disagreements to their own advantage…and feel guilty later. More often, they blame themselves for the argument, inventing fanciful theories to explain how their actions caused their parents to quarrel.

It doesn't take an all-out screaming match to upset children. Hostility between parents that is expressed indirectly through sniping and sarcasm is also disturbing…and lays the foundation for children to develop the same style of behavior when they grow up.

How to handle disagreements:

• Don't deny that an argument occurred. You can't fool children by pretending that you and your spouse are in agreement when obvious discord has upset the emotional atmosphere. They will figure out on their own that something is wrong and likely think it is worse than it actually is.

If parents deny their anger, children learn that anger is unacceptable and begin to bury their own feelings rather than learn how to deal with them in positive ways.

What you should do: Acknowledge the argument and encourage your children to express their feelings about it. No matter how large or small the argument, tell the children who saw it that they can talk to you about it.

What to say: Tell your four-year-old child, "I know you just saw Mommy and Daddy yelling at each other. It was very upsetting for all of us. We're sorry…sometimes grown-ups lose their tempers. It wasn't your fault, and, of course, we still love you as much as ever."

• Don't plead your case to the children or expect them to take sides. It's not your child's job to be judge and jury over your disputes. And if you enlist a child to take your side, it threatens his relationship with your spouse.

What you should do: Explain the content of the disagreement in simple, neutral terms…give just enough information to reassure the child.

Example: Sara and Jeff had a heated argument over accepting Jeff's mother's invitation to

71

dinner. The psychological origin of the dispute is Sara's resentment of Jeff's inability to refuse his mother's requests. Sara should tell the children, "You know how much Grandma likes us to come for dinner, but I would prefer not to go there tomorrow. I'd rather go next week instead."

•Don't trivialize your spouse's anger—or try to humiliate him/her. A child who sees that one parent repeatedly discounts the other's feelings and attitudes will conclude that the second parent need not be taken seriously. But children want two parents they can look up to...and they need to learn that adults take other people's concerns seriously.

What you should do: Find out why your spouse feels the way he/she does, and try to improve the situation with respect, not with ridicule.

•Don't walk out of the house in anger. A child who sees you leave may imagine that you will never come back...and think that if you can leave your spouse, one day you might leave him, too.

What you should do: If you feel so angry that you really can't take it any more, tell the child before you leave...reassure him you'll be back soon. Tell him, "I really must go out for a while, but don't worry. I'll be back to tuck you into bed."

•Don't resort to violence. Dishes should stay in the cupboard...books on the shelves. Violence immediately destroys trust between people ...makes it impossible to resolve disputes sensibly...threatens the physical safety of children caught in the middle...and teaches them to react to their own problems in the same way.

Important: Don't use profanity either...unless you want to hear your children imitating your performance.

What you should do: Learn to recognize the real source of your anger and tell your children about it.

Two basic rules for parents:

•*Rule 1:* Learn to stop a developing argument in its tracks. Plan a strategy with your spouse when you feel a discussion is about to escalate into an angry exchange. One of you might say, "This isn't the place for us to argue. Let's stop now, and we'll discuss it later." Keep in mind,

though, that despite your sincere efforts, you probably won't always succeed in avoiding arguments.

•*Rule 2:* If you do have a major argument in front of your children—let them see when you make up. Show them that grown-ups aren't perfect...but when they make mistakes they own up to them and apologize. You want your children to learn these two rules of adult life.

Source: Lawrence Balter, PhD, professor of applied psychology at New York University. He is coauthor of *Not in Front of the Children: How to Talk to Your Child About Tough Family Matters,* Viking, 375 Hudson St., New York 10014.

Secrets of Happy Couples

The high rate of divorce, combined with the skyrocketing number of dysfunctional families, suggests that there is no such thing as a truly happy marriage...*but my interviews with couples across the country show otherwise.*

The couples I talked to had been married between 7 and 55 years. More than half described themselves as very happily married. Only two or three were actually miserable.

The remaining 35 couples are hanging in there and doing all right.

The happiest couples share a number of characteristics—qualities from which we can learn. And they dispelled several popular misconceptions...

•*Myth:* Be realistic, not idealistic.

Reality: In fact, the most happily married people idealize their spouses. Many of them say they think their husbands or wives are the greatest people in the world. That belief certainly helps bring out the best in their partners. Research has shown that people live up—or down—to our expectations.

Even after the "crazy-in-love" phase has long passed, the happy partners continue to see each other through rose-colored glasses—often more positively than others might see them.

•*Myth:* Happy couples rarely fight.

Reality: Of course, happy couples fight—some more often than others. But happy couples fight by the rules and are able to keep conflicts from escalating.

The rules differ depending on the temperaments of the people involved. Some couples say, "We never go to bed angry." They insist on resolving issues rather than walking away from them.

Happy couples have impulse control. They are willing and able to censor themselves, even in the midst of rage, so as not to say or do the thing that would be "fatal" to the relationship.

•*Myth:* There's no such thing as love at first sight.

Reality: Some romances blossomed slowly. But there were also many who remembered feeling a powerful attraction at their first meeting…and who are still in love with each other years later. There were also cases in which one partner fell in love immediately, while the other partner took longer to come around.

•*Myth:* Friendship, not sex, is the key to a long-lasting relationship.

Reality: Both sex and friendship are important.

While the happiest husbands and wives say they are each other's best friends, they also have very strong sexual bonds. True, the intense infatuation—being ready to jump into bed at any opportunity—fades after a few years. But the sexual chemistry remains, even during periods when a couple isn't making love.

Example: One wife was so exhausted after having a baby that she temporarily lost interest in sex. Nevertheless, she continued to have vivid sexual dreams about her husband.

•*Myth:* Happy couples have independent lives.

Reality: Even if they don't share all the same interests, happy couples spend a lot of time together.

This is another characteristic that has to do with temperament—some couples require less togetherness than others. But the idea that separate identities are essential is completely untrue. These couples have definitely found a shared identity. Over time, they stopped feeling single at heart and came to be married at heart. If that process doesn't happen, the marriage is in trouble.

•*Myth:* The happiest couples raise children together.

Reality: The few childless couples I interviewed are quite happy. What seemed to be important is not whether a couple has children, but whether they agree that children should or should not be part of their lives together.

In fact, children are the subject couples fight about most often—more than sex, money or in-laws. Children can disrupt the unity of a couple, introducing an element of separation and continuous potential conflict.

That doesn't mean that children damage a relationship—far from it. But raising children is very difficult, with a lot to disagree about. Happy couples who are parents face and grapple with these conflicts and learn from each other.

Example: One husband was a severe disciplinarian, while his wife was very gentle with the children. This difference caused an ongoing disagreement between them. Eventually, he realized that she was able to get exactly the response she wanted from the children without screaming or yelling…and he began to temper his own approach.

Why couples get along:

For a marriage to be happy, the partners need to be identical in background but opposite in personality—one woman said.

I saw this truth borne out over and over again. If a couple shares the same background (age, religion, ethnicity, economic status), they are more likely to agree on many of the day-to-day decisions, such as how to raise the children, what vacations to take, what colors to use when decorating the house, etc.

Having opposite personalities is what provides the spark. I saw many couples in which one partner was somewhat depressive and pessimistic and the other was optimistic. They seemed to balance or compensate for each other.

I'm not suggesting that people with different backgrounds can't have good marriages. But shared reference points do make marriages work better.

Source: Catherine Johnson, PhD, author of *Lucky in Love: The Secrets of Happy Couples and How Their Marriages Thrive,* Viking Penguin, 375 Hudson St., New York 10014.

Honeymoon Memory

Ask your spouse to join you for an overnight date at the place where you went on your honeymoon—even if this means staying at a cheap motel. Take the time to recall your honeymoon and the history of your marriage. You may decide to improve on what you did the first time. Make a date to go someplace entirely different to have honeymoon memories.

Source: Dave and Claudia Arp, directors of the Marriage Alive Workshops, a national marriage enrichment network, Box 90303, Knoxville, Tennessee 37990. They are the authors of *52 Dates for You and Your Mate*, Thomas Nelson, Box 141000, Nashville 37214.

Marriage Building

Communicate the good things about your marriage. Most couples express feelings effectively when angry or upset—but not when happy.

Helpful exercise: Write three items that your mate does that please you…three things you would like him/her to do more often…three things you think he would like you to do more often.

Source: *The Ultimate Marriage Builder* by David and Claudia Arp, family-life educators, Knoxville, Tennessee. Thomas Nelson Publishers, Box 141000, Nashville 37214.

Which Type of Marriage Do You Have?

Fifteen years ago, my colleagues at the University of Minnesota and I started a research project to learn how to help couples prepare for marriage more effectively.

The result was the Prepare program for couples planning to marry. Several years later, we started the Enrich program to help couples who were already married increase their satisfaction with their relationships.

Continually refined during the past 15 years, the Prepare/Enrich program includes a 125-item questionnaire that assesses the health of the relationship and two to five counseling sessions that teach proven skills for resolving problems constructively.

To date, Prepare/Enrich has been used by more than 500,000 premarital and 250,000 married couples to enhance their relationships. More than 20,000 counselors and clerics around the country have been trained in its use.

Our research has shown that it's possible to determine the quality of a marriage—or other serious romantic relationship—based on how well a couple rates on *11 relationship dimensions:*

•*Expectations:* Realism about the demands and problems of marriage.

•*Personality issues:* How well you like your partner's characteristics and habits.

•*Communication:* Ability to share feelings and be understood.

•*Conflict resolution:* Ability to discuss disagreements and resolve them.

•*Financial management:* Agreement about budgets, spending, long-term goals and other financial issues.

•*Leisure activities:* Enjoyment of hobbies and other interests, both together and apart.

•*Sexual relationship:* Taking pleasure in sex, and feeling free to talk about sexual topics and preferences.

•*Parenting:* Agreement on the number of children and how they should be raised.

•*Family and friends:* A good relationship with both your own and your partner's family and social circle.

•*Egalitarian roles:* Agreement on decision-making procedures and division of household and other responsibilities.

•*Religious orientation:* Shared values and beliefs.

Five marriage types:

Based on these 11 dimensions, we've identified five different types of marriage—each one representing a different degree of satisfaction or dissatisfaction with the relationship…

•*Vitalized couples*—at the top end of the scale—are strong in nearly all of the above areas. These couples continue to thrive over the long haul because they have so many resources upon which to draw. Even if a problem crops up in one area, their communication and problem-resolution skills are good, enabling them to deal with conflicts before they get out of hand.

• *Devitalized couples*—at the other extreme —have almost nothing going for them. They may be on the verge of splitting up or may stay together for the sake of the children or for religious reasons.

Not only are devitalized couples dissatisfied with their communication, they don't even like each other much. *Sad:* There might have been a time when counseling could have helped these couples to work out their conflicts. But devitalized couples don't even bother to fight anymore. By the time they come in for counseling—if they come at all—there's rarely enough motivation left to save the marriage.

In between those two extremes are three types of couples—conflicted, traditional and harmonious.

• *Conflicted couples* may be unhappy but at least they're fighting—and they are attempting to deal with their problems, if not in the most constructive ways. There's some energy left in the relationships.

Conflicted couples can often be helped greatly by counseling that teaches them better techniques for communicating and resolving conflicts.

• *Traditional couples* are better matched in external dimensions than they are in internal ones.

Traditional couples are strongest in areas such as religion, family/friends, parenting and leisure activities but lack strengths in communication and conflict resolution—and they may not be crazy about each other's personalities.

Traditional couples do fine as long as their external support systems are in place. But if a highly stressful situation should arise—such as a job loss, major illness or crisis with the children—those systems may fail to sustain a traditional couple. They, too, can benefit from communication training.

• *Harmonious couples* aren't quite as happy as vitalized couples, but they do pretty well. Their problems tend to arise during particular situations more than from personality differences. Although their communication might stand some improvement, their skills are basically strong—and if they hit a crisis, they're capable of negotiating it fairly effectively, possibly with the help of short-term counseling. Evaluating your relationship:

Figuring out how your own marriage rates on the 11 relationship dimensions can serve two important functions:

• First, it opens up communication about these issues, which couples too often avoid.

• Second, it can draw attention to trouble spots—before they become too difficult to resolve.

Try this exercise with your spouse or partner:

• Review the 11 dimensions described earlier. Select three areas that you see as strengths in your relationship—and three that could use improvement. We refer to these as growth areas.

Important: Each person should do this part of the exercise independently, without input from the partner.

• Now share your observations with each other, using the following format:

One person describes and discusses a strength area.

Then the other person shares one strength he/she has identified.

Repeat this process until each of you has discussed all three strength areas.

Next, use the same procedure to talk about the three growth areas you chose.

• Finally, discuss whether any of your partner's responses surprised you and where you had the most agreements—and disagreements.

This process can help you acknowledge and capitalize on your strengths and begin to think about what you'd like to improve.

Helpful: Set a date for exploring the growth areas further. At that time, you'll get the best results if you define the problem together. Talk about how each of you contributes to the problem, brainstorm possible solutions, pick one to try and decide how you'll evaluate your progress—together.

If you have so many problem areas that it is difficult to narrow them down to just three—or if you have trouble identifying three strong areas—that's a powerful signal to consider counseling. Almost any couple can benefit from some skill-building assistance, but people who feel this negative about their relationship shouldn't wait.

With outside help, they may be able to rediscover the life in their marriage.

Source: David H. Olson, PhD, professor in the Family Social Sciences Department at the University of Minnesota. He is president of Prepare/Enrich, Box 190, Minneapolis 55440, which trains counseling professionals to work with premarital and married couples.

Family Meetings Resolve Disputes

Family meetings resolve disputes effectively. Schedule council meetings regularly. Operate under rules agreed to in advance. All family members should help run meetings and contribute to them. *Meeting topics:* Solving problems, assigning chores, reviewing responsibilities—also, planning fun activities and expressing appreciation. *Important:* Avoid criticizing anyone's ideas—so everyone feels safe expressing thoughts and feelings.

Source: *Playful Parenting* by Denise Chapman Weston, MSW, licensed play therapist, North Attleboro, Massachusetts. Jeremy P. Tarcher, Inc., 5858 Wilshire Blvd., Los Angeles 90036.

How to Teach Kids Responsibility

Responsibility in children—or anyone—is much more than just remembering to do chores or being obedient. It means caring about how your actions make other people feel and understanding why rules are important.

To teach responsibility:

• Set an example. Kids may not always listen when we lecture them, but they watch us carefully and draw conclusions about appropriate behavior from our actions.

Example I: You and your son are rushing to get to a store before it closes. You stop to help a woman carry her baby stroller up the stairs. Your child learns—it's good to go out of your way to help people.

Example II: At the movies, you lie about your daughter's age so that her ticket is cheaper.

Your daughter learns the nonresponsible message—it's okay to lie.

• Whenever your kids take responsibility, notice it—and express your appreciation. Rewarding desirable behavior encourages this. People often overlook these occasions or take them for granted. Worse, many parents only comment when their kids forget to be responsible.

Parents need to remember to say, "Thanks, that was a big help." Be especially careful to acknowledge behavior that's important to you but that may not be important to your child. *Examples:*

1. "I noticed that you put your books in your room instead of leaving them on the table. That's great—now I can set the table for dinner."

2. "I appreciate that you hung up your jacket when you came home."

3. Give kids choices. Adulthood consists of one choice after another. Making good decisions is a prerequisite to responsible behavior. Therefore a kid who is simply told what to do all the time never learns to make informed choices.

Suggestion: Instead of simply assigning chores to family members, make a list of everything that needs to be done and call a family meeting to decide who will take care of each task. Together, you may be able to divide the duties so that each person is assigned tasks he/she doesn't mind...or work out a rotation system so that no one is always stuck with the most difficult or tedious chores.

Involving your kids in this process shows them that their opinions are valued and gives them experience in finding practical solutions. It also reminds them that they're part of a team, with each member dependent on the others to keep the household running smoothly.

• Help your kids connect privilege with responsibility and vice versa. Too many children believe that they're entitled to whatever advantages they have—as though their parents were here to serve them. These kids have a hard time becoming responsible adults.

A parent who attended one of my workshops uses an ingenious system to prevent this problem. Her family has an annual ritual—each year, each child gets a new privilege and a new responsibility. One is contingent upon the other.

The kids get to discuss their choices with their parents, who then take their concerns seriously.

Example: Your daughter has wanted a dog for several years. She agrees to baby-sit for her brother once a week. For this, she will earn the privilege of getting a dog.

•Impose appropriate consequences. Don't be too quick to "rescue" your children when they make mistakes. Parents often nag and then bail out their children anyway. One of the best ways kids learn is through the impact of reasonable consequences. You need not be overly punitive about mild oversights. Let the consequences speak for themselves...and your child will be less likely to forget next time.

Example I: You asked your son to pick up a carton of milk on his way home from school and he forgot. Instead of rushing to the store yourself, you serve dinner with no milk...and the next morning there's none to put on his cereal.

Example II: Your daughter leaves the house late several times a month and misses the school bus...despite your attempts to get her out the door on time. Each time, you drop everything to drive her to school—lecturing her on punctuality during the trip. Actually, she'll be more likely to change if you stop talking and let her walk to school. If this is not a safe option, tell her you will drive her when you're ready—after you've showered and done your chores. Few kids want to arrive in the middle of the second period.

•Give kids a chance to fix their own mistakes. Let errors be an opportunity for learning and a chance to do better next time. You may be tempted to blow up at your children's failures. But yelling rarely accomplishes anything and is likely to make you, as well as your children, feel even worse. If, instead, you help your kids find ways to set things right, they'll learn much more than they would from scoldings...and you'll feel better, too.

Example: It's your son's turn to make dinner. He forgets, stays late at school to play football and doesn't get home until 6 PM. Instead of snapping at him or starting dinner yourself, try saying, "We have a problem now. What do you think we can do about it?" He may decide to make scrambled eggs...whip up a quick tuna salad...or trade shifts with the person who was supposed to cook the following night's dinner. Even more important than getting dinner on the table, he'll be motivated to take his commitments seriously.

Source: Nancy Samalin, founder and director of Parent Guidance Workshops, 180 Riverside Dr., New York 10024. She is author of *Loving Your Child Is Not Enough: Positive Discipline That Works* and *Love and Anger: The Parental Dilemma*, both published by Penguin Books, 375 Hudson St., New York 10014.

How to Help Your Child Overcome Childhood Fears

While most childhood fears are a normal part of growing up, parents often worry that a particular fear or pattern of fears is abnormal. In such cases, a little information often helps. Common questions:

•*Which fears are normal?* All children are born with innate fears of loud noises and of falling down. As they mature and come in contact with their environment, they typically begin to fear machines, big objects, toilets, animals, strangers, leaving mom and dad.

As their imagination comes to life, children may fear the dark, sleeping alone, monsters, the supernatural, thunder and lightning.

Still later, as children enter their pre-teen years, they'll encounter social fears—fear of looking foolish, speaking in public, doing poorly in school.

•*How should parents treat fears?* Never belittle a child's fear or say that the fear is silly. To the child, the fear is all too real. If you shame children for their fears, the fear may disappear for a brief time...only to explode later on. *Also important:*

•Never force children to confront a fear—for example, by throwing a child who's afraid of the water into a swimming pool. Doing so may intensify the fear.

•Don't cater to a child's fear. Some parents avoid the object of a child's fear altogether, keeping a child from ever having to confront a scary situation. On the other hand, some parents say, "Oh, don't worry about that doggie," but they send another message by holding the child close to them as the dog approaches.

•*How can parents keep a child's fears from snowballing?* Prepare your child for new experiences gradually.

Example I: Before the first day of school, take your child to visit the school and meet the other children. Read books about school and talk about things that children do at school.

Example II: A child who fears dogs may be thinking, "This dog is going to eat me!" Let the child stand back and watch the dog as it interacts with others. Talk about dogs. Explain that tail-wagging and jumping can be signs of friendliness. Pet the dog while your child watches.

• *What if a fear lingers…or becomes very intense?* Whether your child fears spending the night out, bees and wasps, bridges, germs, etc., do not ignore the fear and assume it will just go away.

Danger: Many full-blown adult phobias—including agoraphobia (fear of open spaces or leaving the home), acrophobia (fear of heights) and fear of animals—have their roots in childhood fears that were never addressed.

Take direct action:

There are several strategies for helping your child overcome his/her fear. *Most helpful:*

•Explain that fear is a normal physiological condition. Tell your child that it's part of the fight-or-flight response that arose to protect our ancestors from saber-tooth tigers and other predators.

Assuming your child is in good health, the physical manifestations of fear are not dangerous…whether it's a rapidly pounding heart, "butterflies" in the stomach, fast breathing, lightheadedness or dizziness, trembling, clammy hands, sweating, tingling in hands or feet, etc. Make sure your child realizes this.

•Work together. Say, "We've got a problem, and we're going to solve it together. You've been waking up at night because you're afraid of the dark. Let's work on getting over this together. It's going to be fun."

•Teach positive self-talk. Explain to your child that it's possible to counter fearful thoughts by silently repeating positive ones based on real

information. *Fear:* "That dog will bite me." *Positive self-talk:* "That dog is wagging his tail. He's friendly."

•Give your child correct information…what he needs to know to counteract the fear. *Problem:* Kids have gaps in their knowledge. A child who fears the dark may know something about darkness but may not understand why it gets dark or how long it takes the eyes to adjust. *Typical result:* Panic. As darkness falls, your child starts imagining monsters instead of thinking, "Wait a minute, I'm still in my room. That shape I see over there must be the lamp on my desk."

Educating your child about darkness and its effects on vision and the appearance of familiar objects may help him/her overcome fear.

Similarly, let your child know that not everything she sees or hears is true. If your daughter hears a noise and fears there is a monster under her bed, for example, explain to her, "That's not a monster, that's the water running."

•Teach your child relaxation techniques. Tension causes your child to take short, shallow breaths—and that intensifies the panic. *Fear reducers:* Deep muscle relaxation and "belly" breathing—deep, slow, rhythmic breathing from the diaphragm. Show your child how.

Four-step technique:

In *Monsters Under the Bed*, we present a four-step desensitization process for extreme or persistent fears. Say your son is afraid of the dark…

•*Step one:* Imagination. Use picture books, videos, television programs and "make-believe" games and stories to help your son create fear-reducing positive images. Tell a story in which he wakes up in the middle of the night, looks calmly around and goes back to sleep.

•*Step two:* Information. Give your son helpful facts appropriate to his age and specific fear. Educate him about darkness. Watch sunrises and sunsets together. Use an encyclopedia to study the eye.

•*Step three:* Observation. Use modeling to help him safely come in contact with his fears. *What to do:* Without directly comparing your son to other children, let him observe a child who goes to bed easily in the dark. Say, "Look how the child falls asleep." Or, stand with your son in a darkened room so he experiences his eyes adjusting to the dark.

• *Step four:* Exposure. Slowly familiarize your son to the darkness using a set of graduated activities. First, have him walk into a dark room and stay for a few seconds. Slowly increase the time spent in the dark. Play hide and seek in the dark, follow the leader in and out of darkened spaces, eat dessert in the dark. Do as few or as many of these activities as your son needs to overcome the fear.

Crucial: Set a comfortable pace—don't try to do it all in one day. Have your child use a rating scale of 1 (no fear) to 10 (terrified). If your child signals five or greater, immediately stop what you're doing. Repeat the experience slowly until your child is more comfortable. This gives him/her a sense of control.

When to seek help:

If your child remains extremely fearful despite all your efforts, seek help from a psychotherapist specializing in fears and anxiety disorders. Before the initial visit, make sure the therapist has had previous success treating your child's specific fear.

For a list of specialists in your area, send a self-addressed, stamped, business-sized envelope to the Anxiety Disorders Association of America, 6000 Executive Blvd., Suite 200, Rockville, MD 20852.

Source: Marianne Daniels Garber, PhD, an educational consultant in private practice at the Behavioral Institute of Atlanta. She is the coauthor, with Stephen W. Garber, PhD, and Robyn Freedman Spizman, of *Monsters Under the Bed and Other Childhood Fears: Helping Your Child Overcome Anxieties, Fears and Phobias,* Villard Books, 201 E. 50 St., New York 10022.

Beyond Spanking

When it comes to disciplining children, shouting and spanking are counterproductive. Aside from sending them the message that it's okay to yell and hit to get what you want, these approaches drive bad behaviors underground—kids don't change behavior, they simply become expert at not getting caught.

Alternatives:

• Competition. Children are competitive by nature and love to be "first." Exploit this natural tendency by playing "beat the clock" with your child.

Example: Set a timer for five minutes. Say, "You have to get in bed before the timer rings." Watch your child race to finish.

• Praise. Each time your child does something you approve of, let him/her know. *Key:* Be specific.

Example: Don't say, "You're a good girl for putting your crayons away." Say, "What a neat job you did putting away all your crayons."

• Rehearsing appropriate behaviors. A toddler who gets spanked for running into the street learns to avoid the parent—not the street. *Better:* Repeat lessons about looking both ways, avoiding cars, responding to traffic lights, etc. Once your child masters these skills, he/she will delight in showing them off—and getting your praise.

• Contractual arrangements. The basic principle is that, "When you have done A, then you may do B."

Example: Instead of shouting, "You're in big trouble if you don't do your homework," calmly say, "When you finish your homework, then you may call your friends." Never say, "If you do your homework." If you do, your child might ask, "What if I don't?"

• "Time-out." When your child is out of control, make him/her sit still in a chair for a prescribed period of time (one minute for each year of age is about right). Time-out helps your child cool off by preventing him from receiving any kind of attention (verbal or physical) for an inappropriate behavior. Use a timer so that your child can anticipate when time-out is over.

Source: Jerry Wyckoff, PhD, associate professor of human development, Ottawa University, Ottawa, Kansas. He is the author of *Discipline Without Shouting or Spanking,* Meadowbrook Press, 18318 Minnetonka Blvd., Deephaven, Minnesota 55391.

Better Reprimanding

Preserve a child's dignity by privately discussing his/her behavior and describing how you want him to behave. If the child is not yours, acknowledge that your rules may be different from those at his home—but insist that your rules be obeyed in your house. When dealing with a stepchild, acknowledge that you are not his biological parent but make it clear that there are household rules everyone must obey.

Source: M. Duncan Stanton, PhD, professor of psychiatry and psychology, University of Rochester, New York.

It's Never Too Soon to Foster a Love of Reading In Young Children

Reading adds depth to our lives and offers many hours of excitement and pleasure. Children who learn to love reading at an early age will write and think better as they get older. *Here's how you can encourage your child to read...*

•Don't make reading a chore. You can't simply say, "Sit down and read," and expect your child to read. Some kids will...but most won't. Today you're competing with many distractions that your child may enjoy more—videotapes, CDs, cassettes, video games...and very colorful, dynamic toys.

Reading requires children to think...figure out the meaning of words...determine what's going on in the plot...and use their imaginations. Reading requires more attention than most other activities—so don't treat books as punishment.

•Offer easy-to-read books. People enjoy doing activities that they're good at. Young children will enjoy reading more if they are given books that are fun.

Allow your children to read books that they like rather than those you think will be good for them. If you insist that they read difficult books, reading will become a struggle and they will lose interest eventually.

Older children may opt for what you call trash, such as teen romances. But it is critical that your children enjoy reading and form the habit of reading. Again, allow them to read the books that make them feel like wonderful readers.

•Respect your children's opinions. Show an interest in the books your children read. Engage them in conversation, and treat them like experts, even if it's just a basic book.

By treating children as serious readers and allowing them to choose the books they would like to read, you will be increasing their self-esteem as well as their love of reading.

•Don't censor books. A big part of the fun of reading is choosing your own books. Let your children be the judge of what they should be reading—within reason, since some reading material is truly inappropriate for children.

I don't believe reading can foster bad values or steer a child to a life of crime. More likely, it is the child who doesn't read anything who will be unable to function as a good citizen and is at higher risk for criminal behavior. Avid readers are going to end up with a fairly balanced view of the world, even if for a time they binge on romance or horror novels.

•Recognize that kids go through stages. There may be times when they read a lot and times when they read a little. Children face many pressures these days—at school, in their social lives, on the sports field, etc. Sometimes they use up all their energy just getting through the day.

If your children love reading, they will always come back to it. Leave magazines or books about their current passion around the house to help them keep the habit and love of reading alive until their energy for it returns.

Creating a reading-friendly home:

•Place books wherever children can be found. Keep books out wherever they sit—at the kitchen table, in front of the TV, in the den, in the car, etc. Leaving reading material near food is important—kids especially seem to enjoy reading while eating. You may even want to put a bookcase in the kitchen.

•Remember that reading isn't neat. A reading-friendly home can be downright messy. Avid adolescent readers leave books everywhere—under the bed covers, on the dining-room table, on the floor, on the steps. It's better to find books everywhere than to live with children who leave the books sitting in the bookcase.

•Buy books often. Reading can be an expensive pastime...but by spending money on books, you are showing your kids that you value literature. You might even give your children money to buy books themselves.

Libraries are an alternative, but they may not have the books children enjoy. Also, there are some books that children simply want to own and not have to return in a week or two.

•Give children time to read. If your children are overscheduled and overworked, there won't be time for reading. Readers, especially early readers for whom it's slow going, need time to enjoy books.

A reading-friendly home sees all kinds of reading as legitimate.

Example: It's okay for your daughter to spend Saturday sprawled across her bed surrounded by her favorite magazines.

Source: Mary Leonhardt has taught English in public and private schools for more than 20 years. She is author of *Parents Who Love Reading, Kids Who Don't: How It Happens and What You Can Do About It*, Crown Publishers, 201 E. 50 St., New York 10022.

Questions to Ask When Choosing a Summer Camp for Your Child

•*Is your child really ready for sleepaway camp?* Knowing your child's and your family's needs is the first step to finding the right camp. If your child can't handle being away from home overnight, a day camp is probably a better choice. You may want to have your child sleep overnight at a friend's home to make this determination.

•*Is the camp accredited?* The American Camping Association is the only organization in the US that has a voluntary standards-and-accreditation program for all kinds of camps. These standards cover health and safety, camp management, personnel, programming facilities and transportation. If a camp you're considering is not accredited, ask the camp director why not and then make your decision.

•*What is the camp's philosophy?* Does the camp have a religious background? Is the camp's philosophy one of sports and competition? Sports and instruction? Arts? How does the camp director describe the camp's philosophy? Is that what you want for your child?

•*Who is directly responsible for your child's*

supervision at the camp? Find out the counselor/child ratio to determine whether supervision is adequate. This ratio differs by age group and between day and sleepaway camps. Some offer smaller ratios among younger children.

Ages six to eight: Day camp/one counselor to eight children...*sleepaway camp*/one to six children.

Ages nine to 14: Day camp/one counselor to 10 children...*sleepaway camp*/one to eight children.

Ages 15 to 17: Day camp/one counselor to 12 children...*sleepaway camp*/one to 10 children.

•*Who else besides the counselor can children go to with problems?* Make sure the camp offers a good support system (group or division leaders, counselors in charge of particular activities, head counselors, the director) so your child has more than one person to talk with if he/she is upset about something. Also find out what the camp's policy is on telephone calls home.

•*How are the counselors screened and trained?* If the camp is accredited, you can be assured that the staff is screened and trained. But get specifics on how the counselors are chosen ...what the screening process involves...and what the training covers. Most important is that you feel comfortable that the camp director knows his/her business and is concerned enough to provide the best possible care and supervision.

•*How much instruction is provided during each activity period...and how long do activity periods last?* This will give you a good idea of whether the camp will suit your child's attention span and level of independence. Also find out which activities are required and how many electives your child can choose.

•*Are any trips offered as part of the camp... and what transportation arrangements are made for trips?* Accredited camps will have specific requirements for drivers, vehicles and on-board safety equipment. If you choose a nonaccredited camp, make sure you're comfortable with these arrangements.

•*How does the camp integrate new campers into the group?* If your child is thrown into a group without being properly introduced and made to feel welcome, he won't enjoy himself, no matter how many exciting activities are offered.

• *What medical facilities are available on-site? Nearby?* Any time you have several children together in an active setting, you're bound to have a few injuries here and there. While the majority of these are minor scrapes and bruises, broken bones are not unheard-of.

Most camps have registered nurses or the equivalent on-site and doctors either on-site or nearby. You will want to know what the camp's policies are on medical insurance and notification of parents in the event of illness or injury. You should feel comfortable that the camp is prepared to deal with—and has the ability and experience to deal with—any eventuality.

• *What references can you give me?* Talking to the parents of children who have recently attended the camp can prove invaluable in your decision. Find out what the child and the parents liked best and least about the camp. Also find out whether the reference's child's temperament is similar to that of your child.

Source: Laurie Edelman, executive director of the New York section of The American Camping Association, 12 W. 31 St., New York 10001.

No Summer Job?

Summer jobs teach kids responsibility, provide them with spending money and keep them busy while they're out of school.

More worthwhile: Businesses that kids *start on their own*—since a real business teaches them even more valuable lessons of all kinds.
Before beginning:

A few hours of planning can mean the difference between the success and failure of your child's business.

Important: Help your child work out a business plan. This can simply be notes written on a sheet of paper.

The business plan can determine up-front costs…ongoing costs such as transportation, materials and marketing…income potential… profits…and the competition.

Key: Don't be a know-it-all. Don't do all the planning and decision-making for your child. Part of the value of this endeavor is for your child

to get his/her first taste of running a business—that includes making mistakes. Also, contact the office of the secretary of state, which will provide you with a list of legal and tax requirements.

To market the service, your child could place flyers under doors or on cars during the week and solicit neighbors in person on the weekends.

Here are the most popular jobs that kids are starting this summer…

• Baking:
Opportunities vary according to the neighborhood. But there are probably more organized events in your area this summer than you are aware of—fairs, park gatherings, softball leagues, etc. Sales through local retailers are possible—but trickier.

Beginners' products: Cookies…muffins…and homemade breads. Cakes and pies are usually harder to make and harder to sell.

Requirements: A stove, recipes and ingredients. If your child wants to bake bread, a $120 bread-making machine might be a good investment. Loaves can be made for as little as 15 cents to 30 cents each. If you set up your own selling stand, you may require a vendor license. Contact the event sponsor for information.

Income potential: $5 to $30 an hour. The profit margin on baked goods can be fantastic since they cost so little to make.

• Car care:
Some kids just wash cars…others wax and clean the interiors.

Requirements: Bucket, sponges, towels, soaps, wax and squeegee.

Income potential: $5 to $10 for washing a car. Add another $10 for cleaning the interior. Waxing will add another $15 to $20. Your child could charge $30 for all three services on a car …$60 to $70 on a van or truck.

Keep in mind: Much of this work has to be done in the evenings or on weekends since the clients use their vehicles during the weekdays. This schedule may inhibit a youngster's social life and cut into his income potential, since someone who starts working at 6 PM can't work an eight-hour shift.

• Home-video cameraman:
Many adults would like to film a party or graduation but don't because then they can't enjoy

their guests or the proceedings. That creates a business opportunity.

Requirements: Camcorder, tapes. Also, a demonstration tape to show that your quality is acceptable.

Income potential: Typically $10 to $15 per hour...or a flat fee—sometimes as high as $50 or $75—for chronicling an event that is several hours long.

Important: Make sure that your child promises to deliver only unedited tapes. The venture will become too time-consuming and costly otherwise.

•Lawn care:

Business potential is greatest if the child can use the client's lawn mower. This job can also include removing debris when trees are cut... trimming...and cleanup.

Income potential: $15 per hour, but not all is profit if your child has to supply gas and oil for the mower, which can cost up to $7.50 per job. *Aim:* 20 lawns per week.

Suggest that your child walk the property before agreeing to take the job. The size, roughness and terrain or contour can make some lawns more difficult to mow than the client may think. The child should provide an estimate of the time it will take to complete the job.

If your child uses your mower: He shouldn't work on lawns in terrible condition. Rocks, roots and thin grass can damage your equipment.

If your child needs to buy a mower: First determine the market potential. One young woman I know lined up 45 lawns to do each week before investing $800 in a self-propelling model.

•Design shop:

With a computer, kids can design invitations, announcements, cards, flyers, etc. The market for this includes schools, small businesses and clubs. For example, a visit to the local Rotary Club may help drum up work. The promotion piece should be a great example of your child's work.

Requirements: Computer, a decent graphics program ($50 to $80), color printer. Make copies from your printer or through a local print shop.

Income potential: $5 to $30 an hour.

Source: Ralph Schulz, executive director of Junior Achievement Inc., a national organization that fosters entrepreneurship among young people, One Education Way, Colorado Springs 80906.

How to Teach Your Child Good Manners

Politeness is the cornerstone of any civilized society. In essence, it is respect for other people's feelings.

This respect is reflected in both thought and action...in considering other people's points of view and behaving in sensitive ways.

Unfortunately, the trend toward informality in all areas of our culture has sent children the wrong message about the importance of being polite. Children today stand a good chance of growing up to be rude adults.

Teaching manners takes time and effort, but it is worth treating as a priority.

To teach politeness:

•Display courteous behavior. It's important to teach politeness politely. If we snap at a child for behaving in a rude way, we undermine our message.

Children sometimes *seem* rude even when they don't mean to be. Especially when they're younger than five or six years old, children lack the empathy to know when they might be hurting someone else's feelings. Embarrassing a child by forcing him/her to apologize in such a situation is one of the rudest things a parent can do.

Example: If a store clerk says "hello" to your two-year-old daughter and she looks at the ground instead of responding, it isn't lack of courtesy or deliberate rudeness. It is age-appropriate discomfort with strangers.

Better: Instead of chastising a young child, model polite behavior by replying for her, "Hello, how are you today?" to the clerk. Your child will notice how you act with other adults.

Example: A husband skips watching a televised football game so that he can take care of the children while his wife goes to an evening meeting. When she returns home, instead of saying, "Thank you for looking after the children. I couldn't have attended the meeting without your help," she criticizes her husband— "Why is Janie still up? I told you to put her to bed at 8:30." The children will observe this lack of graciousness. If spouses do not treat each other with basic courtesy, their children will not learn to be considerate.

• Don't reward rudeness. Children often learn unsavory language and other impolite habits from their peers or older siblings. These peers may actively encourage this sort of behavior because they think it is funny. Resist the urge to laugh or explode. Both of these responses give the child a payoff in the form of inappropriate attention.

Better: A matter-of-fact but firm approach—"That language is offensive. You can use it when you're by yourself, but we don't talk to other people that way."

• Help your children to interpret the rude behavior they see. Television and movies today are full of examples of rudeness. I think it's a good idea to watch TV and see movies with your children…and when you see an example of disrespect, point it out—"This kind of behavior is funny on TV, but real life is different. How would you feel if someone treated you that way?"

• Role-play. Children tune out lectures, but they always love to play games. Make-believe is a great way for you to teach kids good manners.

Example: You say, "Let's pretend I'm Aunt Louise. I just gave you an umbrella for your birthday. But what you really wanted was a truck. What would you say?"

Your son: "I hate this stupid umbrella."

You: "I'm Aunt Louise, and my feelings have really been hurt by what you said. I tried to give you something that would give you pleasure. Now, what could you say that would be more thoughtful?"

Your son: "Thank you for the umbrella, Aunt Louise."

You: "That's terrific."

Keep in mind that you are not encouraging your child to exhibit phony or false behavior. There is no deception here—merely a kinder response and respect for Aunt Louise's feelings.

• Expect to be treated with courtesy. Older children may try to impress their friends by being rude to their parents when their peers are around. As with younger children, attacking them publicly for their rudeness will not make your point effectively—but that doesn't mean you need to tolerate inappropriate behavior.

If your son makes a disrespectful comment in front of his peers—"You can't boss me around…"

or "My mother is going to make her disgusting spaghetti sauce tonight"—make it very clear, calmly and in private, that this sort of rudeness will have consequences.

Take your son into another room or wait until his friends leave, and say, "I won't allow you to talk to me rudely. I know that you wouldn't like it if I said something that would embarrass you in front of your friends."

The consequence should always be appropriate to the transgression—"If this behavior continues, your friends will be asked to leave."

• Build politeness into family routines. A parent who attended one of my workshops has a wonderful way to ensure that her children write thank-you notes promptly. The rule in her house is, "When you receive a gift from someone, you can open it and look at it—but you cannot play with it or use it until you have appropriately thanked the person who gave it to you."

Her kids accepted the justice of this approach, and one of the most basic forms of politeness—thank you—became an important part of their vocabulary.

Source: Nancy Samalin, founder and director of Parent Guidance Workshops, 180 Riverside Dr., New York 10024. She is author of *Loving Your Child Is Not Enough: Positive Discipline that Works* and *Love and Anger: The Parental Dilemma*, Penguin Books, 375 Hudson St., New York 10014.

Saying "No" to Kids

Parents can say "no" to their children even when the children complain that "all the other kids have it"…or "*their* parents say it's okay."

Important: Gear your explanation to your child's level of understanding. Preschoolers are prelogical, so avoid a lengthy discussion. For older kids, give your side…and then listen to their side. *Also helpful:* Talking to other parents.

If the disagreement is small, it may be worth giving in and saving your efforts for when it is important. Or negotiate.

Examples: Your son wants a $75 pair of sneakers and you'll spend up to $40—ask him what he is willing to do to earn the difference…

your daughter wants to go to town with friends and you don't think she has the maturity—ask her how she'll show you can trust her.

If your answer is still "no," acknowledge their want but remind them that, after all, you are the parent.

Source: Lawrence Kutner, PhD, is a child psychologist in Cambridge, Massachusetts. He is author of *Parent and Child: Getting Through to Each Other*, Avon Books, 1350 Avenue of the Americas, New York 10019.

Child-Care Placement Agencies

Child-care placement agencies can't do national criminal background checks on caregiver candidates...any such checks are limited in scope. *Reason:* Private citizens and businesses do not have access to national criminal records compiled by the Department of Justice. If an agency claims it conducted a criminal background check, ask how it was done. Be suspicious if the agency claims to have gotten into the national crime computer system. Only law-enforcement individuals have access to this system.

Source: Joy Wayne, director, Nannies Plus, 615 W. Mount Pleasant Ave., Livingston, New Jersey 07039.

Ease Kids' Visits After Divorce

Ease kids' visits after divorce by having clothes at both parents' homes...using a neutral drop-off and pickup place, such as a parking lot or school...displaying the child's art, even if his/her visits are infrequent. If practical, have the family pet travel with the child. Also, let him take along a security blanket or pillow. *Useful:* Let him carry personal belongings back and forth in his own backpack—and make his own decisions about what to take.

Source: Linda Sartori, editor, *Kids Express*, 220 Eye St. NW, Washington, DC 20002.

Secrets of Big-Time Food-Bill Savings

Most of us have had the thought, "I can't believe I'm paying this much for one bag of stuff," as the supermarket cashier finishes ringing up the "few things" we ran to the store for.

"Did I really buy that much?" we wonder. Usually, we haven't bought that much—just paid too much. Here are some ways to save big on the family food bill.
Supermarket savings:

•Shop with a list...or you'll spend more than you save.

•Clip coupons—and keep them organized. Don't throw money away with the garbage. Coupons can easily save you $1,000 a year.

Be willing to give up brand loyalty in favor of a meaningful discount. One brand of tomato paste or dish detergent is much like another.

File coupons in envelopes by category—canned goods, cereals, pet foods, paper products, etc. Put coupons you plan to use right away and those with short expiration dates in the front. Take them with you to the store, along with an empty envelope to put coupons in for the items you select, so you don't have to sort them at the check-out counter.

Shop at a supermarket that honors double the value on the face of coupons. You can also increase your savings by combining in-store sales with coupons. Be sure to calculate the per-unit price of products when using coupons.

Example: A 6-ounce jar of instant coffee may cost $3.29, or 55¢ an ounce, and a 10-ounce jar $4.99, or 50¢ an ounce. Normally, the larger size is the better buy. But with a 75¢ coupon, at a double-coupon store, the 6-ounce jar costs $1.79, or 30¢ an ounce, while the 10-ounce jar is $3.49, or 35¢ an ounce.

•Companion product offers. Companies and supermarkets often issue coupons for a free item, with the purchase of a companion item.

Examples: A free gallon of milk with the purchase of a breakfast cereal...a free box of pasta with the purchase of spaghetti sauce.

•Refund and rebate offers. You may need to clip UPC symbols or save register receipts as "proof of purchase" to send for these offers.

They are worth the trouble—and can be very lucrative, whether you get a cash rebate, additional coupons or free products.

•Senior discounts. Many large chain stores and some independent markets issue senior discount cards that allow cashiers to subtract as much as 5% to 10% off the final bill.

•Generic brands. Not only are they here to stay, they are growing and growing. Generics can provide substantial savings, especially on grooming products, cereals and canned goods.

•Track savings. Most supermarkets total the amount saved with coupons at the bottom of the register receipt. You can deposit monthly savings from coupons, refunds, etc., in an account earmarked toward a goal.

Supermarket alternatives:

•Join a wholesale or warehouse shopping club. These huge operations are springing up in metropolitan areas nationwide. Shopping is a no-frills enterprise, and products must often be purchased in bulk or large sizes. Brand selection may be limited and may change at any given time. But savings can be excellent. *Key:* Know your prices. Some warehouse-club prices are not significantly better than prices at the discounters.

•Shop at farmers' markets, where vegetables and fruits are fresher, tastier and cheaper. Buy in bulk in-season, then can or preserve.

•Shop at bakery outlets and "thrift stores." Thrift stores are one-brand outlets for companies such as Entenmann's, Pepperidge Farm, Arnold's Bakery, Sunbeam Bread and Wonder-Bread/Hostess. Prices run 30% to 50% off retail for day-old goods.

•Food co-ops and buying clubs. Consumer cooperatives are run by members and usually buy food in bulk and then repackage it for buyers. Members can save 15% to 50% on most items, because brokers, middlemen and costly packaging are eliminated from the exchange.

•Do it yourself. Grow a vegetable garden, make your own frozen dinners from leftovers.

Restaurant savings:

•Happy-hour buffets. Between 4 PM and 6 PM, for the price of a drink—not necessarily alcoholic—many restaurants provide free buffets. If you don't mind eating early, many people find these feasts to be filling, fun dinners and a change in daily routine.

•Early-bird specials. Many restaurants offer much lower prices for those who order dinner between 4 PM and 6 PM. You get the same food as on the dinner menu, often with dessert and beverage included, for less than you'd pay for the entrée alone during peak hours. To find specials, check local newspapers or call the restaurants that you are interested in.

•Senior menus. Some restaurants, particularly large chains, have senior menus, which offer smaller portions at lower prices. Carry your identification.

•Two-for-one or free item coupons. Check newspapers and circulars for coupons from area restaurants for "buy one entrée, get the second of equal or lesser value free" or "free wine or dessert with entrée" offers.

•Restaurant discount books.

Examples: Entertainment Publications publishes regional guides for about $35, with about 200 coupons for 2-for-1 meals and discounts at restaurants, fast-food chains and specialty shops (2125 Butterfield Rd., Troy, Michigan 48084, 313-637-8400). The Premier Dining Club qualifies you for 2-for-1 or other discounts at member restaurants nationwide (831 Greencrest Dr., Westerville, Ohio 43081, 800-346-3241).

Invest in savings:

Other companies publish local or regional discount books as well. These can be a wise investment if you like to dine out a lot—but shop around. Prices and services vary substantially.

Key: Make sure the book contains enough discounts you will really use to pay for itself.

Source: Linda Bowman, professional bargain hunter and author of the *More for Your Money* series of guides, including *Free Food & More* and *Freebies (and More) for Folks Over 50,* Probus Publishing Co., 1925 N. Clybourn Ave., Chicago 60614.

How to Cut Your Family's Medical Bills...Now

In an effort to cut waste and reduce the costs of medical care, the Clinton administration and Congress seem set on making sweeping changes to the national health-care system. But whatever legislation passes in 1995, it will be years before the program is fully implemented. *Here are ways that you can reduce out-of-pocket medical expenses right now...*

Hospitals:

•Make sure your hospital stay is necessary. Studies show that only one of every eight hospital admissions is medically necessary and only one of every five operations really makes sense. So when you're told you should have a certain procedure or test, be appropriately skeptical.

•Ask the right questions. The right questions concern both health and money. Often the answer that is best for your health is also best for your wallet. *Ask your doctor the following questions about any recommended procedure...*

•What are the risks of the procedure?

•Which hospital do you suggest—and why? Some are safer than others...some are cheaper ...some are both.

•Are there any less-invasive alternatives to this type of surgery? *Examples:* Clot-dissolving drugs instead of heart bypass surgery...lumpectomy instead of total breast removal for a breast tumor.

•Can I have this procedure done as an outpatient?

•Always get a second opinion. An eight-year study by the Cornell Medical Center found that one out of four second opinions recommends against an operation. The long-term survival rate of people who take such advice is excellent. So even if your insurance company doesn't require a second opinion, get one. And be sure to ask a lot of questions of all doctors, since *you* must make the final decision regarding your treatment.

Studies show that the operations most often considered unnecessary are tonsillectomies, coronary bypasses, gall-bladder removals, cesarean sections, pacemaker surgeries and joint surgeries. Be particularly diligent about getting a second opinion in such cases.

•Pick your hospital. Don't let it pick you. Years ago, no one "shopped" for a hospital. Today, 35% of patients do. Clearly, this is the best option only if you have time before the surgery is necessary.

Opportunity: Community hospitals may be up to 25% cheaper than for-profit hospitals, which order more tests and have bigger markups on procedures and services.

Most doctors are affiliated with more than one hospital, so discuss your options, balancing cost against the success rate for your type of surgery.

•Look for the least-expensive option. Many procedures that traditionally required overnight hospital stays can now be done on an outpatient basis, which can be up to 50% cheaper than a regular hospital procedure. When you discuss outpatient alternatives with your doctor, ask about new "minimally invasive" surgical techniques, which can be considerably less expensive and less traumatic.

Trap: Never assume that your doctor or surgeon will automatically recommend the cheapest way of treating your medical problem. Ideally, you should go prepared to ask him/her about a variety of options that you've already researched.

•Resist unnecessary tests. Always ask your doctor why a hospital test must be given. The tests most frequently over-ordered are urinalyses, chest X rays and two types of blood tests— one that measures white blood cell count and another that measures the amount of time it takes blood to clot. Once in the hospital, insist on advance approval of tests and procedures.

•Save on "incidentals." Check to see what the hospital charges for various services before you check in. The most frequently hidden hospital costs are the $50-to-$100 fees for providing routine information when filling out forms. These charges are levied by 25% to 30% of hospitals. If yours is one of them, ask to fill out the papers yourself—assuming, of course, that you are well enough to do so.

Another example: Fees for health and beauty aids. In some cases, you can save more than $100 by bringing your own toiletries and pills, if you are already on the appropriate medications before being admitted. You may also be able to fill new prescriptions outside the hospital when you are a patient.

•Assume there is a problem with your bill. A new General Accounting Office study found overcharges in 99% of all hospital bills. Why does this matter to someone who has health insurance? Because more and more plans are requiring patients to share hospital costs.

Strategy: Request a fully itemized bill. Then review it carefully. *Look for:*

• Duplicate billings (often for tests).

• Shoddy testing (don't pay for unreadable X rays).

• Unauthorized tests (if you previously specified that you wanted advance approval).

• "Phantom" charges (often for sedatives and other medications that may never have been given to you).

• Bulk charges. If you see a broad heading such as "radiology" or "pharmacy," you can't possibly know if the total is accurate. Ask for a more detailed breakdown of the charges incurred.

Doctors:

• Get your money's worth. Show up as prepared for each doctor's visit as you would for an important business meeting. Bring notes about your medical history, symptoms, medications and questions that you want the doctor to answer. Have your doctor explain what he is writing in your file.

Once you pay the bill, you're entitled to a copy of the lab report—*free*. Ask your doctor to explain it to you.

The more you know, the better able you will be to gauge what treatments are appropriate—and which expenses are worth questioning.

• Phone it in. Take advantage of a doctor's phone hours, which will save you time and money. A Dartmouth Medical School study found that this saved each patient an average of $1,656 over a two-year period.

Warning: There's a difference between avoiding unnecessary visits to specialists and forgoing important preventive measures. People who save money by avoiding flu shots or treatment for high blood pressure are making serious mistakes.

• Avoid the annual physical. Symptom-free adults under age 65 can save $200 to $500 a year by reconsidering whether they really need an annual physical. The American Medical Association's guidelines suggest a full checkup every five years for adults ages 21 to 40—and every few years thereafter, depending on your health. Doctors themselves get physicals much less often than do other professionals of the same age.

Insurance:

• Increase your deductible. Talk with your insurance agent or with the benefits person at your company. The amount you save each year

may be substantial, particularly if you are a healthy adult.

• Avoid being overinsured. Be prepared to absorb some occasional minor expenses rather than seeking a policy that covers every penny of your expenses all the time. This kind of insurance policy is never a bargain.

• If your benefits are ever denied—fight back. Some surveys show that policyholders who contest denials get partial or complete satisfaction 50% of the time.

Drugs:

• Ask your doctor to prescribe generic drugs when appropriate.

• Ask your doctor for free samples of prescribed medicines.

• Cut back on over-the-counter (OTC) medicines. Most OTC remedies for colds, pains and minor problems don't really do any good. In fact, only 30% of all OTC medications can prove their claims.

Source: Frederick Ruof, president of the National Emergency Medicine Alliance (NEMA), an organization that specializes in providing consumers with ways to reduce medical costs. NEMA publishes a booklet called *How to Cut Your Family's Medical Bills by $1,000*, 524 Branch Dr., Salem, Virginia 24135.

How to Be a Better Grandparent

Those of us who are grandparents grew up in a world far different from today's world.

It was a world of stable families…strict rules of behavior…conventional ideas about the roles of men and women…little concern about crime and environmental destruction. As children, we led a slower-paced and far less stressed life than our grandchildren.

With a more complex world full of more choices, only one thing has not changed…the unconditional love and support grandparents can give their grandchildren.

Parents and grandparents:

To be good grandparents, we need to accept that our experience bringing up our own children does not entitle us to second-guess them in their current adult role as parents. They have the right to decide how to run their household and bring up their children.

When your children raise their children differently from the way you raised them, it is because they think their ways are better.

If you are uneasy about their choices, make sure you make any suggestions in a diplomatic fashion…and if they still think their way is right, accept it.

Example: Edna insisted her daughter Gloria follow formal rules of behavior from a very early age. Gloria did not want to be so strict with her own child, Antoinette. Edna feels that Gloria has gone too far in the other direction.

She should not say, "Antoinette is never going to learn how to behave herself unless you teach her some manners!"

A better approach…"Do you feel she's too young to learn to say 'please' and 'thank you'? I know there's a difference of opinion whether to teach children by example or by reminding them."

When you "take out" your grandchildren, don't be afraid to spoil them a little bit. Most parents fondly remember similar experiences with their own grandparents and regard it as part of the grandparents' role.

Exception: Be very strict about following health and safety rules set by your children. Grandchildren have to learn that their parents set the rules to protect them and that unconditional love does not mean dangerous permissiveness. How much help?:

A basic fact of life is that grandparents are older than their children. It is often hard to cope with the demands of lively grandchildren, but it is well worth making an effort to find creative ways to help.

Example: When Eric's wife had to go to the hospital, he called his mother to ask her if he could bring his three young children to stay in her house. Grandma agreed on the spot…and immediately called a nanny agency and hired a full-time babysitter.

Later, she told me, "I love the children, they're very cute. I played with them ten minutes here, ten minutes there—and it worked out just fine!"

A developing relationship:

If you live close to your children, they may expect you always to be ready to drop everything and baby-sit at a moment's notice. Don't feel guilty saying "no" if it's too much for you.

The most exciting part of being a grandparent is watching a new generation grow up, without all the worries and responsibility you had with your own children. *What to expect at different stages…*

•Infancy. Small babies need lots of attention …and the new parents need relief. Grandparents can give some by baby-sitting or providing financial aid and moral support.

•Preschool. The years from two to five are critical to children's development. Grandparents can help them learn to cope with the complexities of language, feelings and relationships.

Example: If your three-year-old grandson calls you a dope, don't just tell him, "It's naughty and rude to say that!" *Better:* "If you're angry at me, you can tell me, but calling me 'dope' hurts my feelings."

•School age. Children become more interested in their peers than their grandparents… but they still enjoy educational adventures. You can read to them…take them to museums and zoos…go on special trips. Show interest in their everyday activities…celebrate their birthdays… express joy at their successes but not disappointment at their failures.

•Teenagers. At 12 or 13 they are likely to feel they have outgrown you and may refuse to come along with the family to visit you. Don't despair…they will come back later. You can provide sympathetic reactions to their problems and gently give advice they will accept more easily than their parents'.

•At all ages. Tell your grandchildren tales about how you grew up. They will be fascinated to learn what the world was like in a different era…and develop a sense of where they came from.

Grandchildren with divorced parents:

With divorce more prevalent than ever before—grandparents can provide emotional support that their grandchildren need to cope with the emotional damage.

Your grandchildren love both their parents. It is best to avoid taking sides in front of the children, regardless of your opinion of who is at fault.

Try to do your best to maintain a good relationship with your child's ex-spouse, particularly if he/she has custody of your grandchildren.

When divorce is followed by remarriage, you may find yourself with a new set of step-grandchildren. You will help keep the new family stronger if you don't demonstrate favoritism to your own grandchildren.

The most important thing you can teach your grandchildren:

According to a Puerto Rican saying: "If someone has to boast about himself, other people say, 'I guess he has no grandmother.'"

By providing unconditional love to our grandchildren just because they were born, we give them a sense of high self-esteem, the key to a worthwhile life.

Source: Eda LeShan, educator and family counselor. The latest of her 25 books is *Grandparenting in a Changing World,* Newmarket Press, 18 E. 48 St., New York 10017.

How to Be a Much Better Long-Distance Grandparent

You may be one of the many grandparents today who live far from their grandchildren. So—it's important to know that there are ways to produce and preserve emotional closeness between grandchildren and grandparents despite geographical distance...and both the older and the younger partners in the relationship can reap rich rewards over the years.
Benefits:

By keeping a close connection with your grandchildren, you can experience once again the joys of watching beloved children grow up ...this time without having to take on the disciplinary role and 24-hour-a-day responsibility of parenthood.

Your grandchildren will gain a sense of love and belonging to a bigger family...and learn to identify with traditions handed down from their forebears. Realizing they are part of a continuing heritage will protect them from the alienation that emotionally cripples so many individuals in today's disconnected world.

Even large distances need not be a barrier to transmitting the warmth you feel for your grandchildren if you take advantage of the different means of communication we possess today.

On the spur of the moment, you can convey your feelings by telephone...at minimal expense, you can send long or short messages by mail...photographs, audio- or videotape can provide a partial substitute for your physical presence...and even relatively infrequent personal visits can provide lifelong memories of happy moments.
Telephone connections:

You can begin to have meaningful communication with your grandchildren over the telephone when they are very young.

Example: I began talking to my grandson Arlo over the phone when he was only about six months. I asked my daughter to put the receiver to the baby's ear, and began speaking the same way I would have if I had been right there..."Where is your nose, Arlo?"..."Where are your eyes?"..."Where are your toes?" My daughter reported his excited reactions to my voice...and within a few months I enjoyed them myself, when he began giggling and repeating words back to me.

Now, Arlo and his brother have learned to expect my regular calls and run to answer the phone and engage in simple conversation.
What do you talk about?:

With preschoolers, express your feelings of love for them openly..."I wish I could put my arms around you and give you a big hug!" They will not be embarrassed to reply in kind. When you ask questions to keep the conversation going, be specific. Don't ask "What are you going to do today?"...but "What toy are you playing with?" When you find a question they like to talk about, use it every time you talk...young children love repetition.

As the children grow up, their conversation will become more sophisticated. They may become less comfortable with effusive displays of affection...but they probably will welcome your willingness to hear their interests and concerns.

One important part of your role as a grandparent is to be a good sounding board to help your grandchildren work things out in their own minds when they feel their parents are unsympathetic or narrow-minded.

Dos and don'ts for good listeners:

•Do listen patiently, attentively and with respect...express your understanding of their point of view.

•Don't insist they talk to you if they don't want to.

•When they want to talk, don't interrupt or interrogate.

•Don't make light of feelings.

•Don't be judgmental.

•Don't offer advice.

•Never criticize either parent.

Save money on long-distance bills by calling when rates are lowest, for example, before 8 AM. *Important:* Make sure your call doesn't interfere with young children's regular schedules...or disturb their parents' sleep.

Communication by mail:

As soon as your grandchildren are old enough to realize that a piece of paper with words on it is a means of communication...not just a potential foodstuff or plaything...they will appreciate receiving their own mail. It shows them someone else thinks they are important.

Postcards: A two-year-old will appreciate a picture postcard with a short personal message.

Example: "Dear Arlo: Can you see this cable car? It runs up and down the big hills here in San Francisco. It has a big, loud bell that goes 'Clang! Clang!' I love you. Grandma."

You don't have to travel to send postcards... every drugstore has a collection with hometown attractions. As your grandchildren grow up, you can make your messages more informative.

Letters: To capture their interest, simply discuss experiences you find interesting...your own, recently or from childhood...or your reaction to their experiences, appropriate for their age.

Example: "Dear Christopher: Your mommy told me you have a new tooth. How many do you have now? You are getting so big I wonder if I will recognize you when I see you. Love, Grandma."

If narrative writing is not for you, send letters with riddles, puzzles, rhymes, pictures...and your grandchildren will respond in kind. Magazines for children have a good selection.

Gifts: Your grandchildren will feel the love communicated by frequent small, inexpensive, but imaginative, gifts.

Young children: Balloons, magnets, flower seeds, old hats for dressing up.

Older children: Stamps, recipes, card or magic tricks.

Photographs: Your grandchildren will probably love old family photos...especially of their parents or grandparents as children. *Hint:* If you don't want to part with your old photos, you can make acceptable copies cheaply on many photocopiers.

Dos and don'ts when visiting:

When parents come to visit grown children with their own families for more than a day or two, some strain is inevitable. *To minimize it...*

•Don't try to take charge of your children's household.

•Don't give unsolicited advice.

•Don't interfere with disciplinary rules.

•Don't agree to help around the house beyond your capabilities or patience.

•Respect your children's privacy.

•Try to fit into the family routine.

•Respect your grandchildren's feelings.

•Make clear your special needs—in advance.

•Try to be a very good guest.

Source: Selma Wassermann, an educator and writer who lives in Vancouver, British Columbia. She is the author of *The Long Distance Grandmother,* Hartley and Marks, Box 147, Point Roberts, Washington 98281.

How to Work at Home Much More Effectively

More than 34 million Americans now work in their own kitchens, basements, spare rooms and garages—doing work that used to be done in high-rise office buildings.

Computers, fax machines, new phone systems and personal organizers are making it possible to do *almost* anything that can be done in a corporate office from your home—or your car.

But running a home office is not like running a corporate office—or like running a home. It has its own unique challenges that you must recognize and address.

Picking your space:

Wherever possible, it's best to set up your office in a separate space, whether it's as small as a closet or as spacious as a spare room. While some people can work in the corner of their kitchens, there's no other place in the home that has more distractions.

Better: Carve out a space in the basement—or even the garage—that is away from household traffic.

When you go to your newly created office, you'll be ready for business. Keep all your supplies there...and keep track of them so that you won't run out of critical items while you're working.

Self-defense: Buy a second set of office supplies for the family (to be kept elsewhere) so they won't raid yours.

If children or pets will be coming into your office, arrange a comfortable area for them with their own playthings.

Trap: Nothing sounds more unprofessional while you're on the phone than a dog barking or a child crying in the background. Try to be alone when you make important calls. And never assume that because you're working at home you won't need child care. Until children are in school all day, you will almost certainly need backup during business hours.

Separating your two worlds:

As a general rule, your business will be much more successful and your tax filing easier if you separate your business life from your personal life. That means having separate phone lines for home and office...using separate credit cards for business expenses...and keeping personal and business papers and records in two different places.

Exception: It's okay to have a column for personal activities in your daily or weekly planner. After all, one of the objectives of working at home is to see your family more often and to be able to fit in your kids' school activities, etc.

It's even a good idea to have your business mail sent to a post office box. This will protect your home address from unwanted commercial contacts. Also, you can leaf through your mail at the post office and discard material that doesn't need to come home.

Taking control:

When you work for a company, you get a day's pay, whether or not you accomplish a day's worth of work.

At home, however, your income is directly related to how productive you are. If you spend 30 minutes on the phone with a friend or 20 minutes looking for a misplaced piece of paper, that's time spent *not* earning money.

At home, you probably won't have a secretary or staff to help you with typing, filing, phone calls and paperwork. You're on your own. Therefore, it is imperative to take control and get your office organized so that you can work efficiently.

Time management:

Good time management is crucial for the home-office professional. Since no one is imposing a schedule on you, you need to discipline yourself. If you can't resist chatty neighbors, working at home may not be for you. Learn to ignore household tasks that need to be done. They can be done later.

• Prioritize. Determine your best time of day ...and schedule important tasks for then.

Throughout the day (about every three hours), ask yourself if what you're doing at that moment is the best use of your time. I call this *structured flexibility*. You've made your to-do list and set your priorities, yet you're aware that your priorities could change at any moment.

Bonus: When you work at home, you have the freedom to work odd hours, nights, weekends or early mornings, when there are fewer interruptions.

• Be willing to change your schedule and *focus* on what seems more important. The word "focus" is key—because you don't want to keep skipping from one thing to another. Then nothing gets finished.

Helpful: Make appointments with yourself to work on certain tasks. Block out time on your calendar to write a report, develop a marketing plan, etc. Turn on the answering machine during that time.

• Set aside some time each week to read. Even spending a half hour or an hour every morning makes a big difference when trying to get through all the newspapers, magazines, professional journals, sales brochures and other material you need to review. Put those articles and brochures that you'll need to refer to again in a *reference* file (distinct from your *current* file).

• Spend at least one full day a week in your office to catch up on paperwork, make phone calls, etc. Choose a day that's most likely to be slow, and try to keep your schedule clear. This will make the rest of your week go more smoothly.

• Learn to say "no"—not only to nonbusiness demands on your time but also to new business that you really can't handle. Clients are more understanding about being turned down than they are about missed deadlines. When you don't set limits on what you can accomplish, the quality of your work will suffer and you will lose business.

• Hire outside help when necessary. One of my clients had a beautifully organized home office but nearly failed because he couldn't type. We solved his problem with an outside secretarial service that picked up and typed drafts. Face the fact that you can't do everything yourself.

Example: If your time can be spent more profitably with a client, perhaps you should hire a high-school student to do some oft-postponed but necessary chore like entering 1,500 names into your computer.

• Group similar tasks together. Make all of your phone calls at once so you don't keep interrupting your work time all day. Write all of your letters during another block of time. Schedule all appointments on the same afternoon. Run several errands in one trip…perhaps at lunchtime when people are not likely to call you back.

• Put everything in its place. It's important to file related paperwork together so that you'll have fewer places to look for something. There are many different filing techniques. You can choose whichever one works for you.

I strongly recommend having at least one high-quality filing cabinet in which you can place hanging files. It is much more efficient to file papers rather than having them in piles that collect dust and are hard to sort through.

Telephone messages: If you're the only one taking messages from your answering machine, use either a telephone log or a plain spiral notebook to keep track of messages. You can write down the date, time, caller's name, company and message. This will provide you with an orderly record instead of dozens of loose scraps of paper. It's also useful to keep a fax-activity logbook for tax and billing purposes.

Another key tool is your Rolodex. File things under the names by which you will refer to them in the future, and keep phone numbers up to date.

Invest in tomorrow:

Just as it takes money to make money, it takes time to save time. Be willing to take a few minutes at the end of every day to clean up your desk, file important papers and set up your schedule for the next day. This maintenance time will save you valuable hours in the long run. Think of it like laundry—if you do a little bit every day, it will never pile up and become a problem.

If your papers are already out of hand and your office mess has become embarrassing, resolve to take several interruption-free afternoons to straighten it out. You'll be much more productive afterward. *Important:* Every improvement will go right to your bottom line, so it's well worth the effort.

Source: Lisa Kanarek, president of Everything's Organized, a consulting firm specializing in paper management, office organization and productivity improvement, 660 Preston Forest Center, Suite 120, Dallas 75230. She is author of *Organizing Your Home Office for Success*, Plume, 375 Hudson St., New York 10014.

How to Sell Your Home Fast

If you need or want to sell your home on your own quickly, you can get a great price in just five days.

Steps to take…

• Lower your asking price. To attract a large number—between 20 and 40—of serious buyers and show that you are flexible, price your home 10% below the price of similar homes in your area. The goal is to price your home as attractively as possible when your ad first appears in the local paper. Free enterprise—having potential buyers bid against one another—will take care of the rest.

•Plan to hold an open house—and offer critical information. Get your home in tip-top shape and gather all the information that will answer buyers' questions over the phone or in person. This information includes a detailed description of your home, an independent inspection report, a radon report and a copy of your property survey. Expect to hear from between 50 and 100 people.

•Run your newspaper ad for the three days before and the two days during the open house. This will attract the maximum number of buyers. The content of the ad is critical. It should mention…

…the location of the home.

…a brief description of the home.

…the asking price.

…you're selling it yourself.

…you'll accept the best reasonable offer.

…the times of the open house.

…you plan on selling the home by the next week.

…your phone number.

When interested buyers call, say your home will be sold to the highest bidder.

•Hold the open house on Saturday and Sunday. On Saturday morning, put up signs in your neighborhood to help guide those who saw your ad for the open house. These signs may also attract some walk-in traffic.

Be absolutely honest about all of your home's flaws. This is not only ethical but smart. Getting interested buyers to make high bids is only part of the reason. You also don't want them to withdraw their bids after they learn the truth about your property.

•Conduct round-robin bidding. You will probably receive many offers. The only way to settle on one offer is to accept the highest bid.

Use *open bidding*. Sealed bidding, which asks people to put their bids in envelopes to keep them secret from others, isn't fair to anyone.

Strategy: Ask interested buyers to submit bids before leaving your home. Then call the bidders on the phone—first the highest bidder, then the next-highest, etc. Be honest and tell everyone exactly how their bid fits in with the others.

Repeat this process for each round. One of the remarkable things about this system is how

its structure maximizes competition. Bids may start at your asking price, but ultimately they will rise higher and higher.

Don't rush the bidders. Expect to spend about five minutes on the phone with each one per round.

When a top bidder emerges, call the other bidders to tell them exactly where they stand.

Tell the top bidder that the house is his/hers. Tell the next two highest bidders that they'll be able to buy your home at their bid price if the higher bidders back out or do not qualify for financing.

Source: William G. Effros, a Greenwich, Connecticut-based computer consultant who sold his own home quickly one year ago using this method. He is author of *How to Sell Your Home in Five Days*, Workman Publishing, 708 Broadway, New York 10003.

Evaluating a Condo… A Checklist

When you evaluate a condominium, consider first the physical appearance of the grounds and the units for sale. Ask yourself these questions…

•Are the building exteriors and the common areas well-maintained?

•Does the development offer the amenities that you enjoy?

•Are there recreational facilities that you will not use but will pay for?

•Are the living units well-constructed, with good quality materials and fixtures? Is there adequate soundproofing?

•Does the floor plan suit your lifestyle?

•Is the location of the unit within the development a desirable one?

•Is the development itself well-situated, with easy access to shops and community facilities?

•Does it offer a safe, secure living environment?

•Will you and your family have sufficient privacy?

•Would you enjoy having the other residents as neighbors?

Source: H.L. Kibbey, author of a series of books for homebuyers and sellers, including *The Growing Older Guide to Real Estate,* Panoply Press, Inc., 15800 SW Boones Ferry Rd., Lake Oswego, Oregon 97035.

Better Home Lighting

- Increase overall lighting to compensate for your need for more light.
- Make sure rooms have uniform lighting from several sources.
- Concentrate light on close work by using adjustable lamps and lights under kitchen cabinets.
- Position reading lights to shine from over your shoulder.
- Use lamp shades that completely shield the bulb and direct light up and down, not into your eyes.
- Replace glaring ceiling fixtures with wall and floor lamps that direct light up.
- Choose matte surfaces instead of shiny table tops and highly polished floors to cut down on harsh reflected light. *Also helpful:* Non-glossy, off-white paint for walls.
- Choose skylights with light wells for reflected instead of direct sunlight.
- Use horizontal window blinds to direct sunlight upward off the ceiling.

Source: Reprinted with permission of the *Mayo Clinic Health Letter* (January 1994), 200 First St. SW, Rochester, Minnesota 55905.

Secrets of Better Lawning & Gardening

Our front lawns and backyards have had a tough winter. Plants and shrubs damaged by severe storms must be removed or replanted properly, and debris must be carefully removed from under plants. *My spring strategies...*
Lawns:
- *Preparing your lawn.* First, clear all debris left behind from winter by using a wire or bamboo rake. Then test your soil's acidity, or pH.

Procedure: Dig down four inches with a hand trowel in four random places across your lawn. Place small samples in a single jar and test them. Some garden centers will test your soil for free...or there are at-home soil testers available starting at approximately $10.

If the soil is highly acidic, it will have a low pH. Spread lime on your entire lawn by following the instructions on the package. Or if the soil has a high pH, spread sulfur over your lawn.
- *Reseed any problem patches.* Be sure to choose a grass-seed mix that contains the highest ratio of *annual* seed to *perennial* seed.

Reason: Annual seed grows rapidly but only lasts a year. It will make your lawn green quickly while allowing the perennial seed to establish itself.

If you recently moved into a newly built house or you are redoing your entire lawn—seed the new lawn as soon as the soil is no longer soggy from the winter thaw. Begin seeding right before another rain hits.
- *Fertilize lawns* once between mid-May and early June. Choose either a natural or synthetic fertilizer that is specifically formulated for lawns.
- *Cut your lawn* as soon as the new green grass has grown about two inches high. *First cut:* For a new lawn, wait until the grass blades are three inches high. *Yearly maintenance:* In the early spring, cut the grass very short—leaving grass blades ¾-inch to 1-inch high. Slowly raise the mower height throughout the spring to more than three inches by the time hot weather arrives.

Bonus: You don't have to bag the clippings. Leave them where they fall to compost. If you cut the top one-third of your grass, you won't even notice the clippings. Just be sure not to cut the grass less than 48 hours before having a party. Otherwise your guests will track the grass clippings into your house.

Important: Never cut your lawn when it is wet. This will damage the grass, ruin the look of the lawn, create messy clippings—and mess up your lawn mower's blades.
Ornamental gardens:
- *Clear away winter mulches and garden debris.* For large areas, use a bamboo rake. For smaller areas, you can use your hands. *Helpful:* Garden gloves.

Hint: Shred the leafy debris by running over it with the lawn mower several times. Use this material to start a new compost pile.
- *Cut off all dead plant material*—blackened tips of rose branches and dead wood from flowering shrubs. Lightly *cultivate*—by turning

up the soil—around perennial plants with a *turning fork* or *hand cultivator.* Watch out for tender, new growing shoots.

•*Apply compost, bonemeal and rock powders* or a light application of balanced synthetic fertilizer to all perennial beds and shrubs. The bag of fertilizer should read *10-10-10,* which signifies the amount of nitrogen, phosphorus and potash in it.

•*Separate any perennials that have become overgrown.* These plants grow rapidly and can overextend the area in which they were originally planted. They need to be cut or divided into smaller plants every three to four years.

To divide: Dig around the plant's root ball with a *garden fork* and/or *straight-edged shovel* until it can be pried loose. Be careful not to cut into any main roots. Some plants may need a lot of encouragement. Remove the plant from the hole and put it on the soil or a tarp. Study it to see where you can divide the plant. Look for areas where there are no branches coming up out of the soil. Then firmly insert *two garden forks,* back-to-back, tines intertwined. Using the forks as levers, pull the handles apart. New plants should measure four to six inches in diameter.

To prepare other plants and trees:

•*Roses.* Remove protective soil around plant stems. Watch for signs of new growth on bare branches and prune them back to give them space. Feed with high nitrogen and phosphorus fertilizer that includes some potassium. Ask the garden center for a recommendation when choosing the ideal fertilizer for your area.

•*New trees or shrubs.* Carefully decide where to put new trees, shrubs and garden beds in advance. Give them plenty of room to grow. Turn the soil deeply and fertilize well.

To plant a tree or shrub: Dig a hole twice as large as the root ball, and save the soil. Fill in one-third of the hole with compost and a handful each of bonemeal and rock phosphate. Mix in some soil. Fill the hole with water and wait until it is absorbed by the soil.

Place the tree in the hole. Remove the burlap covering immediately by jiggling the tree or shrub until you can pull the burlap loose and remove it. Then fill in around the sides of the root ball with soil taken

from the hole, and firm it into place by grasping the base of the tree and moving it gently back and forth until it is solidly standing up straight.

Fill the hole to within one inch of its top with soil, leaving a saucer-shaped moat to catch water, which will slowly seep down to the roots. Water well. Water new trees daily for a week…weekly for a month…then only during periods of drought.

Old adage: A $5 tree will die in a 50-cent hole, but a 50-cent tree will thrive in a $5 hole. In other words, be sure to take great care when planting any tree.

Vegetable and herb gardens:

•*Clear away garden refuse*—if you didn't last fall. Till or cultivate the soil as soon as it is dry—but not too dry. To determine when, take a handful of soil and make a fist. If the soil lightly flakes apart when you open your hand, it is ready to work. Add compost or synthetic fertilizer and cultivate deeply again.

•*Planting bedding plants.* These are those boxes of six to nine little plants. Plant or transplant them on a cloudy, drizzly day—in the early morning or evening—to minimize harm from the sun and maximize the amount of moisture. Water them well.

•*Never walk on wet or soggy ground* to avoid compacting soil.

•*Healthy soil grows healthy plants.* Feed your soil at least once a week by giving it lots of compost. You can't really overdo it.

Source: Bonnie Wodin, owner of Golden Yarrow Landscape Design, a garden consulting firm, Box 61, Heath, Massachusetts 01346.

Secrets of Successful Terrace and Patio Gardens

Tiny yards, patios and terraces are ideal settings for lush gardens. *Key:* Keep your small space simple. Resist overwhelming your setting with too many different types of plants and flowers.

Design elements:

•Begin with the background. Set up a trellis and train small trees or vines to climb it. This will enclose your small space and create ambience and shade.

If you have a wooden fence for privacy, you can attach a foot of trellis to the top to create an airy, open feeling. Cover the fence with climbing plants that attach to the trellis at the top.

•Keep colors simple. Too many colors in a small space is confusing. *Suggestion:* On larger patios, use bright colors, such as orange and yellow, and add some red. On smaller terraces, go with pink, blue or purple, and accent with red.

Alternative: Masses of single colors accented with splashes of a contrasting color. *Very attractive:* A garden of all-white flowers—watch it shine in the moonlight.

•To get the illusion of spaciousness, use finely textured foliage and delicate flowers. Masses of greenery with colorful accents, used sparingly, create a restful scene. Many different plants or large-leaved or unusual plants look cluttered, not soothing.

Ongoing care:

•Water your patio plants daily. They will dry out faster than the same plants in the ground.

•Remove wilting blossoms regularly to keep plants flowering longer. Flowering shrubs should be pruned immediately after blooms fade or die off.

•Use a natural, balanced fertilizer in the spring and again in early summer.

Pest control:

Any plant will attract insects. Do not try to eliminate them by spraying plants wildly with insecticides, many of which are harmful to people.

Strategy: First remove and destroy the affected plant parts. If the plant is in a moveable pot, move it a few feet away from other plants.

Spray the plant and those that were next to it with insecticidal soap, which is available at garden stores. Repeat this process every three to five days until the insects are gone. Then move the plant back to its original location.

For more virulent infestations, blend fresh onion, garlic and hot peppers, and add them to the insecticidal soap spray.

To prevent insects from invading the house, grow tansy in pots adjacent to the house and/or sprinkle bay leaves along the perimeter of the house.

Ideal trees and plants:

•*Trees.* Dwarf fruit trees (plant two varieties of the same fruit to ensure pollination and bountiful fruit), Japanese maple (red- or green-leaved), dwarf conifer, tree roses, bay laurel.

•*Shrubs.* Dwarf azalea, rhododendron, shrub rose, burning bush, dwarf or spreading juniper.

•*Vines.* Perennials—such as climbing roses, firethorn (pyracantha), clematis, ivy, grapes, hops...and annuals—such as morning glory, nasturtium, scarlet runners or any pole bean.

•*Hanging baskets.* Lantana, fuchsia, impatiens, dwarf nasturtium, ivy-leaved geranium, portulaca and vinca.

•*Sun-loving annuals.* Sweet alyssum, candytuft, cleome, dianthus, salvia, geranium, nasturtium, marigold, pansy, verbena and zinnia.

•*Sun-loving perennials.* Dwarf daylily, liatris, thrift (sea pink), English daisy, lavender, sedum.

•*Shade-loving annuals.* Impatiens, tuberous begonia, nicotiana, coleus and vinca. Wax begonia, lobelia and browallia will tolerate partial sun or shade.

•*Shade-loving perennials.* Lady's mantle, hosta, astilbe, Christmas rose, primrose hybrid.

•*Light-shading perennials.* Columbine, blackberry lily, Jacob's ladder, coral bells.

Source: Bonnie Wodin, owner of Golden Yarrow Landscape Design, a garden-consulting firm, Box 61, Heath, Massachusetts 01346.

Better Dog Grooming

Brush dogs before bathing them. Wetting a matted coat tightens tangles, making them harder to remove. The best brushing gets down to the skin without brushing the skin itself. *Technique:* Push the dog's coat back with one hand and brush the hair down, a little at a time, with the other hand. Use quick, deep strokes. Brush one small area at a time.

Source: *Dog Fancy*, Box 6050, Mission Viejo, California 92690.

The Six Principles of Better Dog Training

A dog is much happier and better behaved when he has a clear role in your family. Dogs must be taught to be followers and that every person in the household is a leader.

A well-trained dog eats after you eat... sleeps on your bed only when you grant approval...moves out of your way...follows you out the door...walks by your side with a slack leash. Lunging or straining at the leash should not be tolerated. *Six basic principles:*

•Choose a dog that matches your energy level. All dogs can learn, but some are more active than others.

Example: Most terriers are very frisky, while hounds tend to be low-energy animals.

•Give your dog specific verbal commands. While most dogs can learn up to 30 words, eight commands are adequate for a well-trained house pet. These commands should be simple, concise—no more than three or four words per command—and consistent. If you order your dog to *sit down* while your spouse uses *sit here*, your pet may get confused. The basic commands:

•*Stay.* Keeps your dog from straying.

•*Come.* Releases your dog from a stationary position.

•*Down/sit.* Use this when your dog becomes overly playful.

•*Go to your bed/rug.* Tells your dog that it has its own place to sleep.

•*Leave it/don't touch it.* This will also keep your dog from confronting another dog.

•*Here.* A less-formal version of heel.

•*Take it.* This indicates your permission for the dog to take food from your hand.

•*Free.* This lets your dog know he can go play or relax.

•When giving commands, gear your expectations to the dog's age.

•Build your pet's training around rewards. When training is based on punishment, a dog may become too nervous to learn. Positive reinforcement is far more effective.

Is your dog motivated most by treats? By toys? By petting? Reward each successful performance with whatever makes your pet especially happy.

•Stick to routines for the essentials. Dogs are the most adaptable of all animals. They feel stress, however, when owners are erratic in meeting their basic needs, such as giving them food and water and providing opportunities to relieve themselves. To keep your pet relaxed and self-controlled, set regular convenient times for your dog's meals and outside excursions.

•Review your command code with your pet every few months. All of us—dogs and people alike—need refresher courses to reinforce what we've learned. Practice the commands to be sure the dog follows them each time. You should only have to say your command once.

Source: Maureen Fredrickson, program director for Delta Society, a nonprofit organization that trains people-animal teams to visit patients in health-care facilities, Box 1080, Renton, Washington 98057.

Digestion Problems For Your Pets

Animals have trouble digesting rich, fatty "people food." Feeding your pet table scraps can cause obesity, tooth decay and digestive problems. *Better treats:* Animal biscuits or other snacks that are made to meet your animal's dietary needs.

Source: Linda K. King, DVM, writing in *McCall's*, 110 Fifth Ave., New York 10011.

Cats Must Eat Meat

Cats must eat meat—unlike dogs and people, who can survive on vegetarian diets. Cats' bodies do not make certain crucial nutrients—and meat is a source of these nutrients. *Also:* Cats need a variety of meats. They get bored—and can get sick—if they are always fed the same type.

Source: *101 Questions Your Cat Would Ask Its Vet If Your Cat Could Talk* by Bruce Fogle, DVM, a veterinarian in London, England. Carroll & Graf Publishers, 260 Fifth Ave., New York 10001.

4

Smart Money Management

Smart Money Management:1995...and beyond
Edith Weiner, Weiner Edrich, Brown, Inc.

Working Americans will have to become more and more accustomed to a lifestyle of *income interruptions. Challenge:* Layoffs due to corporate restructuring, technology advancement and mergers and acquisitions will be a growing part of American working life—indefinitely.

Unfortunately, most people are seriously ill-prepared for loss of income. The low savings rate of Americans is no secret. Thousands of hard-working people plod along with minimal financial cushioning in case of emergencies. That will become increasingly risky in coming years.

Money management lesson number one for the next 20 years is therefore: Invest and save aggressively—but not with excessive risk.

Financial markets are becoming more volatile every year.

Part of the reason for this is that the largest single business in the world is currency transfer and trading.

Hundreds of billions of dollars worth of currency are traded daily throughout the world—by a very small number of people. That means that the opportunity for sudden upheaval in financial markets is great—and becoming greater.

The best way to protect your financial assets in this turbulent climate is to use a proven investment advisor. Don't try to become a financial wizard by risking hard-earned dollars in speculative investments—such as commodities, options or other exotic securities. *Also important...*

• *Stay healthy.* This may not sound like good financial advice—or financial advice at all. But it is. Because getting healthy when you're not has become so absurdly expensive—even for insured individuals—a major part of staying financially well-off is staying physically healthy.

•*Know how to acquire information that can be used for financial benefit.* The world is exploding with information about every facet of life. And, most excitingly, this information is getting easier and easier to obtain—via computer, telephone and television. The more you master the media, the more you can save money.

In the health area, for example, it is often possible to get free or inexpensive information about an ailment or disease—via on-line health services, CD-ROM disks from healthcare organizations, etc.

•*Keep acquiring new skills.* Employability will increasingly hinge on your ability to offer skills that are in hot demand. In today's fast-paced technologically oriented environment, it's getting tougher and tougher to keep skills from becoming outdated. This is especially true in computing, accounting, finance, managing globally, etc.

The good news is that there are loads of educational resources available to working professionals—through universities, private vendors and even companies themselves. Take advantage of as many learning opportunities as you can.

Faster Check Clearing

•Don't make deposits through an Automated Teller Machine (ATM). It could add an extra day or two to the clearing process—longer if the ATM is not owned by your bank.

•Deposit checks by 2 PM.

•Use direct deposit if your employer offers it. Paychecks deposited directly are usually available the same day.

•Always make sure that the check is endorsed. A check that is missing the endorsement can be held up by an extra day or two.

•Make sure the written dollar amount matches the numerical amount and that the check is not postdated.

Source: Ed Mierzwinski, consumer program director for the Washington-based US Public Interest Research Group.

Facing Possible Bankruptcy

If facing possible bankruptcy, try to pay off at least one major credit card. A credit card that is paid off before a bankruptcy filing does not have to be included in the bankruptcy and can be used to help reestablish credit afterward. Use the credit card only for small purchases that you can pay off each month to show a positive payment pattern.

Source: *Everything You Need to Know About Credit* by Deborah McNaughton, founder, Professional Credit Counselors, Orange County, California. Thomas Nelson Publishers, Box 141000, Nashville 37214.

How to Get Rich… And Stay Rich

Here are ten strategies that are used by my wealthy clients. Use one—or all—to help yourself become rich.

1. Weigh every purchase based on a cost/benefit analysis.

2. Put discretionary money to work.

3. Prefund life's big expenses, such as a college education.

4. Pay down your mortgage.

5. Participate in your company's 401(k) program if it has one.

6. Sign up for a monthly automatic transfer from your bank account to a mutual fund.

7. Buy a cash-value life insurance policy to force yourself to build up some assets.

8. Take out a bank loan to make an investment.

9. Don't borrow money to pay for assets that have little or no value.

10. Figure out how much money you need to get from here to there. The affluent people I work with do not suddenly wonder how they are going to pay for their 16-year-old's college tuition.

Source: Michael Stolper, president of Stolper & Company, an investment advisory firm for wealthy individuals.

How to Live Within Your Means

You're going to need at least $1 million to retire comfortably, but getting there isn't nearly as tough as you think. All you have to do is save regularly and invest your money intelligently.

To accumulate $1 million, you have to save $600 a month for 30 years. That presumes your money earns 9% a year—a reasonable goal if you have a portfolio that comprises mostly stocks and some bonds. Once you retire, your $1 million will generate an annual income of $50,000 and still give you enough growth to fend off inflation.

Getting started:

So where are you going to find that $600 a month to invest now? The key is to live beneath your means. Stop trying to keep up with your neighbors. Instead start saving for your future.

People who say they cannot save will either have to work until they drop or be willing to live in a state of poverty during the last years of their lives. It is tough to save, but you have to start sometime—and the sooner, the better.

If necessary, start small—saving just $10 a week. Next time you get a pay raise, increase your weekly saving.

Have your bank, credit union or mutual-fund company automatically deduct money from your paycheck or checking account and deposit it in a savings account or mutual fund.

It's easier to save when you never actually touch the money…and you could find that saving becomes addictive. It's comforting to watch your money build up and realize that your finances are finally under control.

Soon you will want to save more and more. How do you do that? Take a close look at your spending—the big-ticket items and the small expenses. You'll find that there's plenty of room to cut down.

Day-to-day savings:

Bring your lunch to work. Join a car pool, or take public transportation. Use coupons—if you don't have time for coupon-clipping, ask your kids to accumulate them. Cut down on eating

out. For most, all these savings can amount to nearly $4,000 a year.

Beware of sales:

No one ever saves money by buying something that's on sale. You're still spending money —not saving it.

Slash your insurance costs:

You could save money on life insurance by buying it directly from a company like Ameritas Life Insurance Corp. (800-552-3553) or USAA Life Insurance Co. (800-531-8000). These companies sell term and cash-value insurance directly to the public, thereby minimizing commissions and fees.

You can also save money by boosting the deductibles on your homeowners and auto insurance policies and increasing the waiting period before your disability insurance starts. Also, consider putting unused valuables in a safe-deposit box at your local bank, where you can insure them for far less than if you keep them at home.

Get your debts under control:

Aside from your home mortgage, keep your debts to a bare minimum. Pay off your credit cards and other personal loans—the interest on these debts is not deductible. With a $5,000 balance on your credit cards, you're paying almost $20 a week in interest.

If you must borrow, consider an investment-related loan or a home-equity loan, both of which usually have tax advantages. Best of all, don't borrow.

Save through work:

Your employer may offer flexible spending accounts that allow you to pay for day care and medical expenses out of pretax dollars. This is a great way to reduce your tax bill and free up money that can be saved.

Cut down on taxes:

Consider three strategies to take money that would otherwise go to Uncle Sam and add it to your savings…

•Buy tax-exempt municipal bonds, if you're in one of the top tax brackets. Municipal bonds will pay you less interest than taxable bonds, but you'll more than make up for the difference in reduced taxes.

•Use tax-favored savings vehicles like 401(k) plans, Individual Retirement Accounts (IRAs) and Keogh plans. These vehicles allow your money to grow tax-deferred, and your contributions may also be tax-deductible.

Best: Fund these accounts as early in the year as possible, so your money has more time to appreciate in value tax-deferred.

•Hunt for further tax deductions. Among the most commonly overlooked tax deductions are miscellaneous ones such as safe-deposit-box rentals and investment-counseling fees…medical expenses including prescribed foods and transportation costs incurred for doctors' visits …employment-related deductions such as the dues paid to professional associations…expenses incurred when looking for a new job in your current field of employment.

For further information on useful deductions, get one of the available tax guides. Alternatively, consider one of the tax-preparation software programs.

Source: Jonathan D. Pond, president, Financial Planning Information Inc., a financial planning group, 9 Galen St., Watertown, Massachusetts 02172. He is the author of *The New Century Family Money Book,* Dell Publishing, 1540 Broadway, New York 10036.

Shop Around for Loans

Banks are now competing for loan business. *Result:* Car loans, credit-card interest rates, even rates on unsecured personal loans can vary by several percentage points at different institutions. A difference of one or two percentage points can save big, big bucks in interest over the term of a loan.

Source: Robert Heady, publisher, *100 Highest Yields* and *Bank Rate Monitor,* writing in *Your Money,* 5705 N. Lincoln Ave., Chicago 60659.

Financial Planner Danger

Some financial planners exploit their clients' passivity or lack of knowledge by pressuring them to follow recommendations blindly. *Self-defense:* Clarify your goals before talking with a financial planner…recognize that the planner is working for you—not vice versa…if you can

tell the planner is being intimidating or condescending, find another.

Source: *Creating Your Own Future: A Woman's Guide in Retirement Planning* by Judith A. Martindale, a certified financial planner, Shell Beach, California. Sourcebooks, Box 372, Naperville, Illinois 60566.

20 Easy Ways to Save Hard Dollars… Year In…Year Out

Small changes in your lifestyle can add up to significant savings over the course of a year. If you adopt just half of these suggestions, you'll save over $1,000 a year…

•Switch from a bank to a credit union. The average checking account now costs $185 a year in service charges to maintain. Credit unions are nonprofit organizations that return surplus funds to members in the form of low-cost services. Larger credit unions offer free checking, low or no annual fees on credit cards and excellent rates on car loans.

Disadvantages: Fewer branch offices, and the branches may not have automatic teller machines. But, remember, not very long ago, we all survived without ATMs.

•Buy your home heating oil in the summer. In my area, prices drop 20¢ a gallon during the off-season, so filling a 275-gallon tank in the summer saves $55. If you are a do-it-yourselfer with extra space, you can buy a used second tank, so you'll have two tanks that can be filled in the off-season. Check local laws about installation and inspection of the second tank. You will have to monitor prices for some weeks to get the best deal in your area, but the bottom should hit sometime between July and early September.

Caution: Don't wait until November, when prices go back up, to get your first fill-up.

•Change the oil in your car yourself.

•Review your insurance policies. Take higher deductibles where you can afford them, and eliminate coverage you don't need for your lifestyle.

Examples: Many people past childbearing age are still paying for maternity benefits. Most car insurance policies cover car-rental reimbursement when the car is in the shop—but will you use this? Maybe you have a second car or friends who will help out. Are there extra drivers listed on your insurance who no longer live with you? Many homeowners' policies cover furs, jewelry, computers or other items you may not own.

Also, check with your agent to make sure you are getting any discounts you qualify for.

Examples: Nonsmoking on health insurance, alarm systems or safe-driving records on car insurance, owning multiple policies with one company.

• Make your own popcorn. A family that pops two batches of traditional generic popcorn a week instead of an equivalent amount of microwave popcorn will save $100 in a year. And it can take less time to make popcorn in a hot-air popper than in a microwave.

• Reduce your smoking by three cigarettes a day. (Or give up smoking altogether and save even more.)

• Rent videos instead of going to the movies. Even better, check them out of the library.

• Make pizza from scratch instead of having it delivered.

• Give personal services rather than store-bought presents. Offer to garden, clean bathrooms or baby-sit for your friend in the hospital. Bring your hostess potted herbs from your kitchen or a homemade casserole. Give the new graduate "free résumé service" or 100 pages of thesis typing. Fill out change-of-address forms for your friend who just moved. Refinish a chest of drawers for newlyweds. And don't forget to make your own greeting cards.

• Share a newspaper subscription with your neighbor. Are you finished with the paper before you leave for work in the morning? Does your neighbor read the paper before supper? Share magazine subscriptions, too. Many public libraries microfilm, then discard, magazines every six months. Request the outdated issues be held for you. Raid recycling bins.

• Hang four loads of laundry a week instead of running the dryer.

• Drink four fewer cans of soda per week—saves $100 a year.

• Tape ten pieces of music from the radio rather than buying commercially recorded audiotapes.

• Cut your family's hair yourself. A child's haircut costs as much as $8 to $10 every six weeks.

An adult haircut at $25 every six weeks adds up to $217 a year. If you learn to trim it yourself you will only need to have a professional job at the hairdresser half the time. This will save you $100.

• Bake one batch of bread (two loaves) once a week.

• Write one good letter a month instead of making an $8 long-distance telephone call.

• Use half your usual amount of cleaning and personal-care products. Find the minimum effective level of shampoo, conditioner, laundry detergent, bleach, dishwasher detergent, toothpaste, shaving cream, lotion, perfume, etc. You may find you can make do with less than half your usual amount.

• Buy articles of clothing from thrift shops and yard sales rather than paying store prices. This is also a fun way to shop.

• Barter for one regular service. Handy with graphics? Arrange to make fliers and do an advertising layout for your massage therapist in return for monthly sessions. Want help cleaning? Offer to take your cleaning person's kids for a weekly activity in return for two hours of housecleaning. Are you an accountant? Trade tax preparation for lawn care or TV repair.

Consider three-party trades to get what you need.

Example: You want ten $10 computer lessons, the computer instructor needs a $100 repair on her car, so you prepare the mechanic's tax return in exchange for fixing the car, in exchange for your lessons.

Be creative!

• Use dry milk. A gallon of whole milk costs up to $2.59 per gallon. Dry milk, purchased in the 20-quart store-brand box, costs $1.60 per gallon. Dry milk is 100% fat-free, while whole milk contains 4% fat. By mixing the two kinds of milk half and half, you can make your own 2% milk. If you use a gallon of milk every three days, you will easily save $100 in a year by substituting dry milk in cooking, homemade cocoa mix and in using the half-and-half mixture for drinking.

Source: Amy Dacyczyn—"The Frugal Zealot." She is the author of *The Tightwad Gazette*, a book of excerpts from her newsletter of the same name, Villard Books, 201 E. 50 St., New York 10022. *The Tightwad Gazette* is published monthly, RR1, Box 3570, Leeds, Maine 04263.

Wintertime Money Savers

Winter is the season of higher electricity and gas bills, car maintenance and repair bills, bills for cold and flu medications and so on. But there are several ways that you can cut down on expenses without sacrificing great comfort. Avoid costly car repairs:

•Keep your gas free of water. The most frequent problems mechanics see in winter are caused by water in the gas. To prevent problems, add a drier (such as Prestone Gas-Drier or Heet) to your gas every few fill-ups.

•Check your radiator fluid and the condition of the radiator hoses. If the fluid is low, add a 50/50 mixture of antifreeze and water. In the coldest parts of the country or when an extreme cold snap strikes, you may want to alter this by using more antifreeze. *Best:* Use a mixture of 70% antifreeze and 30% water. Muddy-looking fluid should be changed. Make sure that the rubber hoses leading from the radiator to the engine are not cracked, brittle, bulging or mushy when they are squeezed.

•Keep your battery terminals clean to avoid starting problems (and costly towing bills). Clean the battery terminals occasionally with baking soda and then reduce the corrosion problem by smearing them with a thin coating of petroleum jelly.

•Promptly repair any nicks in your windshield. Stop those smaller than a quarter from spawning spider legs and ruining the windshield by covering them on both sides with transparent tape (duct tape works, too). Then get the car to a windshield-repair specialist. Cost for a nick ranges from $30 to $50, compared to the $300 to over $600 it can cost to replace the whole windshield.

•Check tire inflation every few weeks with an accurate gauge. Changes in temperature alter tire pressure, and underinflation increases tire wear and gas consumption by as much as 5%. *Important:* Check the pressure while tires are cold. Know how many pounds of pressure they require. Then check them again at the gas station (after they've warmed from being driven on) and add the pounds of pressure that were needed when they were cold.

Save on heating:

•Put on an extra sweater and modify your heating habits. Keep the daytime thermostat at 65 degrees Fahrenheit (rather than 70) and the nighttime temperature at 55 degrees Fahrenheit (rather than 60 or 65). This can reduce your heating bill 15% or more. And turn down the heat when you leave to run errands.

•Keep fireplace dampers closed when not in use. Install glass fireplace doors. Then heat won't escape through the chimney.

•Have your home's insulation checked by your utility company. Many utilities perform this inspection service free or for a nominal fee. Make sure your home's insulation meets the US Department of Energy's recommendations.

•Wrap fiberglass insulation around heating ducts and hot water pipes in basement, attic and crawl space. Putting 2½ inches of insulation around these ducts and pipes will pay for itself in one season.

Save on lighting:

•Replace incandescent lights with fluorescent lights in areas that need light for hours each day. Today's fluorescent tubes produce warmer hues that won't make your home feel like a factory, and they're three to four times more efficient. If you don't want to install the tubes, use compact fluorescent bulbs. They screw into standard sockets.

•Use outdoor light fixtures that turn on and off by means of built-in heat/motion detectors and timers. They're far more economical than those that burn nonstop.

•Don't turn lights on and off frequently. Turning the lights out every time you leave the room for a few minutes may seem like it's doing good, but it shortens the life of the bulbs. So don't turn out the light unless leaving for more than a few minutes.

Grandma's remedies:

•Get an annual flu shot if you're 65 or older or suffer from cardiac or respiratory problems. It's cheap insurance against the major problems a flu can precipitate.

•Have prescriptions filled at a discount drugstore. It is much cheaper than using your hospital's pharmacy.

Miscellaneous money savers:

•Freeze your credit. This is a good idea any time of year, but works especially well around the holiday season. Put your credit cards in a bowl of water and place them in the freezer. It sounds crazy, but by the time the ice melts enough to retrieve the cards, the urge to buy may have passed. And writing checks or paying cash for items forces you to do a "reality check" on how much you really have to spend.

•Put rubber half-soles on the bottom of your shoes. In damp or wet weather, the leather soles of your shoes are constantly absorbing water, which slowly damages the leather and reshapes the shoe. Half-soles cost $12 to $15 and add years of life to your shoes. *Also:* Alternate the shoes you wear each day. Having a day to dry and air between uses greatly extends shoe life.

Source: Andy Dappen, author of *Cheap Tricks: 100s of Ways You Can Save 1000s of Dollars,* Brier Books, Box 180, Mountlake Terrace, Washington 98043.

Don't Leave Home At Higher Cost

American Express gives a $20-a-year senior discount to members age 62 and over—bringing the annual fee to $35 for the green card and $55 for the gold. *To get the lower rates:* Call 800-323-8300 and enroll as a senior member. *Added benefits:* A quarterly newsletter detailing special discounts…a 24-hour travel-information hotline that can arrange fast replacements of prescriptions and eyeglasses or get urgent messages home.

Order Checks By Mail

Order checks by mail rather than from your bank. Two hundred plain checks from a bank can cost $16. Special designs can cost much more. *Much cheaper:* Current, Inc., Box 19000, Colorado Springs 80935, sells 200 checks for $5.95—wide variety available (800-426-0822). Checks in the Mail, Box 17802, Irwindale, California 91706 charges $4.95 for 200 checks—again in many designs (800-733-4443). *Recommended:*

Ask your bank if it offers free checking for seniors—with free checks and no minimum balance. Many banks do this, but not all volunteer the information.

Source: *The Tightwad Gazette: Promoting Thrift as a Viable Alternative Lifestyle* by Amy Dacyczyn, publisher of *The Tightwad Gazette* newsletter. Villard Books, 201 E. 50 St., New York 10022.

The Biggest Questions People Have About Their Money

The stock market has hit record highs…interest rates are rising after hitting 30-year lows …consumer debt is growing again…job layoffs continue…and everyone seems unsure of what to do with their money. Here are the questions that I am most frequently asked about money.

It seems the stock market is the only place to invest now, even though business doesn't look good. What's going on? Most investors think that there's no place like the stock market to beat the 3% yield they get on bank Certificates of Deposit (CDs). Yet there are no guarantees in the stock market. Instead of getting a safe 3% or a hoped-for double-digit return, you could actually *lose* your principal. It is a risk to keep in mind.

The market didn't soar because business is booming. In fact, it has been a pretty slow economic recovery. Higher costs squeeze profits…and since it's difficult to raise prices, companies have to cut costs somewhere, which means laying off employees. These layoffs, in turn, erode consumer confidence. It's a vicious circle—and eventually it could be reflected in sharply lower stock prices.

What are the risks in the stock market? The stock market had a great 10-year performance —a 17.5% average annual return for the S&P 500, including dividends. For the past 30 years, the average return has been 10.6%. But beware of averages.

There have never been back-to-back decades of double-digit returns—tracking the numbers back to the 1920s. The big bear market of 1973/1974 lasted 21 months, and the S&P 500 Index

fell 48.5%. If you bought at the top before the crash, it took more than seven years for the S&P 500 to break even. Most investors and stock-brokers today have never experienced anything like that. Think twice about investing, unless you can afford the risk and have a long-term perspective.

How safe are bonds now? You can lose a lot of money in bonds, even the highest-quality US government bonds. It is not just a question of default—that is unlikely with top-rated bonds. But even when you buy top-rated long-term bonds, they lose market value when interest rates go up.

Example: If you buy a 6.9% 30-year US Treasury bond and interest rates rise just one percentage point, the market value of your bond drops about 12%.

Important: When interest rates rise, the market value of all fixed-rate bonds falls. This applies to government bonds, corporate bonds, municipal bonds and all "packages" of bonds, such as closed-end bond funds or unit investment trusts. So if you think interest rates will rise, don't lock up your money in long-term bonds now.

My bank offers US government bond funds that have much higher yields than CDs. Should I switch? There's no comparison between the two. Even though mutual funds are sold in banks, they are not FDIC-insured. And even if the mutual fund invests in US government bonds, you can lose money if interest rates rise. Deposit accounts pay low rates, but your principal and interest are guaranteed. Stock and bond mutual funds may offer higher returns, but there's no guarantee against loss of principal.

Should I invest in mutual funds or individual securities? Mutual funds are a convenient way to buy diversified investment portfolios that are professionally managed. This is supposed to minimize risk and eliminate confusion. Perhaps it does…but there are now more mutual funds than there are stocks on the New York Stock Exchange.

You still have to do your homework before picking a mutual fund. Also, no matter how good the past performance of your fund or how famous the fund manager, when the stock mar-

ket takes a sharp fall, your fund shares are likely to fall as well.

One other concern: A market correction could trigger panic sales, forcing funds to liquidate some of their holdings, pushing the market down even further. Many investors say they are in for the long term, but they could change their minds as they see prices fall.

What about real estate? It depends. It's a good time to buy a home. Prices are down, and interest rates are still relatively low. *Key question:* Are you secure enough in your job to make the mortgage payments?

As for commercial real estate, we probably have enough to last the rest of the century—without any more building. Investing in rental apartments for income might make sense, but think twice about investing in Real-Estate Investment Trusts (REITs). Many of these newly issued REITs are promising questionable returns.

There is still one tax shelter left in real estate —low-income housing partnerships, which generate dollar-for-dollar tax credits. Value the deal on the tax credits you would get, and don't count on a return on your original investment.

With taxes going up and making it harder to save, how can I protect—and even increase—my assets? The best device is your company's retirement plan. A 401(k) plan offers pretax contributions from current income and tax-sheltered growth over the future. Every worker can contribute up to $2,000 each year to an IRA. You can't deduct it if you participate in a company retirement plan, but your investment will grow tax-deferred. You may deduct the $2,000, however, if you have chosen not to be in your company's 401(k) plan—or if you are not yet eligible for it.

The hottest tax shelter for the rest of the decade will be tax-deferred annuities. These insurance company contracts allow you to put away an unlimited amount of after-tax money that grows tax-deferred until you start to withdraw it after age 59½. They're available in fixed and variable rates—the variable rate offers a choice of mutual funds. Before investing in annuities, understand the costs, including surrender charges and penalties, for early withdrawals. And be sure to choose a strong, well-capitalized insurer.

What are the risks involved in investing overseas? Investing overseas entails not just market and political risks but currency risk as well. Foreign investments are made in each country's currency. You could make a lot of money, but when it's time to translate your profits back to dollars, the gains could be wiped out by currency movements. Many funds hedge against currency fluctuations, but hedging costs eat into profits.

Caution: In recent months, US investors have poured so much money into overseas mutual funds that they have overwhelmed many thinly traded markets. This makes their investments even more volatile.

To speculate on currency moves, the *Franklin/Templeton Global Trust* (formerly the Huntington Currency Portfolios, San Mateo, California, 800-342-5236) allows you to buy a package of foreign currencies. *The Mark Twain Bank* (St. Louis, 800-926-4922) offers FDIC-insured CDs denominated in foreign currencies and paying interest rates offered by foreign banks.

I'm working harder and longer and have less time to tend to my investments. What should I do? It's tempting to turn over your money to a financial planner—but it's still your money and you should approve all investment decisions. No one cares about your financial future more than you do. Make time to learn about the investment alternatives—the opportunities…and the risks.

Source: Terry Savage, registered investment adviser for stocks and commodities and syndicated columnist for *The Chicago Sun-Times*. She is the author of *Terry Savage's New Money Strategies for the '90s*, HarperBusiness, 10 E. 53 St., New York 10022.

Better Budgeting

Track where your money goes by listing every penny you spend for two months. Afterward, review your list and mark each item with an "O" for optional or "E" for essential. *Aim:* Eliminate as many optional expenses as possible without budgeting out your fun.

Source: Personal finance radio hosts Ken and Daria Dolan, writing in *Money*, Rockefeller Center, New York 10020.

How to Be Richer A Year from Now

Many people think they need great and exotic investment strategies to increase their wealth. In fact, the road to greater riches is very simple—especially if you follow these ten steps.

1. *Pay down your credit cards.* This is the single easiest way to boost your wealth. Paying off credit-card balances—on which you may be paying interest rates of as much as 19% to 21%—is like finding a riskless 30% investment. Not only is the interest on credit-card balances no longer tax-deductible, but you're repaying that money in after-tax dollars.

2. *Pay yourself first.* If you can live on your present salary, you can also live on 95% of it. Arrange to save 5% of your gross income each pay period—perhaps through an automatic payroll-deduction program with your bank or mutual fund. What you don't see, you won't spend.

3. *Boost your withholding to reflect your home mortgage expense.* The interest that homeowners pay to the financial institutions that hold their mortgages is tax-deductible. To ease the strain on their budgets, homeowners should adjust their withholding at work and claim exemptions to reflect these deductible expenses and property taxes.

4. *Refinance your old mortgage.* Even though mortgage rates have crept up and many people have already refinanced, there are still millions of people who are needlessly paying interest on their old mortgages of 12% or more. Even those who have refinanced may find that they can benefit if they refinance a second time.

Rule of thumb: You'll come out ahead if your new mortgage rate is at least two percentage points lower than your old rate and you plan to stay in your home for at least two years. When you refinance your mortgage, consider taking a loan for 15 years rather than the conventional 30 years. The monthly payments are similar.

Reason: You'll build your equity in the house faster, thus boosting your individual wealth. Paying off a 15-year mortgage isn't that difficult because the monthly payments are only modestly larger than those of a conventional 30-year loan.

If you really feel you can't handle the bigger monthly payments on a regular basis, consider making extra payments on your 30-year loan when you have extra cash. Every little bit helps a lot.

5. *Maximize your contributions to your 401(k) plan.* A 401(k) plan is one of the best ways to save for retirement, especially if your employer matches your contributions. The employer's contribution provides an instant return on your money, even before you take into account the tax-deferred compounding you get on your investment earnings. The maximum you can contribute for 1994 is $9,240.

Don't be too conservative and confine yourself to safe but low-yielding bonds or Guaranteed Investment Contracts (GICs). Remember, this is long-term money that you won't need until you retire, so invest in no-load stock funds that offer opportunities for capital appreciation.

6. *Don't overlook your Individual Retirement Account (IRA).* Even if your income is too high (more than $35,000 a year if single…$50,000 if married) to deduct your IRA contribution or you are already covered by a retirement plan at work, the power of tax-deferred compounding will allow your IRA investment to multiply faster than through a similar investment outside the IRA. Manage your IRA assertively, and don't be too conservative. Avoid fixed-income investments… concentrate on equity investments instead.

7. *Lighten up on bonds and bond funds.* While we've already had a shakeout, I think the weakest point is still coming. I expect yields to rise and prices to tumble again. If you need income, look into investing for growth—by purchasing stock funds, and then systematically liquidate a portion of your principal to produce spendable cash. Sell off holdings that have increased in price. When people say they need income, they really need cash. Whether that comes from bond interest or principal appreciation in the stock market is irrelevant. By keeping a money-market fund in your growth portfolio and withdrawing from that, you end up with more spendable cash and let stock-fund profits run.

8. *Invest in international stock funds.* Domestic growth funds are not the best place to be. We have an aging, tired bull market in the US that is going through a correction. Foreign markets are surprisingly independent of the American stock market. And recent declines simply mean foreign funds will be much better buys during this period. They tend to get ahead of themselves, correct and start up again. *My favorite mutual funds now:*

•*Oakmark International.* An unusual international fund because it is value-oriented, not growth-oriented. It avoided investment in Japan in 1993, which kept it from suffering the declines other international funds experienced. Oakmark, started on September 30, 1992, was up 28.32% on a total return basis for the 12 months ended March 31, 1994. *Minimum initial investment:* $2,500. *Load:* None.

Oakmark International Fund, 2 N. LaSalle St., Chicago 60602. 800-625-6275.

•*Fidelity Emerging Markets.* This fund selects stocks in countries with developing markets and invests more assertively overseas. It has been a consistent top performer and in the top 30% of its category for the last 3-, 6-, 12- and 36-month periods. *Minimum initial investment:* $2,500. *Load:* 3%. *Performance:* 25.83%.

Fidelity Distributors, 82 Devonshire St., Boston 02109. 800-544-8888.

•*Fidelity Asset Manager.* This is one of the safest of the asset-allocation funds and consistently one of the top performers with less downside risk than other funds. It is flexible and has divided its portfolio evenly between domestic and foreign stocks. It holds emerging-markets debt, junk bonds, foreign stocks, derivatives, European bonds and a wide array of medium-cap issues. *Minimum initial investment:* $2,500. *Load:* None. *Performance:* 19.78%.

Fidelity Distributors, 82 Devonshire St., Boston 02109. 800-544-8888.

9. *Liberate the lemons.* Get rid of financial and nonfinancial assets that no longer fit in with your goals or desires.

Example I: Dump your Christmas club account and bank money-market account. Some Christmas club accounts don't pay any interest at all, and many bank money-market accounts pay such low rates that they're hardly worth mentioning. Furthermore, these holdings are not investments…they're simply temporary parking places for money that is awaiting investment. Take that money and put it into real investments, such as international stock funds.

Example II: If you are considering buying a larger house because you need more room for the stuff you've accumulated over the years, hold a yard sale. It's fun, the kids can get involved… and you'll discover that your present house is much larger once you've cleared out all that junk. Take the proceeds from the sale and invest it.

10. *Don't forget that wealth is measured in ways other than just money.* The greatest riches of all come from your relationships with family and friends. Nurture them with the same care you give your investments.

Source: William E. Donoghue, publisher of *Donoghue's MoneyLetter* (290 Eliot St., Ashland, Massachusetts 01721, 800-445-5900) and author of *William E. Donoghue's Mutual Fund Superstars: Invest with the Best, Forget About the Rest,* Elliott & James, 2212 15 Ave. W., Seattle 98119.

Figuring Out Your Debt

Figure how much debt you can carry by making a list of all your monthly payments on debts that will take at least six months to pay off, excluding your mortgage. Then divide the result by your regular monthly gross income…this is your *debt-to-income ratio.* If monthly debt payments are 15% or less of income, you're doing fine…15% to 20%, take steps to keep debts from accumulating…20% to 35%, you're in a risky area and need to cut back…over 35%, you are in deep enough trouble to ask for help. Most people who hit 50% in debt payment are headed for bankruptcy.

Source: Gerri Detweiler, author of *The Ultimate Credit Handbook,* Good Advice Press, Box 780, Elizaville, New York 12523.

Automated Teller Security

Take your transaction slip with you from an automated teller, instead of throwing it away, to prevent anyone from seeing details of your account and to check against your monthly statement. Notify the bank immediately if you find your ATM card is missing—giving notice within two business days limits your risk of loss to $50…after that it may rise to $500. Check your monthly statement—if an unauthorized withdrawal is reported within 60 days, your risk of loss is limited to $50. Contact the bank immediately if there are any problems with your account. Telephone first and follow up with a written notice. Send it by certified mail and keep the mailing receipt (notice is deemed given to the bank when it is *mailed*).

Source: Edward F. Mrkvicka, Jr., bank consultant in Marengo, Illinois, and author of *The Bank Book: How to Revoke Your Bank's "License to Steal,"* HarperPerennial, 10 E. 53 St., New York 10022.

Time to Take Control Of Your Assets

The only way to truly achieve financial security is to live *beneath* your means. That will give you the extra money you need to pay off debts and begin to save.

Some people think it is impossible to save today. But even in these crazy times, it is not only possible, it is essential to be financially responsible. And it's not as difficult as you may think.

Here's my seven-day plan for getting control of your money. All it takes is 20 minutes a day for one week.

Day 1: Organize your financial records. If you want to dig yourself out of a financial hole, you must figure out how you got there. That means calculating how much money you earn and where it goes. *As a first step, gather the following records:*
- Recent pay stub
- Latest tax return
- Most recent bank statement
- Checkbook
- Current credit-card bills

The pay stub will tell you how much you bring in from work, and the tax return will tell you how much you get from investments and other sources of income.

The bank statement and checkbook will tell you where you are spending the bulk of your money. The credit-card bills will tell you how much additional money you spend that is not being covered by your paycheck.

Day 2: Figure out where your money goes. Once you have compiled your financial statements, you are ready to prepare a summary of your monthly expenses.

Make a list of all your expenses, right down to the smallest item. Pay particular attention to exactly where the cash goes. There's often a lot of room to cut back in this area.

If necessary, keep a journal for a day or two and write down every purchase you make. You will quickly realize that you waste a lot of money—and that there are many ways to save.

Day 3: Categorize your expenses. Slot them into one of the following three categories:

•Regular payments that you have to make, such as for the mortgage and utilities.

•Expenses you must incur but that could be reduced, such as those for food, clothing and transportation.

•Expenses you could eliminate entirely, such as eating at restaurants, going to concerts and buying lottery tickets.

In the last two categories, you will find many areas in which you can cut back.

Day 4: Devise a plan for living *beneath* your means. You have to reduce your monthly expenses so that you spend less than you take in. How much should you cut back? If you are adding $500 a month to your credit-card balance, then you have to cut $500 a month from your spending just to stop your finances from deteriorating.

Even if you manage to do that, you are still not making progress. You must cut more than $500 to get your current debt under control and start building your savings. Make a list of all the expenses that you are eliminating and how much you hope to save.

Day 5: Develop a debt-reduction strategy. Now that you have figured out how to spend less than you earn, what should you do with the extra money?

First pay off your debts. Start with the debts that charge the highest interest rates. These are usually the credit-card bills. Set target dates for when you want each debt to be completely paid. Don't be too ambitious or you will set yourself up for failure.

Day 6: Establish a savings plan. If you don't have any money saved, plan to build up some savings while reducing your debts. But this should not mean that you end up paying off your debts more slowly.

Financially, that doesn't seem to make sense. It's better to pay off credit-card debt at 20% interest than to save money that earns 4% or 5%.

But psychologically, it's a real boost to get some savings under way. In addition, your savings will be helpful in case you lose your job or fall ill.

Day 7: Start an automatic investment plan. It's not only time to think about saving for an emergency but also about investing for the future.

Call your bank, credit union or a mutual-fund company and arrange an automatic investment plan. With this type of plan, money will be deducted directly from your paycheck or bank account every month and put into an investment account.

To arrange for this, you will have to commit to investing $50 or $100 every month. This money can become the basis of your retirement portfolio or your child's college fund.

After you've completed this seven-day plan, you will feel much better…you will get back on track financially…and, most important, you will not lapse into your old spendthrift ways.

Source: Jonathan D. Pond, president, Financial Planning Information Inc., 9 Galen St., Watertown, Massachusetts 02172. He is the author of *The New Century Family Money Book* (Dell Publishing, 1540 Broadway, New York 10036) and developer of *Jonathan Pond's Personal Financial Planner,* an interactive software program (Vertigo Development Group Inc., 58 Charles St., Cambridge, Massachusetts 02141).

Today's Best Credit Cards

Competition among credit-card issuers has driven down the rates and fees they charge consumers. To attract business, some banks are even making it easier for new customers to transfer their other bank credit-card balances.

Important: If you intend to transfer a balance to a lower-rate card, look for a bank that doesn't charge a *balance transfer fee.*

Our favorite cards that offer the most value and don't charge transfer fees*...

Favorite low-rate basic cards:

•Arkansas Federal Credit-Card Services. *Variable rate:* Prime rate** plus 1.75%. *Annual fee:* $35.
Little Rock. 800-477-3348.

•Choice Bank. *Variable rate:* Prime plus 3.9%. *Annual fee:* $20.
Sioux Falls, South Dakota. 800-934-2788.

•Consumer's Best Bankcard. The current variable rate is the London Interbank Offered Rate (LIBOR)** plus 2.6%, but it will jump to LIBOR plus 7.6% on July 1, 1995. *Annual fee:* $29.
Richmond, Virginia. 800-955-7070.

•Consumer's National Bankcard. The current variable rate is LIBOR plus 5%, but it jumps to LIBOR plus 9% on October 1, 1995. *Annual fee:* None.
Richmond, Virginia. 800-955-7070.

•Federal Savings Bank. *Variable rate:* Federal Discount rate** plus 5%. *Annual fee:* $33.
Little Rock. 800-285-9090.

•Oak Brook Bank. *Variable rate:* Prime plus 2.9%. *Annual fee:* $39.
Oak Brook, Illinois. 800-536-3000.

•Wachovia Bankcard Services. *Variable rate for the first year:* Prime. *After the first year:* Prime plus 3.9%. *Annual fee:* $18.
Wilmington, Delaware. 800-842-3262.

Low-rate gold cards:

•Arkansas Federal Credit-Card Services. *Variable rate:* Prime plus 1.75%. *Annual fee:* $50.
Little Rock. 800-477-3348.

•Central Carolina Bank & Trust Co. *Variable rate:* Prime plus 1.5%. *Annual fee:* $20.
Durham, North Carolina. 800-334-1073.

•Federal Savings Bank. *Variable rate:* Federal Discount rate plus 5%. *Annual fee:* $48.
Little Rock. 800-285-9090.

•Oak Brook Bank. *Variable rate:* Prime plus 2.9%. *Annual fee:* $49.
Oak Brook, Illinois. 800-536-3000.

•Wachovia Bankcard Services. *Variable rate for the first year:* Prime. *After the first year:* Prime

*All cards have a 25-day grace period.

**Check *The Wall Street Journal* for current rates on these figures.

plus 3.9%. *Annual fee:* $28.
Wilmington, Delaware. 800-842-3262.

No-annual-fee gold cards:

•AFBA Industrial Bank. *Variable rate for the first year:* Prime plus 3.5%. *After the first year:* Prime plus 6%.
Colorado Springs. 800-776-2265.

•Amalgamated Bank of Chicago. *Variable rate:* Prime plus 4.5%.
Chicago. 800-365-6464.

•USAA Federal Savings Bank. *Variable rate:* Four-week average of the 26-week Treasury Bill** plus 7%.
Tulsa. 800-922-9092.

Source: Ruth Susswein, executive director of Bankcard Holders of America, a national nonprofit consumer group that focuses exclusively on credit education and advocacy, 524 Branch Dr., Salem, Virginia 24153.

Ten Things That Credit-Card Companies Won't Tell You

As competition among credit-card issuers heats up, many people are being bombarded with a wide range of attractive offers from banks and other institutions.

While annual fees and percentage rates on outstanding balances are important, there are many other issues that you need to know about before you apply for a credit card.

Here are ten key points that rarely appear in credit-card issuers' promotional materials but usually turn up in the fine print on credit-card contracts...

•Check your statement carefully each month for error—and fraud. Most people know that if their credit cards are used fraudulently, they are liable only for the first $50 in charges.

But under the Federal Truth-in-Lending Act, if you do not report the disputed charges in *writing* within 60 days of the postmarked date on the bill, you may have to pay the fraudulent charges to avoid being reported to a credit bureau.

Important: Theft can occur without your wallet —or your credit card—ever being stolen. Increasingly, card numbers are being copied and sold to criminals or reproduced on counterfeit cards. Therefore, fraudulent charges can appear while you still have your card in your possession.

Check all your credit-card statements carefully. As soon as you realize that a statement lists questionable charges, call the issuer's 800 telephone number and report it.

Though most problem charges can be handled over the phone, protect yourself by sending a letter to the address that appears on the monthly statement and the credit-card agreement.

Use certified mail/return receipt requested. Then you will have evidence that the issuer received your letter. This precaution protects you in case the issuer fails to recall your original phone call...or denies your claim because you never informed them in writing.

•A credit card with a lower interest rate can save you a lot of money. Even if your card issuer offers a 25-day grace period—during which no interest is charged on new purchases—you will not be eligible for this benefit if you carry over a balance of even $1 from the previous month. Your new purchases will immediately incur interest charges.

Strategy: Carry two credit cards. Use one for purchases that you intend to pay in full each month...use the other—which should have a lower interest rate—for purchases you will repay over time.

If you carry large balances on several credit cards, consolidate debts on the lowest-interest card—provided you have the discipline to refrain from using the other cards and adding to a mountain of debt.

•Pay more than the minimum amount required. A typical credit-card bill of $2,500 can take longer to pay off than a 30-year mortgage. This is because most card issuers require a *minimum payment* of only 2% to 2.5% of the new balance.

Problem: The combination of interest and even a small additional purchase can stretch the debt out for decades if only the minimum is paid each month. Some 12 to 15 million Americans are deeply in debt because they habitually pay only the minimum amount required by the card issuer.

•Not all credit-card issuers calculate interest the same way. There are several methods to calculate interest. Almost 90% of card issuers use the *average daily balance* method, which charges interest on your average balance for the month.

Exceptions: The Discover Card, the Household Bank Card and some cards issued by small banks use the *two-cycle* method. In some cases, this is calculated by adding the average daily balances for the current and previous months. This method can be costly.

Find out which method is used before you apply for a credit card. For those you already own, check the agreement or statement. If it's a two-cycle method, pay off your balance in full each month. Also carry a low-interest card that uses the average daily balance method for charges that you are going to pay over time.

•Using a convenience check isn't the same as using a credit card. Many credit-card issuers send convenience checks to cardholders. These look like personal checks and enable you to write checks against the line of credit on your card. *But there are two traps...*

•You pay interest immediately (no grace period) on the amount borrowed at the cash-advance rate, which may be higher than the interest rate on purchases.

•Convenience checks are not covered by the Fair Credit Billing Act. You do not receive the same protection you would if you had used a credit card and had a dispute over purchased goods.

Recent case: A man ordered a computer from an out-of-state retailer and paid with a convenience check. He never received the computer, and the credit-card company wouldn't help him get a refund.

Use convenience checks only for emergency expenses—paying off balances on cards with higher interest rates...or making a tax payment, if you must borrow to do so.

Important: If you do not need the convenience checks, tear them up. If you simply throw them away, someone may find them and forge your name.

•Most credit cards offer 30-day grace periods for late payments—before the debt is reported on your credit report.

Most issuers do not mention this because they want you to pay quickly—and you should. But many people think that they are reported one day after missing the due date.

Important: Although a late payment may not be reported on your credit report, it will be on file with the card issuer. This could count against you if you request a higher credit limit in the future. Also, some issuers levy fees of $10 to $25 for even one day of lateness.

If it's the first time you were late and you're charged a late fee, call the issuer. You may be able to have it waived—if you prove there were extenuating circumstances, such as being away on a trip…health reasons…or the mail was lost.

If you have lost your job or have another financial crisis and cannot pay, call the issuer and work out an agreement for an extended payment plan. It's always best to discuss late payments with your credit-card issuer *before* you miss the deadline.

• Your card can't be refused because you're not charging enough. A merchant cannot impose a minimum amount of $10 or $25 for those who use American Express, MasterCard or Visa.

What to do: Tell the store clerk that a minimum is not allowed under the merchant's agreement with the issuer. Demand to see the manager if necessary.

Special strategy: If you feel strongly, find something more to buy so that you can charge it. Then write to MasterCard (888 Seventh Ave., New York 10106) and enclose a copy of the charge slip, which will help the credit-card company track down the merchant's bank. For Visa, you must report the merchant to the bank that issued your card. American Express prefers customers to call the 800 number on the back of its cards and discuss it with a representative.

You won't receive credit on your card for the additional items you charged—nor will you receive store credit—unless you return the merchandise. However, if you report the infraction to the issuer, the merchant may be fined up to $1,000 if similar complaints have been filed or are reported in the future.

• Credit-card rates are flexible—if you're a good customer. In this competitive market, a better deal may be yours for the asking. Issuers make money from the merchants as well as cus-

tomers. If you charge several thousand dollars a year, the issuers don't want to lose you. If you pay in full each month, ask that the annual fee be waived. If you carry a balance and pay on time, call and request a lower interest rate. A reduction of at least two percentage points a year is reasonable to expect.

• Turn down offers for higher credit limits. Many issuers offer an initial waiver of fees or low interest rates as incentives. But by saying "yes" to too many offers, you will raise your outstanding credit limit. This can count against you on a credit report. That's because some lenders look not only at debt but also at available credit.

• Do not change accounts frequently. That looks bad on your report. But if you find a card with more favorable terms than you have now—cancel your present card and switch.

Source: Gerri Detweiler, consumer credit consultant in Arlington, Virginia. She is the author of *The Ultimate Credit Handbook*, Good Advice Press, Box 780, Elizaville, New York 12523.

Paying the Monthly Minimum

Paying the monthly minimum on your credit-card account can sink you ever-deeper into debt—even if you stop charging to the account. *Reason:* Some companies' minimum payments are less than the interest due for that month.

Source: *Get Rich Slow* by Tama McAleese, a certified financial planner and syndicated columnist. The Career Press, 180 Fifth Ave., Box 34, Hawthorne, New Jersey 07507.

Do You Need a Debit Card?

Pros: Using a debit card is safer than carrying cash and handier than writing checks. Fees are comparable to using a bank Automated Teller Machine (ATM) card…if you make many purchases, you can get a card from an issuer that charges only a flat annual fee—rarely more than $24. Cons: Many merchants do not yet accept debit cards. Some charge a fee for doing so but since they get their money instantly, this is an extraordinary charge so be sure to ask about it before using your card. If you already have a bank ATM card that works like a debit card in local stores, you won't need a Visa or MasterCard debit card unless you travel.

Source: Gerri Detweiler, consumer credit consultant in Herndon, Virginia, and author of *The Ultimate Credit Handbook*, Good Advice Press, Box 780, Elizaville, New York 12523.

Joint Bank Accounts

Joint bank accounts can trigger inheritance problems. Too often the surviving spouse will treat adult children equally in a will but put one child on bank accounts for bill paying if the parent becomes incapacitated. Upon the parent's death, the joint-owner child becomes sole owner of the parent's bank accounts, contrary to the parent's intent. Even if the joint-owner child voluntarily shares with his/her siblings, there may be a gift consequence for the joint-owner child. *Better approach:* Sign a durable power of attorney naming one or more children as agents. Leave the bank account in your name, and the will provisions will divide it equally. *Note:* This procedure will require a probate proceeding.

Source: Martin M. Shenkman, Esq., in private practice in New York City.

Banking Self-Defense

The fact that the banking industry is getting stronger doesn't mean *your* bank is healthy. Keep deposits under the $100,000 limit that is insured by the Federal Deposit Insurance Corporation…and check your bank's financial statements. Look for one that is making a profit and that has equity exceeding 5% of assets—4% after deducting problem loans in excess of reserves. Now, more than 650 banks—about 5%—are still in a stressed financial condition.

Source: Warren Heller, research director, Veribanc Inc., independent bank-rating agency, 27 Water St., Wakefield, Massachusetts 01880.

How to Get Out of Debt And Stay Out of Debt

Millions of Americans are trying to reduce their credit-card debt. Faced with increasing financial responsibilities, many are looking for ways to eliminate the bills they receive each month and free up some of their income.

Fortunately, most debt is manageable—if it is addressed early enough. Here's what I tell people who are overburdened with debt…

Acknowledge the problem:

Most people deny that they have debt problems. They refuse to admit that the problems exist or believe that they will go away by themselves.

The fact is that if you owe money on your credit cards and cannot pay the entire amount when the bill arrives, you have debt.

If your debt grows too large, you run the risk of being unable to meet your monthly payments and seriously damaging your credit rating.

The biggest drawback to debt is that it uses up income that could have been invested or spent elsewhere. You are also paying more for something over time than if you had paid for it in full right away.

Even if your debt situation is only temporary, immediate action must be taken to minimize interest payments.

Put everything in writing:

To determine how much debt you are carrying monthly, calculate how much you owe. Then determine your monthly income and expenses. If your debt is higher than your monthly income, you should take steps to reduce it.

Strategy: Make two lists—one for expenses that are essential and the other for those that are optional. Some expenses that seem essential may have to be reclassified as optional. Hold a family meeting to plan cutbacks.

While debt may be a difficult subject to discuss with your spouse and children, it is essential that all family members make sacrifices.

Don't slash expenses too dramatically:

Just as total deprivation diets do not help you lose weight permanently, budgets that completely eliminate anything that hints of fun do not permanently eliminate debt. Cutting back is better than cutting out.

Examples: Maybe you can no longer dine out twice a week. But you could go out once a month for special events. Your new budget should accommodate these occasional excursions.

Work hard to stay on course:

Paying debt is an incremental process. Try not to take on new debt or go on a spending binge as a reward for being frugal.

If you're having trouble making payments, don't ignore the bills. That only gets you into deeper trouble.

Instead, contact all of your creditors to work out less onerous repayment plans or to assure them that you will keep making regular payments. That is what your creditors really want to hear from you, since regular lower payments are better than no payments at all.

Source: Alexandra Armstrong, chairman of Armstrong, Welch & MacIntyre Inc., a Washington, DC-based financial advisory firm. She is coauthor of *On Your Own: A Widow's Passage to Emotional and Financial Well-Being*, Dearborn Financial Publishing, 520 N. Dearborn, Chicago 60610.

You Can't Borrow Your Way Out of Debt

Lesson: Don't enter a loan-consolidation agreement that stretches out the term of your borrowing, no matter how attractive its advertising sounds. *Catch:* Even if you obtain lower monthly payments, you'll pay much more interest over the long run. *Exception:* If you can obtain a reduction in the interest rate you're paying on your total borrowing, loan consolidation may make sense. This might be possible if you pay off high-rate, nondeductible credit-card interest with funds obtained through a home-equity loan carrying a lower rate of interest that is deductible.

Source: *Life After Debt: How to Repair Your Credit and Get Out of Debt Once and For All* by Bob Hammond, retired credit-repair consultant. Career Press, Box 34, Hawthorne, New Jersey 07507.

You and Your Money Month-by-Month

The wheels of commerce turn with predictable regularity. The key is timing your purchases.

•February. The season of love brings with it big reductions on china, glass, silver, mattresses and bedding.

•March. Watch for special preseason promotions for spring clothing. Ski equipment is at an annual low as well.

•April. Sales begin again after the Easter holiday, especially on clothing.

•May. Spring cleaning means specials on household cleaning products. This also is a good month to shop for carpets and rugs.

•June. Shop for furniture. Semiannual inventory is on the way in, old items must go.

•July. Most stores liquidate their inventories to make room for fall goods during this month. Sportswear, sporting equipment and garden tools and supplies take noticeable dips.

Source: Kenny Luck, author of *52 Ways to Stretch a Buck*, Thomas Nelson Publishers, Box 141000, Nashville 37214.

Protect Your PIN

The personal identification number (PIN) used at automatic teller machines is the main link between you and your money. *Self-defense:* Do not pick one that includes numbers from your phone number, address or driver's license—if your wallet is stolen, the thief might figure out the PIN. Do not write your PIN down anywhere—memorize it.

Source: Dennis Fertig, editor, *Your Money*, 5705 N. Lincoln Ave., Chicago 60659.

Checkbook Checklist

Your check register is a good record of deposits and spending if you record all transactions in it. Be sure to include date, check number, name and invoice number or date of invoice. More ideas…

• Keep a spare check or two in your wallet.

• Paper clip the checkbook on the page you are working.

• Write check numbers in the register ahead of time.

• Color code in the register. Use red for tax-deductible items.

• Round up check amounts to the nearest dollar.

• Cut addresses off extra deposit slips for address labels.

• Keep a small, thin calculator in your register.

• Use black or blue ink. Light colored ink doesn't copy as well.

• Keep track of monthly expenses at the back of the book.

Source: Heloise, whose syndicated column *Hints from Heloise* appears in more than 500 newspapers internationally. She is the author of a number of books, including *Heloise: Household Hints for Singles,* Perigee Books, 200 Madison Ave., New York 10016.

A Dollar Saved

A dollar saved is worth more than a dollar added to current income. Reducing spending by a dollar lets you save the full dollar. But in order to spend an additional dollar, you have to make between $1.15 and $1.50 (the added amount goes to taxes).

Source: *Make Your Paycheck Last* by Harold Moe, Holmen, Wisconsin, airline captain who got himself out of deep debt. Career Press, Box 34, Hawthorne, New Jersey 07507.

Beware of Loans to Family Members

Fifty percent of loans to family members are never repaid. For loans to friends, at least 75% are not repaid. *Self-defense:* Before lending any money to your family members or friends, think the deal through carefully—as both a business proposition and a personal matter.

Source: Andrew Feinberg, financial columnist and author of *Downsize Your Debt: How to Take Control of Your Personal Finances*, Penguin, 375 Hudson St., New York 10014.

Money Strategies... For Your 20s, 30s, 40s... And Beyond

When managing your money, you should learn to act your age. These are key strategies for investors in three different age groups—those in their 20s and 30s...those in their 40s and 50s...and those who are retired.

20s and 30s:

• Buy a home. It may turn out to be your single best investment, especially if you buy a single-family home rather than a condominium.

• Invest for growth. Those in their 20s and 30s should put 70% of their long-term investment money into stocks and/or stock mutual funds. The remainder should go into bonds or bond funds.

• Plan now if you want to retire early. Almost half of all working-age people hope to retire before age 65. Many of them do it—but they actually can't afford to. Successful early retirees typically established that goal in their 20s and 30s, when they still had plenty of time to accumulate wealth. They sacrificed early by saving 20% or 25% of their income and living in cheaper housing than they could afford.

40s and 50s:

• Keep investing for growth. You should have 50% to 60% of your investment portfolio in stocks and the remainder in bonds. When you're within 10 years of retirement, keep that same mix but change the types of securities you own to reduce your risk somewhat.

• Avoid taxes. Make full use of tax-deferred savings vehicles, including 401(k) plans, Individual Retirement Accounts (IRAs) and variable annuities. Your 40s and 50s are your peak earning years and, hence, your peak tax years, so tax-favored savings are critical.

• Project your retirement income and expenses. Do this once a year, so you know how much you need to be saving and when you can retire.

• Review estate plans every few years.

• Keep loved ones informed.

Source: Jonathan D. Pond, president of Financial Planning Information Inc., 9 Galen St., Watertown, Massachusetts 02172. He is author of numerous books on personal finance, most recently, *The New Century Family Money Book*, Dell Publishing, 1540 Broadway, New York 10036.

5

Insurance Savvy

The Worst Problems You're Likely to Face With Your Insurer

Insurance companies are in the business of selling security and peace of mind. But when it comes to settling claims, most insurance companies are in the business of saving money.

While millions of policyholders have their claims settled with a minimum of fuss, there are many areas in which abuses by insurers are widespread.

Rule of thumb: The higher the cost of your claim, the more likely you are to have trouble with your insurer.

The most common ways insurers shortchange policyholders—and how to defend yourself...

• Unwarranted rescissions. Attempts by an insurer to rescind—or cancel—a policy *after* a claim has been filed are common in all insurance and widespread in health claims. Wrongful rescissions comprise 25% of the cases I handle.

How it works: Many insurers don't investigate your insurance application until you've filed a claim. This procedure is called *post-claims underwriting*. An adjuster audits your medical records, not for the purpose of paying your claim—that's a separate department—but to see if you forgot to include something on your application.

Example: A woman who had cancer hadn't disclosed that she had consulted a doctor several years before about problems with irregular menstrual periods, a normal symptom of menopause. The insurance company attempted to rescind coverage, and a dispute ensued.

Self-defense: Case law on this subject is clear. If you had no knowledge of a medical problem at the time of your policy application, if you failed to appreciate the significance of an omission or if the omission is immaterial or trivial to the underwriting of your policy, your coverage cannot be rescinded.

Example: An insurer can't rescind your policy when you make a claim for knee surgery on the grounds that you didn't disclose an insignificant problem, such as an allergy.

When applying for insurance: Answer all questions honestly, yourself. Insurance agents often paraphrase questions.

Example: The agent says, "Any problems with your blood pressure?" when the question actually reads, "Have you ever been treated for high blood pressure?"

• Failing to fully investigate claims. According to consumer protection laws in almost every state, it is the insurer's duty to investigate policyholders' claims in good faith. But insurers are sometimes adversarial when it comes to paying claims.

Result: Insurers may deny claims without consulting the appropriate experts—doctors, appraisers, contractors—or do so only to find a reason not to pay.

Example: A dying woman who required 24-hour skilled nursing care was denied health coverage on the grounds that the care was custodial. The family sued, complaining that the insurer did not discuss her condition with her doctors or the nurses who cared for her and allowed unqualified claims investigators to make medical decisions. The family won the case— unfortunately, after the patient had died.

Self-defense: If your claim is unfairly denied, enlist the help of your insurance agent and submit statements from experts who can support your claim. If your claim is for property damage, visual documentation—photographs, videotape —can help as well. If the insurer refuses to consider your evidence, contact a trial attorney.

• Overturning medical opinions. Insurers must often review medical questions—Was this treatment really necessary? Is this person really disabled? For this purpose, most insurers use in-house medical examiners or hire "independent" medical examiners who may be biased since they have ongoing business arrangements with the insurers.

Result: Thousands of claims are unjustly denied every year when insurers' "medical experts" override the opinions of policyholders' doctors.

Example: A man was hospitalized with symptoms of a heart attack. After running a series of tests, his doctor found he had a less serious condition. Thus, the insurer decided the hospitalization was "not medically necessary." His doctor contested the decision and won, claiming that it

would have been negligent not to treat the case as potentially life-threatening—not to mention the insurer's bad faith in denying a claim due to hindsight.

Self-defense: Most major medical policies pay for a second opinion—be sure to get one whenever possible. Choose doctors who are willing to go to bat for you if their opinions are contradicted.

• Narrowly defining "disability." Most state laws and employers define "disability" as the inability to perform steadily in a job to which you are reasonably suited by education, training, experience, opportunity and physical and mental capacities.

But most disability insurance policies ignore state law and define disability as the inability to perform any job. By this definition, an executive who suffers a debilitating stroke would not be considered disabled if he/she could still wash dishes and, therefore, could be denied the benefits he expects based on his salary.

Self-defense: Look for a disability policy that covers you for your "own occupation," not just "any occupation." When filing a disability claim, describe the nature of your work to your doctor and precisely how your injuries affect your ability to work. Make sure this information is included in your doctor's report to the insurance company.

• Denying health claims that have been preapproved. Thousands of policyholders follow their insurers' instructions. They call the insurer for "preapproval" of a medical procedure—but are turned down when they file the claim, often on the grounds that the procedure was experimental, not medically necessary or excessive treatment.

Reason: Policyholders may actually have spoken with a clerk who did not approve the procedure but simply verified the policy is active or that a certain procedure is covered. Clerks are not claims adjusters and do not preapprove the amount the insurer is willing to pay or whether the procedure was necessary for you.

Self-defense: Be sure that you speak with a claims adjuster and get preapproval for the specific procedure and amount covered in writing. If you are denied approval of a formerly experimental procedure, such as a bone-marrow transplant for cancer, have your doctor call the insurer and explain why you are a good candidate for such treatment. If necessary, contact an attorney.

•Using low-price contractors. Home and auto insurers often obtain estimates on volume bases from contractors who do inferior work at relatively low rates.

Self-defense: Before accepting repairs to your home or auto by an insurance company's contractor, get several estimates from independent contractors and evaluate any discrepancies. Then, negotiate with your insurer. Most are willing to compromise.

•Refusing to pay full-replacement value on home contents. Many people are careful to buy homeowners insurance that promises to pay replacement costs rather than market value. Costs to rebuild can be far greater than the market value of a home.

Problems: Full-replacement coverage is often capped at an amount that is far less than it would take to rebuild the structure, rendering the coverage meaningless. And many policies are unclear as to whether the replacement coverage extends to the contents of the home as well as the dwelling—since personal belongings are covered in a separate section. Finally, if you do file a claim, the insurer may demand receipts for everything you say must be replaced. Few people are able to thoroughly document all their possessions.

Self-defense: Examine your policy to determine your actual coverage. Check to see that caps are not too low. Keep a current inventory of your belongings in a safe-deposit box or with your agent.

•Using false or deceptive advertising practices. Some insurers train their agents to sell policies based on advertising or brochures that seriously misrepresent the actual contents of the policies.

Example: A self-employed client bought what he believed was a major medical policy with a lifetime maximum of $1 million from a subsidiary of a major insurance company. When he filed a claim for treatment for non-Hodgkins' lymphoma, the company paid only $3,420 of $47,000 in medical and hospital bills.

Result: He sued and showed that the company's brochures radically overstated what turned out to be a bare-bones policy. In the policy, doctors' visits were excluded for the first four weeks following surgery, for example, and only a small percentage of surgeons' fees were paid—not 100%, as stated in the brochure. The jury found the company guilty of fraud and awarded the plaintiff $25 million in punitive damages.

Self-defense: It can't be said too often—take the time to read your insurance policies. If you find there are discrepancies between a company's ads, brochures or booklets and the actual policy, the courts will generally rule in your favor—but it's always better not to have to go that far.

Source: William M. Shernoff, an attorney specializing in consumer claims against insurance companies. His law firm, Shernoff, Bidart & Darras (600 S. Indian Hill Blvd., Claremont, California 91711, 909-621-4935) provides free answers to questions from consumers nationwide about insurance coverage and disputes. Mr. Shernoff is the author of *How to Make Insurance Companies Pay Your Claims,* Hastings House, 141 Halstead Ave., Mamaroneck, New York 10543.

Shrewder Long-Term-Care Insurance Buying

Key features of a good long-term-care policy...

•A prior stay in a hospital is not required before you collect your benefits.

•Coverage for Alzheimer's disease or related illnesses or disorders is guaranteed.

•Home care is included as a regular benefit or available with an extra premium. *Best:* A policy that allows you to alternate between home and a nursing home.

•Benefits are adjusted, at least partially, for inflation.

•The policy is guaranteed renewable for life.

•The policy has a "waiver of premium" clause that allows you to make no payments if ill—and after receiving benefits for a specified period of time.

•There's a "window" that allows you to change your mind and cancel the policy at no cost within the first 30 days.

Source: Daniel Kehrer, a Los Angeles-based business and finance writer and author of *Kiplinger's 12 Steps to a Worry-Free Retirement,* Kiplinger Books, 1729 H St. NW, Washington, DC 20006.

How to Get Your Health Insurance Company to Pay Up

Don't give up if you have trouble getting a fair claims settlement from your health insurance company. There are a number of steps you can take to fight the insurer's decision to refuse your claim.

First: Resubmit another medical insurance claim form about 30 days after the refusal. Very often, a company randomly denies a claim... and just as randomly approves the same claim when it comes in again. It does no harm to try for reimbursement of a doctor's bill by submitting your insurance forms a second time.

Second: If that does not work, contact the insurer and request, in writing, a full explanation of the refusal to pay. Sometimes the denial-of-benefits statement is filled with numeric or alphabetic codes that are undecipherable by a layperson. Request a clear explanation. There should be no ambiguity as to why a health insurer will not pay the benefits that you think are called for in the contract.

Third: Once you are given the insurance company's rationale for turning you down, you have a couple of other weapons in your arsenal...

...The insurer cannot give you an alternative reason for the refusal after you refute the initial one.

...When the refusal is based on a rule against paying for experimental treatment, you can marshal evidence from your doctor and others that the treatment was, in fact, the treatment of choice—and therefore should be covered by the policy.

Fourth: If it becomes necessary to appeal, start within the company. Write directly to the president—whose name can be found in insurance directories at your local library...or call the company and ask.

Enclose copies of all relevant documents... claims forms, medical receipts, responses from the insurer, notes of telephone conversations and any backup materials.

Caution: Never send any originals, since you may need them for future action.

Fifth: If you get nowhere at the company level, write to your state insurance department. Every state now has a section set up to assist consumers with complaints. You can reach them by checking directory assistance for a toll-free number.

With the correct department and address, again mail copies of the relevant documents and ask for a response. The insurance department won't take your side in every dispute, but it can obtain an answer from your insurance company in situations where you have been stonewalled or treated unfairly.

Ultimate weapon: File a suit against the insurer in small claims court, or in a regular court if the amount at stake is too large to be handled by the small claims court. If you go to regular court you'll need a lawyer, preferably one who takes the case on a contingency basis, where the fee is a percentage of what you recover. You can handle a small claims case yourself. If the insurer's behavior is particularly abusive, you may be able to collect punitive damages from such a suit.

Real case: A man was conned into trading in his health policy for another on the basis that the second policy was substantially improved. Yet when he filed a claim, he found the new policy paid 40% less in benefits than the old one. He sued the insurance company for fraud ...and wound up collecting over $1 million in punitive damages.

Bottom line:

Carefully review your policy before filing claims for illness or injury.

Go to your corporate benefits manager or insurance agent with any questions about coverage and costs. By knowing exactly what you can expect from your policy, you won't be surprised when the reimbursement check arrives. And in the event that the insurer sends you the wrong amount, you will be ready to take whatever action is necessary to obtain the money you deserve.

Source: Robert Hunter, insurance commissioner for the State of Texas and former president, National Insurance Consumer Organization, Box 15492, Alexandria, Virginia 22309.

Don't Delay Filing Your Health Insurance Claims

Delays can be costly in submitting health insurance claims. Most policies have a 90-day time limit—and claims will be rejected if filed after that point. Also, in most states, insurers *must* begin action on claims within a set period of time after submission. The sooner a claim is filed with the insurance company, the sooner it will be reviewed and paid.

Source: *Health Insurance: How to Get It, Keep It or Improve What You've Got* by Robert Enteen, adviser on health-insurance policy issues. Paragon House, 401 Fifth Ave., New York 10016.

Faster Filing of Health Insurance Claims

Prepare a master form for each of your policies. Use a blank insurance-company claims form and fill in the policy number…your name and address…insured's Social Security number…additional health coverage carried by the family…the signature of the insured. When you need to file a claim, simply photocopy the master form and add details on the bills you are submitting.

Source: *The Health Insurance Claims Kit* by Carolyn F. Shear, MSW, medical claims agent, health insurance claims processor, Deerfield, Illinois. Dearborn Financial Publishing, 520 N. Dearborn St., Chicago 60610.

Home Health Care Visits

Home health care visits are covered by Medicare provided each of the following four conditions are met: The care includes intermittent skilled nursing care, physical therapy or speech therapy…the patient is confined to home…home care is approved and arranged by a doctor …the agency providing the care to the patient is a Medicare participant.

Source: *Retiring Right: Planning for Your Successful Retirement* by independent retirement and financial management planner Lawrence J. Kaplan, Manhassett, New York. Avery Publishing Group, 120 Old Broadway, Garden City Park, New York 11040.

Insurance Warning

Beware of illustrations from insurance agents that claim to show how much a life insurance policy will grow in value. It's easy for the agent to assume a rate of return that greatly inflates a policy's projected worth. Due to the power of compound interest, even a small increase in the assumed annual rate of return—1% or less—can lead to a totally unrealistic estimate of a policy's future value. *Important:* Compare a policy's projected rate of return to returns that you know you can get from other investments. Remember that you won't get anything for nothing. If the gap seems too big, be skeptical.

Source: *Your Life Insurance Options* by Alan Lavine, financial writer. John Wiley & Sons, 605 Third Ave., New York 10158.

When Both Spouses Have Health Insurance

More employees are being asked to pay more of the cost of health-care coverage at work as health costs keep rising.

But working couples—where each spouse has health coverage—have options. While they can keep their separate health plans, they may save money if they opt for the spouse's plan that offers the most for the family.

Doing the arithmetic:

How to do the economic analysis to determine if switching plans makes economic sense for you…

Using a legal pad, compare the four key costs of health coverage for each plan:

1. Annual premium cost. How much will it cost a year for everyone in the family to be covered?

2. Maximum deductible. How much must you pay before the plan starts to kick in?

3. Co-insurance. What percentage of each bill will the plan pay, and how much must you pay?

4. Plan cap. What's the most you will have to pay out-of-pocket for medical bills each year?

Example: It would cost $500 a year for the family to join John's health plan and $1,000 to join Jane's plan. But the out-of-pocket cap for Jane's plan is $1,000, while John's cap is $3,000.

Maximum possible total cost: $2,000 with Jane's plan, $3,500 with John's plan.

Other considerations:

• Opt-out opportunities. Many companies pay a cash payment if you drop your coverage and shift to your spouse's plan.

Example: Your employer will pay $500 if you don't join your company's medical plan. You can use the money to pay the higher premium required to get family coverage under the spouse's plan.

• What is covered? Money isn't always the only consideration. Consider switching if one plan offers considerably more liberal coverage for services important to your family, such as outpatient psychiatric or dental care, or chiropractic services.

Important: Paying extra to keep both plans seldom makes economic sense today. Working couples once could get 100% coverage for treatment by coordinating plans. Now most plans have a "nonduplication of benefits" provision that makes the employee's plan the primary provider.

Example: Before, your plan might have paid 80% of a $1,000 claim, while your spouse's plan would pay the remaining $200. That's rare today.

Key: Before you switch, determine if the family can rejoin your plan if your spouse is laid off or fired. Most employers will count it as a "change in family status," and let you back in. But double-check, just to be certain.

Source: Tom Beauregard, health-care consultant, Hewitt Associates, 40 Highland Ave., Rowayton, Connecticut 06853.

How to Be Able to Afford to Get Sick

Many employers are cutting back on health benefits—and some insurance companies have grown increasingly ruthless when it comes to paying their policyholders' claims. What you should know to make sure you can afford to get sick...

• Avoid switching health insurance plans...if you're satisfied with your current coverage...if you have a chronic medical condition...or if you have had a recent health problem. *Reason:* A new insurer will exclude coverage for any "preexisting" condition and may find you "uninsurable" if your medical problem is serious. Even if your health is good, many insurers impose waiting periods on new policyholders for certain procedures.

Exception: If your employer changes insurers, state law generally requires that the new insurer provide the same coverage without penalty to you.

• Avoid temporarily dropping out of a health plan. Many companies offer an annual "menu" of benefits to choose from—health and life insurance, paid vacation days, child care, retirement contributions, etc. Healthy employees or those who are included on a spouse's policy are often tempted to temporarily forgo the medical plan in favor of other choices.

Catch: Even if your company tells you otherwise, the insurance company is not obligated to take you back as an individual after you waive group benefits. Even if you provide evidence of your insurability, your coverage may be denied or restricted.

• Don't drop family coverage either...for the same reason. Many companies offer financial incentives to employees who waive family coverage. While at first it may not make sense to pay for double coverage when both spouses work, it is always a gamble to drop coverage. Should the insured spouse die, lose his/her job or become divorced, the family could find itself uninsured. In cases of serious illness or injury, double coverage will be welcome.

• Choose "household name" insurers. Often, companies offer employees the choice of a traditional insurance plan, an HMO-type plan with a limited choice of participating doctors and hospitals and a self-insured trust. *Caution:* Beware of insurance companies you've never heard of. To check the financial status of an insurer, call your state's department of insurance.

• Beware of policies that exclude coverage if you become eligible for Medicare. Anyone disabled by a catastrophic illness or injury becomes eligible for Medicare. Insurers would like to shift the cost of catastrophic care to the taxpayer. But you are paying premiums to ensure better protection than Medicare can provide in case of crisis. Look for a policy that pays costs "over and above" what Medicare will pay.

•Contact your federal representatives and ask them to close the ERISA loophole. In 1984 the Supreme Court held that ERISA (Employee Retirement Income Security Act), a federal law, supersedes state consumer laws governing insurance. This created a loophole that gives health insurance companies immunity from damage suits filed by policyholders insured through their employers—85% of all insured Americans. *Result:* An explosion of bad-faith practices by health insurance companies—unconscionable refusals of claims and policy cancellations—against which insureds have no recourse.

Source: William M. Shernoff, a specialist in consumer claims against insurance companies and author of *How to Make Insurance Companies Pay Your Claims,* Hastings House, 141 Halstead Ave., Mamaroneck, New York 10543. He is a partner in the law firm of Shernoff, Bidart & Darras in Claremont, California.

Canceling Your Life Insurance

Most people who buy life insurance are not aware that they have up to ten days after the policy arrives in the mail to cancel it—and receive a full refund. *Problem:* Policies are often filed away as soon as they arrive. *Strategy:* Use the ten days to discuss with friends, experts and even other agents whether you've made the right decision.

Source: James Hunt, a director of the National Insurance Consumer Organization, Box 15492, Alexandria, Virginia 22309.

Review Life Insurance

Review life insurance needs when you: Get married or divorced...have a child...buy a residence...change jobs and need to assure the family's new level of income and lifestyle. *Other factors that affect insurance needs:* Acquisition of illiquid assets, such as real estate or a private business, on which you will owe estate tax...the

maturing of children for whom you may have less need to provide...accumulations of wealth in retirement accounts.

Source: Suzette Loh, personal financial planner, Richard A. Eisner & Company, accountants and consultants, 575 Madison Ave., New York 10022.

Remodeling and Homeowners' Insurance

Most homeowners' policies should cover any reasonable remodeling, including building material stored on-site. Call your insurance agent to let him/her know that you are making changes that could affect your coverage. If you hire a contractor, it is his responsibility to provide insurance. *Important:* Insist on seeing a certificate of insurance *before* signing a contract. The contractor's insurance should cover any injuries or damage to your home during the job.

Source: *The Family Handyman,* 7900 International Dr., Minneapolis 55425.

Homeowners' Insurance Cost-Cutters

Accept a higher deductible on your policy... install security devices and fire and smoke detectors and alarms in your home—and tell your insurance agent you've done so...comparison shop among three or four different insurance carriers...consider combining different types of coverage—homeowners' and auto—into one policy.

Source: *How to Buy a House, Condo or Co-op* by Michael C. Thomsett, a Washington-state insurance consultant, and the editors of Consumer Reports Books, 101 Truman Ave., Yonkers, New York 10703.

Home-Insurance Trap

Most US homes—possibly as many as two out of three—are underinsured.

Common problems: Insuring for market value rather than replacement cost...giving incorrect information when taking out the policy—so later coverage upgrades are also based on the wrong information…failing to inform the agent whenever changes are made…failing to get extra insurance for special hazards associated with home offices.

Source: John Robertson, director of underwriting, property/casualty division, State Farm Insurance, 112 E. Washington St., Bloomington, Illinois 61701.

How to File an Airtight Insurance Claim

Insurance companies are very happy to accept your premiums and promise you peace of mind. But when it comes to paying claims, it is routine procedure for insurers to comb the paperwork for errors, oversights or other reasons to delay or deny payment.

Best protection: Submit claims that can be handled smoothly the first time through, with no need for clarification or opportunity for refusal. Homeowners' claims:

• Report theft or vandalism to the police. Most insurers will deny your claim if you fail to notify the police of a criminal act. Insurers depend on police reports to determine the circumstances of such claims, including any questions of negligence on your part.

• Photograph damaged property before starting repairs. And—write down the details of the incident leading to your loss.

• Notify your insurance company right away. Ask them to send you a claim form and authorize any immediate repairs you must make to secure your property.

• Take necessary measures to prevent further loss or damage to your property.

Examples: Fix broken windows, doors or locks, plug leaks, etc. *Reason:* If further damage results from your failure to do so, the insurer does not have to cover the loss.

Don't expect to be reimbursed for the repairs you make yourself. Most insurers only pay for professional work. Wait for your insurer's authorization before making major or permanent repairs.

• Read your policy for specific instructions and to check your coverage. Many people find they are covered for more than they realized.

• Keep records of repair and replacement costs. Take notes on why work is done, document the necessity with photographs and keep copies of all bills and receipts. If your home was so damaged you must live elsewhere temporarily, keep those bills as well.

• Fill out the claims form accurately, and keep copies of everything. It is not at all unusual for insurers to lose claims and documentation. But the most common reason for problems with claims is that policyholders omit necessary information. Include your policy number.

• Send in your claim promptly, preferably within 30 days. If there is a part of your claim you can't estimate—a long-term repair, redecorating cost or clean-up cost—notify the insurer that you will be making a further claim later. Auto accidents or theft:

• Check for injuries, call for emergency assistance if necessary—and call the police. Most states require the police be notified if damage exceeds about $300. Again, you hurt your chances of the claim being paid if there is no police report.

• Gather information from any involved drivers, passengers—and especially witnesses. Exchange insurance information with other parties. *Biggest mistake in auto claims:* Failing to get names and addresses of passengers and other witnesses.

• Take photographs or make a diagram describing the accident. Photos of skid marks, impact marks, etc., can be helpful. The police should make a diagram at the scene as well.

• Don't sign anything other than the police report. Your insurer may refuse to pay your claim if you sign a statement admitting fault, agreeing to be responsible for damages or releasing another party from liability.

• Notify your insurer and your state Department of Motor Vehicles. Failure to notify the DMV in cases of injury or damages over about $500 can result in suspension of your driver's license.

• Delay repairs until your adjuster inspects the vehicle. You may be asked to get many estimates for repairs. Keep copies of each.

• If your car is stolen or "totaled," most insurers will offer you the Actual Cash Value (ACV) of your car. Check your insurer's assessment against Blue Book and dealers' estimates. Remember, the value of your car may be higher if you can document low mileage, recent improvements, etc.

Medical claims:

•Have medical procedures preapproved by your insurer whenever practical. In cases of emergency, see that your insurer is notified as soon as possible.

Caution: Preapproval does not mean the insurer agrees to pay a particular amount—only that your coverage has been confirmed.

•Get a second opinion when warranted. Most insurers will pay for a second opinion before surgery, some require you get one before they will pay full benefits. *Aim:* To eliminate any question that your treatment was "not medically necessary."

•Make sure claims forms are filled out completely and properly. This may sound obvious, but health insurance is the area in which you are most likely to encounter problems. Delays can occur from something as simple as omitting the date on which you had a procedure done, or as complex as explaining why complications of surgery necessitated additional procedures. Make sure your doctor gives detailed explanations. *Aim:* To eliminate any question that your treatment or length of hospital stay was "unreasonable."

•If your doctor or hospital submits your claim for you, call your insurer to make sure they have received everything they need. Often, people assume their claim is being processed, when the insurer is waiting for supporting information.

•If your insurer asks for additional information or disputes your claim, make sure your doctor responds immediately, or have the doctor send the information to you so you can submit it to the insurer. Insurers frequently turn down or only partially pay medical claims because the code the doctor fills in for a certain procedure doesn't seem to warrant the charges.

Source: William M. Shernoff, a specialist in consumer claims against insurance companies. He is the author of *How To Make Insurance Companies Pay Your Claims*, Hastings House, 141 Halstead Ave., Mamaroneck, New York 10543. His Claremont, California, law firm, Shernoff, Bidart & Darras, has a staff of insurance analysts who will answer questions regarding insurance coverage and disputes.

Dangerous Insurance

Mail-order insurance frequently offers neither good value nor good coverage.

While it can often be purchased without a physical examination, the price is high and there's often fine print that states the life insurance policy won't pay until death or until several years have gone by.

Health policies that are limited to accidents or hospital indemnity ($100 per day for only a few days) or one disease (cancer) don't take the place of health insurance that covers all situations completely.

Source: J. Robert Hunter, insurance commissioner for the State of Texas.

Travel Insurance Self-Defense

Buy trip cancellation/interruption insurance through your travel agent, not the tour operator. *Reason:* If the operator goes bankrupt, its insurance policies will be worthless. *Usual cost:* $5.50 per $100 in tour charges. *Caution:* Check exclusions and other limitations before buying a policy. *Also useful:* Book tours only with tour operators who belong to a national consumer-protection program, which can intervene in case of a dispute.

Source: S. Burkett Milner, president, National Tour Association, Lexington, Kentucky.

Weather and Your Insurance

Many insurance companies have begun to factor predictions about the weather into their underwriting decisions. *Example:* More severe hurricanes in the South Atlantic US. *Result:* Insurance is becoming more expensive—or even unavailable—for people living in these areas.

Source: *New Scientist*, King's Reach Tower, Stamford St., London SE1 9LLS.

Insurance Insight

It's okay to pay insurance premiums for many years without ever collecting a penny in claims. *Reality:* You've gotten exactly what you paid for —a transfer of the risk for certain types of losses. *Example:* If you purchased a life insurance policy to ensure the financial security of your young children and then failed to die before the children were grown, the children *were* protected against the loss of financial support if you had died.

Source: *The Guide to Buying Insurance: How to Secure the Coverage You Need at an Affordable Price* by David L. Scott, professor of accounting, Valdosta State College, Valdosta, Georgia. Globe Pequot Press, Box 833, Old Saybrook, Connecticut 06475.

Find Out How Much Life Insurance You Need

To find how much life insurance you need: Figure your monthly after-tax take-home pay. Then, determine how much of that your family will need to cover monthly expenses, should you die—a typical figure is 75%. Next, learn how much income your family will obtain from other sources—Social Security survivor's benefits, pension-plan survivor benefits, etc.— and subtract this number to find your monthly cash shortfall. Multiply that number by 12 to reach an annual figure. Decide for how many years you will have to cover monthly expenses— your future financial need may drop greatly after children graduate from college and move out, for instance. Buy enough insurance to provide that many years of income.

Source: *Life Insurance Handbook* by Jersey Gilbert, financial reporter at *Money*. Consumer Reports Books, 101 Truman Ave., Yonkers, New York 10703.

Paying an Insurance Premium

Paying an insurance premium in full each year makes the most financial sense—unless you have cash-flow problems. Then opt to pay monthly by having the premium withdrawn electronically by your insurer from your checking account. *Reason:* The implicit carrying charge is generally lower for monthly payments than for semiannual or quarterly installments.

Source: Glenn Daily, independent fee-only insurance consultant, 234 E. 84 St., New York 10028.

Seven Ways to Cut Home Insurance Costs

Premium savings are available from most major insurance carriers for policyholders who take the following steps…

1. Protect your property. Insurers give discounts for smoke detectors, alarm systems and other security devices.

2. Tell the insurance company when you retire. If you are likely to spend more time at home during the day, the company may lower your premiums.

3. Raise your deductibles.

4. Pay annually. It's usually cheaper than paying semiannually or quarterly.

5. Buy all your insurance from the same company. You may be able to get a package deal.

6. Quit smoking. Many companies give non-smokers discounts on homeowners' policies.

7. Don't hire a public adjuster unless necessary. This person's job is to help you evaluate your losses and settle with the insurance company. In exchange, the adjuster gets 10% to 15% of whatever you recover. To save money, try to settle with the insurance company by yourself first.

Source: Jonathan Pond, a nationally recognized expert in financial planning. He is the author of *The New Century Family Money Book*, Dell Publishing 1540 Broadway, New York 10036.

6

Tax Smarts

Tax Loopholes for Those Over 50

Believe it or not, as we grow older, tax loopholes become easier to find...

•*Loophole:* Escaping a stiff penalty tax on distributions from retirement plans by delaying distributions. If you withdraw money from a tax-qualified retirement plan, such as an IRA, Keogh or 401(k) plan, before the magic age of 59½, you are subject to a 10% penalty tax on early distributions from the plan. By postponing distributions until after that age, you avoid the penalty. However, any money you take out is considered taxable income.

More: Avoid tax on large distributions from retirement plans by speeding up withdrawals. The law imposes a stiff 15% penalty tax on withdrawals from retirement plans that are considered excessive. What's excessive? Annual payments of more than $150,000 and lump-sum payments of more than $750,000. One way around this is to start taking money from your retirement plans as soon as possible after you reach age 59½, in order to reduce the size of your plans and limit your exposure to the penalty.

...and more: If you use some of the distribution money to buy life insurance policies through a life insurance trust, the insurance proceeds will not be subject to estate taxes.

•*Loophole:* Not paying tax on $125,000 in profits from the sale of your house. If you are age 55 or older when you sell your primary residence and you have lived in it for three of the last five years, the first $125,000 of profit is totally tax-free. But since this tax break can be taken only once during your lifetime, it's important to wring the maximum tax advantage from it. Two situations in which you should pass up the exclusion:

•If you're planning to buy another house within two years of the sale. *Reason:* This enables you to defer tax on your profits from the initial sale and preserves your right to claim the $125,000 exclusion on the sale of the second house.

•If the profit on the sale of your home is relatively small. *Reason:* Since the exclusion can be taken only once, you may be better off paying capital-gains tax now on the modest gain—perhaps because you were forced to sell in a depressed real-estate market—and preserving the exclusion for the future, when market values may have rebounded.

More: If you're planning to remarry, and if both you and your prospective spouse are 55 or older, you can make double use of the exemption if you each sell your house before you tie the knot. *Reason:* The exemption can be used only once. If one spouse has taken it previously, it can't be taken again by a newly married couple, even if the other spouse has never used it. So by each using the exemption before marriage, the couple can escape tax on as much as $250,000 in gains on the sale of their separate homes.

•*Loophole:* Making full use of the $10,000 annual gift-tax exemption to reduce estate taxes. The maximum federal tax on estates is 55%. If you live in a state that imposes estate taxes as well, your beneficiaries may wind up getting no more than 40% of what you leave them. One of the easiest ways to cut estate taxes is to give away property during your lifetime.

You can give up to $10,000 a year ($20,000 if you and your spouse make a joint gift) to each of any number of recipients without having to pay gift tax. The advantage of making such lifetime gifts is that they remove assets that otherwise would be included in your taxable estate.

More: Make larger gifts that are subject to gift tax now—to reduce estate taxes in the future. This is a good technique if you don't need all the income from your assets.

Example: You want to make a gift of $25,000 to your grandchild. The gift tax on that would be 50%, or $12,500. So your total cost of the gift would be $37,500. If, instead, you left your grandchild that same $25,000 in your will, the total cost of delaying the $25,000 bequest would be $50,000. *Reason:* When you pay gift tax on a transfer made during your life, the tax itself reduces the size of your estate. But if the transfer does not take place until after death, the estate tax becomes part of your estate. *Caution:* Gift tax on gifts made within three years of death will be added back to your taxable estate.

•*Loophole:* Getting the government to help share the cost of your job-hunting expenses, if you're an executive who has been hit by corporate downsizing. The cost of looking for a job in the same field you're already in is deductible as a miscellaneous expense—once you've exceeded the threshold of 2% of your Adjusted Gross Income. This means you can write off the expenses of retaining an outplacement firm, preparing and printing a résumé, telephone calls, traveling to job interviews and lunches and dinners (subject to the new 50% limit) related to your search.

•*Loophole:* Transferring appreciated assets from an ill spouse to the healthy one to cut capital-gains taxes. The healthy spouse transfers assets that have a large unrealized gain, such as stocks, to the sick spouse. (There's no tax on transfers between spouses.) The sick spouse bequeaths the assets in his/her will to the healthy one. After the sick spouse dies, the healthy one inherits the assets with the tax cost (or basis) increased to their value as of the date of death. The healthy spouse can then turn around and sell the assets without having to pay capital-gains-tax on the appreciation.

Caution: The gift from one spouse to the other must be made more than one year before the date of death or the stepped-up basis will be denied.

•*Loophole:* Escape self-employment tax by recharacterizing payments from a business. If you're in business for yourself, you're subject to a hefty self-employment tax in 1994. It's 12.4% of your first $60,600 in net income...and 2.9% on an unlimited amount of net income above that.

If you're leaving your employer but have been asked to continue in a limited capacity, ask to be appointed to the board of directors rather than be designated as a consultant. *Reason:* Directors' fees are not subject to self-employment tax—consultant's fees are.

Further loophole: If you're selling a business, arrange to receive further income from the company under a "covenant not to compete" rather than as a consultant. This, too, avoids self-employment tax.

•*Loophole:* Escape self-employment tax by recharacterizing payments from a partnership. Partners also face stiff self-employment taxes on net earnings. One way to escape this tax is to have future income from the partnership designated as "guaranteed payments." *How it works:* Say you're a member of a law firm and plan to retire. The agreement calls for you to receive 20% of the profits the first year of retirement, 15% the second year, 10% the third and so on. If this income stream is treated as a series of guaranteed payments, it is not considered earned income and thus not subject to self-employment tax.

Another way to avoid self-employment tax is to convert from general partner to limited partner.

Source: Edward Mendlowitz, a partner in the New York certified public accounting firm of Mendlowitz Weitsen. He is the author of several books, including *New Tax Traps/New Opportunities,* Boardroom Books, Box 736, Springfield, New Jersey 07081.

Appreciated Property… Tax-Saving Tricks

Giving appreciated property to charity:

•You totally avoid capital-gains tax when you give appreciated property to charity.

•You can then deduct the full fair market value of the property as a charitable contribution.

•Under the new law, the untaxed appreciation is no longer subject to the Alternative Minimum Tax.

Caution I: Your contribution deductions cannot exceed 30% of your AGI, but any amount that exceeds the limit can be carried forward to future years.

Caution II: If your income is in the range for itemized-deduction reductions (starting at $111,800 for single filers in 1994), you could lose a portion of your contribution deduction. Check with your tax adviser.

•Giving to your children age 14 or older. This makes sense when you are in a high tax bracket (say 28% on capital gains) and the kids are in a zero or low tax bracket.

Source: Irving L. Blackman, partner, Blackman Kallick Bartelstein, 300 S. Riverside Plaza, Chicago 60606.

Frequently Overlooked Tax Deductions

In the rush to gather information for their 1994 tax returns, many people may miss valuable deductions. Here are the ones that are most often overlooked—and a number of tax-saving strategies for 1995…

Investing:

•Mutual-fund shares. Recheck the cost basis* of the mutual-fund shares you sold during 1994. Income and capital gains earned from the fund that were automatically reinvested in it increase the cost basis and reduce your taxable gain. So your taxable gain may be less than the figure that results from the simple "sale-price-minus-purchase-price" formula.

•Amortize bond premiums. With sharply dropping interest rates, many older taxable bonds now pay more interest than new bonds and thus sell for more than their face values. But these bonds will pay only their face values on maturity. If you have paid a premium to buy one of these older bonds, you can claim a tax break for the resulting decline in the bond's value by amortizing the premium.

Example: You paid $2,000 more than face value for a taxable bond maturing in 10 years. You can amortize $200 per year. *The amortized amount…*

…offsets interest income earned from the bond, if the bond was bought in 1988 or later.

…is an investment interest expense if the bond was bought after October 22, 1986, and before January 1, 1988.

…is a miscellaneous itemized deduction if the bond was bought before October 22, 1986. The deduction is not subject to the "2%-of-Adjusted-Gross-Income" limit, which normally applies to miscellaneous deductions.

•Early withdrawal penalties. If you took money from a certificate of deposit—or any other time deposit—before maturity and therefore paid an early withdrawal penalty, the penalty is fully deductible, even if it exceeds your maximum allowable interest-expense deduction.

*Cost basis is the original price of an asset and is used to determine capital gains.

• Safe-deposit-box fees. If you rent a safe-deposit box to hold securities and other investment items, the cost of renting the box is deductible as an investment expense.

• IRA trustee fees. These are deductible investment expenses if you pay them by separate check instead of having them deducted from your account.

• Bad debts and worthless securities. These produce capital losses in the year in which they become worthless. Review your portfolio, and document the event that made a security worthless or a debt uncollectible during the year.

Note: Pending litigation and bankruptcy proceedings may make it difficult to determine if a security has become worthless. For this reason, the statute of limitations for the deduction of worthless securities is seven years instead of the usual three years. Review your portfolio to find old investment losses that may still be deductible under the extended deadline.

Home:

• Mortgage prepayment penalties. With interest rates at a 20-year low, many people have paid off old mortgages to refinance at lower rates. Any prepayment penalty that resulted is deductible as mortgage interest.

Note: Prepayment penalties on business and investment loans are deductible under corresponding rules for business and investment interest.

• Points. Loan finance fees, or "points," are deductible on a mortgage used to acquire a home. However, points incurred on the refinancing of a mortgage must be amortized (deducted at an even rate over the life of the loan).

Exception: As a result of the continuing decline in interest rates, you may have refinanced a home a second time. In that case, any remaining unamortized points from the first refinancing may be deducted immediately. That, in effect, provides a points deduction for the new loan.

• Real-estate taxes. If you bought or sold a house during the year, review the allocation of deductible real-estate taxes between buyer and seller. Often, the final tax liability for the year isn't known at the time of the sale, so an estimate is used.

If the actual final tax bill for the year is greater than the estimate, the seller is entitled to a deduction that is greater than that shown on the real-estate closing statement.

If real-estate taxes are paid after the year of the sale, the seller's share of the taxes may be deducted either in the year of the sale or in the year in which the tax was paid, whichever produces the greatest benefit.

The situation is different for the buyer. If the buyer is liable for the tax, the buyer's share of taxes are deductible only in the year the actual payment is made. If the seller is liable for the tax, the buyer may deduct his/her allocated share of the tax either in the year of the sale or the year in which actual payment is made.

• Personal property taxes. Local taxes based on the value of personal property may be deductible.

For instance, the following states impose automobile license fees that are based on the value of the car and thus are deductible in whole or part as personal property tax…

Arizona, California, Colorado, Georgia, Indiana, Iowa, Maine, Massachusetts, Minnesota, Mississippi, Montana, Nebraska, New Hampshire, Oklahoma, Washington, Wyoming.

Employee business expenses:

These costs related to the business of being an employee are deductible…

• Job-hunting costs are deductible when you look for a new position in your current line of work—even if your job search is not successful.

Included: Résumé preparation, 50% of meal and entertainment costs, expenses incurred during travel to job interviews, employment agency fees, career counseling fees, advertisement costs, etc.

Job-hunting costs are included among your miscellaneous expenses, the total of which is deductible to the extent it exceeds 2% of your Adjusted Gross Income (your income before taking standard and itemized deductions).

• Moving expenses. In tax year 1995, expenses incurred in a work-related move are deductible only if your new job is at least 50 miles further from your old home than your old job was. Moreover, the deduction is limited to the actual cost of travel and moving household goods.

Limit: You can deduct up to $3,000 of total moving expenses.

•Social Security taxes may have been over-paid during the past year if you had more than one employer during 1994 and your total income from all jobs was more than $60,600. Be sure to claim the credit for overpaid Social Security taxes on your tax return.

•Business gifts made during the year are deductible up to $25 per recipient. Have records documenting the gifts.

Personal deductions:

•Charitable contributions of appreciated property that you have held for more than one year can be deducted from the property's full value, not just the amount you paid for it.

The new tax law makes this type of gift even more valuable by eliminating the risk that such gifts will create liability for the Alternative Minimum Tax (AMT).

•Gambling losses are deductible to the extent that you have gambling winnings. Thus, if you win money in a lottery or at a casino or racetrack, you may be able to shelter your winnings from tax by producing records of your losing bets made during the year. Keep a diary of gambling activities, and save your losing betting slips.

Filing strategies:

•Check all 1099s and W-2 forms, which should be received by the end of January. If they are not accurate, ask for corrected ones before you file.

•Claim all dependents. You may be able to claim a parent who does not live with you as a dependent if you pay most of the parent's support.

Tactic: A multiple support agreement, IRS Form 2120, may make an exemption available when a group of people combine to support an individual, even when no one person provides more than half the support.

•Pick the best filing status. You may cut your taxes by filing a separate return from your spouse or by claiming head-of-household status instead of automatically filing a joint or single return.

Source: Anna Polizzi-Keller, a tax partner at Ernst & Young who specializes in financial counseling, 701 Market St., St. Louis 63101.

How to Talk Your Way Out of IRS Penalties For Late Filing

Showing the IRS that you had a good reason for filing your tax return late may get you off the hook for penalties even if you didn't file an extension form. You must convince the IRS that it wasn't your fault that you filed late, and your excuse must be reasonable. *Excuses that have worked:*

•Your return was mailed on time but was not received by the IRS until after the filing date.

•The return was filed on time but was sent to the wrong IRS office or district.

•You relied on erroneous written information provided by an IRS officer or employee.

•You or a member of your family was seriously ill.

•Your business, residence or records were destroyed by a fire or other casualty.

•Tax forms that you requested in time from the IRS were never received.

•You were unable, for reasons beyond your control, to obtain the records necessary to determine the amount of tax due.

Important: The IRS is not required to accept any of these excuses.

Source: Randy Blaustein, partner, Blaustein, Greenberg & Co., accountants and auditors, 155 E. 31 St., New York 10016.

The Most Common Mistakes People Make When Filing Tax Returns

Many people file their tax returns as early as possible to speed up their refunds. It is very important when preparing those returns to avoid mistakes, which can increase the tax bills or delay the refunds.

Mistakes to avoid:

•Incorrect information. Any misreporting of amounts shown on W-2 or 1099 forms will like-

ly delay the processing of your tax return. IRS computers are very good at matching amounts shown on those forms with amounts reported on tax returns. When the numbers don't match, your tax return may draw unwanted attention from the IRS. *What to do:*

Before preparing your 1994 tax return, make sure that you have received all the W-2s and 1099s that you should have. These forms are supposed to be mailed by payers of income by January 31, 1995, but there's always a chance that some will arrive late—or not at all.

Helpful: To be sure that none are missing, match up the 1099s you received for your 1994 tax return from banks, stockbrokers and other payers of income with those reported on your 1993 tax return.

When you've got all your W-2s and 1099s, double-check them to make sure the numbers reported are accurate. Add up your pay stubs, and check your records for taxable income received from financial institutions. If any are in error, ask for a corrected form from the issuer.

Remember: The IRS assumes that the numbers reported on 1099s are accurate—but mistakes do happen.

List the various 1099s on your tax return individually—do not simply write down one number that totals your 1099 income.

Reason: IRS computers match the numbers shown on specific 1099s with the numbers shown on your tax return. The IRS computer doesn't total entries. If you report only your total 1099 income on your return, the computer will fail to find the match. While inquires are being made, the IRS will delay processing your tax return.

•Paying tax on state tax refunds. Many people make the mistake of automatically reporting state tax refunds as income on their federal tax returns. But a state tax refund is income on the federal return only if the state tax payment previously was deducted on a federal return.

If you claimed the standard deduction on your 1993 return instead of itemizing your deductions—and thus got no benefit from a state tax deduction—a refund of a 1993 state tax payment will be tax-free on the federal tax return.

For high-income taxpayers (1992 AGI over $105,250, regardless of filing status) who itemized deductions in 1993 and received a state tax refund in 1994, the IRS has recently changed its mind about how to compute the taxable portion of the state tax refund. The changes are not favorable. Most affected taxpayers will now pay tax on all of their state tax refunds.

•Paying excess Social Security tax. If you worked for more than one employer during 1994 and your total wages exceeded $60,600, you probably had too much Social Security tax withheld from your salary.

•Overstating mutual-fund gains. Investors who automatically reinvest mutual-fund earnings in extra shares often overstate their taxable gains when they finally sell their shares. This occurs when they neglect to include in the cost of their shares the amount of earnings that were reinvested to help buy them.

By adding reinvested earnings to the cost of the shares, you reduce the profit that results from their sale and cut the tax bill accordingly.

•Improper paperwork on charitable contributions. If during 1994 you made noncash contributions to charity that totaled more than $500, you must file IRS Form 8283, *Noncash Charitable Contributions,* to substantiate your deduction.

Don't wait until the last minute to get the form—it may hold up your return. Get a free copy of it now by calling the IRS at 800-TAX-FORM.

•Underpaying estimated taxes. If you underpaid your estimated taxes during 1994, you'll owe an underpayment penalty. It can be a mistake to simply file your tax return and let the IRS compute the penalty.

Better: File IRS Form 2210 to "self-assess" the penalty, and compute the minimum penalty possible.

Estimated taxes normally are due in four equal quarterly payments. But you also have the option of figuring your tax liability for each quarter on the basis of the amount of income earned through that quarter.

If you received a surge of income late in the year—perhaps through a year-end bonus or a late-taken investment gain—using this option may reduce or eliminate underpayments for early quarters in the year and correspondingly reduce underpayment penalties.

If you let the IRS compute your underpayment penalty, it will probably apply the normal rule since it won't know when you earned your income. Thus, by filing Form 2210 to self-assess the penalty, you may reduce it.

•Not using passive activity losses.* If you have undeducted passive losses from investments in real estate or old-style tax shelters, don't forget that you can carry the losses forward and use them to offset future gains earned from the passive investment properties.

Example: Say you have acquired several apartments for investment purposes and they have generated tax losses that you haven't been able to deduct under passive loss rules. If you sell one of the apartments for a profit, you can use your accumulated losses to shelter your gain on the sale from tax.

•Overlooking the Alternative Minimum Tax (AMT) credit. If you've been liable for the AMT in recent years but won't be liable in 1994, don't overlook the possibility that you might be entitled to a tax credit on your 1994 return.

The AMT applies when people with large incomes use special tax breaks contained in the law to sharply reduce their regular tax bills. But some or all of the AMT paid in one year may support a tax credit in a later year when you are again taxed under normal rules. Consult your tax adviser for details.

•Improper tax treatment of home refinancings. With interest rates at 20-year lows, many people have refinanced their home mortgages. They should be careful to apply the proper tax treatment to loan origination fees, or "points," incurred on such loans. *Such points…*

…are deductible when incurred on a loan used to acquire a home or finance a home improvement because the improvement is considered an "acquisition."

…are not currently deductible when a home loan is refinanced to obtain a lower interest rate. The points must be amortized—deducted at an even rate over the life of the loan.

Opportunity: If you have refinanced a loan for the second time, you may have undeducted

*Passive losses are losses from an activity in which you did not materially participate.

points remaining from the first refinancing. Those points are currently deductible when the old loan is paid off—which effectively provides a points deduction for the subsequent refinancing.

•Overpaying self-employment taxes. This is easy to do if you have sideline income in addition to a regular salary.

Normally, Social Security tax is due on the first $60,600 of earned income in 1994. But income amounts include both wage and self-employment income. Thus, the amount of income upon which self-employment tax is owed is reduced by the amount of wages from which employment taxes have been withheld.

Don't overlook the fact that self-employed persons can deduct 50% of the employment taxes they pay as an adjustment to income when computing AGI. And they generally can deduct 25% of the medical insurance premiums they pay as well.

Filing:

After finding your best tax-filing strategies, take care when going through the steps of filling out your return. The most common causes of return-processing delays…

•Arithmetic errors when tallying columns of numbers.

•Copying wrong numbers when carrying amounts from one tax form to another.

•Forgetting to sign a tax return.

You can head off numerical mistakes by preparing your return with the help of one of the increasingly popular tax-return preparation computer programs that are now available for personal computers. These programs check the numbers for you.

Finally, be sure to file your tax return by certified mail and request a return receipt. If the postmark on the envelope carrying your tax return is illegible or lost, or the return is lost in the mail, a certified or registered mail receipt is the only proof of filing that is accepted under the Tax Code. Messenger and express delivery receipts are not acceptable.

Source: Richard E. Jones, director of tax, Ernst & Young, 999 Third Ave., Suite 3500, Seattle 98104.

How to Deduct The Cost of a Foreign Convention

General rule: Travel expenses incurred to attend a convention are deductible if your attendance benefits your trade or business.

Special tests exist for offshore conventions. First, it must be shown that it was "as reasonable" to hold the convention outside North America as inside. North America includes the US, Canada, Mexico and certain Caribbean Basin and Central American countries. If that can be shown, the costs are 100% deductible if…

• The trip is for seven consecutive days or less, and…

• Less than 25% of the time is spent on pleasure activities, or…

• The taxpayer had no control over the travel— i.e., it was at the behest of and on behalf of his employer—or…

• The taxpayer can substantiate that the trip and convention were primarily for business purposes and not for obtaining a personal vacation or holiday.

Otherwise, you must allocate your trip between business and vacation days, deducting only expenses for business days. The entire trip does not have to be primarily for business. For example, if only five out of 15 trip days are spent at a foreign convention on business, those five days' expenses are deductible.

Source: Irving L. Blackman, partner, Blackman Kallick Bartelstein, 300 S. Riverside Plaza, Chicago 60606.

Recent Taxpayer Victories that Could Be Valuable to You

Use these recent taxpayer victories over the IRS to help plan your tax-cutting strategies for 1995…

• IRS loses. Travel deductible. A self-employed person traveled daily to several work locations.

He deducted his travel costs as a business expense, but the IRS said it was nondeductible commuting expenses. *Court:* The individual also worked at home an average of three hours a week. Although this was a small amount of time, it made his home his one regular, permanent work location. Since the cost of travel between two work sites is deductible, the individual could deduct all the costs of traveling between home and the other work locations. *Philip Alan Boice*, TC Memo 1993-498.

• IRS loses. Smart business owner. Richard Hansen figured out a way to depreciate land used in his business, even though the Tax Code says land is not depreciable. *How:* Instead of having his company buy the land outright, he had it buy a 30-year "right-to-use" the land while he personally bought the remainder interest— which gave him full ownership of the land when the 30 years were up.

Because the right-to-use had a fixed price and a limited term, the company said it could deduct the price over the term, effectively creating annual depreciation deductions for the cost of the land. *IRS objection:* The deal was set up this way solely to create tax deductions that wouldn't be there if the company had bought the land outright. *Court:* It is perfectly legal to structure a property purchase to maximize tax benefits. The deductions were allowed. *Richard Hansen Land, Inc.*, TC Memo 1993-248.

• IRS concedes. Smart investor. An individual who took out a loan on his home and used the money to make an investment was allowed to deduct the interest on the loan as investment interest rather than mortgage interest. The investment interest paid on the loan could then be deducted against investment income, sheltering it from tax. *Point:* This strategy makes sense if further borrowing against a home will not produce deductible mortgage interest because of the $100,000 limit on deductible home-equity financing. By treating the mortgage interest as investment interest, you obtain a second way to deduct it. *IRS Letter Ruling* 9335043.

• IRS loses. Refund is paid. When Peter Mc-Conaughy hadn't received a refund more than a year after requesting it with supporting documents, he was allowed to sue the IRS to compel its payment and he won—and then also collected reimbursement from the IRS for the legal expenses he incurred in the process.

Peter McConaughy, D. Md., No. WN-91-2874.

•IRS loses. Late amended claim is allowed. A refund claim was filed just before the filing deadline. After the deadline, the taxpayer discovered that the refund had been underestimated and filed an amended claim for a larger amount. But the IRS said it was too late. *Court:* The new claim was simply an adjustment of the original, timely claim, so it was allowed.

Mutual Assurance Inc., ND Ala., No. CV-93-H-0952-S.

•IRS loses. Pay rent to yourself. D. Sherman Cox ran his business from an office located in a building that he owned with his wife. He paid himself an annual rent of $18,000—which he deducted as a business expense on Schedule C of his tax return.

He also reported it as rental income on Schedule E—producing a net tax benefit, since passive losses from other real-estate properties could be used to shelter the rental income from tax. But the IRS disallowed the transaction, saying one can't pay rent to oneself. *Court:* Half the rent Cox paid became the legal property of his wife, since she was co-owner of the building. He could claim rental treatment for the $9,000 that accrued to her—even though she filed a joint tax return with him.

D. Sherman Cox, TC Memo 1993-326.

•IRS loses. Inferred theft. A couple followed the advice of their broker and put $300,000 in an investment, which turned out to be a Ponzi scheme.* When the IRS allowed them only a $3,000 capital-loss deduction, they claimed a theft-loss deduction for their full investment. The IRS answered that they hadn't been defrauded because they never had any direct contact with the investment operators—they had simply taken bad advice from their broker. *Court:* The couple had been the victims of fraud, if only indirectly. The theft-loss deduction was allowed.

David Jensen, TC Memo 1993-393.

*A Ponzi scheme is an investment swindle in which some early investors are paid off with money put up by later ones in order to encourage more and more risk.

How to Win the Car Expense Game

Only the business use of your car is deductible. For example, if you drive a total of 20,000 miles in a year and only 8,000 miles are for business, your deduction is limited to 40% (8,000/20,000) of your auto expenses and depreciation.

Better way: Buy a second car to use as your nonbusiness, or personal, car. Keep the second car at home, use it on weekends and drive it to and from your office (where you house your expensive business car).

Assume that each car is driven 10,000 miles a year. The business car is used 80% (8,000/ 10,000) for business. Under the IRS's rules, you can deduct 80% of the expenses and depreciation of the business car. In addition, 100% of business tolls and parking are deductible. The legitimate tax savings are substantial.

To nail down your business car deduction: (1) Keep a log of business and total miles driven, and (2) record expenses in the log and keep receipts.

Source: Irving L. Blackman, Blackman Kallick Bartelstein, 300 South Riverside Plaza, Chicago, Illinois 60606.

Documenting the Business Use Of Your Car

Taxpayers who are salespeople usually put a considerable number of miles on their cars. If you haven't kept a diary showing the business use of your car, the next best approach is to make a list of all your accounts and their location. When audited, this list of accounts can be convincing documentation to support the fact that you traveled in a given territory on a regular basis to visit customers.

Source: Ms. X, a former IRS agent still well-connected.

To Make Your Family's Wealth IRS-Proof

Family wealth is increasingly difficult to shelter from the IRS. The new tax law increases the top income-tax rates, reduces the maximum retirement benefits that can be earned from pension plans, cuts the amount that many of us can save for retirement through Keogh plans and 401(k) savings plans and increases the top estate-tax rate to 55%.

In addition, the $600,000 exemption for estate taxes loses value to inflation every year. If your wealth grows in dollar terms by 10% a year due to a combination of inflation and real growth, the value of the exemption is cut in *half* every 7.2 years.

In 22 years—if the $600,000 exemption remains in place—your exemption will protect only *one-eighth* as much of your estate as it does today.

However, with smart planning you can make your wealth *immune* to the IRS—obtaining current deductions to cut taxes, increasing future retirement income and protecting the assets you wish to leave to your heirs from estate tax.

A combined strategy of charitable giving, intrafamily gifts and life-insurance planning can make this possible.

Self-defense strategy:

The most important tool is the *Charitable Remainder Trust (CRT)*.

How it works: You place assets that will pass to a charity upon your death in a trust. As a result, you retain the income earned from the assets. And you get an income-tax deduction *now* for the value of the gift that will pass to the charity when you die. The amount of the deduction is determined from IRS tables according to the size of the gift and your life expectancy.

Keys:

•You must elect to take an annual percentage payout from the trust. The trust's terms, however, may state that this will be paid only out of current income, plus a makeup factor, enabling the payouts to be *delayed* if the trust invests in low-yield, appreciating assets.

•The trust is tax-exempt, so investment earnings compound tax-free.

•You can be the trustee of the trust and control its investments.

These rules make it possible to use a CRT as a tax-favored *retirement plan*.

Then, when you retire, you switch the CRT to high-yield investments. At that point, the CRT begins making 8% payments to you *plus* makeup payments for past years—giving you a large retirement benefit for the rest of your life.

No limits: Contributions to a CRT are not subject to the dollar limits that apply to other retirement contributions—such as the $2,000 annual limit for an IRA or the $9,240 limit that applies to a 401(k) savings plan in 1994. CRTs are also not subject to the maximum accumulation or distribution limits that apply to other types of retirement plans.

Even better: If you fund the CRT with appreciated property, you avoid paying capital-gains tax on the property.

Bottom line: The CRT's big benefit is capital-gains tax savings and tax-saving deductions now...*plus* higher retirement income later. The cost is that the property left in the CRT ultimately goes to charity instead of to your heirs. But this does *not* mean that your heirs lose out. *Why not?*

•With your estate subject to estate tax, 37% to 55% of the assets left to your heirs—instead of to charity—would actually go to the IRS.

•Life insurance, if placed in a properly structured trust arrangement, is *free* from estate tax. And you can use the current tax savings and increased income derived from the CRT to buy life insurance that will pay your heirs an amount equal to what they would have received after taxes from your estate. The insurance proceeds will be free not only of estate and local inheritance taxes but also of various administration fees that apply to property that passes through an estate.

Bottom line: A CRT can enable everyone to come out ahead—including the charity that ultimately receives a valuable bequest.

The big give-away:

The CRT will protect only part of your family's wealth. You will, of course, have other assets that may be subject to estate tax and that you will want to protect from the IRS.

Key to planning in this area: Remember that while your wealth increases each year due to both real earnings and inflation, the basic tax devices you can use to cut future estate taxes lose value every year to inflation. *The basic tax devices:*

• The lifetime unified estate-and-gift-tax credit for $600,000 of assets.

• The $10,000 per-recipient annual gift-tax exemption ($20,000 when gifts are made by a married couple).

The simplest strategy to cut future estate taxes is to make gifts of appreciating property to the next generation today, so that their growing value is not taxed in your estate when you die.

Every family can use the $10,000 (or $20,000) annual exemption to make such gifts. However, it may pay to use the full $600,000 exemption to make a large gift now and protect it from tax, even though it means your heirs won't be able to use the $600,000 exemption when you die.

Life-insurance trust:

Of course, you may not be willing or able to make large gifts directly to the next generation—perhaps because assets are in the form of a family business or you wish to assure the financial security of your spouse first.

In such cases, the best idea is to establish a *life-insurance trust* that will pay estate taxes for your estate, leaving the estate's assets intact to pass to heirs.

Trap: Don't rely on the unlimited marital estate-tax deduction to protect assets that are left to a spouse from tax. Although the assets will escape tax when they pass to your spouse, they will be fully taxable when your spouse dies.

Smart use of insurance may enable you to pass on a *multiple* of the $600,000 estate-tax exemption amount free of estate tax.

Of course, families with lesser needs can use their $10,000 (or $20,000) annual gift-tax exemption to obtain the same insurance benefit on a smaller scale.

Example: At the time of his death, Malcolm Forbes was reputed to be one of the most heavily insured people in America, having used an insurance trust to pass his $1 billion publishing empire intact to his children.

Planning:

While these tax-saving strategies can provide powerful protection for family wealth, they must be implemented with care and an expert's help. Many technical rules apply. *Examples:*

• A CRT is *irrevocable*. While you can change the charitable beneficiary, you cannot withdraw contributions to the trust principal after they have been made.

• Life-insurance trusts are also irrevocable and must meet technical requirements to be free of estate tax.

• Second-to-die insurance is cheaper than conventional insurance, but it is also less flexible. If you might want to withdraw funds from the policy before your spouse dies, consider other insurance options.

Also, while you can serve as the trustee of your own CRT, you will need to hire a third-party administrator to handle the technical paperwork associated with trust management.

Problem: The typical third-party bank trust department will not be willing to act as third-party administrator for you unless it can act as the trustee of the CRT—exercising control and collecting the related fees.

Source: Arthur A. Wood, CLU and chartered financial consultant in private practice in Kent, New York. He is the author of *How To Create Tax-Exempt Wealth*, Kent Publishing Co., 14684 Roosevelt Hwy., Kent, New York 14477.

The Biggest Traps in Dealing with the IRS… How to Avoid Those Traps

Knowing how to deal effectively with the IRS can prevent little problems from escalating into tax nightmares. Here are the biggest traps taxpayers fall into…

• *Trap:* Failing to respond promptly to IRS notices. Most IRS communication with taxpayers is in the form of a series of notices and/or demands. All too often, taxpayers fail to treat these notices with the sense of urgency that is required. Before they know it, they're facing a big problem—a simple request for information has become a demand for more tax.

The IRS provides a timetable for responding to notices. Usually the deadline is 30 days from the date of the notice. (In some instances it's 60 days.) *Problem:* If it takes the notice a week to get to you, then you have only three weeks to respond.

If you don't respond in time…the next notice you get from the IRS could be a statutory notice of deficiency. This requires you to pay the tax or file a petition with the Tax Court contesting the assessment. That can be a costly proposition, and certainly not necessary since in most instances the problem that prompted the notice can be resolved by correspondence. How you respond to an IRS notice is important. *For an effective response…*

• Mail it by certified mail, return receipt requested, so that you'll have proof that the IRS received it.

• Enclose a copy of the notice you received from the IRS. There are symbols on the notice that will direct it to the right person at the IRS.

• Send your response in the envelope the IRS provides. The envelope is bar-coded so that it will get to the correct IRS destination.

• If you can't accumulate the information requested by the deadline, write a letter asking for more time. Enclose the documents you have collected and ask for an additional 60 days. Usually the Service is receptive to these requests.

• *Trap:* Ignoring incorrect notices from the collection division. The notice you get from the IRS may be based on wildly incorrect information. For instance, I have a client who got a notice saying he had failed to file a Form 942 remitting employment tax for a domestic employee. But the client didn't have a domestic employee. A lot of people would be tempted to ignore a notice of this kind because it was so off-the-wall. But these notices must be answered, too.

If you don't respond to such a notice the IRS will assume that it's right. It will file a return for you and assess your tax. It has the power to do that under Section 6020(b) of the Tax Code.

Bottom line: Never ignore an IRS notice even if it's wrong.

• *Trap:* Getting stuck in the system. It's a mistake to keep writing to the same IRS location over and over again. If, despite your response, you continue to get computer-generated notices from the IRS, contact the IRS's Problem Resolu-

tion Office (PRO). The job of the PRO is to sort out administrative problems taxpayers are having with the IRS.

Every IRS Service Center and District Office has a PRO. A complete listing of addresses and phone numbers for the PRO can be found in IRS Publication 1320, *Operation Link.* This publication is available free from the IRS by calling 800-829-FORM. The PRO is also in the government listings in the phone book.

Before the PRO will take your case: If your problem is notices…you must have responded to two notices and have received a third notice on the same issue which does not acknowledge your earlier replies.

It's usually better to write than call, because the PRO will need to see documentation before it accepts the case. *Include…*

• Copies of all IRS notices together with copies of your responses.

• Copies of documentation you've sent with your replies.

• A concise explanation of the history of the problem you're having.

Cases accepted by the PRO are assigned to individual case officers, so you'll no longer be dealing with the nameless IRS bureaucracy. The case officer will keep you informed about the progress of the case. Experience shows that the PRO is very effective at resolving administrative tax problems.

• *Trap:* Representing yourself at an audit where the issues are complex. If the audit is simply a matter of presenting receipts for your deductions, you can handle it yourself. But if the audit is more involved, and the issues are not simple, you should consider having somebody represent you. *Types of issues you may need help on:*

• Issues of valuation.

• Whether something is a business expense.

• Whether an expense is job-related.

• Deductions for volunteer work for charity.

• Sophisticated stock transactions.

• *Trap:* Most taxpayers who handle complex issues themselves are too talkative at the audit. That can only lead to other issues being raised by the auditor. An audit that was intended to be limited to one or two items on the return may become an across-the-board audit.

• *Trap:* Not reporting miscellaneous income. Companies that pay "miscellaneous income," such as income for freelancing, are required to report it to the IRS on a 1099 if the amount is more than $600. But sometimes the companies don't file a 1099 for items less than $600.

That doesn't mean you can get away with not reporting the income on your tax return. If the IRS later audits the company—and they're doing a lot of auditing in this area—they'll discover that you didn't report income that you were supposed to report. They'll tax you on the income and impose a 20% negligence penalty on the tax you didn't pay.

If the unreported amount is substantial in relation to your earnings, and if the nonreporting continued for a number of years, there's always the chance the IRS will deem the unreporting to have been fraudulent. The penalty for fraud can be jail.

Some people simply don't report miscellaneous income even though they receive a 1099 for it. That's a mistake. The IRS is matching more and more 1099-MISC information forms with taxpayers' income-tax returns—and catching more and more nonreporting. It's clear that the era of not reporting miscellaneous income is quickly winding down.

Source: Pete J. Medina, tax consultant on practice and procedure before the IRS, Ernst & Young, CPAs, 787 Seventh Ave., New York 10019. Mr. Medina is former District Director of the IRS Manhattan District.

Disallowed Deductions

What do you do if the IRS has decided to disallow a deduction you claimed on your tax return and you don't understand why it has taken such action? The first step is to ask the auditor for an explanation. If his/her answer isn't clear, or seems wrong, ask for a written explanation. If your case has already been closed and you have no auditor to ask, request a copy of all the work papers in your file. To get the work papers, you must file a written request with the disclosure officer in the IRS district that handled the audit. Your request should be made pursuant to the provisions of the Freedom of Infor-

mation Act, which requires the IRS to provide you with the information contained in your file.

Source: Ms. X, a former IRS agent still well-connected.

Very Shrewd Ways to Save Taxes in 1995

Recent tax law changes, along with record-high stock prices and historic low interest rates, point to new tax and investment planning opportunities for 1995. To get a head start on this year's tax savings...

• Know what tax bracket you're really in. Many people will owe the bigger Alternative Minimum Tax (AMT), a flat tax levied on some wealthy taxpayers with a large mix of certain deductions and income. AMT taxpayers may need different strategies in 1995. See your tax adviser early in the year if you think you might be subject to the AMT.

Also, tax rates rise as income increases because of phase-outs of itemized deductions and personal exemptions. Plan this year's strategies with your estimated income for 1995 in mind.

• Fund retirement plans fully—and early. A new combined federal-and-state top effective tax rate of up to 50% makes tax-deferral strategies like Keoghs, IRAs and 401(k) plans more valuable than before. By making your contribution at the beginning of 1995 instead of waiting until December, you shelter an additional year's worth of interest from tax.

• Consider investing in municipal bonds and bond funds. Interest paid by issues of states and municipalities can be federal-tax-free. The higher your tax rate, the more valuable the tax break.

Example: A muni bond fund pays 4%. Its taxable equivalent yield for someone in the 36% tax bracket is 6.25%.

Opportunity: Issues used to finance student dormitories and other "non-essential" public projects are free of federal taxes but subject to the AMT. Because of the potential tax liability, private-purpose issues pay slightly more than regular munis. So if you expect to owe the AMT, avoid private-purpose issues and mutual funds that own them. But if you're not going to owe the AMT, you can earn slightly higher yields by owning these bonds.

• Convert income to capital gains to take advantage of the lower tax rate. The 28% cap on capital gains is much lower than the 39.6% top income-tax rate, so look for investments that will generate future appreciation, not current income.

Example: Growth stocks are more valuable tax-wise than stocks that pay high dividends.

Strategy 1: The 28% top rate applies only to investments held one year or more. So if you plan to sell shares, wait until you have owned them at least one year.

Strategy 2: 1995 is an unusually good year for investors to offset their capital gains and losses, reducing the capital-gains tax owed. Because the financial markets have been so strong, many investors have huge unrealized gains. But—because some sectors of the market were hard hit, they may have losses, too. Review your portfolio —and sell profitable shares to offset losers. *Helpful:* Sell $3,000 worth more of losers than gainers, and use the $3,000 to offset regular income from tax.

• Refinance your home and deduct points paid on the original mortgage. Many people refinanced their home mortgages as interest rates have fallen in recent years. Because interest rates have continued to fall, refinancing a second time might pay. Points (upfront charges) paid on a refinanced mortgage are typically not deductible until the loan is repaid. Today competition among lenders has resulted in no-point loans with low interest rates. By refinancing with such a loan, you lower your monthly payments and you can deduct the "points remaining" on your original refinancing.

• Maximize the tax benefits of intrafamily transactions. Gifting cash or property to children removes property from your taxable estate, and any income the property generates is taxed in the child's lower tax brackets if the child is 14 or over.

You can give $10,000 per year to each family member ($20,000 for spouses that "split" gifts). The earlier in the year you make gifts, the bigger the tax savings.

Strategy: If you plan to gift shares of stock, not cash, give the actual shares instead of sell-ing them and gifting the proceeds. That way, proceeds are taxed in the child's lower bracket.

• Consider intrafamily loans among children. A college graduate "borrows" $15,000 from his 14-year-old brother's college fund to buy a new car. He pays 8% interest, a fraction of the cost of a new car loan, and his brother earns substantially more than he would by keeping the cash in a money-market fund.

Caution: Make sure interest paid is a reasonable market-rate interest.

• Review your income sources if you plan to work and collect Social Security. Starting in 1994, 85% of Social Security benefits are taxable (up from 50%) when modified Adjusted Gross Income exceeds $44,000 for married couples ($34,000 for single taxpayers). Working retirees should make sure that they are fully aware of their true "after-tax" salaries.

• Consider investing in yourself in 1995. Before retiring from your regular job, start a sideline business that you develop from a hobby— or another interest—that can create a post-retirement source of income. Uncle Sam will subsidize your business start-up costs in the form of deductions. You can deduct the cost of an office at home, as well as related business expenses, including entertainment, travel, postage, equipment, etc.

Caution: Under the hobby-loss rule, the IRS can disallow deductions when a venture is determined to be a hobby, not a profit-making business. To secure your deductions, make sure the venture is run in a businesslike fashion. Keep income and expense logs, use separate business bank and checking accounts and manage income and expenses, if possible, to show a profit every three out of five years.

Source: George E.L. Barbee, executive director of client services for Price Waterhouse, 160 Federal St., Boston 02110.

When to Amend an Old Tax Return

Most people amend their tax returns because they seek money that they are owed by the IRS.

But knowing when—and when not—to amend a return is crucial, since you run the risk of being audited.

When to amend:

•To correct errors made in your original return. The majority of amended returns fall into this category. *Common errors made in returns:*

•Failing to claim credit for duplicate Social Security taxes that you paid when you switched employers in the middle of the year.

•Mischaracterizing nondeductible child-support payments as deductible alimony.

•Missing deductions on Schedule C for small-business expenses, such as auto expenses or the cost of adding a call-waiting feature to your telephone.

•Reporting a full year's worth of accreted interest for zero-coupon bonds purchased mid-year, an overstatement found in many brokerage interest statements.

•Not claiming the child-care credit for private school tuition costs for children in preschool or kindergarten.

•Calculating depreciation incorrectly for home offices, computers, cars or other business equipment.

•To conform to a court case or revenue ruling that changed the law that was in effect when the original return was filed. Sometimes the tax code is liberalized retroactively, after you filed your return.

Example I: The rule allowing self-employed businesspeople to deduct 25% of medical-insurance premiums from their gross income expired on June 30, 1992. The deduction was reinstated by the new tax law passed in August 1993. Business owners who deducted only 25% of one-half year's worth of their insurance premiums can amend their 1992 returns to claim 25% of the entire amount.

Example II: The city of St. Louis applied its earnings tax to all income earned in that city, including 401(k) contributions, cafeteria-plan contributions and other types of deferred compensation. A state court then retroactively exempted the reductions from the city's earnings tax.

•To deduct this year's casualty losses against last year's income. The IRS allows people with losses from earthquakes, floods or other types of federally designated casualties to generate cash by carrying back the losses.

Example: Taxpayers with 1994 earthquake losses can use them to offset income and reduce the taxes they paid in 1993.

•To offset this year's small-business losses against previous years' taxes. Losses generated by Schedule C businesses or S corporations that exceed other income in the current year can be carried back three years, reducing the taxes owed on previously filed returns.

Strategy: You can speed up your refund by filing a loss-carryback claim within one year of the year of the loss. So amendments based on business losses in calendar year 1994 must be filed by December 31, 1995. Otherwise the amended return will be processed normally by the IRS.

To qualify for the expedited refund, file the loss-carryback claim on Form 1045 instead of the usual Form 1040X.

•To deduct certain investment losses against previous years' investment gains. You can carry back what's called "section 1256" losses for three years and offset any section 1256 income that is not offset by other types of capital losses.

What qualifies: Section 1256 losses include index options, such as options on the S&P 500, commodity futures, currency and other types of commodity transactions.

•To correct an error on the original return that requires you to pay more tax. The IRS matching program compares nearly all of the income reported on individual taxpayers' returns with income reported by payers such as employers, banks, brokerage companies and real-estate brokers. If you make a mistake you'll get caught sooner or later, so you should amend.

Examples: Information matched by the IRS includes wages and other earned income… dividends, interest and proceeds from stock transactions…proceeds from house sales and retirement-plan distributions, etc.

Why to amend: When you correct an error in the IRS's favor, you avoid the additional penalties and interest that would be assessed if the mistake had been found by the matching program or an audit.

•If you haven't reported all your income. Normally the IRS has only three years to examine your return. However, there is no limitation if your return was prepared fraudulently, and the IRS has six years if your return omitted 20% or more of your income for a given year.

When not to amend:

• If income or expenses were reported in the incorrect year. If you reported your income or claimed an expense—even though it was in the wrong year—it may not be worth filing an amended return if you were in the same tax bracket in both years, since the most the IRS will gain is interest for one year.

• If the amounts involved are "insignificant." This judgment must be made by each taxpayer. Consult your tax adviser for guidance.

Reducing the risk of an audit:

Filing an amended return opens up your entire return for audit. *Steps to take...*

• Wait until just before the statute of limitations expires before filing the amendment. Then it is likely only the amended items can be audited, instead of your entire return.

Example: In general, 1991 returns filed by the original due date cannot be audited after April 15, 1995. To protect items on the return that are not being amended, file your amendment on April 10, 1995. Be sure to send the forms by certified mail, return receipt requested, to prove the date of mailing.

IRS Revenue Procedure 92-20 says that when you file before receiving an audit notice, the change is effective as of that year. If you file after an audit notice is received, the change is effective for the earliest year under review. If the error is caught on audit, the change is effective for the earliest year open by statute for examination…creating the biggest tax bill.

• Provide detailed information about the items you are amending. The IRS reviews all amended returns, and the examiners will be unfamiliar with your original return. Make their jobs simple by explaining clearly why the amendment was necessary and providing adequate documentation for the changes.

Deadlines:

You must file an amended return within three years of the date on which the original return was filed or two years from the time the tax was paid, whichever is later. The deadline is extended to seven years for deductions for bad debts or worthless securities and to ten years for foreign tax credits.

Source: Mark A. Dow, tax partner, Coopers & Lybrand, One Metropolitan Square, St. Louis 63103.

Get an Early Start on Your Return…It Pays

Don't wait until April to start putting together what you'll need for your 1994 return. *Start now...*

• Forms and publications. If the IRS hasn't already sent you everything you need, pick up the forms at your local IRS office or order them by phone (800-829-FORM). Don't overlook any new forms you'll need that you didn't use last year.

• W-2s. Your employer must mail W-2s by January 31. If you don't get one, contact your employer. When you receive your W-2, check it for accuracy. If it's wrong, get it corrected immediately.

• 1099 information returns. These, too, should be mailed to you by January 31. You should get 1099s from any persons, companies, banks, financial institutions, etc., that have paid you interest, dividends, freelance income, etc., during 1994. Again, check for accuracy and get any mistakes corrected.

• Deduction data. Sort out your checks, credit-card statements, paid invoices, bills, etc., by category—medical expenses, charitable donations, travel and entertainment and any other items you need for your tax return.

Source: Randy Bruce Blaustein, Esq., partner, Blaustein, Greenberg & Co., 155 E. 31 St., New York 10016.

How to Deduct the Cost Of an Unsuccessful Business Search

There's a way to assure a 100% deduction for all expenses incurred while looking for a new business…and it's easy.

Incorporate, then buy stock from your new corporation equal to the amount of the anticipated search expenses. Then have the corporation, instead of you, pay the expenses of looking for the new business.

This approach puts you in a no-lose position. If you actually start the business, the corporation is set up and ready to go. But if you do not go into business, you at least capture a personal deduction for the expenses paid by the corporation.

How to get the deduction: Liquidate the corporation or sell your stock. A little-known section of the Internal Revenue Code, Section 1244, allows you an ordinary deduction on your stock loss. (Your losses are not subject to the $3,000 limitation on the deduction of capital losses.)

Source: Irving L. Blackman, partner, Blackman Kallick Bartelstein, 300 S. Riverside Plaza, Chicago 60606.

Tax-Saving Ideas for Last-Minute Filers

Here's a list of tax-saving ideas for your personal tax return.
Saving ideas:
•Claim parents as dependents. If you provide more than half of a parent's support, you may be able to claim the parent as a dependent even if the parent does not live with you.

If you and other family members jointly support a parent or other individual, with no one person providing more than half the support, you can file a *Multiple Support Declaration*, IRS Form 2120, to obtain a dependency exemption that can be assigned to one among those providing support. The exemption can be assigned to a different person each year.

•Claim head-of-household status. If you are single with a child or other dependent, you may be able to claim head-of-household status and pay lower tax rates than on a single return.

To do this, you must have maintained a household for more than half of 1994 for a child or dependent relative who lives with you. However, having a dependent parent not living with

you may enable you to claim head-of-household filing status.

•Claim the dependent-care tax credit. If you and your spouse both work, or you are single and work, and you have children or other dependents who have to be cared for while you work, you may be eligible for the child-care tax credit.

Rules: You must have dependent children younger than age 13, or some other dependent who is incapable of caring for him/herself, who you maintain in your home and who must be cared for so that you and your spouse can work or go to school.

The credit equals 20% to 30% of the amount you pay for care—depending on your income level—and is worth a maximum of $720 for one dependent or $1,440 for two.

•Shift the exemption for a child. It can make sense for divorced or separated parents to shift the dependency exemption for a child from the custodial to the noncustodial parent if the noncustodial parent is in a higher tax bracket. Remember, however, that exemptions are phased out for some higher-income taxpayers. Do this by filing IRS Form 8332, *Release of Claim to Exemption for Child of Divorced or Separated Parents.*

•File separate returns. This can make sense if you and your spouse both have income and one of you has large deductions that are subject to a percentage-of-Adjusted-Gross-Income (AGI) limitation.

Example: Medical expenses, which are deductible only to the extent that they exceed 7.5% of AGI.

Point: Combining AGI on joint returns will reduce the deduction. Filing separate returns reduces the impact of the AGI limit on the deduction, since only part of your joint income will be counted.

Separate filings can have many tax repercussions, so work through the figures both ways.

•Take advantage of joint-filer tax rates if you are a qualifying widow or widower. You can do this for two years after the death of a spouse, provided you continue to maintain a home for a dependent child.

•Deduct medical expenses of dependents. If you paid the medical bills of a dependent—including a person for whom you have filed a multiple support declaration—you can deduct those costs. If you paid the medical bills for a former spouse before getting divorced during the year, you can deduct those, too, even though you are no longer married.

•Claim all medical expenses. These are deductible only to the extent that their total exceeds 7.5% of AGI, which can be a high hurdle to jump. However, many surprising items qualify for the deduction.

Examples: Health insurance, the cost of travel to and from a doctor's office or hospital—no matter how far—eyeglasses and contact lenses, prescription birth control, schools for the handicapped and many other items.

Appliances acquired for medical reasons—such as air conditioners and dehumidifiers—can be deducted. So can some medically justified home improvements—such as elevators, central air conditioning and special bathrooms—to the extent that their cost exceeds any increase in value that they add to the home.

•Cut home taxes. If you sold a home in the past year, file IRS Form 2119 to defer your gain on the sale of the home, even if you have not yet acquired a replacement residence. This gives you two years to acquire such a replacement.

Also, you can use Form 2119 to elect the once-in-a-lifetime $125,000 exclusion for gain on a home sale if you are 55 or older.

If you did not sell your home during the year, keep records of all the improvements you made to it during the year—new locks, screen doors, mailboxes, telephone outlets, light fixtures, garbage disposals and anything else that is attached permanently to your home and adds to its value.

You can add the cost of these items to your home's basis (cost), which reduces your profit when you sell your home or its final replacement. Over a lifetime, these items can accumulate to generate huge tax savings.

•Make deductible retirement-plan contributions. Contributions to IRAs, Keogh plans and Simplified Employee Pension plans (SEPs) made for 1994—before you file your return—provide a *double* tax benefit.

They provide a deduction directly…and they reduce your AGI—which can indirectly increase other deductions on your return.

How: Deductions for medical bills, theft and casualty losses and miscellaneous expenses are allowed only to the extent that they exceed set percentages of your AGI. Also, high-income individuals have their total deductions and personal exemptions cut back to the extent that their AGI exceeds certain limits.

Thus, *reducing* your AGI can *increase* the tax benefit you gain from all these items.

•Get Social Security numbers for infants. These are now required for children as young as one year old. The penalty for failing to report a Social Security number for a child has been increased to $50.

To get a Social Security number, file Form SS-5 with your local Social Security office. You can ask for one over the phone. If you file your return before the card arrives, write "applied for" on the space on the return where it is requested.

•Examine "kiddie tax" filing options. Children younger than age 14 who have investment income generally must file their own tax returns to report it.

However, you may be able to avoid the inconvenience of filing multiple returns for children who have income less than $5,000 by reporting their income on your own return. File IRS Form 8814 with your return to do this.

Catch: Reporting a child's income on your own return increases your AGI, which may reduce the availability of certain other deductions, as mentioned above. It may also eliminate the child's ability to take a personal exemption for him/herself on a state tax return. So compare the impact of filing both ways.

•Deduct self-employment tax if you have self-employment income. Fifty percent of self-employment taxes is deductible as an AGI-reducing adjustment to income—one of the most frequently overlooked deductions, according to the IRS.

•Deduct 25% of self-employed medical premiums. The new tax law reinstated this deduction for self-employed persons. Even better, it did so retroactively to June 30, 1992—when this provision previously expired. So you may also be able to file an amended return to claim this deduction for 1992 and obtain a tax refund.

• Avoid estimated-tax penalties. If you underpaid your estimated taxes for 1994, or failed to pay them in equal installments, you can expect the IRS to add a penalty to your tax bill. But you may be able to defeat the penalty...

• If your underpayment resulted solely from the new tax law's retroactive application of higher tax rates, you owe no penalty.

• If you received a disproportionate amount of your income late in the year, you can avoid the penalty for failing to make equal quarterly payments by showing that your payment for each quarter was proportionate to the quarter's income.

Demonstrate that these exceptions apply to you by filing IRS Form 2210, *Underpayment of Estimated Tax*, with your return.

• Defer increased taxes. If your taxes were increased in 1993 by the retroactive application of higher tax rates, you need pay only one-third of the increase this April 15. The rest can be paid in equal installments on April 15 of 1995 and 1996 with no interest due.

Limit: The amount you can pay through installment payments is reduced to the extent that your Alternative Minimum Tax calculation on Form 6251, filed with your tax return, exceeds the tax you would have owed if old tax rates had stayed in effect.

• Get an extension. An automatic four-month filing extension, IRS Form 4868, can give you extra time to find tax-saving strategies and make deductible contributions to a Keogh or SEP.

Remember though, an extension does not give you extra time to *pay* taxes. You must estimate what you will owe for the year and make a corresponding payment with your extension.

• Collect records. Protect against the risk of a future audit by collecting, organizing and attaching explanations to your records *now*, while filing strategies are fresh in your mind.

Remember, an audit is likely to occur two or more years *after* you file, when you may not remember the reasons for actions you took. So have well-organized receipts and records that make things clear.

Source: Jeff Keyser, national director–personal tax, Deloitte & Touche, 250 E. Fifth St., Suite 1900, Cincinnati 45202.

The New Tax Law Affects You

The Clinton Tax Act imposes big new tax increases, but it also creates opportunities to cut the tax bill with smart planning. *Here's what you need to know about the traps and the opportunities in the new law:*

• Higher tax rates. The law's new 36% tax bracket applies to income *exceeding* these amounts...

Status	Income
Married, joint return	$140,000
Married, separate return	70,000
Single	115,000
Head of household	127,500
Estates and trusts	5,500

The law's new top 39.6% tax rate applies to taxable income exceeding $250,000 on a joint return, a single return or a return claiming head-of-household filing status.

It also applies to income exceeding $125,000 on a separate return and income of an estate or trust exceeding $7,500.

Planning: An estate or trust is likely to be in a higher tax bracket than its beneficiaries. By distributing income greater than $7,500 to the beneficiaries, income otherwise taxed at 39.6% will be taxed at the beneficiaries' lower rates.

Also, the 1.45% Medicare insurance tax now applies to *all* wages, instead of just the first $135,000 of wages as it did back in 1993.

The law also permanently extends the 3% phaseout of itemized deductions to the extent that Adjusted Gross Income (AGI) exceeds $111,800 on a single or $167,700 on a joint return in 1994.

Point: When the impact of these tax changes is taken together, the real new top tax rate is greater than 42%.

• Social Security tax. Up to 85% of Social Security benefits is subject to income tax in 1994 when provisional income exceeds $44,000 for married individuals filing jointly...or $34,000 for singles. Provisional income is AGI plus tax-exempt income and one-half of Social Security benefits.

• Retirement benefits. The new law reduces the amount of wages upon which an employer may base retirement-plan contributions for an employee from $235,840 to $150,000, so individuals earning more than $150,000 may see a reduction in the value of their retirement benefits.

In addition, employees who make much less than this—$65,000 or more—and who participate in 401(k) programs may have their maximum elective plan contributions reduced under antidiscrimination rules under the new law.

If you are in either of these categories, review your compensation package with your employer.

•Charities. A canceled check is no longer adequate proof of a contribution of $250 or more to a charity. To claim the gift, you must obtain a written acknowledgment from the charity describing the gift. The acknowledgment must be obtained before you file your tax return.

Also, if you receive anything in return for a gift of $75 or more to a charity, the charity is required to inform you of the value of the item provided to you. You may deduct only the difference between the amount of your contribution and the stated value of the item you received in return.

The new law helps those who donate appreciated property to charity by stating such appreciation is no longer a preference item subject to the Alternative Minimum Tax.

•Investments. Now that the top rate has increased from 31% to 39.6% (nearly a one-third increase), tax-exempt bonds are all the more favorable. The new law sets a maximum 28% tax rate for long-term capital gains. But it also limits the deduction for investment interest by removing long-term capital gains from the definition of investment income. Because investment interest is deductible only to the extent that you have investment income, the deduction available to some investors may be reduced.

Planning: Review the way investments are financed in 1995 to avoid losing interest deductions. Short-term gains are taxed as ordinary income (39.6% rate). Consider holding appreciated property, usually stocks, for at least one year to obtain long-term gain treatment (over 11% savings).

•Moving expenses. The new tax law lets you deduct a job-related move only if your new job is at least 50 miles farther from your old home than your old job was from your old home. The limit used to be 35 miles.

The new law also eliminates the moving-expense deduction for pre-move house-hunting trips, temporary living expenses, the closing costs of selling an old home or buying a new one and the cost of settling an unexpired lease.

New breaks: The new law lets moving expense reimbursements received from an employer be excluded from income starting in 1994. In earlier years, you had to include reimbursements in income, then claim offsetting deductions on your return. Also, moving expenses now are deducted as an "above-the-line" adjustment when calculating AGI, so you no longer have to itemize deductions in order to deduct moving expenses.

•Meals, entertainment and club dues. Under the new tax law, the deductible portion of meals and entertainment expenses is reduced from 80% of cost to 50%...and club dues are no longer deductible.

But you can still deduct the cost of business entertainment that takes place at a club under normal rules, subject to the 50%-of-cost limit.

•Equipment expensing. The new law gives small-business owners a break by increasing the expensing allowance for newly acquired assets used in a business to $17,500 from $10,000. Thus, up to $17,500 worth of equipment purchases made during the year can be deducted immediately, instead of written off over a period of years through depreciation deductions.

•Passive losses from real estate. Under the new tax law, real-estate "professionals" are no longer subject to deduction limitations imposed by the Tax Code's passive activity rules.

Such "professionals" are persons who spend more than half their time engaged in a real-estate-related business such as construction, property development, acquisitions, conversions, rental operations, management, leasing and brokering.

•Luxury tax. The new law retroactively repeals the 10% luxury tax that was imposed during 1993 on the purchase of boats, airplanes, jewelry and furs. If you paid the tax during 1993, you are entitled to a tax *refund* from the retailer who sold the item to you, who will in turn request it from the IRS. Contact the retailer.

•Stock options. *There are two basic types of stock options:* Incentive Stock Options (ISOs) and Nonqualified Stock Options (NQSOs). For many years, when capital gains and ordinary income rates were identical or nearly identical, the employee was less concerned with the type of options held.

*More...*The new law retroactively extends back to June 30, 1992, the tax exemption for up to $5,250 of employer-provided educational assistance...and the deduction for 25% of the cost of health-insurance premiums incurred by self-employed individuals. If these items apply to you, you may be able to file an amended tax return for 1992 to claim them and obtain a tax refund.

Source: Joseph P. Toce, Jr., partner in charge of individual tax and financial consulting services, Northeast region, Arthur Anderson & Co., 1345 Avenue of the Americas, New York 10105.

Even Taxpayers Have Rights

The IRS doesn't have all the advantages in dealing with taxpayers. Taxpayers have rights, too. Here are some of the main ones...

IRS personnel are expected to deal with you in a professional, courteous manner and should...

•Provide you with all the information and help that you need to comply with the tax laws.

•Ensure personal and financial confidentiality.

•Provide clear explanations in any IRS notice or mail inquiry, and supply additional information if requested.

•Collect taxes fairly. *Example:* The IRS cannot sell your home just to collect taxes without the permission of the local district director.

•Give you time to contest an erroneous levy. *Example:* Bank accounts cannot be seized for 21 days after notification and other property cannot be seized for 30 days. But the IRS can freeze these assets during the waiting period.

In interacting with the IRS, the taxpayer has specific rights, too. Most important:

•The taxpayer may consult and/or be represented by a tax adviser, attorney or other professional. Representation must be accompanied by a properly executed power of attorney.

•The taxpayer may record an IRS interview if ten days' notice is given to the IRS. Likewise, the IRS may record a meeting if the taxpayer is informed ten days in advance.

•If the taxpayer accompanies his/her representative, interviews can be suspended at any time to allow the taxpayer to consult with the tax professional.

•Taxpayer meetings with the IRS should be at a time and place that are mutually convenient.

•IRS mail notices can be contested.

•The taxpayer may appeal notices and findings of the IRS examiner and contest penalties.

•The taxpayer may contact the problem resolution officer at the PRO when normal procedures don't work. Contacting the officer will ensure a better response—as the officer must then handle your case him/herself and cannot pass it on to another staff member. When the taxpayer is suffering or is about to suffer significant hardship, a Form 911 can be filed.

•If the taxpayer cannot pay the tax liability in full, an installment agreement can be requested.

Source: Laurence I. Foster, tax partner, personal financial planning practice, KPMG Peat Marwick, 345 Park Ave., New York 10154.

New Interest Deduction

New opportunity: Interest added by the IRS to a business tax liability is *deductible* as business interest even when the tax is reported on a *personal* return.

A federal District Court explicitly overruled the IRS position that interest added to taxes reported on a personal tax return is always nondeductible personal interest.

This creates a new deduction for proprietors, partners and S-corporation shareholders who report business income on their personal returns. They can claim the deduction on the return due this April 15 and on amended returns filed for prior years to claim tax refunds.

Catch: This ruling potentially involves billions of dollars, so the IRS is considered sure to appeal it—and to disallow any such deduction found during an audit before the appeal is resolved. But consider taking it anyway.

Key: The Court's decision is "substantial authority" for the deduction, which should let you avoid any accuracy-related penalty for claiming it erroneously even if the District Court's decision is overturned. So you have nothing to lose by claiming it.

Strategy:

•Claim the deduction this April 15 to get a larger refund for 1994. The IRS only checks *math* before sending out refund checks. By the time the IRS disallows your deduction, *if* it does, the issue may be resolved.

If not, you can file an appeal and even a Tax Court petition later, citing the District Court case as precedent to get extra time.

The worst that can happen is that the District Court will be overruled and you'll have to pay the tax you'd have owed anyway—*plus interest*. But you'll keep use of the money in the meantime. And if the District Court is upheld or your return isn't examined, you'll get to keep the whole refund.

•By filing amended returns that claim the deduction for past years you can keep the statute of limitations open for those years to get refunds if the District Court's decision is upheld.

David Miller, D.N.D., No. A3-92-183.

Source: Randy Bruce Blaustein, Blaustein, Greenberg & Co., 155 E. 31 St., New York 10016.

Checklist: Deductible Investment Expenses

•Fees paid for counsel and advice about investments, including the cost of investment advisory services.

•Investment books and periodicals.

•Management fees for collecting rent, interest and dividends.

•Safe-deposit-box rent (if used to store securities) and fees paid to custodians of securities.

•Transportation expenses to consult with your broker.

•Travel away from home to look after investment property (but not for travel to attend stockholders' meetings).

•Fees charged by lawyers or accountants for investment-related services.

•A portion of depreciation on a home computer used for investment purposes, such as projecting market trends and analyzing yields. *Also deductible:* The cost of investment-related computer software.

•Home-office expenses only if the office is used exclusively to manage your investment affairs and the extent of your investment activities amounts to a trade or business.

Source: Robert S. Holzman, PhD, professor emeritus of taxation, New York University. He is the author of *Encyclopedia of Estate Planning,* Boardroom Classics, Box 736, Springfield, NJ 07081.

How to Turn a Vacation Into a Deduction

The new tax law has implications for those who plan to deduct vacation homes and travel this year—or mix business with pleasure. Here's what you can—and cannot—deduct and the best strategies to use in each case.

Vacation homes:

When tax rates rise—as they did in 1993—vacation homes become less expensive because your deductions are more valuable.

Starting in 1993, your deductions for mortgage interest and taxes became much more valuable because you were subject to new, higher tax rates. *Tax-saving strategies...*

•Rent out your vacation home for less than 15 days this year, and the rental income you collect is tax-free. You can also deduct interest and tax payments on the house for the entire year.

•If you use the vacation home yourself for less than 14 days or less than 10% of the number of days it is rented at a fair market value, your usage is considered minimal and you can claim the full business deductions on all related expenses, such as maintenance, repairs, utilities and depreciation.

Example: When you rent out the property for 150 days, you can use it yourself for up to 15 days and still deduct all expenses.

If you occupy the property for a longer period, you can deduct only part of your expenses. To calculate the deductible amount, you have to allocate expenses based on the ratio of personal and business usage.

Example: You use your vacation home for 40 days and rent it out for 100 days. Rental income equals $8,000. You pay property taxes of $1,600, mortgage interest of $5,200 and the rental portion of your repair and insurance costs were $5,000. Your loss equals $3,800 ($11,800 in expenses minus $8,000 in income).

The *ratio* is calculated by taking the 100 days rented and dividing it by 365 days in the year, according to the Tax Court. After you subtract from the $8,000 of rental income the $1,424 for mortgage interest (100 divided by 365 multiplied by $5,200) and $438 for property taxes (100 divided by 365 multiplied by $1,600), you have $6,138 against which to deduct other expenses.

So you can deduct the full $5,000 for repairs and insurance costs. The remaining portion of mortgage interest and taxes is deducted on Schedule A as an itemized deduction.

Conflict: The Tax Court and the IRS disagree on how to calculate the deduction. The IRS figures the ratio as days of actual rental usage divided by days of *total use,* instead of total days in the year. Both are acceptable, but most vacation-home owners use the Tax Court formula, which always allows them a larger deduction. The Tax Court formula has been approved on appeal to the US Court of Appeals for the Ninth and Tenth Circuits.

Limits: For most taxpayers, the deduction for vacation homes is limited to $25,000. That's because these losses are passive losses that can be used to offset other passive income from rental properties or partnerships, plus up to $25,000 of regular income.

The $25,000 allowance is phased out as your Adjusted Gross Income rises from $100,000 to $150,000, at which point it disappears completely.

Vacation travel:

A deduction for travel expenses depends on whether the trip is primarily for business or pleasure.

Example: You travel to California on business for three days and extend the trip for four more days to visit friends. Because the trip is mostly personal, you can deduct your business expenses but not travel costs.

When a trip is primarily for business, you can deduct travel expenses—but you have to allocate hotel, meal and other types of expenses.

Example: You fly to Chicago for a three-day business trip and stay two days longer. You spend $1,200. Had you not stayed, total costs would have equaled $800. You can deduct the costs of travel plus $800.

When you stay over to take advantage of lower airplane ticket prices, the extra days count as business days.

Example: You fly to New York on Tuesday for business meetings that end on Friday. An airplane ticket home costs $750. You stay until Sunday to see the sights, and your ticket home costs $200. Your weekend hotel and meal costs can be deducted as business expenses.

The extra deductions are available only to the business traveler, not to an accompanying spouse. Most people no longer can deduct the expenses of spouses who accompany them on business trips. Before, spouse expenses could be deducted when there was a legitimate business reason for the trip. Now expenses are deductible only when the spouse is employed by the same company and has a separate business reason for traveling.

Alternative: When you travel by car, you can deduct 29 cents per mile plus tolls—even when your spouse accompanies you. Or you can deduct gas, insurance, maintenance and other *actual* expenses.

Full rental-car costs are deductible. Also, you can deduct the full cost of a double room at a hotel.

Travel outside the US:

Tougher rules apply to travel *outside* the US. You can deduct these travel costs if you pass one of the following four tests...

•You have no "substantial control" over arranging the trip—meaning that you are not management or related to the company but are simply seeking reimbursement for your travel costs.

• You are outside the US for seven consecutive days or less. *Example:* You travel to Europe for a two-day business trip and spend three days sightseeing.

• You spend less than 25% of your time outside the US on nonbusiness activities. *Example:* You are self-employed and travel to Europe for 15 days, three of which you spend sightseeing.

• Personal activities are not a major consideration when planning the trip. This is a strictly factual test that depends on your ability to convince an IRS agent.

Conventions outside the US can be deducted only when there is a legitimate reason to hold the convention abroad.

Cruise trips are even tougher to deduct. Investment seminars are not deductible at all, and legitimate business convention expenses are capped at $2,000.

To deduct the full $2,000, you must travel on a ship that is registered in the US with ports of call only in the US or its territorial possessions. You must prepare a written statement including the number of hours spent each day in meetings. The meeting's sponsor must also provide a statement.

Source: Sam Starr, partner, and William J. Dunn, manager, Coopers & Lybrand, 1800 M St. NW, Washington, DC 20036.

Here's How to Speed Up Your Refunds...

Filing your tax return before the April 15 deadline speeds up your tax refund. Because the IRS is processing fewer returns, early filers can get their refund checks in just 21 days, even sooner if they file electronically.

Here's how to speed up getting your return into the mailbox...*Information needed:*

• Form W-2. Employers must send employee wage statements by January 31. If your W-2 is late, check with your employer. *Last resort:* File

Form 4852 as a substitute. Explain the source of your salary on the form. *Example:* "It matches the figures reported on my pay stubs."

• Form 1099. These "information forms" are used to report dividend and interest income, payments to independent contractors, retirement-plan distributions and Social Security payments. 1099s do not have to be mailed until January 31, but most go out much earlier.

Warning: Do not file early if any of the figures on your 1099s are incorrect. Discrepancies will be caught by the IRS computer, which will flag your return for further scrutiny.

If a payor's name is reported incorrectly— for example, The First National Savings Bank instead of The First National Savings and Loan Association—list it the incorrect way on your tax return, too.

Strategy: Unlike Form W-2, 1099s do not have to be attached to your tax return. So you can file even before you receive them if you are sure that your records are accurate and complete.

• Form K-1. These are used to report income and losses from partnerships—and there is no statutory due date for receiving them.

• Funding your retirement plans. The earlier in the year you fund a Keogh or IRA, the faster money builds up in the account tax-deferred.

Strategy: Cash-pressed taxpayers can file their returns early and then use the refund to make their retirement-plan contributions.

Early filing hazards:

If you will *owe* income taxes, defer filing your return until April 15 to delay paying taxes owed. Don't file early.

The real danger of filing early is that you'll omit items from your return. If you find an error, file an amended return or a corrected Form 1040 before April 15.

Audit risk:

In spite of what many taxpayers believe, early filing does *not* increase the odds that you will be audited. Audit candidates are selected on the basis of certain criteria regardless of *when* the return is filed.

Source: Paul Huth, tax partner, Ernst & Young, 1300 Huntington Building, Cleveland 44115.

How to Deal with IRS Mistakes

Just because you correctly completed and filed your 1994 tax return, don't assume that you're through with the IRS for the year. You may receive an IRS notice asking for additional taxes.

But before paying the extra tax, it is important to check to see whether the notice is correct. The IRS may have made a mistake. *Common errors:* Processing errors:

Most IRS errors originate in the service centers, where more than 115 million tax returns are processed. *Typical mistakes:*

•The IRS is working with an incorrect 1099. The figures on the 1099 don't agree with what the taxpayer reported on his/her return.

•W-2 forms get separated from the returns.

•An IRS clerk who punches returns into his/her computer transposes a number or reports an amount on the wrong line.

Never ignore an IRS notice. And never assume that the problem will be resolved by writing one letter to the IRS. *Always stay on top of the situation until it is resolved.*

Reason: The IRS computer cycle of dunning letters is automatic and ends in enforcement action. If you do nothing, the agency will levy your paycheck or bank account, or place a lien on your home or other property you own.

How to proceed: When you receive an IRS notice, first double-check your tax return to make sure that the error is the IRS's and not yours. If it is the IRS's error, write to the office that sent you the notice, pointing out the error. Include the number of the notice in your letter.

Critical: All your initial contacts with the IRS should be in writing. Always save copies for your files. But suggest in your letter that you discuss the matter by telephone—since the IRS has tried to be more taxpayer-friendly in recent years. Include both your day and evening phone numbers in the letter.

While the IRS tries to respond quickly to taxpayer letters, the volume makes it impossible. *More reasonable:* Expect a response in 30 days.

Warning: Within the 30 days, you probably will receive another IRS notice because the IRS computers are programmed to send them out regularly.

Second notices usually are worded more harshly. Don't panic—again, respond in writing, asking for expedited attention. You won't receive it—but your written response shows that you haven't ignored the second notice.

Within 30 days, you should receive an acknowledgment from the IRS. A postcard stating that the agency is working on your problem is enough to stop the IRS computer from recommending enforcement action.

Key: If you don't hear from the IRS in 30 days, call again. Find the toll-free number for the taxpayer service division of your local service center in the telephone book or IRS publications.

It is often difficult to get through to the taxpayer service division, but keep trying. Staff members can review the status of your account on the IRS computer system. Generally, they will take taxpayers at their word and stop enforcement action. Always write down—and keep—the name of the person with whom you spoke.

More than 90% of all IRS errors are resolved this way. If yours is not, contact your *Problem Resolution Office (PRO).*

PROs are found in every IRS Service Center and district director's office. They act as taxpayer advocates and ensure that taxpayers receive all the rights to which they are entitled under the system.

To get the PRO on your case, you must have contacted the IRS and 45 days must have elapsed without a response. Because PRO staff members have smaller caseloads than other Service Center employees, they can spend more time working with you.

Example: The Brookhaven Service Center has an inventory of 40,000-plus cases, while the typical PRO office has no more than 400 cases.

You will generally hear from the PRO within 15 days of its receipt of your letter. Most problems are resolved within a few weeks.

Audit errors:

Fewer than 1% of taxpayers are audited. About 87% of those audits result in bigger tax assessments. When you believe the auditor has made an error, take your case to his supervisor. If you

151

get no satisfaction there, you can go to the *administrative appeals division*.

Administrative appeals is an independent agency within the IRS. It has authority to settle all cases administratively.

Procedure: Show the facts and records to the administrative appeals officer, and present the information as you believe it applies in your case. About 75% to 80% of appeals decisions come out in favor of the IRS. But on average, the tax liability is cut in half by the appeals division.

Example: An IRS auditor disallows several deductions and sends you a bill for additional taxes owed of $8,500. When you take the case to administrative appeals, the officer upholds the auditor but reduces your tax liability to $4,250.

Cost: When the disputed tax is less than $5,000, it makes more sense to handle the case yourself than to hire a lawyer.

Further appeals: If you disagree with the appeals officer's decision, you can pursue the case in Tax Court...or you can pay the disputed amount and file for a refund in federal district court.

Collection errors:

The IRS collection division takes over when taxpayers do not respond to IRS notices of taxes owed. In this division, most of the IRS errors are judgments about how quickly to proceed against a taxpayer's assets.

Example: A small business owner falls behind on quarterly estimated tax payments when business revenues slow down. The business owner asks for six months to pay off the taxes when business picks up. But the enforcement division puts a padlock on the business's retail store.

Important: Work closely with collection division managers. They are more experienced than field agents and more likely to extend the time for payment before enforcement actions begin.

Otherwise, call the PRO in your district. The officer there has the authority to work out an installment payment plan or an offer-in-compromise and to stop enforcement action.

Source: Cornelius J. Coleman, director, national tax services, Coopers & Lybrand, 1301 Avenue of the Americas, New York 10019.

To Get a Lien Released

Suppose your credit report comes back and it shows that a federal tax lien has been filed by the IRS. You did owe some back taxes a few years ago, but that has long been repaid. Sometimes the IRS fails to issue a *Release of Federal Tax Lien* form or fails to arrange to file this form with the office where tax liens are filed in your state. *Remedy:* Call your IRS district office and ask to speak to the "special procedures" office of the collection division. These are the people who are responsible for issuing and releasing federal tax liens. They will check the computer, and if you have no liability, you can expect them to issue a release of federal tax lien within a few days. Send a copy of the release to the credit bureau.

Source: Ms. X, a former IRS agent still well-connected.

Offer-in-Compromise Strategy

The general rule at the IRS is that it is reluctant to accept an offer in compromise from a young taxpayer. It makes sense, since a younger person—younger than age 50—has many productive years during which enough money can be earned to pay the entire liability. *Recent case:* A single woman, about 28 years old, built up an IRS debt of $30,000. She had no assets and her annual salary was barely enough to cover her necessary living expenses. The argument made to the IRS was that if it did not accept her modest offer she would eventually get married and stop working. In that case, the IRS would receive nothing.

Source: Ms. X, a former IRS agent still well-connected.

Four-Wheel Deduction

A traveling salesman who bought a four-wheel drive vehicle to service customers in rural areas had his depreciation deductions for the vehicle challenged by the IRS. *Court:* The salesman showed that he needed this type of vehicle to reach customers in difficult terrain and had records to prove that he used it for this purpose. His deductions were allowed.

Source: *Stuart L. Reems*, TC Memo 1994-253.

The Filed-When-Mailed Rule

The filed-when-mailed rule applies only when the mailed item is *received* by the IRS. If it is lost in the mail it is deemed *not* filed even if there is convincing proof that it actually was mailed. *Why:* The law specifically states that the *postmark* determines the time of filing—so a taxpayer who can't produce a postmarked envelope doesn't have the required proof that the filing was made on time. *Self-defense:* Always send important documents to the IRS by certified mail.

Source: *James R. Carroll*, TC Memo 1994-229.

Compensation Loopholes: Deferring Pay

The compensation package you get from your employer probably includes some form of deferred compensation whereby money is put away for you but is not available until some time in the future. This form of compensation boosts your pay and offers significant tax advantages. Loopholes:

•Pension and profit-sharing plans. Your employer contributes money to a retirement plan on your behalf and the money accumulates on a tax-deferred basis. You don't pay a current tax on the contribution or on the interest the money earns. No tax is due until you receive a distribution of money from the plan. *More:*

Loophole: Take a tax-free *loan* from the pension or profit-sharing plan. Borrowing is *not* a taxable transaction. You can only do this *if* the plan permits borrowing—not all do. Plans that allow borrowing usually make it easy on the

participant—there's no need to justify why the loan is needed.

Tax law limits: The amount you can borrow is limited to your vested balance in the plan up to the greater of $10,000 or one-half of your vested balance, with a maximum of $50,000.

Loophole: Put some of your own money into the plan—many plans allow employees to make voluntary contributions. Such contributions are not tax-deductible, but the money accumulates on a tax-deferred basis.

Loophole: If your company's plan is inactive —no additions are being made and no benefits are accruing on your behalf—you are eligible to contribute to an IRA.

•401(k) plans. You contribute part of your salary to a company-sponsored savings program. You pay no income tax on the money you contribute until you make withdrawals. Interest, dividends and other earnings accumulate tax-deferred until you take them out.

Many companies "match" employees' contributions by putting additional money into the plan for the employee.

Loophole: Though the amount you can contribute each year is limited by the tax law, it's far more than you can put into an IRA. *Maximum 401(k) contribution for 1994:* $9,240.

•Company-paid life insurance. As long as the coverage doesn't exceed $50,000 worth of insurance, you are not taxed on the premiums the employer pays. But if it is more than $50,000, you are taxed on part of the premiums.

Loophole: The taxable amount is figured from IRS tables and is less than the actual premiums the employer pays. You pay some tax for the extra coverage, but it is far less than it would cost you to buy similar life insurance coverage outside the company.

•Survivor's tax-free benefit. The first $5,000 of death benefits paid by an employer to an employee's surviving spouse or other beneficiary is tax-free. The benefit can come out of deferred salary payments or retirement-plan distributions.

Limit: $5,000 is the maximum amount that can be paid out tax-free regardless of how many beneficiaries there are. The $5,000 can be allocated among any number of beneficiaries.

•Stock options. When a company gives an employee an option to purchase stock that does not qualify as an *incentive stock option* (more relevant information below), the employee must pay tax when the option is exercised. The taxed amount is the difference between the option price and the fair market value of the stock at the time the option is exercised.

Loophole: There is no tax paid when the option is granted. Stock options are a form of deferred compensation. The employee benefits on a tax-deferred basis from the growth in value of the company stock.

•Incentive stock options. These are options that qualify under the Tax Code for special treatment. No tax is levied when the options are issued to the employee.

Loophole: No tax is levied when the options are exercised. Tax isn't payable until the options are sold.

Trap: The difference between the option price and the fair market value at the time the option is exercised is a "preference item" that is subject to the Alternative Minimum Tax (AMT). Employees should be careful not to exercise so many incentive stock options that they fall into the AMT. The exercise of these options must be carefully timed.

•Restricted stock. Sometimes an employer issues stock to an employee that is subject to a "substantial risk of forfeiture." *The most common situation:* The employee will have to give up the stock if he/she doesn't continue working for the company for a specified number of years.

When the restriction lapses, the employee is taxed on the difference between the stock's fair market value at that time and the price paid for the stock.

Loophole: The employee can make an election under Section 83(b) of the Internal Revenue Code to pay tax on the value of the stock when it is originally issued. Then, there is no tax when the restriction lapses. (Tax on any gain is payable when the employee ultimately disposes of the stock.) Employees should make the Section 83(b) election in instances where they expect the company's stock to appreciate considerably.

•Phantom stock, also called *stock appreciation rights*, is sometimes issued to employees. No actual stock is given, but payments are made as if

actual stock had been issued. If any dividends are paid to stockholders, they are also paid to the phantom stockholders. And when the employee leaves the company he/she is compensated for his/her phantom shares. Payments to the employee are taxed as compensation, rather than tax-favored capital gains.

Loophole: The employee doesn't pay tax until there is an actual payment to him as a phantom stockholder. No tax is payable when he first receives the phantom stock. So phantom stock is another form of deferred compensation.

Source: Edward Mendlowitz, partner, Mendlowitz Weitsen, CPAs, Two Pennsylvania Plaza, New York 10121. He is the author of *New Tax Traps, New Opportunities,* Boardroom Special Reports, Box 736, Springfield, New Jersey 07081.

Dealing With the IRS After You're Gone

Estate-tax auditors at the IRS are using special audit techniques to increase the size of a decedent's taxable estate. The first thing asked for by many auditors is a list of every relative, dead or alive, the names of their children and the names of their grandchildren. The auditors want to determine if any gifts in excess of the $10,000 annual exclusion have been made to any of these people during the past 20 years. All gifts made in excess of the annual $10,000 exclusion are added back to increase the size of the taxable estate.

Source: Ms. X, a former IRS agent still well-connected.

How to Get Better Treatment at the IRS

An official at one IRS district office recently told me that a taxpayer would likely receive quicker and more lenient treatment by walking into his/her local IRS office instead of sending in a letter with the same information. The marching orders given to the collection personnel who staff the walk-in areas are to work out partial payment plans with taxpayers as quickly as possible and move on to the next case. Those taxpayers who mail their financial information to the IRS may experience delays because questions that could be resolved with simple answers require detailed correspondence.

Source: Ms. X, a former IRS agent still well-connected.

Avoiding Frustration When Dealing with the IRS

Many times even the people working at the IRS do not know which department or area is best suited to resolve a particular problem. As a result, the taxpayer who wants to resolve his/her problem gets endlessly shifted from person to person. *Better approach:* Call the district director's office and explain your problem to the receptionist. Usually the director's receptionist is sophisticated enough to point you in the right direction. *Alternative:* Call the Problem Resolution Office (PRO) and ask for assistance, even though your case does not yet technically qualify for PRO involvement.

Source: Ms. X, a former IRS agent still well-connected.

When the IRS Assists Foreign Governments

International tax treaties provide that the IRS is available to assist foreign governments in collecting information relating to that government's taxes. It is not unusual for a foreign government to request that the IRS interview a taxpayer in the United States who allegedly was paid money or provided services to a company located in a foreign country. If you or your company is contacted by the IRS based on the request of a foreign government, the immediate suspicion on the part of the IRS is that there may be income that you failed to report.

Source: Ms. X, a former IRS agent still well-connected.

Documenting Charitable Contributions

It is not unusual for people to donate used clothing by depositing it in a receptacle at a shopping center. You don't get a receipt describing the clothes or their value, and you have no way of proving that you donated the clothing. *Best approach:* Write out a list of the articles of clothing you donated. Describe each item, its condition, its original cost (if known) and the approximate fair market value. Estimate the fair market value by browsing in a thrift shop and finding out what similar items sell for there. Mail a copy of this list, together with a cover letter, to the charity. This will create a permanent record of the transaction that you can use if you're audited.

Source: Ms. X, a former IRS agent still well-connected.

How to Organize Your Tax Files To Work for You

Review your 1994 tax return. It will help you create a checklist of topics to consider as you set up your new record-keeping system.

• Use two legal-sized accordion folders. They are available at any stationery store. Label one folder *income* and the other *deductions*. That way, all tax-related receipts can be kept in one place. You can organize these receipts as needed throughout the year.

Examples: Salary statements, mortgage slips, taxi receipts, etc.

• Use a portable receipt keeper. Many people can't find their receipts when they need them.

Solution: Carry a small envelope labeled 1995 taxes in your bag or with your datebook. Use it to collect receipts for tax-deductible restaurant meals, cash donations, tolls or gas. Once a week, file those receipts in your accordion folder at home.

• Use your checkbook and datebook for backup documentation. Try to use checks to pay for all deductible expenses. Every time you do, write the word *tax* and circle it next to the check number in the checkbook. Do the same with your credit-card statements. Tax deductions will be obvious when you review your checkbook and card statements at the end of the year.

• Use your checkbook to document small cash gifts. When you give $10 or $20 in cash to the local Little League or your place of worship, note the amount in your checkbook as a *charitable donation* without figuring it into your bank balance.

Reason: The notation helps prove a gift without a receipt. It also shows when the gift was made. The IRS rarely questions such well-documented cash gifts unless the total is excessive.

• Note deductible expenses in your business diary or datebook.

Store your checkbook stubs, credit-card statements and datebook with your tax return and backup documentation. This will enable you to gather supporting documents quickly in case of an audit.

• Keep the information used to prepare your tax return for at least three years. In general, the IRS cannot audit your tax return after three years. The deadline is extended to six years if 20% or more of your taxes are underpaid. If fraud is suspected, your return can be audited at any time. So use three years as your minimum for keeping complete records.

Better: Retain tax information for ten years or more. Longer holding periods are particularly important when you have unusually large amounts of deductions or expenses that act as red flags, such as home offices. If you decide to throw out any records after your holding period, be sure to keep at least your stock, investment and personal residence records.

Source: George E.L. Barbee, executive director, client services, Price Waterhouse, 160 Federal St., Boston 02110.

How to Use Uncle Sam to Help You Find a Better Job

Today's unsettled economy has turned many people into job seekers.

The good news: Uncle Sam will subsidize your search, even if you're not successful.

To deduct job-hunting expenses, you must be looking for a job in the same trade or business that you're currently in. So, an accountant who takes a job as an accountant with a different firm can deduct his/her expenses. However, an accountant who switches occupations and becomes a bank officer cannot deduct job-hunting expenses.

Other limits: No job-hunt expenses can be deducted for searches for your first job or after a very long period of unemployment.

What's deductible:

You can deduct the costs of typing, printing and mailing résumés to prospective employers…telephone calls…fees paid to employment agencies and career counselors…advertising costs…legal and accounting fees related to employment contracts…and the costs of newspapers or trade journals that you buy for the want ads.

Also: Travel and transportation expenses, such as cab fares to job interviews, are deductible. So is the cost of bringing your spouse to an interview, if the prospective employer requests it.

Caution: Out-of-town travel expenses like transportation, lodging and 50% of meals and entertainment are deductible only if job-hunting is the primary purpose of the trip.

Documentation is critical, especially for unsuccessful job hunts and out-of-town interviews. Keep records of everything you spend and all correspondence, including proof of the job opening and names of the people who interviewed you.

How to deduct job-hunting and education expenses: These are claimed on Schedule A as "miscellaneous itemized expenses," which are deductible to the extent the total exceeds 2% of your Adjusted Gross Income.

Source: Laurence I. Foster, partner, personal financial planning practice, KPMG Peat Marwick, 345 Park Ave., New York 10154.

7

Success in the Office

When Offered a Job

When offered a job, consider all the elements—not just title, salary and responsibility. Decide if you will fit in. If the boss is younger, make sure you'll be comfortable. In a small firm, will you be happy without a large staff? In a large one, will you feel stifled? *Bottom line:* Once offered a job, people tend not to ask questions that might lead them to turn it down. It is better to ask before starting than to take a job that proves to be a bad fit.

Source: Emily Koltnow, founder of the New York-based Women in Networking Workshops and coauthor, *Congratulations! You've Been Fired*, Fawcett Books, 201 E. 50 St., New York 10022.

Secrets of Getting A New Job

After almost 20 years of testing and perfecting, I have developed an amazingly effective process for getting a job. What makes this process so effective is that it is based on the principles of good communication with potential employers.

In these highly competitive and economically strapped times, employers are looking for people with the skills to deliver more—more profit...more customers...more productivity. Here are six steps and why they should work to get you a job offer within 60 days...

•Create a *word bank*. This is a written account of an important achievement in your career. In 200 words or more, describe the task and how you went about it. What problems did you overcome? How? What were the results, in terms of percentage of improvement, dollars saved, etc.?

This is called the word bank because you will borrow from it for each of the following steps. This account of an important achievement is the key to a successful job hunt.

Take your time on your word bank. Go into detail. Include as many of your skills as you can. But stick to just one achievement. If you have a number of notable achievements, you can create other word banks using this one as the model. The more word banks, the more skills. The more skills, the more job opportunities.

What if your work is largely routine? Routine jobs are historically subject to errors and poor performance brought on by boredom and repetition. Write 200 words about your ability to avoid errors and ensure reliability, accuracy and high productivity. These are qualities that are currently in low supply and that employers value highly.

What if you have just finished school and are looking for your first job? Write about the skills you developed in school. Did you get an "A" in a French course after memorizing 500 irregular verbs in just two days? This shows you can learn quickly and handle crash projects—the criteria for many positions. Focusing on how you work, rather than on job titles and descriptions, lets you expand from your current position into new fields that make use of your skills.

•Write a contact letter. As the name implies, the contact letter is written to people who work in your target industry and who you have targeted because they may know of opportunities for someone with your skills. You can find these people by consulting trade directories and publications.

Your contact letter should not include a résumé and should make it clear that you are in search of information—not employment. The heart of your letter is a paragraph of the best ideas from your word bank. The letter informs the contact when you will call for an appointment, during which you will ask just one question and make some notes.

There are three reasons why a contact will probably agree to see you:

1. He/She is a nice person.

2. You're asking for something that this nice person can give you easily.

3. Your word bank convinced your contact that you are worth talking to.

•Begin the contact conversation by asking just one question: "What criteria do you use to hire people in this field?" This is an honest question and one that your contact is qualified to answer. Pay careful attention to the reply. Make a note of each criterion on a legal-sized pad with a black, felt-tipped pen, so that your notes are clear when you review them later.

As the answer unfolds, you will learn a great deal about what your target industry is looking for. When you have learned enough, thank your contact and ask for the names of other helpful industry contacts. Send your contact letter to any new names, mentioning your first contact as a reference.

•Create a competitive résumé. Now, instead of just listing your jobs and titles, focus your résumé on the specific criteria by which people are hired in your target industry. Borrow from your word bank to show how you meet those criteria. The more focused your résumé, the more competitive it is and the better your chances of landing a job interview.

Hints: Don't include any information that does not focus on the criteria. Do send a copy of your competitive résumé and a thank you letter to the contact who helped you write it. It's more than just polite—it could be productive.

•Prepare for the job interview. It will be really anticlimactic when you've done such good homework. Though most decision-makers know their own jobs well, they often have little time to prepare for interviews. Because of your preparation, you'll be in a position to help the interviewer keep the discussion on target. A single question will do it: "By what criteria will you select the person for this job?" This time you're not talking about the industry in general, but about a specific job.

Feel free to suggest the addition of any criteria you have learned during your research. The more criteria, the more chances to draw on your word bank for the necessary skills. After you've shown how you meet a particular criterion, be sure to check it out with the interviewer by asking, "How does that compare with what you had in mind?"

Hints: Before the interview, practice presenting skills from your word bank so that you feel comfortable with what you're going to say. Bring along documentation of your achievements whenever possible.

•Follow up after the interview. Periodically asking how your presentation compared with what the decision-maker had in mind might well result in a decision during the interview.

But if not, write a letter enclosing a summary of your qualifications. If you don't get a job offer, ask for ideas on how to improve your presentation.

Source: Irv Zuckerman, a New York-based communications consultant who has more than 40 years' experience in the field and has taught thousands of people his job-seeking techniques. He is the author of *Hire Power: The 6-Step Process to Get the Job You Need in 60 Days—Guaranteed!,* Perigee Books, 200 Madison Ave., New York 10016.

Better Customer Surveys

Surveys that ask customers to rate how the company is doing in various areas are, for the most part, worthless. *Reasons:* They rarely ask the right questions, and even if they indicate where a company needs to improve, they rarely indicate how. *Better:* Have a third-party interviewer survey past, present and prospective customers on how the company could improve. *Aim:* To get a variety of useful perspectives.

Source: John R. Graham, Graham Communications, marketing consultants, Quincy, Massachusetts, writing in *Sales & Marketing Executive Report,* 4660 Ravenswood Ave., Chicago 60640.

Better Cover Letters

Follow the "three-paragraph rule"—and limit your cover letter to a length that can be read in only 30 seconds. *First paragraph:* Tell who you are and what you want. *Second paragraph:* Explain how you can benefit the employer. *Third paragraph:* Tell the employer exactly what you want him/her to do. *Example:* "When may we get together for a personal interview?"

Source: *Résumés for Re-Entry: A Handbook for Women* by C. Edward Good, president of a publishing and educational services firm in Charlottesville, Virginia. Impact Publications, 9104-N Manassas Dr., Manassas Park, Virginia 22111.

Improve Networking Relationships

Improve networking relationships by getting back to each contact to let him/her know the result of his advice. This used to be called common courtesy, but it is far from common today. *Benefits:* It cements the relationship with your contacts…sets you apart from others…makes them willing to help you again.

Source: Don Lussier, outplacement consultant, 4948 Meadowbrook Lane, Orion, Michigan 48359.

Look for Dissatisfied Customers…

…Then find ways to satisfy them. *Reason:* It costs five times more to replace a customer than to keep one. But complainers are rare. Most people say nothing and go elsewhere. It's good business to find the complainers before they make the switch. *Helpful:* Make it easy for customers to complain, through surveys and toll-free numbers. When you find unhappy customers, satisfy them quickly.

Source: *Save Your Business a Bundle* by Daniel Kehrer, co-owner, Group IV Communications, Inc. Simon and Schuster, 1230 Avenue of the Americas, New York 10020.

A Positive Drug Test Doesn't Equate With Misconduct

A worker fired because of the high level of cannabinoids in his urine can collect unemployment benefits. *Court:* For the firing to have been for cause, the employer would have had to be able to show a job-related reason for its rule against drug use.

Source: *Weller v. Arizona Department of Economic Security,* CA Ariz., 11/15/93.

Recipe for Effective Leadership

Work with your team to develop an understanding of what is really important. Say what's important in three sentences or less—and live it through daily actions and reinforcement. Support your team as it thinks of new ways to get that key job done. Be patient—it may take several years before people realize you take this approach seriously. *Caution:* Don't become so involved in big-picture thinking that you don't see the details.

Source: Robert Mittelstaedt, Jr., vice dean, Wharton Executive Education, writing in *Executive Issues,* 255 S. 38 St., Philadelphia 19104.

Decision Analysis

To measure your skill at identifying priorities and delivering quality work, list all your projects for three months.

Divide the list into two groups—one for significant responsibilities and one for those of little importance.

Rate with a score of 1 each job you complete ahead of time. On-time projects get 2 points. Late work gets 3 points.

Then rate the work's quality. If the way you handled the job was initially correct, give yourself an A. If the approach needed modification, take a B. If you missed the mark, give it a C.

If you prioritize well, you should score better on major projects. But if you score better on tasks of little importance, you're spending too much time on inconsequential tasks.

Source: Catherine Bower, editor, *Working Smart,* 1101 King St., Alexandria, Virginia 22314.

Employee Fraud

More companies than ever are being victimized by employee fraud—dishonest acts going far beyond petty theft or embezzlement. And experience indicates that the loss from employee fraud is continually increasing. The best estimates are that the cost of employee dishonesty now amounts to as much as 5% of the Gross Domestic Product.

The varieties of fraud:

To help deal with employee fraud, first learn the various forms it can take. The types of fraud haven't changed much over the years. There's nothing new in stealing—just variations on old methods. *Some of the most common techniques employees use to steal from a business:*

•Lapping. The employee diverts money from the account of a customer. Checks from that customer may go into a bank account maintained by the employee. The employee may steal from a second customer to cover up the first theft.

This type of theft is widespread. But while the computer has made lapping easier to carry out, it also has made it easier to detect.

•Accounts-payable fraud. The employee may falsify payments to real vendors, or may create phony vendor addresses to which company checks are sent. Alternatively, an employee may intentionally overpay an invoice, take the refund from the supplier and pocket it.

•Payroll ghosts. With so many people being discharged from companies, it is simple for someone in a company that is downsizing to keep a discharged employee on the payroll for a week or two after departing.

The stolen pay goes on the discharged employee's W-2 form, but it never gets noticed. The average worker doesn't know whether he/she has worked 27 or 30 weeks.

•Kickbacks. The employee takes bribes or kickbacks from suppliers and vendors.

This is almost impossible to find, because there are no records—the deals are made in cash.

•Inventory fraud. The employee uses company money to place a phony order, or to order more than the company needs. The merchandise is then sold for the employee's gain.

These days, inventory fraud is more likely to be fraud by management trying to make the financials look better than they are.

•Penny-ante fraud. This is all small stuff—submitting phony invoices, inflating personal expense items, etc.

The amounts involved are small, but it is the most common type of employee fraud—and the type that is growing most rapidly.

Mounting a defense:

The most serious problem at most businesses is the ease with which employees commit fraud and get away with it. When people see they can steal and not get caught, they continue to do it.

The best defense against employee dishonesty is to have an experienced fraud auditor or accountant conduct audits for abnormalities on a regular basis. An ordinary audit is done in enough detail so the accountant can determine that the financial statements fairly represent the company's financial condition and results of operations.

A *fraud* audit is extremely detailed, covering cash, payables and inventory on an item-by-item basis. It is done by someone trained in fraud auditing, for the specific purpose of searching out employee fraud.

Not every accountant can do a fraud audit. Look for someone who is a *certified fraud examiner* (CFE). Most big CPA firms have CFEs on staff, or know how to locate one. Or contact the National Association of Certified Fraud Examiners (716 West Ave., Austin, Texas 78701; 800-245-3321).

The trouble with a fraud audit is that its emphasis on detail makes it too costly for many businesses. It's very expensive to go through the books, transaction by transaction. Some very large companies have internal auditors who continually watch for employee dishonesty. The average middle-sized company—doing under $100 million per year in business—ordinarily doesn't have the wherewithal to retain its own auditor.

Whether a company conducts audits or not, it shouldn't ignore additional defense measures such as sound business practices, rigidly maintained internal controls, fidelity bonding for all employees and insurance coverage that protects against the full range of possible fraud.

Even this, however, won't completely eliminate employee dishonesty. Nothing will do that.

But these steps will give the company some degree of protection.

Preventing fraud:

Basic to controlling fraud is understanding that it can exist anywhere—in the shipping room, the accounting office or anyplace where there is something that can be taken and turned into cash.

The key to employee theft is conversion. People must be able to convert the fruits of their labor into dollars. They can do that by simply taking merchandise and reselling it. Or they can do it by falsifying records. The opportunities for employee dishonesty are almost limitless.

Problem: Spotting an employee likely to turn bad is nearly impossible. It's tough to screen out a new employee who might have been fired elsewhere for stealing. Very seldom will someone intentionally give a negative reference.

Usually, the guilty party is an existing employee with an unblemished reputation. Something happens in his/her life that creates a desperate need for money—maybe an illness or some sort of financial pressure. So the employee steals—usually not a lot of money, just a small amount. Then he/she sees how easy it is. Even when the need passes, the employee continues to steal because it was so simple.

Similarly, the company may inadvertently "invite" otherwise honest employees to steal. By leaving a computer unattended or forgetting to secure a cash drawer, the company may tempt even the most well-meaning employees to take what doesn't belong to them.

Caution: Don't rely on supervisors to control employee fraud because frequently it is supervisors, with their more detailed knowledge of the business, who are the perpetrators.

How to cope:

There are many things you can do—short of a full-scale fraud audit—to combat employee fraud…

•Create a business culture that discourages employee fraud. Implement rigid controls, closely monitor the sensitive parts of the business and let employees know they are being monitored.

•Don't break the rules of sound business practice. Management must set the example of honesty if it expects its employees to act accordingly. It takes very little for this example to be compromised.

Example: If you "open" the warehouse on Saturdays—selling to friends or relatives for cash, off the books, that's a secret that can't be kept. That becomes an invitation for employees to steal.

• Know your employees. Watch for signs that an employee is spending more than his/her salary would seem to allow.

• Get fraud insurance in order. The most important thing you can do to protect the company is to buy a fidelity bond. Be sure all your employees are bonded.

Source: Norman W. Lipshie, senior partner, Weber Lipshie & Co., certified public accountants and certified fraud examiners, 1430 Broadway, New York 10018.

How to Hold on to The Best Employees

A very easy way for a company to save money is to keep talented, productive workers from leaving.

The cost of keeping good workers is slight compared with the expense involved with hiring and training new employees.

The most effective measures for keeping good workers are built around respect for employees and rewards for top performance—practices that reinforce employees' commitment to the company.

American Airlines learned this the hard way. The cause of the flight attendants' 1993 strike was not simply a pay dispute but the flight attendants' perception that management took them for granted.

Hire safer:

• Hire only managers who respect lower-level employees. A good way to gauge their attitude is to talk with the receptionists and secretaries who deal with applicants when they arrive for interviews. If an applicant is unpleasant to a receptionist on the day of the interview, it's a safe bet that, if hired, that person will continue to show little respect for subordinates.

• Train managers to give frequent and conspicuous recognition to workers who perform above their job requirements. Above all, make it a rule that compliments be given in public and criticism in private.

Caution: Don't compliment employees in memos unless you want the statements to become part of their personnel files. *Reason:* If you later must fire a worker, he/she may be able to fight the dismissal with a stack of written commendations.

• Reward good ideas. Suggestion-box systems can be very effective. But they backfire if the company fails to acknowledge each suggestion and reward ideas that save money or time.

• Encourage teamwork whenever possible. An overlooked advantage of teams is that they prevent good employees from becoming discouraged when they see a coworker slack off. On a team, productive employees can tell a slacker to shape up. Teams also build familylike pride among members and in the company. Good workers rarely want to leave a supportive corporate family.

• Use performance reviews to motivate, not to criticize. First compliment the employee on what he/she is doing right. Then get a commitment in areas where performance can improve. And ask the worker how supervisors and the company can improve.

This brings employees further into a feeling of corporate family. Instead of being threatened by performance reviews, the reviews make them feel part of the process of moving the company forward.

• Provide competitive salary and benefits. Don't believe surveys that say employees value a challenging job over compensation. Some might, but the majority want to ease the pressure of making ends meet. To keep good people, pay as much as or slightly more than competing businesses.

Then, reward the top performers with bonuses —and dismiss workers who underperform.

• Explain dismissals to survivors in a compassionate way. If the company must lay off a substantial number of workers, it will have to accept a certain amount of demoralization among the survivors. To prevent the drop in morale from causing good workers to jump ship, explain the move honestly and fully.

In the case of individual firings, a company can't go into nearly as much detail, since there may be personal information that it can't legally reveal.

Instead, the appropriate manager should say that the company regretted having to terminate the employee and that the employee has very good qualities that should make him/her successful elsewhere.

Source: Robert Half, author of *Finding, Hiring and Keeping the Best Employees,* John Wiley & Sons, 605 Third Ave., New York 10158. He is founder and former chairman of Robert Half International, worldwide recruiters headquartered at 2884 Sand Hill Rd., Menlo Park, California 94025.

Controlling Unnecessary Interruptions

Control unnecessary interruptions at work with a *point question.* This is a nonthreatening query designed to get to the cause of the interruption. *Examples:* "How can I help you?" "What brings you around today?" "What can I do for you?" The *point question* transfers "ownership" of the conversation to the interrupting person, in effect asking him/her to justify the intrusion—and preventing him from wasting your time.

Source: *The Ten Natural Laws of Successful Time and Life Management: Proven Strategies for Increased Productivity and Inner Peace* by Hyrum W. Smith, CEO, Franklin Quest, Salt Lake City. Warner Books, 1271 Avenue of the Americas, New York 10020.

Speak More Softly

Speak more softly, not louder, when dealing with an *irate* telephone caller. It is natural to try to speak more loudly so the caller can hear you. But this encourages the caller to keep shouting. *Better:* Speak quietly enough so that the caller has to stop talking to hear what you are saying. People always pay attention to a whisper.

Source: *Your Telephone Personality,* 12 Daniel Rd., Fairfield, New Jersey 07004.

Middle Managers: How to Manage Them, How to Motivate Them

Middle managers have been hit heavily by American business's downsizing revolution. The surviving ranks of middle managers—now much thinner—face intense pressure to adjust to the climate of efficiency, high productivity and innovation that downsizing depends on.

Better motivation:

The message to middle managers often doesn't get through because the brass talks in slogans.

Example: "The world is our market." It might sound like a good vision for the company, but the slogan does little to motivate middle managers.

More effective: Include middle managers in off-site meetings where the upper ranks have traditionally acted alone in establishing the company's vision. When managers with day-to-day responsibility have a chance to help shape the vision, they develop a stake in implementing it.

Once middle managers have a stake in making a vision a reality, they can work with senior executives to devise measurable and achievable goals. For some departments, the goals might be numerical. For others, they could be less quantifiable, such as raising the general level of experience in new hires.

Once goals are set, managers must be held accountable. If even one middle manager gets away with not meeting one of the assigned goals, few managers will take the goals seriously.

Coaching and support:

Too often, senior managers who owe their success to a mentor or a coach forget that their own middle rank needs the same support. In today's business world, especially after downsizing, middle managers can rarely excel without effective coaching from above.

Example: A well-known company recently raised its high financial goals, communicated them well to middle managers, provided people with additional training, bought new equipment and established strict systems of accountability. But it still failed to meet expectations because middle managers felt isolated, as though someone had thrown a problem at them and then walked away.

Effective coaching:

• Get to know each manager individually. That doesn't necessarily mean on a personal level, but well enough to gain a clear idea of his/her problems and resources. In that way, you can anticipate problems and give appropriate help when it's needed.

• Share information. When middle managers discover via the grapevine what they should have learned from the boss, they begin to distrust upper management—and perhaps feel betrayed.

• Build trust by being credible. Nothing destroys the trust of middle managers more than seeing a top executive say one thing but do another.

Example: A CEO tells middle managers, "You are our most important asset." Then six months later half of them are callously fired.

Smarter restructuring:

After downsizing, some companies find that top management's message doesn't get through because they haven't always kept the best people. In fact, many businesses are downsizing only because it's the popular thing to do.

But even companies that have a legitimate reason for downsizing face the problem of being sure they're laying off the right people and keeping just the ones they'll need after restructuring.

To solve the problem: Form task forces to take a fresh look at how work can be done, including new processes, new management structures and a new evaluation of the skills that are needed in the managers. *This exercise will show:*

• Whether downsizing is necessary in the first place.

• If it is, what kind of managers will be needed after the restructuring.

Next step: Lay off *all* the managers in the affected areas. Then, the company asks them to reapply for the fewer remaining jobs that now require higher skill levels. In that way, it's possible to weed out those who lacked the skills needed after restructuring.

To maintain trust, take pains to explain the business reasons for the layoff decision. *Also important:* Adequate severance and outplacement assistance. As needed, give survivors additional equipment, staff and other support.

Source: Lynda C. McDermott, president, EquiPro International, Ltd., a strategic and organizational consulting firm, 424 E. 57 St., New York 10022.

Termination Basics—1995

Downsizing the workforce is difficult, regardless of how much experience you've had at it, or how much you have prepared for it.

It is, however, possible to make the process much less painful, as well as to prevent costly litigation and maintain morale in the organization. My firm has counseled hundreds of companies in this difficult task, and in the process has fine-tuned some of the techniques that help managers in almost any termination situation.

Often, the first reaction to being terminated is shock. That is quickly followed by denial, then by anger and then sometimes a desire for revenge.

Next come feelings of self-doubt and depression—"How can I tell my family?" "How will I ever find another job in this economy?"

It is at this delicate point that the company can turn a painful loss experience into a constructive, forward-looking process by providing professional counseling and outplacement services.

The termination process:

The manager should typically begin with a moment or two of courtesies but then get quickly to the point.

Place the decision within a context ("Because of our recent merger, the company has some redundancies…") and then make a clean, direct statement of the decision. Do not equivocate. Leave no room in the employee's mind for doubt or negotiation.

Example: "As you may have heard, John, the company is reorganizing. As a result, a number

of positions are being abolished. I'm sorry to say that yours is one of them, and that a decision has been made to terminate your employment."
Give reasons:

In any downsizing, it's important to stress that performance, career potential or personality were not involved in the termination decision—that this would have happened to anyone who was in that job.

But people who are being terminated have a right to know the reasons for the decision because, among other things, they will have to answer that question when interviewing for another job. Be prepared, too, to explain why your company couldn't find another position for them within the organization.

If you get angry questions, such as "Why are you doing this to me?" or "How did you come to pick me?" reiterate that it is the position that has been eliminated—or that the job requirements have changed. If true, go on to say, "You are a fine person and have done a good job and we will give you an excellent reference." Again, it's helpful for people to know that they will receive competent outplacement guidance.

If discrimination is claimed, say again, "This process of reorganization had nothing to do with you personally. It is an elimination of *functions*."
Severance package:

Next, it's important to review the highlights of the severance package.

Since even the clearest communication may not penetrate when people are upset, it's crucial to also present a *written statement* of the terms and benefits which can be studied later when reality sinks in.

Tell the terminated employee exactly where he/she should go from your office—whether to a certain individual in the benefits or human-resources department or to an outplacement counselor, who should be on premises if possible.

With people who seem confused or dazed, it's a good idea to personally accompany them to the next location. If they have reacted with tears, offer tissues, show compassion and allow them to regain their composure before moving them along to the counseling process.

Key: Every employee is also a member of a group, a work unit or team—and probably also has other friends in the organization. Consider how and when others will be told. Will there be a meeting or an announcement or a farewell party of some sort? Bear in mind that word gets around pretty fast anyway. Try to let departing employees leave with self-respect and dignity intact. But be sure that appropriate outside contacts and coworkers are informed.

Take all necessary steps to protect company assets by getting back company credit cards, securing proprietary data, etc. In cases where computer access is an issue, arrange to have the person's password blocked from the system.

It's usually best if terminated employees don't return to their desks that day. This protects both the company and the employee from unnecessary emotional strain. Arrange for them to come in later when the office is closed and they can be accompanied by someone from human resources. Human resources, rather than the manager doing the terminating, should also be responsible for the routine of collecting company credit cards, keys, etc.

Important: The company should establish a firm policy about post-termination access to the premises and communicate it clearly. Non-employees should not be admitted unless they are accompanied by a designated person.
Traps to avoid:

A termination meeting is not the time for a performance appraisal. Don't be defensive or feel that you must convince the person that the termination is justified. Just state the decision with conviction. Bargaining or even allowing discussion of alternatives like transfers or demotions is a mistake.

Any personal problems with each other that you may have had in the past are not relevant now. They were not factors in the decision and they won't change the outcome.

Whether or not top management has chosen unsuccessful business strategies, avoid getting sucked into criticizing the company. Just listen. Don't agree or disagree. Never shout or argue, even if the other person does. Stay calm.

If someone seems suicidal, as occasionally happens, offer a measured response like "I'm sure you don't mean that…" *but make sure that professional counseling is made available immediately.*

165

No matter how well intentioned, it's not helpful to say, "I know how you feel." Everyone reacts differently and has a right to his/her own feelings.

Avoid the "blessing in disguise" theme, even though that often turns out to be the case after good counseling.

If the person is a friend, reaffirm that friendship by offering to be helpful in the coming weeks and months, but don't bog down in talk about the good old days.

Let the outplacement consultant or human-resources manager take the lead in discussing difficult questions like how to notify family and friends, and where and how to start looking for another job. Just offer to be helpful and available.

Source: William L. Ayers, Jr., The Ayers Group, Inc., a management-consulting firm that specializes in human-resources management and corporate downsizing, 370 Lexington Ave., New York 10017.

Budget-Based Salary Objections

Budget-based salary objections are often real. The company may not be able to afford to pay more. *Alternative:* Negotiate for noncash benefits, such as hours off or additional vacation days. *Helpful:* Try to get an idea of when the employer expects the budget to improve—then negotiate for future compensation.

Source: *The Smart Woman's Guide to Interviewing and Salary Negotiation* by Julie Adair King, president of an Indianapolis-based marketing-consulting company. Career Press, Box 34, Hawthorne, New Jersey 07507.

Motivation for Home Workers

Convince yourself that you're truly "going to work" by establishing an early-morning routine similar to that of someone who works for a company. *Helpful:* Get up at a normal work-

day hour...dress in sharp business clothes... set aside a certain time to arrive in your (home) office to begin the day. *Also:* It may help to get in your car and drive around the block so you feel as if you've "arrived" at the office.

Source: Allan Cohen, editor, *Working from Home,* Box 1722, Hallandale, Florida 33008.

How to Break Free from Corporate Bondage

It's never easy to leave a career in which you've spent much of your lifetime. It's even harder if you've reached a high level of success and are locked in by the golden handcuffs of a large salary, benefits, expense accounts, perks and prestige.

But I've discovered that many people who seem to have it made are really unhappy. *Questions to ask yourself:*

• Do you harbor a secret dream of doing something else?

• Have you thought about your dream— really thought about it?

• Do you think you're too old to make a major change?

• Do you worry about your mortgage and other financial responsibilities?

Reality: In today's world of corporate restructuring and downsizing, more and more middle- and high-level managers are having the decision made for them. Whether or not you have a clearly identifiable dream, if you are in a corporate management position it is smart to seriously consider what you might want to do instead...and how you can go about doing it.

The dream comes true:

In my case, I wanted to be a writer, my dream since I was a child. I'm now following a ten-year path to realize that dream. Although I have several years to go along this path, I've already published two books and 14 screenplays, and I'm working daily on writing projects.

My family life is considerably richer. I'm even making a fairly good living between my writing, teaching continuing education courses about marketing and running a successful international marketing agency.

I've never worked harder, but it no longer seems like work because I really enjoy what I'm doing. When you add up work-related items, such as preparation, travel time and entertaining clients after hours, your job represents a huge segment of your life. Think how happy you would be if you could spend that time doing something you love to do.

Where to start:

Take a few days off to analyze and visualize how it would feel to actually live your dream. Is this what you really want?

Even if you eventually decide not to change careers, this is a valuable exercise. It refreshes your outlook, allows you to reexamine your strengths and weaknesses and lets you fine-tune your goals.

Caution: Be sure that you're not just experiencing mid-life hopelessness borne of extreme fatigue, stress or career stagnation. Maybe it isn't really the industry or the job, but the particular company or people with whom you're working that have got you down or held you back.

Change for the sake of change, without any planning behind it, is dangerous and sometimes leaves behind a trail of family breakups, wasted dreams, substance abuse and severe depression.

Whatever your age, if your dream is merely to become rich or famous as soon as possible, you're more apt to find restlessness and insecurity than happiness.

I find that most dreamers fall into three basic categories:

• Daydreamers, who are always fantasizing but find all kinds of reasons not to actually do.

• Different drummers, who don't talk much about their dreams but just make them happen (entrepreneurs, inventors, scientists, artists), in spite of obstacles and doubters.

• Procrastinators, who have what it takes in terms of skill and talent but keep putting off their dreams until tomorrow. These people need a push and a plan.

Helpful: Write down exactly how you arrived at where you are today, then make a written commitment to leave your current job and try something new.

Dream assessment:

Thorough research is essential to really know what this new career path would entail. It helps to evaluate whether you can live with the downside that accompanies any evolution.

Research is needed to succeed and understand how long attaining the success might take. To find answers to these questions, you'll have to visit the library—and talk to a lot of people who are in the same or similar businesses.

The right stuff:

Ask yourself—and a trusted friend or counselor, but not a member of your family, if he/she thinks you have the aptitude and talent to succeed at your dream. If so, you can always obtain additional education, training and practice.

It's just a matter of analyzing what is lacking and then determining how you could go about acquiring it and how long it will take.

It's also useful to analyze your weaknesses —including any bad habits that may be bothering you.

Consider your family's financial needs (short- and long-term), such as living expenses, insurance, savings and pension plans. Decide what you can cut out.

A certain amount of fear is healthy because it will force you to figure out how to deal realistically with financial problems and other hurdles. But don't let it paralyze you.

The most difficult fears to handle are those (often disguised) of your spouse, family and friends who want to keep the comfortable status quo. Expect this opposition, and don't let it discourage you. If it does, you may not be ready to make the move.

Set a timetable:

While it's important to set a timetable for your plans, don't expect to make your dream come true overnight. You might, for example, take night courses so you can keep working at your current job. If you've been laid off, you may have to take an interim job to tide you over.

If you are working with an outplacement firm, make it clear to the staff that your goal is to try the new endeavor, not repeat the old one. The staff of the outplacement firm may be able to help you assess your goals and get started on the new path.

As you spell out the various elements of your personal game plan, try to start on a self-improvement program that includes proper diet, rest and exercise.

It is also a good time to concentrate on eliminating or reducing bad habits. Get help if necessary. You must be prepared to go after your dream with all of your determination.

Don't depend on luck. Luck requires being well-prepared when opportunity knocks. An action plan means setting specific programs of what, where, when, how and costs. I suggest making detailed lists, even down to the type of new clothing you may need. Use a monthly calendar to schedule each of the activities required in your plan.

Map out one year. At the end of the first month, you will have a better idea of what you can accomplish on a daily and weekly basis without stretching yourself to the limit. You're striving for a lifetime program, not quick burnout.

At the end of six months and again at the end of a year, review your progress and reevaluate on the basis of your experience. Reassess your plan occasionally to make sure that you're not overloading yourself, neglecting your family or lacking needed relaxation.

If events that are beyond your control have caused a temporary detour, don't panic. Write a new plan for the next 12 months, in which you add or delete parts of your original action program. Build on your strengths and cut down the weeds—those things that you no longer need to do.

Source: Michael Dainard, former director of marketing for CBS television stations and, since 1986, president of Michael Dainard Associates, an international marketing agency in New York. He is the author of *Breaking Free From Corporate Bondage,* Dearborn Publishing Group, 520 N. Dearborn St., Chicago 60610.

Better Organization

Keep only those office supplies that you use constantly on top of your desk. Store the rest of your supplies in a nearby drawer or closet... store extra or infrequently used supplies some-where else...scan the contents pages of magazines and periodicals to determine in advance what you might want to read, and tear out and file any articles to read later. Schedule one hour each week to organize, straighten and refine. *Remember:* Only 20% of all filed paper is ever retrieved.

Source: Stephanie Schur, founder of Spaceorganizers (774 Mamaroneck Ave., White Plains, New York 10605) and creator of the video *How to Organize Your Home.*

How to Ask for a Raise Without Getting Fired

When I was in charge of an office of 250 employees, I had the same problems that all executives have, including one of the most difficult challenges—how to compensate employees. It's relatively easy to arrive at appropriate pay for the very best employees. On the other end of the spectrum, there are marginal employees —those who are at high risk for being let go when they ask for an increase in salary.

When I asked borderline employees why they thought they deserved an increase, their answers followed a pattern:

• *I haven't had a raise for more than a year.*

• *Others at this company who do similar work earn more money.*

• *Employees at other companies earn more.*

• *My expenses are going up all the time.*

All of these answers are inappropriate. Not only will they antagonize the person who grants such raises, they can also work against you— making you someone who is not worth promoting or even a layoff candidate. Here are some rules to avoid offending your employer when you ask for a raise:

• Don't threaten him/her or imply that you might resign—unless you're fully prepared to follow through.

• Don't compare your salary with that of others in your company or other companies. Your skills are probably unique, and presenting them as such will improve your chances of getting that raise.

•Let management know that you like the company and your job. And add a true compliment to your boss, one that's not obviously flattery.

•List your achievements in the past 12 months. It might be difficult to remember them all—which is why it is important to write them down as they happen.

•Ask for what you want, and be prepared to compromise.

Key: Understand that *yearning* for a raise is not the same as *earning* a raise.

Source: Robert Half, founder of Robert Half International Inc. and Accountemps (Box 3000, Menlo Park, California 94026), employment specialists in the financial, accounting and information-systems fields. His newest book is *Finding, Hiring and Keeping the Best Employees*, John Wiley & Sons, 605 Third Ave., New York 10158.

Better Career Advancement

Get ahead through observation. *Examples:* See how employees at various levels dress—if you see differences, dress like people at the level one step above yours. Watch what people do at lunch—such as eat at their desks or go out in groups. Try to do what successful long-time employees are doing. In meetings, try to sit close to people one level above you without actually encroaching on their territory. *Bottom line:* Learn how successful employees rise in the firm and try to follow their pattern.

Source: Kathryn Marion, editor, *Reality-Check Gazette,* 10327 Cabin Ridge Ct., Manassas, Virginia 22110.

Overcome Career Block

Overcome career block by tapping into buried interests. These may give you insights into what new jobs or projects might be right for you. *Ask yourself:* What do you know well enough to teach someone else?…Which newspapers and magazines do you read regularly?

…Where do you like to browse?…Which TV shows do you watch?…Who is the one person in the world you would be willing to change jobs with? Think about a job you would *hate* to do and then recast it into a positive form. *Example:* If being a bank teller sounds awful because you'd be indoors in a very structured situation, look for something that would allow you more freedom and flexibility.

Source: Phyllis T. Ritvo, MEd, a career counselor who runs Directions for Change in Brookline, Massachusetts.

How to Beat the Unspoken Rules of the Workplace

All organizations—business, political and educational—operate under *two* sets of rules today.

Formal rules: These are written to offer official guidance and direction to people. Without such rules—clearly stated and universally understood—an organization would degenerate into chaos.

Unspoken rules: These rules are informal but just as important as the formal ones. While they are never outlined in memos, they are universally understood. These rules are based on fear and mistrust and define what one must do to be accepted and get ahead in the organization.

Abiding by the unspoken rules can be even more critical to one's success than abiding by the formal rules…but there is a high price to pay for following these rules to the letter.
Paying the price:

Those who blindly follow the unspoken rules may achieve success—but they frequently lose their individuality, integrity and sense of personal power.

Job dissatisfaction is widespread today, partly because of all the downsizing and restructuring that is taking place in companies and organizations. But most of the dissatisfaction actually stems from the choices people make each day as they knuckle under and obey unspoken rules at any cost so they can keep their jobs.

Knowing when and how to break the unspoken rules—and with whom to break them—is an art that can be learned. In some cases, challenging the unspoken rules can put your job at risk. But they can be broken without openly challenging and threatening the system.

Staying in an environment in which your self-esteem is constantly being eroded and you aren't allowed to be an individual or express yourself can be a major source of stress. You must weigh your need for integrity and self-esteem against your need for financial security.

Breaking the rules:

The eight unspoken rules—and how to break them:

•The boss is always right and should never be challenged.

How to break it: The key is in presenting your thoughts without alienating or threatening the boss. Don't think of it as challenging the boss—or proving that you're right and the boss is wrong. Think of it as presenting a different perspective. Get away from black-and-white thinking. Look for common ground—points on which you agree so you can both walk away winners. The more points you can agree upon, the more open your boss is likely to be to your ideas.

•The boss is there to be served—not to serve.

How to break it: You must believe that you have a right to have your needs met, too. If you think of yourself as a servant with no rights, you're giving away your power. Ask for what you need in such a way that meeting your needs is seen as a benefit to your boss and the organization. Don't confront your boss. *Aim:* Show your boss how you can better meet his/her needs.

•Appearances are more important than reality.

How to break it: Appearances are important and can't be ignored. But appearances that are not backed up by substance will be uncovered. Instead of always thinking, "How will this make me look to the powers-that-be?" be sure to ask yourself regularly, "Is this in the best interests of my department and the company?"

Decisions made only to enhance your image will hurt you eventually. Decisions based on fact, integrity and good judgment will improve your image—and your value to the organization.

•Never trust anyone but yourself.

How to break it: If you can't trust anyone at work, you will become exhausted and isolated. But be careful in whom you put your trust. Blind

trust can be career suicide. So study people—spend time with them…listen to their opinions. Most important, listen to your gut. It's the best judge of whom you can trust.

You don't have to trust many people. Pick a few whom you can trust. Over time, confide in them as you build relationships with them.

•Never display strong emotions or feelings.

How to break it: Emotions are energy in motion. When you can't find appropriate outlets for your emotions, your energy gets blocked.

Don't express emotions inappropriately, like crying when you feel like it or banging your fist on the table. Find healthy ways to express your emotions so you don't feel like a powder keg. This is when your trusted friends come into play. When you feel like you're going to explode, talk to them.

Be direct with people, but don't alienate them. Tell them why you are angry, but remain objective. Speak from the facts instead of making emotional accusations.

•If you make a mistake, you will be punished.

How to break it: Plan the risks you want to take carefully—weighing the cost of failure against the potential benefits of success.

If you make a mistake—or fail at something—be sure it was not from carelessness. Careless mistakes will give you a reputation for being unprofessional. If you always conduct yourself as a professional, when you make a legitimate mistake it will be looked at differently.

Never try to hide a mistake. Tell your boss before he finds out from someone else. Explain that you are going to remedy the situation—and what you plan to do. Never put the blame on someone else.

•Don't be too different from your peers.

How to break it: The key is to distinguish yourself without alienating others. Don't try to be the star. Find subtle ways of letting your accomplishments be known. If you help and support your coworkers and share credit whenever possible, you will establish yourself as a leader. You may not get full credit on any single project, but the real goal is to get people to trust you, help you and see you as a leader. If your coworkers feel you're in their court, they will want to support you.

• Always be gracious and polite to authority figures, even if they don't deserve it.

How to break it: We lose power and self-esteem by kowtowing to the boss—letting him walk all over us. If someone in authority attacks you unjustly, don't just accept it passively. But don't counterattack either. Let him know as politely and objectively as possible that his behavior is not acceptable.

Don't communicate defensiveness or fear, which will encourage a bully to take greater advantage of you. Let your body language communicate that you will not be beaten down by that type of behavior.

Speak from the facts as you know them. State your willingness to cooperate and help others with whatever the problem is. But politely state that you would appreciate it if he would not speak to you in such a derogatory manner.

Source: Diane Tracy, president of Tracy Communications, a management-consulting and training firm that specializes in empowerment, Box 466, Ramsey, New Jersey 07446. She is the author of *Take This Job and Love It: A Personal Guide to Career Empowerment*, McGraw-Hill, 1221 Avenue of the Americas, New York 10020.

Better Meetings

Ask attendees to evaluate the meeting's content by handing out a questionnaire at the meeting's end. *Helpful:* Phrase questions in positive language to encourage constructive responses. *Example:* Instead of asking "What didn't you like about the meeting?" ask "What would you like done differently next time?"

Source: *The Busy Manager's Guide to Successful Meetings* by Karen Anderson, business consultant in Lexexa, Kansas. Career Press, Box 34, Hawthorne, New Jersey 07507.

If You Hate Your Boss

If you hate your boss but not your job, apply for equivalent jobs elsewhere in the firm. If you hate your *job* but not your *boss*, ask him/her if you can get other work to do. If you hate your boss *and* your job but want to stay with the

company, ask Human Resources if you can get other work with a different manager. *If you still decide to leave:* Try to make sure you do not move to a similar situation at your next job.

Source: Robert Half, founder of Robert Half International Inc. and Accountemps (Box 3000, Menlo Park, California 94026), employment specialists in the financial, accounting and information-systems fields. His newest book is *Finding, Hiring and Keeping the Best Employees*, John Wiley & Sons, 605 Third Ave., New York 10158.

Your Dream Career In Today's Tough, Tough World

During the 40 years following World War II, many Americans believed that if they found jobs with large companies, they would find happiness, career growth, lifetime job security—and be well-compensated and well-respected. In today's intensely competitive global marketplace, that dream has changed.

But if you are willing to think realistically about what you want from life and what can and cannot be achieved, you may still enjoy a career that matches your dreams.

Marketplace realities:

Today, more than ever, employers want to see how you boost the company's productivity. If you hope to advance your career or even just keep your present position, it is up to you to show them that you are productive in your job.

Finding how to do that will require time and effort. So take advantage of the opportunities that exist—even in today's economy—to fulfill both your employer's needs and your own. This approach will combine maximum productivity with self-fulfillment—the definition of a dream career.

Identify your dreams:

If you want to achieve your career dreams in today's marketplace, you must first understand clearly what they are—and know who you are.

Unleashing your imagination is the best way to explore what is really important to you and

171

to find out how you really want to spend your life. *Helpful exercises:*

•Imagine that your favorite rich relative just left you $1 million. How would you use it?

•Imagine that you have won an all-expense-paid trip anywhere in the world but you have to decide where to go within the next 15 minutes. Where would you go?

•Imagine that you have been given the use of a huge billboard in the center of town to display any message you want. What would be your message?

Fantasies like these encourage your imagination and reveal truths that would normally be censored by your internal editor when you raise such serious subjects.

Of course, you will not likely live out the fantasies—but thinking about them will give you better insight into what you enjoy doing, help you determine what your dreams really are and translate them into real life.

Example: Mark was an attorney in the legal department of a large corporation that was involved in industries ranging from cellular phones to cosmetics. He felt his career was at a dead end, with no prospects for promotion within his department.

While working on the firm's acquisition of a mining company, his strong moral sense made him put great effort into making sure that the corporation met all the legal requirements for public disclosure of its plans. It made Mark think that he might enjoy working as an executive in the corporation's mining division rather than as a corporate lawyer.

Assess your skills:

Objective: Find a way to use the skills you already possess—or would like to acquire—in the work environment you prefer.

Suggestion: To uncover all your options, review everything you have done in your life. Think of your whole life experience—both professional and personal—as a series of achievements of all kinds. Identify the skills that helped you carry out each one, and write each skill on an index card.

You should accumulate a huge pile of index cards—my clients typically end up with hundreds. As you review them, you will think of activities that match your interests and skills.

Important: Look for new insights, and make sure your self-assessment is realistic by asking relatives, friends and colleagues for their thoughts.

Example: Mark had a long-standing amateur interest in geology that would enable him to quickly master much of the technical material needed as a mining executive. He had also demonstrated leadership and financial skills as chairman of a successful drive to provide computers for his community's grade schools. He now had concrete evidence that he was qualified to be more than a lawyer.

Choose a target:

With a well-founded idea of who you are and what you want, consider the employer's point of view. Ask yourself where your skills and interests would fit best.

Example: Mark had discovered he had a significant skill used in the course of his community service—convincingly motivating community action in town meetings.

Consider lateral moves: If you are reluctant to leave the security provided by your present employer, think of other positions you might fill within the organization.

Today, lateral moves are not regarded as fatal to your advancement. A position somewhere else within your company might provide an environment in which you can exercise the skills you want to emphasize.

Bonus: Both your initiative and greater breadth of experience will make you more visible to higher management when they make promotion decisions.

Speak to a range of people in your organization and its competitors to find out what is going on in the field you are researching and who the people are who make the decisions. Make contacts at trade association meetings and industry conventions.

Study the trade press, and read the newspapers with an eye to events that will affect your company and your chosen area of interest. If the company gives that area a low priority, think of another area of interest—or another company.

Guides to high priority: If your company has a lot of interest in a particular area or operation, it will probably show up prominently in the annual report, CEO speeches and lobbying activities.

Market yourself:

You have chosen the position that you want to fill by seeing that it fits your skills and desires —and you have identified at least one person whose business needs you are well-qualified to satisfy. Perhaps you have even met that person while doing your research. Contact him/her, and explain exactly how you can contribute. Make a specific proposal.

Example: Mark knew that his corporation had acquired the mining company because a planned new coal mine promised huge profits. But top management was now concerned that community opposition would prevent the new mine from opening.

Mark approached the CEO with his plan for winning public support. Based on Mark's previous success in ensuring that the corporation was scrupulous about full disclosure, he was put in charge of the mining division's public information division.

With the effort that you have put in, your proposal should be convincing, and you are on your way to your dream career.

Source: Nella Barkley, a career counselor and president of Crystal-Barkley Corp., 111 E. 31 St., New York 10016. She is the author of *How to Help Your Child Land the Right Job (Without Being a Pain in the Neck),* Workman Publishing, 708 Broadway, New York 10003.

Employee Surveys... The Common Traps

Annual employee surveys are a useful way to discover how employees view the company's strengths and weaknesses. When designing such surveys, avoid these common traps...

•Asking too many questions.

•Failing to ensure anonymity. Employees will hesitate to be truthful unless they are confident that their responses are confidential. Design the survey so that the questions asked are not specific enough to identify individual employees. Never publish employee comments verbatim. If the survey is conducted in-house,

safeguard completed surveys to ensure their confidentiality. Consider using an outside service for data input, compilation and security.

•Failing to custom-design the survey. The survey is best-designed with the organization's needs in mind. Don't use standardized surveys.

•Asking questions that have no purpose. If you already know how employees feel about a subject, don't bring it up in a survey.

•Asking questions that are relevant only to certain employees. Avoid asking questions that apply only to specific departments, work units or locations, or that reflect the biases of individual managers. *Reason:* Employees won't want to see questions that are irrelevant to them.

•Asking too few—or too many—open-ended questions. Open-ended questions are difficult to respond to and are not easy to tabulate and analyze. Don't avoid them entirely, however. A few well-chosen open-ended questions can encourage candid comments.

•Failing to communicate results. Managers need clear guidelines for communicating survey results and discussing them with employees.

•Failing to address problem areas. An employee survey will indicate where action is needed to improve the company's operations. If there is no follow-up, management risks the loss of credibility with employees, and the next survey won't be taken seriously.

Source: H. F. Hunter, president, Hunter-Thomas Associates, a management-consulting firm that conducts employee surveys and manages quality service programs, Box 9784, San Jose, California 95157.

Preventing Workplace Violence

There were more than 1,000 occupationally related homicides in 1992, the most recent year for which statistics are available. In the 1980s, homicide was the third leading cause of job-related fatalities and accounted for 12% of all workplace deaths.

The National Institute for Occupational Safety and Health (NIOSH) has issued several suggestions to help employers prevent work-

place violence…
- •Install good external lighting systems.
- •Use drop safes to minimize cash on hand.
- •Install silent alarms and surveillance cameras.
- •Increase the staff on duty.
- •Train employees in both conflict resolution and nonviolent response techniques.
- •Arrange for regular police checks.
- •Close the business during high-risk hours—late at night and early in the morning.

Source: Margaret Bryant, editor, *Preventive Strategies for Employers*, Jackson, Lewis, Schnitzler & Krupman, 101 Park Ave., New York 10178.

Curtail Talkative Colleagues During Meetings

There are usually some people who cannot wait to share ideas with the group. But letting them dominate may crowd out less-confident colleagues who have excellent ideas…but are hesitant about expressing them. *Effective:* Gently cut off talkative people by complimenting their ideas…then saying that, before they continue, you would like to hear suggestions from some other people.

Source: Barry Lenson, editor, *Personal Report for the Professional Secretary*, 1328 Broadway, New York 10001.

Sick Leave Savings

Fight sick leave abuse by providing only minimal sick leave benefits—just three to five paid sick days annually.

Don't be worried that this will make it hard to attract or retain employees. The company should not want to attract the kind of employees who like to take a lot of sick days.

Better: Recruit motivated employees and give them incentive bonuses based on performance.

Planning: For employees who are truly sick, establish a 70%-of-pay disability benefit, administered by a third-party insurer, that kicks in after only five days—a generous benefit paid for by sick-day savings, that will be used only by those who really need it.

Source: Robert R. Falconi, chief financial officer, Planning Systems Inc., McLean, Virginia, writing in *Employee Benefit News*, 1483 Chain Bridge Rd., McLean, Virginia 22101.

8

The Winning Edge

The Anger Trap And How to Avoid It

When you are angry, your whole body is alert—poised to act decisively. You are at your most powerful—and most aggressive. *And that is just why anger is dangerous.*

Mishandling that power can create havoc—in your personal life and on the job.

Hurt, frustration or fear generally set this power in motion. Most people develop a pattern of anger at a very early age—a pattern that too often is out of control and ineffective.

Always a penalty:

Anger in the workplace is the most difficult anger of all to use in a constructive way. For executives, there is far less room for patience than there is in most personal relationships. If you don't properly manage anger on the job, you risk seriously damaging your reputation and even your career.

Managers may think they don't suffer any penalty for displays of anger toward those who work for them. But victims of unbridled anger do get back at the boss—through absenteeism, being less productive, criticizing the supervisor whenever they have the opportunity or failing to back up the manager when he/she needs support and is most vulnerable.

Straight thinking about anger:

There is no need to be a hostage to your temper. But it is hard work getting your anger under control to work for you rather than against you.

Basics to managing anger:

• When you are angry, you are in a heightened state of awareness. You must find ways to use that energy to identify what is offending, frustrating or frightening you.

• When you're confident that you have discovered the source of the anger, focus the energy you have generated to achieve the results you want.

There are several effective ways to harness anger-related energy. *Examples:*

• Examine yourself honestly to identify...

1. Whether you enjoy being angry. And if that immediate gratification and its short-term gains are worth the long-term losses.

2. How you want your relationship to end up when you express your anger toward another person.

3. How you feel when you explode with anger.

•Write a letter to yourself answering those questions. Read it aloud to yourself at least once a week. *Aim:* To adopt new standards for self-evaluation to regulate your behavior.

•Stay alert to anger developing within yourself when you are involved in transactions or relationships that you know from experience can lead to trouble. The best way to develop this skill is to spend time as each day moves along writing down your feelings. Pick an exact amount of time—at least half an hour. Record the time and date of the entry and write exactly what you are feeling *right then and there.*

Keep an anger diary. Immediately record pertinent facts about every episode of anger. You cannot record your anger day after day without eventually changing the way you behave.

Simple format: When was I angry? With whom? What was my response? Why was I angry? What did I accomplish with my anger? What strategy did I come up with to deal with my anger under these circumstances? Did I implement my plan?

•Delay your response if you see anger coming. Buy yourself time. Consciously refuse to do what you used to do—remembering that it didn't work. *Do one thing:* Think…

1. Why am I angry? What is the hurt, the fear, the frustration? This arms you with information to confront the next question…

2. What do I want from this encounter? What long-term relationship do I want with this person? Now you can move to figuring out an alternate strategy…

3. How can I get what I want? What strategy should I use instead of exploding or sulking or feeling resentful?

Example: You and an employee discuss a task and jointly agree on a deadline for its completion. As the date the assignment is due approaches, you feel yourself getting angry because you are sure the deadline will be missed. You know your problem is explosive anger. Think about what you want to accomplish when the employee announces that he/she needs another day…week…month. Make it clear, for example, that you rely on the employee to get the work of the department done effectively and that you become concerned—even angry—when that is threatened. You both can then use this understanding to come up with mutually acceptable adjustments to the way you work—to avoid problems in the future.

Source: Neil Clark Warren, PhD, a clinical psychologist and author of *Make Anger Your Ally,* Focus on the Family Publishing, Colorado Springs, Colorado 80995. Dr. Warren is a leader of Anger Management Seminars and founder of Associated Psychological Services, 2 North Lake Ave., Pasadena, California 91101.

Almost Everything Is a Negotiation

To be cooperative—or to be competitive—*that* is the question in winning negotiations.

When workers and management bargain over wages, it's usually intensely confrontational. But if the objective is to land a job with a certain company, the smarter strategy may be not to bargain too hard, but to be super-cooperative.

Example: A former student of mine, after telling us about how he had negotiated badly and had probably paid too much for a used convertible, went on to say that the company he wanted to work for had made him a job offer. He was going to accept it, but had the nagging feeling that the salary should be better. He wanted to ask for more money before accepting the job, but didn't want to alienate anyone at the company.

Instead of making an aggressive demand for more money, as most people would do, he simply accepted the job and said how happy he was to be coming to the firm. But, he added, there was one thing troubling him—the starting salary. It seemed low. Could they possibly do something about it? Now he was part of the team and it was their turn to show fairness. A few hours later, they called him back, offering an increase of $5,000.

Lesson: Different situations require different bargaining strategies. Some call for a competitive approach. In other cases, cooperative bargaining works best. It's important to understand the difference and to pick up on subtle changes in a bargaining situation that demand a different stance.

Know your position:

The drive to win is so deeply ingrained that many of us are unnecessarily competitive in negotiating.

Trap: Trying to beat the other person in a negotiation is usually mutually disastrous.

I've seen many people miss golden opportunities for compromise—and mutual gain—because they're afraid their opponent might do better than they will.

Reality: When you negotiate effectively, you and everyone involved can obtain favorable outcomes. It should be a win-win situation. *Key:*

•Know yourself—what do you really want.

•Know the other person. You may never know what he/she really wants, but try to figure it out.

•Know the situation—how you stand vis-à-vis the opposing party—so that you can put forth your position with maximum positive effect.

Often one party begins negotiations with more power than the other. But that can change.

Example: If a car dealer has a quota to meet by the end of the month, he may be more willing to deal on the 29th or 30th.

By contrast, if you really need an agreement, and the other person doesn't, you may have to concede more. Caring less creates a bargaining advantage.

General rule: Try to do the best you can for *you.* Assume the other person is doing the same. But don't insist on beating the other person. Just try to meet your objectives as nearly as possible. You can concede on things that don't matter to you.

Look for the prominent solution:

Though negotiators often fail to recognize it, there's almost always what I call a *prominent solution* in a negotiation—something obvious, familiar or compelling. *Examples:*

•When quizzing groups of people about the best place to meet in Paris or New York, the answers are always heavily skewed to the Eiffel Tower and the Empire State Building.

•Where numbers are involved, people usually choose something round, like 50–50 or

$1 million. If a used car is offered for $10,650, for example, most people say the final price will be $10,000. When the starting price is $2,650, the dominant choice is $2,500. When it is $2,450, $2,000 is the most popular end point.

Similarly, there is often an underlying structure to a negotiation that makes one outcome more obvious and more reasonable than any other.

Whether or not it is perceived by the bargainers, that's often where the negotiations end up.

Strategy: When you recognize that a prominent solution exists or that there is an underlying structure to the bargaining game, work within that structure to your best advantage. You can even formulate your strategy backward, from the most likely final result to your first strategic moves.

Example: If you want to get $10,000 when selling a car, start by pricing it at $10,650. That way, after negotiation, you'll be likely to end up with $10,000. You may even get lucky and get an opening bid for $10,000, in which case you might finally realize $10,300 or $10,400.

Caution: Don't short-circuit the bargaining process, even if you know up front what the prominent solution will be. This is what happened to the president of a company who knew from earlier contract settlements in his industry that the end point of bargaining with the union would be a raise of $1 an hour. To him, this was the prominent solution, but he failed to use it effectively. Anxious to wrap up the talks, he offered the union $1 right off the bat. The union insisted that this was an opening offer and proceeded to caucus, string out negotiations and finally ended up with a much more generous settlement.

Problem: The president didn't play the game of going to the eleventh hour, with both sides conceding a lot. Reciprocating concessions is an extremely strong norm in the collective bargaining game.

Expand information:

From buying a car to negotiating a merger, most people don't do enough research.

Negotiators can always use more information. Good decision-makers (who are better bargainers) are constantly open to new information.

They also pay close attention to nonverbal signals, such as sweaty palms or an unexpected flush. Though sometimes hard to interpret, these can give you a better reading of how your proposals are being received or in what spirit counteroffers are being advanced.

Expect conflict:

Even with friends and family, you should expect conflict in a bargaining situation. But, conflict only jeopardizes the negotiating process if you don't work for a solution.

Caution: Beware of threats—either making or receiving them. If you make a threat and the other person responds in kind, you may find yourself in a dangerous game of chicken. If both of you are stubborn, if your threats are public or if you're worried that your credibility will be shot if you recant, it may be very difficult to back down. As a result, you may both end up getting your worst possible outcomes.

Best: Avoid making threats at all. And, instead of responding aggressively to threats from the other side, try to get the negotiations back on a positive track to a solution.

Source: J. Keith Murnighan, W. J. Van Dusen professor of management, Faculty of Commerce, 2053 Main Mall, University of British Columbia, Vancouver, British Columbia, Canada V6T 1Z2. He is the author of *Bargaining Games: A New Approach to Strategic Thinking in Negotiations,* Quill/William Morrow & Co., Inc., 1350 Avenue of the Americas, New York 10019.

Ten Ways to Reduce Stress

• Understand that you have some measure of control over your own life. People who sit around feeling like victims will never be able to reduce stress because they don't know they can. Take action.

• Make choices to make stress manageable and learn how to think in a positive way. Abraham Lincoln said: "A man is about as happy as he makes up his mind to be." Take responsibility for your own life.

• Make changes in your life...and your daily routine.

• Keep all elements of your being healthy—spiritual, physical and emotional. If more stress comes along you'll have some breathing room.

• Set attainable goals and make practical choices about your life. Stop being a perfectionist. Be realistic. If you continually set unattainable goals, you're creating your own stress.

• Evaluate and identify the sources of stress. Then minimize or eliminate the stresses. If you know that every time you see your sister it drives you crazy, you have to choose either to resolve whatever difficulties you have or stop seeing her.

• Practice things like reducing your debt. Many marriages fail because of fights over money. If you're stressed because of finances, get some financial counseling and learn how to get out of trouble.

• Take time out to play. Do something fun with friends or a crossword puzzle by yourself. Act silly with your grandchildren. Read a book. Play and stress don't easily coexist.

• Learn to say "no" and stop overcommitting yourself. There are only 24 hours in a day. If you've committed yourself to do too much, you'll be so stressed that you can't finish. The only way to stop overcommitting yourself is to know what you're really committed to.

• Don't be afraid to seek emotional support from family and friends.

Source: Connie Neal, author of many self-help books including *52 Ways to Reduce Stress in Your Life,* Thomas Nelson Publishers, Box 141000, Nashville 37214.

How to Teach Yourself Anything—How to Do Well on Any Test

A super-high IQ is not essential to learn rapidly and efficiently. Whether you're in graduate school, taking continuing education courses or trying to assist a child in high school or college, there are studying techniques that will result in improved understanding, higher test scores and better grades.

Key: Take an active role right from the start. Don't approach the assigned reading passively and assume that if you simply pass your eyes over your textbook and notes enough times, you'll absorb it. Engage in an ongoing dialogue with the reading material.

Key questions to ask yourself:

• *Why I am reading this?* Before you begin reading, ask yourself if you are reading for general ideas or specific facts. And—how deeply you have to probe the material.

You can cut your reading time dramatically if you realize that you can skim much of the book—even skip parts that you will never need to know.

• *What do I already know about the topic?* Before you begin, spend a few minutes jotting down what you know already, what you think about it and what you would like to know.

This will prime you to ask yourself relevant questions as soon as you begin to read the material and you will probably be surprised when you realize how many ideas come from your background knowledge.

Further, thinking for yourself before you give the author a chance to influence you will improve your ability to form original insights and opinions.

Bonus: This exercise gives you practice at quick responses to new material, a valuable skill when you are faced with unexpected test questions or sudden real-life problems that you haven't studied.

After these preparations, skim the whole book. Pay particular attention, though, to the introduction, table of contents and chapter summaries and glance at the author's biography. All this information will help you answer the next question.

• *What's the big picture?* Once you begin reading, find out the main points and ideas conveyed by the book so that you don't get bogged down in details during the next stage, when you actually read the book in depth.

Your aim is to sustain an active dialogue that helps you learn as you read. Learning new material is often hard work that stretches your mind. The process becomes more enjoyable when you approach it like a game.

• *What is the author going to say next?* Try to anticipate the next step in the discussion. Even if you are learning something completely new, you can probably make a reasonable guess.

Example: If you are studying chemistry—a subject about which you know nothing—and you come to a section on "strong acid reactions," you can anticipate that the next topic will be something like "weak acid reactions"—even if it isn't, you will be more interested in following the discussion than you would if you were just reading passively.

Absorbing new material will become even easier when you answer the next question.

• *What are the expert questions?* These are the questions that are typically asked about the subject you are currently studying.

Example: Geology books repeatedly answer questions like "What is this made of?"; "What are its properties?"; "Where is it found?"; "By what process was it formed?" History textbooks deal with other questions like "When did it happen?"; "Who was involved?"; "What were the causes?"; "What were the effects?"

When you know the pattern of these questions, you can anticipate a lot of what will appear in tests.

• *What are my own questions?* To study more effectively, exercise your curiosity by asking general subject-related questions that interest you. Try to answer the questions; don't be afraid to guess.

Example: If you are studying financial planning and read that the amount available to a person in a case study for investment is the difference between earnings and expenditures, ask yourself when is it appropriate to increase earnings and when is it appropriate to reduce spending.

As you go further into the subject, you will find some of your answers are right, some are close and some are way off. Whatever the case, thinking inquisitively and comparing your ideas with the facts will help you master the material as it becomes more familiar and personally meaningful. As you read on, the next three questions will help you take notes that are useful to review the subject and study for tests.

• *What information is important?* That will, in large measure, depend on why you are reading the book. Don't waste time and effort compiling notes that are irrelevant to your real aim. In general, about 20% of the book contains 80% of the useful information.

•*How can I summarize this information?* The shorter you can make your notes, the more useful they will be, especially if you are preparing for a test.

Important: Use your own words. If you are just copying phrases from the text, there's a good chance you don't really understand it.

•*How can I organize the information?* Try grouping it in ways different from those of the text. See what connections you can find, play with the material, summarize with diagrams and sketches, acronyms, rhymes and anything that makes sense to you and helps you remember it. The more you exercise your brain to organize the material, the better you will be able to understand and recall it. Aim to condense the whole subject you are studying until it fits on one page, then study that page until you can reproduce it from memory.

You are now ready for the big test. All the thinking and questioning you did while reading has prepared you to handle any question you are likely to get. Looking beyond the immediate payoff of passing the test, active learning stimulates your continuing intellectual growth.

Source: Adam Robinson, cofounder of the Princeton Review, a program that helps students do well on standardized tests, 2315 Broadway, Third Floor, New York 10024. He is the author of seven books on education, most recently *What Smart Students Know: Maximum Grades, Optimum Learning, Minimum Time,* Crown Publishers Inc., 201 E. 50 St., New York 10022.

Now Is a Very Good Time To Reinvent Your Life And Escape Lifetraps

Many people go through life repeating the same self-destructive behaviors. They may keep forming attachments to the wrong people or sacrifice themselves so much to others that they neglect their own needs or regard themselves as unworthy, no matter how much they achieve.

While these people say that they would like to live more fulfilling lives, they seem unable to change these patterns, which I call *lifetraps.*

Lifetraps are developed in response to emotional damage caused during childhood. Repairing that damage requires three steps:

•Learning to recognize the patterns.

•Understanding what their origins were in childhood.

•Working determinedly to confront and change the destructive behavior.

Origin of lifetraps:

Lifetraps begin when our parents or others stronger than ourselves repeatedly mistreat us in some way. We become emotionally accustomed to the situations, no matter how unsatisfactory they may be. Then, as adults, we continue to create similar situations because that is all we know.

Example: Heather's parents, Holocaust survivors, were terrified that something might happen to their daughter and discouraged her enjoyment of everyday activities by continually warning her of remote dangers like being trapped in the subway, drowning or pneumonia.

Result: At age 42, Heather was a self-imposed prisoner in her own home, dependent on tranquilizers and paralyzed by fear of the outside, and her husband was losing patience.

Eleven common lifetraps:

Lifetrap: Vulnerability. Do you live in fear that disaster—whether natural, criminal, medical or financial—is about to strike? Do you tend to exaggerate the danger in everyday situations? As a child, you were probably overprotected by parents who constantly warned you about dangers.

Lifetrap: Defectiveness. Do you feel flawed —like there is something wrong with you? This is found in those who were constantly criticized as children and never given respect. As adults, they still expect rejection and, therefore, fear love.

Lifetrap: Subjugation. Do you sacrifice your needs and desires in favor of other people's needs for fear that they will reject you or because you will feel guilty if you please yourself instead? This lifetrap stems from childhood subjugation or from a parent who was needy.

Lifetrap: Unrelenting standards. Do you always strive for unrealistically high standards and never feel satisfied with yourself or others? You were probably told as a child that nothing you did was good enough and that anything less than the best was failure.

Lifetrap: Entitlement. Do you feel that you should have whatever you want right now? Impatient adults who disregard others were likely spoiled children who never learned self-discipline.

Lifetrap: Emotional deprivation. Do you feel that nobody truly understands or loves you? This lifetrap affects people whose parents gave them inadequate nurturance. As adults, they tend to be attracted to others who are cold and ungiving or may even act that way themselves. In either case, they form relationships that only fulfill their negative expectations.

Lifetrap: Failure. Do you believe your achievements are inadequate? This lifetrap develops in children who are constantly told—often by their fathers—that they are inferior and are tagged stupid, lazy and untalented. As adults, they tend to act in ways that make them fail, and they cannot admit or identify their actual successes.

Lifetrap: Abandonment. Are you constantly fearful that those close to you will desert you—or die? These fears are a response to loss or separation from a parent at an early age or to an emotionally remote mother or father. People caught in this lifetrap are drawn to partners who are likely to abandon them, and their fear often makes them cling so tightly that they drive partners away.

Lifetrap: Mistrust. Do you expect to be hurt or abused? Mistrustful adults were often abused—physically, sexually or psychologically—during childhood. As adults, they are drawn to abusive or untrustworthy partners, and with good partners, they may themselves be angry or abusive.

Lifetrap: Dependence. Do you feel unable to handle everyday events and problems without a lot of help? This develops in those who were made to feel incompetent whenever they tried to demonstrate independence during childhood. As adults, they seek out strong figures to rule their lives and shrink from showing any initiative.

Lifetrap: Social exclusion. Do you feel different from other people or ill at ease in group surroundings? As a child, you may have felt rejected by others because of some difference. As an adult, though you might feel comfortable in intimate settings, you still may feel uncomfortable in groups.

How to break free:

You can escape from lifetraps. Negative patterns formed in childhood can be changed, provided you make a conscious decision to confront your problem. But you must first decide what positive life goals you are seeking.

When you identify your own needs and aspirations—not those forced on you as a child—you will realize how the negative patterns locked in by your lifetraps prevent you from fulfilling your goals. Then you are ready to change. Steps:

• Identify and address the childhood source. Try to relive the pain you felt as a child—imagine you are that child once again, experiencing a particularly painful event. As a mature adult, reassure your inner child that there are other ways to cope.

Example: Danielle, trapped in the abandonment pattern, had a father who ran away and an alcoholic mother who paid little attention to her. She recalled a typical childhood scene when her mother was drunk and Danielle was trying vainly to get her attention.

The adult Danielle imagined herself entering the scene, taking the child Danielle on her lap and telling her, "Don't worry. Your parents aren't here when you need them, but I will stay with you and help you come out okay."

• Express your pain. Write a letter expressing your feelings to the parent or person who helped cause your lifetrap, even if you tear it up or put it away in a drawer.

• Break the pattern. Identify specific examples of negative behavior that you repeat frequently and work on changing them, one at a time.

Example: Heather, whose vulnerability lifetrap was discussed earlier, noted that before she went to sleep at night, she checked every possible source of danger—the children's room, garage, stove, microwave, toaster, even the hair dryer—five times.

With thought and effort, Heather learned how to estimate more realistically these and other fears of remote risks that were trapping her. She gradually began to engage in more activities, which improved her marital relationship and allowed her to enjoy life.

Important: Don't be afraid to ask for help from friends or therapists.

•Confront yourself. Look realistically at your behavior, write down specific ways in which you surrender to your lifetrap, then use rational thought to counteract them.

Example: Frank, trapped in mistrust, was intensely suspicious of his wife, Adrienne, and constantly accused her of betraying him. When asked to list the evidence, he could cite only one specific circumstance—before they were married, Adrienne had lunch with an old boyfriend without telling Frank. Adrienne had long since explained it was only to say good-bye to the former boyfriend. When he looked at this event realistically, Frank realized that his suspicion was unjustified.

Helpful: Write a reminder on a flash card explaining why the lifetrap is false. Put it in your wallet, and consult it frequently.

Example: After Danielle realized her fears of abandonment were unrealistic, she wrote a flash card saying, "It's not true that everyone will abandon me. I just feel that way because when I was a child my parents abandoned me."

•Keep trying. Breaking a lifelong pattern of behavior is not easy, but the rewards make persistence well worth it.

Source: Jeffrey E. Young, PhD, founder and director of the Cognitive Therapy Centers of New York City and Fairfield County, Connecticut. He is a faculty member of the Department of Psychiatry at Columbia University in New York and author of *Reinventing Your Life: How to Break Free of Negative Life Patterns,* Dutton, 375 Hudson St., New York 10014.

For More Out of Life

If you slow down, you'll enjoy life more. *Key moves…*

•Drive at least five miles per hour slower. Try a new route or simply notice the old one more.

•Take a moment before eating. Say grace or just sit quietly. This reminds us to notice our meal instead of wolfing it down.

•Spend five minutes in your driveway before entering your house. Shift from work to home by listening to music or taking deep breaths.

•Shower after work.

•Wait a few rings before answering the phone.

•Honor the process itself. Slow down, do just one thing and allow yourself a sense of accomplishment.

Source: Stephen Rechtschaffen, MD, cofounder and president of the Omega Institute, an educational retreat center in Rhinebeck, New York.

The Art and the Science Of Making a Complaint

When Martha Crawley, a financial analyst, was studying at the Yale School of Organization and Management in 1992, she purchased a Northgate personal computer that turned out to be a lemon. She did what was logical—she called the company's technical support line… and called…and called again.

Instead of giving up, Ms. Crawley got smart. "It suddenly occurred to me, 'Who has the most interest in keeping me happy?' The company's salespeople, of course. I got through immediately to the sales staff, and the replacement part I needed was in my hands within three days."

A creative approach like Ms. Crawley's goes a long way toward getting help from a company that has sold you a problem. The following are some more guidelines for successful complaining, and a list of whom to call when things go wrong.

Begin at the beginning:

If you are complaining about a product, start by contacting the company. To complain about a service or a nonresponsive company in your state, contact the state's consumer protection agency (look in the government listings in the telephone book). As for the state's attorney's office and the local Better Business Bureau, they will want a record of your complaint to pursue the problem for the public good, but they will not act as your personal problem-solver. Any complaint about a merchant or service provider that requires a city license (for example, taxi drivers, dry cleaners) should be reported to your mayor's office.

Resources:

The *Consumer's Resource Handbook* lists the addresses of several hundred consumer representatives and federal and state agencies that handle consumer complaints. It is available in most libraries, or you can get a free copy by writing to the Consumer Information Center, Dept. 592Z, Pueblo, Colorado 81009.

Another valuable resource is AT&T's directory of toll-free numbers for virtually every business that has any dealings with consumers. To purchase it, call 800-426-8686. A call to your library's reference section can yield a company's phone number and address from *Standard & Poor's Register of Corporations, Directors and Executives*.

Be prepared:

Before you make any calls or write any letters, gather all the necessary documentation. Know the model number of any appliance and dig the warranty out of the kitchen drawer, along with the sales receipt. When you call the company, record the name of the person you talk with and keep careful notes on what was said and how many calls you made before your call was returned.

Knowledge is power:

Know your rights as a consumer before you begin the complaint process. Ralph Charell, author of *Satisfaction Guaranteed* (Linden Press, 1985), offers the following advice: "Call the state or federal agency that handles your type of complaint, and explain to the receptionist that your problem is extremely legalistic and you'd prefer to speak directly with their on-staff counsel. Most of the time, you'll be referred directly to the person most able to help you.

"Ask the attorney if he/she could copy for you any laws that directly outline your rights in this case. Also ask whether you can add his name to the list of people who will receive copies of all correspondence about this complaint. You may get faster results from a company when they see that you've already gotten an attorney from the state's Consumer Protection Agency involved."

Keep cool:

"State simply and reasonably what has happened and how you'd like it resolved," says Barry Reid, director of the Georgia Governor's Office of Consumer Affairs.

Escalating:

Be prepared to escalate. "If it's clear you're being stonewalled, announce where you plan to go next in your hunt for satisfaction," Mr. Charell says. "Reporting the problem to state or federal agencies or even contacting the local news media may well be enough to make sure your claim receives attention."

Special help:

•Credit cards. Bankcard Holders of America, 703-481-1110, provides pamphlets that outline your rights as a credit-card consumer and that help guide the complaint process.

•Travel-agent trauma. The American Society of Travel Agents, 703-739-2782, or the United States Tour Operators Association, 212-944-5727, will mediate if the troublesome agent is a member. If not, your state's consumer protection agency can help.

•Car trouble. The Center for Auto Safety (2001 S St. NW, Suite 410, Washington, DC 20009) can help direct your complaint in the right direction. The National Automobile Dealers Association, 703-821-7000, and the Better Business Bureau's Auto Line (check with your local chapter) provide referrals for mediation for consumers with complaints about cars. Each group handles complaints about a different group of car makers—call for details.

•Mail order. Contact the Direct Marketing Association's Mail Order Action Line, 212-768-7277.

•Stockbrokers. Complaints about a stockbroker should be made to his/her brokerage house, the National Association of Securities Dealers, 212-858-4000, and the Securities and Exchange Commission, 212-748-8053.

Register your gripe about a financial planner with the following trade group: International Board of Standards and Practices for Certified Financial Planners, Inc., 303-830-7543.

Pension or mutual-fund managers must be registered with the Securities and Exchange Commission, 212-748-8053, which handles complaints related to them.

Your state's Board of Accountancy (check state listings in the phone book) should hear about any troublesome certified public accountant.

•Home improvement. Contractors should be licensed by the state. Call your state's consumer protection agency with complaints.

•Insurance. Your state insurance commission will hear your complaint. The National Insurance Consumer Organization, 703-549-8050, can provide you with phone numbers for your state commission.

•Real estate. Problems should be referred to your state's regulatory body.

•Medical mess-ups. Direct complaints to your state's medical licensing board. You can also consult the Medicare Telephone Hotline, 800-638-6833, which can refer you to your state Medicare agency.

And...

Consumer advocacy groups like the Consumer Federation of America, 202-387-6121, and the National Consumers League, 202-639-8140, may not handle your complaint directly, but they'll tell you whom to turn to.

Some government offices that handle complaints are the Consumer Product Safety Commission, 800-638-2772, the Food and Drug Administration, 301-443-4166, and the Federal Trade Commission, 202-326-2222, which deals with unfair and deceptive trade practices or advertisements and complaints about funerary services or used cars.

Source: *The New York Times.*

Get Rid of "Should" Statements

Get rid of "should" statements by asking who says you should do it. This makes you aware that you are criticizing yourself unnecessarily. Once you realize you are making your own rules, you can change them. Reformulate "should" statements into more realistic, less upsetting ones. *Example:* Instead of "I should be able to make my wife happy," say, "It would be nice if I could make her happy."

Source: *Feeling Good: The New Mood Therapy* by David Burns, MD, psychotherapist and University of Pennsylvania professor. Avon Books, 1350 Avenue of the Americas, New York 10019.

Get More Out of Your Dreams— Skills for Unlocking Dreams' Secrets

Dreams can be a rich resource for creativity, decision-making, problem-solving and self-understanding.

We actually do much of our information processing at night. Dreaming helps us integrate emotional and intellectual material from the day —without the defensiveness that characterizes our waking thoughts. Because we're more honest with ourselves when we are asleep, we're often more insightful as well.

Recalling dreams:

You may not remember your dreams, but that doesn't mean you didn't have any. Everyone dreams at least four times a night. You can learn to recall your dreams by trying to "catch" them first thing in the morning.

Opportunity: Keep a pencil and pad by your bed. Jot down the date each night before you go to sleep. Immediately after waking up in the morning, write down a few lines about whatever is on your mind—even if all you write is, "There is nothing on my mind." Within a week or two, you'll find that you're remembering plenty of your dreams.

Using dreams to solve problems:

Everyone has had the experience of "sleeping on a problem"—and waking up with the solution. We can make this process more deliberate by practicing what I call *dream incubation.* Here's how you can do it:

Before you go to bed, write down a one-line phrase that clearly states an issue you want to understand better, a problem you'd like to resolve or the kind of idea you need.

Don't try to solve the problem at this time. Turn out the light and repeat the phrase over and over—as calmly as though you were counting sheep—until you fall asleep. *Bonus:* This will also help you fall asleep more quickly.

As usual, when you wake up, write down what's on your mind. Sometimes the answer will be straightforward—in the form of a simple idea rather than a dream.

The Winning Edge

People have used dream incubation to find ways of resolving conflicts with a friend or colleague, streamlining office paperwork, turning around a marketing campaign and coming up with ideas for a presentation.

Other answers may require more interpretation. You might have a dream that helps you understand the situation better, even if you don't have the information to solve it completely. Or your dream may reframe the question. In rare cases, the dream incubation may not work—if another pressing problem comes up at the same time.

With my clients, I have found that dream incubation leads to helpful insights as much as 95% of the time. It sounds hard to believe, but it's true. Interpreting your dreams:

Many people think of dream interpretation as a system of rigid Freudian symbols. Sigmund Freud and Carl Jung were on the right track in taking dreams seriously, but they drew on their cultural prejudices and attached specific meanings to various dream images.

Actually, each individual's dream metaphors are very private and personal. I encourage people to dismiss their preconceptions about dream symbols and discover for themselves what they think about the images in their dreams. It's not necessary to analyze every detail of a dream in order to understand it. Record the main ideas and themes.

Then set up a *dream interview* with a friend, a therapist—or even yourself as interviewer—to clarify the dream's meaning. *The dream interview has three major steps:*

•Description. Describe each of the major elements—people, animals, objects, setting, action and feelings—in the dream as if you were describing them to someone who comes from another planet and has never heard of them. If you are doing a self-interview, you might find it helpful to write down the descriptions the first few times.

•Bridge. For each element, ask yourself, "Is there anything in my life—or anything about myself—that's like this figure or action in my dream, which I describe as…?"

•Summary. Tie together what you've learned by reviewing each description and its bridge. Think about how the dream as a whole could be a parable about your life.

To use the insights you've gained, consider taking a fourth step:

•Action. Reread your dream several times, and keep it in mind during the day. Your dream may give you the insight and courage to make important changes.

Caution: Never act based on a dream without first evaluating the option in your conscious mind. Dreams aren't commands from the supernatural—at best, they're new ways of viewing issues. Any action you take based on a dream insight should also make perfect sense in waking life and should seem so obvious that you can't believe you didn't think of it before.

Common dream themes:

Though each person's dream symbolism is highly individual, certain themes often have connotations that are common to many people. *Examples:*

•The examination. In the dream, you're about to take an important test and you haven't studied all semester or you can't find the examination room. In waking life, you may be facing a challenge for which you don't feel prepared.

If you are prepared, the dream may reflect simple anxiety. But it could also be a warning that you need to take steps to meet the challenge. Another possibility is that you're living under such pressure that you never feel quite ready for anything. You may need to reevaluate whether you want to keep functioning that way.

•Falling. Dreams in which you are falling often have to do with loss of control. Are there areas in which you're out of control? Does this present a danger to your career or a personal relationship?

•Having sex with a surprising partner. This doesn't usually mean that you harbor a secret attraction for the person you dreamed of making love with. More often, when you describe your dream partner, you'll find you're describing some aspect of yourself or of your real-life partner.

Source: Gayle Delaney, PhD, codirector of the Delaney & Flowers Center for the Study of Dreams, 337 Spruce St., San Francisco 94118. She is the author of *Breakthrough Dreaming*, Bantam Books, 1540 Broadway, New York 10036, and *Sexual Dreams*, Fawcett Columbine, 201 E. 50 St., New York 10022.

Communication Barriers

Being aware of the barriers to communication will help you overcome them.

We live in unique, private worlds of personal experience. Nearly everyone is insecure to some extent—so when we feel threatened, we tend to react with blame and self-defense.

Everyone has trouble handling strong feelings. Feelings are facts to the person experiencing them.

We perceive power imbalance in difficult communications, but rarely confront issues of power directly.

Source: *The Power of Ethical Persuasion* by Tom Rusk, MD, associate clinical professor of psychiatry, University of California, San Diego. Viking, 375 Hudson St., New York 10014.

Lessons in Life from George Washington

George Washington, the first president of the US, taught Americans what to expect from their leaders. He set an example that has served the nation well for more than 200 years. Washington's personality and behavior can teach us many lessons—in statesmanship and also in life.

Strength:

Washington stood 6 ft. 3 in. tall, head and shoulders above most of his countrymen. At that time, the average American male was 5 ft. 6 in. tall, about three inches shorter than now.

Washington had huge hands and took pride in his physical strength. He put that strength to good use throughout his unusually active life. He was a businessman and farmer, soldier and statesman—often simultaneously. But he recognized the distinction between strength and force.

Example: When Washington campaigned for election to the Virginia State Assembly in 1755, one of his speeches offended a proud man named William Payne. The hot-tempered Payne grabbed a hickory branch and knocked the much bigger Washington to the ground. The next day Washington visited Payne's favorite tavern and demanded to see him. Payne thought he was going to be challenged to a duel. Instead, Washington apologized, retracted his offending comment and asked to shake hands in friendship.

Lesson: The true test of strength is not indulging your natural aggressive instincts but being able to conquer them.

Self-improvement:

As a youth, Washington wanted to become a member of the fashionable Virginia aristocracy and win fame and fortune. He observed very closely the way his high-placed friends and relatives acted and dressed. And he read widely to make up for the deficit in his skimpy formal education.

After he inherited a substantial estate at Mount Vernon, Virginia, from a relative and then came into wealth in 1759 by marrying Martha Custis, the richest woman in Virginia, Washington worked to improve the estate by experimenting with new agricultural techniques and machines, and tested 60 different crops.

As he matured, Washington combined his own ambitions for material advancement with continuous efforts to develop his own character.

Example: Washington had a fierce temper that he struggled his entire life to control. As president, one of his worst moments came when he received news of the fate of an army expedition sent to subdue a group of warring Indian tribes in Ohio. Because of the ineptitude of Major General Arthur St. Clair, who commanded the expedition, two-thirds of the 1,400 men had been killed or wounded.

Washington's immediate reaction was a furious outburst of swearing. But within a few minutes, he controlled his temper and declared that St. Clair would be given a fair hearing.

Lesson: Before you can lead others well, you must learn to lead yourself.

Price of fame:

As president, Washington was probably the most famous man of his time. As a general, his small army of colonials defeated the mightiest army in the world. As a statesman, he was charged with leading a newborn nation based on the unprecedented idea of the freedom of the individual.

Everywhere Washington went, he was met by his countrymen's adulation and foreigners' curiosity. He accepted his historic role but suffered because he was unable to enjoy a private life—outside of the one with his closest family members.

Example: Washington's adopted granddaughter, Nelly Custis, described how he would laugh heartily when she described her youthful pranks. But her friends—and even Washington's relatives—were so awed by him that they were afraid to laugh or speak naturally in his presence. When Washington entered a room full of children who were enjoying a lively conversation, they would often be struck dumb. He would stay for a short while and then leave, frustrated and disappointed.

Lesson: Fame is a mixed blessing. A small amount gratifies the ego…but in large doses, it makes life difficult.

Humility:

Washington's military exploits against the French and Indians made him well-known when he was still in his 20s.

However, he was acknowledged as the leader of the American cause against the British 20 years later because of the practical economic measures he sponsored…and the judgment he showed as a delegate to the Continental Congress.

After being unanimously chosen as commanding general of the new Continental Army in 1775, Washington left the meeting room, telling Patrick Henry: "From the day I enter upon the command of the American armies, I date my fall and the ruin of my reputation."

Before his first election to the presidency in 1789, he explained his ambition to "live and die on [his] own plantation." He reluctantly agreed to run for a second term only when it became clear that he was the only person who could hold the country together.

Washington resolutely refused a third term, setting a precedent broken only by Franklin D. Roosevelt and now prohibited by a constitutional amendment.

After he left office in 1797, Washington returned to his beloved Mount Vernon to live the farming life he had always wanted. A constant stream of admirers visited and each was impressed by the same character traits.

Example: English comedian John Bernard, touring the young United States in 1798, came across an overturned carriage with a woman lying beside it, unconscious, on a rural Virginia road. Bernard saw an elderly man straining to help the woman and free the carriage from the half-ton of luggage burying it.

After they had finished their work, the elderly man invited Bernard to recover at Mount Vernon and he realized that the savior was George Washington. Bernard was impressed by Washington's thoughtful remarks—but even more by his behavior, so different from that of most country gentlemen, who would have sent their servants to help. The former president had pitched in himself.

Lesson: Greatness is measured by action, not reputation.

Source: Richard Norton Smith, author of *Patriarch: George Washington and the New American Nation,* Houghton Mifflin, 215 Park Ave. S, New York 10003. He is former director of the Herbert Hoover Presidential Library and now executive director of the Ronald Reagan Center for Public Affairs in Simi Valley, California.

To Ease Mild Depression

Change your environment if certain settings make your mood worse…seek family counseling to resolve conflicts in close relationships…engage in a pleasurable activity every day…get moving—even a 10-minute daily walk can help…join a support group for depressed people.

Source: Robert Guynn, MD, chairman of psychiatry, The University of Texas Medical School in Houston, reported in *The University of Texas Lifetime Health Letter,* 7000 Fannin, DCT 12.012, Houston 77030.

The Simple Secret of Sabotaging Self-Sabotage

If we routinely fall short of our goals and/or make decisions that interfere with our personal, professional or financial growth and/or feel inadequate to meet the challenges in our daily lives—we may be victims of our own self-defeating behaviors.

Self-defeating behaviors are responses that originally protected us and helped us to cope with life but which now work against us.

Example: A child who is subjected to excessive criticism learns to keep a low profile—to avoid notice or possible derision. Such a child is apt to mature into a painfully shy adult, incapable of making friends or achieving career goals.

By coming to understand these negative patterns and the purposes they once served, we can learn to replace our destructive behaviors with constructive ones.

Variety of self-defeating behaviors:

The average person in our culture regularly indulges in a dozen or so self-defeating behaviors.

These range from serious threats to health, such as smoking or drug abuse, to more subtle forms of self-sabotage like perfectionism, procrastination, hostility, compulsive worry or shyness.

Displaying a self-defeating behavior does not mean you're "sick." It simply means that you're still being controlled by negative external forces that have been internalized—family members, church, school, etc. These institutions are too often sources of criticism, prejudice, unrealistically high expectations and even abuse.

We may have been victims of these environmental influences earlier in our lives. But as adults, we victimize ourselves—by continuing to behave in ways that are no longer helpful.

Dangerous patterns:

Because these destructive patterns are learned and reinforced unconsciously, it's sometimes hard to spot the danger they pose. *Two powerful forces keep these destructive patterns alive:*

• A promise of protection. For example, you might think to yourself, "If I worry all the time, I'll be prepared when disaster strikes."

• Fear. This is often expressed as an almost superstitious thought—"If I stop worrying, disaster will surely strike."

Unfortunately, the behavior doesn't deliver on the promise...and people wind up being ruled by the fear.

Example: Chronic worry undermines both your health and your enjoyment of life. When bad things do happen, you're too tied up in knots to deal with them effectively.

Five steps for changing self-defeating behaviors:

Step 1: Identify the behavior. We'll continue to use the example of compulsive worry.

Step 2: Identify the situations that trigger the behavior. You may feel as if you fret constantly. But give the matter some thought and you may notice that you worry only under certain circumstances—for example, when you're trying to fall asleep, when your child comes home late from school or when a major project is due at work.

Step 3: Observe how you build the behavior. Self-defeating behaviors aren't floating around in space waiting to attack us. We create them by following a specific pattern of thoughts and behaviors. Breaking down the parts of this sequence can help us to regain control.

There's always a split-second between the triggering situation and the moment we begin to construct the behavior.

In this instant we choose to think a self-defeating thought, focus on that thought and begin behaving so as to reinforce the thought.

Example: You come home early from work and are enjoying the afternoon paper. *Trigger:* You glance up at the clock and notice that your 13-year-old daughter is 15 minutes late. A split second later you think that something terrible may have happened to her.

You may also hear an inner voice saying, "If I continue to enjoy myself, and something awful does happen to her, it will be my fault."

Panic sets in, and you imagine all of the horrible possibilities—"What if she's been mugged, kidnapped, hit by a car?"

Finally, you cement the behavior by disowning it—you find a way to shift the responsibility for your reaction to a source outside yourself: "If only she would call when she's going to be late, I wouldn't feel this way."

It's nearly impossible to change this pattern once it's been set in motion—one step follows automatically on the heels of another. But—by repeatedly observing the sequence of mental events, you can learn to break this pattern of behavior in the future.

What once happened automatically will gradually become a conscious process—and will therefore lose much of its power.

Key: In the split second before you build the self-defeating behavior, you'll begin to ask yourself, "What can I do instead?"

Step 4: Find a healthy replacement behavior. Simply trying to stop the self-defeating behavior is a recipe for certain failure—you cannot replace something with nothing. Instead, you must substitute another, more constructive action. *Examples:*

•Engage in gardening, weightlifting or another physical activity that leaves you no mental energy for worrying.

•Force yourself to repeat to yourself reassuring, rather than catastrophic, statements.

•Calm yourself with deep breathing exercises.

•Call an upbeat friend.

•Organize a messy drawer.

•Read.

•Take a nap.

•Plan your weekend.

Where to find replacement behaviors:

•Your past. What did you do before negative experiences led you to create the self-defeating behavior?

•Role models. What would one of your "heroes" do in a similar situation?

•Your body. What would feel good physically in this situation?

•Your wiser self. Often, we already have the answers we need—if we can only trust ourselves.

•Feedback from others. Ask friends and other people you trust for suggestions.

Step 5: Practice replacing the old behavior with the new, healthier one. At first you'll need to be vigilant. It will feel unnatural not to slip into the old pattern.

But if you persist, you'll reprogram your unconscious mind and the new, self-enhancing behavior will become as automatic as the self-defeating behavior once was.

Source: Robert E. Hardy, EdD, a licensed psychologist affiliated with Personnel Decisions, Inc., a Minneapolis-based international consulting firm that applies the principles of behavioral science to building successful organizations. He is coauthor, with Milton R. Cudney, of *Self-Defeating Behaviors,* Harper/San Francisco, 10 E. 53 St., New York 10022.

Conquering Forgetfulness

Aging and memory loss do not go hand in hand, contrary to popular belief. The chronic confusion, disorientation and loss of self-sufficiency often associated with growing older are in most cases the result of some specific neurological or psychological disorder.

Memory is not a "something" that we have. It's a skill that can be preserved and developed —no matter what your age.

The first step is to avoid—as much as possible—the things that weaken our memory.

•B-vitamin deficiency. Memory can be impaired by deficiencies in…

•B_1 (thiamine)—found in whole-grain products and salmon steak.

•B_3 (niacin)—found in meat, peanuts, tuna and turkey.

•B_{12} (cobalamins)—found in beef, milk products, eggs and flounder.

Although vitamin deficiencies are rare in this country—where most people overeat—certain people are at risk…

•Heavy drinkers (two or more drinks a day) are at risk of Wernicke-Korsakoff syndrome, a neurological disorder marked by partial or total loss of short-term memory—and associated with inadequate consumption of thiamine. If you drink heavily, it's a good idea to cut back or stop. Otherwise, ask your doctor about thiamine supplements.

•Elderly people who consume fewer than 1,800 calories a day. They, too, can have deficiencies and should ask their doctor about supplements.

•Strict vegetarians. Vitamin B_{12} is found only in meat, fish, eggs and dairy products. People who consume no animal products of any kind should ask their doctor about B_{12} supplements.

•Prescription drugs. Sleeping pills, tranquilizers, some antidepressants, antianxiety drugs and even some prescription painkillers can cause memory loss.

At greatest risk: People 55 years old or older.

If your doctor prescribes one or more of these drugs for you, ask if they are absolutely necessary. In many cases, nondrug approaches are equally effective—psychotherapy, regular exercise, dietary modification, etc.

If drug therapy is essential, ask your doctor if your dosage can be reduced—or if you can switch to another drug that might have less of an effect on your memory.

Example I: Some types of blood-pressure medications—including beta blockers—can reduce the flow of blood to the brain, resulting in temporary or perhaps even permanent memory loss. Other types of antihypertensive medication might pose less of a problem.

Example II: Certain types of antidepressants can exacerbate memory problems in persons already suffering from memory loss. Some of the newer antidepressant medications, including Prozac, might be safer.

Finally, avoid overmedication. Some doctors are in such a hurry to "process" their patients that they may fail to get an accurate picture of their patients' overall health. And, they sometimes prescribe drugs when no drugs are needed—or prescribe higher than necessary doses. This is a special problem for elderly people.

•Bypass surgery. One possible side effect of coronary artery bypass surgery is memory impairment. This impairment seems to be a consequence of reduced blood flow to the brain during surgery, although this remains a matter to be fully investigated.

While a recent study showed that bypass patients had slight memory impairment for up to six months after surgery on neurological testing, some of my patients who underwent bypass surgery experienced memory trouble for even longer periods of time.

Self-defense: Be careful of bypass surgery or any other long, complex operation requiring general anesthesia. (This is especially important for people older than 55.) In some cases, nonsurgical alternatives to bypass are worth trying—for example, adopting an extremely low-fat diet or taking cholesterol-lowering drugs. Or you might have your arteries cleared via balloon angioplasty, which poses less of a threat to your memory. *Ask your doctor.*

Alzheimer's—or not?

Doctors used to blame memory problems in older people on "hardening of the arteries"—or simply on "aging." Now some doctors blame the problem on Alzheimer's disease—even though there's no clear way to diagnose Alzheimer's. In such cases, the real problem might be something far less serious and possibly reversible.

Memory loss might be caused by depression or by numerous tiny strokes, a condition known as Binswanger's disease. Unlike Alzheimer's, depression is treatable—as is the high blood pressure that can lead to Binswanger's.

Self-defense: If you or a loved one is diagnosed with Alzheimer's, insist on a reexamination to rule out other possibilities.

Challenge your brain:

A lazy brain is more apt to forget things than a brain that gets regular "exercise." No matter what your age, certain exercises can help keep your memory keen:

•Balance your checkbook in your head. Adding and subtracting helps boost powers of concentration and attention—and prevents the loss of mathematical abilities.

•Test your power of recall. While stuck in traffic or waiting on line, try conjugating verbs from a foreign language or mentally reciting the titles of Beatles songs.

•Occasionally use your nondominant hand. If you doodle, for example, try using your nondominant hand to reproduce a drawing done with your dominant hand. This exercise helps "transfer" functions and information from one hemisphere of the brain to the other. This is an excellent way to keep your mind "revved up."

•Do brain-relaxing exercises. The more relaxed your mind, the better your powers of concentration—and the stronger your ability both to memorize and to recall information.

Forms of relaxation: Transcendental meditation, self-hypnosis or the simple but effective program developed by Dr. Herbert Benson in his book, *The Relaxation Response.*

•Eat right and exercise. Regular exercise not only promotes physical health, but also helps prevent depression. Excessive consumption of dietary fat and other poor dietary habits can lead to stroke, which of course can cause memory loss.

•Work. Retirement is often viewed as a time to do little or nothing. But the less you do, the less you and your mind will be able to do. If you retire, find something to keep yourself occupied and your mind engaged. *Possibilities:* Explore a new occupation or volunteer work. The only reason to stop working is serious illness.

Source: Vernon H. Mark, MD, former professor of surgery at Harvard Medical School, Boston, and retired director of neurosurgery, Boston City Hospital. He is the author of *Reversing Memory Loss,* Houghton Mifflin Co., 215 Park Ave. S, New York 10003.

Five Days to an Organized Life

Grab just a few moments each day for the next five days, or one day a week over the course of the next five for an organized way to get organized:

•Day one. Develop a list of rewards for yourself—15-minute rewards, two- to three-hour rewards, all day rewards. *Examples:* Phone a dear friend, hike a favorite trail or play 18 holes of golf.

•Day two. Write down goals. Dissect them into manageable, bite-size bits, and develop a plan of action that may include communicating with people, getting more education or doing research. *Example:* A new job might require interviewing friends, taking a résumé workshop and/or doing research at the library.

•Day three. Transfer every task to a pocket notebook, but divide the tasks into calls, errands, things to do and things to write. *Examples:* Call a career counselor, order stationery, set up files, draft a résumé.

•Day four. Buy a pocket calendar and record specific appointments and deadlines, "must do" tasks from your notebook as well as time for planned rewards. *Example:* Thursday: 7:30/breakfast with Ted. 9:30/staff meeting. 10:45/draft new marketing plan. 12:30/lunch in the park.

•Day five. Create a short, daily "to do" list by choosing a few reasonable tasks from your notebook and scheduling them when there is a break in your calendar schedule. *Example:* 7:30/breakfast with Ted. Stop by the post office. 9:30/staff meeting.

Source: Lucy H. Hedrick, time-management consultant and author of *Five Days to an Organized Life,* Dell Publishing, 666 Fifth Ave., New York 10103.

Better Ways to Make Better Decisions

Most people lack confidence in their abilities to make good decisions. Afraid to make a mis-take, they either act on impulse or put off making a choice until circumstances make the decision for them. Either way, they wind up with unsatisfying results. But decision-making is not all that difficult. You just need a system.

In order to find a very effective system, I spent several years observing how people make decisions. During the process, I stopped thinking in terms of *good* and *bad* decisions.

To many of us, *good* means *perfect*—and aiming for perfection immobilizes us. Instead, I strive to make *better* decisions than I used to.

I found that the key to making a better decision is simple—*ask yourself better questions*. If you ask yourself the right questions, you can make an effective decision in very little time.

Better questions rely on both your *head* and your *heart* for guidance. "Head" questions help you determine, "Is this practical?" "Heart" questions ask, "Does this feel right to me?" Most people habitually rely on one of the two—either head or heart—but not both. That's a big mistake. Relying on head *and* heart guides us to choices that are sensible as well as satisfying.

I have identified six questions—three for the head, three for the heart—that can illuminate almost any decision. It's not necessary to ask yourself all six questions. In fact, one question to the head and one to the heart are all you really need.

Focus on the two questions that strike you as most relevant. You will probably be able to answer them quickly.

Head questions:

•Question 1: "Is this something I *want* or something I really *need*?" Wants and needs are easily confused. We would be much happier over the long-term if we made decisions based on what we need, rather than being swayed by temporary or superficial desires.

Example: You've been dating someone for a few months, and you're deciding whether to make a commitment. You may *want* this person because he/she is attractive, wealthy and well-built.

But if you think about what you *need* in a relationship, you may realize that includes a sense of humor, the capacity for honesty and a passion for life. If your attractive companion doesn't have these qualities, getting more involved is likely to leave you disappointed.

Another way of looking at this question—"When I look back a year from now, what would I like to have done?"

•Question 2: "Am I aware of all my options?" A common justification for an unsatisfying decision is, "I had no choice." But people usually have far more options than they first realize. Often, simply asking this question is enough to make you aware of alternatives. But it's also a good idea to gather information. This is a simple process—all you have to do is keep your eyes and ears open. Read, pick up the phone and talk to friends and strangers who have knowledge of the issue and observe how other people have handled similar situations.

Example: My wife and I recently built a home in Hawaii. Before we chose the construction materials, our contractor told us that shipping lumber and supplies from the mainland US would be too expensive. Therefore, we would be limited to what was available on the island.

Instead of taking his word for it, we called lumber mills and shipping companies in the continental US and found that we could build more cheaply and quickly by using their services. We built our home for half the cost—and three times more quickly—than if we had followed the contractor's recommendation.

•Question 3: "What are the probable consequences?" A more detailed version of this question is, "If I choose this option, what will probably happen? And then what will probably happen after that? And then what?" These questions encourage you to think beyond the immediate to the potential outcome of your decision—and whether you will be happy with it.

Example: Your company has been steadily laying off employees in your division. You can't decide whether to (1) start looking for another job or (2) hang on and hope you don't get fired.

Probable consequences of Option 1: You make valuable contacts, learn more about what's going on in your field and eventually land a new, more secure position, though it may not happen right away.

Probable consequences of Option 2: You feel anxious, irritable and resentful. You could keep your job but in an environment that fosters insecurity and frustration, or you could lose your job and experience a crippling setback in your self-esteem—because you let someone else determine your destiny.

Heart questions:

•Question 4: "Am I telling myself the truth?" Too often, the answer is "no." We tell ourselves what we want to hear.

Another way to approach this question is to ask yourself, "What do my friends think?" Not that you should automatically do what everyone else thinks is right, but your friends are likely to be more objective and see pitfalls that you refuse to acknowledge.

•Question 5: "Does this feel right?" "Rightness" is hard to define, but you know it when you feel it. If your mind can't come up with the answer, consult your body. Does thinking about the option make you feel energized or drained?

•Question 6: "What would I do if I weren't afraid?" *Alternative phrasing:* "What would I do if I deserved better?" Our fears may seem realistic, but we often hold ourselves back by imagining things to be worse than they are. Just because a particular option makes you afraid doesn't mean it is the wrong one. Don't let fear make the decision for you—or keep you from making any decision at all.

Source: Spencer Johnson, MD, author of *Yes or No: The Guide to Better Decisions,* HarperCollins, 10 E. 53 St., New York 10022, and coauthor of *The One-Minute Manager,* Berkley Publishing Group, 200 Madison Ave., New York 10016.

Clarify Your Life Values

Clarify your life values by determining what will make your life more worth living. *Ask yourself:* What would you like to have accomplished by the end of your life...what biographical information would you like the newspaper to include in your obituary...what would your spouse, friends, boss or enemies add to that obit? *Also:* In only one or two sentences, describe how you want to be perceived and remembered.

Source: *From Stress to Strength: How to Lighten Your Load and Save Your Life* by Robert S. Eliot, MD, FACC, director, Institute of Stress Medicine in Denver. Bantam Books, 1540 Broadway, New York 10036.

How to Make It in the Needy, Numbing 1990s

Almost 20 years ago, I wrote that anyone who wanted to succeed could do so. That remains true today but it is both more difficult and more important to succeed now than it was then.

Today, management at all levels is less tolerant of those who fail to produce and less generous to those who are merely competent. Corporations are eager to trim workers who do not excel, and company loyalty is not enough to ensure survival.

Even if you do your job well, success is not an automatic consequence. It results from a systematic approach that makes sure you get things done and that others see you as successful. To achieve these two results, you must cultivate a number of specific qualities—energy, competitiveness, realism, memory and communication. Energy:

Success requires a great deal of energy. This does not mean a capacity for long hours of hard work. It means enthusiasm to get things done—combined with the ability to do them right.

•Structuring your time. If you are not a hard worker by nature, structure your time to encourage achievement by following two rules:

•Break up your workload into small, manageable parts.

•Reward yourself as you complete each task.

As you reach each goal, you will develop a sense of accomplishment that will encourage you to continue.

Example: My energy level used to dissipate within two hours of my arrival at the office each morning. I found myself trying to deal with a deluge of phone calls, letters to answer and people waiting to see me.

Solution: I decided to spend my first hour each morning doing nothing but answering mail. By completing this limited but essential chore, I was able to start my day with an "achieving" frame of mind. Then, I rewarded myself with a short coffee break and was ready to go on to successfully tackle the more ambitious tasks of the day.

•Focus on the important tasks. You won't get very far if you stick to small tasks, but it is tempting to put off an important job that will take a few hours or days of hard work.

A simple trick to tackling large projects: Promise yourself a period of relaxation after you complete the necessary hard work. That will help you put in the extra effort to finish the job as quickly as possible and show how much you can accomplish when you work at a high level of efficiency.

•Eat and sleep well. You won't have much energy in the afternoon if you have a heavy midday meal, so stick to a light lunch. If you get drowsy in the middle of the afternoon, don't be embarrassed to take a short nap as long as everyone is aware of how busy you were in the morning and how energetic you are after your nap.

•Look energetic. Promote an image of success, both to others and yourself, by always appearing energetic. Always move briskly, don't slouch—stand straight, with head up, stomach in, chest out, and never keep your hands in your pockets.

Competitiveness:

To get ahead, you must be willing to compete with others and eager to accept responsibility.

Sometimes, competition leads to direct confrontation. Make sure that it is no more brutal than it has to be and that you keep the advantage. *Rules of direct confrontation:*

•Don't sit opposite your opponent—it sharpens the conflict. Try to sit side-by-side. To keep your resolve, look at his/her mouth, not eyes.

•Strike the first blow. Capture the advantage by stating your case rapidly and terminate the initial confrontation as soon as possible.

•Take responsibility for your position. Otherwise, you will get bogged down in a pointless discussion of your personal opinion. Successful people carry out decisions after they have been made, they don't agonize after the fact.

You also must accept responsibility without being asked. This means taking on vital tasks that others avoid because the tasks are perceived to be too trivial or tedious. Within a short time, you will acquire knowledge and skills that nobody else has, and more important responsibilities will begin flowing to you.

Hint: Pay careful attention to routine memos that everyone else ignores. You will find many problems as you search for solutions. If you suggest and volunteer to implement improvements, your reputation for success will grow.

Realism:

To succeed, you must see the world as it is, not as you think it should be. *Some important examples:*

•Be realistic about other people. You can't trust everyone, and those whom you can trust may not always perform the way you want them to.

•Be realistic about yourself. Recognize your good points but be aware of your faults.

•Study your past failures. You may find a way to transform them into successes.

Important: Realism must be balanced by an ability to fantasize. Dreams of success will motivate you to achieve them in reality.

Memory:

You are unlikely to succeed unless you can remember what you have to do and whom you should know.

•Use the best memory aid: Lists. Don't try to memorize every fact you need to know—simply write them down.

•Remember people's names. Get them correct from the start. When you are introduced to someone, repeat his name several times during the first conversation and make sure of the spelling. At the earliest opportunity, write down the name together with other useful memory-jogging information, such as the person's occupation and where you met.

Hint: If you run into someone whose name escapes you, a graceful solution is to announce your own name. The other person will usually reciprocate.

Communication:

Successful people know how to let others know who they are and what they want. Good verbal communication requires you to speak and write clearly in positive terms.

Hint: Try to postpone areas of disagreement until you have demonstrated how much agreement you share.

•Use body language to get attention.

Example: At meetings, don't sit forward with your elbows on the table. Sit back to listen.

When ready to speak, straighten out, move forward and put your arms on the table. You will get everyone's attention.

•Speak in public successfully. Speak in short sentences, touch on a variety of points, be unambiguous and summarize at the end. And always finish sooner than the audience expects.

Source: Michael Korda, editor-in-chief of Simon & Schuster. He is the author of four nonfiction best-sellers, including *Success! How Every Man and Woman Can Achieve It,* Ballantine, 201 E. 50 St., New York 10022 and five novels, most recently *The Immortals,* Simon & Schuster, 1230 Avenue of Americas, New York 10020.

Giving and Receiving Feedback

Giving and receiving feedback is tricky, even for the most happily married couples. *Helpful:* A "feedback contract" negotiated and signed by both partners. *Useful questions:* Are you open to feedback at all times?…Do you want to be asked first, "Do you want feedback about this?"… Would it be more empowering for each of you to ask for feedback rather than to wait for it? Once you've made the agreement, write it down and put it someplace visible, like on the bathroom mirror or the refrigerator.

Source: *Centering and the Art of Intimacy Handbook: A New Psychology of Close Relationships* by Colorado Springs psychotherapists Gay Hendricks, PhD, and Kathlyn Hendricks, PhD. Fireside Books, 1230 Avenue of the Americas, New York 10020.

How to Know Yourself Much, Much Better

We each make our own path through life. To succeed and better understand our behavior, we must be prepared to ask where we are at every stage of the journey. Then we can better decide where we want to go—and how to get there.

Here are guideposts to some of the most important issues we face and questions to ask as we meet life's challenges…

Growth:

The main purpose of life is emotional and spiritual growth. No one really ever becomes fully *grown-up*. Most people are actually emotional children walking around in adults' clothing.

Growth involves pain. Many of us would like to go back to earlier times in our lives—even infancy—when we were protected from the challenges of adult life. That desire causes people to remain fixed in second childhoods—self-centered, whiny and dependent. To know whether you have the basic prerequisite for growth, ask yourself, "Do I accept the impossibility of returning to childhood?"

Courage:

Emotional and spiritual growth demands that you meet the challenges with which life continually confronts you, despite your fear of painful new experiences. Taking on these challenges in the face of such fear requires courage.

When you feel uneasy about an uncomfortable situation, ask yourself, "Will I be better off avoiding—or meeting—this challenge?" If you act only when your inner voice tells you it is the right thing to do, you are truly on the road to growth and maturity.

Anger:

Anger is a necessary emotion and an important self-defense mechanism. But we need to know when anger is appropriate and how to express it.

When a situation provokes you to anger, there are at least five different ways to express it. *Ask yourself:*

• "Should I apologize?" My initial reaction was mistaken…I was at fault.

• "Should I ignore it?" What the other person did was an accident…it was not his/her fault.

• "Should I minimize my anger?" The other person *did* insult me a little…but it wasn't important.

• "Should I express my anger?" I will think about it for a few days. If it is clear that the other person seriously wronged me, I will complain to him/her.

• "Should I lose my temper?" The other person wronged me so badly that I have to express my anger strongly—on the spot.

You can assess your own stage of life's journey to maturity by how often you step back, think through your anger and express it appropriately.

Judgment:

It is impossible to go through life without making judgments about people—whom you should marry, how much freedom to give your children, whom you should hire or fire. How well you make those judgments is critical to the quality of your life. Before you judge someone else, you should judge yourself.

Example: You have to fire an unsatisfactory employee. It has to be done but ask yourself:

• Was I sufficiently concerned with the employee earlier?

• Did I speak to him/her as soon as I could have or did I avoid confrontation until it was too late to solve the problem?

If you answer such questions honestly, you will know how to act in the future to prevent the need for similar painful results.

Uncertainty:

Life is a series of decisions—and there is an easy way and a difficult way to make each of these decisions.

Easy way to decide: Always follow a rigid rule.

Example: Your teenage daughter wants to stay out on Saturday night until 1 AM. Your response may always follow the rule "No! You know that your curfew is 10 PM." or the rule "Of course. Whatever you do is fine."

Difficult way: Analyze every situation as thoroughly as you can.

Example: You think to yourself, "She does have a 10 PM curfew, but we set it two years ago. She is responsible and we trust her but we aren't sure about the boy she's going with."

Then you try to decide the most appropriate reply—"no," "yes" or a compromise, such as coming home by 11 PM.

The *easy way* avoids thinking and allows quick decision-making.

The *difficult way* leaves you in doubt but admits there is no magic formula for the correct answer in every situation. If you take the difficult way, you know that you take life seriously.

Will:

How much you achieve in life depends on how strong a will you possess and on how well you can control it.

A *weak will* is like a little donkey in your backyard. It can't do very much work, and about the worst damage it can cause is to eat your flowers.

A *strong will* is like a dozen Clydesdales. If those massive beasts are trained, disciplined and harnessed, they can help you move mountains. But if you let them run wild, they may knock down your house.

To harness your will, voluntarily subject it to a power higher than yourself. The nature of that power is defined by your religious and moral beliefs.

To understand your role in life, ask yourself, "Am I undisciplined and selfish—or willing to go where I am led by the higher power in which I believe?"

Self-love:

Army psychiatrists once studied the personalities of 12 people in the service. All were very successful in their jobs, their families and their social relationships. They were asked to list the three most important things in their lives.

While they disagreed on their second and third most important priorities, every one of those successful people named the same top priority—*myself*.

This reply did not mean these people were exceptionally selfish. All were loving spouses and parents and caring supervisors. They stressed their self-love because they truly appreciated the value of life and felt a corresponding responsibility to make the most of it, which is why they were successful.

Self-love is consistent with a sense of *humility*, defined by a 14th-century monk as "a true knowledge of oneself as one is."

If you can attain humility—the ability to realistically evaluate both your virtues and your faults—then you own the best compass for guiding yourself along the winding highway of life.

Source: M. Scott Peck, MD, psychiatrist, management consultant and founder of the Foundation for Community Encouragement, 109 Danbury Rd., Suite 8, Ridgefield, Connecticut 06877. His most recent book is *Further Along the Road Less Traveled: The Unending Journey Toward Spiritual Growth*, Simon & Schuster, 1230 Avenue of the Americas, New York 10020.

Only Expressing Criticism

Only expressing criticism, anger and bitterness to your spouse is counterproductive.

Break the negative-feedback cycle by spending 10 to 15 minutes alone with your partner, providing each other with honest, positive feedback. *Examples:* Tell your partner three things you like about the way he/she looks…his three greatest personality or character strengths…at least two things he does particularly well.

Source: *Lethal Lovers and Poisonous People* by Los Angeles psychologist Harriet Braiker, PhD, Pocket Books, 1230 Avenue of the Americas, New York 10020.

How to Get What You Want From Any Bureaucracy

Bureaucracies often are difficult and frustrating to deal with. But you *can* improve your odds of getting what you want almost every time. *Here's how:*

• First you must believe that you are going to win. It sounds simple—but believing that you're going to triumph is *crucial*. It will help you maintain a positive attitude—and keep you from flying off the handle.

• Have your facts in order. Before contacting anyone, *rehearse* your case. It should be clear, to the point and unemotional. A logical, cool, businesslike approach works best.

• Speak to the right person. Don't waste time and emotional energy telling your story to the first person who answers the phone. That person is often just routing calls. Ask for someone who handles your type of problem.

• Mention your credentials. Once you reach the right person, identify yourself and make it clear in a nonthreatening manner that you are serious and well-respected. It doesn't matter whether you are a doctor, a plumber, a nurse or a grocery clerk. Explaining what you do or where you work confirms that you're established and responsible—not a crank.

• Make it clear that you are going to continue to pursue the matter. After being rebuffed initially, you can save yourself a lot of time by calmly making it clear that since you know you are right, you are not going to drop the matter.

This is when a positive attitude really helps. Once the person with whom you're speaking realizes that you believe you are going to win—and that the only unknown is how much time it is going to take—he/she will often relent.

• If you're dissatisfied with the explanation you are given, go right to the top. If you don't get satisfaction from the person who *should* respond, don't waste time inching up the chain of command. Each person along the way will refer you back to the person who initially rebuffed you. Contact the top person in the department or organization—initially by phone. Usually he will tell you to contact him by mail. Send a letter, but follow up about two weeks later with a phone call.

• Get specific promises. Well-meaning double-talk does you no good. You want concrete answers to your problem and a time when it will be resolved.

• If you face further setbacks, don't be afraid to use stronger measures. This is always a last resort, but if there's a traffic light that your city won't fix or a similarly gross oversight by a bureaucracy, tell the person in charge that you plan to inform his superior or even the media. Some people just need a lot of nudging to know that you're serious about the complaint.

Source: Sammy "The Nudge" Fleischer, a New York City community activist who for 60 years has succeeded in convincing the city to rehabilitate parks, fix sidewalks and install hundreds of street lights. In honor of his effectiveness, the city offered to name a municipal park after him. Mr. Fleischer, however, requested that only the pool in the park be given his name.

Lessons in Leadership

Becoming a leader does not require super intelligence or an important-sounding title. It does, however, require the ability to make others respect you and believe in your vision. Leadership is an attitude and a state of mind.

Leadership characteristics:

Here are leadership characteristics that anyone can incorporate into his/her life—qualities you can use to unlock the doors that keep you from achieving your leadership potential:

• Leaders have the authority of knowledge. Every leader develops a business skill at which he is better than anyone else—a demonstrated talent that colleagues admire.

To be a leader, you can't just be a talker. You need to demonstrate that you are deeply involved in whatever you do. You must also bring something special to the party—something that will make other people's jobs easier.

• Leaders are visionaries. They are able to see facts and ideas that others view as ordinary and rearrange them so that they become extraordinary.

Leaders form visions that draw simplicity out of complexity and clarity out of obscurity. By simplifying what is complex, leaders make patterns emerge that become the inspiration for their visions.

How can you become a visionary? By developing the ability to step back from your immediate context. Visionaries can elevate themselves above the minutiae and rearrange all the available facts into a larger whole.

Example: When you're in a crowd, all you can see is what is immediately around you—one person's shoulder and another person's back. But from a helicopter high above the crowd, you can see all the people and buildings. You can see everything from a new perspective.

• Leaders produce change. They are not disoriented by change and don't run from change. They see change not as a threat but as an opportunity and a challenge.

Leaders are able to master change because they have already experienced and managed painful change within their own lives. In fact, they are what I call *twice-born.*

This sounds spiritual—even metaphysical—but it isn't. I am referring to episodes of great stress and trauma. We have all experienced such events. They range from universal episodes, like passing through adolescence, to tragic episodes, like losing a sibling at a young age or surviving a serious illness.

Leaders emerge from these events with a sense of clarity, a feeling of renewal and a need to ask, "Why do things work the way they do?" A leader—as long as he is healthy enough emotionally to master his own tragedies—has the ability to emerge from trauma with the capacity to cope creatively.

While everyone has had twice-born experiences, it is how we handle these experiences —how we integrate them within ourselves— that differentiates leaders from followers.

•Leaders give their all. They are willing to commit themselves to their visions and their success. Leaders do not hold back. They do not *conditionally* dedicate themselves to the success of their visions and let themselves become sidetracked, they *completely* dedicate themselves. Tapping their reservoirs of passion gives leaders the energy to transform the present into a more successful and promising future.

Sometimes giving your all is expensive—to your family and your own personal well-being. Leaders understand this expense but still are willing to pay the price for pursuing their visions.

•Leaders are good listeners. They are able to hear what others are saying about the problems that accompany change. They accommodate the difficulty others experience in the pursuit of that vision. It is one thing to have a vision and another to empower other people to follow your vision. That doesn't mean the road toward the vision will be smooth.

•Leaders are good communicators. They are clear, concise, complete and consistent. Good leaders are able to deliver the messages they want to deliver—and deliver them with enthusiasm and sincerity.

•Leaders are students. They never stop learning and growing. They study the process and are willing to learn from their mistakes. Most people say they learn from their mistakes, but most repeat the same mistakes their entire lives.

Leaders are always thirsty for knowledge, and they seek it from the wisdom of today as well as from the wisdom of the past. Today's problems are so complex that solving them *requires* as many points of view as possible integrated into the solution. How can you gain this knowledge? You read…and read…and read. You listen to great people. You take time to think. You attend concerts. You visit museums. You read biographies of great people.

•Leaders take risks. They create change, which requires risks. They are willing to take risks because they can visualize how things can be done better.

The most important risk is the willingness to expose yourself to the possibility of a negative outcome in order to carry out your vision. Risk does not mean betting on long shots. In order to be a risk-taker, one needs some record of success. People will not take risks if they fail repeatedly.

•Leaders are ethical. People will not follow you if they don't trust you. It's not a matter of morals. It is a matter of mechanics. People may follow you because you con them into doing so. But in the long run, you will get caught.

•Leaders are optimists. They have hope. They trust their gut feelings and other people. That trust and hope are the basis on which leaders empower others.

Believe in yourself as a winner. No one will trust you unless you believe in yourself and demonstrate that you have confidence in your vision of the future.

Source: Howard G. Haas, senior lecturer at the University of Chicago's business school, chairman of Howard Haas & Associates, management consultants, 208 S. LaSalle St., Suite 1275, Chicago 60604, and former chief executive of Sealy Inc. He is coauthor of *The Leader Within: An Empowering Path of Self-Discovery,* HarperBusiness, 10 E. 53 St., New York 10022.

Rely on Internal Cues

Rely on *internal* cues—not external factors— to stay on your diet. Scales may be unreliable— weight can change daily for anyone…and exercise builds muscle, which weighs more than fat. A compliment on how good you look provides temporary reinforcement but can lead you to backslide if you do not get another one soon. *Better:* Look inside yourself. Take responsibility for your actions and thoughts. Only you can decide how you feel.

Source: *Emotional Weight* by Colleen Sundermeyer, PhD, nutritionist and eating-disorder counselor, Rancho Murieta, California. The Putnam Publishing Group, 200 Madison Ave., New York 10016.

How to Be Happy with a Less-than-Perfect Body

It has become "normal" for people to be dissatisfied with their bodies. To varying degrees, most of us are unhappy with what we see in the mirror. We're too fat, our feet are too big, our hair the wrong color, our noses misshapen, our muscles too small. The list of complaints is endless.

We Americans, of course, are especially concerned with our weight. We abhor fat, and we aren't afraid to say so. In a time when most people are careful not to offend members of other racial, ethnic or religious groups, we remain insensitive to the feelings of overweight people. In cartoons and in comedy routines, as in casual conversation, fat people remain a favorite target.

Ridicule isn't the only injustice visited upon fat people. A study conducted recently at the Harvard School of Public Health found that fat women earn less than their thin counterparts and are more likely to have a low socioeconomic status. (Interestingly, fat men do not suffer financial hardship, but short men do.) The eight-year study involved 10,039 randomly selected people.

But it is possible to overcome bodily concerns and learn to live with imperfections—in ourselves and in others.

The meaning of perfection:

Each day, we're barraged by messages from the media, advertisements and even friends and family—all suggesting that we are physically inadequate, that unless we have the "perfect" weight, height, hair, facial features, etc., we are somehow freaks.

But there are many more "normal" people than fashion models—so maybe it's *them* and not *us* who are freakish.

I believe that "perfection" has far more to do with being comfortable with who and what we are than with having the "ideal" body.

Our culture's abhorrence of fat is a recent phenomenon. Throughout most of our history, being portly was valued as a sign of health and wealth. Thinness was equated with illness or poor nourishment—and by extension a lack of success and social standing.

Plump women were considered desirable. Full buttocks were particularly attractive and sexually stimulating—just look at the paintings of Rubens and Renoir.

Obviously, this perception has changed in recent decades. Advertisers spend billions each year trying to convince us that body fat, baldness and shortness are unattractive and even unwholesome.

Has this been helpful? No. All it's done is cause countless self-image problems, and we're spending a huge amount on cosmetic surgery, fad diets and uncomfortable clothing. Is "imperfection" unhealthy?

Not at all. A receding hairline certainly isn't a sign of poor health, nor is a long nose, wrinkles around the eyes or being a bit shorter than friends and coworkers.

Again, let's look at fat. Studies have repeatedly shown that as we reach middle age, our bodies naturally gain weight. A man who weighs 160 pounds at age 25 can reasonably expect to gain at least 20 pounds by age 50. This weight gain is not unseemly or dangerous, although popular culture would suggest otherwise.

Result: To keep the weight off, middle-aged people diet continually and engage in overly strenuous exercise programs. Ironically, these diets and exercise programs can pose greater threats to their health than a few extra pounds.

Lesson: Bodies change over time, and the slow, gradual accumulation of weight is not inherently bad.

In fact, being slightly overweight may be healthier than being thin. A recent study by the Metropolitan Life Insurance Company found that underweight people have considerably higher mortality rates than people who are overweight.

This is not to suggest that it's okay to "let yourself go." Eating indiscriminately and without regard to nutrition inevitably leads to health problems—as does a lack of exercise. And the fear of falling victim to such problems only heightens the stress.

If you have crossed the line to unhealthy weight gain, you should take steps to shed a few pounds. But if your feelings are based only upon what you fear others think about your weight, there may be no need to lose weight.

Caution: Excessive weight gain that occurs despite a sensible diet and regular exercise suggests a glandular problem. See a doctor.

Perception versus reality:

Like most people in our society, I once had a very negative impression of people who are overweight—including my wife. This was especially true because I am quite lean and thought everyone should be like I was.

But about 15 years ago my attitude began to crumble. I started to see my wife not as "fat," but as "pleasingly plump." I stopped criticizing her weight and started to accept her the way she was. I've been happier ever since—and so has she.

What changed me? I began to realize that the people I knew came in all different shapes and sizes, and most were capable, ambitious, intelligent and warm-hearted. With some embarrassment, I realized that it was wrong to criticize these people just because their bodies failed to conform to an artificial image of perfection.

What you can do:

•Focus on how you feel—not on what you look like. Most of us feel better when we eat a low-fat, high-fiber diet, drink alcohol in moderation or not at all, avoid smoking and get regular exercise. But even if you follow this familiar wisdom, there's no assurance that you will look like a model—even if your parents did.

If your ancestors were bald, or had big jowls or protruding ears, it's pointless to blame yourself if you share the same traits. More problems are caused than resolved when people try to repudiate their bodies. Try to accept the natural shape of your family tree.

•Avoid fad diets. Many of the diets advocated today deprive people of wholesome, necessary foods and don't take into account an individual's natural body composition. Instead of picking a diet from a magazine or a bestseller, follow the guidelines of the Department of Agriculture's *Food Guide Pyramid.** Vary the size of the portions according to your desire to lose or gain weight.

Never diet solely to change your body shape. And you absolutely must avoid yo-yo dieting, in

**The Food Guide Pyramid* booklet (HG252) is available from the Consumer Information Center, Dept. 119A, Pueblo, Colorado 81009.

which large quantities of weight are repeatedly lost and regained. Recent studies have found this to be dangerous to your health.

Think: Do you feel comfortable with your body? If you feel no lack of energy, if you feel attractive, if you enjoy sex (studies have shown that so-called fat women have sexual relations more often and enjoy them more than underweight women) and if you feel that you can accomplish personal or career goals, then why attempt to change things?

Source: Charles Roy Schroeder, PhD, professor of exercise physiology, biomechanics, fitness and wellness, Memphis State University, Memphis, Tennessee. He is the author of *Fat Is Not a Four-Letter Word,* Chronimed Publishing, Box 47945, Minneapolis 55447.

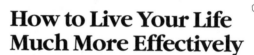

How to Live Your Life Much More Effectively

When Rush Limbaugh began hosting his nationally syndicated radio program in 1988, he was heard on 56 stations. His tell-it-as-he-sees-it on-air delivery made waves across America. Now *The Rush Limbaugh Show* is carried by 630 stations—and has more than 20 million listeners.

Here Limbaugh shares the principles he followed to become successful:

•Find out how winners got to be winners. Unsuccessful people tend to be jealous and suspicious of achievement. They assume that most successful people started out with unfair advantages or got where they are by cheating.

Not true. The vast majority of success in this country was *earned* through hard work. And maintaining success is even harder than earning it in the first place.

I'm not saying that some people do not get help along the way. Doors are opened all the time. But an open door is nothing more than that—it doesn't automatically lead to success.

Instead of being resentful of achievers, try to understand them, study them, find out how they got where they are and learn whatever you can from their experiences.

•Avoid naysayers and negative types. It's easy to find people to talk you *out* of something.

I floundered in radio for 12 years, and all that time everybody told me I should get out of it and that radio wasn't a fair business—because they had failed at it.

So I left the radio industry in 1979 and spent five years feeling miserable in a sales job for which I wasn't suited—and went nowhere. Finally in 1983, I returned to radio—my real love—and began my show locally in Kansas City, Missouri. If I had followed the naysayers' advice, I'd still be stuck in that sales job—still unchallenged, frustrated and feeling empty.

•Believe in yourself. Whatever real success you achieve will result from listening to yourself, believing that your dreams have value and honoring your vision with action.

When I moved to New York five years ago to launch a national version of my radio show, people said, "You have to have guests on your show. Everyone else does it that way." I said, "That's exactly why I don't want to do it that way."

I wanted to do my show the way I enjoyed doing it and find out if I could be the reason people listened. Everybody in broadcasting was convinced that my approach would never work.

•Stick to your principles. I can't think of anything more important than character. If you don't have credibility, integrity and the courage of your convictions, people won't trust you. And if they don't trust you, they won't bother to listen to you, buy a product from you or take your advice.

Talking the talk is not enough—you've got to *walk the walk*. Live by your principles. Even if people disagree with you, they'll respect you.

•Find a career that lets you be yourself. For some reason, most people assume they're not supposed to enjoy what they do for a living. They think a job is, by definition, something they don't like but have to do. They don't realize that, like most limitations, this one is self-imposed. If you approach your job as something you just do in order to earn money to enjoy yourself on weekends, you won't enjoy your weekends much either. A job that lets you be yourself will allow you to become the best you can be.

After all the years I spent stumbling around in radio, what finally gave me the break that led to my success was having a show on which I could be myself. Instead of trying to become a star by figuring out what other people wanted and giv-

ing them that, I did the show my own way—and listeners responded.

I work hard, but I don't find my work arduous or something to dread. I don't even consider it to be work.

•Don't ask anyone to do something that you can't—or won't—do. This is especially important for people who aspire to leadership positions. Someone who is just starting out will often look at an older, more successful person and envy the things that person doesn't have to do—without realizing everything he/she had to do in order to get to his present position.

Example: A CEO of a major corporation may not make sales calls anymore—but when he was in sales, he was probably one of the best at it. When he talks to his sales force now, they know he isn't asking for anything that he has not already done himself or anything he could not do again if he ever had to. He knows what he's talking about, and it shows.

•Be curious. Insatiable curiosity will yield inside information you wouldn't get if you were too quickly satisfied with the answers. It keeps you on the cutting edge.

Don't ever assume that what you've already learned is sufficient—it probably isn't. Continue to dig deeper, no matter what you think you know. Never stop asking "Why?"

•Always align yourself with the truth. I don't claim to have a direct line to the truth. Like morality, it can't be defined by any individual. But in my career, I am engaged in the relentless pursuit of the truth.

When I tell people what I think is wrong with society and about the changes I believe need to be made, my statements are based on the facts as I can best determine them. And if I find out that I got the facts wrong, I make the correction immediately—and as loudly as I can.

•Listen to your elders. *Seasoned citizens* are among the greatest resources we have today. No matter what your age, there is always someone who has lived longer and been through more than you have.

Many people today think that history began the day they were born. They're convinced that the times we live in are the worst ever—that the problems we face have never been dealt with before. This is a pathetically limited perspective.

Take a look at the gadgets that two-income couples are working themselves to death to acquire—cellular phones, air conditioners, microwave ovens. These things that they consider necessities didn't even exist 40 years ago.

Talking to people who lived through markedly different times can really help us put our values in order and our needs in perspective.

•Lighten up. Finding ways to bring a smile to your face is what life is all about. But too many people have wound themselves into fits of rage and obstinacy.

We've become too sensitive and concerned with offending. It's impossible to go through life without offending or being offended. If your objective is to avoid all offense, you're going to lead a very grim existence. Even worse, you won't be honest—you'll be compromising your integrity at every turn.

We aren't meant to go around with clenched fists, gritting our teeth. Human beings are productive, happy and honest when we can relax and let out a good laugh. I laugh at myself all the time.

Source: Rush Limbaugh, host of *The Rush Limbaugh Show,* the nation's highest-rated national radio talk show and the top-rated late-night syndicated TV talk show. He is editor of *The Limbaugh Letter* and author of two best-selling books—*The Way Things Ought to Be* and *See, I Told You So,* both published by Pocket Books, 1230 Avenue of the Americas, New York 10020.

When You Feel Negative Emotions

When you feel negative emotions, ask yourself why you are feeling them…what you can do about them now…whether this is the right time to feel emotional pain. If it is not, take conscious control of the emotions and change them. *Important:* Treat feelings and emotions as messengers, not controllers. They are like internal eyes and ears, reporting how your body is handling a situation. Learn to control your responses to feelings—not be controlled by them.

Source: *Toughness Training for Life* by James Loehr, EdD, president, Loehr-Groppel Sport Science, Wesley Chapel, Florida. E.P. Dutton, 375 Hudson St., New York 10014.

How to Let Go Of a Grudge

Practically everyone has held a grudge at one time or another in their life. Some people hold on to grudges for their entire lives.

But stubbornly clinging to a grudge is counterproductive. It wastes valuable mental energy and prevents us from addressing the issues that originally led to our resentment.

Why we hold on to grudges:

•The belief that resentment will keep us from ever being taken advantage of again. The irony is that a grudge maintains the *illusion* of power without the *reality*. As a result, our resentment can actually make us *more* vulnerable.

Example: A manager refused to read material suggested by an executive against whom he held a grudge. As it turned out, by not reading the material, he was ill-prepared for several key meetings.

•The fear that letting go of the grudge will prevent us from getting the revenge we deserve. In reality, revenge is rarely satisfying because:

•Being poisoned by hatred or paralyzed with rage results in a hollow victory.

•Grudges actually provide convenient excuses for not moving on in our lives. This is what psychologists call *secondary gain*.

Example: A man held a grudge against his employer, barely talking to him for eight months because of a relatively minor slight. In fact, this employee was ill-suited to his job and knew it. Instead of looking for a different job, he used his grudge as justification for not progressing in his career.

How grudges hurt us:

We may have imagined the supposed slight that left us feeling betrayed, it may have been only a misunderstanding or past experience may cause us to see innocent comments as malicious. In some cases, someone really may have meant to do harm.

But whether or not it's based on an accurate perception of another person's motives, holding a grudge often hurts the grudge-holder more than it hurts the perpetrator. *Reasons:*

•Preoccupation with how badly we've been treated causes a tremendous amount of distracting mental activity that keeps us from productive work. It's extraordinary how much time we can spend plotting revenge, worrying ourselves sick about being cheated and feeling angry or sad—all emotions and thoughts that interfere with reaching goals in both our professional and personal lives.

•Anger—induced by your grudge—can cause tremendous physiological stress, potentially contributing to heart disease, ulcers and other health problems.

•An obsession with revenge can lead to vengeful actions that rarely relieve the anger and may create unbearable guilt if these obsessions are acted out.

•Nursing a grudge blocks us from engineering a real solution to the problem—such as expressing our hurt and asking for an apology—and keeps us from practicing good assertive skills that are *more* likely to protect us from future pain.

How to get rid of a grudge:

We *can* get over our grudges and get back to the business of living. *Steps:*

•Determine whether the slight was real or imagined. Review the situation carefully. Generate alternative explanations for what happened to see if there's any room to interpret the experience as a misunderstanding. Was the other person really trying to hurt you? Or did he/she unwittingly touch upon an issue about which you are overly sensitive?

•Challenge all of your irrational and magical ideas. The offense itself is usually not nearly as bad as the exaggerated feelings of hurt and anger that arise in reaction to it. Identifying those automatic reactions can rob them of their power. *Examples:*

•*Irrational belief:* If I'm nice to others, they'll always be nice to me.

Challenge: It would be great if the world worked that way, but it doesn't. It's unrealistic to expect life always to be fair to me, no matter how decent I am.

•*Irrational belief:* I can't stand that this happened.

Challenge: Of course I can stand it. Who needs this resentment?

•*Irrational belief:* This person is evil and horrible and deserves my hatred.

Challenge: This person is human, with all the faults that come with that, and hating him is hurting me more than it hurts him.

•Take any necessary action. Assert yourself if you didn't before. Many people with long-standing grudges suffer in silence—they never even tell the perpetrator that they were hurt. Take responsibility for your feelings, and be authentic in expressing them.

•Perform a ritual to release your grudge. Because grudges involve such powerful feelings, a simple ceremony can help you let go by evoking equally powerful symbolism.

Strategy: Write out the grudge and all your feelings about it on a piece of paper. Bury the paper—literally—in the backyard or in the soil around a potted plant. Resolve not to raise the matter at all for three months. This is more realistic than trying to dismiss it from your mind forever. Whenever it crosses your mind, remind yourself that you've buried it. At the end of three months, dig up the piece of paper and reconsider your grudge. Are you finished with it? If not, what would it take for you to be finished? Is there an irrational belief you haven't effectively challenged? Do you need to take more assertive action? Repeat the ritual if you need to.

This is an amazingly powerful technique. I've seen it work for countless people, from business partners to spouses. It has worked on issues that have festered for years. It allows you to recognize your power to let go of the grudge. Holding on to a grudge feels powerful but it isn't; letting go is real power.

Source: Barry Lubetkin, PhD, director of the Institute for Behavior Therapy, 137 E. 36 St., New York 10016. He is the author of *Why Do I Need You to Love Me in Order to Like Myself?*, Longmeadow Press, 201 High Ridge Rd., Stamford, Connecticut 06904.

How to Take Charge of Life Problems You Thought You Couldn't Change

Most people have difficulty coping with change. But in today's world, change is inevitable—and if you do not take charge of your own life, change will take charge of you. Even if you are content with things as they are, you have to prepare for change since situations shift frequently today.

Performing your job well is not really a defense. If your company decides to downsize or is put up for sale—no matter how well you have mastered your current position—you may need a different set of skills to meet the needs of the future. In the 1990s, life planning is a survival skill.

Avoiding change:

People who cannot face change are in a state that I call *Inner Kill.* Prime symptoms include:

• Always taking the safe way.

• Reacting instead of taking risks.

• Avoiding decisions.

• Daydreaming and talking rather than taking action.

Inner Kill is closely related to fatigue, which may result from overwork and a pressure-filled life or underwork and too little engagement in life.

Examples:

• *Middle-aged people* are often under intense pressure. They must juggle overwhelming work schedules and personal and financial responsibilities that may include aging parents and growing children.

Result: Some middle-aged people just go through the motions of their daily activities— fatigued and unable to think about where they are headed.

• *Early retirees* who have unexpectedly and involuntarily been removed from the workforce may find themselves bewildered and unable to respond to life meaningfully—especially if they never took time during their careers to define themselves in ways other than their occupation.

Result: Many of these early retirees become ill within two years of their retirement.

• *Young adults* graduating from college and beginning their careers rarely think through what their talents and interests are best suited for. Many allow events to control them.

Result: Five, 10 or 20 years down the road, they find themselves in a rut and wonder how they ever got into it.

How to face change:

• *Take the initiative.* To engage life, you must take the initiative when facing change. That requires overcoming a number of very common fears—of criticism, rejection, betrayal, failure, even success. You must *rescript* yourself to trust both your own judgment and that of other people who can help you.

• *Accept that change is inevitable and impossible to avoid.* Decide to change, instead of escape—use change for personal and professional growth.

• *Be prepared to take risks.* It is better to choose the calculated risk of a positive decision for change than to let outside events force other less-welcome risks on you. Prudent risk-taking requires excellent information, so the first step is to acquire the information you need.

• *Take stock.* Before creating a vision of where you want to go in life and how you can get there, you must know yourself. Answer the questions "Who am I? Why am I here? Where am I going?" Finding the truth about yourself requires courage. You must think seriously and answer a series of questions to assess your quality of life in ten fundamental areas.

• *Time.* What is your daily schedule? Do you have time for your real priorities? What is your most important need now?

Suggestion: Keep a journal of your activities, and review it at least quarterly. If your schedule is not consistent with your priorities, be prepared to change it.

• *Values.* What are your top three values now? Can you describe one risk you have taken recently because of your values?

Suggestion: Ask yourself why you do the things you do. Consider what values your actions express and whether you agree with them.

• *Vitality.* How do you spend your leisure time? Do you have fun? If you are tied to a routine and never enjoy spontaneous fun, you are suppressing an important part of yourself.

• *Purpose.* Why do you get up in the morning? Do you have a sense of purpose?

Suggestions: Consider what you would like your epitaph to say. If you learned that you had only two years to live, how would you spend your time?

•*Career.* How did you get where you are? Did you choose your career—or did it choose you? At what point did you come to love what you are doing, and why? If your current job does not match your needs and wants, the mental and physical costs can be high. True career progress requires not continual promotion but continual growth.

•*Talents.* What natural talents do others see in you? Which talents do you most enjoy using?

Suggestions: Consider your ability to handle facts, figures and concepts, deal with people, manipulate objects, etc. Consider keeping a *talents inventory.*

•*Spirituality.* Do you set aside time for contemplation? What principles govern your actions? You will live a more satisfying and fulfilling life if you know you are here for a higher purpose—not just to satisfy your material wants and compete in a rat race.

•*Health.* How is your health and your energy level? Do you exercise enough, relax, smoke, drink? If you take care of your health, you can expect a longer, better life.

•*Relationships.* Do you have friends? To whom do you talk? Do you talk about what is important to you? The single most important source of meaning in our lives is our connection with the people we love—spouse, family and friends. Reflect on how well you are able to communicate with those closest to you.

•*Money.* What annual income do you need to support your lifestyle? How is your financial health? Do you have written financial goals and plans? If your current situation is unsatisfactory, decide whether the appropriate change is to make more money or to need less.

Important: You cannot take stock by yourself. Discuss the questions with the people who know you best.

Taking charge:

After taking stock of your current activities and setting your priorities, you are equipped to decide the changes you want to make for a better future.

•*Write a master dream list* of all the things you would like to do throughout your life.

•*Talk with your partner*—or your family—and make a joint list.

•*Choose four major goals to pursue for the next 12 months*—one each for your personal life, your work, your relationships and your finances. *Key questions to ask yourself:*

•Do the people who matter to me support me?

•Do I have enough time and enough money?

•Am I willing to sacrifice any lower-priority items that conflict with a more important one?

If you can answer each question with a "yes," tell others about your plan to increase your motivation.

•*Develop an action plan for each goal—with deadlines.* Break the plan down into small, measurable steps. Put a date on each step to track your progress. Your action plan will put you on the road to meaningful change.

Source: Richard J. Leider, a partner in The Inventure Group, a personal growth and team-effectiveness consulting firm, 8500 Normandale Lake Blvd., Minneapolis 55437. He is the author of *Life Skills: Taking Charge of Your Personal and Professional Growth,* Pfeiffer and Company, 8517 Production Ave., San Diego 92121.

How to Develop a Positive Attitude… How to Maintain a Positive Attitude

For success in all areas of life, *attitude* is much more important than *aptitude.* People who cultivate consistently positive attitudes expect great things, work hard for those things and are likely to achieve them.

In fact, research by psychologist Martin Seligman of the University of Pennsylvania revealed that optimistic people are happier, healthier and more successful than those with a negative outlook on life.

Health:

A new branch of medicine—*psychoneuroimmunology*—studies the relationship between mental attitude and health. Physicians have found that a positive attitude can result in faster recovery from surgery and burns, more resistance to arthritis and cancer and improved immune function.

Reason: Brain-produced substances—*neuro-peptides*—transmit chemical messages that direct the immune system. When you think positively, these messages are more emphatic. When you are depressed, they tell your body, "Why bother?"

Success:

When you think positively about yourself, you work harder at what you want to do—and give up less easily. You make a better impression on others, which encourages them to help you.

When you think more positively about your colleagues, employees, spouse and children, you build stronger and more productive relationships—leading to greater success at work and at home.

Lesson: If you think you would be happier with your life if you were more successful, you have things backward.

Developing a positive attitude:

A positive attitude does not pop into your mind by itself. How you feel is a decision you make every day. If you don't automatically feel upbeat, look around and find something to feel good about. *Aim:* Start out each day in a positive way:

• Use a clock radio that plays music that is soft and pleasant to wake up to. *Don't* use a loud alarm clock.

• Allow yourself enough time to prepare for the day's activities at a civilized pace. *Don't* get up at the last possible moment.

• Think about the positive things you expect to accomplish today. *Don't* listen to news of the world's problems or worry about your own problems while you are dressing.

• Eat a healthy breakfast. *Don't* drug yourself with coffee or cigarettes.

• Discuss your plans for the day with your partner. *Don't* bury your face in the newspaper.

• Each day, find some positive feature about your partner and compliment him/her on it.

As you go about your day's activities, always expect the best.

Obstacles:

The common obstacles to developing a positive attitude are the types of negative thinking that distort your evaluation of situations. Here they are, and how you can turn them around:

• *Exaggerating.* Overestimating problems and underestimating abilities.

Example: "I'm always late for meetings."

Replace with: "I make it to most meetings on time."

• *Overgeneralizing.* Taking an isolated event and assuming it always happens.

Example: "I'm stupid."

Replace with: "This time I made a wrong turn, but I usually do get where I'm going easily."

• *Personalizing.* Thinking everything revolves around you.

Example: "Everyone noticed that I wore the same dress twice."

Replace with: "I like this outfit, and I am properly dressed for the occasion."

• *Either/or thinking.* Seeing things as mutually exclusive, even when they're not.

Example: "Either I get the promotion or I'm a failure."

Replace with: "My performance has been exceptional, and I have a good chance of getting promoted. If I don't get it this time, there will be other opportunities."

• *Jumping to conclusions.* Drawing conclusions from limited information.

Example: "I wasn't assigned the project because I wasn't at my desk when my manager called."

Replace with: "I'll ask my manager if there's a way I can help out with the assignment."

• *Ignoring the positive.* Focusing on one negative and forgetting about all the positives.

Example: "I did not make my sales quota last month."

Replace with: "I hit my sales goals for 11 of 12 months, and I will hit it again."

Setting yourself up for success:

Nothing enhances a positive attitude more than *success*, so regard success as the normal state of affairs—and the lack of success as the exception.

• *Avoid perfectionism.* Very few things are perfect in this world, so try to recognize that falling short of perfection is not failure.

Helpful approach: Remember that there is no such thing as failure—only outcomes. If your efforts produce an outcome that is less successful than you had hoped, don't say, "I'm a failure." Instead, say, "I'll change what I did wrong and next time I'll do better."

•*Focus on the future.* You can't change the past, but if you decide where you want to go in the future, you will give yourself the best chance of getting there. Always aim high, and you too will make it a winning life.

Source: Wolf J. Rinke, PhD, president of Wolf Rinke Associates, a human-resources development and management consulting firm in Clarksville, Maryland, and adjunct associate professor at Johns Hopkins University and the University of Maryland. He is the author of *Make It a Winning Life: Success Strategies for Life, Love and Business,* Achievement Publishers, Box 1184, Clarksville, Maryland 21029.

Some Ways of Coping with Conflict Are Much More Effective than Others

Whenever we deal with others, some level of conflict is inevitable. In today's world, as we come in contact with an ever-growing number of personalities and viewpoints, it becomes more important for us to be able to handle conflict effectively.

Coping with any conflict requires you to answer the following three fundamental questions:
•Whom do you want to influence?
•What does he/she want?
•How might you change his position?

The following five-step method of answering those questions was developed at Harvard University during a course on international conflict. But it works just as well when handling everyday situations at home, at work or in the community.

Decide on your purpose. You can't expect to reach your goal unless you know what that goal is so you can set off in the right direction.

First, step back from the immediate differences between you and the other person and focus on your long-term goals. Before you say or do anything, consider whether or not what you're about to do will make it easier or harder to get what you want.

Example: If you are negotiating to buy a new car, your goals are to leave the showroom with a suitable vehicle and to spend as little money for it as possible. You are most likely to achieve both goals if you first learn as much as you can about the cars available—so you know which are the best buys—and then focus on getting a good deal rather than trying to prove that you are smarter than the salesperson.

Try to deal with every conflict efficiently, peacefully and with minimal emotional and financial cost to yourself.

Put yourself in the other person's shoes. Conflicts usually arise because two people look at the same situation in different ways. To influence someone to act the way you want him to, you must understand the other person's point of view as well as your own.

In any conflict, try to describe both your perspective and the other side's perspective. Ask yourself, "If I were in his position, how would I feel?"

Example: You want your son to go to college, but he wants to become a rock musician. Before you tell him why he should think about college, remind yourself that he is only 17 years old and firmly convinced that his judgment is just as good as yours.

Your perspective: I know and want what is best for my child.

His perspective: I am not a child any longer. I know what is best for me, and I don't want to be pushed around.

As soon as you put yourself in your son's place, you will realize that if you lay down the law, he will be more likely to rebel and react emotionally than to change his mind.

Focus on the other side's choice. It is not enough just to understand the other side's position…you want to *change* it. This is accomplished by talking and acting in ways that send a three-part message to the other side:
•What you want him to do.
•What will happen if he doesn't do what you want.
•What will happen if he does do what you want.

Example: When talking to your son, the aspiring musician, demonstrate that you understand his side of the argument as well as your own. Discuss his ambitions sympathetically. Then explain why a college degree will create more options for him—whether his musical career succeeds or fails. Also, explain that you would be able to help finance his education now but you might not be able to do so later because of other financial constraints.

When the other side replies to your proposal, emphasize the positive aspects of his message. If it meets some of your concerns but not others, don't respond "Yes, but…" instead, say "Yes, and…"

Example: If your son tells you, "I'll go to college this year if you buy me a new $5,000 sound system for my band," tell him, "It's a great idea to keep up with your music while you're in school, and I can lend you $1,000 to buy the equipment." Important questions to ask yourself:

•Does the other side see my position as a request or a threat?

•How can I state my position so that it is more appealing to the other side's interests?

•Why might the other side not trust my motives?

•Are my claims convincing?

•Does the other side have anything to gain from what I am suggesting?

Generate fresh ideas. If you are involved in a conflict, it is unlikely to get better if you just keep thinking, saying and doing the same old things. Look at the situation in a different framework. Find new ways to handle it. *To generate new ideas:*

•Gather a small group of people who have an interest in the outcome, and ask them for suggestions. Write down the suggestions. Don't criticize the suggestions, no matter how wild they seem.

•Listen to new perspectives about the conflict from people who have different backgrounds.

•Meet informally with those who disagree with you to explore new possibilities.

Put ideas into action. No matter how good your idea is, it won't go anywhere unless it is accepted by the people who make the decisions. You have to know who the decision-makers are and present your ideas in ways that make them realize they will gain more from ending the conflict than from continuing it.

Example: I mediated a conflict that threatened to destroy a family business. The founder and longtime chairman said that he was ready to turn over the reins to his nephew. But he was demanding a price for his share of the company that was three times its true value. After hearing all sides, it became clear that the patriarch was not really motivated by greed. He was psychologically reluctant to abandon his leadership role in the company.

Solution: The nephew proposed that when he became the new chairman, he would retain his uncle as senior adviser and head of research and development. The founder happily accepted this suggestion, and company management changed hands rapidly and smoothly with a realistic financial settlement.

Source: Roger Fisher, Samuel Williston Professor of Law Emeritus at Harvard Law School and founder of the Harvard Negotiation Project. He is coauthor of *Beyond Machiavelli: Tools for Coping with Conflict,* Harvard University Press, 79 Garden St., Cambridge, Massachusetts 02138.

Meditation: The Basics

Meditation is a form of mental exercise in which you develop your ability to concentrate. And just like any exercise, the more you work at it, the easier it gets—and the greater the benefits.

If you practice meditation, your thinking will become more organized and disciplined. By routinely meditating, you will strengthen your will, sense of purpose, goal-oriented behavior and ability to bar distractions.

There are many different meditation techniques, but at their core—wherever they originated—they are based on the same principles. Choose a technique with which you are comfortable, and change techniques if necessary. The basics:

•Commit to 10 to 15 minutes per day, five to seven days per week for the first two weeks, then increase to 20 to 30 minutes.

•Set a timer or put a clock within easy view.

•Pick a quiet place and get into a comfortable position.

•Anytime you become aware of stray thoughts interrupting the meditation, push the thoughts aside and resume the technique.

•Close your eyes.
Three techniques:

•The Meditation of Breath Counting—Methodically, count to four and repeat, again and again, slowly.

•The Meditation of the Bubble—Visualize yourself at the bottom of a crystal-clear lake where bubbles are rising slowly to the surface. Each bubble contains one isolated thought, feeling or perception as it drifts into and out of range. Switch to another bubble roughly every seven seconds, about the time it takes for the bubble to pass from view.

•The Mantra Meditation—Create a one or two syllable word and repeat it quietly aloud.

Examples: Om, shareem, tooray.

For personal instruction or to explore other forms of meditation techniques, check the Yellow Pages under "Meditation Instruction." Ask your doctor. Ask at a health food store. Check local papers.

Source: Lawrence LeShan, PhD, author of *How to Meditate,* Bantam Books, 1540 Broadway, New York 10036. *Meditating to Attain a Healthy Body Weight,* is also by Dr. LeShan.

Life Lessons from Thomas Alva Edison

Last year, IBM received more patents in the US than any other domestic or foreign company. It is hard to believe, but for nearly a decade *several* Japanese companies have topped this list.

With technology and innovation playing a bigger role in the US economy, the life of Thomas Alva Edison (1847–1931) takes on new meaning. Edison held 1,093 patents—more than any other individual in US history. His invention of so many things—including the phonograph, electric light bulb and motion picture camera— is still the standard by which all inventors compete. The lessons of Edison's life can suggest to us all how we can make the most profitable use of our talents and time.

Self-education:

Edison had an incredible amount of curiosity and eagerness to learn. He only had a few months of elementary school before his formal education ended, but his mother, a former teacher, continued his schooling at home. The love of reading and knowledge that Edison learned from her continued throughout his life.

Edison recalled, "My mother taught me how to read good books quickly and correctly, and as this opened up a great world in literature, I have always been very thankful for this early training."

Lesson: Education is an attitude...not just an acquisition.

Using time wisely:

Edison's education did not stop when he went to work at age 12 selling candy and newspapers on the railroad. When the train was laid over in Detroit, he raced to the public library to read for a few hours.

While working on the train, Edison also took the opportunity to study business practices. He soon discovered that by wiring ahead to the next train station that there was news about a Civil War battle, he could increase the sales— and price—of his papers when he arrived. He started his own newspaper that featured news and gossip about the railroad and the towns along the line.

Edison printed his newspaper in the baggage car. He also set up a small chemistry laboratory in the car and spent his remaining free time conducting experiments described in a chemistry textbook.

Lesson: Lack of time and space doesn't have to stop you from doing what is important.

Persistence:

When Edison made his famous statement that "Genius is 1% inspiration and 99% perspiration," he wasn't joking. When he set out to develop a new device, he never gave up. If one approach failed, he would try another...and another... and another...until he succeeded. In the early 1900s, Edison set his lab staff to work to develop a new storage battery. After testing a huge number of possible compounds—50,000, by one account—one of his workers asked the great inventor if he was discouraged by so many failures and the lack of results.

Edison's response: "Why, man, I have gotten a lot of results. I know several thousand things that won't work."

Lesson: Failure is a state of mind...if you approach it positively, it's just a learning experience along the road to success.

Taking the broad view:

Edison had to focus on the finest details as he perfected his many inventions. But despite his focus on detail, he never lost sight of the big picture. *Some examples of his broad vision:*

•Commercial vision. After four years as a roving telegraph operator, Edison applied for and received his first patent in 1869, when he was only 22. It was for an electric vote recorder. When nobody wanted to buy one, he resolved that he would never try to invent anything unless he could identify a commercial demand for it.

•Industrial lab. Within a few years, Edison had earned enough money to build a machine shop where he could manufacture the various improved telegraphs and other machines he constructed. He soon realized that he would not be satisfied with his life just as a successful manufacturer—he had too many ideas and knew he could not develop them all by himself.

That problem led him to conceive of one of his greatest inventions—a major laboratory with state-of-the-art chemical and electrical equipment and a skilled staff of expert technicians and scientists, all dedicated to developing new profit-making devices. In short, Edison invented an "invention factory."

•Competition. Edison realized that in a competitive world, it was not enough just to make a good product. He kept making minor improvements to everything he invented. And even after mastering one way to do something, he continued to search for other, better ways.

•Electric light. Edison was not the only inventor who was trying to develop the electric light at the time. But he was the only one with the vision and financial backing to solve the practical problems of creating a world lit by electricity. This vision involved developing not just a superior light bulb but a whole *system* that included improved generating and distribution equipment.

Example: Edison first made an intensive study of the well-established gas-lighting industry. He decided that his system would be more acceptable to the public if he developed an underground transmission system—parallel to that used for piping gas—to avoid adding to the tangle of overhead wires from telegraph and telephone poles that were beginning to disturb the public.

Lesson: To be a winner, you have to do more than simply keep your eye on the ball. You have to understand the rules…and the forces that have an impact on your work.

Source: Paul Israel, PhD, associate editor of the Thomas A. Edison Papers at Rutgers University. The papers are available in *Volume I: The Making of an Inventor (1847-1873)*, *Volume II: From Workshop to Laboratory (1873-1876)*, and *Volume III: The Early Menlo Park Years (1876-1877)*, Johns Hopkins University Press, 2715 N. Charles St., Baltimore 21218.

9

Investment Savvy

How to Make Money In the Hot Asian Stock Markets

As investors seek higher returns on their investments, many are looking abroad to diversify their portfolios. Few areas of the world offer as much explosive potential as Asia.

About this hot region, Rissa Seigneur, an investment manager and market analyst who lived in Singapore for nearly a decade and is in constant contact with Asian business and political leaders, money managers and bankers gives her outlook and investment strategy.

Given the current high levels of the Asian stock markets, is now a good time for US investors to invest there? Yes, because the long-term picture is clearly upward. If you had made a small investment in the Japanese stock market 25 years ago, when Japanese stocks were cheap, and stashed it away, it would be worth a small fortune today. The emerging markets of China, Hong Kong, Indonesia, Malaysia and Singapore present the same opportunities for long-term wealth accumulation. As a result, Asian investments belong in every investor's portfolio.

The key is to have your strategy mapped out in advance and know what to watch for in each market. Always have in mind a manageable selection of stocks that you can monitor so that you will be ready to implement your plan through your stockbroker when there is a sell-off.

How can an individual in the US keep up with the news in these markets to make better investment decisions? By reading *The Asian Wall Street Journal Weekly* and *The Far Eastern Economic Review,** and by watching CNN's "Business Asia," which airs each weekday at 8:30 PM Eastern Standard Time.

If someone already owns Asian stocks or stock mutual funds, should he/she continue to hold them? Yes, because fundamentally, you should be invested in Asia for the long-term—seven years or more. Of course, when stocks have posted the kind of dramatic gains we have seen

The Asian Wall Street Journal Weekly, 200 Liberty St., New York 10281; *The Far Eastern Economic Review*, 36 W. 36 St., New York 10018.

in Asia recently, investors should take some profits.

Strategy: Set profit targets before you invest. If a stock or mutual fund has doubled, take profit on half of your position to get your money back and continue to hold the other half. Similarly, for a stock or fund that is up 30%, particularly if the run-up has been fast, you take profit on one-third of your position.

If you were to sell off your entire position, there is always the risk that you will lose out if the market advances again. This is the downside risk of fine-tuning versus long-term commitment.

What should be in an individual's Asian portfolio? It should be structured to obtain the obvious benefits of diversification by country —and by industry sector.

In addition, if you buy individual stocks, you should hold positions in companies at different stages of their development cycles. The ideal mix is a portfolio made up of predominantly well-seasoned, well-positioned companies while continually adding some younger companies— those that offer unique products or services.

As these younger companies mature, add new companies that can be purchased at lower costs. Companies in the early stages of their development promise faster growth and higher returns.

While smaller- and medium-capitalized stocks do not have the liquidity and are not as easy as blue-chip stocks to sell in a down market, a stock's immediate lack of liquidity should not be a deterrent to the long-term individual investor.

The dual goal of this investment strategy is to build core positions in today's excellent companies as well as to identify, accumulate and hold the stock of companies that are good candidates to become the blue chips of tomorrow. Here are my favorite Asian markets...

China:

The immediate concern for US investors is whether the Chinese government will be able to control the country's overheated economy. High inflation has resulted from overbuilding in Guangdong (the southern province near Hong Kong), along the coast and in urban areas.

The Chinese government is well aware of the political and social unrest that high inflation can create, and it is actively working on this problem with monetary controls and a policy of pushing investment into new regions.

Example: The government has created an industrial zone outside Shanghai (Pudang) that is the size of Singapore, with all the necessary infrastructure—transportation, telecommunications, schools, hospitals, etc.

China will succeed in evening out pockets of feverish growth by directing investment into the more than 6,000 zones that the government has earmarked for development, offering fiscal and other advantages to promote investment.

Considering that 80% of the population lives in rural areas of the country, there is vast potential for developing new growth areas. The longer-term concern for investors is how the transition of power will take place after Deng Xiaoping is gone and how his departure will affect business development and the liberalization of China's "socialist market economy."

Forecast: China will prosper, so it is wise to build up strategic investments there now. I recommend buying into China through "China concept" stocks. These are companies in other Asian markets such as Hong Kong and Singapore that do business in China.

Hong Kong:

Don't be alarmed about the political sparks between Britain and China as Britain prepares to turn over Hong Kong to China.

The Chinese will do what they want, and they want the economic benefits of a prosperous Hong Kong. What happens when the British leave is not the main issue. After 1997, the British will be out of the picture.

As a result, Hong Kong has to be viewed within the context of Greater China. Hong Kong is a dynamic and resilient economy, and I expect it to remain that way.

Yet the political uncertainty adds an element of volatility to a market that has tremendous potential for further appreciation. It is important to be prepared by carefully monitoring your investments there—and keeping up with Hong Kong news. When the market finds a political excuse to catch its breath and consolidate, use that as an opportunity to buy more shares.

The strongest stocks on the Hong Kong exchange are those involved in the infrastructure of

Greater China. They can be purchased through your stockbroker.

• *Wharf* (WARFY) is involved in a range of businesses, including property and hotel management, telecommunications and warehousing services.

• *China Light and Power* (CHLWY) supplies electricity to the new territories in Hong Kong.

• *Citic Pacific Ltd.* (C) has interests in Hong Kong and China, including airlines, a chemical-waste treatment company and industrial properties.

• *Hopewell* (HUWHY) has operations in construction, engineering and property investment.

These stocks all will be key players in the massive long-term development of China.

Singapore:

This is a strong economy and a well-run country with good infrastructure and virtually no political risk.

In such a sustained bull run, with earnings prospects continuing to look very healthy, what might precipitate a buying opportunity?

The big news on the horizon is the first privatization of a government-owned utility in Singapore—the Telecoms issue, which has been anticipated with equal enthusiasm by local and foreign investors. Singapore Telecoms will be a good core holding when the price/earnings ratio settles down after the excitement of the initial listing. My other favorites are the Big Four banks—Development Bank of Singapore, Overseas Chinese Banking Corp., Overseas Union Bank and United Overseas Bank, each of which has gained between 50% and 100%.

Singapore-based companies, both big and small, also offer entrée into China. *My favorites:*

• *Keppel Corp.* (KEP), primarily a ship repair and building company. Also has holdings in real estate, banking, financial services, transportation, telecommunications and engineering.

• *QAF* (QAF), a food manufacturer, specifically bread and baking products.

• *Singapore Computer Systems* (SCS).

• *Fraser & Neave* (F&N) manufactures and sells soft drinks, beer and dairy products.

Malaysia:

In this market, the gains are very much the same as those in Singapore—but the investment environment is very different. This is a much more speculative market, and I do not suggest investing in speculative stocks.

Pursuing my philosophy of strategic investing—building long-term positions that will grow as this economy continues along its rapid path of industrialization—I recommend concentrating on stocks that focus on infrastructure and telecommunications, and some stocks that reflect the rich natural resources and expanding consumer market. *My favorites:*

• *Telekom* (Telekom Malaysia), the phone company, and *Tenaga,* the power company, which are both up 30%.

Caution: The Malaysian market can be volatile, so use dips to initiate or add to positions in these two major companies.

I also like smaller companies—particularly *CHG* (CHG) in the timber industry, for its strong exports, *Malaysian Oxygen* (MOX) in industrial gas and *Nestlé Malaysia* (NESZ) as a regional food-company play.

Indonesia:

Since this market is already up 60%—the biggest gain in Asia so far in 1994—I'm for blue-chip stocks now:

• *P.T. Astra* (ASIN), a diversified holding company that specializes in the automotive industry.

• *Hero Supermarkets* (HOST), a huge grocery chain.

• *P.T. Ever Shine Textile* (EVST), a garment manufacturer.

Source: Rissa Seigneur, founder and president of Tactics Financial Services, an investment-management and advisory firm, 10 E. 40 St., Suite 1300, New York 10016. She is also international adviser to the new stock mutual fund Austin Global Equity Fund (*Minimum investment:* $10,000).

Five Signs of A Good Stock

1) Earnings per share show an upward trend over five years…2) Increasing earnings are accompanied by increasing dividends…3) A Standard & Poor's rating of A– or better for the

firm's financial strength…4) At least 10 million shares of stock outstanding, to assure liquidity if you decide to sell…5) A price/earnings ratio that has not been bid up to much above market averages—which would indicate that investors have already discovered the stock and run up its price so that it is no bargain.

Source: *How to Invest $50–$5,000* by Nancy Dunnan, financial analyst. HarperPerennial, 10 E. 53 St., New York 10022.

What Everyone Should Know About Bonds

While most investors have a good understanding of how the stock market works, too few are even remotely familiar with bonds—or the bond market.

As a result, many individuals invest blindly and are unaware of the risks. That's unfortunate, because bonds deserve a place in every portfolio. Over time, they can produce higher returns than other fixed-income investments—if you understand what you are doing.

Bond basics:

The face value of a bond is fixed at the time it is purchased. It is the amount a bondholder can count on getting in cash on the date the bond matures, which could be anywhere from one year to 100 years, depending on the particular bond.

The market value—the price at which you can sell a bond any time before maturity—is profoundly affected by changes in interest rates. These rates are driven by expectations about the course of inflation. The longer the amount of time until a bond comes due, the more vulnerable it is to these expectations on a day-to-day basis.

When interest rates go up, the prices of bonds held by investors go down. *Reason:* Newer issues offer higher yields. For example, investors won't pay the $1,000 you paid for a 7% bond if they can get 8% now.

A guess about the probable course of inflation is built into a bond's interest rate—or "coupon"—at the time it is issued. For example, a bond paying 7% may assume a 4% inflation rate, for a real return of 3%.

But if inflation turns out to be much higher, you will take a beating if you have to sell a bond before it reaches maturity. You can, of course, hold a bond to maturity and collect its face value—but the dollars you will get back may have a lot less purchasing power than they did when you invested them.

How to play interest rates:

•If you think interest rates will rise—buy bonds with short or intermediate maturities, generally not more than eight to ten years. A spurt in interest rates after you buy the short or intermediate bond will not affect its price as much as it would a long-term bond because the substandard return lasts for a much shorter period. In other words, you will get back your principal sooner and be able to reinvest it at the new, higher interest rates.

•If you think interest rates will fall further—buy bonds with low coupons and long maturities (more than ten years) that are selling below their face values.

•If you have no idea about which way interest rates are heading—"ladder" your investments. Buy bonds of different maturities—short, intermediate and long—to give you some protection against rate movements in either direction.

Common problems and solutions:

•Bonds can be difficult to buy at fair prices. Bonds have always been a game for major players—commercial banks, insurance companies, pension funds and mutual funds—which buy and sell them in huge quantities and pay less for them than you could. *Self-defense…*

1. Buy new issues. Initial offerings by governments, agencies and corporations usually sell for set prices. Commissions are generally paid by the seller, not you.

2. Buy US Treasury securities directly from the government. The Treasury "auctions" one-year bills every month. Other bonds and notes are auctioned at various times during the year.*

*For information on the direct purchase of Treasury securities, check with your local Federal Reserve Bank or write to the Bureau of the Public Debt, Division of Consumer Services, 300 13 St. NW, Washington, DC 20239; 202-879-4000.

•Bonds can be hard to sell at fair prices. Many issues rarely trade in the secondary market. Dealers don't like to handle small numbers of bonds and often cut prices to move them quickly. If you have to sell, the bid price may shock you. *Self-defense...*

1. Hold bonds to redemption. This is almost always the best strategy for individuals. Invest in bonds with the intention of holding them to maturity.

2. Buy bonds that are likely to have an active secondary market. If you feel the yield on long-term bonds is too good to pass up, choose those that are part of large offerings from well-known issuers. Find out if they are actively traded by asking your broker.

•Bonds can be retired early—or "called"—years before their scheduled maturity. Issuers can call bonds when interest rates fall if a call feature is part of the original issue. Just as home owners rush to refinance mortgages, bond issuers reduce interest expenses by replacing old, high-interest bonds with new ones at much lower rates.

Even though the call price is usually slightly above a bond's face value, early redemption is almost always a blow to bondholders. They lose the high returns they've expected to earn for years and must then reinvest the principal at lower market rates.

Even worse: An investor may have paid a premium for a high-yielding bond and so will lose income when it's called. *Self-defense...*

Buy bonds that can't be called. Read the prospectus on a new issue carefully to check for call provisions. If a bond is already trading in the secondary market, ask your broker whether it is callable before you commit. If you decide to buy a callable bond for the increased yield, you should understand the call provisions and how they may affect your investment.

•Interest and principal may not be paid. Corporations and municipalities sometimes do go belly-up. When they do, you may lose most of your investment. *Self-defense...*

Look for quality. Unless you have good reason to think a company that is facing hard times is due for a comeback, forget it. Invest in conservatively managed companies that are leaders in growing industries.

•Insist on collateral. Don't rely on an issuer's revenue stream to service a bond. If the assets pledged to secure the debt are valuable, chances are you'll get most or all of your money back if disaster strikes. Bondholders can force the sale of these assets to pay their claims.

•Invest in US Treasury securities—the ultimate security, since our government isn't going out of business.

A case for bond funds:

Unless you have large amounts of money to invest in bonds (more than $100,000 for municipals, $50,000 for corporates), beware of buying individual issues. You are bound to sacrifice diversification—either in terms of issuers or maturities—and it is easy to get lost in the intricacies of some of the markets.

Generally, individuals are probably better off investing in bond funds.

Drawback: Mutual funds don't "mature," so there is no guarantee that you will get back your investment on any specified date.

Be sure to match a fund with your own investment standards and invest in at least two of the following types of bond funds:

•Longer term—13 years or more—for the higher yield.

•Intermediate term—from two to 12 years—to reduce risk.

It's important to know a fund's fee structure before you invest, so read the prospectus carefully. *Look for:*

•Low expense ratios. This is critical. An expense ratio of more than 1% is a big drag on your yield.

Example: A bond fund with a gross return of 7.5% yields a net return of 7.2% if the annual expense ratio is 0.3% of assets, but yields only 6.5% if the ratio is 1.0%.

•Loads. Some funds charge a front-end load —or fee—when you invest. Others charge a back-end load when you sell. Back-end loads are generally reduced over time, for example, from 6% of net asset value on shares held less than a year to no fee at all on shares held five years or more. Clearly, it is more costly to sell before the fees phase out.

•12b-1 fees. Many bond—and stock—mutual funds charge 12b-1 annual fees to cover their distribution and marketing costs. The amount is small (0.25% to 0.50%), but over the long haul these charges mount up.

Source: David L. Scott, PhD, professor of accounting and finance at Valdosta State University in Valdosta, Georgia. He is author of *The Guide to Investing in Bonds,* Globe Pequot Press, Box 833, Old Saybrook, Connecticut 06475.

Beware of Fund Descriptions

So-called "balanced" and "equity income" funds are presumed to be less risky than growth funds but actually are often *more* risky than investors think. This is because many fund managers who wish to push their funds up in the performance rankings are tempted to invest in high-yield, high-risk investments that boost performance statistics—*short-run.* People who choose "balanced" funds on the basis of high returns may wind up buying more risk than they wanted to take.

Source: *Barron's Guide to Making Investment Decisions* by John Prestbo, editor, *The Wall Street Journal.* Prentice Hall, Rt. 9W, Englewood Cliffs, New Jersey 07632.

Before Buying High-Yield Bonds

See if they are subject to a call provision that allows the issuer to pay them off before maturity. Call provisions reduce the potential for gain on any kind of bond by giving the issuer the power to redeem them if interest rates decline, which is just when a bond will go up in value. But they are especially onerous on high-yield "junk" bonds because of the greater risk investors incur with them. Investors have their potential gain limited by the call provision, while still incurring the full risk that if

interest rates rise, their bonds will plummet in value.

Source: Ben Weberman, financial columnist, *Forbes,* 60 Fifth Ave., New York 10011.

Broker Beware

If your broker plies you with requests to sell a stock, ask for solid reasons why. *There are only two reasons to sell a stock:* Something fundamental about the company has changed for the worse, or the price of the stock has run up to a high level without good reason. Insist that the broker explain which is true. Remember that brokers make money from commissions, so they gain when you churn your account even if you don't. Listen to your broker, but be your own expert—trust yourself more than anyone else.

Source: *Fire Your Broker: Straight Talk on Managing Your Money from the Financial Analyst Who Defied Donald Trump* by Marvin B. Roffman, president, Roffman Miller Associates, money managers, Philadelphia. Carol Publishing Group, 600 Madison Ave., New York 10022.

Five Questions to Address Before You Develop a Business Plan

I have reviewed thousands of business plans from people who were seeking to raise funds for their business ventures.

Very few of these would-be entrepreneurs had thought through the major considerations that interest potential investors.

Before they spend thousands of dollars preparing business plans, I advise my clients to write executive summaries that answer these key questions, then use the summary to create a formal business plan.

•*How much money is needed?* The worst offense for any new business venture is to be undercapitalized. Enough money is usually needed to cover all expenses until the company becomes cash-flow positive—that is, has a profit above and beyond all of its expenses. It's better to err on the high side than to leave yourself short and have to raise more money later.

Alternative: Some biotech and high-technology companies deliberately raise money in stages. First they raise enough to develop ideas and create prototypes or viable products. Then they raise additional rounds of financing to enter production and sell the products. For these businesses, each stage requires a separate plan.

• *On what will the money be spent?* This is determined according to your experience in the field or, failing that, by comparison to similar entities. In every new venture, there will be some guesswork, but get expert help in calculating expenses to reduce that guesswork.

Ideally, talk with someone who has been a financial officer in a comparable business. Be sure to say that the figures were prepared with the help of this expert, and attach his/her résumé for added clout. *Remember:* In order to attract investors, you'll need to present an intelligent financial rationale for your business.

• *Who will own and who will operate the business?* Usually in a new company, one of the owners is the operating manager, but that's not always the case. Don't try to hide ownership. Investors like to see that key people, such as inventors or scientists who will be critical to future growth, have bigger stakes than mere promoters.

Investors also look for quality board members who own significant shares so that they are not just window dressing. If you are looking for a strong financial officer, say that up front—you may get suggestions from those who read your summary plan.

Investors are more likely to invest when they know that a trusted financial executive will be supervising how their money is spent.

• *What are the projected financial results for the company?* Investors want to know what kind of returns they may see and when. Be as specific as possible—monthly for at least the first 12 months, and go out as long as five years. The second and following years might be projected quarterly. A summary of the projections is helpful.

Example: With $2 million—in 18 months, we will have a company doing $3 million in sales, which represents 1% of the market.

By advertising, reinvesting cash, etc., at the end of the second year, we expect to have $14 million in sales and a profit of $2 million.

At the end of five years, we anticipate sales of $28 million and profits of $4.2 million.

Important: Most venture capitalists seek a ten-to-one return over five years. So potential investors will figure that your company will be worth roughly $42 million, or 10 times $4.2 million in profits.

If, for their $2 million investment, you gave one-third ownership, after five years their investment is presumably worth $14 million, seven times what they put in.

• *Do I really know enough about this business?* Readers of your executive summary will conclude whether or not you know what you're talking about. If you have trouble answering any of these questions, it's a signal that you need more expert help before moving ahead.

Source: Dan Brecher, Esq., a lawyer specializing in representing investors and underwriters of public offerings of securities, 909 Third Ave., 17th floor, New York 10022. He is the author of numerous articles on securities law and raising venture capital.

What to Do with Your Money in These Times Of Low Returns

The big question on most people's minds today is: "What should I do with the money I have in bonds that have been called...or the CD that is about to mature?"

The problems, of course, are the low interest rates that fixed-income investments are earning now. These rates are particularly stressful because they make it harder for investors to outpace inflation when saving for long-term, big-money items—college tuition, health care and retirement. Though inflation is running about 3%, inflation for these major life expenses is about 10% a year.

Result: In an attempt to find more attractive investment returns than are currently available in the bond market, investors are forced to speculate in the stock market.

Selective stock picking:

Just because we are being forced to speculate doesn't mean we can't speculate intelligently.

This means selectively picking stocks that will generate good, reliable dividends while offering the prospect of future price appreciation. In looking for such companies, I follow three basic rules:

• Focus on companies that pay respectable dividends. These days that means yields of more than 3% annually.

• Focus on companies that are trading at prices somewhat close to their lows of the year —rather than close to their highs.

• Focus on top-quality companies that have demonstrated the ability to thrive under all kinds of economic conditions.

My favorite stocks:

With these rules in mind, I have settled on a handful of attractively priced, top-quality stocks that are ideal for income-oriented investors who are dissatisfied with the puny yields offered by fixed-income vehicles. *They are:*

• Ball Corp. This manufacturer of metal and glass food-and-beverage containers acquired a can company and is phasing out its aerospace business. The packaging industry should prosper as the recovery continues.

NYSE:BLL. *Recent share price:* $27¾.

• Bell South. By the end of 1994, I expect all the Baby Bells to be involved in cable TV in an attempt to get in early on the information superhighway. Although the takeovers may not produce what we are expecting, the phone companies have no choice but to become involved or be left behind. This telephone company provides service to the south and south-central regions of the country.

NYSE:BLS. *Recent share price:* $57⅞.

• Bristol-Myers Squibb. This drug maker's price has been clobbered by health-reform fears. It now yields about 5%, and, in my opinion, has nowhere to go but up.

NYSE:BMY. *Recent share price:* $58¾.

• CPC International. The old Corn Products, this is an international food processor that is the first major food company to invest overseas with heavy emphasis on Europe. There is a tremendous demand for American brand products abroad, and the company, with such brands as Hellmann's Mayonnaise and Mazola Corn Oil, is well-positioned for future growth there. Currently yielding 3%, it is a well-run company that could be selling at $70 within the next few years.

NYSE:CPC. *Recent share price:* $47⅛.

• Merck. It's a money machine that had its price beaten down by the Clinton administration's health-care reform plans. But now it's so low that it isn't likely to be hammered any further. I'm buying it for the first time in 11 years. I think it will be selling at $45 in another year, so investors who want to take their money and run at that point will realize well over 20% in appreciation.

NYSE:MRK. *Recent share price:* $35¾.

• Southwestern Bell. Another Baby Bell, it serves Texas and states in the southwest and is currently yielding 3.6%.

NYSE:SBC. *Recent share price:* $40⅝.

A word on utilities:

You'll notice that I didn't mention any utilities, which are the traditional equity investment suggested for investors seeking income. The problem with utilities now is that they are interest-sensitive and can only decline in price when interest rates go up, as rates are bound to do sooner or later.

In fact, utilities are like bonds. By purchasing them now, you are, in effect, taking a stand that interest rates must stay down. I think that is unlikely, given the long downtrend in rates.

If you absolutely must go to fixed-income investments, then I suggest that you purchase a high-quality, long-term bond mutual fund. But be sure to dollar-cost average your purchases—spreading out the money you invest over several months—to minimize the impact of future interest-rate increases.

Source: Louis Ehrenkrantz, president of Ehrenkrantz King Nussbaum, a brokerage firm with $148 million under management, 635 Madison Ave., New York 10022. *Minimum account size:* $50,000. His stock recommendations in *The Ehrenkrantz Report,* a newsletter for clients, have risen an average of 23% annually for the past five years.

Mutual-Fund Past Performance

Claims often are very misleading. Be especially wary of long-term claims stating that an amount invested in the fund 20, 30 or more years ago would be worth a huge amount today. *Reality:* A large portion of long-term gains expressed in dollar terms is due to inflation and the much reduced value of today's dollar. Also, if you really had invested all your money in one fund so long ago, by now you'd probably have spent much of it on children's college costs, vacations, retirement costs and other items.

Source: *Straight Talk About Mutual Funds* by Dian Vujovich, former stockbroker. McGraw-Hill, Inc., 1221 Avenue of the Americas, New York 10020.

Beware of Bloated Inventories

Beware of bloated inventories when investing in a company. High inventory levels may mean that the company's products are unattractive or growing obsolete…the company is wasting money on storage costs rather than investing in operations…prices will have to be cut to move stocks, reducing future earnings. *Key:* Look at the company's turnover ratio —its annual sales divided by the amount of inventory on hand. A high turnover ratio is a good sign that inventories are moving quickly. Compare the company's turnover ratio with those of its competitors and with its own

turnover ratio in past years to get an idea of the business's competitive standing.

Source: *Blue Chips & Hot Tips: Identifying Emerging Growth Companies Most Likely to Succeed* by W. Keith Schlitt, PhD, and Howard M. Schlitt, PhD, New York Institute of Finance, 2 Broadway, New York 10004.

Annuity Opportunity… Not Just for the Wealthy Under the New Tax Law

Now that tax reform has boosted the top marginal tax rate for wealthy individuals to nearly 40%, people are searching for investments that will shield some of their income from the tax collector.

One way to do this is through a *variable annuity.* It allows you to invest in a wide range of mutual funds and defer the accumulated earnings until you begin to withdraw your money, presumably when you have retired and are in a lower tax bracket.

Like any annuity, a variable annuity is basically a contract with an insurance company. In return for paying a lump-sum premium today or making several subsequent premium payments, you will receive a stream of payments— the annuity—from the company in the future.

• *Traditional fixed annuity:* Your premium is invested by the insurance company in fixed-income instruments such as bonds. Your account grows at a fixed rate of interest (which these days is rather low and generally unappealing) until you begin to withdraw your money.

• *Variable annuity:* You—not the insurance company—call the investment shots. The size of your account at retirement depends on your acumen when choosing investments.

Each insurance company that sponsors annuities offers its own menu of mutual funds (called subaccounts). You, the policyholder, decide which funds to invest in. If the funds do well, the value of your account swells and you get to retire in style. If they do poorly, you may wish you had stuck with a bank CD.

Questions and answers:

•Who should buy an annuity? Even though earnings within an annuity accumulate tax-free until they are withdrawn, annuities are not for everybody. The combination of charges that variable annuities impose makes them much more expensive than the alternative mutual funds that are available on the open market.

Result: Because the tax advantages of annuities don't come cheap, you should be in at least the 28% tax bracket to benefit.

If you're young and on the fast track at work, it probably doesn't make sense to purchase a variable annuity. That's because a few years from now your tax rate will probably be higher than it is today, due to promotions and salary increases.

The tax-deferral privilege of an annuity only makes sense if you expect to be in a lower, not higher, tax bracket at retirement. That's because when you withdraw the money, you'll want to be taxed at a lower rate—not a higher one.

It also takes years for some charges that annuities impose to disappear. You want to be absolutely sure you won't need the money you invest for at least a decade.

If you think you might need to tap into your funds for a new car or other purchase, invest your money elsewhere so you won't be hit with a stiff penalty for early withdrawal, including a 10% tax penalty for investors under age 59½.

If you're so conservative that you can't stand fluctuation in the value of your mutual funds and you plan to invest in a money-market fund because it doesn't fluctuate, don't do it through any type of annuity.

Reason: The yields on these funds are so low that the costs of the annuity will swamp your investment returns.

Variable annuities are best for those who are prepared to take some risks so they can reap the rewards of adventurous investing.

•What kinds of charges do annuities impose?

•*Surrender charge.* Sometimes called a *contingent deferred sales load*, this charge is imposed if you decide to cancel your annuity within a certain time. The charge generally starts out at 8%, drops to 7% during the second year and continues declining by one percentage point per year until it finally disappears. But with some insurers, the surrender charge continues until the tenth year. Some insurers do not have surrender charges.

•*Insurance expense ratio.* This charge reflects a company's cost of providing the death benefit and may also cover administrative expenses and distribution costs. The average annual ratio is 1.27% of assets. The ratio ranges from a high of 1.75% to a low of 0.33%.

•*Mutual-fund expense charge.* Paid by the insurance company to the managers of the mutual funds it offers, this charge reimburses managers for the cost of operating the funds. Most funds charge less than 1% annually, although the costs of operating international funds are higher and run up to 1.24%.

•*Annual account charge.* This contract fee is paid to sponsors of the variable annuity and generally runs about $30 a year.

•Which annuities are best? It all depends on your investment goals and tolerance for risk. My favorites now:

•*Guardian Investor Variable Annuity.* Has three subaccounts—mutual funds offered under an annuity product—that are suitable for people who want to invest in growth stocks.

Two are growth funds—*Guardian Stock Fund*, which had an average total return of 27.89% for the three-year period ended October 31, 1993, and *Value Line Centurion*, which was up 24.82% for the same period. *Value Line Strategic Asset Management* was up 25.96%. An added plus is that the insurance expense ratio of these annuities is a very low 1.15%.

Sponsor: Guardian Life & Annuity Co.; 800-221-3253.

•*Franklin Valuemark II Variable Annuity.* Good choice for income-oriented investors. Offers 18 different funds. I like the *Income Securities Fund*, which feasts on unusual bond offerings—such as preferred stocks and foreign bonds. It was up an average of 12.49% for the three-year period. I also like the *Rising Dividends Fund* (not old enough to have a three-year history) and the *Utility Equity Fund*, up 15.54% for the period.

Sponsor: Allianz Life Insurance Co. of North America; 800-342-3863.

•*The Variable Fund of Aetna–Variable Annuity Account B.* Low-risk growth-and-income fund that was up an average of 10.78% for the past five years. It's not a flashy performer but rather follows a slow and steady route and is a good choice for conservative investors. It is managed by Aetna's own portfolio managers rather than an outside mutual fund and has produced a handsome return of 13.21% during the past decade.

Sponsor: Aetna; 800-525-4225.

• *Fidelity VIP II Asset Manager Portfolio.* People assume the performance of a variable annuity subaccount matches the performance of a similarly named mutual fund, but that's not always the case. The popular *Fidelity Asset Manager Fund,* for example, has a three-year total return of 21.2%, compared with 18.7% for the annuity subaccount *Fidelity VIP II Asset Manager Portfolio.*

Important: The mutual fund is deriving much of its current growth from increasing its investments in foreign markets, up to 50% of assets. But the annuity subaccount, until recently, was limited to investing only 35% of its assets overseas. Now it can go as high as 50% and has done so. The two funds should perform more alike going forward.

Sponsor: Fidelity Retirement Reserves; 800-544-8888.

Source: Jennifer Strickland, editor of *Morningstar Variable Annuity/Life Performance Reports,* a publication that tracks performance figures for more than 1,500 variable-rate investment products, 53 W. Jackson Blvd., Chicago 60604.

What Every Mutual-Fund Investor Must Know Now

Investors are pouring money into mutual funds at an unprecedented rate. Many are buying funds for the first time. Here are ten basic facts that mutual-fund investors should know:

1. Government-bond funds aren't risk-free. These days, a lot of people are moving money out of certificates of deposit (CDs) and into government-bond funds. They see "government" in a fund's name and think the returns are somehow guaranteed. While they are safer than non-government funds during periods of rising interest rates, even well-run government bond funds have posted double-digit losses.

The same holds true for municipal-bond funds. Just because a fund owns bonds issued by state and/or local governments doesn't mean there isn't a risk.

2. Money-market funds aren't investments. They masqueraded as investments during the early 1980s, when 10%-plus yields were available. But that was an aberration. Money-market funds are really just a temporary parking place for cash. Once you add taxes and inflation, you probably won't make any money with these funds. You would be much better off in stock and bond funds, providing you have a reasonably long-time horizon—seven or more years.

3. Everyone should own stock funds. That includes retirees. If you've made it to age 65, the actuarial tables indicate there's a good chance you'll live another 20 years. That's plenty of time to successfully invest in stocks. The idea that you retire, buy bonds and clip coupons for the rest of your life is very dangerous. Because of the threat to your standard of living from inflation, you've got to own some stock funds.

4. Load funds don't perform better. Just because a fund charges a sales commission, or "load" as it's known in mutual-fund lingo, doesn't mean you're going to get superior performance. The commission is there to compensate the broker who sells you the fund. If you don't need that service, you can save some money by going the no-load route and buying funds that don't charge a sales commission.

5. High expenses can mean low returns. In the 1990s, investment returns are likely to continue lower than they were in the 1980s. As a result, it's critical that you don't shortchange your investment returns by buying funds with high annual expenses. Right now, stock funds charge average annual expenses of 1.5%, taxable bond funds levy an average of 1% and municipal-bond funds and money-market funds charge about 0.75% annually. Any time you see a fund with above-average expenses—beware.

6. Fund investment minimums aren't set in stone. The highly regarded Clipper Fund (800-776-5033), for instance, has a

regular $5,000 minimum, but this no-load fund will let you open an IRA with just $1,000.

The Janus Group of Mutual Funds (800-525-8983) and the Strong Funds (800-368-1030) each usually require a $1,000 minimum. But these two top-notch no-load fund groups will waive their minimums if you sign up for an automatic investment plan—so that every month at least $50 is withdrawn from your bank account and put directly into a fund.

Other fund groups offer similar services. *Warning:* If you use automatic investment plans, it becomes tougher to figure out your capital gain or loss when you sell your fund shares, so be prepared for some tax headaches.

7. Selling a mutual fund isn't always painless. Unless you're selling a money-market fund, you can never be sure what share price you are going to get. You might need a signature guarantee from a bank before you can redeem your shares. And you may have to pay certain fees when you sell—a back-end sales charge.

8. Good funds can have bad fund managers. Before buying a fund, you should find out how much of the fund's record is attributable to the current fund manager. Some funds are run by individual managers, and some are run by committee. If a fund is run by a single portfolio manager, a change of manager may have a big impact on how the fund performs.

9. No fund performs well all the time. That's why you should own a mix of different funds. A lot of people look at the lists of leading fund performers and buy a bunch of funds just because they've been at the top of the performance charts for the past year or the past three years.

But if you do that, you are likely to end up buying funds that have been on a hot streak—and that have all used essentially the same investment style. If that style goes out of favor, all your funds could get battered at the same time.

Most investors should own a variety of funds that use different investment styles. To find out how a fund manages money, look at its annual report and see what sort of securities the fund buys. Alternatively, talk to one of the fund's phone representatives or look in the financial press and see if you can find an interview with the fund's portfolio manager.

10. There are some top-notch funds you may want to avoid. These funds may take more risk than you're comfortable with.

In addition to knowing how well a fund can perform, it is also important to know how badly the fund can do. Even the best funds go through rough patches. The severity of these losses can affect your ability to stick with a fund and thus enjoy the wonderful returns that it boasts about in its advertising. Look at the fund's year-by-year results and see how much you could have lost—and how long it took for the fund to recoup those losses. If the fund's past losses seem unbearable, don't buy it.

Among stock funds with good long-term records, I favor Nicholas Fund (414-272-6133) and Fidelity Contrafund (800-544-8888). Both have a history of holding up well in bear markets. Nicholas is a no-load fund. Fidelity Contrafund charges a 3% commission, but you can avoid the load if you buy the fund for your retirement account.

Source: Don Phillips, publisher of *Morningstar Mutual Funds,* a newsletter that evaluates and ranks mutual funds, 53 W. Jackson Blvd., Chicago 60604.

Better Mutual-Fund Prospectus Reading

To find the fees charged by the fund, turn to the section marked "Summary of Fees and Expenses" or "Expense Information." Then look for...*Shareholder Transaction Expenses:* Here you'll find the amount of any front-end load, back-end or deferred load, redemption fee and transfer or exchange fee. *Annual Operating Expenses:* You'll find the management fee, 12b-1 fee and custodial, auditing and shareholder service fees. These will be added up on a line labeled "Total Fund Operating Expenses." Remember that a fund with lower expenses than others has a head start on providing a higher return.

Source: *Jay Schabacker's Winning in Mutual Funds* by Jay Schabacker, Schabacker Investment Management. American Management Association, 135 W. 50 St., New York 10020.

Mistakes People Make Picking Mutual Funds Today

Mutual funds are an easy way to invest in stocks and bonds, but watch out for these common mistakes:

1. *Paying a sales load to buy funds.* Investors don't need to pay up to 8½% of their investment—there are always excellent no-load funds to choose from.

2. *Failing to diversify a fund portfolio.* Diversification controls risk and boosts investment returns. Start with a core of conservative funds, then add stock funds that use a "growth" approach to picking stocks and some using a "value" approach. Growth managers look for companies with above-average earnings prospects—value managers look for bargain shares.

Finish up with funds that own large-capitalization stocks, small-capitalization stocks and overseas issues.

3. *Buying tax-free funds without reviewing the tax implications.* While municipal bonds usually yield less than taxable bonds, the after-tax return is often higher because income earned by munis is tax-free. But not always. Figure taxable equivalent yield before buying shares by dividing the actual yield by 1 minus your tax rate.

Example: The taxable equivalent yield for a muni fund paying 4% for a 31% tax bracket taxpayer equals 5.8% [4 divided by (1–.31)].

4. *Paying too much attention to the headlines.* Most news has already been discounted by the market.

5. *Emphasizing too long-term performance figures.* By concentrating on 10- and 15-year track records, you miss too many good funds with shorter records. Five years is enough.

6. *Failing to set up a procedure to quickly redeem your shares.* Funds will not mail you a check or wire money to your bank unless authorized in advance.

What to do: Ask for and complete the application for wire privileges. Or open up a money-market account with the fund group and ask for a checkbook. You can sell shares, have the proceeds deposited in the money-market account and write yourself a check.

Source: Sheldon Jacobs, editor and publisher, *The No-Load Fund Investor,* Box 318, Irvington, New York 10533.

How to Bullet-Proof Your Mutual-Fund Portfolio

During the most recent turmoil in the stock and bond markets, many mutual-fund investors panicked. Prompted by fears that the markets were in a free fall, many abandoned their stock and bond funds in favor of money-market funds.

Bad move—the time to sell your stock-and-bond-fund shares is when the market is doing well. If you sell *during* a correction, you forfeit all chances of making up your losses when the markets rebound.

Better: If, during the recent correction, you discovered that you really don't have the stomach for sharp declines, consider reallocating some of your investments to protect your portfolio's overall return in the future.

Important: I am not advising that you cash out of everything you own and shift assets into other investments, but you should consider one or more of the following strategies to reduce your risk in a bear market. Which strategies you choose depends on your current holdings and tolerance for risk.

Strategy: Buy a bear-market fund.

Some funds are designed to perform well when stock prices are declining. These are among the only funds that can choose to "go short"—by betting that stock prices will fall. Bear-market funds also invest in gold, which tends to do well when the markets are in turmoil. By adding a bear-market fund to your portfolio, you'll have a buffer in case stock prices drop. But I wouldn't put more than 10% of a portfolio in these funds. *Current no-load favorites:**

*All performance figures in this article are three-year annualized rates of return for the period ending March 31, 1994, unless otherwise noted.

•Lindner Bulwark Fund. *Minimum initial investment:* $3,000. *Performance:* NA (This fund was just started in February, 1994).

Ryback Management Corp., 7711 Carondelet Ave., St. Louis 63105; 314-727-5305.

•Robertson Stephens Contrarian Fund. *Minimum initial investment:* $5,000. *Performance:* 15% (from its inception on June 30, 1993, through May 2, 1994).

Robertson Stephens and Company, 555 California St., Suite 2600, San Francisco 94104; 800-766-3863.

Although these funds are new, their managers have extensive fund experience.

Important: Don't buy a gold *fund.* They are volatile and generate poor long-run results. You're better off buying funds like those recommended here, for which the decision to invest in gold is left up to the manager.

Strategy: Switch into low-volatility stock funds.

Because they specialize in dividend-paying companies, out-of-favor stocks and often some bonds, these funds tend to hold up better in bear markets while still generating decent bull-market performance. A conservative investor could easily put 50% of his/her portfolio into these funds. *Current no-load favorites:*

•Fidelity Puritan Fund. *Minimum initial investment:* $2,500. *Performance:* 15.18%.

Fidelity Investments, 82 Devonshire St., Boston 02109; 800-544-8888.

•Lindner Dividend Fund. *Minimum initial investment:* $2,000. *Performance:* 11.91% (for five years ending March 31, 1994).

Ryback Management Corp., 7711 Carondelet Ave., St. Louis 63105; 314-727-5305.

•Mutual Beacon Fund. *Minimum initial investment:* $5,000. *Performance:* 21.10% (for three years ending December 31, 1993).

Heine Securities, 51 John F. Kennedy Pkwy., Short Hills, New Jersey 07078; 800-553-3014.

Strategy: Shift long-term bonds to short-term bonds.

Rising interest rates hurt Treasury-bond funds the most, especially those that invest in bonds with 30-year maturities. If all of your bond investments are in funds with long maturities, consider switching half of them into short-term (seven- to ten-year) corporate-bond funds or GNMA funds, which invest in mortgage-backed securities. *Current no-load favorites:*

•Fidelity Spartan Ginnie Mae Fund. *Minimum initial investment:* $10,000. *Performance:* 7.19%.

Fidelity Investments, 82 Devonshire St., Boston 02109; 800-544-8888.

•Vanguard Short-Term Corporate Portfolio. *Minimum initial investment:* $3,000. *Performance:* 7.85%.

The Vanguard Group of Investment Companies, Box 2600, Valley Forge, Pennsylvania 19482; 800-662-7447.

Aggressive investors might want to buy high-yield junk-bond funds, which aren't as sensitive to rising interest rates and should benefit as the economy makes it easier for indebted companies that issue junk bonds. *Current no-load favorites:*

•Fidelity Capital & Income Fund. *Minimum initial investment:* $2,500. *Performance:* 23.63%. *Redemption fee:* 1.5% of shares held for less than one year.

Fidelity Investments, 82 Devonshire St., Boston 02109; 800-544-8888.

•Vanguard High-Yield Corporate Portfolio. *Minimum initial investment:* $3,000. *Performance:* 15.39%.

The Vanguard Group of Investment Companies, Box 2600, Valley Forge, Pennsylvania 19482; 800-662-7447.

Strategy: Diversify into foreign stocks.

Foreign markets do not always move in sync with the US market, so owning a foreign-stock fund may provide a cushion if the US market continues to slide. Right now, I especially like European stocks because European economies are coming out of a recession.

Meanwhile, I'm nervous about Japan because stocks there have recently performed well and there's a lot of political uncertainty. As a result, I'd steer clear of Japan-specialty funds and buy either a Europe-specialty fund or a well-diversified international fund. About 15% to 25% of your portfolio should be in these funds. *Current no-load favorites:*

•Invesco European Fund. *Minimum initial investment:* $1,000. *Performance:* 6.99%.

Invesco Funds Group, Box 173706, Denver 80217; 800-525-8085.

•Oakmark International Fund. *Minimum initial investment:* $2,500. *Performance:* 53.81% (from its inception on September 30, 1992, through April 30, 1994).

Oakmark International Fund, 2 N. LaSalle St., Chicago 60602; 800-476-9625.

Strategy: Buy a market-timing fund.

Some funds engage in market timing, which involves trading in and out of the stock market in an effort to catch bull markets while sidestepping bear markets. I suggest putting up to 15% of your portfolio into one of these funds. This fund should limit your bear market losses while getting you back into stocks so that you'll benefit when prices start to rise once again. *Current no-load favorite:*

•Merriman Capital Appreciation Fund, which is currently 90% in cash and 10% in international stock funds. *Minimum initial investment:* $1,000. *Performance:* 5.8%.

Merriman Investment Management Co., 1200 Westlake Ave. N., Suite 700, Seattle 98109; 800-423-4893.

Strategy: Do nothing.

When all else fails, this is a viable strategy. In the case of mutual funds, what goes down tends to come back up.

Example: In the months following the 1987 stock-market crash, mutual funds recouped their losses in an average of 18 months. In the 1990 market drop, it took six months.

Source: Sheldon Jacobs, editor of *The No-Load Fund Investor,* Box 318, Irvington-on-Hudson, New York 10533. He is author of *The Handbook for No-Load Fund Investors*, which is available through *The No-Load Fund Investor.*

Investment Strategies For Clinton Times

The headline-grabbing feature of the 1993 tax law was the 39.6% top bracket—retroactive to January 1, 1993. But the law hurts even if you aren't in the top bracket. Tax changes threaten everyone building a retirement nest egg.

Checklist to rethink retirement planning:

1. Build your investment strategy on capital gains. The new rates for higher-bracket tax-payers make income a "punishable offense." Keeping the capital-gains rate at 28% favors retirement investments that offer long-term capital gains over high current income.

Invest retirement funds more aggressively. The further from retirement you are, the more aggressive you can be. Growth stock funds seem riskier than funds that generate income. But income will be taxed at the new, higher rates. Gains from growth stocks will be taxed at the 28% capital-gains rate.

Caution: Beware of mutual funds with lots of unrealized capital gains. In a correction, they might take those gains—hitting you with unexpected tax. *Morningstar Mutual Funds*, a mutual-fund tracking and ranking service, now calculates unrealized capital gains for funds. Ask funds about their tax situations before investing.

2. Capture capital gains in fixed-income investments. Investors have built up big gains in most long-term bonds—including CMOs (collateralized mortgage obligations) and zero-coupon bonds—and in bond funds and unit trusts. When interest rates inevitably go up, much of your appreciation will vanish. So—consider selling now. Be wary of new fixed-income investments.

Caution: Capital gains are seen as a benefit for the rich, so today's 28% rate may go up in the future—another reason to take gains now.

3. Consider taking capital losses now. Dump losing investments as part of restructuring your portfolio. Use your losses to offset long-term capital gains, so you don't pay taxes on at least part of the gains. Large capital losses can be carried forward to offset long-term capital gains in future years.

4. Invest the maximum in all tax-sheltered accounts. IRAs and 401(k) plans let you trade in your portfolio without worrying about tax consequences. You should invest retirement savings more aggressively than nonsheltered savings. Higher tax rates make it more advantageous than ever to invest in an IRA or Keogh. Keep transaction costs low by investing in mutual funds that waive loads and transaction fees for tax-sheltered accounts.

5. Contribute the maximum to your employer-sponsored retirement savings plan. Such plans let you invest more than the $2,000-a-year limit for IRAs, are fully deductible and often provide for employer matching contributions. Invest to the maximum in your plan before you invest in an IRA.

6. Ask for more choices in your 401(k). The investment option most frequently missing is an international stock fund. That is exactly what you need now. You can invest in an old bull market in the US or in a young bull market internationally. Ask your employer for a wider, more sophisticated choice of investment options. It is to your employer's benefit for you to take responsibility for your retirement plan.

7. Explore variable insurance products. Variable annuities are a way to shelter unlimited amounts of money for retirement. But given their current structure—up-front load and high expenses—they can be an expensive way to turn long-term gains into ordinary income. You pay taxes on money when you withdraw it. When you die, taxes are due on unrealized gains before anything goes to your heirs.

If you want a variable annuity, go for the lowest costs. Vanguard and Fidelity offer no-load variable annuities. Look for a wide range of investment choices. An investment with a good recent track record may not be good in the future.

Alternative: Consider variable universal life insurance. If you fund it properly—through four substantial equal payments over a seven-year period—you can borrow out the cash value tax-free. Whatever value is left when you die passes to your heirs—also tax-free. As with variable annuities, go for the lowest fees and a wide array of investment choices.

8. Don't overpay your state taxes. It isn't just federal taxes that are going up. State taxes are, too. Don't pass up ways to cut your state tax bill. Income from federal government obligations—including Treasury bills, bonds and notes and savings bonds—is exempt from most state and local taxes. Report the income on your federal return, but not on your state return. Mutual funds holding US government issues will tell you what portion of your income came from sources exempt from state taxes.

9. Take advantage of any taxes paid by a mutual fund to foreign governments. Taxes paid by global and international mutual funds can reduce both your federal and state tax bills. Expect the fund to report any foreign tax credits on your 1099. If you have foreign tax credits, don't take them as deductions. Take them as credits, where each $1 of credit cuts your tax bill by $1.

10. Don't let your tax situation steer you to unsound investments. Even with the new law, tax considerations come second to sound investment choices. Tax-exempt securities—municipal-bond funds and tax-exempt money-market funds—do generate tax-free income. Using only tax considerations as your guide, tax-exempt bond and money-market funds will seem to be a top choice.

But long-term municipal bonds are extremely interest-rate sensitive, and bond prices have risen dramatically. If interest rates rise, the values of municipal-bond funds will go down. It could become a bloodbath, if funds have to sell bonds at fire-sale prices.

The small advantage you get from tax-free income isn't worth the risk. Invest in taxable investments. Pick a money-market fund that invests 100% in US government securities. Given the exemption from state and local taxes, you'll make as much as in a tax-free money fund—in a higher-quality investment.

Source: William E. Donoghue, publisher of *Donoghue's Moneyletter,* 290 Eliot St., Box 9104, Ashland, Massachusetts 01721.

A Mutual-Fund Stock Split Or Dividend Payout

A mutual-fund stock split or dividend payout has no financial impact on fund investors. Although the number of shares owned will change, their total value remains the same and there are no tax consequences.

Source: *Straight Talk About Mutual Funds* by Dian Vujovich, former stockbroker. McGraw-Hill, Inc., 1221 Avenue of the Americas, New York 10020.

Steady-As-You-Go Investing

Good old-fashioned fundamental investment analysis—finding companies most likely to prosper under a given set of economic conditions—has given Princor Growth Fund a 14.83% average annual rate of return over the past five years.

That's more than four percentage points (or about 40%) better than the Standard & Poor's 500 stock index has done over the same time.

Outlook: But what's ahead for this growth-oriented fund—and for investing generally? Steady-as-you-go is how the fund's senior manager, Michael Hamilton, characterizes the major influences on fund stock selections right now…

•A stock market that is likely to return just 7% to 8% a year to investors for the next two or three years. That's compared with the market's century-long average real rate of return of about 10% a year—and the double-digit premium growth rates of the past decade.

•Modest economic growth—with a relatively low rate of inflation.

Strategy: The best investment values in this slow-but-steady market, says Hamilton, are in companies that…

•Sell products and services to other companies that make those buyers more productive.

•Sell successfully not only in the US but can compete in the rest of the world. Hamilton calls that international competitiveness "having a tailwind."

Hamilton's top picks…

•Clark Equipment Co. A restructured truck and machinery producer. NYSE:CKL. *Recent share price:* $64⅜.

•Ingersoll-Rand Co. Still a strong world competitor in heavy equipment. NYSE:IR. *Recent share price:* $36⅞.

•Lukens, Inc. A steel producer in upward transition as a result of substantial capital spending. NYSE:LUC. *Recent share price:* $33⅜.

•Tecumseh Products Co. A well-run pump/compressor/refrigeration equipment company. NASDAQ:TECUB. *Recent share price:* $46¼.

Source: Michael Hamilton, senior manager, Princor Growth Fund, Princor Financial Group, Des Moines, Iowa 50392. The fund has a 5% up-front sales charge, a 0.24% 12b-1 fee and no redemption charge. *Minimum investment for a regular account:* $300.

New Tax Break for Small-Business Investors

As an incentive to channel capital into new small businesses, the 1993 Tax Act created a tax break for investors.

One-half of the gain from investments in certain small businesses is tax-free when the following IRS criteria are met…

•Shares must be bought in an initial offering, not on the secondary market. *Exceptions:* Shares acquired by gift or death of the purchaser, or distributed by a partnership (in either case acquired as an initial offering).

•Shares must be held for at least five years to qualify for the tax break.

Impact: In most cases, one-half of the profit when the stock is sold will not be subject to capital-gains tax.

Example: You buy shares for $5,000 and sell them for $20,000 six years later. One-half of your $15,000 gain—or $7,500—is tax-free. Because the top tax rate on capital gains is 28%, the net effective tax rate on your profit equals only 14% —a big savings.

Limit: You cannot exclude from taxation more than $10 million ($5 million for married filing separately) or ten times the tax cost (basis) in your shares—whichever is more. The limit is applied separately to each eligible company in which you invest.

Caution: One-half of the amount of the excluded capital gain will be a tax preference item in calculating the Alternative Minimum Tax (AMT).

Example: You buy shares for $5,000 and sell them for $20,000 six years later. You can exclude $7,500 from capital-gains tax, but $3,750 is a tax preference item for AMT purposes.

Because the top AMT rate today equals 28%, the net tax rate is potentially 21%.

Nearly all types of regular corporations can issue shares that qualify for this tax break. They must be active businesses, meaning that at least 80% by value of their assets must be used in the active conduct of their trade or business and no more than 10% of their assets can be tied up in securities or real estate.

Exceptions: Financial companies, real-estate investment trusts, personal-service corporations, S corporations, "possessions" corporations and oil and gas producers, among others.

When a company issues stock, its cash plus its adjusted basis in other property (including the amount of the stock issue) must be $50 million or less.

To qualify, shares must be issued after August 10, 1993, the date the new Tax Act was signed into law.

Note: The tax break applies to newly issued stock of an existing company as well as stock issued by a new company.

Downside: New start-ups of small companies are extremely risky investments. The risk is magnified because if you bail out of your shares when you see signs of trouble in the business, you forfeit the tax break.

Source: Richard J. Shapiro, tax partner, Goldstein Golub Kessler, 1185 Avenue of the Americas, New York 10036.

To Set Up an Investment Club

Have at least 15 members to share the work and create enough investment volume to obtain reduced commissions. Draw up a partnership agreement that specifies meeting schedules, required contributions, member duties and how departing members are paid off. Draw up by-laws detailing investment philosophy, etiquette and procedures for resolving disputes—and dismissing disruptive members. *Helpful:* Join the National Association of Investors (810-543-0612) to obtain practical advice on running the club as well as investor's manuals, stock analysts' charts and

company reports. *Cost:* $35 per club—plus $11 per member annually.

Source: *Smart Money,* 250 W. 55 St., New York 10019.

The Questions to Ask Before Investing in Rental Property

Now is still a great time to invest in a rental property. Though interest rates are rising, they are still low, housing prices are soft and the rental market is strong. However, it is easy to make a mistake if you don't ask the right questions. Bad news doesn't have to scare you away, but you should know *all* the bad news before you buy.

•*What are the local real-estate market conditions?* How much are other property owners charging renters? How are the local water and school systems? What are the economic trends for the neighborhood?

Opportunity: Get to know real-estate brokers who have worked in the neighborhood for a long time. Ask them what they think will happen to the area. How are properties selling in this neighborhood compared with other properties nearby?

•*How much work does the property need?* Have an engineer inspect the property you are interested in. You need to know more about the condition of a rental property than the condition of your own home. *Reason:* With an investment property, you won't be able to put off making repairs just because you don't have the funds available immediately.

•*What are the local income and expense ratios?* What kind of rent can you command, and what vacancy level should you expect? The local tax assessor usually has such information.

•*Can you make any cosmetic changes that will allow you to increase the rent?* Check with the local zoning board.

•*Are there any hidden "time bombs"?* These problems can include pending legal action against the property, bad title, existing code violations or contracts that would obligate you to pay for leased equipment, employment contracts, etc. Watch out for obsolete equipment, environmental problems, false income and expense statements from the previous owner, etc.

•*Do you know everything about existing leases and tenant records for the property?* Pay a certified property manager to research this for you. Watch out for leases that give tenants the option to renew in several years…allow them to paint the interior of an apartment without your approval…permit any kind and number of pets…allow them to have as many people as they like living in their apartments…or have no penalty for late payments.

Source: Jack Cummings, a real-estate broker in Fort Lauderdale. His most recent book is *The Real-Estate Investor's Answer Book: Hundreds of Money-Making Ideas for Today's Market*, McGraw-Hill Professional Book Group, 11 W. 19 St., New York 10011.

A Family Investment Club For Fun…and for Profit

Betty and Bob Taylor started the *Taffy Investment Club* in 1987 to teach their children and grandchildren about money.

Along the way, the Taylors themselves learned a few things about money—and about ways in which family members can work together as investment partners.

So far, the club has done astonishingly well. Taffy—which stands for *Taylor Financial Family*—has had an average annual return of 28.9% for the past seven years, compared with 11.26% for the S&P 500. It is one of the top investment clubs in the country.

Also impressive is the fact that the club's 18 family members live in five different states throughout the US.

Despite the distance between them, each member—from 19-year-old granddaughter, Jennifer, to Betty's 94-year-old father, Ester—has an equal say about how and in what the club invests.

What do the club's members look for in a company before investing in its stock, and what

are the club's secrets for working so well together? Betty Taylor shares some insights…

Picking stocks:

•Read as much as you can to spot hot companies. Everyone in the club reads the financial pages each day, but Bob and I do the most reading and clipping since we're retired and have more time on our hands. We always read *Barron's, Investor's Business Daily, The Kansas City Star, USA Today, The Wall Street Journal* and six or seven financial magazines. We comb through news articles about industries in which we're interested, looking for mentions of hot companies. Then we clip them and research the companies' fundamentals.

We subscribe to *Value Line,** which provides us with most of this financial information. *Standard and Poor's*, which can be found at local libraries, and company annual reports give us information on companies that *Value Line* does not cover.

We look for companies with dominant market shares and earnings that have grown by at least 15% a year and that are expected to continue this pattern.

We particularly like companies that have little or no competition. They tend to be either niche players, such as Worthington Industries, a specialty steel producer, and Automatic Data Processing, a payroll processor…or they are industry leaders, such as Home Depot, Intel, McDonald's and Wal-Mart.

•Thoroughly research the company's finances before purchasing its stock. We analyze more than 100 stocks each year and use rigorous criteria to examine them. To qualify for our portfolio, which has 12 stocks, a company must have:

•*Steadily growing earnings*—about 15% a year. This and the following information can be found in *Value Line*.

•*Steadily growing sales*—also about 15% a year.

•*A price/earnings ratio* that is lower than the average of the stock's high and low price/earnings ratios for the past five years.

**Value Line* is a weekly survey that is available by subscription. *Cost:* $525 per year, or $55 for a 10-week trial subscription. 800-833-0046.

•*Little or no debt.* If the debt load of a company is more than one-third of its capitalization, we won't buy the stock.

•*Profit margin* that is larger than those of its competitors in the same field.

•Hold management accountable. We study the last two annual reports of any company whose stock we're thinking of buying. We look at the earlier report to see what the CEO promised and read the new one to see if he/she delivered.

•Make sure you understand what you're buying. Although we don't care what kind of business a company is in, we like to understand what it does.

Example: We like to have in our portfolio some stocks in companies that our nine grandchildren—who range in age from 10 months to 21 years—can easily understand. In many cases, children are the biggest consumers of the products that are manufactured by these companies.

McDonald's and Wal-Mart are two big winners for the kids. We bought McDonald's stock in 1988 and 1989 at an average price of $24, and it's now $60⅞. We bought Wal-Mart stock in 1987 for $7½, and it's now $23¾.

•Have a clear investment strategy. We believe in dollar-cost averaging—investing regularly—two or three times a year. We also reinvest our dividends and we like to have a diversified portfolio to reduce risk.

We invest for the long-term and have sold only two stocks during the past eight years. We believe that the longer you hold your stocks, the more valuable they become—and so far we've been right. The only time we sell is if our reasons for buying the company's stock change.

If one of our members wants to sell shares, another member usually buys them. Although this is a taxable event, the shares remain within the club.

•Continually reassess your portfolio. We re-evaluate our stocks at least every six months. The question that we ask is "Would we still buy the stock today?"

Strategy: If the fundamentals deteriorate, we sell the stock. We check earnings in the quarterly results.

Example: We bought stock of TCBY, the frozen-yogurt chain, in 1987 because our grandchildren loved the dessert. We paid $7½ at the time. In 1989, we noticed that frozen-yogurt outlets were popping up all over our community. We thought it was probably happening throughout the country. Even McDonald's was selling frozen yogurt.

Given the increased competition in this industry, we assumed that earnings growth would slow dramatically. We sold the stock later that year at $22, right after we noticed that earnings had declined quarterly. TCBY now trades at $5¾.

Secrets of staying together:

Because our members live so far apart, almost all our "meetings" are conducted by mail. We like to keep the phone for family talk, not our investment strategies. We compile our own stock studies and send them to one another along with company information packages. Bob and I are responsible for that. We ask members to put their buy, sell or hold votes in writing, which keeps things more formal.

•Follow the one-person, one-vote rule. We don't think that the club members with the largest holdings—in our case, the grandparents—should get a disproportionate share of the votes. Grandchildren should have an equal say. That's how they learn.

•Choose a low minimum monthly investment. This makes it easier for all our members to invest regularly, which is part of our investment philosophy. It also encourages those members who have less money—such as our grandchildren—to participate consistently. The minimum monthly investment is $5, but the average amount is $200.

•Set rigid deadlines. In our club, all votes and monthly contributions have to be received by the seventeenth of each month. There are no exceptions. This helps diminish griping and special pleading. If you don't play by the rules, you don't get to vote or invest.

•Encourage all members to suggest possible purchases. We give our members monthly progress reports. This keeps everyone involved and increases the chances of finding investment gems.

Example: Our best investment has been Home Depot, which we bought in 1987 and

1989 at an average price of $4. It's now $44¾. Interestingly, it wasn't suggested by great-grandpa, grandpa or grandma. The idea came from our son-in-law, Joseph, who is a do-it-yourselfer in Georgia.

Source: Betty Taylor of the Taffy Investment Club, Overland Park, Kansas. To get its start, the club followed many of the guidelines in *Investors Manual: The Handbook for Learn-by-Doing Investing*, The National Association of Investors Corp., 1515 E. Eleven Mile Rd., Royal Oak, Michigan 48067.

When You Invest Abroad

When you invest abroad, you invest not just in the foreign stocks or bonds you purchase—but also in the foreign currency. If the currency drops in value, so will your investment. When selling a currency that will keep its value, remember that over the long run countries with high savings and productivity rates together with low interest rates have the strongest currencies. When selecting foreign investments, examine the fundamentals of the country you invest in as well as those of the business.

Source: *Getting Rich Outside the Dollar* by Christopher Weber, investment consultant, Ormond by the Sea, Florida. Warner Books, 1271 Avenue of the Americas, New York 10020.

Quick Securities Analysis

You don't need an MBA to judge the financial health of a business in which you might invest. First get its latest financial statement. Then figure its *quick ratio*—cash and marketable securities divided by current liabilities. If this is more than 1.0, the company can pay its debts. If not, don't invest. Also figure its debt-to-capital ratio—total long-term debt divided by total capital, which consists of long-term debt plus the total value of all outstanding common stock. Long-term debt is part of the company's capital, so it is counted on both

sides of the equation. Typical debt ratios vary by industry, but a ratio of more than 25% may be risky.

Source: *Barron's Guide to Making Investment Decisions* by John Prestbo, markets editor, *The Wall Street Journal*. Prentice Hall, Route 9W, Englewood Cliffs, New Jersey 07632.

Adding International Stocks to Your Portfolio

Adding international stocks to your portfolio reduces risk. Every monitored investment newsletter that recommends a blend of US and international investment has increased its return and lowered its risk by doing so. *Why:* International stock markets do not move in lockstep with US markets, so when US markets are down foreign ones are likely to be up and vice versa. Thus, buying international stocks reduces the risk that your whole portfolio will decline in value at one time. And international markets have equaled or surpassed the performance of the US market in recent years. Investments in international stocks are easily made through high-quality mutual funds.

Source: Mark Hulbert, editor, *Hulbert's Financial Digest*, 316 Commerce St., Alexandria, Virginia 22314.

The Biggest Stock-Picking Blunders...And How to Avoid Them

When the stock market begins to rise significantly, many people who have been sitting on the sidelines with cash will likely rush to invest. But as we have learned from the correction, it's better to look—and then look again—before you part with your money. Here are the biggest mistakes people make when investing in stocks...

•*Blunder:* Not using critical stock-selection criteria. Most investors are unaware of the fundamentals that make up a successful stock.

Instead, they buy fourth-rate stocks that are not market leaders.

A common method touted by experts is to choose stocks with low price-to-earnings ratios (P/Es). This strategy is a mistake. It's like saying you want to hire lousy players for your football team because they won't cost as much as great ones.

Reality: The better stocks almost always have P/Es that are higher than the market average—which is now 18. As a result, these stocks look expensive.

I have studied the stocks that have done best during the past 40 years over all different types of market cycles. Because of their superior earnings records, most of them had P/Es that were higher than the market average at the time.

To differentiate between the great stocks with high P/Es and the lousy ones with high P/Es—read on.

•*Blunder:* Buying a stock whose price is declining. We are a nation of bargain hunters. Individual investors are always looking for stock bargains and shopping for stocks that have reached new lows for the year.

Reality: This is a good way to ensure miserable returns. A declining stock seems like a true bargain because it is cheaper than it was a few months ago. But the company may also be headed for an extended period of poor performance or even bankruptcy. Institutional investors occasionally buy these stocks because they have lots of money invested elsewhere to minimize the risk—and can make up any loss somewhere else. An individual with a handful of stocks in his/her portfolio cannot afford to bet that a stock has hit its absolute bottom.

•*Blunder:* Using the dollar-cost-averaging method to buy shares of a stock whose price is declining. Dollar-cost-averaging involves investing the same sum of money at consistent intervals, such as once a month, regardless of the stock's price. The logic here is that you will be buying more shares as the stock price declines.

Reality: Investors who follow a stock down can lose big. If you buy a stock at $50 and buy more at $40, your average price per share is

$45. If it continues downward, you are just throwing good money after bad.

Exception: Using dollar-cost-averaging to buy shares of a growth mutual fund whose price is declining is a good strategy.

Reason: A mutual fund's portfolio is well-diversified and will almost always come out of decline when the general market eventually recovers.

•*Blunder:* Buying second-rate stocks because they pay high dividends. Dividends are not as important as increasing earnings per share. In fact, the more the company pays in dividends, the weaker it may be. That's because the company may have to pay high interest rates to replenish the money that was paid out to shareholders. Realistically, you can lose the amount of a dividend in one or two days' fluctuation in the stock's price.

•*Blunder:* Continuing to hold on to declining stocks because the losses are small. It's human nature to become emotionally involved with stocks and to keep waiting and hoping for a turnaround.

Reality: In most cases, your loss will get much bigger.

The only way to prevent a huge loss is to take a small loss. The best way to do that is to set a loss limit. We sell when the stock has declined 8% from our purchase price. If you're indecisive, have your broker put in a stop-loss order at 8% below the purchase price. The stock will then be sold automatically.

Example: If you buy a stock at $40 and it drops to $36¾, sell it.

This strategy is like taking out a little insurance policy. Otherwise, if you take a big loss, another stock will have to produce an even bigger return to make up for it.

Conversely, you should also avoid cashing in small, easy-to-take profits while holding on to losers. Many investors sell stocks with profits before they sell those with losses. The move helps them feel like winners rather than confirming that they've made a mistake.

Source: William J. O'Neil, a trader and stock analyst who is the founder and chairman of *Investor's Business Daily,* a national business and financial newspaper, 12655 Beatrice St., Los Angeles 90066 (800-831-2525). He is author of *How to Make Money in Stocks,* McGraw-Hill, Inc., 1221 Avenue of the Americas, New York 10020 (800-338-3987).

10

Retirement Planning

How to Be Prepared When Your Spouse Retires

One of the greatest mistakes a couple can make is to assume that retirement will simply be a continuation of married life as they have known it.

Retirement has its own rhythm, just as the honeymoon years, child-rearing years and empty-nest years had theirs.

Most likely change: You will spend much more time together. *Result:* Trouble spots may arise in the smallest areas of daily life. Many newly retired couples, even those who agree on the major issues of their retirement—where to live, how to handle the finances—are surprised by how infuriating they may suddenly find their comfortable, cherished mate.

Most common trouble spots:

•Lack of retirement planning. Many a husband has been shocked to learn that his wife has no desire to move to the fishing village he always pictured as a retirement home. Failure to communicate expectations about retirement, or to do the preplanning necessary to make your plans a reality, can cause terrible conflict in retiring couples.

To offset clashes over major issues: Attend a retirement-planning workshop at your local Chamber of Commerce, community college or senior center. Workshop leaders say that no session is conducted without each person making at least one amazing discovery about their spouse's retirement goals.

•Failure to appreciate the psychological impact of retirement. Couples must realize that retirement can be a traumatic passage, particularly for men. Even men who look forward to retirement may feel fearful and "lost" when they no longer have a routine and the familiar identity of their working selves. Concerns with mortality and self-worth may loom large for the first time.

Best course for women: Respect the grieving period. Don't crowd or smother your husband with suggestions, opinions, questions or demands or push him into a full schedule before he is ready. But do let him know that you are there. This is a good time for extra cuddling, affection and reassurance. Let him percolate a bit, and shift the focus to your own feelings.

Many women feel that they have spent their entire lives deferring to the needs of their husbands and families. They expect retirement to be "their turn" and fear being trapped again by their husbands' needs.

Best course: Have compassion for your husband's feelings, but be very firm regarding your own needs.

Once the transitional period passes, women can help their husbands back into active life. Men are badly needed as community volunteers. Some may just want to "play" awhile, others may enjoy part-time work or a second career.

•Alcoholism/clinical depression. Alcoholism is under-recognized and badly under-treated in seniors, even though treatment has a high likelihood of success in this age group.

Depression, with or without alcohol, can afflict either sex, but is especially common among those forced to take "early retirement." Depression can also be triggered by many medications. If you suspect either problem in your family, don't hesitate to seek professional help.

Small stuff—but major gripes:

•Grocery shopping. It sounds hilarious—but this is a top area of conflict cited by retired couples. Often the wife has been shopping for years, and finds it insulting when her husband suddenly questions every choice and examines every tomato.

I have met many couples who have had bitter arguments over who gets to push the cart!

Solution: Decide that one of you will do all the shopping. Or shop with two lists. He can select the produce, while she does the rest.

•Territorial strife. With two people in one house, problems often arise over rooms and routines.

Examples: She wants the spare room as a sewing room, he wants a den. He used to leave for work, so she could drink coffee and watch *Good Morning, America* before starting her chores. Now he wants to watch CNN and complains when she starts the housework.

Solution: Communication, compassion and compromise. It's your retirement as well as your spouse's. Wives must be willing to cede some domestic territory—it's his kitchen, too. Husbands must face the necessity to "get a life," and not expect their wives to provide one.

•Comings and goings. Insecurity often manifests as controlling behavior…Where are you going? When will you be home? Who's on the phone?

Solution: Stay calm and considerate. Reassure your mate, but don't be bullied. *Essential:* Keep your sense of humor.

•Division of labor. He expects her to perform the same chores she always has, even if she's still working part-time. She expects that now that he's retired, he'll take on some household chores.

Solution: It's time to be fair.

Men: You may have retired from work, but not from the partnership of a marriage. Offer to take on the vacuuming. Don't force her to ask.

Women: Acknowledge the work he does do—caring for the yard, garbage, car, etc. Then ask for the help you need from your spouse. But if you ask him to vacuum, let him do it his way. *Helpful:* List chores you each hate, and negotiate for the other to take them on. Hire help for chores you both hate.

•Sex. Many men find sex a means of self-proof as well as pleasure. So a pleasant side effect of the anxieties retirement can produce is that many men discover a renewed enthusiasm for sex. Older men often have a stronger sex drive in the morning—so don't be too quick to leap out of bed. You don't have to—you're retired!

Wives: Enjoy it, buy some new lingerie and be willing to try new things.

Caution: Some couples experience the opposite, and shy away from intimacy after retirement. If your sex life is unhealthy, this is a problem that needs to be resolved through frank discussion or counseling.

•Television. Get two!

Source: Gloria Bledsoe Goodman, author of *Keys to Living With a Retired Husband,* Barron's Educational Series, Inc., 250 Wireless Blvd., Hauppauge, New York 11788.

Retirees Who Need Cash

Retirees who need cash should dip into taxable investments before spending tax-sheltered retirement funds. *Reason:* Tax-sheltered investments grow more quickly than comparable taxable investments. *Caution:* Beware of early withdrawal penalties from any account.

Source: George E.L. Barbee is executive director, client services, Price Waterhouse, 1177 Avenue of the Americas, New York 10036.

Answers to the Most-Asked Questions about Money And Retirement

It's not easy building a strong, well-rounded retirement portfolio, given today's high stock prices and low bond yields. Each step of your planning raises questions about how and when to invest.

Here are answers to ten of the questions that retirees—and those saving for retirement—are asking most often today:

• *What's the best overall allocation of assets for a retirement portfolio—stocks vs. bonds vs. cash?* My rule of thumb is that your age equals the percentage of your portfolio you should be putting in bonds. Reasonably affluent people planning for retirement should have half to 60% of their assets in stocks, the rest in bonds. Whatever the split is, I recommend you further break down your retirement portfolio this way:

• *Stocks or stock mutual funds:*
  • 30% income
  • 20% growth
  • 20% small cap
  • 30% international.
• *Bonds or bond mutual funds:*
  • 40% municipals
  • 20% treasuries
  • 20% corporate
  • 20% mortgage-backed.

Obviously, keep the municipals outside the tax-sheltering of your retirement funds (they're already tax-free).

• *What's the best allocation of assets in a 401(k) plan for someone over 50?* Follow the same rule-of-thumb as above, your age equals the percentage of 401(k) assets that should be in bonds. Again, affluent people can put 50% to 60% of their 401(k) assets in stock.

But don't put any of your 401(k) money into the stock of your own company. I don't care how optimistic you are about that company's future; you never know what's going to happen to that stock. It's just too risky. I would also avoid money-market funds and Guaranteed Investment Contracts (GICs). Over time, bond funds will probably outperform GICs.

The range of choices in a 401(k) tends to be abysmally narrow. That's why it's important to coordinate your 401(k) plan with your other investments.

• *Are utility stocks still good retirement investments?* As a long-term investment, utilities do have a role in a portfolio. Just don't go too heavily into them. At current valuations they aren't providing a lot of income. Putting more than 20% of your wealth into utility stocks is placing too much of a bet on a sector that is reasonable but not spectacular.

• *Is it wise to invest in Real-Estate Investment Trusts (REITs) today?* REITs have been very hot lately. But I think the people who are getting into them lack a sense of history, because REITs have gone through protracted periods of grievous downturns. I think they're trading at very high values, given the fact that there's nothing that suggests that our national real-estate outlook is ebullient. REITs could play a role in a portfolio, but it should fall on the speculative side.

• *Is there one type of mutual fund that you particularly favor for retirement planning?* I refer to balanced funds as the one fund to own if you own only one fund. A balanced fund requires the manager more or less to stay within a fairly narrow parameter of stocks and bonds. Almost universally that is 60% stocks, 40% bonds.

Maintaining that balance forces the manager to do the right thing. If stock prices have risen, he/she is forced to sell stocks. If stock prices drop, he's forced to buy stocks. It's that enforced discipline that has given balanced funds, over the long term, just about as good a performance as the aggressive stock funds with considerably less risk.

• *How much of someone's retirement savings should be invested overseas?* I think 30% of the stock side of your portfolio could be invested overseas. I think there's an opportunity in the international bond market. I could see as much as 20% of the bond side of a portfolio going into the foreign-bond sector.

If you're going to invest in foreign stocks, invest in an international fund that only invests overseas, not in a global fund that can invest in the US stock market as well. Avoid single country or single region funds. When you invest in an international fund, you're paying the manager not only to pick good stocks, but to decide which countries those stocks should be in.

• *What role should a variable annuity play in retirement planning?* It's certainly a vehicle to put money aside for retirement in a tax-advantaged form. But only buy a variable annuity after you've contributed the maximum to a 401(k) or 403(b) plan—and only after you've contributed the maximum to an IRA or to a Keogh plan if you have self-employment income.

The higher the fees on a variable annuity, the more your return will be reduced. You probably can save some money by going to one of three major no-load mutual-fund companies that offer variable annuities. In alphabetical order, they are Fidelity, Scudder and Vanguard.

They have good underlying funds, and their fees aren't as onerous as the fees of many of the annuities that are sold by insurance salespeople. Weigh the allocations in favor of stocks, because you're going to need a big return to offset those annual fees you're paying.

• *How much of a retirement portfolio should be in bonds—and what are the rules for buying bonds today?* The way to play bonds is to "ladder" maturities—spreading your money over different maturities. That's easy to do with bond funds because you have short-term funds, intermediate-term funds and long-term funds. Intermediate bonds, or intermediate-bond funds, give you 85% of the yield of a long-term bond with a lot less volatility.

Interest rates in real terms aren't that low because inflation is quite low.

But you can't let bonds play a major role in your retirement portfolio, even with low inflation, or you're going to run out of purchasing power before you die. Even in retirement, you need to keep investing for growth.

In lieu of bonds, I would look for stocks that have a good record of increasing their dividends over the years. There are plenty out there.

• *Should you try to invest for life in your retirement portfolio—or should you actively manage this money?* It's crucial to actively manage a portfolio, even when it's a retirement portfolio. After all, you're still a long-term investor when you're 65 or 75. The world changes and you have to be alert to that. In retirement you have the time to do it.

• *What can help someone overcome inertia and fear—and start actively saving for retirement?* You have to face reality, and the reality is that you've got to beat inflation by 3% after taxes in order to provide an income that's going to just keep up with inflation.

People have to realize how important this is —and that's the stick. The carrot is obviously that the more preparation you do for retirement, the more you are preparing a financially comfortable, worry-free retirement.

Source: Jonathan Pond, author of *The New Century Family Money Book*, Dell, 1540 Broadway, New York 10036. He is president of Financial Planning Information, Inc., 9 Galen St., Watertown, Massachusetts 02172.

Ensuring Retirement Income

Individuals have to take more responsibility to ensure retirement income than ever before, says trend analyst Arnold Brown. Many retirees are finding that their pensions amount to as little as 10% of their salaries. Companies that used to provide "defined-benefit" plans—guaranteeing a set payment amount after retirement—have been switching to nonguaranteed "defined-contribution" plans, or else requiring that employees invest on their own, and this means they are likely to build up far smaller pensions.

Source: Arnold Brown is chairman of Weiner Edrich, Brown, Inc., trend analysts, 200 E. 33 St., New York 10016.

You Can Crash-Proof Your Retirement Investments

Your retirement money has to last the rest of your life—unless you're prepared to risk doing without, or sponging off the kids. That means building the right mix of retirement assets to begin with, and shuffling them around when changing circumstances dictate.

That's not so easy in a time of constant change and uncertainty in the economy and in the financial markets. But you can do it, if you follow this eight-step guide:

1. Don't forget your rainy-day fund. You can get so absorbed with planning for retirement you forget to keep money set aside against the unexpected, like illness or job loss.

The first step in crash-proofing is to keep at least three months' living expenses safe—and readily accessible. Many people now keep a higher cash reserve than they used to because they're worried about job stability. If you're 50, and planning to retire at 60, consider a higher cash reserve because if you lose a job, it may not be so easy to find another.

The problem, given today's low interest rates, is where to put the money so that it earns money and is safe. I favor a money-market mutual fund, or a credit union which may pay a little more than a bank. For anyone above the lowest tax brackets, you'll earn a higher after-tax return from a tax-exempt money fund.

Retiree Alert I: The cash-reserve rule may not apply to you if you are retired and have a steady income stream from Social Security, a pension or regular withdrawals from an IRA.

Alert II: Even if you are retired, you may be in a high-enough tax bracket that a tax-exempt money fund makes sense for what cash you do keep.

2. Don't put all your investment eggs in one basket. Don't put all your money into bonds or stocks or money in the bank. If you spread your retirement money over a wide array of assets, a setback in one market won't wipe you out.

Our current asset-allocation model for someone who wants the best blend of risk and return: 40% stocks, 30% fixed-income investments, 20% real estate, 5% cash, 5% "other" investments. Adapt that model to your own circumstances—and be sure to diversify.

3. Go for growth over fixed income. The worst mistake for someone who is retired, or about to retire, is to invest money only to earn income. Many retirees invest for income because they think that this strategy is safe. Crash-proof your retirement money by investing it for total return—dividends plus capital appreciation—for as long as you can. You want the principal to grow and the income stream to grow so you are able to combat both inflation and taxes adequately.

You must invest your retirement money with the idea that it is going to last another 40 to 50 years. If you invest only for income, and not for growth, it may not.

Retiree Alert: Keep investing for total return, rather than for income alone, even after retirement. You should find that your need for current income diminishes in retirement. After age 65, most people don't spend money as they did earlier.

4. Balance stocks vs. stock mutual funds. There's a lot to be said for picking the best mix of common stocks—as opposed to putting all your money into mutual funds. Mutual funds distribute gains yearly—hitting you with an annual tax liability. You don't pay taxes when individual stocks appreciate until you sell the stocks. The right mix of individual stocks will usually outperform a mutual fund. High performance and low taxes is a wonderful way to crash-proof your retirement money.

But, with communication as rapid as it is today, I think many mutual funds get information—and act on it—faster than investment advisers, stockbrokers or individual investors. Also, there are over 4,000 mutual funds around today. I think putting together portfolios of mutual funds makes sense. *Bottom line:* Invest in mutual funds over stocks unless you are in a position to lose money.

Finally, too many individuals get emotionally attached to stocks. They say, "I can't sell my IBM" or "I can't sell my Philip Morris," and they don't sell when they should. Mutual-fund managers can sell at the optimum time because they don't have the same affection for a stock.

5. Build a defensive mutual-fund mix. Consider "hybrid" funds—which invest in a range of securities——for crash-proofing at least part of your mutual-fund investing. For instance, there are bond funds which invest in a mix of US corporate bonds, high-yield bonds and international bonds.

"Balanced" funds split pretty evenly between stocks and bonds. Asset-allocation funds shift among stocks, bonds and cash—seeking the best combination of risk and reward for given market conditions.

In every case, diversification is your most important crash-proofing tool. With these funds, you're buying a lot of diversification in one fund, since it's rare for both stocks and bonds to lose in a single year.

You could build a total portfolio around income, balanced and asset-allocation funds. But I still favor dividing your fund investments three ways:

- One-third in bond funds.
- One-third in balanced funds.
- One-third in good-quality growth-stock funds.

6. Follow a low-risk bond strategy. Too many people—retirees and those planning for retirement—are being sold bonds based on the record of the past ten years, which saw rates steadily falling and prices steadily rising.

Things are likely to be different in the future, with rates going back up and bond prices coming down. Crash-proof your retirement funds by taking those changing market forces into account. As a general rule, the shorter the maturity of a bond, the less the price of that bond will fall when rates move up.

Exactly how you apply that depends on how much money you have. With a portfolio of good size, look into a "ladder" of maturities—have a series of individual bonds—with another bond maturing every couple of years. Prices of your other bonds may be down, but you can invest money from the maturing bond at the new, higher interest rate.

With less money, go with a mix of bond funds—split 50–50 between intermediate-term and short-term. You can use taxable bonds if they're for a tax-shielded account, such as an Individual Retirement Account. Consider tax-exempt bonds if they're in your own name. Tax-exempt bonds now return 85% of what taxable bonds return, and you pay no federal taxes on the income. Single-state tax-exempt bond funds free you from state and local taxes.

7. Send some money on an overseas vacation. I think it's important to have some of your retirement money in international investments outside the United States. That may not sound like a conservative tactic, but I think it's a good hedge if you're concerned, as I am, about the high level of prices in the US stock market. International securities do pose more risk than US stocks or bonds. But you can find better values in international markets today, and interest rates are higher overseas than they are in the US.

I recommend that 10% to 20% of your total portfolio be internationally oriented. It would be in international stock or bond mutual funds according to your investment objectives and your tax bracket.

8. Don't put your stocks away and never look at them again. Market timers try to pick the ideal time to buy an investment and the ideal time to sell. If you could do that perfectly, you wouldn't have to worry about crash-proofing your retirement money.

Unfortunately, trying to time your investments seldom works out, except for very short periods. Usually, you can do a better crash-proofing job if you concentrate on choosing investments wisely, invest on a regular basis and hold on for the long term. That's because, in a growing economy, most investments show gains over time. What you hope, in selecting a mutual fund, is that the portfolio manager will make wise investment decisions for you.

This *doesn't* mean you can buy stocks or mutual funds for your retirement fund and never think about them again.

Look at IBM and Philip Morris. Investors are so nervous it seems that every day they take out another stock and shoot it. One company recently reported earnings down by only four cents a share and the stock immediately lost 20% of its value.

Don't neglect your investments. You can't say, "I've taken care of all contingencies," and go happily about your life. You must review your investments regularly yourself, or you must sit down with an adviser at least twice a year just to check that you're on the right track. There are too many things that are changing, that have to be watched.

Source: Alexandra Armstrong, certified financial planner, and chairman of Armstrong, Welch & MacIntyre, Inc., 1155 Connecticut Ave. NW, Suite 250, Washington, DC 20036.

Pros and Cons Of Borrowing

Pros and cons of borrowing against your retirement savings: If you participate in an employer's 401(k) plan, you may be able to borrow half of your account value—up to $50,000—without incurring taxes. Borrowing is easy—nobody checks your creditworthiness and you pay interest on the loan to yourself. *Drawbacks:* You may end up with less money at retirement because the interest you pay yourself may be less than the earnings had you left the money in the account—and because you may be tempted to make loan repayments with amounts that you would otherwise use to make deductible plan contributions…if you leave the employer, you may have to repay the whole loan at once …and if you can't repay the loan, it will become a taxable distribution to you.

Source: Neal J. Solomon, CFP, Solomon Associates, financial planners, 15 First Ave., Gloversville, New York 12078.

What to Do with Your Money Now to Enhance Your Retirement

While many people who are nearing retirement age are planning to take it easy, their money has to keep working. These are the steps to take before you quit the workforce to ensure that you are prepared financially…

• Review your debts. If you're still paying off the mortgage on your home, see if it's worth refinancing at the current low interest rates. Do it now, before you retire. Once you are no longer employed, you may find banks don't want to refinance your mortgage because your income will be lower than when you were still working.

When refinancing, don't extend the length of the loan and don't get an adjustable-rate mortgage. If anything, you want to shorten your mortgage and get a fixed-rate loan. Your mortgage payment is often your biggest expense, so be sure to determine how much you'll be paying each month. A fixed-rate mortgage will give you that peace of mind.

While you're at the bank, consider arranging a home-equity line of credit. Once again, it is better to do this while you're still working because you may have difficulty setting this up once you have retired. You can use this line of credit to pay off any consumer debt, especially high-interest credit-card debt.

Otherwise, don't plan on touching the money. This credit line is to provide emergency funds.

• Update your pension benefits fully. Write to the Social Security Administration to get an estimate of the benefits you are likely to receive.

You should also contact your company's personnel department to find out what you'll get from its defined-benefit pension plan. There aren't that many people who are covered by defined-benefit plans any more. Unlike Social Security, most company pensions don't increase every year with inflation.

• Simplify your finances. Move all your individual retirement accounts to one brokerage firm or mutual-fund company. This will help simplify the paperwork and enable you to better track your investments.

My clients have found that a Charles Schwab brokerage account (800-435-4000) is very effective. Schwab makes it easy to build a well-diversified portfolio because it sells mutual funds managed by a host of different fund companies. And your Schwab account will allow you to buy individual securities as well.

When you retire, this new account will be the receptacle for the rollover money that you will receive from your company's defined-contribution plan. Similarly, you should try to consolidate your non-IRA money. Again, I favor a Charles Schwab account. I would also combine all bank accounts into one or two accounts at one bank—if the total will be less than the FDIC-insured limit.

• Calculate how much income your portfolio will generate. Once you've got all your assets consolidated, add them up. Then have a competent financial planner calculate how much income your assets will generate, taking inflation into account.

If you set up a portfolio with 60% stocks and 40% bonds, you will have only $5,000 a year to spend for every $100,000 in your portfolio. Your $100,000 should generate more than $5,000 in gains each year. But if you spent all your gains, your portfolio would stop growing and its real value would be badly eroded by inflation.

• Figure out how much you currently spend, and how that's likely to change when you retire. It's important to know your annual expenses so you can see if your retirement plan is feasible.

If your lifestyle is too lavish to be sustained by the money you're likely to get from Social Security, your company pension and your portfolio, then you may have to delay retirement while you save more money.

To calculate your current spending, total your canceled checks and ATM withdrawals for the past year. Then think about how that spending may change once you quit your job. A common rule of thumb is that retirees generally need 75% of their preretirement spending money.

• Build a well-balanced portfolio. Our grandparents bought bonds when they retired and lived off the income. Now, that doesn't work because we have higher inflation and are living longer. Plan to keep a hefty chunk of your portfolio in stocks, so that you can earn some capital gains. Once you have retired, stocks should comprise 40% to 60% of your portfolio.

Target 20% of your portfolio for foreign investments, including stocks and bonds. For-eign stocks and bonds perform similarly to US stocks and bonds over long periods—more than seven years. But foreign securities often behave differently over the short term, so they tend to smooth out performance if they're added to a US stock and bond portfolio.

Small-company stocks can be 25% to 50% of your US stock-market allocation. By including the small-capitalization stocks, you should be able to increase returns and reduce volatility.

Consider shifting out of long-term bonds. Intermediate-term bonds—those that mature in five to ten years—tend to perform as well as long-term bonds but don't fluctuate as much in price. With interest rates at historical lows, this is no time to be in long bonds.

• Use your tax shelters wisely. Concentrate your stock-market investments in your IRA and other tax-sheltered accounts. Put bonds in your taxable accounts. Tax sheltering is more beneficial with stock-market investments because stocks tend to generate larger gains than bonds.

Important: Once you have retired, plan to spend your non-IRA money first. Then your IRA savings can continue to enjoy tax-sheltered growth. Since you will be spending non-IRA money, which is allocated more toward bonds, you may need to rebalance your portfolio by gradually placing more bonds in your IRA.

• Plan your medical insurance. This is critical for people who retire before age 65 and need medical coverage before Medicare kicks in. Your employer may continue to provide your insurance. If that is not the case, consider your local health maintenance organizations or a Blue Cross and Blue Shield policy. Avoid smaller or lower-rated insurance companies, which sometimes cancel policies suddenly.

• Consider canceling your life insurance. In many cases, there's no longer any financial reason to protect a nonworking spouse from the death of the family's breadwinner. You'll need the premiums for other expenses.

Source: Robert Bingham, a partner at Bingham, Osborn & Scarborough, an investment advisory firm, 351 California St., Suite 1250, San Francisco 94104.

Avoid Including Retirement-Plan Assets

Avoid including retirement-plan assets in a Qualified Terminable Interest Property (Q-TIP) trust. *Problem:* Even though this trust shields most assets from estate taxes while controlling how the assets are paid out, retirement plans and IRAs payable to Q-TIPs are estate-taxed if these arrangements are not required to pay out all of their annual income once a year. *Better:* To avoid estate taxes, have your retirement assets payable directly to your spouse.

Source: Seymour Goldberg, partner in the law firm of Goldberg & Ingber, PC, 666 Old Country Rd., Garden City, New York 11530.

New Job Opportunities For Retirees

Finding a job after retirement requires a different kind of strategy from the career tactics you used earlier in life. For many, the key move is taking advantage of the vast, but often little-known, resources that can lead to satisfying jobs. The inside track:

Many companies hire retirees, but a few actively seek older people to employ. Applying to the "seekers" can be a shortcut to employment:

- Days Inns of America
- Hewlett-Packard
- Kentucky Fried Chicken
- Travelers Corp.
- Walt Disney

Of Travelers' 34,000 employees, for example, 6,500 are retirees.

Groups that track these companies and offer other employment help to retirees include:

- *American Association of Retired Persons*, 601 E St. NW, Washington, DC 20049, 202-434-2277.
- *Forty Plus*, 1718 P St. NW, Washington, DC 20036, 202-387-1582.
- *Operation Able*, 180 N. Wabash Ave., Suite 802, Chicago 60601, 312-782-3335. Able also holds "job fairs" that put employers together with job-seeking retirees. Increasingly, employment and temporary agencies attend the fairs.

- *Senior Career Planning & Placement Service*, 257 Park Ave. S., New York 10010, 212-529-6660. This group has had great success in helping retired managers find jobs at companies such as Polaroid and Seagram's.

It generally makes more sense to apply to small rather than large businesses. Small companies often have difficulty finding the type of expertise that comes only with years of experience.

Best places to look:

Today's hot businesses for retirees: Financial services, health care, the hotel and hospitality industry, pharmaceuticals, restaurants and catering, sales and marketing, travel.

Many retirees overlook nonprofit corporations because of the mistaken belief that they rely chiefly on volunteers. As a matter of fact, most nonprofits have a good track record of hiring retirees, especially in part-time and temporary positions.

Try to take advantage of the network you built up during your earlier career. Many retired network members may be working again. If they are, some are likely to know of positions for other retirees.

Unconventional opportunities:

- *International Executive Service Corps*. This group places retired American executives as volunteer consultants to overseas businesses and governments. Box 10005, Stamford, Connecticut 06904, 203-967-6000.
- *Peace Corps*. Some 12% of the Corps is over 50—the oldest is 81. Like the Service Corps, the Peace Corps can be more emotionally than monetarily rewarding. 1990 K St. NW, Washington, DC 20526, 800-424-8580.

Upgrading skills:

To make yourself more marketable, be prepared to beef up your skills with additional training. That's especially necessary in jobs where new technology, such as word processing, has been introduced.

Other types of training may be needed to help you use old knowledge in new ways.

Example: Many people who worked with a product during their earlier career may now be able to find a job selling the product, provided they acquire training in sales.

Where to go for training: The same groups that help retirees find jobs are usually excellent resources in recommending local organizations and schools that offer training courses to retirees.

Companies that offer training to older workers include AT&T, GE and Pitney Bowes.

Playing to strength:

In your résumé and job interviews, show how you can help a company meet two of today's biggest needs in employees—*experience* and *stability:*

• Stress experience by highlighting specific accomplishments in previous jobs.

• Use words that convey how your past performance has contributed to profit and growth —*launched, pioneered, created, generated, streamlined, tripled, expanded.*

• Omit your age and irrelevant dates on the résumé, but be frank about your background. (It's illegal for employers to ask your age.)

• Frame your responses to an interviewer's questions in terms of your seasoned judgment and lifetime experience of working with people. When asked about your last job, for instance, talk about projects that demanded your ability to get along with others. Cite examples of your good judgment.

• Avoid self-deprecating comments about old age. The most common are, "When you get to be my age"…and "Back then we did things differently."

• Never set limits on how many years you plan to work. Some companies believe that retirees are only interested in working for a year or two.

• Dress well for interviews, but don't try to look younger than you are. Rehearse for interviews with a friend.

• If an interviewer says you're overqualified, say something like this, "If overqualified means I have a lot of experience, you're right. But I'm willing to work at the going rate and would enjoy bringing my experience and skill to the job."

Your rights:

Sadly, "overqualified" is often used as a euphemism for "too old." Under the federal Age Discrimination in Employment Act, it's illegal (with several exceptions) to discriminate against workers on the basis of age.

If you believe that a prospective employer is guilty of discrimination, you might want to contact an office of the US Equal Employment Opportunity Commission. To find the nearest office, phone 800-669-4000.

The self-employment trap:

Don't be tempted to go into business for yourself if you lack the right combination of skills to make it a success.

To be a successful freelance consultant, for instance, you first have to be a good salesperson. And running your own company also requires a broad range of skills including administrative skills.

Frequent solution: Team up with other people, one who's talented in administration and another who's skilled at selling. Many regional *Forty Plus* offices are especially good at building entrepreneurial teams of retirees with different skills.

Advantages:

The advantage to health in finding a job after retirement can be surprising. Not only do employed older people live longer, but studies show they also recover faster from ailments. And keeping active may even improve your looks and attitude.

Source: Robert S. Menchin, former vice president of the Chicago Board of Trade and author of *New Work Opportunities for Older Americans,* Prentice Hall, 440 Sylvan Ave., Englewood Cliffs, New Jersey 07632. He's now president of Wall Street Marketing, 401 N. Franklin St., Chicago 60610, consultants in selling to older consumers.

Exceptions to the 10% Early Distribution Penalty

Early distributions from retirement plans are subject to 10% additional tax. But there are exceptions to this penalty. The 10% penalty does not apply to distributions that are:

• Made on or after the date the employee reaches age 59½.

• Made to a beneficiary (or to the estate of the employee) on or after the death of the employee.

• Attributable to the employee's being disabled.

• Part of a series of substantially equal periodic payments (not less frequently than annually) made for the life (or the life expectancies) of the employee or the joint lives (or joint life expectancies) of such employee and his/her designated beneficiary.

• Made to an employee after separation from service after attainment of age 55.

These exceptions to the penalty are found in Section 72(t) of the Internal Revenue Code.

Source: Randy Bruce Blaustein, Esq., partner, Blaustein, Greenberg & Co., 155 E. 31 St., New York 10016.

How to Make the Most of Your Retirement Plan

Chances are that for many workers, the difference between a financially comfortable retirement and a financially strapped one will depend in large part on whether or not they've made good use of their 401(k) plans at work.

If you start contributing early in your career and make wise investment choices, you will probably do well. But if you postpone making contributions and are too cautious in your investment strategy, you may find yourself coming up short.

The 401(k) plans—which allow employees to postpone receiving part of their pay to put it into tax-deferred retirement accounts—will be the dominant form of corporate retirement savings by the end of the century.

How to make the most of your 401(k):

• *Before you sign up, review a summary plan description.* The plan sponsor is legally required to provide this document, which explains the plan in terms that are easy to understand. It spells out what percentage of your salary you can contribute to the plan, how much—if at all—the company will match your contributions, the investment choices you have and how often investments can be redirected. Reading this material and calculating what will be going into your plan will help you determine how aggressive your retirement savings outside the plan should be.

• *Check out your plan's investment choices.* A good plan should give employees at least four options—a stock fund, a balanced fund of stocks and bonds, a fixed-income fund and a money-market fund.

While three or four choices may be fine for small 401(k) plans, mature plans (those with more than $100 million in assets) should offer workers a menu of eight to twelve choices.

• *Beware of oddball investments made by the plan.* If any of the plan's investments don't make sense or seem unusual, ask the benefits person at your company to request more information from the group that is managing the plan.

Selection of a retirement-plan investment must be based solely on the interests of the plan participants. An investment must be able to be readily liquidated and its market value readily determinable.

• *Voice your concerns* if you feel that the investment choices in your retirement plan are limited or, even worse, inappropriate. This should be done first informally over the phone and then, if you're not satisfied, in writing to the person handling benefits at your company.

Unfortunately, some companies may not be open to suggestions from employees. Remember, no one is forcing you to participate in a 401(k) plan. If the choice comes down to keeping your job or improving the investment choices in your plan, you will have to do some hard figuring to determine which is more beneficial in the long run.

• *Beware of investing everything in your company's stock.* This could make you overly dependent on your employer's fortunes. If your company does poorly, you could lose your job as well as the money you've invested.

Problems: Some plans may not give you any choice but to invest in your company's stock if you want to participate in its 401(k) plan or a company will offer to match your contribution dollar-for-dollar only if you funnel it into company stock.

Strategy: Look at the volatility of the company's stock. If you are comfortable with it, then it is generally better to put your money into company stock rather than lose out on the higher match...but switch it to another investment at the earliest possible moment, often after a certain time has elapsed or once you reach a certain age.

Important: Make sure your plan permits such transfers before you invest in company stock.

• *Compare your plan's costs and expenses with those of other plans.* This information can be hard to find, since expenses are often buried. Ask the plan representative. Annual expenses in large plans typically range from about 0.3% to 0.7% of assets. Expenses of smaller plans are often higher. While the difference may seem small, they add up to big money over several decades.

In smaller plans, administrative expenses are typically paid by the employer. In larger plans, it is more likely that some of these costs are passed on to employees. If you feel expenses are too high and there is no matching contribution, you may not want to participate.

• *If you leave your job, don't assume that you must immediately withdraw your 401(k) balance from your former employer's plan.* The law says that if your balance is at least $3,500, your old plan must allow the money to remain there. Many companies don't reveal this, perhaps because they face administrative problems in keeping track of former employees' 401(k) accounts. Instead, they allow departing employees to mistakenly think they must pull out their money.

Preserving your old 401(k) plan allows you to qualify for income averaging. This spreads across a five-year period the taxes on the 401(k) funds if you later take a lump-sum distribution. It may also allow you to make use of loan provisions if the plan allows borrowing by former employees.

You may also be able to roll over the money into your new employer's 401(k) plan—but you may have to wait until you are eligible for the new plan. In the meantime, you can keep it with your old employer's plan or put it into an IRA rollover account, which would not be subject to tax or regular IRA contribution limitations. You may prefer to keep the money in the rollover IRA, which gives you *total* control over your investment options.

• *Double-check the plan's math.* This is to make sure that you are being credited correctly for your contributions, your employer's contributions and your investment earnings. You don't have to calculate it exactly, but you need to get a feel for whether the numbers are in the ballpark.

Under the law, plans must provide a statement of contributions and earnings at least annually. Most provide such information quarterly, and some even provide it monthly. Paying attention to such details could save you thousands of dollars.

Example: A company failed to process instructions by employees to invest their 401(k) plan contributions in the stock market in a timely manner. By the time the payroll department got around to executing the workers' investment decisions, six months had passed and those employees missed a big rally in the stock market. A few savvy workers caught the company's mistake when they questioned why their investment returns lagged behind those of the broad stock-market averages.

Result: The company had to pay more than $100,000 to compensate employees for their missed investment gains.

Source: Ted Benna, who in 1980, as a benefits consultant, discovered a little-noticed provision in the tax law that opened the door to the creation of the 401(k) plan. He is now president of The 401(k) Association, an organization that helps members, through newsletters and workbooks, make the most of their plans. One Summit Square, Doublewoods Rd. and Rte. 413, Langhorne, Pennsylvania 19047.

Early Retirement Choice

Employees often are offered the choice of an enhanced pension or a lump-sum severance payment as an incentive to take early retirement. It can be difficult to decide which is most valuable. *Rule of thumb:* Multiply the increase in your pension by 100 and compare it with the cash payment. Thus, an extra $500 per month added to your pension would be the equivalent of a severance payment of $50,000. *Note:* The 100 multiplier is based on a series of complex calculations that take into account such factors as life expectancy, age of retirement and present value of the payment.

Source: Bill Mischell, principal, Foster Higgins, benefits consultants, Princeton, New Jersey.

What Retirees Should Withdraw...and When

People nearing retirement are often confused about which assets to tap first, which to leave alone and how to avoid penalties and lessen taxes.

The basic rule: Avoid withdrawing tax-deferred money for as long as you can. This includes IRAs, 401(k) assets, deferred annuities, etc. *Strategy:* Tap your "life savings"—stocks, bonds and other investments in taxable accounts—before invading tax-deferred retirement accounts.

The distribution rules and tax consequences for various retirement assets:

• Annuities. Payouts are subject to income tax —and there is generally a 10% penalty when they are withdrawn before you reach age 59½. Also, some annuities charge a surrender fee if you withdraw funds too early.

• 401(k) plans. Withdrawals are usually subject to normal income tax, plus a 10% penalty for those under age 59½, although some exceptions apply.

Everyone *must* begin withdrawals by April 1 of the year after they turn 70½ or face a 50% penalty on the difference between what was paid out and what should have been paid out.

• IRAs. All deductible contributions and earnings are subject to regular income tax upon withdrawal, plus a possible 10% penalty if taken before age 59½. Withdrawals must begin by April 1 of the year after you turn 70½.

• Pension from current or former employers. Your company may require you to begin taking payments at retirement, and you must always do so by April 1 of the year after you turn 70½. Regular income tax usually applies.

• Social Security. Payments can begin as early as age 62, but monthly checks will be greater the longer you wait—*until age 70.* Currently, there is no benefit to delaying Social Security payments past age 70.

Source: Jonathan Pond, president of Financial Planning Information Inc., 9 Galen St., Watertown, Massachusetts 02172. He is the author of *The New Century Family Money Book*, Dell Publishing, 1540 Broadway, New York 10036.

It Pays to Be an IRA Early Bird

The earlier in the year you make your IRA contribution, the better. It gives you a head start on tax-deferred growth. Consider two savers, one who makes his IRA deposits as early as possible (January 1) and the other who waits until the last minute (April 15 of the following year). Assume each IRA earns at a pace of 10% a year. After 20 years, each will have contributed $40,000. But the early bird's IRA will be up over $125,000 while the procrastinator's will be about $110,000.

Source: Daniel Kehrer is a Los Angeles-based business and finance writer and an executive with the publisher, Group IV Communications. He is the author of *Kiplinger's 12 Steps to a Worry-Free Retirement,* Kiplinger Books, 1729 H St. NW, Washington, DC 20006.

All About Bonds' Place Now In Retirement Planning

Basic rule: Bonds and bond mutual funds should be at the core of your retirement portfolio. The right bonds will give you a steady stream of income for life.

Extra benefit: The run-up in interest rates that began in February of 1994 enhances the case for bonds. Short run it adds to the risk because bond prices fall when interest rates go up. Longer run it makes bonds more attractive because investment dollars buy a higher income stream.

Looking ahead: Long-term rates could go up another half-percentage point over the next year.

• *What kinds of bonds?* Super-safe US Treasury issues, or corporate bonds that pay more? Taxable bonds—or tax-exempt issues that return less, but shield income from Uncle Sam?

• *What about funds that invest in securities of the Government National Mortgage Association (Ginnie Mae)?* They were all the rage for retirees a couple years ago, but cooled off.

• *Why bonds and not a bank account?* Bonds pay more than bank accounts. A bank CD still only pays around 3%. A short-term bond fund yields close to 5%. A long-term fund yields about 6½%.

Problem: Bonds aren't insured the way CDs are, which exposes you to a little more risk.

Solution: Bonds in most funds average AA credit quality (with AAA the very highest quality). The AA bonds are considered safe, very secure.

•*If bonds are so good, why invest in anything else?* Your financial assets should be heavily in bonds as you near retirement. But it's important to keep at least 30% to 40% of your assets in stocks to protect them against the ravages of inflation.

•*Should I invest directly or buy a mutual fund?* You can customize your portfolio if you buy bonds directly. But most individuals don't have access to the information that market professionals have. They don't have the assets to diversify as completely as an institutional investor.

Helpful: Leave the management to professionals—and buy bond mutual funds.

•*What are the risks of investing in bonds?* Two types of risk are of special concern to retirement accounts:

Credit risk: That a specific bond will default or have its credit rating downgraded.

Market risk: That perceptions of inflation will send interest rates up and bond prices down.

•*How can I minimize these risks?* Protect against *credit risk* by buying bond funds. Funds are diversified among hundreds of separate bonds, so the risk of a specific issue going bad is pretty much diversified away. Protect against *market risk* by avoiding long-term issues. Market risk is graduated by maturity, meaning the longer the maturity, the more prices will fall when interest rates go up.

Helpful: Invest your money in short- or intermediate-term bond funds (those with maturities of ten years or less). They provide a good level of income and don't fluctuate as much in price as longer-term issues.

•*Am I rich enough for tax-exempt bonds?* Intermediate- and long-term tax-exempt municipal bonds now yield up to 85% of what Treasury bonds yield. It doesn't take much of a tax bracket to make you better off picking a municipal-bond fund.

Helpful: The breakeven tax rate that tips the balance to municipal bonds over Treasuries now is below 20%. If your tax bracket is 20% or above, there's a strong case for municipals.

•*Are Ginnie Mae funds coming back?* Funds that invest in the Ginnie Mae securities were very popular until a year or so ago. They paid a relatively high return that made them very attractive for retirement portfolios. Then mortgage rates fell, and Ginnie Mae funds only produced returns in the low single digits in 1993.

Helpful: With the backup in interest rates, the return on Ginnie Mae funds should improve. The return should climb to the mid-single digits in 1994, and maybe a little higher in 1995.

•*What are the pros and cons of "junk bonds"?* A junk bond is any bond rated below BBB. The stronger economy has improved both corporate earnings and the quality of junk bonds—which yield about 8% against 5% or so for a fund that invests in US Treasury issues. As long as the economy remains relatively strong, junk bonds probably will do pretty well. Some of the risk of junk bonds can be diversified away through a broad mix of holdings—which is what you get from a mutual fund.

Helpful: I like junk bonds. But junk bonds aren't for the weak of heart.

•*Where should I invest my money?* The best relative opportunity right now is municipal bonds, followed by "investment-grade" corporate securities (BBB or higher). Depending on the intestinal fortitude of the investor, the high-yield or junk-bond markets should have a place in the portfolio. I'm neutral on Ginnie Mae and Treasury issues.

"Ladder" your bond investment by buying two or three funds with varying maturities—say a short-term fund with an average maturity of 2½ years, an intermediate fund with an average maturity of five to ten years and a long-term fund with an average maturity of 20-plus years. That gives you the higher rates of long bonds and the risk-protection of shorter bonds. *How should I invest it?* There's a compelling logic to dollar-cost averaging into a bond fund, so you're not putting all your new money into bonds at the same time.

Source: Ian MacKinnon, senior vice president, bond investing, for the Vanguard Group of Investment Companies, one of America's biggest family of no-load mutual funds, Box 2600, Valley Forge, Pennsylvania 19482.

11

Enjoying Your Leisure

Ex-*Jeopardy!* People Picker Tells How You, Too, Can Be a Game-Show Contestant

After years of watching game shows and knowing most of the answers, you may want to become a contestant.

More than 650,000 potential contestants audition every year, so if you want to be a winner you must master your game and develop your personality.

Select your game:

Every TV game show is different, so for the best chance target the one for which you are most suited. Spend time watching as many game shows as possible. Determine which of the four types most interests you and which game most closely fits your skills and personality.

•Trivia/quiz games test your knowledge of topics including people, current events, history, religion, business, sports, entertainment, products and how quickly you can recall your knowledge.

Examples: Hollywood Squares, Jeopardy!, The Price is Right.

•Word/puzzle games test your vocabulary and language skills.

Examples: The $100,000 Pyramid, Scrabble, Super Password.

•Personality games test your spontaneous responses and emotional reactions to your personal experiences and real-life situations.

Example: Love Connection.

•Kids/teens game shows feature contestants who are less than 18 years old.

Examples: Where in the World is Carmen Sandiego, Jeopardy!-Junior/Teens Division.

Focusing:

If you can't decide immediately, try playing board/computer/video games that duplicate the shows you think you might want to try for. See which you enjoy most, are quickest at and win most often.

Choose a particular game: After watching all the shows of that type, study their formats.

Zero in on your final choice by asking yourself what you want in a game show. Do you want money? Goods? A great date? Do you want to play individually or with teammates? Other contestants? Celebrities? How fast-paced is the game? How far are you willing to travel for the audition?

Know your game:

Become an expert: If you want to win or even to get through the audition, you must be thoroughly familiar with your chosen game. You need to know the playing format.

Example: On *Jeopardy!,* contestants provide a question to the host's answer.

You must know the rules cold.

Example: On *Wheel of Fortune*, after spinning the wheel, you must supply a consonant to put in the puzzle.

Learn your game's jargon and the particular phrases favored by the game show. If you don't use them at the audition, you're unlikely to get on the show.

Example: Contestants on *Wheel of Fortune* waiting for the wheel to stop always urge: "Come on $5,000!"

Practice, practice, practice until the game becomes second nature. *To play along while watching it:* Cover up the answers on the screen or turn your chair around while you answer, write down your answers and check your score, use the game's language and expressions and talk and act like the contestants.

Sharpen your skills with board games or videos, broaden your knowledge of a subject by reading books, magazines and newspapers and compete with family members and friends who play the game well.

Helpful: Set up a mock game-show set in your own home using your own furniture and simulate studio distractions with bright lamps and a noisy radio in the background.

Develop your personality:

Imagine you were auditioning yourself. What would you notice about your appearance and personality? What have other people told you are your five strongest points?

Examples: Winning smile and quick wit.

Those strong points will show in your audition if you have spent hours practicing the game in front of the TV so it feels natural to you.

Work on your verbal skills, enunciate clearly and loudly, speak in complete sentences using words you are comfortable with, maintain eye contact, always show enthusiasm and smile.

When you feel you have practiced enough, call or send a postcard to the show to say you want to be a contestant. Ask if you can audition in your own area. If you must travel to the show's hometown, schedule it when you have time.

When audition day arrives, make sure you look your best and let your sparkling personality shine through. Be prepared to fill in forms and take a written puzzle test.

Those who pass, go on to a second audition where the game is actually played in competition with others. If you do well enough, you will be one of the chosen few.

Important: Shows have many legal restrictions. *Example:* Knowing anyone who works at the studio will disqualify you.

The show:

If you are chosen, you will get about a month's notice, with instructions on where to go and what to bring.

Example: Five shows are typically taped in one day, so take five outfits in case you are a multiple winner.

How well you do depends on your skills, practice and competitors. You may win big money and/or valuable merchandise. Even if you end up with only a consolation prize, you'll have a memorable experience and lifetime recollections of your few moments of fame.

Source: Greg Muntean, a former contestant coordinator for *Jeopardy!* He is the coauthor of *How to Be a Game Show Contestant*, Ballantine Books, 201 E. 50 St., New York 10022.

How to Start a Stamp Collection

Stamp collecting is often pursued primarily for pleasure. But the most satisfying stamp collections are those built with an eye toward value. Chief considerations:

•Quality over quantity. Beginners are often dazzled by the opportunity to buy a lot of cheap stamps to fill holes in an album. *Drawback:* Because these stamps are so common, they have no value to other collectors.

To put together a higher-quality collection, focus on *rarity* and stamp *condition*.

•Used vs. unused. This is strictly a matter of collector preference. Used stamps are generally cheaper and can be obtained from everyday mail. Simply cut off the corner of the envelope, soak in water and wait for the stamp to float to the surface after its gum dissolves. Hinges are perfectly acceptable for affixing used stamps.

Exceptions: If the piece of mail was sent before 1940, ask an expert to inspect the stamp before you soak it off. It may have far more value still on the envelope than it would by itself.

Warning: Some dealers defraud collectors by regumming uncanceled stamps. Collectors do not want regummed stamps. To be safe, purchase only from members of the American Stamp Dealers Association.*

•Centering. Most stamps are printed off-center within their margins. Perfect (or *superb*) centering can make a ten-fold difference in value.

Example: The US ten-cent stamp from 1869 is worth just $25 if the perforations are cut into the design on one or two sides. With superb centering, however, the same stamp is worth up to $400.

•Cancellations. A stamp's value drops if the black postal marks are heavy and deface or obscure the design.

•Condition. Over the years, many collectors have affixed stamps to albums with moistened hinges. When a hinge is removed, it leaves a mark on the stamp's gum—a flaw that reduces its value.

Alternative: Protect your unused stamps with mylar plastic mounts before placing them in an album.

•Perforations. One or two missing "teeth"— the notches along the edge—have only slight importance to US collectors. But a stamp that

*American Stamp Dealers Association, Three School St., Glen Cove, New York 11542. 516-759-7000.

is torn or missing a piece of its design is lower in value.

•Specialty. Collections are more satisfying— and valuable—when their focus is narrow. Follow your own interests.

Examples: A collector might begin with stamps of the world, then move to US stamps, 19th-century US stamps, US stamps before 1870, stamps from 1869 and finally the ten-cent 1869 stamp. A doctor might collect medical stamps— pictures of famous physicians, medicinal herbs or medical equipment. A car fancier might focus on race cars—or Volkswagens. A Philadelphian might look for stamps relating to that city.

First-day cover envelopes are colorful souvenirs. They are now produced in such volume that they are worth less than the stamp's face value.

Source: Michael Laurence, editor and publisher of *Linn's Stamp News*, the world's largest newspaper dedicated to stamp collecting, Box 29, Sidney, Ohio 45365.

Secrets of Quick Cooking

Knowing your way around the kitchen will help you get your meals on the table in minutes. Here are some hints to help you along the way:

•To use your food processor more efficiently, first chop all dry ingredients, such as bread crumbs, in the processor, then wet ones, such as onions. This way it will not be necessary to stop in the middle of a recipe to wash the processor bowl.

•To make ten-minute rice, cook it like pasta. Place the rice in a large pot of rapidly boiling water for ten minutes, drain and add sauce, oil or butter. No need to cover it, but stir the rice once to ensure that it doesn't sit on the bottom of the pot.

•If you make your own salad dressing, mix it in the bottom of your salad bowl. Add salad and toss. You won't have to use extra mixing bowls.

•Use a few small chopping boards. They can be carried to the stove or pot with the ingredients—and you won't have to stop and wash boards while working.

•To speed up stir-frying, place each of the ingredients on a plate or chopping board in order of use so you'll easily know which ingredient to add next.

•To get a quick high- or low-heat response from *electric* burners when sautéing or stir-frying, keep two burners going—one on high, one on low—and move your pot back and forth.

•To help meat marinate quickly, poke holes in it with a skewer or knife. Use high temperatures to brown, broil or stir-fry in order to seal in the juices.

•To peel garlic quickly, firmly press the clove with the side of a knife and the paper skin will fall off or peel away easily.

•To wash watercress or fresh herbs quickly, immerse the leaves in a bowl of water for several minutes. Lift them out of the bowl. Sand and dirt will be left behind. For quick, easy chopping, cut them with scissors.

Source: Linda Gassenheimer, executive director of Gardner's Market, a chain of gourmet supermarkets in Miami. She is the author of *Dinner in Minutes: Memorable Meals for Busy Cooks*, Chapters Publishing, Ltd., 2031 Shelbourne Road, Shelbourne, Vermont 05482.

How to Buy at Flea Markets

Flea markets can be a bargain-hunter's dream—*but let the buyer beware*. Here are the best ways to make great deals at flea markets—and have fun while you're hunting.
How to find the best deals:

•Evaluate a variety of flea markets to find your favorites. Flea markets are unpredictable—anyone can rent a table and sell whatever was in the attic, closet or basement. But no matter where they are located, the best flea markets offer a wide range of used and new merchandise, antiques, collectibles and good, old-fashioned "junque." Many include a farmer's market as well.

To evaluate a flea market: Look for diversity. Cruise the market quickly before deciding to stay. Do you see merchandise that interests you? Or is it just a show of cheap socks and knock-off designer watches?

Example: I visited a flea market in North Carolina that was stocked almost entirely with used computer equipment, office supplies and

stationery overruns—good deals, but not what I was interested in at the time.

•Familiarize yourself with market values of collectibles and antiques. Flea markets are not geared for people who know exactly what they are looking for—they're for fun and surprises. But the more you know about the values of many types of items, the better you will be able to identify and bargain for a treasure when you see it. If you are serious about antiques and collectibles, check price guides and retail dealers regularly to develop an eye for authenticity, condition and prices.

•Be prepared to bargain for the merchandise—but don't feel obligated to bargain. Most vendors will bargain, some won't. Usually, if a flea-market vendor senses you know what you are talking about, he/she will move on the price. Many dealers "build in" a cushion so they can come down in price, so that you feel as though you are getting a deal and both you and the vendor get what you want.

•Talk to the vendors—especially if you have an item to trade or are looking for something special. It is boring to sit at a table all day, and flea-market vendors generally love to gab. Most vendors network among themselves and exchange merchandise and business cards. Many are knowledgeable antique professionals or collectors themselves. Most of them buy as well as sell and know what everyone else has to offer. Many vendors have a shop or store items at home that they would be happy to bring to the market the next week.

•Come early and stay—or return late. As a general rule, you can find the best buys very, very early in the day. But if an item is unsold at the end of the day, you may be able to negotiate a better price. *Best strategy:* Visit your favorite markets regularly. Go early in the morning and pass through quickly, to scout out anything new and interesting. Swoop down on the treasures you must have immediately or that you believe will sell by the end of the day. Then return for the last-minute bargains near closing time. The strongest buyers arrive when the booths are being set up—and bring flashlights with them.
What to avoid when shopping at flea markets:

Mistake: Thinking you are getting a steal. Most flea-market vendors are reputable, well-informed on the value of their merchandise and want happy, repeat customers. But there are always a few who intend to thrive on credulous tourists.

Mistake: Buying the first thing you see. This may sound as if it contradicts the "come early" rule—but flea-market vendors often have overlapping wares. That is, you may buy a "unique" Maltese falcon statue, only to find a whole tableful further on.

Buyers can often find real steals at small, out-of-the-way markets that are not hit regularly by bargain-hunters. But there are also excellent deals to be found at the large, well-publicized markets.

My favorite flea markets:

•Rose Bowl Flea Market. In the parking lot of Rose Bowl Stadium, this is one of the largest flea markets in the world and certainly one of the most fun.

Rose Bowl Stadium, Pasadena, California. Rosemont & Arroyo. Second Sunday of every month, 9 AM to 3 PM. 213-588-4411.

•First Monday Trade Days in Canton. This small Texas town overflows on the first Monday of every month and the long weekend preceding it. A very colorful market, one of the largest in the US.

On Highway 19 at Kaufman St., Canton, Texas. Daylight to dusk. 903-567-6556.

•Ft. Lauderdale/Thunderbird Swap Shop. Florida is flea-market paradise—and this is one of the best, a megamall indoors and hundreds of vendors set up outdoors as well.

3501 W. Sunset Blvd. at 31 Ave., Ft. Lauderdale, Florida. Daily, 7:30 AM to 5:30 PM. 305-791-7927.

•Renninger's #1 Antique Market. Huge antique market.

Rte. 272, a half-mile north of Exit 21 off the Pennsylvania Tpke., Denver/Adamstown, Pennsylvania. Sundays, 7:30 AM to 5 PM. 717-336-9997.

•Green Dragon Farmer's Market & Auction. A smaller, country market with a nice variety of merchandise and auction sales of livestock.

955 N. State St. (spur of Rte. 272), between Rte. 322 and the Pennsylvania Tpke., Ephrata, Pennsylvania. Fridays, 9 AM to 10 PM. 717-738-1117.

Source: Albert LaFarge, author of *The Confident Collector: US Flea-Market Directory,* Avon Books, 1350 Avenue of the Americas, New York 10019.

Crucial for Better Biking

A comfortable fit between bike and rider. *Helpful:* Set seat height by placing one foot on the pedal in its lowest position so the heel is slightly off the top of the pedal. Make sure there's a slight bend in the knee to avoid complete extension. Adjust the handlebars so you can comfortably rest your hands on the handles. Handlebars should be as wide as your shoulders. Adjust the handlebars' stem height so it's two to five centimeters below the tip of the saddle.

Source: Davis Phinney, 1991 US pro champion from Santa Cruz, California, quoted in *Men's Fitness,* 21100 Erwin St., Woodland Hills, California 91367.

What to Do When You Win the Lottery

Many people assume that winning the lottery would automatically solve all their problems.

In fact, winning the lottery creates a whole new set of problems. Steps to take if you're ever among the lucky ones:

•*Tell no one outside your immediate family that you've won.* Your silence—and the freedom from pressure that it buys you—will allow you to think about how to invest your windfall in privacy. If you are interviewed by the media, be an uninteresting, dull and boring interviewee. In the long run, that will discourage others from bothering you.

•*Don't assume that you've won.* Some people choose to buy a "quick pick" ticket, for which the numbers are chosen for you at random. If this was the case with your winning ticket, there is the possibility—although a slim one—that you may not have won at all.

Reason: Under the rules of most state lotteries, only a certain number of quick-pick tickets can hit the jackpot in a single game. If more than the intended number of big winners are mistakenly printed, all may be disqualified—leaving their owners with no more than a refund of the amount spent on the ticket.

•*Secure your winning ticket.* Start by signing the back of your ticket, which seals your right to the proceeds. Then photocopy both the front and back of the ticket to protect yourself. Type up a separate statement of authenticity with your signature, and, as an added precaution, have this statement notarized. You must surrender your lottery ticket to have it validated, and copying it will protect you in case the original is lost by the lottery bureaucracy. Keep the photocopies in a safe-deposit box until you are ready to turn in your ticket and claim your prize.

•*Claim your prize correctly.* If you neglect to mail in an official claim form (available from your lottery retailer) within a set number of days or fail to appear in person and have your winning ticket validated, you may be disqualified.

Deadline: Usually from 6 to 12 months after the winning drawing, depending on the state.

•*If you have indeed won big, get an unlisted phone number.* Database marketers, reporters, charities and curiosity-seekers obtain lists of lottery winners' names through the Freedom of Information Act. Though addresses and phone numbers are not so readily available, they may leak out eventually. Be prepared to change your phone number two to three times within the first nine months after you win—the period in which pressure to seek you out will be greatest.

•*Don't assume you've won the total jackpot.* Approximately one-third of the time, several winners share a prize.

•*If you've won as part of a group, set up a partnership* by drafting a simple agreement using one of the *Do-It-Yourself Fill-in-the-Blank* legal kits (available from TitleWaves and many bookstores). Call the IRS at 800-829-3676 and ask for the SS-4 Form to obtain a federal employer identification number. Validate your ticket under the name of the new entity. This will add another line of defense between you and the mail that is soon to come your way.

•*Get a post-office box*—preferably one from the US Postal Service instead of a mail-service company—rather than receiving mail at home. Winners often receive solicitations for business schemes, media deals, marriage proposals, etc.

•*Buy a home-security system.* It should include perimeter contacts on all doors and windows, interior infrared motion detectors, motion-sensitive lighting, audible on-site alarm *plus* a 24-hour monitoring service that connects your home to a central station alarm.

Consider: A drive-by armed-guard service. Request high-visibility protection for the first nine months after you win. Several lottery winners have had their homes burglarized even before they received any cash.

•*You may have to quit your salaried job.* It may not be practical for you to keep working at your company when you earn far more than your bosses. Resentment can arise, and bosses may assume that you will eventually quit, making promotions unlikely and limiting your responsibilities. In addition, many "jackpot chasers" will phone you at work, causing even further disruption of the workplace.

•*Be a little frivolous—and then a lot cautious.* Blow 10% of your first lottery check. Be mindless and irresponsible—and get it out of your system. Put the remaining 90% away for at least three months. Park it in a money-market mutual fund or a 90-day CD to avoid temptation. Few people are accustomed to dealing with large sums of money, and they need time to adjust. In either case, make sure your money is adequately insured by investing no more than $100,000 at a single bank.

•*Get out of town.* Take an inexpensive trip—and treat it like a business trip. Go where you will have the solitude you need to plan the next steps in your new life.

Source: Rob Sanford, certified financial planner based in Malibu, California. He is the author of *Infinite Financial Freedom: What to Do Before and After You Win the Lottery*, TitleWaves Publishing, Box 943, Malibu, California 90265.

Camcorder Pitfalls

Every autofocus system makes errors under certain filming conditions. *Common problem areas:*

•Objects that are shiny, horizontally striped or diagonally slanted.

•Subjects that move rapidly, are set behind glass or railings or have little contrast—such as a white wall.

•Two or more subjects at different distances that occupy the same zone in the viewfinder.

•Dark subjects.

•Night scenes.

Self-defense: Switch to manual focus before shooting in situations where the system is error-prone.

Source: *John Hedgecoe's Complete Guide to Video* by John Hedgecoe, professor of photography at the Royal College of Art in London, England. Sterling Publishing Co., 387 Park Ave. S., New York 10016.

Better Dating: A Checklist

•Never talk about an "ex" on a first date. Try to talk about life—not your former lovers. If the subject of past relationships does come up, be careful to tread lightly and don't dwell on the negatives. Betrayal, misery and anger are not ideal themes for dinner conversation. These topics can only diminish—not improve—your standing with your date.

•Be accessible. Don't try to impress a date with your busy schedule. Availability is very comforting. If you give the impression that you are a workaholic, your date will probably believe that he/she will end up lonely in a relationship with you.

•Don't reveal too much about your past on the first or second date. Save that for future meetings. It's important to keep the mystery alive.

•Be warm and familiar. If you're having a good time and feel comfortable, let your date know it—touch his/her shoulder, arm or hand, laugh.

•Have confidence. Everyone admires those who are sure of themselves. But beware—there is a fine line between confidence and arrogance. Try to show that you are comfortable with yourself, but don't rub it in—and don't tell exaggerated stories about yourself. This makes you seem insecure.

•Maintain a fluid exchange of conversation. Pay attention, be alert and be responsive. Neither of you should dominate the conversation. If your partner continues to do so despite your attempts to strike a balance, he/she may not be the right person for you.

•Don't rate your date on the basis of one two-hour meeting. Men are particularly guilty of this, especially if the women are not super-attractive in the way that they prefer. Yes, you need chemistry, but the first few dates don't have to set off fireworks. Get to know the person before you make up your mind.

•Date against your "type." Both men and women miss out on countless opportunities by responding only to those types they've dated in the past. If the person you're with is kind and considerate, give yourself time to appreciate those qualities. You may be surprised.

•Don't talk about your physical—or mental—health problems. This will make you seem old and frail—even if that is not the case. Besides, such conversation is seldom interesting. Of course, you should mention these problems if the other person should know about them up front.

•Beware of dates who are commitment-phobic. People of this type have personalities that work against any long-term relationships.

Examples: A man tells you on the first date that he hates his mother or makes you feel uncomfortable by talking about his dreams for your future together—after spending only an hour with you. In both cases, the person did not set out to sabotage the evening—it was simply his psychology at work. Think of such comments as an advance warning system.

•If you have children from an earlier marriage, don't talk about them all night. It is perfectly fine to mention your children and tell your date how much they mean to you. But your time together should be about the two of *you*—not about your children.

•Be wary of someone whose lifestyle is the opposite of yours. Tennis players don't have to date tennis players, but an athletic person is not likely to be happy with someone who is always sedentary or who thinks that exercise means walking through a mall when you shop. Don't assume that this won't matter. It probably will.

Source: Denise Winston, president of Denise Winston Professional Matchmaker and Love Coach Inc., a matchmaking service, 200 E. 61 St., New York 10021.

All About the Trees and Shrubs that Attract Birds

Bird-attracting trees:

•Alder trees attract chickadees, warblers, redpolls and other small birds in the late fall and winter. These moisture-loving trees have smooth trunks and graceful foliage and must be watered regularly in areas that have dry summers.

Planting: Roots are shallow and invasive, so use these trees in backgrounds or grove plantings.

•Ash trees produce large quantities of aerodynamic, single-winged seeds in late summer that attract a variety of seed-eating birds, such as titmice and juncos. Ash trees are fast-growing, tough and undemanding. Most varieties turn bright yellow or purple in autumn.

Planting: Since most varieties grow big and round-headed, put them near plants that will benefit from the ash trees' shade. *Examples:* Joe-pye weed, American cranberries, elderberries, rhododendrons and azaleas.

•Beech trees drop nutritious little nuts in the fall and winter that attract wood dwellers (grouse, wood ducks and wild turkeys) as well as seed lovers (evening grosbeaks). These majestic, imposing trees have ground-sweeping lower branches that provide heavy shade and rule out plantings beneath.

Planting: Set in the lawn or at the background of a garden.

•Cherry trees bear fruit that attract a variety of songbirds in summer. The deciduous varieties are known for their spring flowers on leafless limbs.

Planting: Use as accents to the patio or garden. But keep far enough away from the pavement to prevent the fruit from staining or making a mess.

•Holly trees provide wonderful nesting sites in the spring, berries in the winter and good, dense cover all year long.

Planting: Hollies make wonderful background screens or barriers and also work as accent trees for lawns, gardens and patios.

•Russian olive trees are one of the best bird-attracting plants around, due to the abundant crops of olivelike berries they produce from fall well into winter. Narrow, willowlike, silvery-gray leaves cover an upright and angular branch structure that reaches no more than 25-feet high.

Planting: Use as a background tree or a windbreak hedge.

Bird-attracting shrubs:

•Barberry bushes produce hanging, reddish fruit that sustains birds throughout the winter. They also provide good, dense cover. Japanese barberry is a particularly pretty variety, with purple and yellow leaves and gorgeous scarlet fall color.

Planting: Use in sun or light shade for a screen, hedge, border or barrier.

•Viburnums of many types produce lots of berries for a variety of songbirds. They are showy and fragrant when in bloom.

Planting: These medium to large plants are best when used for background, screen and accent situations.

•Woody vines like climbing roses, honeysuckle and English ivy are also good choices for birds. Roses provide edible red fruit (hips), and honeysuckle has masses of red or purple fruit. Both produce fragrant flowers for the yard and house. Sparrows, house finches and cardinals all love nesting in ivy and feasting on the insects it harbors.

Planting: Ask your local nursery, as each variety has different needs.

Source: Jeff Cox, host of PBS television's 26-part series *Your Organic Garden.* He is the author of nine books, including his latest, *Landscaping with Nature: Using Nature's Designs to Plan Your Yard*, Rodale Press, 33 E. Minor St., Emmaus, Pennsylvania 18098.

Favorite New Cameras

Disposable:

•*Polaroid Talking Sidekick.* This single-use 35mm camera talks. Press the "talk" button and the camera makes one of two different comments. There are four cameras with different messages, including "What's so funny?", "You're not smiling" and "C'mon, look happy." Each camera comes with two messages. *Other features:* Built-in flash and built-in roll of 24-shot color film. *Size:* 6¼" x 2¼" x 1¾." *Weight:* 4 oz.

Polaroid Corporation, 575 Technology Square, Cambridge, Massachusetts 02139. 800-343-5000.

Panorama:

•*Minolta Panoramic Zoom 28.* Allows you to take both panoramic pictures (3.5" x 10") and regular-sized shots (4" x 6") on the same roll of film. *Important:* Alert film processors so that they can make the proper adjustments before developing the film. There's no need to keep track of the size of each shot. *Other features:* 28mm to 70mm zoom lens, built-in flash, "red-eye" reduction, auto focus and date/time stamp that can be turned on and off. *Size:* 5.5" x 2.15" x 2.3." *Weight:* 10.6 oz.

Minolta Corp., 101 Williams Dr., Ramsey, New Jersey 07446. 201-825-4000.

Point-and-shoots:

•*Ricoh RW-1.* Includes many basic features found in more expensive point-and-shoot models. Fits easily into a shirt or pants pocket, and the sliding lens protector makes it easy to take pictures quickly. *Other features:* Automatic flash, panorama and standard modes, automatic film rewind and red-eye reduction. *Size:* 4.8" x 2.6" x 1.8." *Weight:* 8 oz.

Ricoh Corp., 180 Passaic Ave., Fairfield, New Jersey 07004. 800-225-1899.

•*Olympus Infinity Stylus Zoom DLX.* The easiest-to-use, pocket-sized 35mm camera on the market. *To operate:* Slide open the weather-resistant cover, look through the viewfinder to frame your subjects and shoot. *Features:* Auto flash, red-eye reduction, 35mm to 70mm built-in zoom, built-in date/time stamp and auto timer. The camera weighs only 7.8 oz. and has excellent picture quality. *Size:* 4.9" x 2.5" x 1.8."

Olympus America, Inc., 145 Crossways Park, Woodbury, New York 11797. 800-622-6372.

Sport/underwater:

•*Canon Sure Shot A-1.* The smallest, lightest underwater camera. Can be used to depths of 16 feet and floats to the surface if dropped. Red-and-white body makes it easy to see the camera underwater, and it automatically switches to a focus-free mode. Large viewfinder and oversized buttons make use easy when you're wearing a scuba mask and gloves. Double-layer glass plate prevents the lens from fogging. *Other features:* Built-in flash and red-eye reduction. *Size:* 5¼" x 3½" x 2⅛." *Weight:* 10.6 oz.

Canon USA, Inc., One Canon Plaza, Lake Success, New York 11042. 800-828-4040.

Single-lens reflex:

•*Canon EOS A2E.* The first camera to offer *eye-controlled focus* technology. *How it works:* Simply press the shutter button halfway and the camera automatically focuses on what you are looking at in the viewfinder. This feature is particularly helpful when shooting fast-paced action, such as a sporting event. The viewfinder follows your eye as you watch the players—keeping the lens focused on them. Or if you want to focus on someone behind another player, simply look at him/her in the viewfinder. Also has built-in flash. *Size:* 6¹⁄₁₆" x 4¾" x 2⁵⁄₁₆." *Weight:* 23.6 oz.

Canon USA, Inc., One Canon Plaza, Lake Success, New York 11042. 800-828-4040.

Source: Andy Pargh, an independent product reviewer who writes "The Gadget Guru," a nationally syndicated newspaper column. He is also a contributing correspondent to the NBC *Today* show.

Better Fireworks Photographs

Use a camera with adjustable shutter speed —automatic cameras will not work. *Make time exposures*—hold the shutter open for several seconds to get the effect of lights blooming in the air. *Use a tripod* to keep the camera steady. *Shoot with print film*—better for this purpose than slide film. *Use a flash* for ground displays or the faces of children watching—but remember that most camera flashes illuminate only eight to ten feet.

Source: Photo experts at Eastman Kodak Co., quoted in *Woman's Day*, 1633 Broadway, New York 10019.

How to Take Much Better Photos Outdoors

You don't need magical skills to be a nature photographer. Even without sophisticated equipment, you can come away with wonderful pictures of landscapes, plants or animals. *What you need to take great photos...*

Patience:

Nature photography is a contemplative activity. You cannot rush nature. You cannot make animals or a landscape do anything. For the best pictures, you must settle in and observe.

Types of questions to ask yourself: How is a flower affected by the play of sun and clouds or by passing breezes? How does a landscape change with the light from dawn to dusk?

Example: When I recently visited the Grand Canyon, I watched one person after another march up to the rim, stand with their backs to this marvel, have a friend take their picture and then move on. I sat on the rim of the canyon for the entire day, photographing at intervals and watching the play of light and clouds. I took the best pictures at sunset.

Love of the subject:

The first challenge is to become familiar with your subject through repeated exposure. African safaris and trips to Yellowstone National Park are wonderful opportunities, but you can also profit from less expensive trips.

Where to start: A local park, zoo or woodland. For plants and flowers, a nearby botanical garden will do fine. Choose the subjects that most fascinate you, and "stalk" them like a hunter.

Caution: Avoid the woods during deer-hunting season. My own career was almost ended by a potshot in the Allegheny National Forest.

Awareness of light:

The best time to take photographs of nature is during the early- or late-day hours, when the low sun enhances the subject. *How to take advantage of the low-angle light:*

• To produce dramatic pictures from even the simplest camera—position yourself so that the light is coming diagonally over your shoulder onto the subject.

• When shooting a landscape or the texture of animal fur, bird feathers, fish scales or flower petals—position yourself so that the light is hitting the subject from the side. Side lighting reveals texture.

• When you want to create a halo of light around animals or flowers or show the translucency of insects and plants—position yourself so that the low sun is behind the subject. Be careful that the sun doesn't hit the camera lens directly.

Useful for all nature photos: Soft light that is diffused by thin clouds or light mist anytime of day.

To be avoided: "Top" light from overhead summer sun, which casts shadows that record almost black on film. As a rule, I will not shoot if my shadow is shorter than I am.

Equipment:

You can take good nature pictures with virtually any camera as long as you know its limitations. In fact, I have seen very good shots from point-and-shoot and even disposable cameras.

For serious nature photographers, a good tripod is an important accessory. It is absolutely essential for use in low light with long exposures or for close-ups made with slow small apertures and shutter speeds for maximum depth of field. It will minimize blur caused by camera shake when shooting with telephotos and zoom lenses.

Overcome your limitations:

It is valuable to look at nature photographs taken by the masters to see the elements of great pictures.

Even more important is experience. Like driving a car or playing the piano, nature photography requires physical skills and quick reflexes. As you practice and experiment, those skills will become second nature—allowing you to seize those magical photographic moments.

Most common error: Viewing a subject—such as a landscape—through your eyes, and then barely glancing through your viewfinder before taking the picture. The camera's translation from three to two dimensions will change the view.

Exercise: Train yourself to look at everything through your viewfinder, closing your other eye if necessary.

Source: Susan McCartney, an international freelance photographer who conducts workshops at the School of Visual Arts in New York. She is the author of *Travel Photography: A Complete Guide to How to Shoot and Sell* and *Nature and Wildlife Photography: A Practical Guide to How to Shoot and Sell,* Allworth Press, 10 E. 23 St., New York 10010.

Collecting Autographs

You can often collect autographs from celebrities just by asking. *Best approach:* Writing a letter to create a conversation with the celebrity —and show a genuine interest in his/her work —in order to stimulate a reply. *Example:* Richard Berman got an autograph from astronaut Neil Armstrong by asking for his view on the theory that the world would be better if we blew up the moon. *To reach a celebrity:* Write in care of the institution with which he is affiliated (book publisher, movie studio, etc.) or join the Universal Autograph Collectors Club, Box 6181, Washington, DC 20044. It publishes a bimonthly magazine with the addresses of famous people. Include a large, self-addressed, stamped envelope with your letter.

Source: Richard Berman, a media consultant in Chappaqua, New York, and an avid autograph collector.

How to Enjoy Zoo Visits Even More

Over the past ten years, most of the nation's zoos have become entertainment centers. Shows, rides and restaurants have been added. To make your next visit to the zoo more rewarding…

Before you go, plan your trip in advance by calling the zoo for the following information:

•Admission prices and hours. You may be surprised by their fees. You'll have more fun if you know the cost in advance.

Range: Free to $12 for adults, $4 for children.

The best time to arrive at the zoo is when the gates first open in the morning. This will allow you to enjoy your visit before the zoo gets crowded and while the animals are most active.

•Zoo map and brochures. These help you plan your visit—and decide how much time you'll need to see everything.

•Special programs. In addition to the regular exhibits and shows, there are many events scheduled around the holidays and major vacation times.

•Restaurants. Though most zoos offer fast food, a few on-site restaurants serve truly excel-

lent cuisine and have excellent views. *Examples:*

•The AfriCafe at Portland, Oregon's Metro Washington Park Zoo (503-226-1561) has a complete menu and a salad bar.

•Cypress Knee Cafe at Audubon Zoo and Zoological Garden in New Orleans (504-861-2537) serves Cajun specialties.

Other restaurants serve satisfactory food but provide great views. *Examples:*

•Durham's Treetop Restaurant in Omaha's Henry Doorly Zoo (402-733-8401) allows you to watch the animals in the world's largest re-created rain forest.

•Caldwell Zoo's dining area (903-593-0121) in Tyler, Texas, overlooks a re-created East African savanna.

•Star attractions. Many zoos today specialize in a particular rare breed or showcase an especially noteworthy animal. *Examples:*

•The Metro Washington Park Zoo's elephant museum will tell you everything you want to know about elephants. Afterward you can visit the largest breeding herd of elephants outside of Asia.

•The Cincinnati Zoo's Big Cat Canyon (513-281-4700) offers a bridge that encircles the habitat where more than half the world's existing white tigers are bred.

Other zoos offer more than just animals. *Example:*

•The Texas! Exhibit at the Fort Worth Zoo (817-871-7050) re-creates a pioneer town, complete with an operating blacksmith, one-room schoolhouse and native animals such as wolves, prairie dogs and wild turkeys.

Once you are there:

•Keep the kids excited by playing games. This will make your visit more enjoyable. *Examples:*

•Animal alphabet. Children compete by finding as many animals as possible with names beginning with different letters of the alphabet. The one who names the most animals wins. Keep track on a sheet of paper.

•Postcard search. As soon as you arrive, buy five postcards that depict different animals from the zoo's gift shop. The first child to spot all five animals wins.

•Zoo grid. On a sheet of paper, draw a grid with seven rows and four columns. Head the four columns mammals, birds, reptiles and amphibians. In each of the rows, list the world's continents—Africa, Asia, Australia, Europe, North America, South America and Antarctica. The player who fills in the most boxes with animals spotted during the visit wins.

•Leave time to see a zoo show. They are often entertaining, educational and are usually free.

Rule of thumb: The larger the outdoor theater, the better the show.

Best shows: Cincinnati, Indianapolis, Oklahoma City, San Diego.

•Expect to spend money on a few rides. Monorails, sky rides, boat and train rides save you some walking and offer views of animals that may not be available elsewhere. At some zoos, they're the only way to see certain animals. *Examples:*

•New York's Bronx Zoo (718-367-1010) has the Bengali Express, a monorail trip through a Wild Asian preserve.

•Sedgwick County Zoo (316-942-2212) in Wichita has a boat ride that takes you through part of a wild river where you will see bison, elk, lemurs and birds.

For a better view, bring binoculars or a camera with a telephoto lens.

Source: Allen W. Nyhuis, who has visited the 53 top zoos in the US. He is the author of *The Zoo Book: A Guide to America's Best*, Carousel Press, Box 6061, Albany, California 94706.

How to Throw a Very Successful Party

A successful party isn't hard to put together once you get the formula down. Unforgettable parties are the result of the clever mix of:

•A legitimate reason (or plausible excuse!) for a get-together.

•A carefully orchestrated plan.

•Creativity.

Be a director:

Your party will be different if you direct it, rather than just invite folks and hope for the best. *Examples:*

•If you host a baby shower, make it a toys only or baby's bath only shower, and your guests will head eagerly to the stores now that you've eliminated guesswork.

•Center a retirement party on the retiree's hobby—say, golf and have guests wear golf clothes.

•Turn a going-away party into a movable feast where friends pick up and travel together from house to house for each course. Meet at the first house for drinks and hors d'oeuvres. Move on to the second for soup and salad. Travel to the third for the main course. Wind up at the fourth house for dessert and coffee and a fond farewell.

Party checklist:

Once you have chosen the reason for a party, you must get yourself organized.

You don't want to be expecting your first guest to come through the door, only suddenly to remember you forgot to buy ice. To avoid that kind of catastrophe, develop a "things to do and things to buy" checklist that is divided into four sections that help you organize your time and effort as the day of the party approaches:

Section 1: Three weeks before the party. Develop a guest list, create the invitations (and mail them), decide the menu, write a grocery list and hire any serving help you might need.

Section 2: A week before the party. Call guests who didn't RSVP, buy the food and drinks, prepare food and decide what you're wearing.

Section 3: One day before the party. Clean the house, arrange the party room, pull out the serving dishes and confirm deliveries and caterers.

Section 4: The day of the party. Decorate, finish cooking, set up everything, mentally "travel through" the party and get dressed.

Invitations:

Make your invitation a show stopper. *Best:* Homemade invitations. *Examples:*

•For a birthday party, go to your library and get a photocopy of the front page of a newspaper from the day and year your birthday guest was born. Design your invitation to the size of a column in the paper, paste your column over an old column and photocopy as many invitations as you need.

•For a baby shower, cut out small footprints on which you've written party details.

• For a Christmas party, make gingerbread people, each one decorated with a guest's name and a card tied around the neck.

Theme food:

Offer theme food—and serve it with flair. *Examples:*

• For a graduation party, serve high-quality food cafeteria-style—on trays.

• For dessert at a family reunion, have each family contribute an eight-inch-square cake decorated with the contributor's name on it, and place the squares together to form a show-stopping pièce de résistance.

• Break out the wicker baskets, old-fashioned tins and large seashells to serve food, rather than using ordinary or dull serving dishes. Food looks and tastes better when it is served creatively.

Activities:

Plan unusual activities. No charades. No board games. Sustain the mood of the party. *Examples:*

• For a baby shower, buy eight jars of baby food, remove the labels and have each guest taste and write down the flavors she thinks she has just tasted. The guest with the most correct answers wins a prize—perhaps a home pregnancy kit or a stuffed toy.

• Create a great birthday videotape by having guests relate funny anecdotes about the honoree. Play the tape during the party, and give the tape to the birthday boy or girl as a souvenir.

• For a family reunion have the oldest relatives tell their life stories.

Decorations:

A party without decorations is like a movie without a musical score—something is missing. Done well, decorations add immeasurably to the atmosphere and to the enjoyment of the people at the party.

And here's where the kids, a spouse and friends come in. Pass out assignments, for example to cut out legs and boots from felt and hang Santa's legs in the fireplace at Christmas, to create a basket of honeymoon items (cologne, mints, body paint, silk panties, videos) as a centerpiece at a bachelorette party or to collect and hang photos of the guest of honor from past to present (complete with captions) at a birthday party.

Unusual themes:

Every month of the year, there is a ready-made excuse to throw a party...

• January 9, Sherlock Holmes' Birthday.
• March 24, Harry Houdini's Birthday.
• June 7, Day of the Rice God.
• July 14, Bastille Day.
• September 26, Johnny Appleseed's birthday.

Any excuse can be the perfect excuse for a party. *Examples:*

• An international evening where the guests bring dishes from the old country.

• A fashion-victim party where guests wear the unwearable.

• A ski party far from the slopes where the guests dress in snow bunny or ski bum apparel.

• An invite-a-friend party where each guest brings someone new to the group.

Put your imagination to work:

Parties don't have to be held in someone's house or in a rented hall. You can also create your own car road rally or biking party by designing your own map and clues along the way with a favorite restaurant as the ultimate destination.

You might also consider having everyone meet at a bowling alley, espresso bar or at a nearby dance studio.

Source: Penny Warner, author of *The Best Party Book— 1001 Creative Ideas for Fun Parties,* Meadowbrook Press, 18318 Minnetonka Blvd., Deephaven, Minnesota 55391.

Make an Ordinary Home Dinner Special

Make an ordinary home dinner *special*—invite an unusual guest—someone outside your normal circle. *Examples:* A business associate you admire or someone you would like to get to know better, a neighbor or someone who has done you a favor. *Benefits:* You'll dramatically change your routine dinnertime interactions—and your relationship with your guest.

Source: *How to Be Happier Day by Day* by Alan Epstein, PhD, California-based cofounder of True Partners, an introduction and relationship counseling service. Viking, 375 Hudson St., New York 10014.

The President's Greeting

Did you know that President Clinton will send a greeting card to anyone over age 80—and those who have been married for 50 years? Send a postcard at least one month in advance of the birthday or anniversary to: President William J. Clinton, c/o Greeting Office, The White House, Room 39, Washington, DC 20500.

Interactive Gambling on TV

Interactive gambling on TV will let viewers take part in bingo, horse-racing and poker. A test will start in the fall of 1994 on a Pittsburgh cable channel. If successful, it could be one of the most profitable multimedia applications—Americans spent 70 times as much on gambling last year as they spent on movies.

Source: Nelson Goldberg, president, Gaming Entertainment Television, Pittsburgh, quoted in *The Economist*, 111 W. 57 St., New York 10019.

New Game of Tennis

Forget about the boundary lines...forget the number of bounces. Just keep hitting. It's much more aerobic, much less stressful. *Much more fun:* Start with at least a dozen balls—two dozen is better. Everybody wins.

12

Estate Planning

Shrewder Estate Planning

If you have a pattern of making gifts and want that pattern continued even if you're incapacitated, your power of attorney should explicitly include the power to continue making gifts on your behalf. Such gifts can be used to reduce the taxes that will be imposed on an individual's estate by removing property from the estate before the individual dies. *Trap:* The IRS recognizes such gifts for tax purposes only when the power of attorney expressly authorizes them. The IRS does not recognize gifts made under a mere "general authority" to handle another person's affairs.

If you want your power holder to continue making gifts, make sure that an explicit authority to make gifts is included in any power of attorney drafted to protect your own affairs.

Source: David S. Rhine, partner, BDO Seidman, CPAs, 15 Columbus Circle, New York 10023. Mr. Rhine specializes in estate planning.

Ten Biggest Estate Planning Mistakes... And How to Avoid Them

A good estate plan can slash your estate-tax bill so you can leave more to your heirs and less to Uncle Sam. As you fine-tune your estate plan, watch out for these common mistakes:

•*Mistake:* Failing to use the annual $10,000 gift-tax exclusion. The IRS lets you give away up to $10,000 a year per donee free of gift tax to an unlimited number of people. Spouses who make joint gifts can give each donee $20,000 a year.

Solution: Set up an annual gifting program to reduce the size of your estate. Consider making gifts at the beginning of the year so that the income being produced by the sum will no longer be your tax problem.

•*Mistake:* Overusing the estate-tax marital deduction. The IRS lets spouses leave each other property free from estate tax. But leaving everything to your spouse increases the family's estate-tax bill. You forfeit one of the $600,000 estate-and-gift-tax exclusions available to you when you die.

Example: Jack leaves property worth $1.2 million to his wife, Mary. No estate tax will be owed because of the estate-tax marital deduction. When Mary dies, one-half of her property will be sheltered by her $600,000 exclusion. Taxes owed on the other $600,000 will be about $250,000.

Solution: Jack puts $600,000 for Mary into a trust that does not qualify for the estate-tax marital deduction. When Jack dies, no estate tax will be owed because the $600,000 remaining in his estate will be sheltered by his $600,000 lifetime exclusion. Mary will receive income from the trust for life and when she dies, the children will receive the property in the trust. No estate tax will be due on Mary's estate because the $600,000 she owns outright will be sheltered by her exclusion.

•*Mistake:* Making no plans to shelter taxable life insurance proceeds. Many people are not aware that life insurance proceeds in their estate are taxable if they push the estate over $1.2 million. After taxes, your heirs receive the remainder.

Solution: Transfer ownership of the insurance policy to your children or other beneficiaries, or if you are planning to buy an insurance policy, make your heirs the owners. *Another option:* You can fund a trust with a life insurance policy. Your spouse can receive income for life, and the trust proceeds can pass to your children when your spouse dies.

Important: If you die within three years of transferring an insurance policy, that asset is still considered part of your taxable estate. So make any necessary changes as soon as possible.

•*Mistake:* Making gifts to someone who uses the money to pay for medical or educational expenses. When you pay a medical or educational institution directly on someone else's behalf, you can exceed the $10,000 annual limit on tax-free gifts.

Solution: By paying medical or educational costs yourself, you can reduce the size of your estate by more than the $10,000 allowance—without owing any gift taxes.

•*Mistake:* Setting up a living trust to reduce your estate-tax bill. Living trusts—trusts set up during your lifetime—have no impact on estate-tax liability.

Solution: Understand that estates of people who have living trusts bypass probate, thereby eliminating those costs. Living trusts also prevent the public inspection of your estate. But don't rely on them to save estate taxes.

•*Mistake:* Saving the unified credit to shelter estate assets at your death. The $600,000-per-person estate-tax exclusion also applies to gifts that are made during your lifetime.

Solution: In some cases, it makes more sense to make large gifts of property during your lifetime than after your death. This will shelter gifts from taxes by reducing the $600,000 lifetime estate-and-gift-tax exclusions.

The reason for making such gifts is that you can remove all future appreciation on the gifted property from your taxable estate. *Good assets to consider:* Interest in a family-owned business, partnership shares, real estate, growth-oriented stocks and mutual funds.

•*Mistake:* Not keeping your beneficiary designations up-to-date. Beneficiaries must be named on many assets. *Examples:* Life insurance, retirement plans, bank and brokerage accounts. That's why it is easy to inadvertently leave valuable insurance proceeds to a former spouse, for instance.

Solution: Check beneficiary designations whenever there have been major changes in your life. *Examples:* Marriage, death, birth of a child.

•*Mistake:* Holding all assets jointly. Houses, brokerage accounts and other assets held in joint names pass by law to the survivor when one holder dies. As a result, carefully constructed estate plans are rendered ineffective.

Example I: When a married couple's jointly held assets pass automatically to the surviving spouse, the $600,000 lifetime exclusion for the deceased spouse is forfeited. *Better:* Set up a credit-shelter trust, which shelters this lifetime exclusion from estate taxes.

Example II: John has remarried, but wants his children from his first marriage to inherit his assets when he dies. If the accounts are held jointly, his second wife would automatically inherit them. John can set up a trust to give his second wife income over her lifetime and then distribute the assets to his children after her death.

Solution: Consider how assets are held before developing an estate plan and make changes, if necessary.

•*Mistake:* Constructing an estate plan that uses the marital deduction to reduce estate taxes when a spouse who is not a US citizen inherits property. No estate-tax marital deduction is available for noncitizen spouses.

Solution: While the marital deduction does not apply, the annual exclusion for tax-free gifts is raised from $10,000 to $100,000 for noncitizen spouses. Consider a lifetime gift program or set up a qualified domestic trust, which would be eligible for the estate-tax marital deduction.

•*Mistake:* Omitting foreign-owned assets from your estate plan. Assets owned anywhere in the world by US citizens are subject to the US estate tax.

Solution: Review your estate plan, taking into account all assets owned worldwide. Look into the estate-tax credit for foreign taxes paid and the impact of any tax treaties between the US and countries where you own property.

Sources: David Gerson, tax partner and regional director of estate planning, and Charles R. Cangro, senior tax manager, Ernst & Young, 787 Seventh Ave., New York 10019.

Living Wills—Traps And Opportunities

Suppose you became comatose after a stroke, serious accident or surgery. Without a living will or other health-care directive, you could spend months or even years being kept alive by a mechanical ventilator.

In this dire situation, you might prefer to be allowed to die or maybe you'd like to live no matter what and fear that someone would pull the plug. Either way, consider putting your wishes into a living will *now*.

In most jurisdictions, you can also create a *proxy directive* or *health-care proxy*, which designates someone to make health-care decisions for you if you become incapacitated. Another health-care document called a *medical directive* or *living will* makes specific stipu-

lations regarding your wishes concerning your care if you are incapable of expressing them.

A simple mistake in preparing these documents could nullify your wishes. Sloppy or incomplete preparation of your living will, for example, could prevent the document from being legally binding, especially if the directions are challenged in court and a videotape or hastily scribbled note does not suffice. Other mistakes to avoid:

•*Mistake:* Failing to comply with state law. Each state has its own medical decision-making legislation. To obtain a free set of sample forms for your state, contact Choice in Dying, 10th Floor, 200 Varick St., New York 10014, 212-366-5540. The group also answers questions about patients' rights.

•*Mistake:* Being stricken in the "wrong" state. You can't be sure exactly where you'll be "hit by a bus," but certain precautions will help protect your wishes no matter where you become sick or injured. If you work or vacation regularly in states other than your home state, prepare additional health-care decision-making documents that adhere to those states' requirements. Of course, it's unreasonable to make 50 different documents. Deciding how many living wills to prepare is a judgment call.

•*Mistake:* Choosing the wrong proxy. Your papers should designate one or more people, ranked in order of authority, to make medical decisions for you if you become incapacitated. Be sure to notify everyone on your list and make sure they fully understand your wishes. Some states allow only one designated proxy to serve at a time, but alternates can be named. Avoid choosing someone whose moral, ethical or religious outlook might preclude them from doing what you ask of them.

•*Mistake:* Choosing the wrong witnesses. When choosing people to witness the signing of your health-care document, look for adults over age 18 and make sure they can be contacted quickly in case they're needed. *Caution:* Health-care providers and anyone who might conceivably stand to benefit financially from your death should not be used as witnesses. Otherwise, the document might not be valid.

•*Mistake:* Having too few witnesses. Obtain the signatures of three witnesses, even if your state requires only one or two. The seal of a notary public makes the document appear more official, although it is seldom required.

• *Mistake:* Misplacing the living will. Your living will should be accessible immediately when needed. File a copy with other important personal papers at home. Be sure to tell family members, your doctor, lawyer, etc., where to find it. Also, insert a card in your wallet describing this location. Do not store your living will in a safe-deposit box or at work—these locations are not easily accessible. And consult the law in your state. In Minnesota, driver's licenses indicate whether the holder has a living will. In Mississippi, living wills must be filed with the state board of health.

Send copies of your living will to your family physician and any medical specialists who might be involved in your care, a close family member or friend and anyone designated to make medical decisions for you.

• *Mistake:* Failing to update your will. In some states, living wills must be periodically renewed. Even if your state does not, it's a good idea to review your living will every three to five years—more frequently if your state laws are revised, if you move to another state or if your medical, financial or marital status changes. *Issues to consider:*

• Have your wishes changed?

• Have any recent changes in state law affected the document?

• Are the names and addresses listed on the living will still correct?

• Have you changed doctors or lawyers?

If you make changes, be sure to distribute copies of the updated living will.

• *Mistake:* Omitting important details. In some cases, the only "plug" to pull is to withhold food and water (typically artificial nutrition and hydration through tubes). In some states, this treatment will be withheld only if the patient's living will says to do so. Some religions forbid such a step, while others forbid blood transfusions. If any of these issues pertain to you, make sure your living will covers them thoroughly.

• *Mistake:* Vague wording. The dark side of living wills is the prospect of having medical care withheld when recovery might have been possible. Your living will should not attempt to eschew all medical care.

• *Mistake:* Failing to include a "severability clause." This indicates that the provisions of the living will remain binding even if one or more parts of the living will are invalid for some reason and thus protects your interests even if laws concerning living wills change.

Source: Sanford J. Schlesinger, JD, a partner in the law firm of Kaye, Scholer, Fierman, Hays & Handler, New York City. He is coauthor of *Planning for the Elderly or Incapacitated Client*, Commerce Clearinghouse, 4025 W. Peterson Ave., Chicago 60646. The book was written for attorneys, accountants and other professionals but is easily understood by the general reader.

Living Wills Save Money

Living wills save money during patients' last hospitalizations. Hospital charges for those Medicare patients who did not have living wills during their final hospital stays averaged more than $95,000. For patients with living wills, the average was $30,000. *Reason:* Living wills prevent patients from receiving any unwanted treatment—such as life-prolonging therapy.

Source: Study of almost 500 Medicare patients, led by Christopher Chambers, MD, Thomas Jefferson University, Philadelphia.

Living Trusts

Living trusts, in many situations, can be more trouble than they're worth. In the first place, living trusts don't save estate taxes. The same estate-tax savings can be accomplished through your will. And you still need a will to dispose of property that isn't covered by the trust. Probate time can be saved with a living trust, but speedy distribution of your property isn't always wise. A smart trustee will make sure estate taxes are paid before distributing assets to heirs. There are, however, a number of valid reasons for using a living trust. See your estate planner.

Source: David S. Rhine, a partner with the accounting firm BDO Seidman, 15 Columbus Circle, New York 10023.

Estate Plan Redo

Change your estate plan when any of these events occur:
- Change in marital status.
- Birth or adoption.
- Serious illness, disability or special support needs of an heir.
- An heir's request for gifts while you're alive instead of under your will.
- Forgiven loans.
- Change of residence.

Caution: Watch carefully for changes in estate value. If you are leaving specific amounts to some people and the balance to your surviving spouse, your spouse could be shortchanged if stocks or other assets drop in value.

Source: Robert Carlson, editor, *Bob Carlson's Retirement Watch,* 8245 Boone Blvd., Suite 700, Vienna, Virginia 22182.

Smarter Estate Planning

It *may* make sense to use your $600,000 estate-tax exemption *now.* Give away assets that you can afford to give. *Problem:* Several members of Congress have been trying since 1992 to reduce the estate-tax exemption from $600,000 to $200,000. A switch to a $200,000 threshold would hit as many as 25% of primarily older Americans. To reduce your taxable estate—in addition to using the $600,000 estate-tax exemption—set up a life insurance trust to remove insurance proceeds from your estate. Adopt a program to make current $10,000 gifts to children and other beneficiaries. Use trusts to remove appreciated property from your estate.

Source: Stephen Rosenberg, a certified financial planner in Warner Robins, Georgia. He is the author of *Keep Uncle Sam From Devouring Your Life Savings,* The Career Press, 180 Fifth Ave., Hawthorne, New Jersey 07507.

Shrewd Way to Save Estate Taxes

A shrewd way to save estate taxes is to set up a family partnership to own assets. It is a way to move wealth to the next generation at low gift-tax cost. What you do is form a partnership with family members, with yourself as the general partner—you have 99% of the shares and the rest of the family has 1%. Every year you transfer parts of your interest to other family members.

Source: David S. Rhine, a tax partner with BDO Seidman, CPAs, 15 Columbus Circle, New York 10023.

Trusts Are Not Only For the Rich

Few people realize how valuable trusts can be for their own estates. Too many mistakenly assume that trusts are only for the fabulously rich and not for those with just a family home, a company pension and a life insurance policy. But even these people can benefit substantially from trusts.

Reason: Trusts save thousands of dollars in gift and estate taxes *and* provide a way to manage these assets when the original owners are no longer around. They also can protect assets from creditors and malpractice suits.

Trusts need to be set up properly if they are to be effective, so be sure to consult an attorney. *Here are five of the most basic types of trusts and what they can do for you…*

Life insurance trust:

Let's say you own your home and have some modest investments, a pension and a $500,000 life insurance policy. If your children are the beneficiaries of the insurance policy, your family could owe the government hundreds of thousands of dollars in estate taxes.

Reason: Life insurance proceeds, while not subject to federal income tax, are considered part of your taxable estate and are subject to federal estate tax with rates of 37% to 55%.

Solution: Create an irrevocable life insurance trust, which will then own the policy and receive the cash payout upon the policy owner's death. *Benefits:*

- Income for the beneficiaries. The irrevocable life insurance trust can be structured so that your survivors receive some or all of the annual income generated by the trust. The survivors can even receive the principal—subject to certain restrictions.

• Avoidance of estate taxes. If it's properly structured, such a trust ensures that insurance proceeds escape taxation in your estate as well as the estate of your surviving spouse.

In addition, because the proceeds are not included in your taxable estate or your spouse's taxable estate, they are not part of the public record and escape publicity. They also are not affected by probate costs.

• Protection of assets. The trust protects the insurance proceeds from creditors and malpractice actions.

• Reliable management. By naming a family member and an outsider, such as a bank or an accountant, to manage the trust assets, you eliminate the problem of inexperienced or incapable beneficiaries investing the trust's money.

Credit shelter trust:

The primary purpose of a credit shelter trust is to preserve the $600,000 tax exemption—*the unified credit*—that all individuals get in their estates.

Under the law, everyone can give away $10,000 a year to individuals and $600,000 during his/her lifetime or upon death tax-free. Most couples own all their property jointly and have wills in which the husband leaves everything to the wife and the wife leaves everything to the husband. This may not be the best arrangement.

Example: Let's assume that a couple jointly owns an estate worth $1.2 million. When the first spouse dies, there will be no estate tax because of the unlimited marital deduction. But when the second spouse dies, the estate, which is now larger, will owe about $225,000 in estate taxes.

Solution: When your joint estate exceeds $1.2 million, divide all joint property equally between you and your spouse. For example, change a joint brokerage account into two separate accounts with half the assets in each. Then create a credit shelter trust under each spouse's will. The trust will allow the estate of each spouse to escape tax by taking maximum advantage of the $600,000 unified credit.

Example: Going back to the couple mentioned earlier…when the first spouse dies, $600,000 of his assets goes into a credit shelter trust for the benefit of the second spouse. (When the second spouse dies, $600,000 of her assets passes directly to the children or other heirs—with no estate tax).

Whichever spouse survives can have the right to receive all the income produced by the trust. That spouse also has the right to take principal from the trust to maintain his/her standard of living. It's almost like having the assets in your own name.

Important: It's not enough to just create the trust. You may also retitle your joint property in separate names so that upon your death the property can be transferred to the trust in order for it to save your family estate taxes.

Q-TIP trust:

A *Qualified Terminable Interest Property (Q-TIP)* trust defers taxes and helps you attain a personal goal. Its aim is to ensure that after a spouse's death, assets exceeding the $600,000 unified credit pass first to the surviving spouse tax-free and then to the individuals for whom they were ultimately intended.

Without a Q-TIP trust, the assets could pass from the surviving spouse to his/her children from a different marriage.

Benefit: The trust is often used in second marriages to provide lifelong support for a current spouse. Then it funnels assets to the children from the first marriage after the stepparent's death.

Under this arrangement, your current spouse receives all of the income annually from the trust for life.

After your current spouse dies, *your* children—not your spouse's children from a previous marriage or any other beneficiary that your current spouse may have—inherit the principal. Even though your spouse's interest in the trust property terminates upon death, the initial transfer of property to the trust still qualifies for the unlimited marital deduction.

Children's trust:

This trust is designed to provide for your children and addresses a problem that occurs with gifts to children under the Uniform Gifts to Minors Act (UGMA) and Uniform Transfers to Minors Act (UTMA).

Problem: Under UGMA and UTMA, once children reach age 18 or 21, depending on the state in which they reside, they can do whatever they wish with the money in their custodial accounts.

If they want to use it to support a commune or buy a sports car instead of finishing college, there's nothing you can do about it.

Benefit: By transferring assets to any children's trust, such as a *Crummey trust,* the trustee can determine how the money in the trust is used and how much the child can receive.

Grandparents' trust:

This is similar to the children's trust, except that the grandparents establish it to help pay for their grandchildren's college expenses.

A separate trust can be created for each grandchild. The limit that can be placed gift-tax-free in the trust each year is $10,000 per grandparent. Otherwise, the grandparent begins to eat into his $600,000 credit.

As with a children's trust, the trust document and the trustee define how much money is used and for which purposes.

Important: Avoid setting up a single trust that names more than one grandchild as the beneficiary. Otherwise, you will run into the expensive generation-skipping transfer tax, which in many cases applies to transfers of more than $1 million.

Source: Martin M. Shenkman, a tax and estate attorney who practices in New York and New Jersey. He is author of several books, including *The Complete Book of Trusts*, John Wiley & Sons, 605 Third Ave., New York 10158.

Savvy Estate Planning

List your miscellaneous personal property and the people you want to inherit it in a letter—not in your will—and keep it with your important papers. Then you can avoid the expense of revising your will each time your property changes. The executor must report all miscellaneous property to the IRS and pay any estate or gift taxes on them.

Source: Martin Shenkman, an attorney in private practice in New York and New Jersey who specializes in estate, tax and financial planning.

Before Naming an Executor

Before naming an executor to handle your estate, ask yourself if the person you have chosen is experienced in handling investments, has the organizational skills to handle the paperwork and tax filings or the ability to retain and control professionals to perform their functions, has the time to give the estate the attention it will need and is likely to become involved in intrafamily conflicts concerning control of the estate or distribution of assets. *Trap:* The first person you think of to handle your estate may not be the right person. To learn of the problems that may be encountered, ask acquaintances who have administered an estate about their experiences. If the estate is complex, consider taking steps to minimize future problems—consolidate investment assets into a limited number of brokerage accounts. For businesses, prepare shareholder agreements that all heirs sign and that address succession of management, how profits will be divided between heirs who are in the business and those who aren't and write a detailed letter of instructions for your family and executor.

Source: Martin Shenkman, New York attorney and the author of *The Complete Book of Trusts,* John Wiley & Sons, 605 Third Ave., New York 10158.

To Keep a Will From Being Challenged

To keep a will from being challenged, have it drawn up by an experienced, competent attorney, have independent witnesses who can vouch for your mental state, videotape the signing and a follow-up chat with your lawyer and witnesses as evidence of your mental competence and state of mind, have a clean document—avoid deletions, notes in margins, erasures and anything else that could be cited as evidence of confusion or tampering and have each page of the will signed or initialed by yourself and your witnesses. *Also:* Consider putting valuable property in a trust that will pass it to designated beneficiaries on your death. Trusts are more difficult to break than wills.

Source: Alexander Bove, estate and trust attorney, Boston, quoted in *Money,* 1271 Avenue of the Americas, New York 10020.

Estate Planning Tool

A *durable power of attorney* gives a person you choose the power to act as your agent and legal representative for specified purposes in case you become disabled or incompetent.

Needed: Language in the power of attorney document specifying that the holder of the power may continue to act on your behalf in case of your disability or incompetency. Without that language, a power of attorney automatically ends in case of disability or incompetency.

Source: *Retiring Right: Planning for Your Successful Retirement* by Lawrence Kaplan, PhD, professor of economics, City University of New York. Avery Publishing Group, 120 Old Broadway, Garden City Park, New York 11040.

13

Very, Very Personal

Hysterectomy Hype— 90% Are Unnecessary

Of the 600,000 hysterectomies performed in the US each year, only 10% are medically necessary. The other 90% are done for the surgeon's convenience or profit…to let a surgical resident practice his/her technique…or simply because removing the uterus is assumed to be the best solution for many different gynecologic problems.

Most disorders that lead to hysterectomy are not life-threatening. They should be treated in other, less invasive ways.

Why are so many hysterectomies performed? Most gynecologists genuinely believe that women benefit from the surgery. Relieving a woman of her reproductive organs, they say, frees her from menstrual cramps and heavy bleeding, the need for birth control and any possibility of developing cancer of the endometrium (uterine lining) or ovaries.

Maybe so, but the procedure will most likely leave her with troublesome side effects—if she lives. One in 1,000 women die undergoing hysterectomy.

Complications and side effects:

About half of all women who undergo hysterectomy develop postoperative complications —often because of sloppy surgical technique.

Examples: Severe vaginal bleeding…injury to the bowel, bladder or ureters (the tubes that carry urine from the kidneys to the bladder) …opening of the wound (dehiscence)…adhesions (internal scars formed when tissue surfaces stick together).

Such complications are especially common following complete hysterectomy, in which both the ovaries and uterus are removed. Roughly 40% of hysterectomies are complete hysterectomies.

In addition to these complications, many women who undergo hysterectomy experience side effects.

Most common: Fatigue…aching joints…urinary-tract disorders…depression…decreased sexual desire…reduced vaginal lubrication.

Because these side effects aren't easily measurable, doctors have traditionally dismissed women's complaints as being "all in their heads." But when every woman says the same thing, that cannot be the explanation.

One reason that hysterectomy has such far-reaching effects is that removing the ovaries also robs the body of…

• Endorphins. Without the ovaries, the body tends to produce less of these natural pain-killers, which create a feeling of well-being.

• Androgens. Androgens boost the sex drive and raise the energy level. (The ovaries supply roughly half of the body's supply of androgen. The other half is supplied by the adrenal glands.)

• Estrogen. Absence of this natural compound has a negative effect on cholesterol levels, raising the risk of heart attack—the leading killer of older women.

Even if the ovaries are left intact during a hysterectomy, the operation may cause them to malfunction.

When to have a hysterectomy:

Hysterectomy is appropriate for only three conditions…

• Endometrial or ovarian cancer.

• Hemophilia, von Willebrand's disease or another bleeding disorder.

• Heavy menstrual bleeding that fails to respond to other forms of treatment.

Safer alternatives are available for all other conditions, including…

• Fibroids. Up to 40% of women have one or more of these benign uterine tumors. They're especially common in women 35 or older. More hysterectomies are done for fibroids than for any other reason. But no matter how many fibroids there are or how big they might be, fibroids never necessitate removal of the uterus.

A fibroid should be removed only if it causes heavy or painful menstrual periods…if it's likely to interfere with pregnancy…or if it presses on other organs, preventing them from functioning properly. In such cases, the surgical method of choice is not hysterectomy, but myomectomy.

In this procedure, the surgeon—working through a small horizontal incision—meticulously cuts out the fibroid. Any competent gynecologist who performs surgery could learn this procedure. But because myomectomy takes more time and requires more skill than a hysterectomy, few gynecologists bother to learn it.

They figure that most of their patients won't know the difference anyway.

• Endometriosis. In this disorder, tissue lining the uterus spreads to other parts of the body, causing bleeding and cramps.

There are several appropriate ways to treat endometriosis.

Examples: Laser surgery or electrocautery to remove the troublesome tissue…tubal ligation (sterilization)…and treatment with Danocrine, Lupron, Synarel or any of the other excellent drugs now available.

• Uterine prolapse. This condition—marked by weakened vaginal muscles that let the uterus slip through the vagina—is most common in older women and in those who have had several children.

It can be treated with Kegel exercises to strengthen vaginal muscles…surgery to tighten the vaginal muscles or to resuspend the uterus …or use of a pessary, a rubber implant that holds the uterus in place.

• Menstrual disorders, including ovarian cysts, pelvic inflammatory disease (PID), pelvic pain and premenstrual syndrome (PMS).

Cramps usually respond to pain-killing medication and heat.

Cysts usually disappear on their own or can be removed via laser or conventional surgery.

PID, a sexually transmitted disease, is generally curable with antibiotics.

Pelvic pain may have another source entirely, such as a slipped disc.

Finally, many books, articles and self-help groups are available to assist women with premenstrual syndrome.

• Precancerous conditions. Endometrial hyperplasia and other precancerous conditions can usually be controlled with the hormone progestin or via dilation and curettage (D&C), a minor surgical procedure in which the endometrium is scraped with an instrument called a curette.

Obtaining a myomectomy:

If your gynecologist recommends a hysterectomy—for fibroids or any other condition other than cancer or uncontrolled vaginal bleeding—don't accept this advice. *Instead, ask your doctor…*

• *Can you do a myomectomy instead?* If he/ she says your fibroid is too big, find another doctor. An experienced surgeon—one who performs at least 20 myomectomies a year—can remove all fibroids via myomectomy.

• *What will you write on my surgical consent form?* A doctor who plans to write "myomectomy, hysterectomy if indicated" is probably more likely to do a hysterectomy than a doctor who writes simply "myomectomy." If your doctor insists on specifying both options, consider finding another doctor.

• *Will you stand up to my health insurance company if it resists paying for my myomectomy?* Most insurers pay when pressed—but in many cases only after harassing doctors and patients with endless paperwork and phone calls.

Basic rule: Don't go under the knife without getting a second opinion. Your health insurer may insist on it. Make sure you're comfortable with the doctor and treatment plan.

Needed—public outcry:

After preaching the value of alternatives to hysterectomy for 25 years, I'm treated like a fanatic by the medical community. Physicians run the other way when they see me coming.

But I really don't care. I just want to spread the message that women are being needlessly disfigured. That's why I wrote my book. If women start screaming, "You can't take my uterus!" doctors will eventually listen.

Source: Stanley West, MD, chief of reproductive endocrinology at St. Vincent's Hospital and an infertility specialist in private practice, both in New York City. He is coauthor of *The Hysterectomy Hoax,* Doubleday, 1540 Broadway, New York 10036.

Hot Flashes

Hot flashes and other symptoms of menopause may be minimized by eating a diet rich in soybeans. Eating a soy-rich diet may also reduce the risk of breast cancer. Soy and other legumes (beans, yams, etc.) contain *phytoestrogens,* compounds that may mimic estrogens in older women and act as a natural estrogen-replacement therapy for menopausal symptoms. Phytoestrogens may also lower younger women's risk of breast cancer.

Source: Barry R. Goldin, PhD, associate professor of community health, Tufts University School of Medicine, Boston.

X-Rated Videos

X-rated videos help men with fertility problems produce better sperm for use in artificial insemination. In a recent study, those who masturbated while watching the videos produced semen with more than double the sperm counts—and with higher proportions of healthy sperm. *Theory:* Sperm quality and fertilizing potential improve with increased sexual excitement.

Source: Nikolaos Sofikitis, MD, PhD, assistant lecturer in urology, Tottori University School of Medicine, Yonago, Japan.

Trichomoniasis

Trichomoniasis, the sexually transmitted bacterial disease, affects men as well as women. Any man whose sex partner has been diagnosed with trichomoniasis should seek treatment. Some infected men have no symptoms. Others develop a painful penile discharge and/or minor penile irritation. *Problem:* If untreated, the male partner can pass the infection back to his female partner, reinfecting her. Condoms help prevent transmission of the disease, although just how effective they are remains uncertain. There are 73 million cases of trichomoniasis each year.

Source: John Krieger, MD, professor of urology, University of Washington School of Medicine, Seattle. His study of trichomoniasis in nearly 500 men was reported in *Annals of Internal Medicine,* Independence Mall West, Sixth Street at Race, Philadelphia 19106.

Bicycle Seats

Bicycle seats can cause numbness, temporary impotence or even a painful permanent erection (priapism) in men who ride often or for long distances. *Reason:* The traditional narrow, one-piece design puts too much pressure on the internal erectile chambers of the penis. *Self-*

defense: Pedal as smoothly as possible to avoid bouncing…or fit your bike with a newer split seat that has one side to support the right buttock and another to support the left. Stationary exercise bicycles do not seem to pose a threat.

Source: E. Douglas Whitehead, MD, director, Association for Male Sexual Dysfunction, 520 E. 72 St., New York 10021.

Urinary-Tract Infections

Urinary-tract infections are twice as common in hot weather. *Self-defense:* Do not hold off going to the bathroom—and be sure to empty the bladder fully when you go. Drink plenty of water and other fluids every day. Urinate after sex. Change wet bathing suits—moisture helps bacteria grow. Wear cotton underwear—to improve ventilation of the skin. Avoid tight pantyhose—it promotes perspiration that nourishes bacterial growth. Women with a history of urinary-tract infections may want to test themselves periodically for underlying infection. Screening tests such as Biotel are available over-the-counter in drugstores.

Source: Bruce Shepard, MD, clinical associate professor of obstetrics and gynecology, University of South Florida, Tampa.

Understanding Endometriosis

Although severe cramps and irregular periods are sometimes considered "normal" features of the menstrual cycle, these problems are often evidence of *endometriosis.*

This ailment occurs when "renegade" cells from the uterine lining (endometrium) spread to and begin growing in or around the ovaries, pelvic cavity, colon, appendix, vagina and other parts of the body.

Increasingly common, endometriosis now afflicts an estimated ten million American women.

Many, perhaps most, of these women don't even know they have the disease. One-third of women diagnosed with endometriosis have no symptoms at all. These cases are typically discovered during surgery for an unrelated problem.

Benign—but not harmless:

While endometriosis is technically a "benign" illness (meaning no cancer is involved), its effects are often far from benign.

Besides severe menstrual pain and menstrual irregularities, endometriosis can cause pain during sex…infertility…and in severe cases obstructions of the bowel or urinary tract.

In a healthy woman, endometrial cells are shed from the body each month in the menstrual blood. But for some unknown reason, these cells sometimes migrate to other parts of the body. There, stimulated by the hormone estrogen, they form thriving masses.

Endometriosis typically starts during a woman's teenage years—and keeps getting worse. *Problem:* The condition often goes undetected for years. Even when they suspect endometriosis, doctors often fail to perform the tests necessary for a definitive diagnosis.

In my view, *any* suspected case of endometriosis requires both a definitive diagnosis *and* immediate treatment, especially in women who someday wish to bear children.

Reason: Once the reproductive organs are involved, the proliferating endometrial tissue makes conception less likely. Women with endometriosis should be aware that delaying childbirth might jeopardize their chances of ever becoming pregnant.

Prevention and risk factors:

The causes of endometriosis are poorly understood, so there's no way to prevent it. All women can do is acquaint themselves with the usual symptoms and risk factors…and seek expert medical advice at the first hint of trouble.

Endometriosis risk factors:

• Heavy menstrual periods lasting five days or longer.

• Family history of endometriosis.

• Narrowed cervix (cervical stenosis) or another anatomical problem that blocks normal flow of menstrual blood.

Women who are taking estrogen following radical surgery for endometriosis (hysterectomy and removal of both ovaries) should have their blood monitored for estrogen content. Too much estrogen in the bloodstream can cause endometriosis to reappear.

Recent research on lab animals suggests that chronic exposure to dioxin, PCBs and other toxins can promote endometriosis.

Theory: These compounds mimic the action of estrogen in the body...and estrogen is a known trigger of endometriosis.

Unfortunately, it's very hard to limit your exposure to these chemicals. Trace amounts of several different toxins are found in the air and water and in many foods. You could drink bottled water...but it's usually sold in plastic bottles, and plastic contains PCBs.

What your doctor will do:

Endometriosis often cannot be detected during a routine pelvic exam, or by ultrasound, X rays or magnetic resonance imaging (MRI) scans.

Consequently, women suspected of having endometriosis generally must undergo *laparoscopy*, a surgical technique in which a long, narrow viewing tube is inserted through a tiny incision in the lower abdomen.

Laparoscopy provides quick, accurate diagnosis. But like any surgical procedure, it leaves a scar (tiny in this case)...and involves certain risks. *Cost:* $2,500 to $5,000.

Recently, I've begun screening for endometriosis using an experimental blood test called the *anti-endometriosis antibody assay.*

At $100, the test is remarkably inexpensive compared with surgery. However, it's by no means foolproof. While a positive result on this test indicates a 95% likelihood of endometriosis and may therefore require surgery, a negative test is inconclusive.

In its current form, the test is helpful in determining which women are at greatest risk of endometriosis. Someday it might eliminate the need for surgical diagnosis altogether.

Drugs vs. surgery:

Hormonal changes that occur during pregnancy and breast-feeding help keep endometriosis under control. At other times, endometriosis sufferers need help—either from drugs or surgery—to boost fertility and reduce symptoms.

Several endometriosis drugs are now available. Many cases of endometriosis can be controlled with very-low-dose oral contraceptives. More severe cases may require treatment with other synthetic steroids or with an especially potent class of drugs called *gonadotropin-releasing hormone (GnRH) agonists.*

GnRH agonists temporarily halt the production of estrogen in the body. This prevents new endometriosis deposits...and gives the immune system a chance to "clean up" existing deposits.

If abdominal discomfort or infertility persists despite treatment with these drugs, surgery is necessary. In some cases, all the endometrial deposits can be removed via laparoscopy. More severe cases may require *laparotomy*, in which the surgeon makes a larger incision and performs "open" surgery.

If you opt for surgery, make sure to pick an experienced reproductive surgeon—particularly if you hope to preserve your fertility. Ask that he/she remove endometrial tissue only—and that all healthy tissue be spared.

Danger: Some surgeons remove the uterus and both ovaries along with endometrial deposits. This procedure—hysterectomy and bilateral oophorectomy—is necessary only for the most severe cases of endometriosis.

Important: Even if your surgery is successful in relieving pain or restoring fertility, there's no guarantee that its effects will be permanent. In many cases, endometriosis deposits grow back within a manner of months or years.

For more information: Contact the Endometriosis Association, 8585 N. 76 Place, Milwaukee 53223. 800-992-3636 or 414-355-2200.

Source: Gary S. Berger, MD, medical director, Chapel Hill Fertility Center, and clinical associate professor of obstetrics and gynecology, University of North Carolina Chapel Hill School of Medicine, and adjunct associate professor of maternal and child health in the university's School of Public Health. Dr. Berger is coauthor of *The Couples' Guide to Fertility,* Doubleday, 1540 Broadway, New York 10036. The book contains a section on endometriosis and a directory of 1,000 fertility specialists in the US.

How to Have a Safe Mammogram

By detecting breast tumors too tiny to be seen or felt, mammograms do save lives. But many women worry about being exposed to X rays… and wonder if this exposure might cause cancer.

In fact, the benefits of early detection of breast cancer far outweigh the risks—in women 40 years of age or older. Because cancer is rare in women younger than 40, there is no real public health justification for mass screening of these women. However, for women younger than 40 *who have breast asymmetry or other symptoms,* mammography is essential.

Women *should* be concerned about inaccurate mammograms caused by faulty equipment or technique. To minimize your chances of such problems, have your mammogram done only at a center accredited by the American College of Radiology (ACR).

Beware: About 3,000 mammography centers in the US are not accredited, although some of these may be in the process of being accredited. To find an accredited center in your area, call the American Cancer Society at 800-227-2345. Also essential for a safe, accurate mammogram:

• A board-certified radiologist.

• Technicians specially trained in mammography. For an accurate mammogram, the woman's breast must be positioned with absolute precision. The X-ray exposure settings must be carefully chosen and the breast-compression device correctly applied. A technician without specialized training might be unfamiliar with these nuances.

• Specialized equipment. X-ray machines specifically designed for radiography of the breast produce detailed images at a level of radiation lower than is possible with conventional X-ray machines.

To further ensure accurate results, avoid having a mammogram during the days just prior to your menstrual period. Breasts are tender and more dense then, thus making breast abnormalities harder to spot.

Also, avoid using talcum powder or deodorant the day of your mammogram. Traces of either of these products may show up as a calci-fication and consequently confuse a radiologist's interpretation.

Good news: Women whose breast tumors are diagnosed and treated before reaching one centimeter in size have a five-year survival rate of 93%. The American Cancer Society urges women to have a mammogram every other year between the ages of 40 and 50…annually after age 50.

Source: Gerald Dodd, MD, former chairman, division of diagnostic radiology, University of Texas M.D. Anderson Cancer Center, Houston.

Breast-Cancer Danger

Tamoxifen, a drug taken by breast-cancer patients to prevent recurrence of the disease, raises the risk of uterine cancer. *Self-defense:* Breast-cancer patients already taking tamoxifen should continue to do so, in consultation with a doctor. But they, and those who've taken tamoxifen in the past, should be especially vigilant about getting regular gynecological checkups *and* watching for symptoms of uterine cancer. Symptoms include bleeding between periods or after menopause…unusual vaginal discharge.

Source: Gregory Burke, MD, director, division of oncology and pulmonary drug products, Food and Drug Administration, 5600 Fisher's Lane, Rockville, Maryland 20857.

Breast Milk And Allergies

While breast-feeding helps protect infants from food allergies, it can sometimes cause allergic reactions in them. *Problem:* The mother herself may show no signs of the allergy. *Most common infant allergies:* Milk, egg or peanut products. Breast-feeding mothers should avoid these foods if they notice signs of eczema—red, itchy blotches—on their baby's skin. If the rash continues, blood tests can help identify the problem food.

Prenatal protection: If food allergies run in your family, avoidance of these foods in the last trimester may be beneficial.

Source: Richard B. Moss, MD, associate professor of pediatrics, Stanford University Medical Center, Stanford, California.

Breast Cancer— If Only I Had Known...

I was 46 when I was first diagnosed with breast cancer. My tumor was 1.5 centimeters in diameter and had spread to the lymph nodes. I underwent a lumpectomy, radiation and six months of chemotherapy. Only a few weeks ago, I passed my five-year checkup with a clean bill of health.

My story has a happy ending. Looking back, though, I would have been greatly helped and comforted had I received certain information, not just from physicians but also from women who had undergone the same experience.

•Having cancer is not your fault. No one knows exactly why women develop breast cancer, but it's certainly not because they have a "cancer personality." That idea is a lot of bunk. I've seen happy, optimistic cancer patients die very quickly after their diagnosis...and I've seen negative, hostile people live long after they "should" have been dead.

Lesson: Never view cancer as your own fault. I once overheard two therapists talking about a woman whose cancer was not responding to therapy. One said, "If she could only visualize better, she could cure this." What a ridiculous notion!

There's nothing wrong with trying alternative methods of healing, such as visualization, if they make you feel happier or more in control. But no one should ever blame you for your cancer.

•You have more time than you think you do to make decisions about treatment. Like most women newly diagnosed with breast cancer, I felt I had to decide immediately about whether I'd have a mastectomy (removal of the breast), a lumpectomy (removal of just the tumor), radi-

ation, etc. I was afraid that if I delayed treatment, my cancer would spread like wildfire.

Truth: In most cases, it's safe to take a couple of weeks to consider your options—and come to terms with your diagnosis.

Waiting also gives you the opportunity to get a second opinion—and that could help you avoid making a big mistake. Some old-school surgeons, for example, continue to recommend mastectomy even though in many cases it's just as effective—and far less emotionally wrenching —to have a lumpectomy followed by radiation.

•You'll find yourself resenting the doctor who diagnosed your cancer. Being diagnosed with breast cancer is so unnerving that women often find themselves resenting the doctor who made the diagnosis...and many find a new doctor. It's the old shoot-the-messenger feeling. You want the floor to open up and swallow him/her. But if the doctor is compassionate and competent, changing doctors at this stage is often a mistake.

•Coping with your fear is the hardest part of having breast cancer—but the fear doesn't last forever. At first, the fear that the cancer will spread and that you will die is almost overpowering. It affects everything you say, feel or do.

Eventually, the fear subsides. Although you might occasionally lapse back into fearful thinking, you get on with your life.

•Breast-cancer surgery isn't painful. I was afraid my operation would cause a great deal of pain. As it turned out, neither the surgery nor the recovery period was particularly painful physically—although the drainage tube inserted in my armpit for a week or so following surgery did cause a little discomfort. I was also weepy, depressed and maybe even a little irrational after surgery...but that quickly passed.

•The timing of breast-cancer surgery affects your chances of survival. Recent studies have shown that premenopausal women survive longer when tumors are removed during the second half of their menstrual cycles. Although this finding remains a matter of debate among cancer specialists, ask your doctor about scheduling surgery during the second half of your cycle, after ovulation.

•Chemotherapy affects your memory. During the months I was undergoing chemo, I experienced several memory lapses. I'd be trying to write and suddenly find myself unable to remember what it was I wanted to say next. At first I thought I had a brain tumor. I was terrified. Only later did I learn that temporary memory problems were a common side effect of chemotherapy. When they stop pouring the poison into your body, your memory returns to normal.

• Breast radiation is generally not very debilitating. Compared to chemotherapy, it's a piece of cake. It leaves you feeling a little tired, but not sick.

• Support groups are a tremendous source of emotional comfort during your recovery. Having cancer is a lonely, isolating experience. After my diagnosis, one or two longtime friends suddenly stopped calling and visiting. If your friends abandon you, realize that it's because of their fears—not because of something you did.

Even if your friends don't abandon you, they may be uncertain of how to behave in your presence. This can cause a lot of awkwardness. You may feel, for example, that you have to crack jokes or tell funny stories just to lighten the mood. After a while, these kinds of feelings become an enormous burden.

Joining a group of other women with breast cancer can lift this burden. When you're among peers, you don't have to take care of anyone else. You're free to laugh or cry—just be yourself.

• It's important to be kind to yourself. Guilt is a constant companion when you have cancer. If you eat too much fatty cheese or don't exercise one day, you feel you're contributing to your demise. But that's just not true.

Bottom line: Chemotherapy is hard on your body and will make you feel tired and cranky. If watching the soaps and eating popcorn will make you feel better, then do it. There is no need to feel guilty.

• You don't feel like celebrating at the end of treatment. I thought that when I eventually finished my chemotherapy treatment I would be ecstatic. But when that day finally came, I found myself pleased—but also sad to say goodbye to all the doctors, nurses and technicians who had been my "teammates" for so long. Suddenly, I was alone with my enemy and no longer doing anything to fight it. Fortunately, I had a great support group to make me feel less vulnerable.

• Life after cancer can be more satisfying than it was before. Although I would never have wished cancer upon myself, I must admit that having the disease has helped me understand my real priorities in life. I no longer worry about rejection, nor am I driven to spend time trying to gain prestige and status in the business world. I want to be with my 15-year-old daughter, Anna, and make my writing as strong and beautiful as it can be.

Cancer has also made me tougher and more gutsy. After all, what can hurt me after I've had cancer? But I'm also a much nicer person now. I'm more apt to send a sympathy card or visit someone in the hospital because I know how much such gestures mean to someone who is sick and frightened.

Source: Juliet Wittman, an award-winning reporter for the *Boulder Daily Camera,* Boulder, Colorado. She is the author of *Breast-Cancer Journal,* Fulcrum Publishing, 350 Indiana St., Golden, Colorado 80401.

How to Get the Love You Want

There is hope: A deep and long-lasting love and companionship in marriage is possible.

The secret: Couples must change from an unconscious marriage to a conscious marriage.

Almost all couples start their relationship as an unconscious marriage just by falling in love. In this state of romantic love, infatuation or "love at first sight," you feel your union is "magical"— and that your beloved is "the perfect one"…"the answer to your dreams."

What you do not realize is that this "person of your dreams" has qualities—voice tone, posture, facial expression, mood and character traits— that match an "image" in your unconscious mind of important people from your past (parents, other childhood caretakers). You actually fall in love with someone similar to those childhood caretakers.

More often we unconsciously choose mates who have similar negative rather than positive traits, that become obvious and disturbing after the "glow" of romance fades. They also have positive traits but the negative traits are more apparent.

Examples: Picking a husband who ignores you like your father, or a wife who nags like your mother.

The marriage becomes "unconscious" because both people try to recreate—in order to repair—their childhood.

They feel more or less in love depending on their unconscious anticipation of getting early needs met in the marriage.

Problems emerge when the partner, similar to the past figure, does not repair the initial hurt or give them the love they never got from their parents, leading to disillusionment, distrust or divorce.

Instead of love notes, back rubs, avid listening and time together, now each "escapes" into separate interests, friends, activities.

This unconscious repetition of the past to satisfy unmet needs—wanting from your spouse what you did not get from your parents—explains why spouses sometimes get more furious at their partners than the situation warrants.

Example: If your husband isn't at the office when you call, you panic, fearing he's having an affair or will leave you, triggering old feelings of abandonment when your mother left you with a baby-sitter, or was sick and unavailable—or worse—died.

Another common problem emerging from the unconscious marriage is the power struggle, where spouses react like children toward each other or as their parents reacted toward them.

While couples may panic over such conflicts, there is a hidden gain: The end of romantic love and being numb to each other's negative traits can be the beginning of more realistic reappraisals and growing up.

This is where "Imago Relationship Therapy" comes in ("imago" means "image"). This is a synthesis and expansion of ideas and techniques from other schools—including psychoanalysis, social learning theory, transactional analysis, gestalt and systems theory—to help couples move from repetitions in an unconscious marriage to a constructively conscious marriage.

The conscious marriage brings an end to romantic attachment and power struggles. The couple makes a commitment to uncover the un-

conscious needs that ignited their initial attraction, to heal their wounds and to move to a more evolved relationship based on personal wholeness and accepting and appreciating each other as separate beings. The spouse goes from being a surrogate parent to a passionate friend.

The steps to create a conscious marriage can be done alone—or with the professional help of a therapist. *Important:*

•Learn the dialogue—an essential communications skill that *enables couples to heal each other's emotional wounds by...*

Mirroring—repeating back what each other says about needs.

Validating—telling your partner you understand the logic of his/her needs given his/her childhood frustrations.

Empathy—experiencing your partner's feelings.

•Use the dialogue process, mutually identifying unmet needs and the corresponding specific request underlying a complaint.

Example: "You come home late" reveals "I need to feel loved" and the resulting request, "I would like you to come home by 7 PM on Tuesday nights."

•Identify the unmet agenda, the one from childhood that repeats in the marriage (attention, praise, comfort, independence) and how it sabotages the current relationship.

Examples: "Isolators" need "space" out of fear of being smothered by a spouse as they were by a parent. "Fusers," abandoned as children, want to merge with a spouse.

Helpful: Imagine addressing each important person in your childhood home, noting their positive and negative traits, what you liked and didn't like, wanted but didn't get. Ask then for what you want—and imagine them giving it. And—to separate yourself and your partner from parents, compare positive and negative traits, what you enjoy most, what you want and don't get.

•Develop personal wholeness—instead of seeking a mate to fill in your "holes." Find your "lost self."

Example: Because your father drank, you learned to ignore feelings of shame and sadness.

Drop the facade or "false self" that protects you from hurt. Reclaim your "disowned self" that was criticized and denied.

Example: Your mother always said you're not as smart as your brother, so you don't act smart even if you are.

Change your own negative traits without projecting them onto a partner (complaining, "He's bitter, not me," when you are really bitter) or acting them out.

• Validate and support each other's efforts.

• Communicate your needs instead of clinging to the childhood belief that your partner instinctively knows your needs. Fulfill some needs on your own.

• Meet your partner's needs more often than putting yourself first—in healing his/her wounds, you heal your own.

Example: When an emotionally unavailable man marries a woman with a similar-type father, the husband heals her wound and his own by becoming more sensitive to her needs.

Stretching exercise: Do something that your partner wants that is difficult for you to do.

Make a verbal or written commitment to stop "exits"—escapes from intimacy like overworking, over involvement with children, shopping, drinking, lying, picking fights—and to work together for a defined time. Set aside an hour of uninterrupted time together for a defined time.

Write a personal and joint relationship vision —"We are affectionate with each other," "We are loving parents," "We have fun."

Communicate better by taking turns as deliverer who describes a thought, feeling, anger or complaint, starting with "I" ("I felt anxious today at work")—and as receiver who paraphrases the message and asks for clarification. ("This morning you woke up wanting to stay home. Did I understand you right?").

"Re-romanticize" by sharing what pleases you now—"I feel loved when you call me from work…and when you massage my back…and when you listen when I'm upset"—what once pleased you—"I used to feel loved when you held my hand, wrote love notes, whispered sexy things in my ear."

What would please you—"I would feel loved if you took a shower with me…watched my favorite TV show…slept in the nude."

Do two each day for the next two months—and keep adding to the list.

Surprise each other with one new pleasure each week and one fun activity—walking, tennis, dancing, showering.

Visualize your love healing your partner—visualize your partner's love healing you.

This new conscious love will create a stable and passionate bond between the two of you and improve physical and emotional health. This new conscious love will also help you strengthen your immune system. It will flower into broader concern for others, the environment and a spiritual union with the universe.

Source: Harville Hendrix, PhD, educator and therapist who is the founder and director of the Institute for Relationship Therapy in New York. He is the author of the best-selling book *Getting the Love You Want: A Guide for Couples,* Harper/Perennial, 10 E. 53 St., New York 10022, and *Keeping the Love You Find: A Guide for Singles,* Pocket Books, 1230 Avenue of the Americas, New York 10020.

Prostate News

The prostate has been called the gland that always goes wrong—at least after age 50 or so, when prostate problems rise dramatically.

Yet new diagnostic and treatment techniques mean that more and more prostate problems can be caught early—and cured or successfully controlled. Certain lifestyle changes may even help to prevent prostate problems in the first place.

The prostate gland is located behind a man's pubic bone, at the mouth of the bladder. It is normally walnut-sized but tends to become larger with age. The gland is important during a man's prime reproductive years—it produces prostatic fluid, which makes up about 80% of semen and helps sperm to survive in the vagina after intercourse.

From men's 20s through their early 40s, prostate problems are usually limited to occasional infections. After the late 40s, however, problems may become more chronic or serious. But even prostate cancer, which strikes one in 11 American men, is treatable—the success rates are highest when the disease is diagnosed early.

The most common prostate problems and what can be done about them:

Prostate infection:

Symptoms of prostate infection, or prostatitis, include frequent and/or painful urination. The most common cause is bacteria spread through sexual activity...the more sex partners you have, the greater your chance of getting a prostate infection. The condition can usually be cured by antibiotics.

Prostate infections take longer to clear up than many other kinds of infections—patients must sometimes stay on antibiotics for several weeks—or even months. If your doctor prescribes antibiotics, be sure to keep taking the medication as long as your doctor advises—even if your symptoms have subsided.

Benign prostate enlargement:

Also called Benign Prostatic Hyperplasia, or BPH, this condition occurs when a mass of tissue begins to grow on the prostate. This benign tumor may cause pressure on the urethra, leading to an increased need to urinate (especially at night), a weak urine stream and the feeling that the bladder is never completely empty.

Not everyone with BPH has these symptoms. We don't know what causes BPH, but it seems to be related to testosterone production and to age. Nine out of ten men who reach the age of 80 experience some form of BPH, usually mild.

BPH is not a cancerous condition—a benign tumor doesn't spread—but that doesn't mean it should be left alone. Uncontrolled prostate growth can lead to kidney or bladder damage —as it did for Howard Hughes, who died of complications brought on by benign prostate enlargement for which he had refused to seek treatment.

Options for treating BPH:

Surgery: Since the 1940s, the surgical treatment of choice for BPH has been transurethral prostatectomy/TURP. The excess tissue is removed by means of a resectoscope, a narrow device inserted through the opening of the penis. The procedure takes less than an hour and has a very high success rate. *Disadvantages:* TURP can lead to infertility...and fewer than one in five men may be impotent after the surgery. However, many new techniques are available to overcome impotence. *Promising*: Laser surgery. It is also performed via a scope inserted through the penis. Last year, lasers accounted for 10% of prostate surgeries performed in the US. Whereas TURP requires several days in the hospital and up to eight weeks of recovery time, laser surgery can be performed on an outpatient basis under local anesthesia...with the patient back at work after a few days.

Losing popularity: Balloon dilatation, a technique that received a great deal of publicity several years ago. In this nonsurgical procedure, a balloon is inserted through the penis via a catheter, inflated to widen the urethral channel, then withdrawn. Although many patients report temporary relief of discomfort related to urination after this procedure, long-term follow-up suggests that symptoms tend to recur.

A number of other treatments, including one using heat from microwave radiation, are undergoing experimental trials.

Medication: Finestride (*trade name:* Proscar) received FDA approval in 1992. It shrinks the prostate by acting on an enzyme involved in the production of testosterone—without affecting testosterone levels elsewhere in the body. The drug must be taken for six months before the prostate begins to shrink. Finestride can be very effective but should not be prescribed blindly—it doesn't work for about 50% of patients.

Certain alpha adrenergic blockers, normally prescribed for high blood pressure, have also been shown to provide relief from prostate enlargement. One of these, terazosin (*trade name:* Hytrin), received FDA approval as a BPH treatment. Terazosin works not by shrinking the prostate but by relaxing muscles at the neck of the bladder, making urination easier.

Prostate cancer:

A spate of recent celebrity deaths from prostate cancer—including rock musician Frank Zappa and actor Bill Bixby—have made many more Americans aware of this disease. About 165,000 new cases of prostate cancer occur each year, but by no means is it always fatal.

Because early detection is so important to successful treatment, every man over age 50 (over 40 for a man whose father, grandfather or brother had prostate cancer) should see a urologist at least once a year. The annual visit should include both a rectal exam and a relatively new test called the Prostate Specific Antigen (PSA). This simple test measures the level of a chemical produced only in the prostate. If the level is higher than normal, it may be a sign of prostate enlargement and/or cancer.

Though the PSA test was a real breakthrough in early diagnosis, it's no panacea. It's estimated that 20% of men with elevated PSA readings do not have prostate cancer while 20% with low PSAs do have prostate cancer. That's why the rectal exam is so important. The doctor may be able to feel an abnormality not detected by the test. If either method suggests possible cancer, ultrasound should be performed to confirm the diagnosis.

The traditional treatment for prostate cancer is radical prostatectomy—surgical removal of the prostate. In many cases, this method allows the patient to live a long and full life. However, it is a drastic treatment that can result in impotence and incontinence.

One promising new treatment, known as "seeding," involves surgically implanting tiny radioactive capsules in the prostate. Radiation from the capsules kills cancer cells for about a year, with few side effects.

A study I've participated in for the past four years has found normal PSA levels in 93% of early-stage cancer patients after seed implantation treatment, using Palladium 103 as the radioactive source. The treatment is not generally effective for later-stage cancers, however.

In the past, castration was often recommended as part of prostate-cancer treatment, in order to reduce testosterone production. A more recent alternative is hormonal therapy. Leuprolide (trade name: *Lupron*) is one of the newer medications. Injected by the urologist once a month, it blocks the action of testosterone, with fewer side effects than would result from taking female hormones such as estrogen.

Source: Steven Morganstern, MD, director of urologic services at Metropolitan Hospital in Atlanta. He is coauthor of *The Prostate Sourcebook,* Lowell House, 2029 Century Park E., Los Angeles 90067, and *Love Again, Live Again,* Prentice Hall, 113 Sylvan Ave., Englewood Cliffs, New Jersey 07632.

Sex Myth

It is a myth that older men are dissatisfied with the quality of their sex lives.

It is true that more than half of men between 40 and 70 experience some difficulty in obtaining and maintaining erections. But they expect a decline in performance to occur as they age, so their level of satisfaction with sex remains the same as when they were younger.

Source: John McKinlay, PhD, an epidemiologist with the New England Research Institute, Nine Galen St., Watertown, Massachusetts 02172.

Pap Smears

Continue getting pap smears, even if you have had a complete hysterectomy. Women who have lost their uterus, cervix and ovaries can still develop other gynecological problems. *Example:* Cancer of the vagina, which can be detected by pap smear. How often a woman needs to be screened depends on the reason the hysterectomy was performed in the first place. *General guidelines:* A woman who had a benign condition—such as fibroids—should continue to have a pap smear every two or three years for the rest of her life…a woman who had abnormal cells or was diagnosed with cancer should be screened every year.

Source: Isaac Schiff, professor of gynecology, Harvard University Medical School, Boston.

For Menopausal Women

For menopausal women, "combined hormone therapy"—estrogen taken together with progestin—has several advantages. *Important:* It significantly reduces premature heart disease by dramatically lowering cholesterol levels. Combined therapy reduces LDL (bad) cholesterol by 30%. At the same time, hard-to-raise "good" cholesterol (HDL) goes up by 19%. *Helpful:* The important but less well-known risk factor Lipoprotein-a is reduced by as much as 50%. Overall cholesterol levels are reduced by 15%.

Source: Joel Morrisett, PhD, professor of medicine and biochemistry, Baylor College of Medicine, Houston.

Estrogen Pros and Cons

Taking estrogen after menopause has many benefits, but data about its possible risks are confusing—and changing all the time.

It will probably take ten years for studies to give a clearer picture of when estrogen replacement therapy (ERT) is and isn't a good idea. In the meantime, women must weigh the available information, discuss it with their doctors and keep watching for new data.

Important: If a postmenopausal woman has not had a hysterectomy, estrogen is nearly always prescribed along with progestin. Estrogen given alone raises the risk of cancer of the endometrium (uterine lining), but the estrogen-progestin combination seems to erase that risk. (A woman whose uterus has been removed cannot get endometrial cancer.)

Based on the most recent data, we now believe that estrogen protects against the following:

•*Heart disease.* ERT reduces risk of heart disease by as much as 50%, according to several recent studies. Estrogen appears not only to boost blood flow to the heart, but also to raise HDL (good) cholesterol and lower LDL (bad) cholesterol levels.

Problem: Most of these studies measured estrogen taken alone. It's still unclear whether an estrogen-progestin combination lowers heart-disease risk.

•*Osteoporosis.* Broken hips and other broken bones are a leading cause of death among older women.

•*Symptoms of menopause.* ERT helps prevent hot flashes, vaginal dryness, incontinence and possibly mood swings.

Estrogen should be *avoided* by women who…

…have had breast cancer. Estrogen's relationship to breast cancer remains uncertain, but women who have had breast cancer may want to avoid estrogen until more information is available.

…have had a thrombo-embolism (blood clot in the lung). Women who take estrogen may be at slightly higher risk of this type of clotting.

…can't tolerate estrogen's side effects. These may include bloating, weight gain, nausea, headaches, vaginal spotting or bleeding and mild depression.

Despite sometimes frightening reports in the popular press, the risks posed by estrogen appear too small—especially when compared to its potential benefits.

Example: The average 50-year-old woman has a 45% chance of getting heart disease at some point in her life...and about a 30% chance of dying from it. That same woman has a 10% chance of getting—and a 3% chance of dying from—breast cancer. As for endometrial cancer, the incidence is only 3%, and the death rate less than 1%.

Since we have no conclusive data showing that estrogen with progestin raises the risk of endometrial or breast cancer, estrogen's protective value against heart disease seems to far outweigh the possible cancer risk.

Other risks to estrogen therapy may yet be discovered. But based on what we now know, estrogen therapy can be recommended for most menopausal women.

Source: Howard A. Zacur, MD, PhD, director of the Johns Hopkins Estrogen Consultation Service and associate professor of gynecology and obstetrics at the Johns Hopkins Medical Institutions in Baltimore. He is coauthor of *Estrogen Replacement Therapy: The Johns Hopkins Guide to Making an Informed Decision,* The Johns Hopkins University Women's Health Center, 550 N. Broadway, Suite 1100, Baltimore 21205.

Impotence: What to Do Before You See the Doctor

Achieving an erection is nothing less than a feat of hydraulic engineering. Sexual arousal dilates blood vessels in the penis. The hydraulic fluid (blood) flows in, causing the penis to become engorged.

Anything that disrupts the flow of blood interferes with the process.

Result: Impotence. It's a problem that affects 30 million American men—one in five.

Causes of impotence:

Until recently, impotence was considered primarily a *psychological* problem. Over the last two decades, however, we've learned that psychological factors—including, paradoxically, the fear of being unable to perform sexually—account for less than 25% of all cases of impotence. *Far more common is impotence caused by physical problems, including...*

• Arteriosclerosis. The same sorts of fatty deposits that build up in the coronary arteries build up in the arteries supplying blood to the penis. Instead of a heart attack, however, the result is impotence.

• Smoking. Toxins in smoke damage blood vessels in the penis, preventing the free flow of blood needed to produce an erection. Some have overcome impotence by giving up tobacco.

• Prostate trouble. Some cases of impotence are associated with an enlarged, inflamed or infected prostate. *Symptoms:* Frequent urination, especially at night...burning or pain during urination or ejaculation. If you experience any of these symptoms, get a prostate exam.

• Drug use. Many cases of impotence are caused by drug or alcohol abuse. Drinking can trigger impotence by raising blood levels of the hormone estrogen (produced by men as well as women) and lowering testosterone levels. Testosterone levels can also be lowered by marijuana. Cocaine, heroin and other illicit drugs can cause nerve damage.

Impotence can also be a side effect of tranquilizers, antidepressants, anti-anxiety drugs and diuretics ("water" pills) used to treat high blood pressure.

• Nerve damage. Getting an erection is difficult or impossible without healthy nerves leading to and from the penis. These nerves can be damaged during surgery on the prostate, bladder, rectum or even on the aorta, the large artery leading from the heart. The nerves can also be damaged by injury.

• Diabetes and kidney disease. Roughly half of all diabetic men become impotent within ten years of the onset of the disease. Uncontrolled diabetes limits blood flow and causes nerve damage.

Hormonal disturbances caused by kidney disease can lead to high blood pressure, which necessitates use of medication that can cause impotence.

• Obesity. Being overweight is associated with diabetes, hypertension and high cholesterol—all of which are factors in impotence.

Solving the problem:

Once you've considered the possible cause of your problem, you can take steps on the road back to full enjoyment of sex.

Here are some simple things you can do to determine what might be causing your impotence. Take your findings to the doctor and you'll speed up the return of your sex life.

• Make sure you really are impotent. If you have trouble achieving or maintaining an erection less than 30% of the time, you're probably not impotent. Occasional failure is perfectly normal. More frequent problems, however, suggest that it's time to check further.

• Review your sexual history. Jot down the specifics of your sex life during the past several months—when, where and how often you had sex...how often you were impotent...what you had to eat and drink beforehand, etc. If you find a pattern to your impotence, you may be able to find a way to break it.

• Keep a sex log. Write down all the specifics of your *current* sex life. Such a log can help you pinpoint possible causes of impotence... and it can also be a big help to your doctor.

Caution: Some men find that keeping a written log makes them anxious—which, in turn, can make it even harder to get an erection. If this is the case, try making mental notes and reviewing them with a physician.

• Test your "apparatus." If you're impotent during sex but can achieve a full erection while masturbating, you're probably okay physically. Odds are it's a psychological problem.

If you cannot achieve a full erection during sex or while masturbating, try the "postage stamp" test. This is a crude but effective version of a common laboratory method.

Procedure: Before going to sleep, encircle your soft penis with a ring of postage stamps. Moisten one of the stamps on the end, then press it against the stamp on the other end until the ring is secure. It should be snug, but not tight.

During a normal night's sleep, you should have three to five erections. If any of the perforations is torn when you awaken, you've probably had at least one erection. Your impotence is probably psychological in origin. If the stamps are intact, your impotence probably stems from a physical cause.

•Examine your relationship. Be honest. Are you and your partner having problems? Have you stopped communicating? Are you depressed? Is your partner? Have you developed a bad case of "performance anxiety?"

If you answer "yes" to any of these questions, your impotence may stem from a psychological cause. In some cases, though, psychological problems are the *result* of an impotence problem—caused by a physical problem.

The best way to deal with psychological impotence is to discuss the problem as candidly as possible with your partner, doctor—and possibly a psychotherapist. If talking about the problem fails to help, ask your doctor about self-injecting your penis with *papaverine* or *prostaglandin E₁* prior to sex. In some cases—roughly 10%—the answer may lie in a surgically implanted prosthesis.

•Take a "drug inventory." Consider all the drugs you're taking. If you suspect that one might be causing your impotence, ask your doctor about alternatives. Another drug might be just as effective without causing impotence …or there might be a drug-free option.

Caution: Do not stop taking any prescription medication without first consulting your doctor.

Finally—relax. Your problem is probably not as hard to solve as you might think. In some cases, simply learning to adopt a more relaxed approach to life and sex is all it takes. Or take a relaxing vacation with your partner.

Enjoy the pleasures of intimacy. It's one thing to become a workaholic and throw oneself fully into a job. But to enjoy the pleasure of a loved one's company or the physical caring of sexuality is a very different thing.

If your problem persists, see a urologist who specializes in the treatment of impotence. The information you've already uncovered will speed the return of a fulfilling sex life.

Source: Steven Morganstern, MD, director of the Morganstern Urology Clinic, Atlanta. He is coauthor of *Overcoming Impotence,* Prentice Hall, 113 Sylvan Ave., Englewood Cliffs, New Jersey 07632.

Between-Period Spotting

Between-period spotting is not normal—even after strenuous exercise—and should be discussed with a gynecologist. Spotting could signal polyps, fibroids, infections, inflammations, hormonal problems or cancer. *Helpful:* Use a calendar to record every episode of spotting. This will help determine whether you are spotting at certain times during each of your menstrual cycles.

Source: Mona Shangold, MD, professor of obstetrics and gynecology at Hahnemann University, Philadelphia, and coauthor of *The Complete Sports Medicine Book for Women,* Simon & Schuster, 1230 Avenue of the Americas, New York 10020.

Birth Defects News

New research on birth defects provides evidence that environmental factors play an important role. According to the latest study—involving more than 370,000 women in Norway and published in *The New England Journal of Medicine*—a woman whose first child has a birth defect has a substantially higher risk of having a second child with the *same* defect…and she has a slightly higher risk of having a second child with a *differerent* defect. *Surprising:* If a woman who had a child with a birth defect moves to a different community or changes partners between pregnancies, her risk of having another baby with a similar defect drops—though it is still higher than other women's risk. *Unknown:* Exactly which environmental factors are responsible for birth defects.

Source: Jennifer L. Howse, PhD, president of the March of Dimes Birth Defects Foundation, 1275 Mamaroneck Ave., White Plains, New York 10605.

Lemons Beat Morning Sickness

Fresh lemons are an old cure for seasickness. They often prevent morning sickness, too. *Alter-*

natives: Sniff fresh lemons…suck wedges plain or sprinkled with salt…drink lemonade. Experiment to find the most effective approach. *Other natural aids:* Anise…ginger or ginger ale.

Source: *No More Morning Sickness: A Survival Guide for Pregnant Women* by Miriam Erick, RN, affiliated with Brigham & Women's Hospital, Boston. Plume, 375 Hudson St., New York 10014.

Gonorrhea Causes Infertility

Gonorrhea isn't the only sexually transmitted disease that causes infertility in women. *Trichomoniasis*—infection with the *Trichomonas* protozoan—can also cause the problem. Compared with healthy women, those with trichomoniasis were 1.9 times more likely to have tubal infertility…while those with gonorrhea were 2.4 times as likely to be infertile.

Source: Francine Grodstein, ScD, research fellow, department of epidemiology, Harvard School of Public Health, Boston. Her study of more than 4,000 women was reported in *Family Planning Perspectives,* 111 Fifth Ave., New York 10003.

Decreased Sperm Count

Decreased sperm count and motility—common in heavy smokers—may be reversible. *Key:* Vitamin C. Male smokers who received 200 or 1,000 milligrams of ascorbic acid daily for four weeks produced more healthy sperm than did heavy smokers who did not take the sup-

plements. The larger dose produced a greater improvement.

Source: Earl Dawson, PhD, associate professor of obstetrics and gynecology, University of Texas Medical Branch, Galveston. His study of 75 male smokers was published in *Fertility and Sterility,* 1209 Montgomery Highway, Birmingham, Alabama 35216.

Drugs and Infertility

Women who have used tranquilizers for more than two years—or antidepressants for more than six months—are *three times* more likely to be infertile due to ovulatory problems than the general population. *Twice as likely:* Women who have used asthma medications before the age of 21 or thyroid replacement hormones. *Yet to be established:* Whether infertility is caused by the drugs…or the underlying disorders. *Advice:* When planning a pregnancy, consult your physician to determine safe medications.

Source: Study led by Marlene B. Goldman, ScD, associate professor of epidemiology, Harvard School of Public Health, Cambridge, Massachusetts.

Vaginal Infection

Vaginal infection early in pregnancy increases the risk of premature labor. Women with *bacterial vaginosis* were five times more likely to have early labor than uninfected women. *Self-defense:* Any woman who experiences abnormal vaginal discharge should see a doctor. Antibiotic treatment is 80% effective against bacterial vaginosis.

Source: Catherine Ison, PhD, lecturer in medical microbiology, St. Mary's Hospital Medical School, London. She coauthored a study of 783 pregnant women, which was published in the *British Medical Journal,* Tavistock Square, London WC1H9JR, England.

14

Nutrition, Fitness and Exercise

Nutrition, Fitness and Exercise: 1995…and beyond

Edith Weiner, Weiner Edrich, Brown, Inc.

Personal health became a hot part of American culture in the 1970s and 1980s. It has stayed that way ever since. There's no reason to believe that Americans' obsession with health, fitness, nutrition and longevity—especially longevity—will wane in the next ten years. As part of this groundswell of health consciousness, there has been a great proliferation of alternative therapies for all sorts of ailments…

•Aromatherapy for the treatment of anxiety, stress and panic has gotten more and more attention in recent years.

•Hypnosis to help smokers quit and to treat emotional disorders continues to thrive.

•Acupuncture, holistic medicine and herbal treatments continue to draw the attention of medical researchers *and* potential patients.

The ultimate result of this explosion of choice is favorable. It will help exert downward pressure on prices, and provide a higher chance of successful treatment when aggressive medicine is not called for or has too many side effects.

Meanwhile, Americans' concern with staying healthy will result in increasing demand for healthful foods—organic products, low-fat foods, chemical-free foods, etc.

The national fight against obesity and heart-threatening cholesterol will continue to build momentum in coming years. And with this, the well-established compulsion for fitness will flourish, with sales of athletic equipment burgeoning, and the popularity of all kinds of sports and fitness activities increasing. But the less-impactful and less-stressful activities will do the best.

A good part of the reason for this phenomenon relates to the aging of the huge baby-boom generation, and their intense desire to lengthen their healthy lives.

This is also good news for professionals who specialize in relieving people of their dis-eases—as distinct from their medical diseases. Dis-eases common among American baby boomers today include aging skin, excessive fat, receding hairlines and loss of memory.

Result: Plastic surgery is big business…liposuction is a term for the first time familiar to an entire generation…drugs promising to restore hair growth on bald heads are huge profitmakers and all sorts of herbal and vitamin formulas for improving memory and other brain functions are widely reported on in popular consumer magazines.

Mistakes People Make Walking for Their Health

The most common mistake people make in walking for their health is not walking often enough or fast enough. *Frequency:* Walking three times a week yields a bare minimum of overall fitness. Significant cardiorespiratory benefits really kick in starting at four days a week. So does weight loss, for which it's best to walk every day. *Important:* Consult with your physician before beginning any new exercise regimen.

Speed: The faster you walk the more calories burned and the more time saved. How it works…

Three miles per day is the optimum distance for fitness. If you stroll along at a 20-minute per mile pace, it will take you one hour per session to do your walking. At this speed a mostly sedentary person can expect about a 4% improvement in cardiorespiratory fitness over several months. But if the same person works his/her speed up to 15-minute miles, he/she gets more than double the improvement (9%) and saves time—cutting down from an hour to 45 minutes per walk.

True aerobic walking—12-minute miles—gives four times the cardiorespiratory improvement (16%) and takes only 36 minutes per three-mile walk.

Mistake: Taking it easy, walking too slowly. If your doctor says it's okay to walk, then try to walk within your individual training range.

This means walking fast enough to reach the ideal exercise heart rate for your age. To find your individual ideal and safe heart rate take the number 220 and subtract your age. Between 65% and 85% of this figure is the heart rate you want to attain.

Example: At age 50, subtract 50 from 220 to get 170: 65% of 170 is 110. This is the desired, minimum target pulse rate.

Mistake: Taking it easy to avoid injury. Walking has proven to be virtually injury-free. And if it's done fast enough it can yield even better benefits than jogging—at any age. (Fast enough usually means going at least a bit faster than the speed at which you would naturally break into a jog.) From sedentary, start out at a comfortable pace. Over several months you should be able to walk a 15-minute mile. Three miles in 45 minutes is a good goal for a moderate fitness level. Then try to work it slowly down to 36 minutes.

The chances of injury from jogging are about 40% in any given year. The chances of injury from walking are near zero over a lifetime.

Mistake: Not stretching. It's safe enough to walk without stretching. But a daily, gentle stretching of the major muscle groups of the leg gives a walker the flexibility to move more easily and more powerfully. Without stretching, the walker is likely to have a short leg swing, giving a choppy or even shuffling gait. Older walkers in particular should stretch to maintain maximum flexibility.

Caution: Do not bounce when you stretch. Instead, stretch the leg muscles slowly as though pulling on a thick rubber band—you should feel the pull but not experience pain. Take 15 to 20 seconds per stretch and repeat three times. *Best advice:* The hamstrings (the muscle group in the back of the thigh) are the most important ones to stretch. Stretch when your muscles are warm after your walk.

Mistake: Poor posture. Most people do not have good walking posture. Many walkers tilt the head down and slump the shoulders. Keep shoulders back, head up and chin level to the ground.

Source: Casey Meyers, a health and fitness authority and author of *Aerobic Walking*. Most recently, he wrote *Walking: A Complete Guide to the Complete Exercise*, Random House, 201 E. 50 St., New York 10022.

Best Room Temperature

Best room temperature for exercising indoors is 68° to 72°F. It's better to feel a bit cool at the beginning of your workout. As you warm up, you won't be overwhelmed by the rising heat. *Also:* To help dissipate body heat and humidity, exercise only in a well-ventilated room with controlled humidity.

Source: American College of Sports Medicine, 401 W. Michigan St., Indianapolis 46202.

Health-Club Threat

The sweaty heat, humidity and confined space make most health clubs perfect breeding grounds for bacteria, fungi and other nasty microbes. *Self-defense:* Use hot tubs only if the water is crystal clear. Wear rubber thongs when showering, and dry feet thoroughly and dust them with antifungal powder before putting on your shoes. Use a clean towel. Dry off from head to feet—not vice versa—to avoid spreading germs from your feet to your upper body. Avoid touching your face, especially your nose and eyes, while working out.

Source: Tobias Samo, MD, clinical associate professor of internal medicine, Baylor College of Medicine, quoted in *Men's Health*, 33 E. Minor St., Emmaus, Pennsylvania 18098.

Stair Climbing

Stair climbing promotes fitness just as effectively as running—and it's less likely to cause injury. Women who worked out on stair-climbing machines got just as fit as women who jogged. But not one climber experienced serious injury, compared to 29% of runners. Stair climbing may be especially appropriate for runners interested in cross-training and for those in need of post-injury rehabilitation.

Source: Steven Loy, PhD, associate professor of kinesiology, California State University, Northridge. His study of 25 women was published in *Medicine and Science in Sports and Exercise*, 428 E. Preston St., Baltimore 21202.

Avoiding Crime While Walking or Running

•Whenever possible, do your walking or running with others.
•Know your route, including the locations of telephones and open businesses along the way.
•Carry coins to make a telephone call.
•Avoid running or walking when your route is deserted.
•Stay away from doorways, alleys and other places where an attacker might hide.
•Stay away from trails surrounded by trees or dense foliage.
•Vary your routine so you can't be counted on to be in a certain place at a certain time.
•Let someone know where you're going and how long you plan to be gone.
•Carry identification, an emergency phone number and a police whistle or other noise-maker that can be used to call for help.

Source: Susan Kalish, executive director, American Running and Fitness Association, 4405 East-West Highway, Suite 405, Bethesda, Maryland 20814.

Hot Weather Exercise Basics

Drink at least eight 8-ounce glasses of water a day. Be sure to have some before…during… and after exercising. Take frequent breaks. Quit if you feel weak, dizzy or faint. Wear a hat and lightweight, brightly colored clothing to reflect sunlight. To boost your body's retention of water, speak with your doctor about increasing your salt intake during summer months.

Source: Robert Levine, MD, assistant professor of medicine, Baylor College of Medicine, Houston.

Better Workouts

It's not how long you exercise at a time that counts, but your *cumulative* workout time. *Example:* Two 10-minute runs are nearly as valuable as one 20-minute run—provided you run at comparable speeds. *Lesson:* If you have only ten minutes free during the day, then run for only ten minutes. *However:* Workouts lasting longer than 35 minutes *do* significantly boost endurance and aerobic capacity.

Source: Owen Anderson, PhD, publisher of *Running Research News*, Box 27041, Lansing, Michigan 48909.

How to Stick to an Exercise Program

•*First:* Find an exercise program you enjoy. If you enjoy it, the chances are you're going to want to stick with it.

•*Second:* Find something that fits your lifestyle. For example, something that doesn't require you to go to the mountains to hike, or require special equipment that you don't have or can't afford.

•*Third:* Make an appointment with yourself to exercise so there's always time that's scheduled in. Without that reminder, it's easy to run out of time.

•*Fourth:* Psych yourself up. You have to recognize the benefits of exercise. By doing something you like to do and getting into some consistency, if you're on a program for a while, you'll start to feel the results. You'll feel better, have some pride when you finish your workout, maybe reduce some stress. And you may notice you've gotten a little stronger or lost some weight. You can use these things and really dwell on them to help reinforce your positive mental attitude for exercise.

•*Fifth:* Morning is a good time to exercise. It helps get your day started and you get it done and out of the way.

•*Sixth:* Exercise at least three times a week. And try to incorporate activity that exercises the cardiovascular system as well as strengthens your muscles. Things like taking a brisk walk for 20 or 30 minutes, cycling, playing recreational sports or exercise classes are all valuable workouts for the cardiovascular system.

•*Seventh:* Exercise in moderation. Some people, when they get on a program, get fanatical for a few weeks, then they stop. The key is consistency, not how intense you are per session. It's much more important to have a moderate session and do it consistently over a long period of time.

Source: Jake Steinfeld, personal trainer to Hollywood stars and the author of *Don't Quit*, Warner Books, 1271 Avenue of the Americas, New York 10021.

Better Mall Walking

Carrying a purse or wearing a shoulder bag interferes with free arm swing. Get a small fanny pack for your wallet and car keys instead. Pick the longest straightaway for your walk so you can sustain a strong pace with few turns—a quarter-mile-long mall would allow a half-mile walk with only one turn. To cool down, when pace is not important, walk the mall's perimeter.

Source: *Walking: A Complete Guide to the Complete Exercise* by Casey Meyers, walking consultant, St. Joseph, Missouri. Random House, 201 E. 50 St., New York 10022.

The Best New Shape-Up Equipment

Cycle:

•*Precor M8.2E/L.* This heavy-duty recumbent cycle trainer has an ergonomically designed seat for a comfortable workout that is easy on the lower back. Also good for people with high blood pressure, seniors, pregnant women or anyone who is out of shape and is just beginning an exercise program. *Features:* Built-in heart-rate monitor, programmable computer, frictionless, magnetic-resistance mechanism, adjustable seat, padded handlebars and wheels for easy portability. *Dimensions:* 63" x 27" x 43".

Precor Inc., Box 3004, Bothell, Washington 98041. 800-477-3267, ext. 105.

Heart-rate monitor:

•*Polar Edge.* EKG-accurate and unobtrusive. Most attach to fingers or earlobes, so they measure only the pulse and, depending on body movement, often give inaccurate readings. This two-part unit consists of a monitor that attaches to the chest and an LCD wristwatch that receives readings from the monitor via wireless technology. The watch keeps track of the amount of time you're in your proper heart-rate zone for a more effective workout. Comfortable for both men and women.

Polar CIC Inc., 99 Seaview Blvd., Port Washington, New York 11050. 800-262-7776.

Help for minor injuries:

•*Wrapz* provides either cold or hot compression therapy in one well-fitting package so you can continue to train and compete even while nursing minor sports-related injuries. The reusable and removable gel pack can be stored in the freezer to provide cold relief or heated in the microwave for hot, moist compression. Breathable and comfortable stretch-fabric wraps come for knees, back, shoulder, wrist, ankle, elbow and neck.

Wrapz Inc., 111 E. Chestnut St., Suite 54C, Chicago 60611. 800-289-9727.

Stair climber:

•*Fitness Master 570.* This is a true breakthrough in home stair-climber design. Unlike most club-quality stair machines, which are bulky and institutional-looking, this is sleek and compact enough to fit into any home decor. (It's won two international design awards.) *Features:* Independent stepping action, smooth operation, adjustable motor speed and both programmable and manual operation. *Floor dimensions:* 29" x 21" x 53."

Fitness Master Inc., 504 Industrial Blvd., Waconia, Minnesota 55387. 800-328-8995.

Tennis trainer:

•*Tone Trainer* teaches budding tennis stars one of the most important aspects of developing a winning stroke—the ability to hold the racquet with a light grip during preparation and a firm grip at the moment just before contact with the ball. Tone Trainer consists of a small monitor that fits into its racquet throat and an electronic strip embedded in the grip. The unit generates an audible tone whenever the player's grip is tight, training him/her to relax and tighten the grip at the appropriate moments. Particularly

effective for intermediate players who want to improve their game.

Tone Trainer Inc., 4720 SE 15 Ave., Suite 203, Cape Coral, Florida 33904. 800-677-4858.

Treadmill:

•*Precor M9.20S.* This high-tech treadmill features a proprietary technology that allows the running surface to "float" on a specially formulated shock-absorbing material. *Result:* Running or walking is less stressful, your feet won't wobble and the tread feels realistic—firm and not mushy. *Features:* Built-in programs including weight-loss and interval course; digital readout including calories burned, time, distance, speed, incline; motorized incline and the no-maintenance bed never needs lubricating. *Dimensions:* 67" x 28.5" x 43."

Precor Inc., Box 3004, Bothell, Washington 98041. 800-477-3267, ext. 105.

Weight system:

•*Body Lift 1000.* A true weight-training home gym without the weights. Using a cleverly designed pulley system, the machine uses the lifter's body weight to provide variable resistance ranging from three pounds to 129% of the user's weight. It's easier to use and less threatening than bulky weight-stack machines. It accommodates a complete range of biomechanically correct upper- and lower-body workouts. The machine is compact, well-built and offers smooth operation. *Dimensions:* 48" x 42" x 72."

Pacific Fitness Corporation, 6600 W. Katella Ave., Cypress, California 90630. 800-722-3482.

Source: Patrick Netter, an independent home fitness-equipment expert and consultant, 10480 Kinnard Ave., Los Angeles 90024.

Frozen Gel Packs

Frozen gel packs can treat injuries more gently than ice packs. To make one—*partially* fill a *heavy-duty* plastic freezer bag with a mix of ¼ rubbing alcohol and ¾ water. Seal the bag, then seal it inside of a second plastic bag. Place in the freezer. Because of alcohol's lower freezing point, the gel will remain soft.

Source: *University of California–Berkeley Wellness Letter,* 5 Water Oak, Fernandina Beach, Florida 32034.

Secrets of Exercise Stick-To-It-Iveness

Seventy-five percent of people who start an exercise program quit within a year. *To be an exercise veteran...*

•Choose a program that is fun for you. *Best:* Lifetime sports—hiking, swimming, walking, dancing, gardening, volleyball, tennis, golf (no golf carts please). Add appropriate conditioning exercises once you are comfortable with the regimen.

•Pick a motivating role model—someone you've seen on the tennis court or in your aerobics class.

•Join—or create—a team to add fun, competition and socializing.

•Treat exercise times like "appointments." Those who miss three consecutive exercise sessions are more likely to abandon the program altogether.

Source: Robert Hopper, PhD, who gives seminars on health and fitness nationwide. He is based in Santa Barbara, California.

Real Cause of Flabby Muscles

Lack of exercise—not aging. Muscle mass does decline between ages 30 and 70. But isotonic—strength-building—exercises can reverse the decline. Half an hour of isotonics two or three times a week can increase strength within two weeks and double it in 12 weeks—by changing the ratio of muscle to fat. *Bonus:* Increased bone density—helping prevent fractures caused by osteoporosis.

Source: William J. Evans, PhD, Director of Noll Laboratories of Human Performance Research, Pennsylvania State University, University Park. He is coauthor of *Biomarkers: The Ten Determinants of Aging You Can Control*, Simon & Schuster, Inc., 1230 Avenue of the Americas, New York 10020.

Treadmill Traps

Setting the speed too fast or the incline too steep...keeping your ankles too stiff, which can lead to shinsplints...flailing your arms, which can twist your torso and stress the back...locking your arms in one position, which prevents your body from making subtle adjustments to better absorb impact. *Helpful:* Keep your gait smooth, upper body loose and arms close to your torso, moving them back and forth in a relatively straight line.

Source: Mike Motta, president, Plus One Fitness in New York City, quoted in *American Health*, 28 W. 23 St., New York 10010.

Health-Club Secrets

More than ten million Americans work out in 15,000 health clubs and spas across the country. They pay substantial amounts for the privilege—but things don't always turn out as planned. Health-club members face three common pitfalls—insolvency, incompetence and injuries. To protect yourself:

•Check with consumer watchdog groups. Call your state or local consumer protection agency and the Better Business Bureau. Ask whether any negative reports have been filed against the club you have in mind. At least 36 states have enacted legislation designed specifically to protect the interests of health-club members.

For additional information, contact the Association of Physical Fitness Centers, 600 E. Jefferson St., Rockville, MD 20852 (301-424-7744). This trade group monitors member clubs to ensure that they meet minimum standards.

Caution: Never join a health club before it opens, no matter how sterling its prospects or how luxurious its facilities. Look for a club with at least three years of continuous operation—or a new branch of an established chain.

•Conduct a thorough inspection of the club. Go at peak time—at lunch, for example, or after work. If the place is wall-to-wall with people, there is probably a lack of equipment or instructors. If it's empty, something else is wrong. *What else to look for:* The pool, bathrooms, locker rooms and weight rooms all should be clean and well-maintained. Equipment should be in good repair. Faulty or worn equipment can cause injuries. As you walk around the club, find out what members like most about the club—and what they like least.

•Make sure the club is bonded. Some states require health clubs to post a minimum bond of $500,000. While that's hardly enough for a large club, it suggests at least some financial security on the part of the owner. Request evidence of bonding from the club or from the consumer protection agency.

•Insist upon qualified instructors. Though many fine trainers lack formal credentials, competent ones often will be certified by one of three sanctioning bodies…

•American Council on Exercise, 800-825-3636.

•American College of Sports Medicine, 317-637-9200.

•Aerobics and Fitness Association of America, 800-445-5950.

•Resist hard-sell tactics. An eager salesperson may offer you a special membership contract that expires "at midnight tonight." Don't take the bait—no matter how interested you are in the club. Instead, request a one-day trial membership. *Cost:* No more than a few dollars—perhaps free. If possible, try a sample session with a personal trainer.

•Negotiate your membership fee. Annual fees range from several hundred dollars for a family all the way up to $3,500 for an individual. Some clubs tack on a nonrefundable initiation fee of several hundred dollars. But no matter what the initial quote, membership fees and conditions are almost always negotiable.

•Insist on a short-term contract. Sad but true —90% of health-club members stop coming after three months. To avoid paying for workouts you never get, arrange to pay on a monthly basis…or sign up for a 90-day trial membership. *Important:* Don't sign on the spot. Take the contract home and review it with a friend or family member.

•Read the fine print. A typical contract is two pages. Each portion must be scrutinized not only for what it includes, but also for what it omits. Make sure you will have full access to all facilities that interest you…swimming pool, squash courts, etc. Avoid contracts that limit the hours you can use the club—unless that fits your schedule.

If the contract does not include an "escape" clause, insert one. It should stipulate that you will get a prorated refund if you move or become disabled before the term is up. *Caution:* Watch out for the club's escape clause—a waiver of liability in case you are injured. Such clauses are illegal in many states, but cross it off and initial it before signing just to be sure. If possible, get the club to guarantee that it won't move.

Finally, make sure the contract covers everything that you've discussed with club employees. Never rely on verbal agreements.

If you have second thoughts about joining a health club, ask for a full refund. Most states mandate a three-day "cooling-off" period, during which consumers can back out of contracts and major purchases.

Source: Stephen L. Isaacs, JD, professor of public health at Columbia University and a practicing attorney in New York City. He is coauthor of *The Consumer's Legal Guide to Today's Health Care: Your Medical Rights and How to Assert Them,* Houghton Mifflin, 215 Park Ave. S., New York 10003.

Immunity-Boosting Diet Strategies

Surely, the best way to build resistance to infections, as well as cancer, is to eat lots of fruits and vegetables, especially garlic and those rich in beta-carotene and vitamin C. *Other strategies…*

•Go easy on meat—especially fatty meats.

•Restrict omega-6 fatty acids of the type in corn oil, safflower oil and sunflower seed oil.

•Eat seafood, especially fatty fish and shellfish, as well as other foods high in zinc.

•Eat yogurt regularly.

•Go easy on sugar. Evidence suggests that it lowers immunity.

Packaged Foods

Packaged foods often contain far more calories than their labels indicate. *Recent survey:* Foods distributed *regionally* contained up to 25% more calories than specified on their labels…and *local* brands averaged about 85% more calories than stated. *Better:* National food products, possibly because of better quality control. Their calorie content was understated only by an average of 2%. *Self-defense:* Dieters and diabetics should stick to national brands…recalculate for regional or local brands…or prepare their own food.

Source: David Allison, PhD, fellow, Obesity Research Center, St. Luke's/Roosevelt Hospital, New York City.

Fruit vs. High Blood Pressure

The more fruit you eat, the lower your chance of developing high blood pressure. In a recent study, men who ate the least fruit were almost 50% more likely to develop hypertension than men who consumed the most fruit. Of course, an even more important factor in determining hypertension risk is body weight. In the same study, the men who weighed the most were four and a half times more likely to develop high blood pressure than the men who weighed the least.

Source: Meir J. Stampfer, MD, DrPH, associate professor of epidemiology, Harvard School of Public Health, Boston. His study of 30,681 men 40 to 75 years of age was published in *Circulation*, 7320 Greenville Ave., Dallas 75231.

Blood Pressure

Blood pressure is more likely to remain at healthy levels in people who eat a diet that is rich in beans, rice and other sources of vegetable protein…higher than usual in polyunsaturated fat… and low in saturated fat and cholesterol.

Source: Kiang Liu, PhD, professor of preventive medicine, Northwestern University Medical School, Chicago. His study of more than 1,800 men, ages 40 to 55, was reported in *Internal Medicine News* and *Cardiology News*, 12230 Wilkins Ave., Rockville, Maryland 20852.

Chinese Food

Chinese food can contain surprisingly high amounts of fat. One dinner-size take-out order of *kung pao* chicken (chicken and peanuts in hot pepper sauce) has 76 grams of fat—more than the 60 or so grams the average person should eat in an entire day.

Self-defense: Order steamed or stir-fried vegetables or Szechuan shrimp—they contain one-fourth the fat of kung pao chicken. Eat a cup of rice for each cup of entrée…mix entrées with steamed vegetables…before eating, lift individual food pieces onto the rice, leaving behind excess sauce, egg and nuts. Then eat directly from the rice bowl.

Source: Jayne Hurley, RD, associate nutritionist, Center for Science in the Public Interest, Washington, DC. She is coauthor of a study of Chinese food published in *Nutrition Action Healthbletter*, 1875 Connecticut Ave. NW, Washington, DC 20009.

Cancer and Food Preparation

At least ten different kinds of carcinogens are released when meat, poultry or fish is grilled or fried. Some of the compounds are the same ones found in cigarette smoke. *Self-defense:* Stew or roast these foods. *Also:* Eat more carrots and green, leafy vegetables. They contain vitamin A and carotenoids—substances shown to inhibit cancer in animals. Grilling vegetables does not release carcinogens.

Source: Clinton Grubbs, PhD, director, nutrition and carcinogenesis laboratories, University of Alabama, Birmingham.

Zinc and Heart Disease

Taking zinc supplements can reduce levels of copper in the body…which reduces levels of HDL (good) cholesterol, apparently boosting the risk of heart disease. Copper and zinc have similar chemical properties, so an excess of one interferes with the metabolism of the other. Because many people do not get sufficient copper, zinc supplements should be avoided unless needed for a specific ailment.

Source: Leslie M. Klevay, MD, human studies research leader, Human Nutrition Research Center, US Department of Agriculture, Grand Forks, North Dakota.

Foods...Bad and Good

Bad foods most think are good:

•Apple juice. Very sugary. Unlike orange juice, it doesn't contain vitamin C unless it's fortified. Can cause diarrhea in some youngsters.

•Carob products. Added butter and oils make most carob-based products just as fattening as the chocolate items they're meant to replace.

•Cottage cheese. Contains about 40% fat by calories with little of the calcium found in most dairy products. *Self-defense:* Buy no-fat cottage cheese, although there's still not a lot of calcium.

•Cream cheese. As fatty as butter or margarine but with little dairy calcium. Also low in protein.

•Processed dried "fruit" snacks. Contain more sugar than actual fruit.

•Iceberg lettuce. Has little of vitamins A and C and is low in fiber. *Better:* Romaine lettuce.

•Muffins. May contain more fat and calories than the donut or Danish they are meant to replace.

Good foods most think are bad:

•Eggs. High in protein with half the fat of a tablespoon of most salad dressings. *Important:* Limit yourself to three or four a week.

•Jelly. Contains half the calories of butter or margarine—and is fat-free.

•Pancakes. But only when eaten with low-fat toppings such as yogurt, brown or powdered sugar, fresh or dried fruit, jam or jelly.

•Pizza. A fairly well-balanced meal—when topped with low-fat mozzarella cheese, tomato sauce and vegetables. *Avoid:* Sausage, pepperoni and ground-beef toppings.

•Pretzels. Contain one-tenth the fat and fewer calories than potato chips. Pick unsalted varieties to reduce sodium.

•Red meat. In moderation, a good source of iron, protein, zinc and several B vitamins.

•White bread. Contains plenty of complex carbohydrates and little fat.

Source: Lawrence Lindner, executive editor of the *Tufts University Diet & Nutrition Letter*, 203 Harrison Ave., Boston 02111.

It's Never Too Late to Lower Your Cholesterol

Despite all the information we've been seeing in the media about the health benefits of a low-fat diet and regular exercise, not enough of us are translating this information into action.

Current estimate: Even now, almost one out of every two Americans will die of a heart attack or stroke.

Those who are lucky enough to survive a heart attack can attest that the experience is painful and incapacitating. But most heart attacks don't kill people—at least not right away. They just cause pain and incapacitation for a time.

A heart attack requires a long stay in a hospital's intensive-care unit...bypass surgery or angioplasty, neither of which are pleasant or comfortable...and may be accompanied by angina, the repeated, intermittent lesser pains that can be very frightening when they strike in the midst of normal activity. In short, if a bad heart doesn't kill you, it can drastically interfere with your enjoyment of life.

Given the frightening odds—and the dramatic potential of proper diet and exercise to improve them in our favor—why aren't more people switching to healthier habits?

Common excuses:

Excuse: It's too late for me to change. In fact, much of the damage to arteries from years of poor diet is reversible. Studies conducted by Dr. David Blankenhorn, Dr. Dean Ornish and others have shown that strictly controlling the intake of saturated fat and cholesterol can start to open up arteries that were clogged by years of plaque buildup. This reversal process may take several years...but it's never too late to change your habits and improve the health of your heart.

Excuse: I avoid foods that contain cholesterol—so I don't have anything to worry about. Cholesterol is only one dietary contributor to poor heart health. Saturated fat is worse. Even if you shun cholesterol, your body will manufacture it if you eat saturated fat. Labels can be misleading—a bag of potato chips may be correctly labeled "cholesterol-free," but the chips are loaded with heart-damaging saturated fat.

My experience: I thought I was doing all I needed to do by eating more fish and less red meat...and then I experienced angina while jogging. Tests showed that my coronary arteries were 98% blocked. I was a heart attack waiting to happen, and was scheduled for bypass surgery. I'd given up hamburgers and ice cream—but the fish and chips I was eating instead were soaked in fat and continued to contribute to plaque buildup.

Excuse: I'm a busy person—I don't have time to look up everything I eat in an index and count grams and percentages all day. This is certainly a frequent complaint. The recommended guidelines seem so complicated that most people don't bother to use them—at least not after the first week or two.

That's why I teamed up with the renowned Dr. William P. Castelli, who directed the famous Framingham Heart Study sponsored by the National Institutes of Health, to develop a formula for heart-healthy eating that's easy to use and won't occupy a person's entire waking hours.

I also wanted to find out how to make changes in eating habits that didn't result in diets that were so boring no one could stick to them. I discovered that you can switch to low-fat eating without feeling tortured or deprived.

Simplified guidelines:

Most reports recommend that people cut fat intake to a percent of total calories. But who has time to figure daily calorie intake, total fat grams and what percentage that represents? At first, I facetiously thought I'd have to hire a full-time dietitian and accountant to follow me around if I were to meet these standards.

Dr. Castelli and I worked out the math and arrived at a general formula that applies to a very broad number of people. Originally, we developed daily limits for cholesterol, saturated

fat and total fat...but we found that this was too much for most people to keep track of.

Our solution: Cut back on all fats—but count only the grams of saturated fat you eat each day. *Not calories, not cholesterol*...just saturated fat. Limit saturated fat to 20 to 22 grams per day.

For someone who routinely takes in 2,000 calories a day, 20 to 22 grams of fat represent about 10% of calories from saturated fat.

We think those at greater risk for heart disease should limit saturated fat intake to 10 to 12 grams, or a little less than the usually recommended 7% of total calories. *Risk factors include:*
- Previous heart attack.
- Bypass surgery.
- High blood pressure.
- Smoking.
- Strong family history of heart attack.
- High cholesterol.

Although the official guidelines consider a blood cholesterol level of 200 to 240 to be "borderline," half of heart attacks occur in that range. More meaningful is the ratio of total cholesterol to HDL (the so-called "good cholesterol"). To find this figure, just take your total cholesterol count and divide by your HDL count. Even if your total cholesterol count is not in the high range, you are at a high risk for a heart attack.

Even if you aren't considered at risk for heart disease, it's still a good idea to cut the amount of fat—especially saturated fat—in your diet.

Watching fat intake is also a good way to lose weight without going hungry...and it will improve your overall energy level—and many people on a low-fat diet just feel better.

How to do it:

How do you go about reducing dietary fat in general...and saturated fat in particular?

There's no mystery to it. As new labeling regulations take effect, more and more packaged foods are listing detailed nutritional information—including grams of saturated and other kinds of fat per serving—on their labels.

For foods without such labels, you can use tables found in many books on nutrition available at your bookstore or library.

Think about eating a variety of wholesome, minimally processed foods—such as grains, fruits, vegetables and legumes. Cut back on meats and animal-derived products (such as butter), which are high in saturated fat. Fortunately, there are good substitutes for butter and ice cream.

This doesn't mean you have to go without meat forever—that prospect is what keeps many people from improving their diets. Just eat less of it, and choose your cuts more carefully.

Instead of buying US choice grades of beef, which are heavily marbled with streaks of fat, choose the very lean cuts called "select grade."

Look for the leaner cuts of pork now on the market.

Trim the fat and skin from chicken.

You don't have to give up your favorite recipes, either—just learn to substitute low-fat ingredients. There's hardly any recipe for which that can't be done. (I'm still working on a really good pie crust without much saturated fat, and I'm almost there. I haven't found the secret yet, but I'm convinced I will.)

Example: Mushroom and beef on pasta, using only one teaspoon of canola oil and three ounces of thinly sliced extra-lean beef. Stir in eight ounces sliced mushrooms. Don't overcook. Salt and pepper to taste and serve on angel hair pasta for a gourmet meal for two.

If you enjoy a hearty breakfast, try making French toast using *Eggbeaters* or *Simply Eggs* in the batter in place of eggs…and frying the toast in a nonstick pan lightly coated with canola oil rather than butter.

Oatmeal is another satisfying breakfast dish. Pour nonfat milk over it…or if, like me, you're not a fan of nonfat milk, just top the cereal with jam or maple syrup and skip the milk.

(Commercial granola is not a low-fat breakfast choice—it tends to be high in coconut and palm oils, which are loaded with saturated fat.)

You don't even have to give up dessert. One of my favorite treats is an orange freezie. Peel and section three oranges and place them in a heavy-duty blender with ¼ cup water and ¼ cup sugar. Gradually add crushed ice and puree until smooth. Turn off the blender periodically and mash the ice in with the rest of the ingredients. Keep adding ice until the texture is the way you like it—thick enough to eat with a spoon or thin enough to drink. I used to think a day wasn't over without a milk shake or ice cream sundae…but since I discovered orange freezies, I don't miss those high-fat desserts.

What about exercise?

Diet is only part of the healthy-heart lifestyle —exercise is also important in improving the total-cholesterol-to-HDL ratio. Like diet, exercise has been treated as far more complicated than it needs to be…causing people to get discouraged and give up.

Some guidelines will tell you that you need to work out until you achieve a certain pulse rate, which must then be maintained for a certain period of time, for a given number of sessions a week.

But you don't need fancy measurements or an elaborate regimen to benefit from exercise. I think it's more practical—and equally effective—to make sure you get some form of moderate to vigorous physical exercise every day. That exercise can be walking, hiking, jogging, swimming, bicycling—anything that gets your heart pumping.

How long and intense should each session be? Common sense is the best guideline. Start at a pace you can handle…keep going until you're challenged but not completely exhausted…and gradually increase the challenge. If you haven't been on an exercise program recently, *check with your doctor* before beginning a workout regimen.

Don't discount "natural" forms of exercise that are already a part of your life—walking a reasonable way to work, digging vigorously in the garden and so on. Do more of the physically demanding activities you already enjoy—even if they aren't officially designated as "exercise."

Source: Glen C. Griffin, MD, who was a practicing primary-care physician for 29 years before becoming editorial director of McGraw-Hill Healthcare Publications. He is editor in chief of the medical journal *Postgraduate Medicine*, writes a newsletter column on healthful gourmet cooking and is the coauthor (with Dr. William P. Castelli) of *Good Fat, Bad Fat: How to Lower Your Cholesterol & Beat the Odds of a Heart Attack*, Fisher Books, Box 38040, Tucson, Arizona 85740.

How is Your Diet?

The 40 questions below will help you focus on the key features of your diet. The (+) or (−) numbers next to each set of answers instantly pat you on the back for good habits or alert you to problems you may not even realize you have.

The "Grand Total" analysis on page 299 rates your overall diet, on a scale from "Great!" to "Arrgh!"

The quiz focuses on fat, saturated fat, cholesterol, sodium, sugar, fiber and vitamins A and C. It doesn't attempt to cover everything in your diet. Nor does it try to measure precisely how much of these key nutrients you eat.

What the quiz will do is give you a rough sketch of your current eating habits and, implicitly, suggest what you can do to improve them.

And don't despair over a less-than-perfect score.

Instructions:

•After each answer is a number with a (+) or (–) sign in front of it. Circle the number corresponding to the answer you choose. That's your score for the question. (If you use a pencil, you can erase your answers and pass the quiz along to someone else.)

•Circle only one number for each question, unless the instructions tell you to "average two or more scores if necessary."

How to average: In answering question 19, for example, if you drink club soda (+3) and coffee (–1) on a typical day, add the two scores (which gives you a +2) and then divide by 2. That gives you a score of +1 for the question. If averaging gives you a fraction, round it to the nearest whole number.

•If a question doesn't apply to you, skip it.

•Pay attention to serving sizes. For example, a serving of vegetables is half a cup. If you usually eat one cup of vegetables at a time, count it as two servings.

•Add up all your (+) scores and your (–) scores.

•Subtract your (–) scores from your (+) scores. That's your grand total.

Quiz:

1. *How many times per week do you eat unprocessed red meat* (steak, roast beef, lamb or pork chops, burgers, etc.)?
a. 0 (+3)   d. 4–5 (–1)
b. 1 or less (+2)   e. 6 or more (–3)
c. 2–3 (0)

2. *How many times per week do you eat processed meats* (hot dogs, bacon, sausage, bologna, luncheon meats, etc., not including products that contain one gram of fat or less per serving)?
a. 0 (+3)   d. 2–3 (–1)
b. less than 1 (+2) e. 4 or more (–3)
c. 1 (0)

3. *What kind of ground meat or poultry do you usually eat?*
a. regular or lean ground beef (–3)
b. extra-lean ground beef (–2)
c. ground round (–1)
d. ground turkey (+1)
e. Healthy Choice brand (+3)
f. don't eat ground meat (+3)

4. *Do you trim the visible fat when you cook or eat red meat?*
a. yes (+1)   c. don't eat red meat (0)
b. no (–3)

5. *How large is the serving of cooked red meat that you usually eat?* (To convert from raw to cooked, reduce by 25%. For example, 4 oz. of raw meat shrinks to 3 oz. after cooking. There are 16 oz. in a pound.)
a. 8 oz. or more (–3)   d. 3 oz. or less (0)
b. 6–7 oz. (–2)   e. don't eat red meat (+3)
c. 4–5 oz. (–1)

6. *What type of bread, rolls, bagels, etc., do you usually eat?*
a. 100% whole wheat (+3)
b. whole wheat as first or second ingredient (+2)
c. rye, pumpernickel or oatmeal (+1)
d. white, French or Italian (–1)

7. *How many times per week do you eat deep-fried foods* (fish, chicken, vegetables, potatoes, etc.)?
a. 0 (+3)   c. 3–4 (–1)
b. 1–2 (0)   d. 5 or more (–3)

8. *How many servings of nonfried vegetables, including potatoes, do you eat per day?* (One serving = ½ cup.)
a. 0 (–3)   d. 3 (+2)
b. 1 (0)   e. 4 or more (+3)
c. 2 (+1)

9. *How many servings of cruciferous vegetables do you eat per week?* (Count only kale, broccoli, cauliflower, cabbage, brussels sprouts, greens, bok choy, kohlrabi, turnip and rutabaga.)
a. 0 (–3)   c. 4–6 (+2)
b. 1–3 (+1)   d. 7 or more (+3)

10. *How many servings of vitamin A-rich fruits or vegetables do you eat a week?* (Count only can-

taloupe, apricots, carrots, pumpkin, sweet potatoes, spinach, winter squash and greens.)
a. 0 (−3)   c. 4–6 (+2)
b. 1–3 (+1)   d. 7 or more (+3)

11. *How many times per week do you eat at fast-food restaurants?* (Include burgers, fried fish or chicken, croissant or biscuit sandwiches, topped potatoes and other main dishes. Omit plain baked potatoes, broiled skinned chicken or low-fat salads.)
a. 0 (+3)   d. 2 (−1)
b. less than 1 (+1)   e. 3 (−2)
c. 1 (0)   f. 4 or more (−3)

12. *How many servings of grains do you eat per day?* (One serving = 1 slice of bread, 1 large pancake, 1 cup cold cereal or ½ cup cooked cereal, rice, pasta, bulgur, wheat berries, kasha or millet. Omit heavily sweetened cold cereals.)
a. 0 (−3)   d. 6–8 (+2)
b. 1–3 (0)   e. 9 or more (+3)
c. 4–5 (+1)

13. *How many times per week do you eat fish or shellfish?* (Omit deep-fried items, tuna packed in oil and mayonnaise-laden tuna salad—a little mayo is okay.)
a. 0 (0)   d. 3 or more (+3)
b. 1 (+1)   e. 0 (vegetarians) (+3)
c. 2 (+2)

14. *How many times per week do you eat cheese?* (Include pizza, cheeseburgers, veal or eggplant parmigiana, cream cheese, etc. Omit low-fat or fat-free cheeses.)
a. 0 (+3)   c. 2–3 (−1)
b. 1 (+1)   d. 4 or more (−3)

15. *How many servings of fresh fruit do you eat per day?*
a. 0 (−3)   d. 3 (+2)
b. 1 (0)   e. 4 or more (+3)
c. 2 (+1)

16. *Do you remove the skin before eating poultry?*
a. yes (+3)   c. don't eat poultry (0)
b. no (−3)

17. *What do you usually put on your bread or toast?* (Average two or more scores if necessary.)
a. butter or cream cheese (−3)
b. margarine (−2)
c. peanut butter (−1)
d. diet margarine (−1)
e. jam or honey (0)
f. 100% fruit butter (+1)
g. nothing (+3)

18. *What kind of milk do you drink?*
a. whole (−3)   d. ½% or skim (+3)
b. 2% fat (−1)   e. don't drink milk (0)
c. 1% fat (+2)

19. *Which of these beverages do you drink on a typical day?* (Average two or more scores if necessary.)
a. water or club soda (+3)
b. fruit juice (+1)
c. diet soda (−1)
d. coffee or tea (−1)
e. soda, fruit "drink" or fruit "ade" (−3)

20. *Which flavorings do you most frequently add to your foods?* (Average two or more scores if necessary.)
a. herbs or spices (+3)
b. garlic or lemon juice (+3)
c. olive oil (−1)
d. salt or soy sauce (−1)
e. margarine (−2)
f. butter (−3)
g. nothing (+3)

21. *What do you eat most frequently as a snack?* (Average two or more scores if necessary.)
a. fruits or vegetables (+3)
b. yogurt (+2)
c. crackers (+1)
d. nuts (−1)
e. cookies or fried chips (−2)
f. granola bar (−2)
g. candy bar or pastry (−3)
h. don't snack (0)

22. *What is your most typical breakfast?* (Subtract an extra 3 points if you also eat bacon or sausage as part of your breakfast.)
a. croissant, danish or doughnut (−3)
b. whole eggs (−3)
c. pancakes or waffles (−2)
d. cereal or toast (+3)
e. low-fat yogurt or cottage cheese (+3)
f. don't eat breakfast (0)

23. *What kind of cereal do you eat?*
a. whole grain (like oatmeal or shredded wheat) (+3)
b. low-fiber (like Cream of Wheat or cornflakes) (0)
c. sugary low-fiber (like Frosted Flakes) (−1)
d. regular granola (−2)

24. *What do you usually eat for dessert?*
a. pie, pastry or cake (−3)
b. ice cream (−3)
c. fat-free cookies or cakes (−1)
d. frozen yogurt or ice milk (0)
e. nonfat ice cream or sorbet (+1)

f. fruit (+3)

g. don't eat dessert (+3)

25. *How many times per week do you eat beans, split peas or lentils?*

a. 0 (–3)   d. 3 (+2)

b. 1 (0)   e. 4 or more (+3)

c. 2 (+1)

26. *Which items do you choose at a salad bar?* (Add two or more scores if necessary.)

a. nothing, lemon or vinegar (+3)

b. fat-free dressing (+2)

c. low- or reduced-calorie dressing (+1)

d. regular dressing (–1)

e. croutons or bacon bits (–1)

f. cole slaw, pasta salad or potato salad (–1)

27. *What sandwich fillings do you eat most frequently?* (Average two or more scores if necessary.)

a. regular luncheon meat (–3)

b. cheese (–2)

c. roast beef (–1)

d. peanut butter (0)

e. low-fat luncheon meat (+1)

f. tuna or chicken salad (+1)

g. fresh turkey breast or bean spread (+3)

h. don't eat sandwiches (0)

28. *What do you usually spread on your sandwiches?* (Average two or more scores if necessary.)

a. mayonnaise (–2)

b. "light" mayonnaise (–1)

c. ketchup, mustard or fat-free mayonnaise (+1)

d. nothing (+2)

29. *How many egg yolks do you eat per week?* (Add one yolk for every slice of quiche you eat.)

a. 2 or less (+3)   c. 5–6 (–1)

b. 3–4 (0)   d. 7 or more (–3)

30. *How many servings of a rich source of calcium do you eat per day?* (One serving = ⅔ cup milk or yogurt, 1 oz. cheese, 1½ oz. sardines, 3½ oz. canned salmon (with bones), 5 oz. tofu made with calcium sulfate, 1 cup greens or broccoli or 200 mg of a calcium supplement.)

a. 0 (–3)   c. 2 (+2)

b. 1 (+1)   d. 3 or more (+3)

31. *What do you usually order on your pizza?* (Vegetable toppings include green peppers, mushrooms, onions and other vegetables. Subtract one point if you order extra cheese.)

a. no cheese with vegetables (+3)

b. cheese with vegetables (+1)

c. cheese (0)

d. cheese with meat toppings (–3)

e. don't eat pizza (+2)

32. *What kind of cookies do you eat?*

a. don't eat cookies (+3)

b. fat-free cookies (+2)

c. graham crackers or ginger snaps (+1)

d. oatmeal (–1)

e. sandwich cookies (like Oreos) (–2)

f. chocolate-coated, chocolate chip or peanut butter (–3)

33. *What kind of frozen dessert do you usually eat?* (Subtract a point from your score for each topping you use—whipped cream, hot fudge, nuts, etc.)

a. gourmet ice cream (–3)

b. regular ice cream (–2)

c. frozen yogurt or ice milk (0)

d. sorbet, sherbet or ices (+1)

e. nonfat frozen yogurt or fat-free ice cream (+1)

f. don't eat frozen desserts (+3)

34. *What kind of cake or pastry do you usually eat?*

a. cheesecake, pie or microwave cake (–3)

b. cake with frosting (–2)

c. cake without frosting (–1)

d. unfrosted muffin, banana bread or carrot cake (0)

e. angel food or fat-free cake (+1)

f. don't eat cakes or pastries (+3)

35. *Which of the following "salty" snacks do you typically eat?* (Average two or more scores if necessary.)

a. potato chips, corn chips or prepopped popcorn (–3)

b. tortilla chips, reduced-fat potato chips or microwave popcorn (–2)

c. salted pretzels (–1)

d. light microwave popcorn (0)

e. unsalted pretzels (+1)

f. fat-free tortilla or potato chips (+2)

g. homemade air-popped popcorn (+3)

h. don't eat salty snacks (+3)

36. *What do you usually use to sauté vegetables or other foods?* (Vegetable oil includes safflower, corn, canola, sunflower and soybean.)

a. butter or lard (–3)

b. margarine (–2)

c. vegetable oil (–1)

d. olive oil (+1)

e. broth (+2)

f. water or cooking spray (+3)

37. *How many times a week does your dinner contain grains, vegetables or beans, but little or*

no animal protein (meat, poultry, fish, eggs, milk, cheese)?

a. 0 (–1) c. 3–4 (+2)
b. 1–2 (+1) d. 5 or more (+3)

38. *With what do you make tuna salad, pasta salad, chicken salad, etc?*

a. mayonnaise (–2)
b. light mayonnaise (–1)
c. nonfat mayonnaise (0)
d. low-fat yogurt (+2)
e. nonfat yogurt (+3)

39. *How many times per week do you eat canned or dried soups?* (Omit low-sodium, low-fat soups.)

a. 0 (+3) c. 3–4 (–2)
b. 1–2 (0) d. 5 or more (–3)

40. *What do you typically put on your pasta?* (Add one point if you also add sautéed vegetables. Average two or more scores if necessary.)

a. tomato sauce, with or without a
   little Parmesan (+3)
b. white clam sauce (0)
c. meat sauce or meat balls (–2)
d. Alfredo, pesto, creamy or oily sauce (–3)

Your grand total:

+59 to +117	Great!	You're a nutrition superstar. Give yourself a big pat on the back.
0 to +58	Good	You're doing just fine. Pin your quiz to the nearest wall.
–1 to –58	Fair	Hang in there. It is time to brush up on daily nutritional needs.
–59 to –116	Arrgh!	Empty your refrigerator and cupboard. It's time to start over.

Better Restauranting

Read between menu lines to find the fat: *À la mode*—with ice cream…*au fromage, au gratin*—with cheese inside it or in a cheese sauce…*bisque*—cream soup…*casserole, escalloped, hollandaise*—in cream sauce…*au lait*—with milk. *Basted, buttered, creamed, crispy, pan-fried, hash, sautéed* all mean extra fat is used.

Better: Entrées grilled or poached in wine, lemon juice or tomato sauce…baked potato or pasta in red sauce. Make "on the side" and "no butter" part of your vocabulary.

Source: A Better Tomorrow, 404 BNA Dr., Suite 600, Bldg. 200, Nashville 37214.

Garlic and Immunity

Although enthusiasts claim that eating garlic boosts the immune system, there is currently no solid scientific evidence to support such a link. However, garlic does contain beneficial compounds that, taken at high doses, are powerful antioxidants that can help to lower cholesterol, prevent blood from clotting and may help fight cancer and heart disease. *Dosage:* As a preventive measure, eat three medium-sized cooked garlic cloves daily. *Important:* Eating the garlic raw doesn't help. If you find there is no improvement in your immunity or cholesterol levels after one month, discuss the matter further with your doctor.

Source: Ron Rudin, MD, internist in private practice, 121 E. 84 St., New York 10028.

Sweet News About Chocolate

Chocolate is not so bad for the heart. It gets its unique mouth-feel from the stearic acid in highly saturated cocoa butter. Unlike other saturated fatty acids, stearic acid does not harm blood vessels. The body rapidly converts it to a form that neither raises nor lowers cholesterol. *Bottom line:* Two or three chocolate bars a week will not hurt the heart as long as you don't gain weight. Dark chocolate is best—milk chocolate also contains butter fat, which does clog arteries.

Source: Research led by Margo Denke, MD, University of Texas Southwestern Medical Center, Dallas.

Storing Fresh-Squeezed Juice

Store fresh-squeezed juice in a container just big enough to hold it. Juice deteriorates in a container that is too large.

Source: *How to Absolutely, Positively Maintain Weight Loss in Spite of Everything* by Martin F. Schwartz, PhD, research professor, New York University Medical Center, New York. National Center for Weight-Loss Maintenance, 200 E. 33 St., New York 10016.

Even Healthier Salads

Pick lettuces with rich color. Although all lettuces are about 95% water, the greener or redder the leaves, the more nutrients they contain. While pale-green iceberg lettuce is only minutely more nourishing than tap water, romaine contains double the calcium, five times the vitamin C and eight times the beta-carotene. Spinach contains 20 times as much beta-carotene. *Try other greens, too:* Oak leaf...watercress...curly endive...arugula...lolla rossa...radicchio...mizuna.

Source: Wahida Karmally, nutritionist, Columbia-Presbyterian Medical Center, New York, quoted in *Health*, 301 Howard St., San Francisco 94105.

Green Tea Magic

Green tea may help prevent throat cancer. Men who drank it regularly were 20% less likely to develop the cancer than those who didn't...and women who drank it regularly faced a 50% lower risk. *Possible hero:* Polyphenol. In tests on animals, this compound found in green tea has been shown to lower cholesterol and protect against cancer by neutralizing enzymes that produce cancer-causing substances.

Source: Joseph K. McLaughlin, PhD, former deputy chief of the National Cancer Institute's biostatistics branch and cofounder of the International Epidemiology Institute, Rockville, Maryland.

Monounsaturated Fats Study

Monounsaturated fats (canola and olive oil) may be no better than polyunsaturated fats (corn oil) at helping people reduce elevated cholesterol levels. In a recent study, a group of volunteers limited their saturated fat intake to less than 7% of total calories. During one five-week period, the volunteers ate a diet rich in corn oil. During another, they ate a diet rich in canola oil. And during a third period, they ate a diet rich in olive oil. *Result:* Their LDL (bad) cholesterol levels were not significantly different from one period to the next—between 13% and 17%. And contrary to previous studies, monounsaturated oils are no better at sparing HDL (good) cholesterol than polyunsaturated oils.

Source: Alice H. Lichtenstein, DSc, assistant professor of nutrition, Human Nutrition Research Center on Aging, Tufts University, Boston. Her four-month study of 15 individuals with elevated cholesterol levels was published in *Arteriosclerosis and Thrombosis*, UCLA School of Medicine, 47-123 CHS, 10833 Le Conte Ave., Los Angeles 90024.

Safer Seafood

For expert advice on handling and storage of seafood, plus nutritional information and seafood safety, call the FDA's 24-hour Seafood Hotline at 800-332-4010. Information will be mailed or faxed to you. Or—speak to a seafood specialist, noon to 4 PM Eastern Standard Time, Monday through Friday.

15

Very, Very Smart Education

Clever College-Aid Strategy

Parents turned down for a federal Parent Loan for Undergraduate Students (PLUS) due to a poor credit rating have another financing option. Have your child apply to the Stafford Student Loan program. *Example:* A college freshman can borrow $4,000 over the normal $2,625 limit for dependent students. The student will be charged interest on the additional amount, but the variable rate is relatively low—now 7.43%.

Source: Kalman A. Chany, president of Campus Consultants, Inc., a firm that advises families on financial-aid eligibility, 968 Lexington Ave., New York 10021.

The 30-Year College-Loan Repayment Plan

The new 30-year college-loan repayment plan from the government will be offered first to those graduating in the spring of 1995. It is of little importance to students now borrowing money from the government since the option will not be available until graduation, when repayment begins. The new repayment plan reduces monthly payments by extending the payback period and is aimed at graduates who expect to take low-paying jobs.

Source: Kalman A. Chany, president of Campus Consultants, Inc., a fee-based firm that advises families on financial-aid eligibility, 968 Lexington Ave., New York 10021.

Common College-Savings Mistake

Using only a growth-stock mutual fund, which is too conservative for expenses that are ten years or more away. *Better:* A mix of two or three aggressive no-load stock funds. *Recommended asset allocation:* The 20th Century Gift Trust Fund/800-345-2021…and Oakmark International/800-476-9625. Both have excellent management and track records.

Source: Robert Markman, president of Markman Capital Management, which invests client assets exclusively in no-load mutual funds, 6600 France Ave. S., Minneapolis 55435.

Mistakes People Make When Applying for College Financial Aid

Most parents need financial help when they are paying for their children's college educations. Unfortunately, many parents are not familiar with the best ways to apply for and receive financial aid.

Result: They pay more out of their own pockets and enroll their children in colleges that they can *afford*—rather than colleges that are ideal for their children.

Here are the most common mistakes people make when applying for financial assistance from a college:

•*Mistake:* Assuming that you're not eligible for financial aid. Many people don't even apply because they believe they are not eligible if they earn more than $75,000 a year or own their own homes…or they've heard that their neighbors applied and were turned down.

Reality: There is no real income cutoff. Sometimes families with incomes in excess of $125,000 receive financial aid. Financial aid is awarded based on a complex formula that factors in many variables, including the number of members in the household, the number of children in college and the age of the oldest parent.

•*Mistake:* Failing to do any advance planning for the application process. Eligibility is determined by taking a snapshot of your family's financial situation. If you are applying for your child's freshman year of college, the year that is scrutinized is from January 1 of your child's junior year in high school to December 31 of his/her senior year. Any financial transactions you make during that year could help— or hurt —your child's chances of getting aid.

Example: If you had accumulated some stock investments to pay for college and sold them during the first half of your child's senior year in high school, the capital gains on the stock would increase your income and reduce your eligibility for aid.

To give your child the best chance of receiving financial aid, you must plan ahead to accelerate income into earlier years and minimize discretionary income items during the key tax years that affect your eligibility for aid.

•*Mistake:* Missing the deadlines. Many people believe that the time to apply for financial aid is after the child has been accepted to a college.

Reality: It's crucial to apply for aid at the same time that your child is applying to colleges. There is a limited amount of aid available, and priority is given to those who meet the deadlines. Deadline extensions are rarely granted.

The best source of information about deadlines is the school itself. Be certain to find out if the material is to be postmarked, received or processed by the deadline.

•*Mistake:* Not keeping track of the process. Many families simply fill out the financial aid forms and hope for the best. They are not assertive enough and do not keep track of things. They also don't check in with the colleges.

Reality: You have to assume that things are going to go wrong. Check with the school and make certain it has everything it needs. Find out if there is anything else you could send to improve your chances. Make photocopies of all the forms in case you are asked any questions.

Important: Although instructions on the application forms will tell you not to send them by certified mail, I recommend you do so for your own protection. If your forms are lost or misplaced, the processing center of the college may try to claim that you never filed them. Using certified mail/return receipt requested gives you proof of mailing and delivery.

•*Mistake:* Assuming the college will help you get the most financial aid possible.

Reality: It's important to understand that the college is apportioning a pot of money…and demand exceeds supply. Therefore, it is not in the school's best interest to help you figure out how to maximize your child's financial aid.

•*Mistake:* Assuming financial-aid packages are set in stone.

Reality: It is often possible to negotiate a better package than the one you are initially offered by the college. One of your strongest bargaining chips could be a better financial aid package from a comparable school. You might say, "I'd really love to have my child attend your school, but money is an issue. We've been offered a more generous package from College X." Be honest about this, though, since you may be asked to provide a copy of that package.

Trend: The first offer that a college makes to parents is often not its best offer. The college wants to see if you will blink—and it is leaving room for bargaining. College officials will deny this vehemently, but every year I see colleges change the sizes of their awards.

•*Mistake:* Rejecting student loans when they're offered as part of a package. Many parents say "I don't want my child to borrow or to have debt when he/she graduates from school." Meanwhile, these parents have thousands of dollars in credit-card debt outstanding.

Reality: Student loans are great deals and compare favorably with other borrowing options.

Better: Take the student loans, use current income to pay off other debt and then, if you want to pay the student loans off in a lump sum after graduation, you can do so with no repayment penalty. In this way, you might save hundreds—or even thousands—of dollars in interest.

•*Mistake:* Being unaware of other attractive borrowing options.

Reality: Even if they don't qualify for need-based student loans, virtually all students qualify for *unsubsidized* Stafford Loans. The colleges' financial-aid offices can tell you how to apply for these loans.

Some colleges have their own loan programs, which may have very attractive terms. There is also the federal Parent Loans for Undergraduate Students (PLUS) program, which allows you to borrow the total cost of education less any aid offered.

Example: If the tuition costs $25,000 and your child is getting $10,000 in financial aid, he can borrow up to $15,000.

Borrowing strategy: Take out a Perkins Loan first, then a Stafford Loan, then a PLUS Loan.

•*Mistake:* Assuming that outside scholarships are where the *real* money is. People are always hearing about awards from fraternal associations, unions and private foundations. They're told all they have to do is find these untapped resources.

Reality: These awards represent less than 1% of all financial aid available and, as many families find out, may not save you money.

Reason: The school reduces your aid package by the amount of the scholarship.

Strategy: If your child wins an outside award, try to convince the school to reduce the loan and work-study portions of the package rather than the grant money dollar for dollar.

•*Mistake:* Misunderstanding the federal rules for divorced and separated parents. Federal rules require that the parent with whom the child resided most during the 12 months prior to completing the application submit the financial information. Custody and dependency for income-tax purposes are not relevant.

Some colleges may also require disclosure from the other parent. Even in this case, state and some federal aid programs will still be based on only one parent's financial data.

•*Mistake:* Misunderstanding the definition of an "independent student." Many parents believe that if they don't claim a child on their income-tax returns for several years, the child will qualify as an independent student and the parent's financial situation will *not* be relevant for obtaining financial aid.

Reality: The parents may be paying several thousand dollars in additional taxes and accomplishing nothing. The requirements for independent-student status are straightforward. The student must meet any one of the following criteria...

•24 years old as of January 1 in the academic year for which aid is sought.

•A ward of the court or have both parents deceased.

•A veteran of the US Armed Forces.

•Married.

• A graduate-school or professional-school student.

• Have legal dependents other than a spouse.

• *Mistake:* Failing to understand the implications of every financial decision you make during the years you are seeking aid.

Reality: From January 1 of your child's junior year in high school to January 1 of his junior year in college, any decision you make could ruin your chances for aid the next year. *Common mistakes:*

• Withdrawing funds from a pension.

• Taking capital gains on securities.

• Overpaying state and local taxes so that you receive a large refund the following year.

Note: Widowed or divorced parents who remarry during a child's college years are sometimes unpleasantly surprised to find that the income of the new spouse is factored into the financial-aid formula.

Source: Kalman A. Chany, president of Campus Consultants, Inc., a fee-based firm that assists families in maximizing financial-aid eligibility, 968 Lexington Ave., New York 10021. He is the author of *The Princeton Review Student Access Guide to Paying for College,* Villard Books, 201 E. 50 St., New York 10022.

How to Make the Most of a College Visit

• Talk to an alumnus before you tour the campus. If you know someone who graduated from the college you plan to visit, call him/her. Ask what he would advise you to see.

If you don't know any graduates, ask the admissions department for the names of alumni who live in your area and who might be willing to chat with you.

• Speak with the department head. When making an appointment for an interview with an admissions officer, also set up an interview with the head of the department in which you're most interested. This will give you a chance to evalu-

ate the quality of the education that you would be receiving.

Be prepared to discuss the curriculum…or, in the case of the arts, to be asked to audition.

• Tour during the summer. Life is more relaxed on campuses in the summer…but you can still get a feel for the college's student life without having to compete with the crowds of touring high-school students.

The summer is also ideal because you'll have more quality time with the college's admissions staff. In the fall, half the college's admissions staff is on the road interviewing students while the other half is interviewing one candidate every 45 minutes.

• Dress neatly. Do not wear jeans, cut-offs, tank tops or sweatshirts—you will look irresponsible in such attire. Instead, boys should wear chinos and collared shirts…girls should wear skirts and blouses. *Important:* Wear comfortable shoes. You do a lot of walking when you visit a college campus.

• Ask for directions—*frequently*. This will give you a chance to find out how receptive and friendly the students are. Do they go out of their way to help? Give accurate directions? Offer to show you around or answer other questions? The more you talk to the other students on campus, the better you will get to know the school.

• Scan the school newspaper. Ask in the admissions office for copies of the past year's issues. The more, the better. The stories will give you a sense of what was important to students last year and how the university responded. They will also tell you which arts are strong on campus—and what types of entertainment and speakers the school attracts.

• Check the bulletin boards around campus. Bulletin boards show what is really happening on campus on a daily basis. Everything will be there—plays, parties, where to buy used textbooks, etc. They'll also indicate what the students do on weekends.

• Eat in the cafeteria. At most colleges, visitors can pay to enter the dining hall. Sometimes the admissions department provides passes. This is important because it gives you a chance to sample a food plan that you would have to pay for later. It also lets you see whether students feel comfortable enough to linger or study there.

• Look for signs of crime prevention. Regardless of where they are located, most colleges in the US today are experiencing higher crime rates than in the past. Alarm boxes on poles and numbers to call to request police escorts show that the college is taking this matter seriously. Ask the admissions officer what other steps are being taken.

• Make sure you get the interviewer's name and send him a thank-you note. Few candidates do this. In addition to just being good manners, it will leave the administrator with a better impression of you.

• Keep a diary. Since you'll probably be seeing anywhere from three to ten campuses, it's easy to forget the good and bad points of each. This diary will give you a clear idea of what you saw and will be particularly helpful if it comes down to a choice between two alternatives.

Source: Arthur Mullaney, director of College Impressions, a fee-based group that takes students on seven-day trips to 12 Northeastern colleges and coaches them on the admissions process, Box 507, Randolph, Massachusetts 02368; 617-843-8033. He is director of guidance at Randolph High School in Randolph, Massachusetts.

Beware of Senior-Year Slump

Instead of slouching toward graduation, high-school and college seniors should spend their senior years building their job-hunting momentum. Their résumés should show that, instead of simply puttering along during the final year of school, they revved up for entry into the world of work. *Helpful:* Increasing school activities... taking on short-term projects...acquiring new skills or polishing current ones. Many interviewers focus on senior-year activities because they feel that people who don't slack off have superior work habits.

Source: Marilyn Moats Kennedy, editor, *Kennedy's Career Strategist*, 1150 Wilmette Ave., Wilmette, Illinois 60091.

Ten Surprise Expenses You Face When Your Child Goes to College

• Books and supplies. Costs of $500 to $700 a year are common.

• Health insurance. If your child isn't covered on your policy, the college may require you to buy a policy. *Cost:* $300 to $500.

• Furniture/appliance rental. It can cost $50 to $100 to rent a refrigerator for a dorm room. Students living off-campus may need to rent furniture. *Annual cost:* At least a few hundred dollars.

• Damage assessments. Even if your child didn't do anything to damage school property, he/she may be liable for a share of the fix-up costs. Such charges are most common in freshman dorms.

• Activity and lab fees. Many schools assess students a per-semester activity fee (typically $20 to $50). Some science courses may impose lab fees of $10 to $50 per semester for aprons, disposable glasses, etc.

• Sports can be an important aspect of campus life—for which you'll have to pay. Student admission to football and basketball games is seldom free these days. Students who join club teams may have to pay for uniforms and equipment.

• Parking. Semester fees can range from $10 to several hundred dollars.

• Administrative fees. You want your child to take the right courses, but the cost of changing after the semester begins can add up. Many schools assess drop/add charges of $10 to $20. Many charge $100 or more for late registration.

• Late fees. For the student, these are most likely to be for library books. But parents may also be hit with extra fees if they file loan applications late or don't get tuition payments in on time.

• Noshing. Regular meal service is included in the room and board charges. Between-meal pizza and other snacks are not. College students are notorious snackers and partiers—for which you can expect to pay.

Source: Kalman A. Chany, president of Campus Consultants, Inc., a fee-based firm in New York City that assists families in maximizing financial-aid eligibility. Mr. Chany is the author of *The Princeton Review Student Access Guide to Paying for College,* Villard Books, 201 E. 50 St., New York 10022.

Better College Applications

Include a self-addressed, stamped postcard with your college application and ask that the admissions office send it back to you as a record that they've received the application. As cards arrive, file them with the copies of each application. If you still haven't received a postcard a week or two before the application deadline, call the college to check.

Source: *Cash for College* by Cynthia Ruiz McKee, cofounder of College Resource Materials, a company in San Antonio, Texas, that helps people find scholarship money. Hearst Books, 1350 Avenue of the Americas, New York 10019.

What College Graduates Need to Know About Health Insurance

Most college students are covered by their parents' health insurance or school-sponsored plans. But when they graduate, there may be a gap between the expiration of their student coverage and the time they land jobs.

Defensive tactics:

•Check your policy to see when the coverage of your children lapses. Many families believe that their dependents are covered as long as they are in school. But most group policies require students to be *full-time* (generally considered 12 or more credit hours per semester) to qualify for coverage after age 19…and even the most comprehensive policies stop covering students at ages 22 to 25. So don't assume that your children are covered through law or medical school. Many policies extend coverage through the summer following graduation but lapse in the fall. Check with your insurance company.

•If your child is covered on your employer-sponsored plan, he/she has 60 days from graduation—or from the time that coverage lapses —to apply for benefits under COBRA. According to the federal COBRA law, anyone covered by an employer-sponsored group plan is eligible for an additional 18 months of post-policy coverage by paying the individual rate, pro-vided there are at least 20 employees in the firm. *Note:* Individual insurance companies and states may provide better benefits than what's required by law.

Important: An employer is not required to notify an employee that coverage has lapsed for one of his dependents.

COBRA advantage: The child remains covered for preexisting conditions. But extending benefits under COBRA is an expense—usually at least $150 a month.

•Consider a short-term insurance policy. Graduates who feel secure in their job prospects might make do with short-term policies. These policies are written for terms of 30 days to six months and are generally rewritten once.

Advantages: Short-term policies are easy to qualify for. The premiums may be as low as $50 a month, depending on the size of the chosen deductible and the age, gender and state of residence of the policyholder.

Disadvantages: These policies are written by few companies and are not available in all states. Coverage is rarely comprehensive. Pre-existing conditions and travel outside the US are generally not covered. *Companies offering short-term policies:* Golden Rule Insurance Co./317-297-4123…Time Insurance Co. (a unit of Fortis, Inc.)/800-800-8463, ext. 8335.

•Consider converting existing coverage to an individual major medical plan. This is an excellent option that is underused. Within 18 months of the expiration of group benefits or at the end of the 18-month COBRA period, your child has the right to *convert* his coverage to an individual policy at the same insurance company.

Advantages: Consistency of coverage. The reality is that it takes time to find work, and not every job comes with benefits. Also, some employer-sponsored plans don't start for three to six months. If your child expects to change jobs a lot, travel or freelance, individual coverage will go with him.

Disadvantages: Converted coverage may not be as good as an employer's group plan. Premiums can be high but usually less costly than those charged by a COBRA plan.

Helpful: Take a high deductible. Your child needs protection in case of a $20,000 illness, not a $2,000 one.

•Investigate opportunities for group coverage. Many private organizations offer group health insurance plans to members.

Examples: College alumni associations, National Organization for Women.

Helpful: Check the rating of the company with which the organization has its contract. Visit your local library to check A.M. Best, Moody's or Standard & Poor's directory. Look for ratings of A and above.

•Pay premiums annually to get the best value for your money. Your child's annual premium may be higher if he chooses to pay it monthly or quarterly. Also, he should pay premiums toward the end of each grace period so he can hold on to his money for as long as possible—or keep it, should he find a job with benefits or marry and qualify under his spouse's plan.

Source: Sam E. Beller, CLU, ChFC, president of Diversified Programs, Inc., an insurance sales organization, and Diversified Advisory Services, Inc., a financial-services organization, 450 Seventh Ave., Suite 500, New York 10123. He is the author of *The Great Insurance Secret*, which is available from Diversified Programs, Inc.

Check a College's Safety Record

Check a college's safety record by asking to see the annual security report required by federal law. Each college must report all crimes on its campus, from sex offenses to murders. In 1993, robbery, assault and motor-vehicle thefts increased at colleges. Burglaries and murders declined. *Caution:* Critics say some schools deliberately underreport campus crime.

Source: Survey of more than 750 schools by *The Chronicle of Higher Education*, 1255 23 St. NW, Washington, DC 20037.

Best Time to Meet Teachers

The start of the year, when your child's slate is clean and no problems have arisen. Open-house meetings usually take place six weeks after school starts. By then, a pattern has already been set—and these meetings are not for extended talk. *Better:* At the end of the first week of school, ask the teacher for a talk the following week. At the meeting, express general support and say that you will help if problems arise.

Source: *Save Our Schools: 66 Things You Can Do to Improve Your School Without Spending an Extra Penny* by Mary Susan Miller, PhD, a former teacher and administrator who now teaches at William Patterson College, Wayne, New Jersey. Harper San Francisco, 1160 Battery St., San Francisco 94111.

Secrets of Learning Any Language

No matter how poorly you did when you had to study French or Spanish in school, you can still learn any foreign language now…*if you really want to.*

Teaching myself to speak 23 foreign languages during the past 46 years has helped me develop a method that maximizes language proficiency while minimizing the pain involved. It still takes a lot of work…but this method lets you have a lot of fun as well.

Tools to learn a language:

The secret of learning a language is to use all the tools available. Find a bookstore that offers a broad selection of learning materials in your chosen language. Then acquire the following…

•Language textbook. A basic text that covers grammar thoroughly. Before beginning any study of your new language, read the first five chapters over and over—until you understand as much as you can. If some sections remain incomprehensible, leave them…you will be able to understand them later.

•Phrase book. A phrase book for travelers contains many practical words and phrases… and tells you how to pronounce them.

•Dictionary. Get a two-way dictionary that has both English-foreign and foreign-English sections.

•Language courses on cassettes. The best are formatted courses that follow the Pimsleur method. This method doesn't simply repeat phrases in English and the other language, but it forces you to recall what you learned earlier.

• Flash cards with English words and phrases on one side and translations on the other side provide a convenient method of rapid review.

• Newspaper. Get a copy of one newspaper in the language you are studying…preferably one from the country itself rather than one published in the US.

How to learn a language:

Spread out your newspaper and begin reading the first paragraph of the first article. Highlight every word you don't know with a marker. Look up these words in your dictionary.

Whenever you find a new word—or whole phrase—write it and the translation on opposite sides of a blank flash card.

If you find a word that looks similar to one that you already know, it is probably a different grammatical form of the base word found in the dictionary. Try to figure out the meaning in the newspaper from the context and the grammar you have acquired so far.

Put the dictionary word on a flash card. Write the words you don't understand on question cards to carry with you so you can ask their meaning from someone who knows the language.

Now go on and try to decipher the next paragraph.

If possible, set aside a block of time every day for language study. In addition to studying the grammar and the newspaper, start to learn the conversational phrases in your phrase book so you can try them out whenever you meet someone who speaks the language.

Listen to your cassettes…but not passively. Test yourself by hitting the pause button after an English phrase and trying to translate it yourself before you switch the cassette back on.

Wherever you go, carry a pack of flash cards. Review the cards in every spare moment—waiting for an elevator or phone connection, at the checkout counter, etc.

Source: Barry Farber, the nationally syndicated radio talk-show host and founder of The Language Club, Box 121, Times Square Station, New York 10036. He is author of *How to Learn Any Language*, Citadel Press, 600 Madison Ave., New York 10022.

Seventh Grade

Seventh grade is a watershed year for most students.

Reason: School days are structured differently, with a different teacher for each subject. Many children have a hard time adjusting and grades may suffer. *When a child's grades slip:*

• Find out how your child perceives the situation and ask him/her to suggest solutions.

• Don't be surprised if he blames the teachers for being "too hard" or claims they don't "like" him.

• Explain that he has to do the work nonetheless.

• Talk to your child's teachers and ask for their thoughts on the problem.

• A child who forgets assignments or turns them in late simply may need a notebook to keep track of his schedule.

• Get your child to agree to a study schedule to complete each day's work.

• Instead of focusing on grades, focus on the quality of day-to-day work. If the work is done right, the grades will follow.

Source: Laurence Kutner, PhD, child psychologist in Cambridge, Massachusetts, and author of *Parent and Child: Getting Through to Each Other*, Avon Books, 1350 Avenue of the Americas, New York 10019.

16

Consumer Savvy

Better Home Building

Don't pay too much of the contractor's price up front. Home building is a volatile field, and cash can disappear with the project still not completed.

Best: Make a modest cash deposit when you sign the contract, then provide progress payments at agreed-upon points to meet the contractor's cash-flow needs. Save a sizable final payment to be made *after* the successful completion of the project—when a certificate of occupancy is obtained.

Safety: Hire a builder who has been in business in the area for a long time and has developed a good reputation. Have a real-estate lawyer review any contract you sign.

Source: Philip Springer, editor, *Executive Wealth Advisory*, 1101 King St., Alexandria, Virginia 22314.

Three Principles Of Saving Money

Buy cheaper—look for sales, rebates, generics, bonus sizes and discounts...*make it last longer*—take care of it, repair it instead of replacing it, use it longer...*use it less*—overusing almost anything limits its life span.

Source: *Dollar Wise Newsletter*, Box 270924, Fort Collins, Colorado 80527.

Wrinkle-Free Shirts

Wrinkle-free shirts are not. Although they are advertised as never needing ironing, these shirts nonetheless carry additional care instructions.

Source: Survey of menswear experts in *The Wall Street Journal*.

Consumer Savvy

Moving and Storage Auctions

Moving and storage auctions can be good sources of functional household and office items at low cost. Movers and mini-storage companies hold auctions whenever they have enough unclaimed inventory—often every two to three months. Cash is usually required for these purchases. Often items must be picked up within five days. Items are sometimes grouped by function—but more often, bidders pay for the entire contents of a storage compartment or container at the discretion of the auctioneer. *To find auctions:* Check listings in newspaper classified ads, or contact local storage or auction companies.

Source: Jack Fuchs, owner, Whitehall Storage, New York.

Insulation Cuts Bills

Heating and cooling can account for 60% of a home's energy use. Insulation can lower costs significantly. In cold climates, doubling the thickness of insulation on the attic floor can cut 40% of the heat seeping up through ceilings. In warm climates, the same insulation can prevent 40% of the heat trapped in the attic from coming into living areas.

Source: *Solving Your Financial Problems* by Richard L. Strohm, attorney, Scottsdale, Arizona. Career Press, Box 34, Hawthorne, New Jersey 07507.

Buy Something of the Highest Quality

Buy something of the highest quality every once in a while. If you love to read—buy a beautifully embroidered bookmark...If you write a lot of letters buy some very handsome stationery that will make you feel like royalty when you sit down to write. Price doesn't always have to be your prime concern. Some-

times it's wise to treat yourself to something that's going to make you happy for years to come.

Source: *How to Be Happier Day by Day: A Year of Mindful Actions* by Alan Epstein, PhD, California-based co-founder of True Partners, an introduction and relationship counseling firm. Viking, 375 Hudson St., New York 10014.

Great Buys by Mail and Phone

Why settle for the best deal in town when you can get the best deal in the United States? You can save big, big bucks off the price of major appliances, top-of-the-line furniture and large equipment by telephoning a price-quote company.

For a broad spectrum of items—lingerie, high-quality art supplies and name-brand sporting goods, you can thumb through a wide variety of very attractive, specialized direct-mail catalogs, mail or phone in your order and save.

Big-ticket items:

The average consumer doesn't know much about price-quote companies because they don't spend a great deal of money advertising—but their salespeople are eager to receive your call. They require that you know what you want, the name of the manufacturer, model number and other descriptive details of the item you intend to buy.

Here's a sampling of the kind of merchandise offered by price-quote companies handling calls from around the country:

•Furniture. Cedar Rock Furniture carries all major brands of furniture at up to 50% below retail.

Cedar Rock Furniture, Box 515, Hudson, North Carolina 28638. 704-396-2361.

•Appliances. EBA Wholesale offers dozens of products from more than 50 top-name manufacturers, including Admiral, Panasonic, Litton, KitchenAid, Westinghouse and General Electric at up to 60% less than list price.

EBA Wholesale, 2361 Nostrand Ave., Brooklyn 11210. 718-252-3400.

•Automobiles. Nationwide Auto Brokers will send you a form ($9.95) showing all the operational equipment available for the car you want and then arrange delivery with a local dealer. You save from $150 to $4,000 by allowing the broker to negotiate a dealer-to-dealer price break that eliminates the salesperson's commission.

Nationwide Auto Brokers, 17517 W. 10 Mile Rd., Southfield, Michigan 48075. 800-521-7257.

•Computers. CMO offers name-brand computers like IBM, Epson and Hewlett-Packard as well as systems and software at savings as great as 40% off retail.

CMO, 2400 Reach Rd., Williamsport, Pennsylvania 11701. 800-233-8950.

•Fitness equipment. Better Health and Fitness will help you complete your fitness center with name-brand equipment at savings of up to 25%.

Better Health and Fitness, 5302 New Utrecht Ave., Brooklyn 11219. 718-436-4801.

To locate a price-quote firm in your area, turn to the Yellow Pages for the type of item you're looking for, but understand that there are tiers of discounters, with those who do the highest volume buying getting the best prices. Your best bet by phone will be a company with nationwide delivery. But shop discounters, too.

Example: If you want a new stove, look in the Yellow Pages under a major heading such as *Appliances:*

•Household.

•Major dealers.

You often will find promotions for "top brand names" at "wholesale prices to the consumer." Smaller items:

There are hundreds and hundreds of fabulous catalogs you'll never know about unless you watch for their rare ads in the back of newspapers or magazines or you learn about them through word of mouth.

Yet, these catalogs offer you the opportunity to buy your favorite brand of merchandise at a great price without spending money on gasoline and sacrificing hours out of your day to trek to the mall.

There are catalogs for just about anything you might want—from the mundane to the exotic. Here's a sampling of nontraditional catalog types:

•Art supplies. Cheap Joe's Art Stuff. Save 30% on paint, canvas, brushes, mat cutters, books on art. Free catalog.

Cheap Joe's Art Stuff, 300A Industrial Park Rd., Boone, North Carolina 28607. 800-227-2788.

•Fragrances. Essential Products Company lets you save up to 90% on perfumes. Essential Products buys them from a company that copies designer scents. Free brochure.

Essential Products Company, 90 Water St., New York 10005. 212-344-4288.

•Bed and bath. Harris Levy, Inc. Save up to 50% on Wamsutta, J.P. Stevens, Springmaid and Fieldcrest, etc. Free catalog.

Harris Levy, Inc., 278 Grand St., New York 10002. 212-226-3102.

•Collectibles. Quilts Unlimited. Save 20% to 30% by buying from "America's largest antique quilt shop." *Catalog:* $5.

Quilts Unlimited, 440-A Duke of Gloucester St.,Williamsburg, Virginia 23185. 804-253-8700.

•Boating supplies. Goldberg's Marine Distributors. Save up to 60% on boating equipment and nautical clothing, and receive your shipment in three to seven days. Free seasonal catalog.

Goldberg's Marine Distributors, 201 Meadow Rd., Edison, New Jersey 08818. 800-BOATING.

•Camera equipment. Porter's Camera Stores. Save up to 35% on equipment, cameras. Free catalog.

Porter's Camera Stores, Box 628, Cedar Falls, Iowa 50613. 800-553-2001.

•China. Greater New York Trading Co. Save up to 60% on Lenox, Waterford, Wedgwood and just about every other major manufacturer of fine china. Free brochure.

Greater New York Trading Co., 81 Canal St., New York 10002. 212-226-2808.

Basics:

•Whether you are calling a price-quote company or a direct-mail marketer, always know the return policy before you make a commitment— sometimes there is a charge for returned items.

•Use a credit card so you have recourse if you need to return an item.

•Keep records of your transaction by noting the date the order was placed and the name of the order-taker.

•Save your receipts.

•If you ask for a price quote through the mail, it will help to send a business-sized, self-addressed, stamped envelope to speed the response.

Armchair shopping pays off:

Not only do you get great convenience by checking with price-quote firms and ordering through direct-mail catalogs, but you get big savings. Sometimes those calls are free with the 800 number, and with high-ticket items or quantity purchases, shipping charges may be waived.

Source: Sue Goldstein, author of *Great Buys by Mail (And Phone!)*, Penguin Books, 375 Hudson St., New York 10014.

Do Not Buy Extended Warranties

They are high-cost insurance against small risks that you can cover out of your own pocket. *Beware:* Salespeople push the warranties hard—they are a major profit center for retailers. *Reality:* Only 10% of camcorders bought between 1987 and 1992 ever needed to be repaired.

Source: *Consumer Reports*, 101 Truman Ave., Yonkers, New York 10703.

How to Take Back Anything You've Bought... Or Been Given

Most shoppers would like to return many more purchases than they actually do—for many reasons.

The single biggest reason people avoid returning items they don't want is that they are afraid someone will say "no."

But why tie your money up in useless possessions?

Here's how to take back almost any unwanted purchase or gift—even when rude sales clerks insist you can't:

• Have a valid reason for making the return. There are many valid reasons for making returns, including "I just don't like it."

You do not need to invent a complicated story to return an item, nor must you justify yourself to a sales clerk. But for people who are uncomfortable making returns, it helps to be clear on your reason ahead of time. The clerk will probably ask for a reason to fill in on the store's return form. In most cases, this is not a challenge to your right to make the return. It is simply the clerk's job.

Common valid reasons for returns:

• Item doesn't fit well.
• Item faded, bled, shrank.
• Color is wrong.
• Item is defective.
• Item does not perform as promised.
• Item arrived too late.
• Parts are missing.
• Item was an unwanted gift.
• Changed mind, don't like it.
• Ordered two, want to return one.
• Have one just like it.
• Found one for a lower price.
• No longer need it.
• Toy/item is dangerous.

• Save proof of purchases. It is always easier to make returns if you have the sales receipt. But a credit-card slip or statement is usually enough to prove where you bought an item and how much you paid for it. *Good policy:* Staple tags or credit-card slips to sales receipts and keep them for a while after making purchases.

• Charge your major purchases. Charging allows you more "return leverage" because you have a record of your purchase, even if you lose the receipt. If a store refuses to honor a reasonable return request, you can threaten to withhold payment.

Caution: The store may use such action to file a negative credit report against you, so be sure to consult the credit-reporting company's rules before doing this.

• Shop at stores that have favorable return policies. Generally, large department stores are matter-of-fact about returns. Small shops and boutiques are likely to have more conservative return policies. We have found a wide disparity in store policies. *Common variable factors:* Window of time allowed for returns…whether cash refunds or store credits are issued.

Caution: Always ask about the return policies at small businesses.

• Return merchandise promptly—in good condition. If you know you want to return something, do it promptly, as some stores limit the amount of time from the date of purchase they will accept returns. Whenever possible, return merchandise in the original box or bag, clean, refolded or polished.

• Deal with the person in charge. Often, store clerks do not have the authority to accept a return. If you meet with a reluctant or rude store clerk, ask to speak with the manager. Most stores want their customers to be satisfied, and will try to please you—so don't take "no" for an answer.

• Be prepared to compromise. In the event you have exceeded a store's return policy, be flexible. You may not get exactly what you want—a cash refund—but you may be able to negotiate for a store credit, partial refund or exchange.

• Don't feel—or act—guilty. Returning merchandise is neither immoral nor illegal—so don't keep unwanted items.

Stores can resell merchandise returned in good condition…stores can usually return used or damaged merchandise to their suppliers for credit…losses incurred for merchandise that can't be returned are a legitimate cost of doing business that stores build into their prices.

You are already paying for your right to return —so use it!

• Know your legal rights. Manufacturer's warranties generally provide for repairs at no charge if an item doesn't work. Most merchants will exchange defective items for new ones. But even if an item you purchase has no warranty, all merchandise is sold by law under an "implied warranty."

This unwritten warranty provides that the product you buy will do what you bought it for, for a reasonable amount of time.

Example: A shirt is made to be washed or dry-cleaned. If it shreds, bleeds or shrinks, it is not performing as a shirt.

• Know your recourse. Most problems with consumer products can be resolved by speaking to the store manager. When this approach fails, you should write a letter of complaint both to the retailer and to the manufacturer.

Helpful: Call the Better Business Bureau, a local action line, hot line or consumer action panel or your state consumer-protection agency.

If a substantial amount of money is at stake, you may wish to file a claim in small claims court. Finally, you may wish to complain to a federal agency, such as the Consumer Product Safety Commission.

Don't fall for these myths:

• *Myth:* I've already worn it, so I can't return it. While you can't return something because you ruined it yourself, you can certainly return any item that does not do what it is supposed to do.

Example: A popcorn maker that doesn't pop.

• *Myth:* I can't return it—it was a gift. Even if you don't have a receipt, most stores will accept returns of gifts that can be identified as theirs from a label or packaging.

• *Myth:* The receipt says "All sales final." Could be—but it's always worth a try. You may be able to exchange the item for store credit.

Exception: Personal items, such as bathing suits or underwear, are generally not returnable unless the original packaging is undisturbed.

• *Myth:* I can't return it—I bought it months ago. A defect may not appear for some time, but this doesn't mean that you can't ask to have it repaired or replaced at no charge.

Example: I bought a VCR which broke down after four months. Even though the 90-day warranty had expired, the store replaced it anyway, because it contained a defective part.

• *Myth:* I can't return food. Most supermarkets will gladly accept returns of unopened canned foods or foods that are spoiled or defective.

Example: After my cat went on a "diet," I returned several cans of a brand of cat food I no longer wanted.

• *Myth:* It's my tough luck if I found one cheaper after I already bought this one. If an item goes on sale soon after you bought it for the regular price, or if you find the same item elsewhere for a lower price, by all means, take it back! Many stores will refund the difference.

Source: Arlene Singer, a professional buyer in the advertising field, and coauthor, with Karen Parmet, of *Take It Back! The Art of Returning Almost Anything,* National Press Books, Inc., 7200 Wisconsin Ave., Bethesda, Maryland 20814.

Start a Gift Shelf

Start a "gift shelf" by setting aside gifts bought on sale throughout the year. When you need a gift, check the shelf before going shopping. You may find that you've already bought the perfect gift—and at a great price.

Source: Roxanne M. Logan, editor, *Frugal Connoisseur*, Box 290-183, Waterford, Michigan 48329.

Listing Food Items

List the food items that you discard every time you clean out your refrigerator. If, after several cleanings, you see a pattern of under-used items that often spoil, change your buying habits accordingly.

Source: Lynn Parrinella, editor, *Dollar Wise*, Box 270924, Fort Collins, Colorado 80527.

Better Buying

Get the simplest, well-built product that will do the job you need done. *Example:* If you sew a few simple items a year, such as curtains and napkins, you do not need a computerized sewing machine with multiple attachments.

Source: *Woman's Day*, 1633 Broadway, New York 10019.

Save on Directory-Assistance Charges

When you move to a new town, take your old phone book with you in case you need to call former associates or businesses.

Source: Jackie Iglehart, editor, *The Penny Pincher*, Box 809, Kings Park, New York 11754.

How to Pinch Pennies… Twenty Ways to Save

It's always easier to spend less than it is to earn more. And given our current income-tax structure, spending $10 less is worth nearly twice as much as earning $10 more. So pinch those pennies—they can really add up. *Here are 20 simple strategies that add up—and up…*

• Shop when supermarkets are least crowded. It's hard to calculate the best buy on peanut butter when anxious people are shoving past you in the aisles. Avoid hours when most working people shop—between 5:00 and 6:00 PM, on weekends and on the fifteenth and thirtieth of the month. *Better:* Shopping early in the morning or later at night. *Added benefit:* By avoiding long checkout lines, you also minimize the temptation to make impulse purchases.

• Drink more water. Stop buying sugary drink mixes and soft drinks. Squeeze a lemon into a pitcher of ice water instead. It's better for you.

• Store food in reusable containers. You can reduce your need for costly plastic wrap, plastic bags and aluminum foil to almost nothing by using plastic containers and glass jars to store food.

• Reduce butter, salt and sugar. The amount of sugar, salt and fats called for in most recipes is usually much higher than needed for consistency or taste. Each time you prepare a recipe, gradually reduce these ingredients, keeping penciled notes in the cookbook or recipe card.

Example: Use ¾ of a stick of butter instead of the whole stick. Try mixing half butter, half margarine.

• Use skim or powdered milk. Gradually switch from whole or 2% milk to 1%—then switch to skim. Use powdered milk in baking. Mix skim or powdered milk to extend and lower the fat content of other products—such as chocolate milk, buttermilk or eggnog.

• Replace ground beef with ground turkey. It's less expensive, high in protein and lower in fat. Many people find they like the taste as well as, or even better than, beef, because it is less greasy. Start with flavorful dishes, such as meat loaf, chili, spaghetti sauce.

•Use expensive ingredients sparingly. Create main dishes that use small pieces of meat, seafood or poultry as part of the dish, in combination with rice, pasta, potatoes, couscous or other grain. Your family and guests will be impressed by your culinary artistry, and your grocery bills will drop. *Helpful:* Get new recipes from cookbooks in your local library. Explore vegetarian, seafood, Indian, Middle Eastern, Asian and other specialty cuisines.

•Shop for clothes at end-of-season sales. You won't have to wait long. A fashion season usually ends earlier than the actual season, so the store can clear the floor for the next season's wares.

Example: Bathing suits usually go on sale around the Fourth of July, not the end of August.

•Use tie spray. Expensive silk ties are almost impossible to clean without spotting, unless they have been sprayed with a food and drink repellent. A spray-protected tie will wipe clean, eliminating the need for dry-cleaning or replacing it.

•Don't overdry your clothes. All that lint in your dryer's filter comes from your clothes, towels and bedding. Overdrying causes fabrics to wear thinner and shrink more, and helps elastic deteriorate.

•Reduce dryer time even more. Put full loads of wash through an extra spin cycle to remove as much moisture as possible. The dryer uses more than twice as much energy as the washer. Do consecutive loads of laundry, rather than single loads throughout the week. *Reason:* Much of the initial energy a dryer uses goes to heat it up. Once it's heated, it can keep going efficiently.

•Buy furniture at discount. You may not want a used sofa as the centerpiece of your living room—unless it is an antique. But when looking for lamps, end tables, side chairs, chests and other furnishings, you can find high-quality merchandise at department-store and furniture-store showrooms, where pieces that have been floor models, reconditioned or repossessed are sold at discount. Estate sales are another good source for high-quality used furniture.

•When building a home or addition, ask contractors to reduce their rates if you agree to do the cleanup at the end of each day. You'll have to sweep up sawdust and remove scrap wood to meet safety regulations. But you'll save on construction crew time.

•Stop buying costly cleansers. Generic brands of ammonia and bleach will clean almost everything in your home. Follow dilution instructions. Don't ever mix them together. Use bleach to kill mildew in bathrooms, or pour it down drains once a month to keep them clear. Use vinegar or lemon juice as a glass cleaner. Add either to hot water to cut grease in drains and pipes, or freeze either into ice cubes, then run through the garbage disposal.

•Stop buying costly cosmetics. Most moisturizing creams are petroleum jelly and added scent. Look for a discount brand with the same ingredients as the expensive type you usually buy.

Astringents and "toners" are usually composed of alcohol and water, with added scent. *Just as effective:* Witch hazel and distilled water. For men, rubbing alcohol or witch hazel with a drop of cologne is an excellent aftershave. Cologne is usually a better buy than perfume. *Rule of thumb:* Use less. Lemon juice will eliminate unwanted freckles and lighten hair.

•Use natural pesticides. Put bay leaves in cupboards to keep away bugs. Peppermint will deter mice. Boric acid will kill roaches. Ants dislike cloves and red pepper. Fleas hate salt water. Surround vegetable gardens with marigolds to repel insects.

•Install ceiling fans to cut air-conditioning bills. A ceiling fan will make up to a six-degree difference in comfortable temperature in the summer. Fans use less energy than air conditioners, and they are quieter.

•Finance your car through a home-equity loan rather than a car loan, so you can deduct the interest. Don't purchase the extended warranty when buying a new car. The new car warranty should be adequate. If it's not—you're buying the wrong car.

•Eat out at lunch. The menu is usually the same as at dinner, but prices are lower. And—if you aren't satisfied, at least you haven't spent a fortune.

•Choose hobbies wisely. Many pastimes can turn into money-savers, money-makers or skills to be bartered for other services you want.

Examples: Woodworking, knitting, music lessons, tutoring reading or mathematics, etc.

Source: Rochelle LaMotte McDonald, a former US Air Force electronics expert, and Anchorage, Alaska, mother of three. She is the author of *How to Pinch a Penny Till It Screams,* Avery Publishing Group, 120 Old Broadway, Garden City Park, New York 11040.

Plan Major Purchases In Advance

Plan major purchases in advance. This gives you time to look for sales on specific items you need—especially big-ticket ones. You will be less likely to shop for the best price after your present machine breaks down completely and perhaps causes household havoc.

Source: Larry Roth, editor, *Living Cheap News,* Box 700058, San Jose, California 95170.

Grace-Period Reductions

Grace-period reductions ranging from 25 days to 20 days—or even zero—are being instituted by some credit-card companies. A zero-day grace period means interest is charged from the date you make a purchase. Companies must notify cardholders of changes in writing—but the notices are easy to miss. *Self-defense:* Read any notice sent by your credit-card issuer.

Source: *Cheapskate Monthly,* Box 2135, Paramount, California 90723.

How to Save Money on Almost Everything

It's easy to cut costs by taking advantage of discounts and freebies. One woman we know saved enough in a few years to buy a new car!

Worthwhile: Keep track of your savings—and enjoy watching them grow.

Utilities/energy:
- For free evaluation of your energy usage, call your local utilities company. In addition, many utilities companies give away free energy-saving devices, such as low-flow shower heads, water-heater blankets and fluorescent bulbs.
- Repair major appliances yourself instead of paying for a costly service call. *How:* Call manufacturers' customer-service repair hotlines for instructions.
  - General Electric, 800-626-2000.
  - Whirlpool, 800-253-1301.
  - White-Westinghouse, 800-245-0600.
- Gather free firewood from any of our 155 national forests. Contact your regional office of the US Forest Service for a permit, which allows you up to six cords of downed or dead wood. At the going rate of about $150 a cord, this will save almost $1,000.
- Install a water restrictor for your shower head. That saves an average family thousands of gallons of water a year. Check with your local utility for a free water-restrictor head.

Home- and health-care products:
- Coupons are not just for food. Some of the very best coupon savings are for cleaning supplies, tissues, toothpaste, shampoo, batteries and other home-care and health-care products. Keep an eye out for "Free with Purchase" offers… stores that pay double coupon values…coupons printed on product packaging.
- Take advantage of refund/rebate offers. You must take the time to save UPC symbols, labels and receipts, but the savings can easily reach hundreds of dollars a year. *Good source of offers:* Supermarket and drugstore bulletin boards.

Refund request forms are often mounted as tear-off pads where products are shelved. Don't overlook offers in hardware and home-building stores, pet stores and appliance stores.
- Ask for free samples at department store cosmetics counters. Just say you need to try products before you buy, and you'll walk away with handfuls of high-priced makeup, skin-care products and fragrances.

Watch for: Fine print in magazine ads offering free samples of perfume or moisturizer simply by writing or calling an 800 number.
- Have your hair cut, colored, permed or styled at a cosmetology school. Students have spent hundreds of hours working on mannequins and each other, and are closely supervised by expert instructors. Customers are usually pampered.

Savings: About 60% less than a salon. The average American woman spends $238 a year at hair salons, so expect to save $143.

•Get routine dental care at a dental school. Services at the country's 57 dental-school training clinics, including orthodontics, are high-quality and 60% less expensive than normal dentists' fees. To find one, check the phone book for your local dental society.

•Ask your doctors for free samples of medications whenever you are given a prescription. Most doctors have plenty to give away.

Home entertainment:

•Take advantage of free magazine offers. Don't throw away subscription invitations from periodicals. Most publications will send you a free issue, then begin your subscription unless you cancel.

Key: Remember to write "cancel" on the invoice they send, and mail it back to them. The postage is almost always paid, and you owe nothing.

•Use your public library to borrow books, records, audiotapes, videotapes, even posters and artwork.

•Order free publications from your favorite manufacturers. Almost every food product company offers a free cookbook, including Quaker Oats, Dannon, Kikkoman, Goya's Seasonings and Nestlé…as does almost every trade organization, including the American Mushroom Institute in Kennett Square, Pennsylvania, the California Raisin Advisory Board in Fresno and the Idaho Potato Commission in Boise.

Examples: Eastman Kodak of Rochester, New York, offers three free booklets on photography…the Chicago Roller Skate Co. has two free booklets on roller skating how-to's…United Van Lines of Fenton, Missouri, offers a free booklet called *How to Hold a Garage Sale.*

To find offers…check package labels for the location of company headquarters, or call 800-555-1212. Then contact the company's customer-service department.

Source: Linda Bowman, author of *The More for Your Money* series of guides, including *Free Food & More* and *Freebies (and More) for Folks Over 50,* COM-OP Publishing, Box 6661, Malibu, California 90265.

Electrical Cost of A Refrigerator

Electrical cost of a refrigerator for 15 to 20 years can be more than three times its original purchase price. *Best:* A top-freezer model. Side-by-side models let more cold air pour out when they are opened. Consider manual-defrost models—they cost less and use only half the energy of automatic defrosters.

Source: *The Earth and You: Eating for Two* by April Moore, a Broadway, Virginia writer. Potomac Valley Press, 1424 16 St. NW, Washington, DC 20036.

Buy Dry Instead of Wet Pet Food

The higher price you pay for moist or semi-moist pet food is for extra water. Add your own water to the dry variety and save. *Also:* When buying pet food in bulk, don't purchase more than a one-month supply to avoid spoilage.

Source: Linda K. King, DVM, veterinarian based in Atlanta, writing in *McCall's*, 110 Fifth Ave., New York 10011.

Better Furniture Cleaning

You can get stains out better by using materials from around the house than with commercial preparations.

•White rings left by drinking glasses on wood furniture. This is the most commonly asked question about household stains. To remove, simply rub with plain white toothpaste (not a gel), then polish with floor wax—it's thicker and easier to work with than furniture wax. If the rings aren't too old, you can rub with cigarette ash—ask a friend to save some for you.

•Cigarette burns on wood. First, gently scrape away the black stain with a small knife. Then paint the cavity with clear nail polish. Allow to harden, then repeat…Apply as many coats as it takes to restore a level surface.

•Scratches on wood furniture. These will fill in if rubbed with camphor oil (you may have to go out to the drugstore to get some).

Some quick cures:

•Adhesive furniture-delivery labels. Rub with a washcloth dipped in cooking oil.

•Candle wax on wood surfaces. Harden with an ice cube then scrape away with a table knife.

•Rust on chrome furniture. Scrub with fine steel wool (#0000), then protect by applying sealer used to prevent copper or brass from pitting.

•Picture frames scratched during moving. Apply shoe polish.

•Scratches on dark woods. Tint with iodine.

Source: Carol Rees, a home-care adviser, author of *Household Hints for Upstairs, Downstairs and All Around the House,* Henry Holt & Co., by mail from Carol Rees Publications, 1310 Atlantic Ave., Waycross, Georgia 31501.

How to Solve Consumer Complaints

To help you get the results you deserve when lodging a consumer complaint:

•Evaluate the problem and decide what action you want taken, whether it's repairing or replacing the faulty product, getting a full or partial refund, etc.

Cars: Get a receipt every time the car is serviced. Without a record of the car's problems, your complaint will be worthless.

•Call the person you dealt with initially and explain your problem and what you'd like done. If he/she is unable to help, proceed to the store manager. If he/she can't help, go to his/her boss, and so on.

Important: Be assertive, not aggressive. Aggressiveness puts the other person on the defensive and never helps your case in the long run.

•Keep a detailed record of everything that transpires, including the name, phone number and title of each person you talk with, and the date and content of each conversation.

•If your problem still isn't solved, explain it in writing and include a summary of what you'd like to have happen and a record of all the steps you've taken so far. Send it to the person ranked above the last person you've talked with, and follow up by phone.

•If the company refuses to respond, contact your local consumer hotline, the consumer protection office in your city or state or small claims court.

Fraudulent companies:

•Ask for your money back with the realization that you probably won't get it. Many of these companies operate for a short time in one area before moving on to another location and changing their name.

•If they don't respond in a timely fashion (in a few weeks), you should report them to the postal authorities, the Federal Bureau of Investigation, the Federal Trade Commission or any other state or federal organization that can put them out of business.

•Protect yourself from fraudulent companies by avoiding prize offers with a price attached, offers that sound "too good to be true" and offers that are only good if you send your check or money order "today."

Source: Shirley Rooker, president of Call For Action, a Washington, DC-based international consumer hotline.

Ten Questions to Ask When Hiring a Nanny

• *Why do you wish to be a nanny?* Look for someone whose answers show a love of children. Taking care of children involves a very big commitment. Don't hire anyone who is unsure about being a nanny.

• *What is your child-care experience?* Ask about past jobs, formal nanny training, degrees in child education and classes in child care. If the applicants have worked as nannies before, ask why they left previous positions. Ask about baby-sitting jobs or other child-related work such as working as camp counselors, play-group leaders or tutors. Get the names and numbers of three or four references.

Also helpful: Personal recommendations from teachers or clergy members.

• *What are your child-rearing philosophies?* You want to hire someone who can be firm yet gentle and nurturing. Offer specific examples of difficult behavior, such as "It's time to go to school but Robin is throwing a tantrum and won't put on her coat. What would you do?"

Key: Look for someone with patience.

• *These are the job requirements. Does this sound like something you can handle?* List the specifics of the job, including hours, responsibilities, days off, salary and benefits (such as health insurance). If the applicant expects to do only child care and you expect cooking too, you'll both end up frustrated.

• *What are your hobbies/interests?* Look for a nanny with varied interests, such as sports, art, music, travel, etc. Try to find an active nanny for a household of athletic youngsters or a musical nanny for a child who takes piano lessons.

When hiring a live-in nanny:

• *What qualities are you looking for in a family?* When hiring live-in help, chemistry is very important. You want someone whose personality meshes with your own. Some live-in nannies expect to be part of the family, while others view the relationship as that of employer/employee.

Discuss: Will the live-in nanny travel with you on vacations? Eat with you?

• *What was your upbringing like?* Was the applicant's childhood stable? Look for someone who can be a wonderful role model for your children. You want someone with similar values and morals.

• *Do you smoke?* Describe your house rules about smoking. If you are a smoker, make the applicant aware of it.

• *Can you drive?* Does the applicant have a good driving record? Check with the Motor Vehicle Department. The applicant can authorize release of this information at the Motor Vehicle Department.

• *Do you have any dietary or other restrictions?* Does the applicant have any allergies or other medical problems? You may want to ask for a doctor's release attesting to good health.

Source: Joy Wayne, director of Nannies Plus, a nanny-placement service, 615 W. Mount Pleasant Ave., Livingston, New Jersey 07039.

The Best Places to Buy Wholesale...by Mail

The convenience of shopping by mail can't be beat—a brief call to a toll-free telephone number saves gas, tolls and parking fees as well as time. And—there are usually well-trained order takers. But why pay catalog prices? *Places to buy what you want by mail at great discounts...*

The basics:

• Many "wholesale" mail-order firms charge from $1 to $5 for their catalogs, but most deduct the catalog price from the first order.

• Some don't issue catalogs, but sell by "price-quote." The customer calls with the manufacturer's name, specific stock or model number, pattern name and color.

Price-quote companies often have the best deals on electronic equipment, furniture and appliances. *Caution:* These firms usually only accept returns on defective goods.

• I use the word "wholesale" to mean discounts of 30% or more on list prices. But some mail-order companies offer genuine wholesale terms to customers who can show they are running a business.

• In some cases, customers can get higher discounts with larger orders. *Helpful:* Buy with friends.

• When comparing prices, always compute the delivered price of a purchase...and compare that with what it would cost to shop at a store, mail a gift yourself, etc.

• Be wary—operators will try to sell you additional products while you're on the phone—it's part of the job.

Electronics & appliances:

• *Crutchfield Corporation.* Save up to 55%. One Crutchfield Park, Dept. WH, Charlottesville, Virginia 22906. 800-955-9009. Informative free catalog features product comparisons.

• *J&R Music World.* Save up to 50%. 59-60 Queens-Midtown Expressway, Maspeth, New York 11378. 800-221-8180. Free catalog.

• *LVT Price-Quote Hotline, Inc.* Save up to 30% on more than 4,000 products. Box 444-W94, Commack, New York 11725. 516-234-8884. Free brochure.

• *Percy's, Inc.* Save up to 40%. Gold Star Blvd., Worcester, Massachusetts 01605. 508-755-5334 or 800-922-8194. Price-quotes on large appliances, audio, video and TVs.
Clothing:
• *Chock Catalog Corp.* (Louis Chock). Save up to 35%. 74 Orchard St., Dept. WBMC, New York 10002. 212-473-1929. Catalog of name-brand men's and women's underwear, sleepwear, hosiery, infant's sleepwear and clothing is $1.
• *Paul Fredrick Shirt Co.* Save up to 50%. 223 W. Poplar St., Fleetwood, Pennsylvania 19522. 215-944-0909. Catalog of high-quality men's dress shirts, ties, accessories is $1.
• *The Ultimate Outlet.* Save up to 65%. Box 88251, Chicago 60680. 800-332-6000. Spiegel's discount outlet. *Catalog:* $2.
Health, beauty and medical supplies:
• *The American Association of Retired Persons* mail-order pharmacy, a benefit of an $8 AARP membership. Call 800-456-2226 for price quotes.
• *Beautiful Visions.* Save up to 90%. 105 Orville Dr., Bohemia, New York 11716. 516-244-2010. Free catalog of name-brand cosmetics and perfumes.
• *Bruce Medical Supply.* Save up to 60%. 411 Waverly Oaks Rd., Dept. 10736, Waltham, Massachusetts 02154. 800-225-8446. Free catalog of dozens of ostomy, diabetic, medical products and aids.
• *Creative Health Products.* Average 30% off. 5148 Saddle Ridge Rd., Plymouth, Michigan 48170. 800-742-4478. Free catalog of fitness equipment and medical devices.
• *Retired Persons Services, Inc.* Save up to 80%. Dept 493000, 500 Montgomery St., Alexandria, Virginia 22314. Call 800-456-2277 for catalog.
Home furnishings & linens:
• *Albert S. Smyth Co., Inc.* Save up to 50%. Dept. WM94, 29 Greenmeadow Dr., Timonium, Maryland 21093. 800-638-3333. Free catalog of tableware, giftware and jewelry.
• *China Cabinet, Inc.* Save up to 50%. 24 Washington St., Tenafly, New Jersey 07670. 201-567-2711. Price quotes on fine china, crystal, flatware.
• *The Furniture Showplace.* Save up to 55%. 1190 Hwy., 74 Bypass, Spindale, North Car-olina 28160. 704-287-7106. Home furnishings and accessories. Free brochure with self-addressed, stamped envelope.
• *Harris Levy, Inc.* Save up to 60%. 278 Grand St., Dept. WBM, New York 10002. 800-221-7750. Free catalog of luxury bed, bath and table linens as well as kitchen and closet accessories.
• *Interior Furnishings Ltd.* Save up to 50%. Box 1644, Hickory, North Carolina 28603. 704-328-5683. Home furnishings and accessories. Free brochure.
• *Murrow Furniture Galleries, Inc.* Save up to 50%. Box 4337, Dept. WBMC, Wilmington, North Carolina 28406. 910-799-4010. Home furnishings and accessories. Free brochure.
• *Nat Schwartz & Co., Inc.* Save up to 50%. 549 Broadway, Bayonne, New Jersey 07002. 800-526-1440. Price quotes on fine china, crystal and flatware.
• *Open House.* Save up to 40%. 200 Bala Ave., Bala Cynwyd, Pennsylvania 19004. 215-664-1488. Price quotes on name-brand tableware, cookware, cutlery.
• *Triad Furniture Discounters.* Save up to 50%. 3930 Hwy. 501, Myrtle Beach, South Carolina 29577. 800-323-8469. Price quotes on home and office furnishings from almost 100 major manufacturers.
Leather goods:
• *A to Z Luggage Co.* Save up to 50%. 4627 New Utrecht Ave., Brooklyn, New York 11219. 718-435-6330. Free catalog of leather goods, luggage and pens.
• *The Luggage Center.* Save up to 50%. 960 Remillard Court, San Jose, California 95122. 800-626-6789. Price quotes on name-brand luggage, briefcases, travel accessories.
Tools & hardware:
• *Tool Crib of the North.* Save up to 50%. Box 13720, Grand Forks, North Dakota 58208. 800-358-3096. *Catalog:* $3, or price quotes on tools and hardware.

Source: Prudence McCullough, executive editor of *The Wholesale-by-Mail Catalog® 1994,* HarperCollins, 10 E. 53 St., New York 10022.

17

Your Car

Side-Impact Air Bags

Side-impact air bags designed to protect the chest, shoulders and head will begin appearing in Volvo automobiles in 1995. The bags are located in the seat cushions themselves, not in the door panels, for more complete protection as seats are adjusted. The bags have a relatively small air capacity—only 12 liters—and can be fully deployed within no more than 12 milliseconds of impact.

Source: *Road & Track*, 1633 Broadway, New York 10019.

Beware of Oil Additives

Many oil additives have no proven benefits for an engine —and may cause engine damage or faster engine wear. The chemistry of automotive oils is delicate. Additives disrupt it— with potentially costly results. *Best:* Do not use them…but if you do, make sure the additive is approved by the manufacturer and won't void your engine warranty.

Source: David Solomon, editor, *Nutz & Boltz*®, Box 123, Butler, Maryland 21023.

Car-Jacking Self-Defense

If you suspect you're being followed while driving, make four right turns—essentially driving in a circle. If, after the four turns, the same car is still behind you, drive to the nearest police station or busy gas station. *Important:* Do not drive home.

Source: *Secure from Crime: How to Be Your Own Bodyguard* by bodyguard Craig Fox Huber in Richmond, Virginia. Path Finder Publications, 1296 E. Gibson Rd., E-301, Woodland, California 95776.

Garage Parking Lowers Insurance

Garage parking lowers insurance by as much as 20%. Few thieves try to steal a car from a garage, and the chances of being sideswiped are dramatically reduced. If you park on the street or in a parking lot, check out garages—their higher cost may be offset by savings on insurance premiums.

Source: Rick Longueira, insurance agent, Flushing, New York, quoted in *Smart Money*, 250 W. 55 St., New York 10019.

Un-Overheating— Secrets of Keeping Cool

What do you do if your engine is drastically overheating, steam has started to spurt from the hood area and the "hot" warning light is on? *Steps to take…*

1. Pull over as soon as possible. Another mile or two can turn a minor repair into a blown head gasket or, even worse, a cracked block. In some cases, the damage can cost more to fix than the value of the car.

2. Unless the engine is smoking or on fire, don't turn off the ignition. If allowed to idle, the engine can throw off more heat because the engine's coolant is circulating. Shutting off an overheated engine can turn the oil to varnish, which can cause engine seizure.

Helpful: Turn the heater to its "high" setting and open the windows. This draws heat away from the engine and helps to cool off the radiator.

3. If you have access to a hose, spray water into the grille of the car, in the area of the radiator. Make sure you cool down the hood area as well to avoid getting burned when you lift it. *Note:* The engine should still be running.

4. When the water has cooled off the radiator to a point where it is cool to the touch, *carefully open the radiator cap.* Pour water into the radiator until it is full. Then replace the cap tightly.

5. If water isn't available, leave the engine on but use gloves or towels to open the hood. Remove the oil filler cap carefully—it's hot—

and add a quart or two of oil. You should do this even if the dipstick indicates that it is full. It can handle the excess, and the oil will help cool the internal engine parts.

Wait until the engine/radiator is cool—about an hour—before driving again. Have the oil changed as soon as you can.

Important: If you do not have water or oil and turning on the heater doesn't help, turn off the engine. Wait until it is cool before trying to start it again.

Source: David Solomon, editor of *Nutz & Boltz®*, Box 123, Butler, Maryland 21023. He is the author of *The Automotive Panic Button*, available through *Nutz & Boltz®*.

Intimidating/Aggressive Driver Self-Defense

Don't be provoked into driving dangerously or responding to another driver's actions… move aside to allow dangerous drivers to pass …avoid eye contact…never make an obscene or otherwise aggressive gesture as the driver passes…if you have a car phone, dial 911 or the appropriate emergency number and report the driver to the police.

Source: Ronald W. Kosh, general manager, AAA Potomac, writing in *AAA World*, 1000 AAA Dr., Heathrow, Florida 32746.

Air Bags Save Lives

Air bags save lives but leave you vulnerable to other injuries. *Reason:* Even when an air bag deploys during a crash, the driver's lower extremities can be injured by the instrument panel or floor. *Possible results:* Ankle fractures …crushed feet…broken legs and hips. *However:* While such injuries can be serious, victims may have died *without* the air bags.

Source: Study of victims of automobile crashes by J. Augenstein, MD, PhD, trauma surgeon, Wm. Lehman Injury Research Center, at the Ryder Trauma Center, University of Miami.

Hidden Driving Danger

Drivers take more risks as cars get safer.

Example: Drivers who know cars with anti-lock brakes are safer may drive more aggressively…or go out in bad weather more often.

Result: Accident rates can actually increase as cars get safer—as driver behavior offsets the benefits of safer cars.

Source: Robert Chirinko, economics department, University of Illinois at Urbana-Champaign.

It's Easy to Avoid Having An Auto Accident

Most drivers think they are safer than other drivers, according to surveys. Obviously they can't all be right. *Problems:*

•Many motorists have an *inflated* sense of their skills.

•Many have misconceptions about traffic safety.

We tend to fear inclement weather. As a result, we drive more carefully in snow and rain. The great majority of fatalities, however, occur in good weather, when people are *not* trying to compensate for difficult driving conditions.

In my 36 years of driving, I have never crashed. This record may be due to good luck …or it may be the result of adopting safe driving practices.

Tailgating:

•Don't follow too closely. Strictly regarded on a risk/reward basis, tailgating is one of the most unappealing driving practices. Many of us tailgate simply out of habit.

Strategy: Allow at least a two-second headway between your vehicle and the vehicle that you are following. *How to control:* Note when the lead vehicle crosses some identifying feature on the road, such as a crack or the shadow of a tree. Count seconds—*one thousand, two thousand.* If your vehicle reaches the same location in less than two seconds, you are following too closely.

•Minimize your exposure to a tailgater. Try your best to get away from the tailgater…or do things that will attract his/her attention.

Strategy I: Tap your brake lights and then speed up. If the other driver thinks you're crazy —*terrific.* He may save you a lot of grief by trying to avoid *you.*

Strategy II: Do the exact opposite of what the tailgater wants you to do—slow down. Then he will be pleased to pass you.

•Be especially wary of a tailgater when you're entering a freeway. Preparing to merge when someone is on your tail is a high-risk situation.

Strategy: Slow down dramatically as you approach the highway. Then accelerate quickly to get into the lane. At all costs, you want to avoid the worst-case scenario—trying to merge, then suddenly having to abort the attempt.

•Approach a traffic light strategically. When another vehicle is on your tail, even a predictable stop at a traffic light can put you at risk.

Strategy: Slow down gradually, thereby lowering the likelihood of being forced to come to a complete stop. Then accelerate when the light changes. This also minimizes vehicle wear and tear and saves fuel.

Lights, intersections, turns, etc.:

•Don't be a slave to the traffic light. One common accident involves a driver who hits the accelerator the instant the light turns green. Unfortunately, this is exactly when he/she is most likely to collide with someone who is trying to make it through a yellow light or is running a red light.

Strategy: When the light turns green, look both ways before proceeding. Ideally, make sure there's a stopped car in each lane.

•Even when a U-turn is legal, it can be dangerous. If you must turn around, pull to the side of the road or pull into a driveway and come to a complete stop. This takes you out of the flow of traffic and removes the pressure of making a quick, perfect U-turn. It also increases the amount of time you have to survey the traffic coming in both directions.

•Be wary of blind spots. Obviously, you should never forget that you have two blind spots—directly behind you on both the left and the right. Also be sure to avoid someone else's blind spots. When you can't be seen, you're at greater risk.

Your mental state:

•Not driving when drunk is *not* enough. Even if you've had just one beer or have taken one antihistamine, it is not a good idea to drive.

In New York and Michigan, which have typical US intoxication standards prohibiting 0.1% or more alcohol in the blood—a driver can be legally sober and still be ten times more likely to crash than a driver who has had nothing to drink.

Many states are now lowering the limit to 0.08%. California adopted this level in 1990. Yet this level is still much higher than in the rest of the world. For example, in Sweden the limit is 0.02%.

•Respect your mental state. An accident is more likely to occur if you're tired, incredibly stressed or angry. Instead of increasing your speed—which automatically boosts your chances of having an accident—calm down and collect yourself.

If someone cuts in front of you improperly, don't let yourself become enraged. He has probably delayed you by less than two seconds. Tell yourself to forget it, and remind yourself of exactly how little time his high-risk maneuver has cost you and how much his behavior will cost him in the long run.

•Know your passengers. Don't be paranoid, but realize that a passenger can often be a distraction.

Strategy: When you're driving, keep your priorities straight. Always remember that driving is a bigger priority than your conversation.

•Watch out for children. All kids represent potential internal disruptions. So be prepared to be hit by a flying sandwich or assaulted by various shrieks and cries. Don't be shocked, and keep your cool. You should also be less attentive to a child's everyday pleas and yowls than you might be if you were in the safety of your home. After all, you're *not* in the safety of your home.

Source: Leonard Evans, DPhil, principal research scientist at the Automotive Safety and Health Research department of General Motors Corp., Warren, Michigan. He is the author of *Traffic Safety and the Driver,* Van Nostrand Reinhold, 115 Fifth Ave., New York 10003.

Auto Accident Checklist

•Move all involved cars safely off the main roadway. Many injuries can occur *after* an accident as people mill around on a busy road.

•Call for medical help for the injured people. If someone appears to be injured but says he/she is okay, call for help anyway.

•Call the police and stay put until they arrive. *Important:* Never admit guilt or negligence. Just relay the facts and let the police determine who —if anyone—was at fault.

•Get data from each driver involved—no matter how minor the accident. *Important:*

- •Name •Address
- •Phone number •Driver's license number
- •Insurance information

Also: Get names, addresses and phone numbers of the witnesses, including passengers in the cars that were involved.

•Write down the details of the accident while they're still fresh in your mind. *Describe:* Car directions, speed, whether signal and brake lights were functioning and used, etc.

•Draw a map of the accident. Note the location of any stop signs, traffic lights, objects in the road, etc.

•If you carry a camera in the car, photograph the accident from all angles and get good shots of any damage to each car.

•Remain calm and follow all police instructions.

Source: *Reality Check Gazette*, 8667 Sudley Rd., MS-270, Manassas, Virginia 22110.

New Tire Self-Defense

Allow the tire-mounting lube sufficient time to dry by avoiding high speeds (over 45 mph) for at least four hours after getting a new set of tires. Tires that are driven too fast and too soon can rotate on the rim, throwing them out of balance and causing the car to shake and shimmy at typical highway speeds.

Source: David Solomon, editor, *Nutz & Boltz*, Box 123, Butler, Maryland 21023.

Registering Your Car

Register a car in the name of the primary driver only. *Reason:* If the car is owned jointly and one spouse has an accident, the victim can go after both spouses' incomes and assets in a lawsuit. In most states, if the vehicle is owned only by one spouse, the other's assets are protected.

Source: Bert Whitehead, Franklin, Michigan, tax attorney and fee-only financial planner.

Cheaper Car Insurance

Discounts are available in many states if drivers complete a defensive driving course. Ask your insurer if discounts apply in your state ...call the National Safety Council, 800-621-6244.

Source: *Auto Insurance Alert!* by financial writer Andrew Tobias, Simon & Schuster, 1230 Avenue of the Americas, New York 10020.

Make It Tough For Car Thieves

Always lock up. Never leave keys inside, put packages out of sight. Park in well-lit areas. At commercial lots and garages, give the attendant only the ignition key—keep the glove box locked. On streets, park with emergency brake set and front wheels turned all the way to left or right—to make towing hard. *Bottom line:* Experienced thieves spend only three to five seconds trying to break into a car. If anything slows them, they move on.

Source: Lynn Ferrin, editor, *Motorland*, 150 Van Ness Ave., San Francisco 94102.

Cars Help Kidneys

The National Kidney Foundation of New York/New Jersey will cart away older and late model cars, whether or not they are in working condition. Proceeds benefit the foundation's programs. The foundation sends a letter acknowledging each gift. Donors may be entitled to a tax deduction equal to a car's fair market value. *More information:* 800-633-6628.

Selling Your Car Yourself

Selling your car yourself makes you more money than you would get selling or trading it in to a dealer...but it is also riskier. *Trap I:* The prospective buyer could steal your car during the test drive. *Self-defense:* Get information—name, address, phone number—on him/her before handing over your keys...go on the test drive or hold his car keys and another item, such as a credit card or driver's license...turn away anyone who makes you uncomfortable. *Trap II:* Erroneous problems identified by the buyer's mechanic to lower the car's value. *Self-defense:* Know what is wrong with your car... be there for the mechanic's inspection. *Trap III:* In many states, the license plate stays with the car. If the new buyer doesn't transfer the title right away, you are still the legal owner and he is driving under *your* insurance policy—you could be liable for any violations or accidents. *Self-defense:* Go with the buyer to the county registrar's office or Department of Motor Vehicles to make the title change.

Source: Paul Brand, a former racing-car champion, instructor in emergency driving and automotive columnist for the *Minneapolis Star/Tribune* and many automotive magazines.

Common Mistakes Using Child-Safety Seats

•*Mistake:* Seat faced in the wrong direction. Infants up to 12 months or 20 pounds should face rearward. Toddlers to age four and between 20 and 40 pounds should face forward.

•*Mistake:* Seat reclined incorrectly. Rear-facing seats should recline at a 45° angle. Forward-facing seats should be upright.

•*Mistake:* Seat belt routed improperly. Child seats that face both rearward for infants and forward for toddlers have two different seat belt paths. Rear-facing-only seats usually have another path. Follow directions carefully when installing the seat.

•*Mistake:* Seat improperly anchored. Test to make sure that the seat is firmly attached. It should not move even if pulled very hard.

•*Mistake:* Harness straps incorrectly positioned. With a rear-facing seat, straps should come from below the child's shoulders. With a forward-facing seat, they should come from the highest slot. If the straps are too loose, tie them together with the plastic harness clip that comes with the seat. In cars with continuous-loop seat belts, use the metal locking clip to hold the shoulder and lap belts together.

•*Mistake:* Booster seats used too soon. These seats—which help correctly position the child for the car's seat and shoulder belts—are only for children between 40 and 60 pounds.

Source: American Academy of Pediatrics, 141 Northwest Point Blvd., Elk Grove, Illinois 60009.

Car Exhaust and Hay Fever

Exposure to nitrogen dioxide from car exhaust doubles the chance that a hay fever sufferer will develop the classic symptoms—sneezing and a runny nose. This chemical appears to damage the mucous membranes lining the nose, making them more sensitive to airborne pollen. *Self-defense:* When pollen counts are high, hay fever sufferers should avoid city streets during rush hour.

Source: Robert Davies, MD, professor of respiratory medicine, St. Bartholomew's Hospital, London.

To Avoid Pedestrian-Vehicle Accidents

Watch out for drunken pedestrians when driving at night near bars and nightclubs…expect children to behave unpredictably and be prepared to slow down or stop quickly when driving near kids…teach your children how to behave safely around traffic…alter your driving route to avoid unfenced playgrounds, nightlife strips and other risky locations.

Source: David K. Willis, executive director, American Automobile Association Foundation for Traffic Safety, 1440 New York Ave. NW, Suite 201, Washington, DC 20005.

18

Self-Defense

How to Keep Your Neighborhood Safe From Crime

The key to making any neighborhood safe from crime is the willingness of its residents to play a role in crime prevention.

Most people believe that this task should be accomplished by law-enforcement officers. Unfortunately, the criminal justice system—police, courts, jails, etc.—is designed to deal with crime only after it has taken place.

Though the police are better able to root out criminal activity, neighbors have far more power to stop crime from happening in the first place.

Examples: A neighbor is usually the first to spot someone breaking into a house...or to call for help if someone is attacked near his/her home.

Criminals acknowledge that their jobs are easier in neighborhoods where people live in isolation...and are much tougher when neighbors watch out for each other.

In my experience as a crime-prevention consultant, the best way to reduce crime is to form a Neighborhood Watch-type of group. These groups—also known as Block Watch, Home Alert or Neighborhood Alert—now protect more than 20,000 neighborhoods in the US.

Neighborhood Watch groups are most effective in stable neighborhoods where most residents own their homes. But with enough persistence, they can also work in apartment buildings.

How to start a group:

• Ask your police department for pamphlets and other instructional materials. In neighborhoods with significant gang or drug activity, a strong relationship with the police is important.

Be aware, however, that most police departments will encourage individual home security —door and window locks, alarm systems, ID numbers on personal property.

Though these are all sensible measures, without neighborhood unity and organization, home-security systems promote a "locked-in" feeling, which encourages crime since criminals know that they probably won't be spotted or reported.

327

• Start small. Find one neighbor who shares your concern about crime and wants to do something about it. See if each of you can bring another neighbor to a preliminary meeting to discuss the Neighborhood Watch concept.

• Define your neighborhood boundaries. It is generally best to cast a small net at the start, then expand as membership grows. My watch group covers a cul-de-sac with 20 homes.

• Conduct a door-to-door Neighborhood Concerns survey. This written survey serves several purposes—it brings the neighborhood's crime problem into focus…it is a key step in enlisting help from the police…and it recruits new members. *Basic survey questions:*

• What do you consider to be our neighborhood's biggest crime problems now?

• What are our neighborhood's biggest potential problems?

• How do you feel the police are handling these problems?

• What do you think the police should be doing?

• Do you have any ideas about what we could do to prevent crime?

• Make it clear that a Neighborhood Watch group is not a vigilante organization. Though some neighbors will quickly rally to support a watch group, others may be reluctant to commit themselves because of apathy, fear or a misunderstanding of the concept.

Key selling point: Neighborhood Watch groups look for suspicious activities, compile data and report information to the police. They do not intercede in potentially dangerous situations.

• Return to the police department to share your surveys and obtain further crime data. Check statistics for neighborhood crime rates—and see what times and days of the week crimes are most likely to occur. Ask about police patrol patterns, duties, response time…and how your group can be of assistance.

To reduce crime:

• Target the criminal population. One myth about crime is that most of it is committed at night by strangers to the neighborhood.

Facts: The typical burglary occurs between 10 AM and 2 PM, when most people are out of their homes. Most crimes are committed by males between the ages of 13 and 22. Quite often, neighbors observe these youths getting into trouble—committing vandalism, writing graffiti—as young as ages seven or eight. They often receive inadequate parental supervision.

These young people can be helped to change —but only if the community takes collective responsibility for them. *How a watch group can intercede…*

• Truancy can be reported to the school when the youth is of school age.

• One or two delegates from the watch group can approach the youth's parents and ask how they might help to resolve this problem together. A group is more likely to be taken seriously than a single irate individual. Be sure the group representatives express a positive attitude and do not blame the parents.

• Train group members to recognize and report suspicious activity. Criminals are more likely to be stopped and apprehended when neighbors trust their instincts and call the police.

Many people are reluctant to make that phone call, fearing they might appear foolish. Most crimes, in fact, are not reported.

"Safe" strategy: Next-door neighbors could agree to call each other first if they see something suspicious around the other person's home. If they find no one at home, they would then call the police.

• Distribute crime-report forms. These forms are to be sent to the police when a group member observes possible criminal activity. Members would describe the suspect and any weapon or vehicle.

In addition to heightening awareness, a watch group can help reduce crime by:

• Distributing decals or window signs to members for their homes. *Note:* To be truly effective, the signs must be backed up by alarms, lights and other security measures.

• Promoting a "Light the Night" effort, in which everyone in the neighborhood agrees to keep their porch lights on after dusk.

Alternative: An agreement to install motion-sensitive lights by all porches and walkways.

• Conduct a neighborhood security survey to identify physical features that make the community vulnerable to crime. Again, local law-enforcement agencies may be of aid. *Most helpful:* An officer trained in Crime Prevention

Through Environmental Design (CPTED), the concept of manipulating building design, landscaping and traffic flow to fight crime.

Source: Stephanie Mann, who helped start the Neighborhood Watch concept in 1969 in Orinda, California. A crime-prevention consultant to police departments and businesses nationwide, she is coauthor, with M.C. Blakeman, of *Safe Homes, Safe Neighborhoods: Stopping Crime Where You Live,* Nolo Press, 950 Parker St., Berkeley, California 94710.

To Avoid Danger On the Street

To avoid danger on the streets, *stay alert.* When walking between car and home or car and store, focus on the area between you and your destination. Walk with a quick, confident step…keep your head up…tune out all preoccupations. *Bottom line:* Your immediate priority is to get there safely.

Source: *The Danger Zone: How You Can Protect Yourself from Rape, Robbery and Assault* by crime-prevention police officer Patricia Harman, Parkside Publishing, 205 W. Touhy Ave., Park Ridge, Illinois 60068.

Self-Defense for a Child Who Is Being Followed

• Safely cross the street.

• Walk or run to the nearest well-lit public facility—restaurant, store or gas station. Go to a trusted neighbor's house and wait there.

• Call or wave to an imaginary friend.

• If caught, scream, "Help"…"Fire"…"He's not my father"—or anything else to attract the attention of passersby.

• Report any unusual situation to parents, teachers, a neighbor or the police by dialing 911 or the operator.

Source: *Fifty Ways to Keep Your Child Safe* by Susan K. Golant, Los Angeles-based parenting author. Lowell House, 2029 Century Park E., Suite 3290, Los Angeles 90067.

Where to Hide Your Valuables

To decide where to hide valuables, you need to understand exactly how burglars operate. The worst room to use is the master bedroom—the place where most people like to hide things. Thieves are likely to start right there. Burglars usually know just where to search both in the master bedroom and in other rooms—including the kitchen, where they are almost sure to check the cookie jar.

But thieves are in a hurry. They rarely spend more than 20 minutes in a house. You can take advantage of a burglar's haste to get away before he is detected by storing valuables in stealth devices. These hiding places take a thief a long time to locate.

• The Wall Outlet Safe* has a tiny compartment, and it requires installation. But if you choose a color and style indistinguishable from your real outlets, there's little likelihood of its being detected. The sockets accept plugs, so you can plug in a combination battery/outlet clock radio with a light-up dial and actually run it on batteries. Or, you can install the outlet safe in a child's room. This is usually the last place thieves look, but also the place people don't like to hide valuables lest children get at them. They won't, though, if the fake outlet is behind a piece of furniture. And a thief probably won't, either—especially if you insert convincing child safety clips in the sockets.

• The Flower Pot Safe. A real, plastic flower pot with a hollowed out hidden compartment within. The compartment is no larger than a small juice glass, but it makes a pretty safe place to keep a necklace and earrings or other valuables, as well as a few large bills.

• Book Safe. Especially effective if you have lots of real books to hide it among. *Helpful:* Models hollowed out from actual books. You can't order these by title, but unlike a wooden fake book this model will age exactly like a real book.

*These and other stealth devices are available at home improvement centers, some hardware stores and from a number of security catalogs. *One of the best:* Knock-Out Security Products, 800-394-7233.

•Safe Cans. These are facsimiles of popular canned products: Shaving creams, cleansers, spray cans, etc. As stealth devices they are well-known to thieves. But they come in a wide variety of designs, and new ones appear all the time. *Best:* Spend extra money for a weighted model, since one that feels too light could betray its real use.

Source: Bill Phillips, a lock expert who writes on security and safety issues. He is the author of *Home Mechanix Guide to Security: Protecting Your Home, Car and Family,* John Wiley & Sons, 605 Third Ave., New York 10158.

Scam Avoidance Checklist

Don't be a participant in your own financial downfall. *Avoid...*
•Anything that requires up-front cash to get rich quick.
•Anything that requires you to pay for the secrets of someone else's success.
•Anything that promises to make you or your house the envy of your neighbors.
•Anything that costs you money in order to save you money.
•Anyone who tells you that rather than working for your money, you should let your money work for you.
•Anyone who doesn't tell you in plain English what it is you're putting your money into.
•Anyone who doesn't have the time, inclination or willingness to let you get a second opinion about the proposed investment idea.

Source: Jonathan Pond, president of Financial Planning Information, 9 Galen St., Watertown, Massachusetts 02172. He is a nationally recognized expert on financial planning. Mr. Pond has written many books, including *The New Century Family Money Book,* Bantam Doubleday Dell Publishing Group, Inc., 1540 Broadway, New York 10036.

How Not to Be Swindled

To help you steer clear of swindlers:
•If any offer sounds too good to be true, you can be virtually certain that it is.
•Never rush or impulse buy. Swindlers don't want to give you any time to think the deal over because your common sense might prevail.

•Responses to help separate the good guys from the bad guys: "Well, let me talk this over with my attorney."..."I'll check this out with the Better Business Bureau and get back to you."
•If an offer is in person or by phone, insist on getting details in writing before making a decision.
•Check out any offer or recommendation thoroughly. Call your local Area Agency on Aging or Better Business Bureau.
•Investigate and comparison shop as you would with any major purchase. Check it out with knowledgeable people.
•Don't sign anything until you've done your investigation.
•Use credit cards, or at least checks—never cash. With credit cards and checks there is a legal record of your payment.
•Never give out your credit card, Medicare, Social Security, telephone calling card or bank account numbers to solicitors.
•The fact that an offer appears on network TV or in a respected magazine or major newspaper means nothing. Acceptance standards for ads are notoriously lax and virtually anyone can buy advertising.
•Beware of anyone touting "little or no risk."
•If you get taken, don't be too embarrassed to report it to the police, your local attorney general, the Better Business Bureau and any relevant professional association. You might help save others from being hurt.

Source: J.L. Simmons, PhD, author of *67 Ways to Protect Seniors From Crime,* Henry Holt and Co. Inc., 115 W. 18 St., New York 10011.

Crime Victim Fight-Back Strategies: Beat the Criminals...Beat the System

Six million Americans are struck by violent crimes each year. Too many crime victims are victimized twice—*first* by the criminal, *then* by a system that denies them justice or financial redress. But victims *do* have rights—and it's important to know how and where to assert them.

•First step: *Contact your local victim assistance program.* They are in all large counties and many smaller ones. In counties lacking such programs, help can often be found from informal victims' advocates in the district attorney's office or police department. *Your victim-assistance representative will:*

•Steer you to counseling—either short- or long-term, depending on your needs.

•Help you get emergency financial assistance.

•Supply information about support groups, such as the National Organization for Victim Assistance (NOVA) and the National Victim Center (NVC).

•Help you apply for longer-term financial assistance. To become eligible for aid from your state's crime-victim compensation board, you must report the crime to the police within 72 hours, then file a claim by the state's deadline—in most cases within one year. The criminal need not be convicted, or even identified.

Covered losses:

Most states cap compensation at between $10,000 and $25,000. Two states—New York and Washington—set no limits. Medical bills, lost wages, replacement-service costs (for services the victim can no longer perform) and funeral costs are often covered. In addition, victims can help themselves financially through a variety of means:

•*Check your insurance policies.* The fine print in homeowner's and health insurance policies may offer more coverage than you're aware of.

•*Check with your employer* about your company health insurance, disability insurance (which allows for extended leaves at reduced pay), sick leave (with pay) and extended sick leave (without pay).

•*Seek restitution from the defendant.* If the defendant is found guilty, the judge may order restitution at the time of sentencing.

Alternate route: The victim may file a civil lawsuit for damages, whether or not the defendant was convicted of a crime. The burden of proof is much lighter in civil courts than in criminal courts. And even poor defendants may have assets ranging from insurance policies to future wages.

Drawbacks: Civil courts are painfully slow, and few victims collect. According to a South

Carolina study, only 10% of crime victims received any money from the perpetrator in a civil suit—and these were cases with guilty defendants.

•*Sue a liable third party.* If you can prove that a third person or company negligence is responsible for your loss or injury, you may win a substantial award.

Example: After leaving a shopping mall at night, a woman is assaulted in a poorly lit outdoor parking lot without security guards. She sues the company that owns the mall for failing to provide adequate security—a customer's reasonable expectation.

Other possible liable third parties include hotels, landlords, businesses, schools and colleges, law-enforcement officials and the manufacturers of crime-prevention devices.

•*Ask your creditors for a less burdensome payment schedule.* Most creditors will be sympathetic, partly because they want to avoid the bad public relations of foreclosing on a crime victim.

•*If you've been injured in a crime, negotiate for a reduced hospital or doctor bill—and for increased insurance coverage.* Both strategies have worked, but only when the person asked.

Legal needs:

Many crime victims seek to put the incident behind them and steer clear of the criminal justice system.

Others feel a need to get involved and help ensure that justice is done. Depending on your wishes, your victim-assistance representative can guide you in working with the district attorney's office, escort you to and from court and prepare you to be a witness.

If you fear the person accused of the crime, you might ask the district attorney to ask the judge to deny bail. While bail is rarely denied, victims often succeed in obtaining *conditions* for bail.

Examples: No contact with the victim or witnesses, staying out of the victim's neighborhood and work areas.

More legal strategies:

•*Never assume that charges will be filed.* If the district attorney believes there is insufficient evidence, he/she may drop the entire matter—even after an arrest. Victims can explain the facts of the case as they know them and urge that charges be brought.

• *Ask the district attorney's office to consult with you before striking a plea bargain.* If a deal is made without your knowledge, you can write to the judge or speak in court on plea-bargaining day. (Ask the clerk or probation officer in advance for permission to speak out.) No plea bargain is final until approved by a judge.

• *Give your views on what sentencing should be to the judge, by letter or in person, if the defendant is convicted.* Only victims can convey the true impact of a crime or their fear of a defendant set free with a suspended sentence.

Source: Charles G. Brown, former attorney general of West Virginia and founder of the Victims' Rights Political Action Committee, 908 King St., Suite 300, Alexandria, Virginia 22314. He is also author of *First Get Mad, Then Get Justice,* Birch Lane Press, 600 Madison Ave., New York 10022.

Driving with Big Trucks

One of the most stressful and frightening aspects of driving is sharing the road with big trucks.

But if you have better insight into the world as seen through truckers' eyes, you may understand more about the way they perform and can avoid tangling with them. Here's what you need to know.

Sharing the road with big trucks:

• *Mirrors:* Most trucks have a multitude of mirrors, both flat and convex. Because of their size, they can distort the picture or leave out whole sections of the lane beside the truck. For this reason, the most dangerous place to drive is beside a big rig. To get an idea of big-rig blind spots, try to see the trucker's face in his/her mirror. You'll quickly learn how limited his visibility is.

• *Lanes:* A trucker's turn signals are most important. Always watch for them. If a trucker signals to change lanes and you are in the way, move out of his way as fast as you can.

• *Escape:* Seasoned truckers know they must have an escape path if they need to get off the road quickly—in case the air pressure fails and

the brakes suddenly lock up. If a trucker is in the left-hand lane, he will always be looking for a path to the right so he can get off the road before the brakes cause the truck to come to a skidding halt.

• *Blind spot:* One thing all trucks have in common is a blind spot directly behind the trailer. If you want to slip in behind a truck to save gas by being pulled along in the truck's wake, you'll find the trucker very uncooperative. Truckers hate it when a four-wheeler hangs back there. It makes them nervous. This is one of the reasons truckers like to drive in caravans, so the trucker behind can watch the "back door." They try to discourage you from slipping in between.

• *Passing:* Truckers hate passing. It is one of the most risky things they have to do. They have to plan their approach, speed, exit and re-entry back into their lane. Anytime they must change lanes, there is a risk of hitting someone hiding in the blind spot. So avoid passing, slowing down and forcing him to pass you.

Consider how much energy a truck uses to speed up and pass. The trucker typically must break the posted speed limit to gain enough momentum to pass. In a trucker's mind, there are two rules to live by—deliver the load on time and use as little fuel as possible. When you get in his way, you become the enemy.

• *Hills:* Truckers like to gain speed while going down hill so they have more momentum to go up the next hill. If you are in their way, you either force them to pass you or to ride on your tail. Sometimes it is better to give up the right-hand lane so the truckers can speed up and slow down when going up and down the hills. *Remember:* Give them room—lots of room.

• *Wet roads:* The water splash from a truck can be overwhelming. Stay away from big rigs when it is raining hard or when there are large puddles in the road. The splash can blind you, especially at night. If your vehicle, trying to pass the truck, is covered with the spray, the truck driver won't be able to see you. Also, trucks have better traction than cars in the wet weather and can stop much faster than cars. Don't follow too closely.

• *Snow and ice:* Because of their awesome weight, trucks can drive on ice and snow long after four-wheel-drive vehicles have lost traction. Don't be deceived into thinking you can continue driving in this weather just because trucks are traveling. If anything, you might become a hazard when you spin out right in front of one.

Dangerous trucks:

In the perfect world, no trucks would have faulty brakes and no trucks would be driving with more than they were designed to carry. But in the real world of everyday driving, many trucks are loaded beyond their rated capacity and many have brakes that are not functioning properly.

For example, the federal formula for bridges dictates the maximum amount of weight that trucks can carry over highway bridges (you've seen the signs along the sides of smaller bridges). Even though there is a federal formula, some states allow trucks to legally exceed this limit by 25%.

The more axles and tires a truck has, the better its stopping ability. If you consider the actual amount of braking ability a truck has in relationship to the weight of its load, you can get an idea of how effective the truck's brakes are. Once the truck's front wheels lose traction, the truck becomes a huge, deadly projectile.

Because dump trucks (also known as "sand haulers") don't have to cross state lines, they don't have to stop at the weigh stations. They only run short distances from the rock pits to the construction sites. Because they are not closely checked for overloading, some may exceed the safe gross vehicle weight limit by as much as they can.

A majority of the single-axle dump trucks in use are designed to carry a maximum of 16.5 tons. But most states do not limit them to the manufacturer's gross weight limit, allowing them to carry in excess of 20 tons. It is estimated that 95% of all single-axle dump trucks are running over the manufacturer's specified safe-load limit.

Some container haulers fit into this category. They run from the shipyard or railroad loading docks to local warehouses, and don't go very far on the highway.

In some states, container haulers are allowed to exceed the manufacturer's safe-load limits. Some owners of container haulers use old, run-down trucks with tires that are unfit for use.

Their extra-heavy loads break up streets and bridges faster than anything else on the road.

Source: David Solomon, editor of *Nutz & Boltz*®, Box 123, Butler, Maryland 21023.

How to Find a Missing Person

When a private investigator is hired to trace a missing person, he/she doesn't immediately put on his trench coat and head for the closest seedy waterfront bar.

The first move is to do some simple research into easily accessible public records. If you want to find your long-lost uncle...old college roommate...someone who owes you money... runaway spouse...childhood sweetheart...or anyone else, you can do the same. *Here are the most useful sources of information...*

Motor vehicle records:

Write to the Commissioner of Motor Vehicles of the state where the missing person last lived and ask for his/her driving record. First call the driving record division to ask the fee for this service—it's usually about $3 to $7.

In your letter, give the subject's date of birth ...or the year you guess is closest to it. If the Department of Motor Vehicles (DMV) informs you that many people in their file share that name and age, write back specifying which part of the state the subject lived in.

If you still get back driving records for a number of individuals, don't give up...these records list valuable information that may help you pin down your target, *including some or all of the following:*

- Address
- Social Security number
- Height
- Date of birth
- Weight
- Dates and locations of accidents
- Eye color
- Dates and locations of traffic tickets
- Hair color
- Restrictions (eyeglasses, etc.)

Disadvantage: Driver's licenses may be renewed as infrequently as once in eight years, so you may find that the address on the record is outdated. If that happens, write again for the motor vehicle registrations on file for your subject's name and date of birth. The address will be more current, because registrations must be renewed annually. Don't forget to enclose a check for the service.

If you still don't track down a current address, you may find more clues by writing to the tag department of the DMV. Quote the title number and vehicle identification number from the registration of a vehicle he previously owned, and request the vehicle history (sometimes called "body file").

This is a packet of up to 30 pages that includes paperwork with the subject's signature, as well as previous addresses listed on yearly registrations. The people who live at those addresses now…and/or the current owner of the subject's old car…may be able to give you more current information about your missing person. *Records of vital statistics:*

State departments of vital statistics will provide records of birth, death, marriage and divorce. In some states, divorce records must be obtained from the clerk of the court in the jurisdiction that granted the divorce.

Birth records contain much valuable information, including:
- Complete name
- Exact date of birth
- Parents' names
- Place of birth
- Parents' ages
- Parents' occupations
- Parents' address
- Mother's maiden name
- Parents' places of birth

Using your knowledge of the family names of both parents of the missing person, you can try to contact relatives who may be in touch with him. Start looking for relatives near the subject's place of birth.

Master death file: This file kept by the Social Security Administration lists all deaths since 1962…including Social Security number, first and last names, dates of birth and death and place of death (by zip code).

How to use it: From the death record of the missing person's parent, find the place of death and write there for a copy of the death certificate.

Contact the funeral home listed on the certificate and ask for the next-of-kin of the deceased, who will be your subject or a close relative. You can obtain access to information on the Master Death File from private companies. The one I use is Research Is Company, 7907 NW 53 St., Suite 420, Miami 33166.

Running someone's Social Security number: The Research Is Company will put through their computers any Social Security number you provide to give you addresses that someone has used for the past several years. If they do not give you at least one address from that Social Security number your money will be refunded.

Federal Parent Locator Service: If you have a child-support order against a missing person, this government agency will search through government records to find him/her at no cost to you.

Important: You must first approach your state's Child Support Enforcement Division to contact the state's Parent Locator Service. *Other sources:*
- Abandoned property files
- Bankruptcy records
- College records
- Military records
- Corporation records
- Small claims court
- Boat registrations
- National cemeteries
- Bar associations
- Medical boards
- Foreign embassies
- Passport records
- Workers' compensation records
- US Postal Service
Good hunting!

Source: Joseph J. Culligan, licensed private investigator. He is the author of *You, Too, Can Find Anybody: A Reference Manual,* available in book or video from the author at 4995 NW 79 Ave., Miami 33166.

Index

337